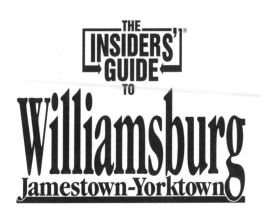

# THE INSIDERS'® GUIDE TO
# Williamsburg
## Jamestown-Yorktown

# THE INSIDERS' GUIDE TO

# Williamsburg
## Jamestown-Yorktown

by
*Cheryl Cease*
and
*Susan Bruno*

The Insiders' Guide®
An imprint of Falcon® Publishing Inc.
A Landmark Communications company
P.O. Box 1718
Helena, MT 59624
(800) 582-2665
www.insiders.com

Sales and Marketing: Falcon Publishing, Inc.
P.O. Box 1718
Helena, MT 59624
(800) 582-2665
www.falconguide.com

Advertising: Falcon Publishing, Inc.
150 W. Brambleton Ave.
Norfolk, VA 23510
(757) 446-2933
rwalsh@infi.net

•

NINTH EDITION

•

©1999 by Falcon Publishing, Inc.

•

Printed in the United States
of America

•

Publications from *The Insiders' Guide*® series are available at special discounts for bulk
purchases for sales promotions, premiums or fundraisings. Special editions, including
personalized covers, can be created in large quantities for special needs.
For more information, please contact Falcon Publishing.

**ISBN 1-57380-092-9**

# Preface

Vacationers who try to take in all - or even most - of the sights and riches of Virginia's Historic Triangle in just one visit probably come away a bit dazed. Like time travelers, they may feel enthralled but confused by jumbled glimpses through the kaleidoscope of eras and attractions. In the morning they stroll down an 18th-century lane. Blacksmiths' hammers ring; horse-drawn carriages clatter by. By afternoon they find themselves on board a futuristic, inverted roller coaster at Busch Gardens. Come dinnertime, they face the same perplexing diversity in terms of menu: new American cuisine at the Trellis or distinctive Colonial fare at Shields Tavern?

While hurried trips to the Williamsburg area are definitely not recommended, even those with luxurious amounts of time to spend in the Historic Triangle will find that paradoxical transitions between past and present abound. The Triangle includes, after all, Jamestown, where Captain John Smith and his determined crew landed in 1607 and arduously established the first, continuous English-speaking settlement in North America. A bit up the road (and away from those marshy riverbanks) lies Williamsburg, capital of the Virginia Colony and center of Revolutionary War fervor. At Yorktown, site of the American Revolution's last battle, British General Cornwallis surrendered to forces led by Washington and French General Rochambeau. With so many historic sites so close to one another, it's small wonder the past not only echoes here but resounds and booms like cannon fire. The sights and sounds of the Historic Triangle can stir visitors' blood in the same manner that young Patrick Henry's speech denouncing taxation without representation must have inflamed the hearts and minds of his listeners in the Hall of the House of Burgesses.

But turn away from the historic districts now and step forward in time. Just across the street is modern, thriving "Billsburg," as locals

affectionately call Williamsburg. This area isn't just about tourism, after all: It's also an increasingly popular place to live, particularly among retirees. According to recent census figures, Williamsburg boasts close to 12,000 residents within its limits, including a college student population of about 7,000. While those numbers may seem small, consider that the city also draws on the suburban populations of James City County and York County, which amounts to roughly 100,000 residents.

Increasing numbers of residents bring with them more of everything else - more neighborhoods and services, scores of new businesses including antique emporia, bargain outlets, ethnic restaurants and video stores. Thus, the present encroaches on the past in the Historic Triangle and vice versa. After a day spent renewing an acquaintance with the dramas, hardships and dreams of 18th-century colonists, visitors can tap their foot to the contemporary rhythms of jazz at J.M. Randalls Restaurant & Tavern. Or you can head over to Water Country USA for a rousing ride on the heart-stopping Double Rampage or a family splash aboard a giant tube at Big Daddy Falls. Or, perhaps when darkness descends, you can join in a chilling, thrilling, Ghosts of Williamsburg night tour.

Such diversity of activities can entice, stimulate and overwhelm. Our guide exists to help visitors and newcomers stay out of the overwhelmed category. We've explored, researched and compiled. What we offer here is a guide to the Historic Triangle's brightest and best of, well . . . just about everything.

So put on your walking shoes, fasten your seat belts, and come journey with us through the glories and, yes, the evils of past and present day Williamsburg, Jamestown and Yorktown. The glories of the past are self-evident - the colonists' struggle for freedom and independence, for example. The evils, you say? Well, slavery and massacre to mention but two. History isn't all a laugh a minute, unfortunately. Then, neither is the present, as anyone who drives Richmond Road during tourist season can tell you.

Take advantage of the decades of Insiders' experience we've accumulated while living, working and learning in the area. Even those visitors who are returning for the third or fourth time will find our guide helpful, as exploration, research and discovery are ongoing processes here. New museums and exhibits open; archaeological digs unearth new remnants of the past; new perspective on historical events is gained each year. Newcomers will find valuable information for helping them get acquainted with the area.

We wish you the most memorable of experiences in the Historic Triangle. We hope our book helps you feel right at home, right away.

**--Cheryl Cease and Susan Bruno**

# About the Authors

## Cheryl J. Cease

Cheryl Cease, born and raised in northern Pennsylvania, first discovered the charms of southeastern Virginia when she moved to the area in 1985. Won over by sunny days and balmy sea breezes, she now admits to a bona fide Southern conversion.

Her eight-year career as a freelance writer and editor has provided ample opportunity to explore this multifaceted pocket of the Old Dominion in great depth; she has written at length on business, healthcare, parenting and travel and has profiled many of the area's more prominent residents. Her articles have appeared in *Virginia Business* magazine, the *Daily Press* newspaper and *Port Folio* magazine. On occasion (all too infrequently, alas), her work has run in national publications. She also prepares newsletters, annual reports, press releases and other types of writing projects for a number of clients.

Prior to flying her freelance flag, Cheryl was an associate editor with both *Virginia Business* and *Tidewater Virginian* magazines. Before coming to Virginia, she served as news editor for the *Centre Daily Times* and as reporter and copy editor for the *Pottsville Republican*, two Pennsylvania daily newspapers. Her writing has earned her awards from both the National Federation of Press Women and Virginia Press Women.

Cheryl holds a bachelor's degree in journalism from Penn State University (go Nittany Lions). In her spare time, she enjoys reading, traveling, baking, skiing, gardening and bellringing in her church choir. She and her husband, David, live in Hampton with their daughters Jessie, who is 8, and Alaina, who is 5 and a half.

## Susan Bruno

Susan Bruno has been writing and editing professionally since 1972, when she joined the staff of Woman's Day magazine in New York City. But signs of her proclivity for writing manifested themselves from the moment she could read and write.

As a youngster, she spent hours perched on the back of a chair in a relative's home, fascinated by an old newspaper that had been framed and mounted on the wall of their family room. It was the front page of *The New York Herald* published the day Abraham Lincoln was assassinated. That front page, which since has come down through the family to her, remains one of her most prized possessions and is the cornerstone of a growing collection of notable front pages from American history she has collected.

Then, a cousin on shore leave from the Navy during the Vietnam War came to visit one evening. After hearing what he did as a war correspondent, Susan decided on journalism as a career.

In high school, she was editor of the yearbook and student newspaper. Susan earned a bachelor's degree in journalism from Ohio University, where she majored in magazine feature writing and public relations, which she later studied further at New York University.

Before landing the job at *Woman's Day*, Susan worked as a Bell Telephone operator on Long Island and then as a bonded stock runner for a small brokerage on the New York Stock Exchange. Answering an ad in *The New York Times*, she was hired by Fawcett Publishers as an assistant to the creative crafts and needlework editor at *Woman's Day*, Theresa Capuana, now a contributing editor at Home magazine. While there, she also trained as a copy editor.

Footloose and unattached, Susan traveled whenever possible, including trips to England, Ireland, France and Canada. She left the magazine four years later when she married her husband, Michael, and joined him in Williamsburg. From there, the newlyweds took the summer off and traveled across the United States, touring 38 states and Mexico. Since then, they've traveled abroad, including time spent in Nova Scotia.

Settling down in 1976, she joined the staff of the Newport News, Virginia, *Daily Press*, where she was a feature writer and, later, a reporter covering tourism in Virginia's Historic Triangle of Williamsburg, Jamestown and Yorktown. During this time, she covered visits by Prince Charles, French President Francois Mitterand, the Shah of Iran and U.S. Presidents Richard Nixon, Gerald Ford, Jimmy Carter and Ronald Reagan, among other notables. She recounts among the most memorable of her assignments the three hours she spent interviewing President Nixon after his resignation, time spent with Vietnam War prisoner Jeremiah Denton after his release and, later, touring the battleship Iowa after the infamous gun turret explosions.

Three months prior to the 1983 Economic Summit of Industrialized Nations held in Williamsburg, Susan joined the Colonial Williamsburg Foundation's press bureau as manager of news and information services, a post she held until the arrival of her son, Evan, in 1988. While there, she wrote the first edition of *The Insiders' Guide to Williamsburg* with her sister, Donna Magoon.

When her son was an infant, she worked as a correspondent for the *Richmond News Leader*, covering local government, schools, business and tourism. She also worked as a freelance writer, with articles appearing in *Country Living*, *Sunset*, *Early American Decorating* and *Southern Living Traveler*, among others. She has freelanced as a correspondent for *The Catholic Virginian*, published by the Diocese of Richmond.

After a one-year stint as acting manager of *The Virginia Gazette* in Williamsburg, she returned to the *Newport News Daily Press*, where she was assistant features editor for two years. Offered a deal she couldn't refuse, especially with her son entering elementary school, Susan returned to Williamsburg to work full-time as managing editor of *The Virginia Gazette*, where she won Chesapeake Publishing's highest editorial award, Editor of the Year. The same year, the paper garnered the Virginia Press Association's coveted Copeland Award for outstanding community journalism.

Susan now operates her own full-service editorial agency, The Williamsburg Wordsmith, and keeps busy in the community, where she is a member of the boards of directors of the Williamsburg Area Chamber of Commerce and the United Way of Greater Williamsburg. She also works as a fundraiser for Walsingham Academy and Child Development Resources.

For relaxation, the Brunos spend time in their beachfront condominium on the Outer Banks of North Carolina, traveling whenever possible, but mostly fishing.

# Acknowledgments

## Cheryl . . .

Putting together a book as all-encompassing as this guide would not be possible without the gracious help of countless "official insiders." Although their names are too numerous to mention here, I would like to extend a special thank-you to Lorraine Brooks of the Colonial Williamsburg Foundation, Amy Jonak of the Hampton Convention and Tourism Bureau, Suzanne Pearson of the Newport News Tourism Development Office, Peggie Gaul of the Colonial National Historical Park and Debbie Padgett of the Jamestown-Yorktown Foundation.

Thanks also to all the business owners, PR reps and event coordinators who took the time to answer questions and deliver timely information to make my updates complete.

But the most heartfelt thanks goes to my husband, David, and daughters Jessie and Alaina for being willing explorers (I didn't have to twist too many arms to get the family to Busch Gardens or Water Country USA) and patient observers of the back of my head on the days I spent glued to my trusty computer in an effort to meet all of my deadlines.

## Susan . . .

Maybe I'm prejudiced, but, if I could, I would thank every one of the thousands of people I contacted in updating this book. Overall, everyone went out of their way to make sure I had updated accurate information. They were forthcoming not because I twisted arms, or threatened to leave them out, or abbreviate their entries if they weren't helpful. No, here in Williamsburg a spirit of camaraderie exists that is unlike anything I've experienced elsewhere.

Visitors are truly appreciated. Repeat visitors are treasured. And, in an effort to render all who travel here repeat visitors, most folks go out of their way to be helpful - even to locals like me.

Williamsburg is truly the epitome of hospitality. People are helpful to a fault, something for which they can be proud.

Just yesterday I stood outside a grocery store chatting with a friend when I witnessed a teenager trying his darndest to help direct a lost family back to the interstate. Their van stuffed to the gills with packages, I imagine they had spent the afternoon Christmas shopping at the Pottery or the outlet malls and, exhausted, they had lost their way. Where else on earth would you find a teenager so intent on making sure this family was headed in the right direction, safely?

In all honesty, I can't possibly thank each person who helped me during this revision. But a few heartfelt thanks are in order.

Thanks first and foremost to all the wonderful people at the Williamsburg Area Chamber of Commerce. These kind people - from Executive Vice President Bob Hershberger on down the line - fielded questions on every conceivable topic related to our area with patience and good humor. Equally patient were the kind folks at the Williamsburg Area Convention & Visitors Bureau. Executive Director Dave Schulte, master of the dry wit, remained unflapped when queried on obtuse aspects of touring the Historic Triangle. When he wasn't around, questions were handled with ease by his able staff. These are true tourism professionals, and we are very lucky to have them here at our disposal.

Thanks, too, to the kind folks at the Williamsburg Hotel-Motel Association, who checked and rechecked questions on area accommodations.

Bed and Breakfast owners - ladies and gentlemen to the last - and hosts at area guest homes couldn't have been more cooperative. Special thanks to Marty Jones, Bill Cole, Ike Sisane, Laura Stet, Sandra and Brad Hirz, John and Kathy Millar (and yes, we all miss Sassafras!), Steve and Maria White, Brian Goordineer, Inge Curtis, Martha and Hugh Easler and the many others who answer questions and kept their senses of humor when I simply didn't understand some of the finer points of operating these truly unique accommodations.

Thanks, too, to some of the special newcomers to these pages. It was great meeting them and adding them to the ranks of our "Best and Brightest." This includes Carol and Todd Arnette at Williamsburg Coffee and Tea; Harry and Jean Matthews at the Alice Person House; Karen Moor at The Whitehall Restaurant; and Dave Wingfield at Yukon Steak Company.

A special thanks to my friend and sister, Donna Magoon, who helped me make sure all the major subdivisions in the area were included in our fast growing chapter on neighborhoods. No easy task!

And hugs and kisses to the two men in my life, who survived on cold sandwiches, leftovers and carry-out food when I was on deadline - which seemed to last for months. To kind and understanding Michael, my husband of 24 years, and my wonderful son Evan, who has been the light of my life for the last eleven. They know how much I love doing this book, so they bent over backwards to indulge me. For this, I love them even more.

Warm thanks to Lianne Lurie and Paul Pittman, dear friends of nearly a quarter-century, who were on hand weekends at the beach with good food and hugs when I was burned out on writing, editing and generally fusing with my laptop.

Thanks, too, to Chuck and Elaine Butler, the ultimate beach people, who kept my son out of trouble when I was so focused on the book, I didn't know if he was in the ocean, in the pool, fishing at the pier or lost on a nature trail.

Thanks to all the good people at the Rundown Cafe in Kitty Hawk, North Carolina, who fed my family and friends on evenings when I was too busy to shop, slice, dice or prepare meals - even when I had planned to do so earlier in the day before getting lost in this revision.

Thanks to Terry Capuana, my first editor and New York connection, who got me involved in the crazy world of journalism at an early age and cheers me on today as I wonder how and why I continue.

A special thanks goes to my associate Kem Putney, who waded through the Golf chapter and rewrote, rechecked and translated it into golfspeak for our duffer friends.

Thanks to my coauthor Cheryl Cease. A true professional in every sense of the word. It's smooth sailing with a co-captain like Cheryl aboard. Someday we are going to have time to meet for lunch.

Thanks to editor Amy Baynard for putting up with scribbles, lost mailings, temporary omissions and bloopers. Thank goodness she's young. Someday she'll look back on all this and giggle, I hope.

And last, but not least, a heartfelt thanks to Beth Storie and Michael McOwen of Insiders' Publishing. They brought me on board 17 years ago to do the very first *Insiders' Guide to Williamsburg* and allowed me the luxury of returning to the book I hold so dear after my retirement from full-time journalism. It was a labor of love done on a typewriter in 1984 - and the love affair grows more mellow (and easier) with age (and computers, fax machines, e-mail and the like).

# Table of Contents

History ........................................................................................ 1
Getting Around ......................................................................... 13
Accommodations ..................................................................... 25
Bed & Breakfasts and Guest Homes .......................................... 47
Regional Cuisine and Wines ..................................................... 67
Restaurants ............................................................................. 79
Nightlife ................................................................................. 107
Shopping ............................................................................... 117
Native American Culture .......................................................... 133
Myths and Legends ................................................................. 139
Colonial Williamsburg ............................................................. 147
Attractions ............................................................................. 169
Jamestown and Yorktown ........................................................ 191
Kidstuff ................................................................................. 213
The Arts ................................................................................. 221
Annual Events ........................................................................ 231
Daytrips ................................................................................. 245
Parks and Recreation .............................................................. 269
Golf ....................................................................................... 277
The Environment ..................................................................... 283
Neighborhoods and Real Estate ............................................... 293
Retirement ............................................................................. 305
Healthcare ............................................................................. 311
Education and Child Care ........................................................ 317
Worship ................................................................................. 327
Our Military Heritage ............................................................... 331
Media .................................................................................... 339
Newport News and Hampton ................................................... 343

# Directory of Maps

Williamsburg and Surrounding Areas ......................................... xii
Williamsburg Historic District .................................................... xiii
Jamestown ............................................................................... xiv
Yorktown .................................................................................. xv

# Williamsburg
## AND SURROUNDING AREAS

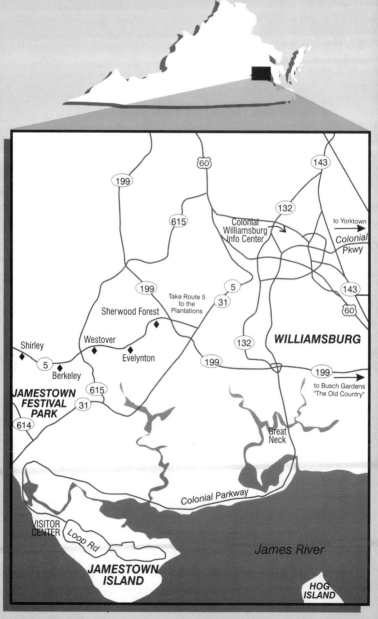

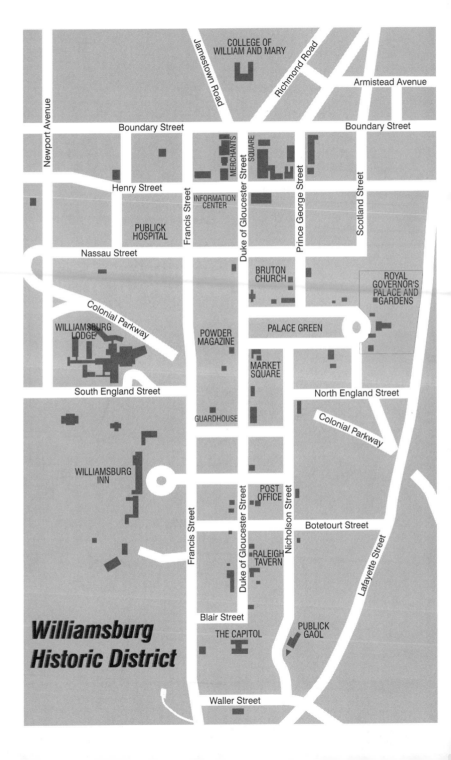

# Williamsburg Historic District

# Jamestown

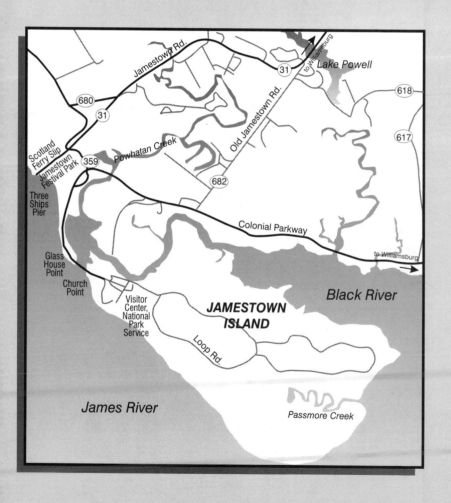

# Yorktown

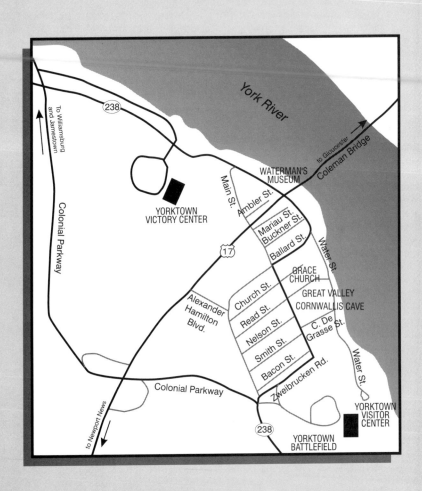

# How to Use this Book

After months of research and writing, we proudly present to you the ninth edition of *the Insiders' Guide to Williamsburg*. This venerable veteran certainly has seen a lot of changes over the years, but as they say, we're pretty confident we're getting better rather than simply older.

In this edition you'll see several changes. We've consolidated a few chapters - Norfolk and Virginia Beach became part of our Daytrips discussion - while divvying up our Accommodations information to include a separate chapter on Bed and Breakfasts and Guest Homes. We also added a section on local media and deleted our service directory, placing the information from that chapter in each of the separate chapters where we think it is more easily accessible to you. We followed that up with a considerable amount of tweaking and polishing. We're pleased with the results and hope you will be, too.

The book still flows in a logical sequence, allowing you to find out anything and everything about Williamsburg without thumbing through nearly 400 pages and calling us less-than-flattering names. But we also give you a good idea of what else lies out there beyond the confines of the Historic Triangle, should wanderlust consume your soul and send you out in pursuit of the delights that the rest of southeastern Virginia has to offer.

As you read the book, keep in mind that the telephone area code used throughout the guide is 757 unless otherwise noted, as is the case in several of our daytrips and many of our excursions to historic attractions located between Williamsburg and Richmond. But be aware, if you are dialing long distance within the same area code - from Williamsburg to Virginia Beach, for instance - you must still dial 1 and the area code as you would for any other long-distance call.

We begin the guide by telling you how to get to Williamsburg, the book's raison d'etre. Once you've arrived, subsequent chapters provide a detailed history of Virginia's Colonial capital and a pronunciation guide for some of the more unusual place names your tongue may trip over (more like a major stumble in some cases) as you encounter them. The result is a book that focuses on Williamsburg in the majority of its content but also provides considerable detail on attractions in nearby Yorktown, Jamestown (the other two points of the Historic Triangle) as well as Hampton, Newport News and potential daytrip destinations such as Richmond, Norfolk and Virginia Beach.

This book is not designed to be read from front to back. We have tried to organize it in a way that you can flip directly to the topic that piques your interest. We've also included plenty of Insiders' tips and a number of special close-ups to share our local insight on the Williamsburg and greater Virginia Peninsula scene.

Our detailed guide to shopping is divided geographically and then in alphabetical order within neighborhoods so you can carefully plan your excursions in this true shopaholic's mecca. Williamsburg restaurants, also in alphabetical order, are divided between those owned and operated by Colonial Williamsburg and the more than 85 eateries of all types located within Williamsburg and nearby areas. So you don't strain your budget, we have included an easy-to-use pricing guide. To help you decide where to rest your weary head - and full stomach - our Accommodations and Bed and Breakfasts and Guest Homes chapters give you a choice of more than 100 places.

(Truly, as long as you make reservations in advance, there should always be room at the inn.) All entries are in alphabetical order within these categories and include a pricing key. Keep in mind that these are not meant to be comprehensive listings but a sampling of the area's best offerings.

Our attractions chapters begin with a separate chapter on Colonial Williamsburg in all of its 18th-century splendor, then follow with a chapter highlighting Yorktown and Jamestown. We conclude with an Attractions chapter, with information on both the area's other side - the Busch Gardens theme park and Water Country USA - and more on its less well-known, but no less popular, historic destinations, from beautiful plantation houses to churches that are centuries old. For family outings, see our Kidstuff chapter, which gives helpful hints for answering the omnipresent query of childhood, "But what is there to do?"

If you're interested in exploring nearby locales, our Daytrips chapter can tell you how to get to points of interest outside the Historic Triangle and what to do once you reach them. This year we've added Virginia Beach, one of Virginia's most popular destinations.

Once again we have dedicated considerable attention and space to Newport News and Hampton, adjacent cities on the Virginia Peninsula that are just a short jaunt east of Williamsburg on Interstate 64. This in-depth chapter includes information on attractions, restaurants, accommodations and shopping. In essence, it's a microcosm of the information we give you on Williamsburg and certainly enough data for planning a separate vacation to the area - dubbed the lower Peninsula - if you so desire.

We also have provided special chapters on other topics of interest including Native American Culture, Myths and Legends, The Environment, Media and Regional Cuisine and Wines. And our chapters on Neighborhoods and Real Estate, Retirement, Education and Child Care and Worship give you some solid leads if you're considering pulling up roots and moving to the Williamsburg area.

We hope you enjoy using the guide as much as we enjoyed putting it together. From our perspective, at least, it was quite a learning experience. We trust that once you read over the information printed on its pages, you will say the same.

If you would like to offer any suggestions as to how we can improve the Williamsburg guide in future editions, we'd be delighted to hear from you. Write to us care of:

The Insiders' Guide to Williamsburg
Falcon Publishing, Inc.
P.O. Box 1718
Helena, MT 59624

Believe it or not, you can thank the lowly mosquito for getting Williamsburg off the ground

# History

Ask anyone what comes to mind when you mention the word Williamsburg, and nine times out of 10 the answer will be history. (The other 10 percent probably will say the Busch Gardens amusement park, but we know what their minds were on during high school discussions of Colonial America.)

It is history that draws (and awes) vast numbers of visitors to the renowned and curious 18th-century buildings and brick-paved streets of Williamsburg from January through December. Most find themselves moved and inspired by this living, breathing example of America's earliest days spread out right in front of them. In town recently to discuss his latest documentary on Thomas Jefferson, filmmaker and historian Ken Burns called his visit to Williamsburg "the highlight of my professional life."

Speaking at the College of William and Mary's 1997 Charter Day convocation, David McCullough, biographer of Harry Truman's and Teddy Roosevelt's younger years, told why we should pay attention to the lessons taught by the past. History, he said, "is a source of strength because we learn by example." And although exploring the past may provide more questions than answers, McCullough noted, it is "an antidote to self-pity" because it teaches us that "no matter what, others have had it worse."

Of course, we don't think that for one minute you're here in Williamsburg to gloat over your forefathers' tough life and other misfortunes. We do believe, however, that if you have come to town to seek a little respite from the cares and speed-of-light pace of 20th-century life, you're in the right place. After all, to say it as succinctly as we can, Colonial Williamsburg is history.

## Why Williamsburg?

Did you ever wonder how it all began? Why the early colonists chose Williamsburg as the seat of government for Virginia? Believe it or not, you can thank the lowly mosquito for getting Williamsburg off the ground. When English settlers set foot on New World soil in 1607, they made their homes in Jamestown, which became the center of the Virginia Colony's government. But, as luck would have it, Jamestown lay on a low, marshy island that was also home to a well-established (and quite nasty) population of stinging and biting insects. Some settlers, fearing island conditions could lead to disease epidemics and finding the current site not quite grand enough for the capital city of America's largest colony, lobbied for relocation to a place called Middle Plantation, which was 5 miles inland. This settlement, which had grown up around a 17th-century palisade built as a defense against Indian attack, by 1690 was a small village composed of stores, mills, a tavern, a church and an assortment of homes. In reality, there was nothing grand about it, but it sat on relatively high ground and had access both to the James and York Rivers via navigable creeks.

Serendipity for those who advocated moving struck in the form of fire, when the Jamestown Statehouse burned for the fourth time in 1698. Thus, the basically unformed village of Middle Plantation became the locus for colonists who envisioned a capital city equal to their aspirations. The name Middle Plantation, more rural than regal, was changed to Williamsburg in honor of William III, King of England, and building began.

The new capital was laid out in a distinctly geometrical fashion, dictated by the colonists' current ideas about proper urban planning. The Market Square, or town commons, and a main street stretching from the Capitol building to the newly established College of William and Mary were the key structural elements of the plan. The Capitol and the college, along with Bruton Parish Church, which lay west of the Square, represented stability and continuity to early settlers. It's not hard to imagine why such symbols were important to colonists who had braved crossing the Atlantic Ocean, facing the unknown in their search for economic advancement and better living circumstances.

By the mid-18th century, Williamsburg was a thriving center of commerce and government. Close to 2,000 people, half of them slaves, called the city home on the eve of the American Revolution. Tailors, carpenters, bakers, gunsmiths, wheelwrights, merchants, clerks and slaves all worked to form the support system for the capital city's growing number of - what else - politicians and lawyers. While the latter two professions wielded power and enjoyed considerable prestige, there are those who would argue that the most important persons in town were the tavern keepers. Taverns were not just for drinking; after all, they were the political, social and cultural heart of Colonial life. If the walls of the Raleigh Tavern could speak, surely they would tell of the times Virginia's burgesses, disbanded by Lord Botetourt, held clandestine sessions there. They could also tell tales of a more scandalous and less heroic sort, for Thomas Jefferson didn't brand the town "Devilsburg" for nothing.

The prominent role Williamsburg played in events leading to the Revolutionary War is well known. In 1765 Patrick Henry delivered his rousing (some said treasonous) Stamp Act Speech at the House of Burgesses here. The First Continental Congress was called from here in 1774. And, for all intents and purposes, the Revolution ended not a dozen miles away, with Cornwallis' surrender to Washington on the fields of Yorktown in 1781.

# From Riches to Rags

But as the Revolutionary War wound down, Williamsburg's days as a center of government were over. In 1780, shortly after Jefferson was elected to succeed Patrick Henry as Virginia's governor, the capital city was moved to Richmond. Jefferson, who came from the western part of what is now the state of Virginia, had long advocated moving the capital west to lessen traveling distances for officials coming from the far reaches of the colony (then stretching as far as Illinois). Richmond also was judged a safer site, in terms of both climate and military defense.

As Richmond moved into the spotlight, Williamsburg suffered through a decline and loss of prestige and vitality. Taverns closed; public buildings fell into ruin. The number of residents dwindled to about 1,400. Shortly after the Revolution, the empty Governor's Palace and Capitol burned. Only two institutions of note remained: the college, with enrollment greatly diminished, and the Public Hospital for the Insane. (Town wags liked to say that the only difference between the two was that the latter required some proof of improvement before letting you leave.)

The Civil War did little to enhance Williamsburg's fortunes. Though most of the 18th-century buildings survived, Federal troops occupied the town for three years, and the college was forced to close after its Wren Building was burned. In 1862, McClellan's Union forces battled through

---

**INSIDERS' TIP**

To provide better and more convenient service to the traveling public, an AAA branch office was opened in the Williamsburg area. Located at 260 McLaws Circle (the Festival Marketplace) in James City County, the office is open 8 AM to 5 PM Monday through Friday and 8 to 11 AM Saturdays. Call 564-7711.

in their attempt to reach Richmond, the Confederate capital.

The arrival of the railroad in 1880 revived the town a little. The C&O's Fast Flying Virginian, also called the Cannonball Express, ran daily out of Newport News to the south, through Williamsburg and on to Toledo, Ohio. (Dinner in the dining car cost less than a dollar, and that included whiskey.) New houses sprang up near the C&O depot, roads were paved, William and Mary added dorms, a library and a gymnasium. But Williamsburg remained a quiet college town, rather insulated, until the mid-1920s when a Rockefeller came to town.

# And Back To Riches Again

Luckily for Williamsburg, Dr. W.A.R. Goodwin, rector of Bruton Parish Church, was a man of imagination. He saw past the shabby exteriors of the many old buildings and dreamed of restoring the town's faded heritage. Goodwin also was a persuasive fellow and was able to interest philanthropist John D. Rockefeller, Jr., in his vision of a vibrant Williamsburg. The two men teamed up and, in 1926, work on the restoration of the Colonial capital began. Rockefeller not only provided funds but also personally devoted himself to the ambitious project by directing the measurements of buildings under cover of darkness and spearheading ambitious research efforts.

Fittingly, the Raleigh Tavern was the first restored building opened to the public in 1932. Soon the Governor's Palace and reconstructed Capitol also were ready for viewing. Colonial Williamsburg, repository of the American past, was well on its way to becoming the fascinating domain that it is today. Tourists arrived in small numbers at first, but after Queen Elizabeth's visit to the Historic Area

in 1957, the public began coming in droves. Hotels, motels, restaurants and shopping centers sprang up to serve them. Visitors to the area today find no lack of dining or lodging alternatives, from the superior to the merely adequate and pretty much everything in between.

Benefiting from the ready audience Colonial Williamsburg provided, a number of nearby Historic Triangle attractions decided in the 1960s and '70s to put on the ritz. National Park Service properties at Jamestown and Yorktown were improved. Jamestown Festival Park (now called Jamestown Settlement), adjacent to Jamestown Island, opened. Yorktown Victory Center opened in 1976. Anheuser-Busch arrived in the area, first with a brewery, then with the enormously popular Busch Gardens theme park, which marked its 20th anniversary in 1996. The Williamsburg Pottery Factory grew from a roadside stand into a vast and somewhat indescribable retail complex that draws millions of shoppers annually from across the nation. Water Country USA opened its doors in 1984 and was purchased by Anheuser-Busch in 1992, and Old Dominion Opry, a country music and entertainment hall, arrived in the summer of 1991. Not one of these attractions has been content to rest on its laurels. Busch Gardens has been adding rides at the rate of about one a year. The park's latest thrill is the Alpengeist, the nation's tallest roller coaster. The Williamsburg Pottery Factory added two new buildings last year. Water Country recently got the go ahead from government officials to add 37 acres of attractions to its 168-acre complex. Old Dominion Opry has reinvented itself as the Music Theatre of Williamsburg, changing its theme from country to a musical mix, and is building a new 20,000-square-foot theater on Richmond Road next to the Williamsburg Soap

## INSIDERS' TIP

**This year's good national neighbor award goes to Anheuser-Busch's James City County brewery. In March 1998, the brewery packaged and shipped more than 2.4 million 12-ounce cans of drinking water for victims of the Midwest floods.**

and Candle Factory. And on May 10, 1997 Jamestown Settlement launched a decade-long countdown to 2007, the 400th anniversary of America's first permanent English colony.

Over the years, numerous groups have organized special events to celebrate the city's heritage or to show off its many resources. Annual events such as the Williamsburg Scottish Festival and An Occasion for the Arts now are part of the regional fabric. Other celebrations - including First Night festivities and the Williamsburg Film Festival - have been added in recent years. And the list undoubtedly will continue to grow.

www.insiders.com
See this and many other
**Insiders' Guide®**
destinations online.
**Visit us today!**

## About The Economy

Although sometimes it may seem like it, attracting tourists isn't the only business of the Historic Triangle. Industry, commerce and professional services have grown hand in hand with tourism, if not always at the same pace. Hard industry is represented by Ball Corp. Metal Container Group, Owens-Brockway Glass, Phillip Morris and a relative newcomer, MergeTech Inc., a manufacturer of heating and air-condition systems. Other major employers include Eastern State Hospital, the College of William and Mary, Anheuser-Busch, Colonial Williamsburg and the Williamsburg Pottery Factory. Unemployment in the area remains low and job growth continues at a slow but steady rate.

When discussing economic development in the area, it's important to remember that Williamsburg is part of the greater Virginia Peninsula, a region that stretches to the south and embraces York and James City counties as well as the cities of Hampton, Newport News and Poquoson. The fortunes of these communities are inextricably linked, and the addition or expansion of a business in one locality is considered good economic news for the entire region. With that thought in mind, it's easy to recognize how the decision of Canon - a major Japanese enterprise - to move to the Peninsula in 1987 opened the door to subsequent international investment and provided a major boost to the economy of the whole area. The fact that Canon continues to expand and open subsidiaries on the Peninsula is further testament to the region's economic health.

A well-known newcomer on the local economic scene is Gateway 2000, one of the nation's largest manufacturers and distributors of personal computers (think black-and-white spotted cows). Since cranking out its first computer at its Hampton plant in 1996, Gateway twice has announced plans to expand and hire more workers.

Doing the high technology of computers one better, the wonders of science are explored at the $600 million Thomas Jefferson National Accelerator Facility (Jefferson Lab for short) in nearby Newport News. It is here that scientists from around the world gather to further research on the mystery and potential of the atom. The city has developed a research park nearby to attract high-tech enterprises. In early 1997, Muhlbauer Inc., which makes machines for producing "smart cards"

# A Williamsburg Chronology

1683: Bruton Parish completes its first church building.

1693: King William III and Queen Mary II grant a charter for the College of William and Mary in Virginia; bricks are laid in 1695.

1699: The Colonial capital moves from Jamestown to Williamsburg, previously called "Middle Plantation." On June 7, 1699, the city officially was renamed Williamsburg when the General Assembly passed the act to build the Statehouse.

1715: The second Bruton Parish Church structure replaces the first.

1765: Patrick Henry gives his Stamp Act Speech in the House of Burgesses.

1774: The First Continental Congress meets in Williamsburg.

1780: Thomas Jefferson becomes the elected Revolutionary Governor; the capital moves to Richmond for better security.

1781: The "Frenchman's Map" of the city, later used in restoration of Colonial Williamsburg, shows the city streets and structures after Lafayette's troops help Revolutionary forces win the Battle of Yorktown.

1862: Williamsburg falls to Federal forces that garrison at the College of William and Mary.

1880: The C&O Railroad (now CSX) arrives in town, bringing with it some recovery from the economic damages of war and decline.

1924-1927: The Reverend W.A.R. Goodwin obtains John D. Rockefeller, Jr.'s, support in restoring Williamsburg's 18th-century heritage.

1932: The Raleigh Tavern, Colonial Williamsburg's first completed restoration, opens to the public. The Governor's Palace follows in 1934.

— continued on next page

Photo: Colonial Williamsburg Foundation

The Christopher Wren Building, c. 1695, is the oldest academic structure in continuous use in America.

1957: Queen Elizabeth II tours the Historic Area; Colonial Williamsburg's Information Center and the Jamestown Festival Park (now Jamestown Settlement) open.

1975: Anheuser-Busch develops its Busch Gardens theme park.

1976: Network television carries the debate between President Gerald Ford and Democratic nominee Jimmy Carter, held at William and Mary's Phi Beta Kappa Hall.

1983: The Summit of Industrialized Nations meets here, bringing together heads of state from the United States, Japan, France, Germany, Italy, Great Britain, Canada and the European Economic Community. President Ronald Reagan serves as host.

1988: Democratic presidential candidates debate in Phi Beta Kappa Hall.

1993: The College of William and Mary celebrates the 300th anniversary of the year it was chartered in England.

August 1995: The College of William and Mary throws a 300th birthday party for the Christopher Wren Building, the nation's oldest academic building in continuous use, built two years after the college was chartered.

October 1995: Defense ministers from each of the 16 North Atlantic Treaty Organization (NATO) nations meet in Williamsburg. It is their first meeting in the United States in four decades.

December 31, 1998: Williamsburg begins its 300th anniversary celebration at annual First Night festivities.

All of 1999: Williamsburg commemorates its 300th anniversary with a big birthday bash and ongoing events throughout the year.

---

(credit cards with personal information that ATM machines read), announced plans to build a facility in the park. About the same time Bell Atlantic opened a telecommunications mega-center in Hampton to offer everything from cellular service to Internet access to the entire mid-Atlantic region.

Tourism counts as industry, of course. In fact, in Williamsburg - ranked as one of the country's top five tourist destinations by the Travel Industry of America - the two most appropriate words for tourism are "big business." Close to one million visitors tour the Colonial capital annually, spending between $600 million and $1 billion and sustaining thousands of jobs.

Special occasions and memorable attractions - and with a few centuries under its belt, Williamsburg has plenty of them - always seem to lure big crowds. The College of William and Mary's 300th anniversary celebration drew huge throngs to the area in 1993. Attendance at Carter's Grove, Colonial Williamsburg's historic James River plantation, has been on the rise also, due in part to the popularity of the fascinating Winthrop Rockefeller Archaeology Museum, which opened in June 1991 and added interpretations of the life of the slaves who lived there. Attendance at both Jamestown Settlement and Yorktown Victory Center increased in 1993, mostly because of group sales. And both Jamestown Settlement and nearby Jamestown Island enjoyed attendance increases of more than 30 percent in 1995, thanks to the widespread popularity of the Disney blockbuster *Pocahontas*. The Yorktown Victory Center and Yorktown Visitor Center experienced similar growth of about 25 percent in 1995. Officials also attribute the area's increased allure to a popular Revolutionary Fun ticket, which offers visitors five-day admission to Jamestown Settlement, Yorktown Victory Center, Colonial Williamsburg, Busch Gardens and Water Country USA. That marketing campaign, one of the first cooperative marketing efforts of its kind in Virginia, sold more than 32,000 tickets in 1994 and influenced visits from more than 37,000 tourists in 1995. A new promotion, "Jefferson's Virginia," offers tours of William & Mary and Colonial Williamsburg as part of a statewide exploration of how the Old Dominion shaped the life of the nation's third president. Turn to our Colonial Williamsburg chapter under tickets for more information.

Revenues and attendance are up for

Photo: Colonial Williamsburg Foundation

The Governor's Palace was home to Virginia's first two governors, Patrick Henry and Thomas Jefferson.

Anheuser-Busch, which employs nearly 4,860 people at its brewery, theme parks, corporate center and residential and resort properties and boasts a payroll of more than $83 million. In 1992, Anheuser-Busch acquired Water Country USA, where attendance is soaring. Jobs at the Busch Brewery, by the way, are considered plums because of high wage scales, good benefits and overtime potential.

The Williamsburg Pottery Factory continues to thrive, with annual sales of $60 million and hundreds of seasonal employees.

Smaller businesses, such as the award-winning Williamsburg Winery, featured in our chapter on Regional Cuisine and Wines, also find the economic climate of the area salubrious, as witnessed in the expansion of shopping centers and outlets on Route 60 west of the city. The upscale Berkeley Commons on Richmond Road, for example, has grown to become the largest outlet center in a 100-mile radius. And a 300,000-square-foot shopping center, called Monticello Marketplace, is open in James City County, not too far from the Williamsburg line.

While the Williamsburg area experienced the same real estate slump as the rest of the country a few years back, falling interest rates and the area's endless appeal to retirees have generated brisk sales at The Governor's Land at Two Rivers, a vast, 1,444-acre residential community with private country club, golf course, nature trails and sanctuary at the juncture of the James and the Chickahominy Rivers in James City County. Another new development, Holly Hills of Williamsburg, a stone's throw from Walsingham Academy, was the site of the 1995 Parade of Homes, a first for the city. Each year this event showcases a neighborhood of premier custom-built and custom-decorated houses selected by a local builders' group from across the Virginia Peninsula.

All told, there are more than 130 neigh-borhoods in and around Williamsburg where home prices range from $80,000 upwards to several million dollars. House-hunters have their choice of contemporary or historical designs, planned communities or out-in-the-country, recluse-style living. And although the average price of a home is somewhat high ($171,000), the Williamsburg tax rate is one of the lowest in the nation.

Residents of the Historic Triangle are blessed in other ways as well: The rich lessons of the past surround them, and the best of the present is just as close at hand. For those in need of a little R and R, Williamsburg hosts the prestigious PGA Michelob Championship Golf Tournament (moved from July to October in 1997). To get the word out that golf courses here rank with the best in the world, the Williamsburg Area Golf Association was formed in 1996. The group must be doing something right: Golf Digest recently named Stonehouse Golf Club in James City County the nation's best new upscale course. If swinging a club isn't your bag, parks in the area offer boating, fishing and hiking. Cultural activities abound - everything from the Virginia Shakespeare Festival at the College of William and Mary to an evening at the opera across the James River in Norfolk - but down-home fun isn't hard to find either.

While many (but certainly not all) would agree that growth is good, keeping up with the rapid pace of development is a challenge for those who plan and construct the region's infrastructure. A key component in Williamsburg's future is the construction of the Route 199 beltway around the city. First discussed by planners some 30 years ago, the highway gradually is becoming a reality. The first phase, an extension of Route 199 in York County to the north, opened in 1996. The last piece of the puzzle, in James City County northwest of Williamsburg, should be completed by spring of the year 2000. When that is finished, the beltway will curve from the Lightfoot exit off Interstate 64 west of Williamsburg to Route 5 and on to I-64 near Busch Gardens and Water Country USA in one giant loop around the parameters of the city.

Another way local leaders and residents concerned about protecting the city's historical and natural resources hope to manage growth is through a community group called the Williamsburg Regional Commission on Growth. The group held its first forum in the fall of 1996 to look at current and past community milestones and to come up with suggestions for managing growth through the year 2050.

## Big Birthday Bash

In the meantime, one of the biggest events on the horizon is Williamsburg's observation of its 300th birthday. The big year is 1999, just one shy of the new millennium, and the city is planning a major bash. A 38-member commission began meeting in March 1997 to toss around ideas for the commemoration. Among them: inviting NATO, which marks its 50th anniversary the same year, to share in the festivities; re-enacting the day in May 1699 when students from the College of William and Mary convinced burgesses to make Williamsburg the Colonial capital; and compiling a locally written book to tell Williamsburg's story.

Virginia's General Assembly already has honored Williamsburg by designating it Virginia's historic city of the year for 1999.

The tercentennial celebration began December 31, 1998, with the city's annual First Night celebration and continues into the year 2000. "It is a celebration for all residents," said former Mayor and City Councilman Trist McConnell, chairman of the 300th anniversary celebration committee. Williamsburg Mayor Jeanne Zeidler, W&M President Timothy Sullivan and Colonial Williamsburg President Robert Wilburn are honorary co-chairman of the event.

Among the special events and promotions already planned are a reenactment of the meeting that led to moving the capital of Virginia from Jamestown to Williamsburg. The Na-

tional Symphony, under the baton of Leonard Slatkin, will perform a live concert. The city will issue a special 300th anniversary calendar. A special Williamsburg license plate is being designed by the Department of Motor Vehicles. A celebratory book, *The History of Williamsburg*, which features writings by 23 authors, will be published.

Special events on the 300th anniversary celebration calendar include, but are not limited to, the following. If you wish to learn more about special events, you can access the calendar in its entirety on the World Wide Web at www.300th.ontheline.com Note that the calendar is constantly updated as new events are planned – so be sure to check it regularly, if possible. Here are the highlights with numbers you can call for more details on each event.

Feb. 21-24: "The Town Before the Town: Exploring Williamsburg's 17th Century Roots." A seminar. (800) 603-0948.

March 1-31: Women's History Month. Colonial Williamsburg will look at women's contributions to the 18th century life during this month-long tribute. (800) HISTORY.

March 7: "The Pied Piper of Hamelin" performed by the Virginia Opera at the Williamsburg Regional Library Arts Center, 4 PM (757) 259-4070.

March 14-17: "The Soul of the Master: Interpreting Religion at Museums and Historic Sites." This seminar is sponsored by the Colonial Williamsburg Foundation. (800) 603-0948.

March 28 & 30: Bruce Hornsby Solo Piano Concerts, benefiting the Williamsburg Land Conservancy. 7:30 PM Phi Beta Kappa Memorial Hall, College of William & Mary. (757) 221-2655.

March 28-31: 53rd Annual Colonial Williamsburg Garden Symposium. (800) HISTORY.

April 15: Simultaneous opening of three

archival exhibits:

18th century Williamsburg at Colonial Williamsburg. (800) HISTORY.

19th century Williamsburg at Swem Library, College of William & Mary. (757) 221-4636.

20th century Williamsburg at Williamsburg Regional Library. (757) 259-4070.

April 17-24: 66th Annual Historic Garden Week in Virginia. Williamsburg Garden Club Tours will be held on April 20. (757) 229-4915.

April 24: "Tales, Trades and Treasures," an active seafaring day in the Port of York. (757) 890-3300.

May 1-January 2000: Opening of Exhibition: "Williamsburg 1699 – When Virginia was the Wild West!" at the DeWitt Wallace Decorative Arts Gallery. Colonial Williamsburg. (800) HISTORY.

May 1-2: 300th Birthday Celebration. Commemorative ceremony recalling historic events of May Day 1699 at The Wren Building, College of William & Mary. 10 AM May Day Picnic/Community Block Party, new Municipal Center. 11:30 AM National Symphony Concert at William & Mary Hall, College of William & Mary. 7:30 PM (757) 671-8100. A Celebration in Song. Afternoon and evening performances by various vocal Groups, William & Mary Hall. May 2, 1-10 PM (757) 220-6104.

May 2: Dance Workshop by the Virginia Academy of Historic Dance at the Williamsburg Regional Library. (757) 259-4070.

May 15: Jamestown Landing Day, Jamestown Settlement. (757) 253-4838.

May 15-16: Jamestown Founding Weekend, Colonial National Historical Park. (757) 229-1733.

June 4-January 2000: "The Washingtons of Colonial Virginia," exhibit at the Yorktown Victory Center. (757) 253-4838.

June 7-18 & June 28-July 9: Learning Weeks in Archaeology. Colonial Williamsburg. (800) HISTORY.

June 19-20: "Brothers in Arms: The African-American military experience at Colonial Williamsburg." (800) HISTORY.

June 25-30: Twelfth Annual Bike Virginia Tour: 2,000 cyclists, traveling 300 miles in five days, plan to visit Williamsburg on June 28-29. Campsite at James Blair Middle School.

June 26-27: "Under the Redcoat: Lord Cornwallis occupies Williamsburg." Military re-enactors at Colonial Williamsburg. (800) HISTORY.

July—August: "Freedom Song." Special ice skating and last show celebrating Williamsburg's 300 years. In the Royal Palace Theater at Busch Gardens, Williamsburg. (757) 253-3350.

July 4: Biggest Ever Fourth of July Celebration in Williamsburg! Children's marching parade, Williamsburg Community Hospital Auxiliary Ice Cream Social in the Wren Yard, Air Force Heritage Band concert and fireworks by Colonial Williamsburg. (757) 253-1862.

July 9-11: Gourmet Weekend: Fine Food & Exceptional Wines with Kevin Zraley, Windows on the World. Sponsored by Colonial Williamsburg. (800) 603-0948.

## INSIDERS' TIP

**The region enjoys a prime East Coast location: Within a radius of 750 miles lies two-thirds of the nation's population. This includes the cities of Boston, Washington, D.C., Baltimore, Philadelphia, New York and Atlanta.**

July 9-Aug. 1: Virginia Shakespeare Festival, Phi Beta Kappa Memorial Hall, College of William & Mary. (757) 221-2660.

July 12-18: Virginia State Open. Golf tournament at Ford's Colony. (804) 330-2470.

Aug. 25: National Park Service Founders' Day. Colonial National Historical Park. (757) 229-1733.

Sept. 4-5: "A Call to Arms and Action," a muster of troops and the 1st Virginia Convention at Colonial Williamsburg. (800) HISTORY.

Sept. 24: "Gala at the Gallery: A Celebration of 300 Years of Music" at the DeWitt Wallace Decorative Arts Gallery, Colonial Williamsburg. 6:30 PM (757) 220-7724.

Oct. 3: An Occasion for the Arts. 30th annual sidewalk visual and performing arts show. Noon to dusk. Merchants Square, Colonial Williamsburg. (757) 229-1736.

Oct. 4-10: Michelob Championship at Kingsmill. PGA Tour.

Oct. 24: "Williamsburg: The Capitol Years," a Virginia Symphony Concert. Jamestown High School. (757) 623-2310.

Nov. 7: 225th Anniversary of the Yorktown Tea Party. Colonial National Historical Park. (757) 898-3400.

Nov. 25-27: "Food and Feasts of Colonial Virginia." Jamestown Settlement and Yorktown Victory Center. (757) 253-4838.

Nov. 29: Opening of the Holiday Season in Colonial Williamsburg.

Dec. 3: Lighted boat parade. Yorktown Waterfront. 8 PM (757) 8887-2641.

Dec. 4: Williamsburg Annual Christmas Parade. (757) 229-6511.

Dec. 5: Grand Illumination. Colonial Williamsburg. (800) HISTORY.

Dec. 11: Yule Log Ceremony. College of William & Mary. (757) 221-4000.

Dec. 13: Gian Carlo Menotti's *Christmas Opera & Other Beloved Classics*, performed by the Williamsburg Symphonia at Phi Beta Kappa Memorial Hall. 8:15 PM (757) 2299-9857.

Dec. 17-19: *The Nutcracker*, performed by The Chamber Ballet. Phi Beta Kappa Memorial Hall, College of William & Mary. (757) 229-1717.

Dec. 31: First Night of 2000. Conclusion of Williamsburg's 300th Anniversary Celebration. (757) 258-0015.

Since every aspect of the celebration is sure to draw big support, we advise you to mark your calendar and make your plans now as accommodations will be filling up fast.

Although we can't begin to list all of Williamsburg's brightest and best characteristics in this introduction, we hope we've whet your appetite for all this historic town and environs has to offer. For much, much more, look ahead to our many other chapters and listings. While no city or region can really be contained within the pages of a book, we trust our guide will serve as a stepping stone for you during your visit to - or your life in - Virginia's Historic Triangle.

Since the chaotic days prior to the American Revolution, Virginians have been marching to the beat of their own drummers. That tradition continues today when it comes to naming Virginia's roadways.

# Getting Around

Repeatedly, those of us who live in the greater Williamsburg area have heard complaints from visitors about how difficult it is to navigate around our town. Admittedly, it can be confusing, but it isn't impossible.

Our first bit of advice is: Don't throw away those road maps. While this chapter can bring you to us and orient you so that you'll have a sense of where things are in relation to each other, finding a specific destination may require the appropriate map and possibly your willingness to admit that, yes, you're lost, and it's time to ask someone for assistance. Don't think twice about asking for directions. Locals are accustomed to helping visitors find their way. And we actually get a certain amount of satisfaction knowing we can get you where you're going. And the fewer confused motorists on the road, the safer for all who travel them.

Before you can hope to find your way around, it's essential you get this brief geography lesson. The terms we'll be throwing at you are enough to confuse many Insiders, let alone a visitor to our fair corner of the world. To help you get your bearings, let's start small and work our way up. If you have a regional or state map handy, it might help to refer to it as we move through our explanation.

Williamsburg is the northwestern-most city in a region called the Virginia Peninsula. The Peninsula also includes the cities of Hampton, Newport News and Poquoson and the counties of James City and York. Surprisingly, Gloucester County also has official status as a Peninsula municipality, even though it sits across the York River from Yorktown and, technically, is not part of the same peninsular landmass.

Across the James River to the south lies an area Insiders call, appropriately enough, South Hampton Roads or Southside. This region comprises the cities of Norfolk, Portsmouth, Chesapeake, Suffolk and Virginia Beach. Taken together, the Virginia Peninsula and South Hampton Roads make up a geographic area dubbed Hampton Roads, which is also the name of the harbor at the mouth of the James River around which most of these cities are arranged.

Now, here's where it gets a little confusing. Hampton Roads is also the name given to our metropolitan statistical area (MSA). For close to a decade, the MSA included only those communities we've listed above. But in 1993, the MSA was expanded to include Matthews County to the north and Isle of Wight County and Currituck (that's "Curry-tuck") County, North Carolina, to the south - primarily because of their work ties to the rest of the region. Technically, that expanded Hampton Roads to include three additional municipalities, although locals haven't entirely gotten it straight just yet, and the viewpoint may change depending upon whom you ask. No matter. The bottom line is that Hampton Roads, with about 1.5 million people, is the nation's 27th-largest MSA, ranking right between Sacramento and Indianapolis, and the fourth-largest MSA in the southeastern United States.

# Getting Here

## By Automobile

### A Word About Routes

Since the chaotic days prior to the American Revolution, Virginians have been marching to the beat of their own drummers. That tradition continues today, it seems, even when it comes to naming its roadways.

While it is the *Insiders' Guide* style to completely identify a state highway as such, using the state highway designation, in Virginia many state highways are simply referred to as "routes." Thus, in this guide, Va. State Highway 5 will simply be called Route 5. Why? Because if you ask anyone on the street directions to Va. State Highway 5, they'll look at you as if you just landed on the planet. Route 5 is called just that, Route 5. Please pardon us this idiosyncrasy. You'll find it's one of many.

Since we're near the southeastern corner of Virginia, most of our visitors travel here through Richmond, which we have to keep reminding ourselves is north of us. Actually, it is northwest of us and therein lies some confusion for direction seekers. Because the Virginia Peninsula on which we are located runs northwest to southeast, it is helpful to think of Richmond as the northwest end of a diagonal line extending to Virginia Beach in the southeast. The line itself is Interstate 64, the backbone of motor transportation in the area.

Most visitors from the north and south head toward our area on Interstate 95. From there, they connect with I-64 East in Richmond, or the Interstate 295 eastern bypass around Richmond, which brings them closer to Williamsburg. Further west, another major north-south connector is west of Charlottesville, where I-64 intersects Interstate 81 in the Shenandoah Valley.

The speed limit on I-64 is 65 mph most of the way from I-95 to Williamsburg, but it can be a monotonous drive, often in heavy traffic. One alternative route is U.S. Route 60, which also intersects I-295 and is a four-lane, virtually traffic-free highway. Route 60 runs parallel and slightly to the south of I-64. A third option is Virginia Route 5, the old plantation route between Williamsburg and Richmond. Protected as a Virginia Scenic Byway, Route 5 is a two-lane road through some of our prettiest countryside. It is especially picturesque during autumn and provides a cooler, tree-shaded option during the heat of summer.

Traveling at legal speed on any of these three highways, you are within an hour of Williamsburg from downtown Richmond.

Northern travelers coming down the Delmarva Peninsula on U.S. Route 13 must take the Chesapeake Bay Bridge-Tunnel to Virginia Beach and follow signs for I-64. That crossing costs $10 each way, a worthwhile investment because you avoid the traffic on I-95.

Travelers on U.S. Route 17 from the north will have to cross the Coleman Bridge over the York River from Gloucester County to Yorktown. This bridge can be the scene of maddening northbound commuter traffic on weekday evenings, though the southbound route is usually good to go except during morning rush hours.

### INSIDERS' TIP

Travelers on I-64 who must cross the Hampton Roads Bridge-Tunnel from Norfolk will find it helpful to call 727-4864 or to tune their car radios to 530 AM before approaching the bridge. These services might recommend saving time by crossing on the I-664 Monitor-Merrimac Memorial Bridge-Tunnel (The M&M), a $400 million, state-of-the-art harbor crossing named for the ironclads that dueled near its northern end during the Civil War. I-664 connects with all major Southside destinations.

Photo: Norfolk Convention and Visitors Bureau

The Hampton Roads Bridge-Tunnel connects the Peninsula and Norfolk.

Travelers from the south on Route 17 rarely have problems. James River Bridge traffic usually runs smoothly into Newport News. A scenic alternative approach from the south is to cross on the James River car ferry from Surry, Virginia (see our entry on the Jamestown-Scotland ferry in our Daytrips chapter).

For shore folk, there's no way around it: If you're traveling to Williamsburg from the east you will have to cross water. That means bridges, tunnels or a combination of the two, which also frequently means traffic delays. From Norfolk and the Virginia Beach resort area, the majority of visitors reach us through the Hampton Roads Bridge-Tunnel. There is no charge for this route, though you might pay a toll in time and patience. Delays are common due to accidents and slowdowns in the tunnel, especially on holiday weekends. The best alternative route is the Monitor-Merrimac Memorial Bridge-Tunnel, which is part of Interstate 664.

From the Hampton Roads Bridge-Tunnel or the Monitor-Merrimac Bridge-Tunnel to Williamsburg, I-64 is undergoing widening and improvements that will last almost to the turn of the century. Bottlenecks occur where the road narrows. In the summer, heavy traffic heading east toward the beaches can wreak havoc on anyone's plans. Always add "if traffic cooperates" after saying "We'll be there Friday evening early" to a Southside friend.

## By Plane

Three commercial airports provide service to the area. All offer a choice of major airlines with a combined total of more than 350 flights daily.

### Newport News/Williamsburg International Airport
**I-64, Exit 255B  877-0221**

The Newport News/Williamsburg International Airport (formerly "Patrick Henry International" and known locally as "New-New Willy") is only 17 miles from the heart of restored Williamsburg. A $26 million passenger terminal opened in the fall of 1992, housing loading bridges, service counters and all the standard amenities of larger airports. The airport is serviced by such airlines as United Express, (800) 241-6522; US Air, (800) 428-4322; and AirTran, (800) 247-8726.

Once you're on the ground, you can catch a taxi (the fare will run about $20), or you can take the Williamsburg shuttle, 877-0279, ($17 one way/$27 round trip). Both options are located outside the terminal. It's a 25-minute ride to Williamsburg.

Of course, you can also rent a car. Several car rental companies have desks in the airport terminal, including Budget, (800) 527-0700; National, (800) 227-7368; Thrifty, (800) 367-2277; and Avis, (800) 831-2847.

## Norfolk International Airport
I-64, Exit 279 • 857-3351

Norfolk's airport lies 50 miles southeast of Williamsburg. It offers major connections, particularly to New York City. Expect an hour's drive from Norfolk to Williamsburg (allowing for traffic and roadwork). Insiders know, however, to allow extra time when trying to make flights or pick up arriving passengers. Snarls at the Hampton Roads Bridge-Tunnel can wreak havoc if you're running on a tight schedule. Norfolk is the major airport in Southeastern Virginia and offers dozens of daily flights to all major destinations, and most minor ones. Flights come and go regularly, so you can make good connections at hubs.

Airlines servicing this airport include: American (800) 433-7300; Continental, (800) 523-3273; Delta, (800) 221-1212; Northwest, (800) 225-2525; United, (800) 241-6522; TWA, (800) 221-2000; AirTran, (800) 247-8726; and Corporate Express, (757) 858-0020.

Rental car companies have desks on the lower level of the airport near the baggage claim area. Among those represented are Alamo, (800) 327-9633; Hertz, (800) 654-3131; National, (800) 227-7368; Avis, (800) 831-2847; Dollar, (757) 857-0500; and Thrifty, (800) 367-2277.

Ground transportation to Williamsburg from here includes several taxi services and a ground shuttle service (857-1231). The shuttle to Williamsburg leaves every 30 minutes and costs $28. When you're heading back to the airport, call the day before to schedule pickup at the door of your hotel. Cab fare will run about $75, cash in advance. Insiders know, however, that if you inquire at the baggage claim area or just outside the terminal at the taxi stand, you can usually find someone else heading for Williamsburg with whom you can share the expense.

## Richmond International Airport
I-64, Sandston • (804) 226-3000

About equidistant from Williamsburg as Norfolk's airport is Richmond International Airport (formerly Byrd Airport). It is 50 miles west of Williamsburg and offers more than 140 nonstop or connecting flights daily. The plus for using this airport, especially if you're renting a car or can't abide a delay on the highway, is that it is a fairly quick, albeit benign, route to the Williamsburg area. The only delays are the occasional highway accident that ties up traffic. Even during rush hours in the morning and evening, this leg of I-64 moves along with few delays.

## Williamsburg-Jamestown Airport
100 Marclay Rd. • 229-9256

Owners and pilots of private planes can land at Williamsburg-Jamestown Airport. This facility, only three miles from town, was greatly upgraded several years ago. A conference room is available, as are a pilots' lounge and a surprisingly good restaurant, Charly's, which serves lunch from 11 AM to 3 PM daily (see our Restaurants chapter).

Williamsburg-Jamestown has a 3,200-foot runway with a right-hand traffic pat-

---

**INSIDERS' TIP**

Beach lovers: I-664, "The M&M" bridge-tunnel, is the route of choice for Peninsula travelers heading to and from the Outer Banks beaches of North Carolina. If your timing is right, however, you may want to stay on I-64 and use its HOV (High Occupancy Vehicle—two or more passengers in a vehicle) lanes through Norfolk to travel beachward after 7 PM on Friday and homeward any time on Sunday.

tern to runway 13 and a standard pattern to runway 31. Noise abatement procedures are in effect on 13. The airport subscribes to PAN AM Weather Systems and can be reached on radio frequency 122.8. They sell Phillips Fuel (100 low lead and Jet-A). Taxi service, rental cars, catering and air tours are available, as are tickets to local attractions. The airport staff, always congenial and willing to assist, is happy to make hotel or restaurant reservations and provide information on aircraft rental, flight instruction or just give friendly advice about the area. A landing fee is charged for commercial, corporate and charter flights. Overnight parking for single-engine aircraft is $4 on grass, $6 on asphalt.

# By Railway or Trailway

## Amtrak

**The Williamsburg Transportation Center**
**468 N. Boundary St. 229-8750 • (800) 872-7245**

Many of our visitors choose to come here by train. The Amtrak terminal, housed in what is now called The Williamsburg Transportation Center, is just three blocks from the historic district. If you're energetic and travel light, it's even possible to walk from the train station to some nearby hotels, though taxi service, provided by Colonial Cab (565-1240), is available.

Train service consists of the daily run of Amtrak's New England Express, which departs New York with several stops, including Washington, D.C., and Richmond, to arrive here in the evening (6:10 PM Monday through Saturday at present, but always check for timetable changes). A second train runs on Friday and Sunday, currently arriving at 9 PM. On Friday only there is a third arrival from Washington, D.C., at 1:02 PM. In July 1997 Amtrak added a new sleeper service, the Twilight Shoreliner, offering overnight trips between New England and Virginia, with stops in Williamsburg, Newport News and five other Virginia cities.

Amtrak provides good connections through Washington, D.C., to all points north and west. Connections to the north and south are frequent from Richmond as well.

Westward trains depart Williamsburg daily at 9:08 AM, with stops in Richmond and Washington, D.C. Because this early schedule can inconvenience tourists who must check out of hotels and return rental cars, Amtrak offers a special late departure on Friday and Sunday, currently at 4:53 PM. And on Friday a third train departs at 10:53 PM. Vacationers who don't want to rush back to real life can thus enjoy one last walk around town, or perhaps linger over brunch.

Amtrak's rates are surprisingly affordable. A one-way fare from Washington, D.C., to Williamsburg starts at $26, for example. Children age 2 to 15 travel for half-fare. Club-car seating is available on some weekend trains, but advance reservations are required for these seats.

A final word of advice for train travelers: Since the major car rental companies' offices are several miles from the station, and since they may close before Amtrak's evening arrival, Colonial Rent-A-Car Inc., a locally owned company, has one of its three offices in the Transportation Center. If you make a reservation with them, a company representative will meet your train with keys and a contract for a rental car in hand. Colonial Rent-A-Car offers rates comparable to national companies and uses only late model Fords in good condition. Their services may save visitors taxi fare to hotels and an overnight wait for a car. Call 220-3399 or (800) 899-2271 for specifics.

## Greyhound/Trailways Bus System

**The Williamsburg Transportation Center,**
**468 N. Boundary St. • 229-1460**

Greyhound/Trailways offers nationwide service to and from the Williamsburg area. Arrivals and departures are from the Williamsburg Transportation Center. Buses to major destinations such as Washington, D.C. ($41 one-way), Philadelphia ($60 one-way) and New York City ($55 one-way) leave throughout the day with as many as six departures in a 24-hour period. No reservations are required, but passengers are asked to arrive at the station at least one hour ahead of departure time to allow ample time to buy tickets, stow baggage and get ready for boarding.

# By Motorcoach

An estimated 95 percent of major motorcoach companies offer charter service and specialized tour packages to the Historic Triangle. Large groups can contact these companies to arrange visits that focus on special interests, and there are many standard tour options that last from three to eight days. The National Tour Association's Consumer Information Line, (800) 755-TOUR, is a good place to begin researching what tours are available from companies nationwide. Each company offers something a little different to highlight its tours - visits to Busch Gardens, the Williamsburg Pottery Factory, the Norfolk Harbor Cruise, free-time days or colonial plantation dinners, for example. Many include the cost of a Pass to Colonial Williamsburg in their package prices.

Listed below are names and numbers for some of the major tour companies servicing the Historic Triangle.

**Beckham Tours/Mississippi**
(617) 821-5990
**Maupin Tours/Kansas**
(913) 843-1211
**Mayflower Tours/Illinois**
(630) 960-3430
**Shenandoah Tours/Virginia**
(540) 885-1528
**Star Tours/New Jersey**
(609) 586-6080

Local tour companies also specialize in assisting groups of tourists or individual visitors. Itinerary suggestions, tours, step-on guides, airport transfers, shuttle service to attractions and help with bus maintenance are some of the services provided by the following enterprises.

**Newton Bus Service Inc.** 874-3160
**Colonial Connections** 258-3122
**Tidewater Touring Inc.** 872-0897
**Williamsburg Limousine** 877-0279
**Gray Line of Williamsburg** 220-2866
**Maximum Guided Tours Inc.** 565-4821

# By Water

It's ironic that the most historic way to arrive in the Triangle - by water - is the least feasible today. While owners of pleasure boats do dock at Yorktown, Jamestown, Smithfield, Hampton or Norfolk to undertake tours of the region, few cruise ships now come to call. The Royal Odyssey of Royal Cruise Line docks several times a year in Newport News so that passengers may tour Colonial Williamsburg during its New York-San Juan run. The Caribbean-bound QE2 also docks occasionally at Newport News, and Covington Cruises' Meridian leaves from Newport News for Bermuda twice a year. Officials hope this increase in pleasure cruise traffic will revitalize plans to build a classier cruise terminal to complement the city's industrial cargo pier facilities.

Yorktown, as part of its Tercentenary revitalization project, also hopes to attract cruise lines with better docking facilities.

---

**INSIDERS' TIP**

It pays to have a destination in mind when you ask a local for directions. Most local directions are not given in terms of east or west, north or south. Instead they are given in terms of "toward" someplace, i.e., "Is that Route 60 toward the Pottery or Route 60 toward Busch Gardens?" or "Are y'all looking for I-64 toward Richmond or toward Norfolk?"

Photo: Colonial Williamsburg Foundation

Visitors can enjoy carriage rides throughout the Historic Area.

*The Nantucket Clipper*, operated by Clipper Cruise Line Inc. of St. Louis, does include a Yorktown overnight on its seven-day Chesapeake voyage, which leaves from Norfolk's Waterside. Call (314) 727-2929 for details.

Coming up the James River from either the ocean or the Intracoastal Waterway, private boaters will find a dearth of public marinas convenient to Williamsburg. One that accepts transient boaters on a space-available basis is the Queen's Lake Club Inc., associated with the Queen's Lake sub-division. Call 229-9127 for information on space, services and rates.

## Once You're Here

There is no better orientation to the area than that provided at the Colonial Williamsburg Visitor Center, roughly at the center of a cross formed by important routes. The Colonial Parkway, the upright portion of the cross, has Yorktown at the top and Jamestown at the bottom. U.S. 60, the crossing arm, has Toano, Lightfoot and the outlets to the left and Busch Gardens to the right. For getting around Williamsburg on your own, it might help to orient yourself by thinking of U.S. 60 as the spine of the city, since there is no motor travel on Duke of Gloucester Street until late in the evening. Toward the north and west from downtown Williamsburg, U.S. 60 is named Richmond Road, the major commercial artery. From the William and Mary campus eastward, Route 60 travels Francis Street to York Street, where it turns east and is the route to Busch Gardens. A parallel Bypass Route 60 north of the center of town features several major motels and restaurants and is a good route for avoiding traffic when traveling from Busch Gardens to Richmond Road locations.

# Pronunciation Guide

**Close-up**

The last thing newcomers need to add to their lists of things to do is to learn a foreign language. English is spoken here, of course, for a longer period than it has been anywhere else in North America. Yet some Historic Triangle local talk may sound downright foreign at first. There are two main reasons for this phenomenon: American Indians and Colonials. Many area geographical terms draw on the region's broad Indian heritage. And a goodly portion of the early settlers' Shakespearean English lingers stubbornly in the pronunciation of places and family names.

We've listed the words that are most likely to confuse, followed by tips for saying them like locals do and short explanations of origins.

Botetourt: bot-a-tot. Lord Botetourt was the Virginia Colony's governor from 1768 to 1770. You'll see his name on area streets and the occasional room or hall of a public building.

Chickahominy River: chick-a-hom-i-nee. This Indian word means "land of much grain." The river is in New Kent County.

DOG street: Students and locals use this acronym for Duke of Gloucester Street, Colonial Williamsburg's central pedestrian thoroughfare.

Fort Eustis: fort you-stess. An Army base in northern Newport News. Irreverent locals sometimes call it Fort Useless, though the post's active participation in the

— continued on next page

Photo: Colonial Williamsburg Foundation

Correct pronunciation of Historic Area streets and attractions can occasionally stump even the locals.

Persian Gulf War has proven them wrong. See our Newport News and Military chapters for more information on this fort and its transportation museum.

Gaol: jail. At the Publick Gaol behind the Capitol on Nicholson Street in Colonial Williamsburg, visitors can see the small, dank cells where 18th-century criminals and debtors were incarcerated. The English are to blame for the funny spelling.

Gloucester: glaw-ster. This county north of the York River is named after an English city.

Isle of Wight: ile-of-wite. Named after an English island, this county lies south of the James.

Mattaponi River: mat-ta-pa-ni. The name of this York River tributary is derived from an Indian language.

Monticello: Thomas Jefferson's estate outside Charlottesville may be mont-a-chel-lo, but Monticello Road in Williamsburg should be pronounced mont-a-sell-o.

Norfolk: naw-fok. Even natives sometimes disagree about the right way to say this city's name, which is another borrowing from the British, who have a Norfolk county. No matter how you say it, be careful! The best advice probably is to say it quickly.

Pamunkey: puh-mun-key. An Indian tribe whose reservation is in King William County.

Poquoson: puh-ko-sen. Derived from the Indian for low ground or swamp, this Peninsula city (next to Yorktown) is actually quite a pleasant place to live.

Powhatan: pow-a-tan. This famous Indian chief, father of Pocahontas, might be surprised to see his moniker used not only on streets but also as a name for a timeshare development.

Rochambeau: row-sham-bow. This French general was Washington's ally at Yorktown during the Revolutionary War.

Taliaferro: tol-liv-er. This old Virginia family, originally Italian, saw their name anglicized. Gen. William Booth Taliaferro was a wealthy planter and greatly aided the devastated College of William and Mary after the Civil War.

Toano: toe-an-oh. This city in James City County takes its name from an Indian believed to have been a member of Powhatan's tribe.

Wythe: with. George

Wythe signed the Declaration of Independence, was William and Mary's first professor of law and eventually became chancellor of Virginia. The Wythe House in Colonial Williamsburg was once his property.

# Automobile Rentals

Don't be fooled by what seems to be a small distance between the Historic Triangle's three corners - it's roughly 23 miles from end to end - or by the fact that many attractions must (and should) be explored on foot. A vehicle is mandatory for a full experience of the area's wealth. Several nationally known car rental companies have offices in Williamsburg or at area airports. Check the phone book for complete listings. Here we mention two local companies offering convenient service and reasonable prices.

### Colonial Rent-A-Car

**The Williamsburg Transportation Center, 468 N. Boundary St. • 220-3399**

If you take alternative transportation to Williamsburg, there is no more convenient rental agency than this one, with service at the gateway for rail and bus access. Various services are offered, including free delivery, free pickup and the availability of car phones. Ask about lower rates for various ages of autos and about "car-in-shop" rates.

### Little Cheeper Car Rentals
**722 Merrimac Tr. • 253-0123**

This small, local agency is in the James York Texaco service station. You will have convenient, courteous service and clean, well-maintained cars to choose from at competitive rates. It's worth an inquiry if you're comparing prices.

Photo: Busch Gardens Williamsburg

The Loch Ness Monster drops its passengers 114 feet, winds them through interlocking loops and hurls them into a dark cave.

# By Bus

A car is an invaluable asset in enjoying the full scope of the area, but parking limitations can make it more of a liability when touring Colonial Williamsburg. Note that the city police take parking restrictions seriously and regularly patrol all signed parking areas and lots in and around the Historic Area. Parking fines average $10, depending on the violation, but it is an expense you can avoid by parking at no charge in the Visitor Center lots provided by Colonial Williamsburg.

Or if Colonial Williamsburg is your main focus, the easily accessible bus service, which leaves the Visitor Center and circulates throughout the restoration from 8:30 AM to 10 PM, is a great advantage for ticket holders. And two other bus systems, described below, round out your options for traveling to and within the Historic Triangle.

## Williamsburg Area Tourist Shuttle
**109 Tewning Rd. • 220-1621**

For those among you who are intrepid and adventuresome, there is the Williamsburg Area Tourist Shuttle, launched in the spring of 1997. It's definitely a bargain: an all-day ticket is $1 per person. The route connects the Williamsburg Pottery in the western part of the area to Busch Gardens in the east with multiple stops in between. En route you will encounter many restaurants, outlet malls, downtown shops, attractions, restaurants and more. It runs from 9 AM to 9 PM Memorial Day through Labor Day, so it has its advantages, not the least of which is that you don't have to worry about parking or paying for parking at any attraction at which you stop.

## James City County Transit
**109 Tewning Rd. • 220-1621**

James City County Transit offers limited local transportation stopping at Merchants Square, the College of William and Mary, the Williamsburg Pottery Factory, the Outlets Mall, the Soap and Candle Factory, Berkeley Commons, Busch Gardens, and major shopping centers in town. The fare is $1 each way, with children younger than 6 riding free. A connection to the Hampton-Newport News bus system is available. Call the previously listed number for specific route information.

# Four Points
#### HOTELS
**BY ITT SHERATON**

## Check out the Most Exciting
## Place to Check in!

Come visit the exciting new Four Points Hotel &
Suites by ITT Sheraton, located adjacent to Colonial
Williamsburg and just minutes from Busch Gardens
and Water Country USA! Settle for nothing but the best
in one of our classical styled hotel rooms or distin-
guished 2 bedroom suites where you can enjoy all the
comforts of home. Here at the Four Points we cater to
our guest's every need offering not only the friendliest
service in town, but also amenities galore!

Bones Grand Slam Eatery & Sports Bar
The area's hottest sports bar and restaurant

Call and inquire about our special packages, including Golf
and Romantic Weekend Getaways. We can also accommodate
your needs for Meetings, Banquets, Weddings, Reunions, and
Parties. Let us help you create memories to last a lifetime!

**Four Points Hotel Williamsburg**
**Historic District**
351 York Street, Williamsburg, VA 23185
Telephone: (757) 229-4100, Fax: (757) 229-0176

# Accommodations

You will have an easier time finding a welcome in the Williamsburg area than some of your predecessors: the British, the French, the Continental Army and, later, Yankee soldiers, who once were quartered in the city, some under less-than-friendly circumstances.

Today's hosts and hostesses want to provide Southern hospitality at its finest, continuing a long tradition dating in this century to the beginnings of the restoration of Colonial Williamsburg when the "come-heres" began to arrive. The habit of hospitality actually goes back much further, however. The Colonial inns and taverns in the Historic Area are in fact the true antecedents of today's hotels, motels and inns.

You'll be pleased to know that your sleeping arrangement will be nothing like that pictured in Colonial Williamsburg's movie, *The Story of a Patriot*, in which wealthy planter John Frye resides in a dreary room and shares his bed with a huge, snoring, vermin-infested "slugabed." Nowadays you will enjoy privacy, spaciousness and comfort, with such amenities as indoor plumbing, which the good Mr. Frye could only dream about.

The history of motor travel in the last 80 years can be traced in the variety of lodgings available to visitors. You'll find charming motor courts composed of individual cottages (think of Clark Gable and Claudette Colbert in *It Happened One Night*) kept up-to-date and spit-spot. Or you might choose one of our motels, whose layout and appearance are reminiscent of the golden mom 'n' pop days of 1950s and '60s highway accommodations before the generic chain hotels came to dominate the interstate culture. Of course, you can always stay in one of the chains themselves — although the generic has given way to individualized decor appropriate to the area's attractions.

In any case, you'll have no problem wondering in which city you're awakening. There are the fine accommodations that truly carry on the best traditions of Christiana Campbell's Tavern, the Raleigh Tavern and the King's Arms Tavern, which, in their heyday, offered the best service and accommodations possible.

A toll-free reservation service, (800) 446-9244, is operated by the Williamsburg Hotel/Motel Association and can advise you on a choice of accommodations as well as make your reservation with member properties. Most accommodations will make dinner reservations for you, and tickets to Colonial Williamsburg and Busch Gardens can be purchased at the check-in desks.

Many visitors to our area choose to camp in one of our several first-rate campgrounds rather than use hotel accommodations. If this is your preference, we list your options in this chapter, too. Williamsburg's bed and breakfast inns are such a special treat that we've put those in a chapter of their own.

Remodeling and variations in services take place frequently at lodgings in the Historic Triangle. We recommend you determine your specific requirements for satisfaction and discuss them with the host's representatives when you phone for reservations.

A timely inquiry can make a big difference in your satisfaction when you arrive in town. While we give you up-to-date details on amenities at the time of publication, some things can change abruptly. For specifics on ground-floor rooms or elevator access to higher floors, nonsmoking rooms, separate heating and cooling controls, feather or synthetic pillows, mattress sizes, shower or tub bathing, age of the establishment, whether your four-footed family members are welcome, and provisions for cable TV service, you might wish to double check at the time you make your reservation.

You might also inquire about proximity to highways, CSX railroad noise and even the condition of the room or rooms you are offered. Other considerations to ask about are actual distance to your local touring destination and directions from Interstate 64 or whichever route you plan to travel.

When making a reservation, also ask your reservation clerk about special discounted rates for AAA members, children, senior citizens, members of the military and government travelers, package and commercial rates under various conditions. That is also the time to inquire about changes in pricing between in-season and out-of-season periods. These periods are defined by the individual lodging, but generally in-season or peak-season is from late March to November and again during the winter holiday season. Off-season months are generally January, February and much, if not all, of March, though this can change, depending on when Easter Sunday falls. We cannot stress enough that reservations made well in advance are almost a necessity in peak-season.

## Price Guidelines

Based on information available at the time of publication, we offer the following price code (for an average charge for double occupancy rates in peak-season) as a general guide, with the warning that fluctuations in price and availability, and even chain allegiance, of lodging often occur.

| | |
|---|---|
| $ | Less than $45 |
| $$ | $45 to $60 |
| $$$ | $61 to $75 |
| $$$$ | $76 to $100 |
| $$$$$ | More than $100 |

The accommodations listed below accept major credit cards unless otherwise noted. And, unless we tell you differently, assume that the lodgings allow smoking and children, and that the facility is handicapped accessible. Although it's certainly possible to find a pet-friendly hotel or motel in the Historic Triangle, it's not the norm. If pets are not mentioned in a hotel's description, assume that you and your family are welcome there, but your furrier relations are not.

# Hotels and Motels

## Colonial Williamsburg

The benefits associated with lodging in one of Colonial Williamsburg's properties are numerous. For instance, they are the closest to the Historic Area, so you won't need to use your vehicle once you get to town. You can charge anything you buy — from tickets to tricorns or just about anything else — to your room and pay for everything at one time when you check out. All properties offer concierge service. You get to ride the Historic Area buses for free, and they have stops convenient to all their hotel properties.

In addition, your children can participate in special summer activities held for guests only and need only pay a nominal fee. Adults can use the Tazewell Club Fitness Center (with only a small charge for guests lodging at the Woodlands or Governor's Inn). But the three best perks include priority for tee times and dining reservations — and the convenience that anything you purchase during your stay will be delivered free to your room so you don't have to carry packages around all day.

### Colonial Houses and Taverns
**$$$$$ • E. Francis St., adjacent to the Williamsburg Inn, Williamsburg**
• (757) 229-1000, (800) HISTORY

**If your windshield wipers are on, your headlights should be, too. It's the law in Virginia.**

If you've ever wished you could wake up in the 18th century in a Colonial residence, the Williamsburg Inn offers the closest fulfillment of that wish you're likely to find. These actual Colonial houses and taverns are the only accommodations within the restored area, and they can comfortably accommodate two to a room. Furnishings vary; some rooms have fireplaces, and some have canopy beds. Some have private gardens. All rooms are furnished with antiques and period reproductions and afford recreation privileges at the Williamsburg Inn. Since these offerings are part of the Historic Area and are very popular, we recommend that you inquire very early about availability and about the accommodations unique to each. There are 84 rooms total, and many book as much as a year in advance.

## The Governor's Inn
$$$$ • 506 N. Henry St., Williamsburg • (757) 229-1000, (800) HISTORY

This 200-room motel — formerly a Sheraton — is a convenient four-block walk from Merchants Square between the Historic Area and the Colonial Williamsburg Visitor Center. Offering shuttle bus service to its guests, the inn is a good economical option among the Colonial Williamsburg hotel properties. Other amenities include tennis privileges, golf, a pool, pet accommodations and babysitting. If you arrive by rail or by commercial bus line, you will be just steps away from this facility.

## Providence Hall
$$$$$ • E. Francis St., adjacent to the Williamsburg Inn, Williamsburg • (757) 229-1000, (800) HISTORY

In this elegant accommodation, next door to the Williamsburg Inn, you will find spacious suites decorated with a blend of 18th-century and Oriental decor. Although there is an extra charge for children, families will enjoy the combination of king-size beds, queen-size sleep sofas and the separate vanity and dressing area. Private concierge service and daily club service breakfast in the executive lounge are among the amenities afforded guests in the 48 rooms,

and they also enjoy the same privileges extended to guests of the Williamsburg Inn. And it's wonderful at the end of the day to be able to wander along the brick sidewalk to the Inn's piano bar, where you can order a nightcap and enjoy some live music before hitting the hay.

## The Williamsburg Inn
$$$$$ • 136 E. Francis St., Williamsburg • (757) 229-1000, (800) HISTORY

This is arguably the premier accommodation in Tidewater, justly proud of its tradition of excellence. The main structure — with its grand Regency design — is in a dignified, beautifully landscaped setting with the Historic Area and the Golden Horseshoe Golf Course on its periphery. All public and private rooms are richly and tastefully appointed — no two rooms are alike — and uncommon touches, such as a door attendant and valet parking, are taken for granted at The Inn. It's all part of the highly professional, discrete pampering the staff offers guests in the 95 rooms. During a visit a few years back, one Insider was delighted to find a delicate trio of tea roses on her room-service breakfast tray.

Three golf courses, a bowling green, a croquet court, tennis courts, a pool, babysitting, accommodations for the physically disabled, a piano bar, a gift shop and meeting and banquet rooms are among amenities you will find here. We refer you to our Restaurants chapter for information on the dining offered here, but please excuse us if we whisper just three words on that subject now: "The Regency Room." Enough said.

## The Williamsburg Lodge
$$$$$ • 30 S. England St., Williamsburg • (757) 229-1000, (800) HISTORY

This hotel is very popular for tourists and for conferences and other large gatherings. It is across S. England Street from the Craft House and the Abby Aldrich Rockefeller Folk Art Collection. (Enjoy the beautiful sunken garden there. It's one of our favorite settings for a quiet stroll.) The Golden Horseshoe golf course and clubhouse also are across the street, and the

Powder Magazine and the center of the Historic Area are within a short block's distance. While the arrangement of the Lodge's accommodations suggests an intimate scale, the facility is much larger than it seems. Its 314 rooms are in a beautiful, rambling structure representing several periods of growth. The Lodge offers some traditional Colonial appointments, but public and private rooms also feature tasteful modern design and decor in keeping with the folk art of the Abby Aldrich collection. We particularly like the warmth of the wood paneling in the reception lobby.

Babysitting, a health club and fitness facility and provision for the needs of physically disabled individuals are other conveniences. Many of Colonial Williamsburg's recreation facilities are available to Lodge guests, and so are very fine dining facilities (see our Restaurants chapter). In cool weather it's a treat to sit in front of the lobby's fireplace and enjoy quiet conversation. In cold weather, the warm, cozy piano bar is a must.

## Williamsburg Woodlands
$$$$$ • 102 Visitor Center Dr., Williamsburg • (757) 229-1000, (800) HISTORY

Nicely appointed rooms (and suites in the Woodlands Suites) with exterior entrances are featured at this 315-room facility in a park-like wooded setting. These are the closest accommodations to the Colonial Williamsburg Visitor Center, which is adjacent to the complex and offers ticket-holding guests of Colonial Williamsburg free bus service into and around the Historic Area. With the amenities and convenient access this lodging offers, it is entirely possible not to require your car during your entire stay. Williamsburg Woodlands offers golf, meeting and banquet rooms and a pool. Handicapped persons can be accommodated especially comfortably here as the rooms are spacious and many are on the ground level. The Cascades restau-

rant is on the premises (see our Restaurants chapter).

# Other Favorites

## Anderson's Corner Motel
$ • 8550 Richmond Rd. (Exit 227 from I-64), Toano • (757) 566-0807

Who would expect a tiger as your first greeter in the Williamsburg area? There he has stood, however, for many years announcing the Exxon gas available at this intersection just off I-64's first Williamsburg exit from the west (the Toano Exit). Exxon, having altered its image, tried to get the tiger removed, but the community became incensed, and the company made an exception in this case and allowed him to stay. Anderson's Corner Motel is part of a complex here also including the Exxon gas station and a restaurant (see Welcome South in our Restaurants chapter). Twelve units are offered. While the motel dates back a couple of decades, you will find the rooms updated, clean, comfortable, well maintained and nicely appointed, though there are no phones in the rooms. Three two-room family units are available for a slightly higher rate.

## Bassett Motel
$-$$ • 800 York St., Williamsburg • (757) 229-5175

At this motel, you are three short blocks from the eastern end of the Historic Area. Being 2 miles away from Busch Gardens, it is also very popular with those planning to spend time there. The 18 large, clean rooms provide individual heat and air conditioning controls and full-tile baths and showers. Be aware that, from mid-November through the middle of March, this motel is closed.

## Best Western Colonial Capitol Inn
$$$$ • 111 Penniman Rd., Williamsburg • (757) 253-1222, (800) 446-9228

Even today the spirit of Williamsburg is visible.

You are only two blocks from the eastern end of the Historic Area at this motel, and its 86 rooms are just steps away from a restaurant. Tucked away off the beaten path, it nevertheless is convenient to dining, several major roads and the Williamsburg Area Chamber of Commerce and Williamsburg Convention and Visitors Bureau, in case you have a question. Its location also makes it convenient for those who wish to include a visit to Busch Gardens in their plans. The playground, outdoor pool and kiddie pool are centers of activity, and a second-story deck overlooking the pool offers a place to enjoy viewing the fun while staying dry. Elevators are provided for reaching upper rooms, and there are accommodations for the handicapped. Children younger than 12 stay for free. Pets are welcome. Discounts are offered for senior citizens and the military.

### Best Western Patrick Henry Inn

$$$$$ • **York and Page Sts., U.S. Rt. 60 E., Williamsburg • (757) 229-9540, (800) 446-9228**

This hotel, the closest to Colonial Williamsburg's easternmost edge, is especially convenient to Busch Gardens as well. The Patrick Henry Inn and Conference Center, with its meeting and banquet rooms for groups of up to 480 people, might be perfect for your business or party require-

ments. More than 300 rooms are available, with suites and king or whirlpool rooms upon request. Physically disabled individuals will find convenient, safe accommodations here. Also on the premises are a heated swimming pool, game room, laundry, babysitting, dining room and lounge. Vacationing pets are welcome (if accompanied by their masters, of course). Check on discounted rates for senior citizens and others.

### Best Western Williamsburg

$$$$ • **7411 Pocahontas Tr. (U.S. Rt. 60 E. at Va. Rt. 199), Williamsburg**
• **(757) 229-3003, (800) 446-9228**

This facility closes in Busch Gardens' off-season, so please check those dates with the reservation clerk. At other times, its accessibility from the Route 199 exit of I-64 and its proximity to Busch Gardens make its 134 rooms particularly attractive, as does the fact that it is also less than 2 miles from the Historic Area's easternmost boundary. The casual, cafeteria-style restaurant, sun deck and pool are very popular. In sight of the pool is a nicely equipped playground. Handicapped accessible rooms are available. Children younger than 12 stay free with their parents. Discounts are available for senior citizens and others. Small pets are allowed.

## Best Western–The Williamsburg Westpark Hotel
$$$ • 1600 Richmond Rd., Williamsburg
• (757) 229-1134, (800) 446-1062

This hotel's 163 rooms are popular with group tours as well as individual travelers. The indoor heated pool is a welcome relief at the end of a day traveling or touring, and complimentary coffee is one indication of the hospitality. The on-premises restaurant is open year round. In addition, a large variety of dining options extends two blocks in either direction. Children younger than 18 stay for free, and small pets are welcome. Senior citizen and other discounts also are available.

## Capitol Motel
$$$ • 924 Capitol Landing Rd., Williamsburg • (757) 229-5215, (800) 368-8383

This motel offers 59 guestrooms. An outdoor pool, a gift shop, rooms for physically disabled individuals and some suites and kitchenettes are additional features. This part of the city does not have the highway-strip character of Richmond Road, and its quieter and slower pace may be attractive to you. Children younger than 18 stay free with their parents. Also inquire about the family plan, senior citizen discounts and special rates for AAA members.

## Captain John Smith Inn
$$$ • 2225 Richmond Rd., Williamsburg • (757) 220-0710, (800) 933-6788

Free in-room coffee is a feature this 67-room motel offers its guests. You will find yourself a five-minute drive from the Historic Area and within easy walking distance of a variety of dining choices. A game room and an outdoor swimming pool offer opportunities for relaxation after a day of sightseeing. This lodge bills itself as "the best little motel in the world," and the staff works hard to live up to that claim. While not fancy, it's a good, well-kept, convenient choice for economy-minded travelers. Children 12 and younger stay free, and senior citizen discounts and many others are offered. One semi-handicapped accessible room is available.

## Carolynn Court Motel
$$ • 1446 Richmond Rd., Williamsburg
• (757) 229-6666

There are 65 comfortable rooms here, and complimentary coffee is always available for guests. While this is one of the area's older properties, it is kept in tip-top shape, and the staff takes customer satisfaction seriously. There is an outdoor pool on the grounds. The option of parking near your door and the nearby picnic area are amenities you also may find attractive. There are many restaurants and gift shops close by in either direction on Richmond Road. Senior citizen discounts and others are offered, and children younger than 17 stay for free. The price is right, and the place is very clean.

## Colonel Waller Motel
$$$ • 917 Capitol Landing Rd., Williamsburg • (757) 253-0999, (800) 368-5006

Families like the inexpensive, all-suite configuration of this 28-room motel's large, comfortable offerings, conveniently located near the eastern edge of the Historic Area. After supper, if you have a ticket, you can wander over to the Colonial Williamsburg Visitor Center and catch the free bus into Merchants Square for an ice cream cone or fresh roasted Virginia peanuts. The pool will take your mind off your sore feet while you review your day's touring. Senior citizen, AAA and many other discounts are offered, except on holidays.

## Colonial Motel
$$ • 1452 Richmond Rd., Williamsburg
• (757) 229-3621, (800) 232-1452

This privately-owned and -operated motel is within walking distance of restaurants and short driving distance of all major attractions and shopping. This older, nicely remodeled property offers 35 clean and quiet rooms, a continental breakfast of hot morning beverages and homemade muffins or scones. Cable TV, an outdoor pool, picnic and play areas and parking at the door are attractive features. Each room has individual air conditioning and heat con-

trols. Connecting rooms, cots and cribs are available upon request, and children younger than 2 stay free.

## Colonial Parkway Inn
**$$ • 800 Capitol Landing Rd., Williamsburg • (757) 229-2374**

There are 38 rooms at this older but very popular motel. Guests will enjoy the tree-shaded grounds and the outdoor swimming pool. You may have to compete for accommodations with repeat customers, especially senior citizens who favor this place. Pets are accepted, and children younger than 16 stay for free.

## Comfort Inn & Suites
**$$$$-$$$$$ • 1420 Richmond Rd., Williamsburg • (757) 229-2981, (800) 444-HOST**

Satellite TV is provided at this location, a five-minute drive from the Historic Area and the Richmond Road outlets and a 10-minute drive from Busch Gardens and Water Country USA. Price includes deluxe continental breakfast. For other meals, there are many restaurants conveniently located nearby. An outdoor pool is available. Facilities for the physically disabled are offered, and senior citizen discounts apply.

## Comfort Inn–Central
**$$$ • 2007 Richmond Rd., Williamsburg • (757) 220-3888, (800) 221-2222**

An indoor, heated swimming pool is available for guests of this motel, which is within easy walking distance to a variety of restaurants. There are 128 comfortable rooms waiting for you, some with a Jacuzzi and some with king-size beds. Facilities for the disabled can be arranged, and nonsmoking rooms are also provided upon request. The facility is five minutes by car from the Historic Area and outlet shopping and a 10-minute drive from Busch Gardens and Water Country USA. Senior citizen and other discounts are offered.

## Comfort Inn–King George Historic
**$$$$ • 706 Bypass Rd., Williamsburg • (757) 229-9230, (800) 358-8003**

There are 157 rooms in this four-story hotel that is a short drive from all area attractions, especially the Colonial Williamsburg Visitor Center. The indoor-outdoor heated pool, exercise equipment, Jacuzzi, sauna and lounge are highlights, and the rooms have HBO and cable for those who need a rest after a day of touring. Jacuzzi suites, honeymoon suites and combinations of connecting and meeting suites can be obtained upon request. Special rooms accommodating the handicapped are also offered. There is a restaurant on the premises. Senior citizen and other discounts are offered.

### Comfort Inn–Outlet Center

$$$$ • 5611 Richmond Rd., Williamsburg • (757) 565-1100, (800) 964-1774

Just between the city and the Williamsburg Pottery Factory, this newly renovated motel is convenient for travelers planning to season their touring with a bit of shopping — or is there such a thing as "a bit" of shopping? The Richmond Road outlets are a short drive in either direction, and the lobby's Outlet Information Center can advise you about particular shopping offerings. Free in-room movies, meeting rooms, a swimming pool and accommodations for the disabled are provided with the 80 rooms. Free continental breakfast and 24-hour free coffee (and evening cider in the colder season) are offered. There is a restaurant on the premises, and children younger than 18 stay for free. Senior citizen, AAA and military discounts are available.

### Commonwealth Inn

$$-$$$ • 1233 Richmond Rd., Williamsburg • (757) 253-1087, (800) 344-0046

It's small and not particularly fancy, but you can't beat this motel's location, less than a mile from the Historic Area. A few years back, it even served as a dorm for some William and Mary students whose dorm burned. Today, this motel is open to visitors and offers 68 rooms, cable TV, free morning coffee, king-size or double beds, a game room, nonsmoking rooms, senior citizen and other discounts and an outdoor swimming pool. Children younger than 12 stay for free. Pets can be accommodated.

### Days Inn–Downtown Colonial

$$$-$$$$ • 902 Richmond Rd., Williamsburg • (757) 229-5060

This two-story, 100-room Days Inn is very popular due to its location within walking distance of both the Historic Area and the College of William and Mary. Park in the motel's spacious lot and walk to Colonial Williamsburg, Merchants Square or anywhere on the William and Mary campus. It also has the amenities expected from this national chain — clean rooms, friendly service, cable TV, an outdoor pool and meeting rooms. It's a good choice if your destination is any of the in-town attractions. Yet, it's also a short drive to all area attractions. Nonsmoking rooms and rooms for the physically disabled are available. Pets are welcome. Children younger than 18 stay for free, and senior citizen discounts apply.

### Days Inn–East Williamsburg

$$$$ • 90 Old York Rd., I-64 and Va. Rt. 199, Williamsburg • (757) 253-6444, (800) 635-5366

This eight-story hotel, across from the entrance to Water Country USA, is the closest to I-64 and offers 202 rooms, each with cable TV. Colonial tavern surroundings in Robert's Restaurant provide an appropriate setting for leisurely dining. The hotel has an outdoor pool as well as fitness, banquet and meeting rooms. For those looking for a little exercise, a volleyball court is always set up. The Historic Area and Busch Gardens are within a five-minute drive, and the outlets and the Williamsburg Pottery Factory are about 10 minutes north on I-64. The Colonial Parkway, with its beautiful drive to Yorktown and Jamestown, is very

---

**INSIDERS' TIP**

Virginia law states that all children younger than 4 years old or less than 40 pounds must be in federally approved child safety seats. The penalty for noncompliance is a $50 fine.

close — and especially lovely when the redbud and dogwood are in bloom each spring. Senior citizen discounts and others are offered, and children younger than 18 stay for free. Facilities for the physically disabled also are available.

### Days Inn–Historic Area
$$$$ • 331 Bypass Rd., Williamsburg
• (757) 253-1166, (800) 759-1166

If you are traveling with children age 17 or younger, they will stay for free at this 120-room motel, just a short drive from the Historic Area, Richmond Road shopping, Busch Gardens and Water Country USA. AARP members receive a 10 percent discount. Free coffee all day is a nice touch. Small-group meeting rooms, a heated outdoor pool and spa, cable TV, nonsmoking rooms and rooms for the disabled are available. The entire fourth floor is a penthouse with a king-size brass bed in the master bedroom. Several popular dining choices and a shopping center are close by.

### Days Inn–Pottery
$$$-$$$$ • 6488 Richmond Rd., Williamsburg •
(757) 565-0090,
(800) DAYSINN

If you're a shopaholic, this 73-room lodging has a view of the Williamsburg Pottery Factory in one direction and the Williamsburg Outlets Mall in the other. And within a square mile, there's more shopping than anyone could handle in an entire weekend. The hotel offers an outdoor pool, continental breakfast, covered parking and accommodations for physically disabled guests. Best of all, you can shop till you drop and be within crawling distance of your room. There are several restaurants within a block in either direction, though you'll have to drive to the finer dining establishments. Children younger than 18 stay for free. Pets are welcome with a $5 deposit. Senior citizen, AAA and military discounts are offered.

### Days Inn–West
$$$$ • 5437 Richmond Rd., Williamsburg • (757) 565-2700

This motel, which isn't fancy but is clean and conveniently located, offers a swimming pool and cable TV to guests in its 122 rooms. It is just west of the city line on U.S. Route 60 W., convenient to outlet shopping, the Historic Area and the Williamsburg Pottery Factory. Busch Gardens and Water Country USA are within a 15-minute drive. Senior citizen and other discounts are offered.

### Econo Lodge Central
$$$-$$$$ • 1900 Richmond Rd., Williamsburg •
(757) 229-6600,
(800) 828-5353

An outdoor pool and pancake restaurant on premises are convenient for guests in the 140 rooms at this motel close to the Richmond Road outlets and restaurants. It is within a 10-minute drive to the Historic Area and a five-minute drive to the Williamsburg Pottery Factory. Children younger than 18 stay for free. Senior citizen and other discounts apply.

### Embassy Suites–Williamsburg
$$$$$ • 152 Kingsgate Pkwy., Williamsburg •
(757) 229-6800,
(800) EMBASSY

One hundred percent satisfaction is guaranteed at this plush suites-only hotel. Tucked away behind the Kingsgate Greene (Kmart) shopping center, this hotel enjoys quiet seclusion but quick access to all attractions and shopping. The 168 suites feature a king-size bed or two doubles in the bedroom and a sleep sofa, wet bar, refrigerator and microwave in the living room. Full complimentary breakfast buffet and a daily evening manager's reception are included in the rate. You also can enjoy the whirlpool adjacent to the indoor heated pool. Suites for the physically disabled, a lounge, a full workout room and a restaurant also are on the premises. A laundry facility and a meeting room for parties of up to 65 people are available. The hotel is five minutes from the Historic Area and 10 minutes from all other attractions around the city. Group, corporate, military, AARP and government rates are available. Children younger than 17 stay for free. The price you will be quoted is for two adults, with each additional adult costing $15 per night extra.

## Family Inns Of America

$$-$$$ • 5413 Airport Rd., at U.S. Rt. 60 W., Williamsburg • (757) 565-1900,
(800) 521-3377

A quick drive from the Richmond Road shopping attractions and 2 miles west of the Historic Area, this motel has 63 rooms. Cable TV, meeting rooms and a swimming pool are provided, and Jacuzzis, waterbeds, kitchenettes and suites are available. Rail traffic on the adjoining CSX tracks may require some adjustment for light sleepers, but our visiting relatives — the severest of critics — attest that the rooms are acceptably quiet. Senior citizen and military discounts are offered. Pets are accepted.

## Five Forks Motel and Campground

$ • 4360 John Tyler Hwy., Williamsburg
• (757) 229-5026

While it may seem a bit off the beaten path, this tidy, small complex along Va. Route 5 about 3 miles outside the city limits shouldn't be dismissed. The complex includes campsites and trailer accommodations, a small motel that offers refrigerators in every room and 12 units with kitchenettes. Children younger than 5 stay for free. Pets are permitted. A laundry room, a swimming pool and a playground are provided. It's a five-minute drive to Jamestown and a 10-minute drive to the Historic Area. A restaurant is adjacent.

## Fort Magruder Inn

and Conference Center
$$$$$ • 6945 Pocahontas Tr. (U.S. Rt. 60 E.), Williamsburg • (757) 220-2250,
(800) 582-1010

With 303 rooms, this is one of the larger lodgings in the area and an extremely popular conference location. If you're a Civil War buff, you'll enjoy this hotel. It is built on the site of the Williamsburg Battle of 1862, and names given to the public rooms honor the site's importance in the War Between the States. We like Lee's Redoubt and Grant's Redoubt as meeting-room names and especially like to watch first-time visitors react to the sign for Hooker's Redoubt — named for the Union general. Saunas, a gift shop, a fitness center, lighted tennis courts, a fine restaurant (the Veranda Room) and JB's Lounge (see our Restaurants and Nightlife chapters) are here for guests, and you will enjoy the indoor pool, the attractive landscaping and proximity to the Historic Area and Busch Gardens. Children younger than 18 stay for free. Senior citizen and AAA discounts offered.

## Four Points Hotel by Sheraton

$$$$-$$$$$ • 351 York St., Williamsburg • (757) 229-4100, (800) 962-4743

There are 141 deluxe guestrooms here, all a very short walk from the eastern end of the Historic Area. Busch Gardens and Water Country USA are within a five-minute drive. Your pets are welcome. You — without your pets — will enjoy the indoor-outdoor heated pool, Jacuzzi, game room, dining room and lounge (see Bones listed in our Nightlife and Restaurants chapters). Three meeting rooms can accommodate up to 250 people for banquets or meetings. Handicapped persons will find comfortable rooms here. Children younger than 18 stay for free. Senior citizen and other discounts are offered. This lodging also offers 55 two-bedroom suites that can accommodate up to six people. Each suite has three color TVs, VCRs and a full-size living room, dining room and well-equipped kitchen. This arrangement is particularly good for visitors planning extended visits. A heated, indoor pool and miniature golf are provided.

## Governor Spottswood Motel

$$ • 1508 Richmond Rd., Williamsburg
• (757) 229-6444, (800) 368-1244

The single-story arrangement and at-your-door parking at this motel are popular with guests, as is its convenience to a wide variety of restaurants and its five-minute drive from the Historic Area, Richmond Road outlet shopping centers and the Williamsburg Pottery Factory. The sunken garden affords privacy and quiet for guests using the outdoor pool, and the beautifully shaded grounds also feature a children's play area and picnic facilities. Other attractive features are a meeting room accommodating up to 125 people, full kitchen units and accommodations for the disabled. There are 78 rooms, all with in-room coffee, and options that include king, queen or canopy beds, freestanding cottages, larger family-size rooms and suites. Senior citizen discounts are offered in the fall, and infants stay for free.

### Hampton Inn–Historic Area
$$$$ • 505 York St., Williamsburg
• (757) 220-3100, (800) 368-8006

The 85 rooms here include access to a large indoor swimming pool with spa and sauna. Rooms have remote-controlled cable TV, interior access or exterior courtyard access and free local telephone calls. Rooms for the physically disabled are also available. The motel is less than a five-minute walk from the eastern part of the Historic Area and is 2.5 miles from Busch Gardens. A free continental breakfast is offered. Lifestyle-50 discounts are offered.

### Hampton Inn & Suites–Williamsburg
$$$$-$$$$$ • 1880 Richmond Rd., Williamsburg
• (757) 229-4900, (800) 346-3055

One of the newest and more convenient motels in town is this imposing property on Richmond Road just at the edge of the city. Aside from a choice of rooms and suites in a spanking new motel, this property is about as convenient to local dining, shopping, eating and sightseeing as any on the map. It's a couple of miles west of the Historic Area, and a couple of miles east of the outlet shopping malls. The standard rooms offer queen- and king-size beds, as do all the suites. There is an indoor pool and exercise room available for use by guests year round. The motel offers a deluxe continental breakfast each morning from 6 until 10 AM, and nonsmoking

rooms are available for those who prefer them.

### Hampton Inn–Williamsburg Center
$$$$ • 201 Bypass Rd., Williamsburg
• (757) 220-0880, (800) HAMPTON

This inn offers an indoor pool, free continental breakfast and contemporary decor. It is also a convenient drive (within 10 minutes) to the Historic Area, Busch Gardens, Water Country USA and — in the other direction — the Richmond Road outlets and the Williamsburg Pottery Factory. There are 122 rooms. You'll also enjoy free in-room movies. Price includes a free continental breakfast. Senior citizen and other discounts are offered.

### Heritage Inn
$$$ • 1324 Richmond Rd., Williamsburg • (757) 229-6220, (800) 782-3800

This stately hotel is a 10-minute walk from the Historic Area and convenient to all Richmond Road shopping and dining. An outdoor patio and pool area, secluded from the busy street, is a wonderful place to relax, socialize and reflect on your day's touring. There are 54 rooms, each decorated with Colonial-style furniture, that feature cable TV. A nice range of room prices makes it likely you'll find something to meet your requirements. Children younger than 18 stay for free. Pets are welcome. The restaurant on premises is operated by an independent catering company that also prepares a wonderful $5 continental breakfast. Senior citizen, AAA and other discounts are offered.

### Holiday Inn Downtown–Williamsburg & Holidome
$$$$-$$$$$ • 814 Capitol Landing Rd., Williamsburg • (757) 229-0200, (800) 368-0200

You will enjoy the indoor pool, exercise room, sauna and whirlpool in the Holidome at this inn. Video games, shuffleboard and a putting green also are offered. If you're in the mood for a stroll, the eastern end of the Historic Area is a short walk away. The 139 rooms, all with cable TVs and in-room coffee, include provisions for physically dis-

A Busch Garden river boat ride is a great  way to relax while staying in and around Williamsburg.

abled persons. Modern and Colonial decor, five meeting and banquet rooms, a lounge and an on-premises restaurant, E.J.'s Landing, are other conveniences for guests. Package accommodation rates and a family plan are offered, so inquire about them when making reservations. Senior citizen and other discounts also are offered.

## Holiday Inn Express
**$$$$-$$$$$ • 119 Bypass Rd., Williamsburg • (757) 253-1663, (800) 283-1663**

Quick in and quick out with all the conveniences of home is what this motel is all about. Conveniently located on the edge of town, Bypass Road offers a quick route to the Historic Area and Richmond Road shopping as well as Busch Gardens and Water Country USA. The 132 rooms feature cable TV. Guests are treated to a free continental breakfast. A swimming pool and rooms for physically disabled persons also are featured. Senior citizen, AAA and military discounts are offered. Children younger than 17 stay for free.

## Holiday Inn Patriot and Conference Center
**$$$$-$$$$$ • 3032 Richmond Rd., Williamsburg • (757) 565-2600, (800) 446-6001**

This inn is on the western border of Williamsburg and very convenient to the outlets and the Williamsburg Pottery Factory. It is a short drive to Colonial Williamsburg and to Busch Gardens as well. Inquire about family rates for the 168 rooms. Small pets (up to 25 pounds) are welcome, and you will find babysitting, golf and tennis privileges, seven meeting rooms, The Sports Bar and Grille and the Plantation Dining Room. An indoor pool and hot tub also are available to guests. Physically disabled persons can be accommodated comfortably. Senior citizen and other discounts are offered, and children younger than 18 stay for free.

## Holiday Inn 1776–Williamsburg
**$$$$$ • 725 Bypass Rd., Williamsburg • (757) 220-1776, (800) HOLIDAY**

You might feel like you're approaching a manor house when you take the drive past the duck ponds and manicured landscaping at this resort-like hotel. Tennis and outdoor swimming are available for guests (with a separate children's pool). There are 203 rooms with cable TV, and meeting rooms are provided for conferences of various sizes. Vic Zodda's Restaurant and Lounge is on the premises (see our Restaurants chapter), and rooms for the physically disabled are offered. This hotel is a five-minute drive from the Historic Area and convenient to shopping, Busch Gardens and the Williamsburg Pottery Factory. Children younger than 18 stay for free. Senior citizen and military discounts are offered.

## Homewood Suites Hotel
**$$$-$$$$$ • 601 Bypass Rd., Williamsburg • (757) 259-1199, (800) 225-5466**

Opened in mid-July 1998, this is a stunning new addition to the Williamsburg hotel scene. The property prides itself on being "a hotel that's like home," and it is. This most unusual, especially attractive property features true suites, with "rooms within each room," including two- and three-room suites with queen and king-size beds, many with wood-burning fireplaces, separate dressing areas and residential-style bathrooms. And that's just the beginning. In addition, each suite features a fully equipped kitchen with oven, microwave, refrigerator and dishwasher as well as TVs in the living area and the bedroom. Honeymoon suites offer fireplaces and Jacuzzis. A well-equipped fitness center features a swimming pool and whirlpool. An on-site business center offers the convenience of a computer, copier and fax machine. Also on the premises is a shop, where guests can buy anything they might need while in residence, including groceries. Guests are invited to a daily pantry breakfast, and evening social hours by the pool or on the patio deck, which has a splendid view of two idyllic ponds. A full laundry facility is provided. Handicapped accessible rooms are available, as are nonsmoking suites. This exquisite property is conveniently located on the U.S. Route 60 bypass, about a mile from the city's Historic Area, Merchants Square shopping and the College of William and Mary. Other attractions, including Busch Gardens, Water Country USA and the Williamsburg Pottery Factory are within a short drive. AAA and AARP discounts are available.

## Hotel Colonial America
**$$$$ • 6483 Richmond Rd., Williamsburg**
**• (757) 565-1000, (800) 922-9277**

If your party includes a dedicated shopper, this will be a very convenient lodging. The famous Williamsburg Pottery Factory is within sight up Richmond Road, and the Williamsburg Outlets Mall is next door. A lounge offers evening refreshments, and a full-service restaurant is also in the building. Whirlpools are available in 168 rooms and another 20 rooms offer Jacuzzi tubs. Suites are available. Persons with physical disabilities can be accommodated. Pets are accepted with a $50 deposit and extra $10 per night. Ask about provisions for babysitting services. Children younger than 18 stay for free, and senior citizen and other discounts are offered.

## Howard Johnson Central
**$$$-$$$$ • 300 Bypass Rd., Williamsburg • (757) 229-6270, (800) 284-4466**

At this motel — formerly the Francis Nicholson — you are a five-minute drive from the Historic Area or the outlets, and 10 minutes by car from Busch Gardens, Water Country USA and the Williamsburg Pottery Factory. Jacuzzi suites are avail-

able among the 115 rooms, as are rooms for the physically disabled. Children younger than 18 stay for free. Small pets are allowed for an extra $5 per night. Cable TV, a video game room, meeting rooms, a laundry, an outdoor heated swimming pool and Jacuzzi and a restaurant are features. Other dining choices are a convenient walk away. Senior citizen discounts are offered.

## Howard Johnson–Historic Area
**$$$$ • 7135 Pocahontas Tr., Williamsburg • (757) 229-6900, (800) 841-9100**

Halfway between the Historic Area and Busch Gardens and a five-minute drive from Water Country USA is this motel offering a complimentary coffee and tea room, 24-hour guest laundry and an outdoor pool. A restaurant is adjacent to the 100-room hotel. Children younger than 18 stay for free. Senior citizen and other discounts are offered.

## Kingsmill Resort
**$$$$$ • 1010 Kingsmill Rd., Williamsburg • (757) 253-1703, (800) 832-5665**

The setting and design of this accommodation are truly stunning and unique as area offerings go, and they promise to be even better with an expansion to the resort, including a large ballroom-banquet room and health facilities. The structure overlooks the beautiful James River on one side, and the famous Kingsmill Golf Course surrounds the property, something to consider if you plan to visit during the annual Michelob Golf Classic (see our Golf and Annual Events chapters). As a guest of the resort you will

---

### INSIDERS' TIP

A beautiful secluded setting for conferences, receptions and overnight lodging is Airfield Conference Center, south of the James River near Wakefield, about an hour from Williamsburg, including the ferry ride. The 218-acre site features a variety of recreational activities including tennis, canoeing, paddleboats and walking trails in the woods. Call (757) 899-4901 or write the center, 15189 Airfield Road, Wakefield, VA 23888, for information and reservations.

have golf privileges at any of the three 18-hole golf courses. All area attractions are a short drive away, but Busch Gardens is the closest. The center offers 400 rooms for guests. One- two- and three-bedroom suites are available, some providing working fireplaces with complimentary wood during the winter. A marina, kitchenettes, babysitting (children younger than 18 stay for free), swimming, tennis, racquetball and other health facilities, billiards, a card room, a lounge, meeting rooms and wonderful restaurants and grills are available to guests. There are various packages available, so inquire about them in your initial contact. We say without any reservation — no pun intended — that this is one of the most pleasant accommodations in the Williamsburg area.

### The King William Inn
**$$-$$$ • 824 Capitol Landing Rd., Williamsburg • (757) 229-4933, (800) 446-1041**

This motel is a half-mile from the Historic Area and is very convenient to Busch Gardens and Water Country USA as well as the Colonial Parkway to Jamestown and Yorktown. Of the 183 rooms, some have microwave ovens and refrigerators. An outdoor pool and an adjacent restaurant make this a comfortable home base for a stay in the Historic Triangle. Rooms are offered to accommodate the physically disabled. The price range is an attractive feature for the economy-minded. Children younger than 17 stay for free. Senior citizen and other discounts are offered.

### Motel 6
**$$ • 3030 Richmond Rd., Williamsburg • (757) 565-3433, (800) 466-8356**

We advise booking a room as much as two months in advance of a peak-season stay at this motel. The bargain price is the main attraction, but the location — 3 miles west of the Historic Area and 3 miles east of the Williamsburg Pottery Factory — makes it even more desirable. The Richmond Road outlets are just west of the motel. There is a swimming pool on premises. Facilities for the physically disabled are offered. Children younger than 18 and pets stay for free. AARP members receive discounted rates here.

### Princess Anne Motor Lodge
**$$$$ • 1350 Richmond Rd., Williamsburg • (757) 229-2455, (800) 552-5571**

In 1994 this motel completed major renovations that, while assuring your comfort and enjoyment, did not detract from the charm of the place — a nostalgic, cottage-style motel within walking distance of the restaurants and shops along Richmond Road. All 71 rooms are on ground level with parking at the door. It's a 20-minute walk to the Historic Area and a 10-minute drive to the Williamsburg Pottery Factory (with all of the outlet shopping attractions along the way). Busch Gardens and Water Country USA are within a 15-minute drive. All rooms have access to the outdoor swimming pool. You will appreciate the Breakfast Room with its full continental breakfast available for three hours every morning. Children younger than 18 stay for free.

### Quality Inn–Colony
**$$$$ • 60 Page St., Williamsburg • (757) 229-1855, (800) 443-1232**

This small motel offers 59 rooms with shower baths and remote-controlled TVs. An outdoor pool provides a spot for relaxation in warm weather. All rooms are modestly furnished but clean and well-kept, and the continental breakfast starts the day well. Senior citizen and other discounts are of-

---

**INSIDERS' TIP**

Some area dry cleaners pick up at area hotels and then return clothes when they are done. It's cheaper than having clothes cleaned by the hotel. Check the Yellow Pages for listings.

fered. After a day of touring, the quiet you find here is a blessed welcome!

## Quality Inn Historic

$$$$ • 1402 Richmond Rd., Williamsburg • (757) 220-2367

This 149-room motel is a few blocks' walk from the eastern boundary of the Historic Area, a short drive from the Colonial Williamsburg Visitor Center and within easy driving distance of Busch Gardens and Water Country USA. Children younger than 18 stay for free, but also inquire about the family plan. Senior citizen and military discounts offered.

## Quality Inn at Kingsmill

$$$$ • U.S. Rt. 60 E. and Va. Rt. 199, Williamsburg • (757) 220-1100, (800) 296-4667

This motel is convenient to I-64 as well as to Busch Gardens, Water Country USA and the Historic Area. There are 99 rooms, including provisions for handicapped guests. Continental breakfast, a swimming pool, some king-size beds and an adjacent restaurant are amenities at this hotel. Children younger than 18 stay for free. Senior citizen and other discounts are offered.

## Quality Inn–The Lord Paget

$$$$ • 901 Capitol Landing Rd., Williamsburg • (757) 229-4444, (800) 537-2438

The 94 rooms, including suites, in this motel are furnished in Colonial and traditional decor. The inn is a 10-minute walk from the Historic Area. You will find a putting green and fishing lake as options for your entertainment, and a coffee shop is on the property for your convenience. Babysitting, accommodations for the handicapped and an adjacent restaurant are features to consider. Senior citizen and other discounts are offered.

## Quality Inn–Outlet Mall

$$$$ • 6493 Richmond Rd., Williamsburg • (757) 565-1111, (800) 524-1443

Guests will find a variety of accommodations here, with king-size and two double-bed arrangements, some units that can sleep six, free continental breakfast, an outdoor pool and free HBO. There are 129 rooms, and the Williamsburg Pottery Factory and the Williamsburg Outlets Mall are within sight in opposite directions. Kids younger than 18 stay for free. It is a 10-minute drive to the Historic Area and about 20 minutes to Busch Gardens.

## Quality Suites–Williamsburg

$$$$$ • 1406 Richmond Rd., Williamsburg • (757) 220-9304, (800) 444-4678

This accommodation is near the intersection with Bypass Road and all of the Richmond Road shopping. Microwaves and refrigerators are available in some of the 112 two-room suites at this lodging, and there is a restaurant adjacent. Also offered are rooms for physically disabled individuals, executive suites and indoor and outdoor swimming at a shared entertainment facility. Senior citizen and other discounts are offered.

## Quarterpath Inn

$$$ • 620 York St., Williamsburg • (757) 220-0960, (800) 446-9222

This inn offers 130 rooms a short walk from Colonial Williamsburg's eastern boundary and five minutes by car from Busch Gardens and Water Country USA. Complimentary coffee and free lodging for children younger than 18 are indicators of the hospitality you will find here. An adjacent restaurant, rooms for physically impaired individuals, an outdoor swimming pool, king suites and whirlpool tubs make the Quarterpath Inn a comfortable place to stay. Senior citizen and other discounts are offered as well as free lodging for children younger than 18. Small pets are welcome.

## Raleigh Economy Inn

$$ • 1624 Richmond Rd., Williamsburg • (757) 229-1297

The 68 rooms in this motel have accommodated visitors and their pets comfortably for many years. The wooded site is very convenient to all Richmond Road in-town shopping and is a five-minute drive from the Historic Area and the Williamsburg Pottery Factory. There are many nearby restaurants for your dining requirements.

### Ramada Inn–Central Williamsburg
$$$ • 5351 Richmond Rd., Williamsburg • (757) 565-2000, (800) 446-9200

This 163-room hotel has an outdoor swimming pool, a restaurant, a lounge and meeting rooms. This motel is in the heart of outlet country but is also very convenient to the Historic Area and to the Williamsburg Pottery Factory. Busch Gardens and Water Country USA are a 15-minute drive away. Children younger than 18 stay for free. Senior citizen and other discounts are offered.

### Ramada Inn & Conference Center–Historic
$$$$-$$$$$ • 500 Merrimac Tr., Williamsburg • (757) 220-1410, (800) 666-8888

The all-you-can-eat dinner smorgasbord and Sunday brunch here are popular with town residents, and there are many other features that might sway your choice as well: the indoor, three-quarter Olympic-size heated pool, game room, health club facilities, George's Tavern, seven meeting rooms of various sizes, suites, rooms for the physically disabled and a welcome mat for pets. In addition to the restaurant inside, the adjacent Martha's Plantation Breakfast offers morning meals. A variety of dining options is within a short drive, and convenient shopping and automobile services are nearby as well. If you stay in one of the 250 rooms, you are within five minutes of Busch Gardens and the Historic Area. Senior citizen and other discounts are offered.

### Rochambeau Motel
$$ • 929 Capitol Landing Rd., Williamsburg • (757) 229-2851, (800) 368-1055

Let's not forget the French General whose assistance to General Washington assured victory at Yorktown! This small, older, 22-room motel offers its guests pool privileges and provisions for babysitting. Pets can be accommodated, but a $25 nonrefundable charge applies. AAA and senior citizen discounts are available.

### Sleep Inn
$$$$-$$$$$ • 220 Bypass Rd., Williamsburg • (757) 259-1700, (888) 228-9698

Opened July 4, 1998, this is one of the town's newest and most attractive properties. From its pristine roadside appeal — with its handsome brick exterior and neatly landscaped albeit newly planted gardens — this attractive motel has fine accommodations in a range of prices. In addition to 63 typical rooms, this property offers two Jacuzzi rooms, each with two king-size beds and, yes, a Jacuzzi for two. All rooms here provide guests with cable TV, phones, alarm clocks, walk-in showers and tasteful, traditional decor. Everyone who stays here is treated to a full continental breakfast as part of the deal. And the indoor swimming pool is open year round. Room specially outfitted to accommodate the disabled are available, and they feature queen-size beds. Most rooms are for nonsmokers, though a few rooms have been set aside for those who do smoke. While there is no restaurant on the premises, several good family restaurants are literally steps away, easily within walking distance. Also nearby are the Colonial Williamsburg Visitor Center, Busch Gardens and Water Country USA to the east, and the Pottery Factory and limitless outlet store shopping to the west. No pets are allowed. AAA and AARP discounts are available.

### Southern Inn
$$-$$$ • 1220 Richmond Rd., Williamsburg • (757) 564-0100

This 21-room establishment has the feel of a motor court, with all ground-level rooms, at-door parking and an outdoor swimming pool as its centerpiece. It is three-quarters of a mile from Merchants Square and is family-owned and operated. Dogs are accepted. Senior citizen discounts are offered.

### Thomas Jefferson Inn
$$$ • 7247 Pocahontas Tr., Williamsburg • (757)

220-2000, (800) 763-3344

This inn offers 55 rooms a mile from Busch Gardens and just a bit more than a mile from Colonial Williamsburg's Historic Area. Babysitting, rooms for the handicapped, kitchenettes, a swimming pool and a restaurant are available. Senior citizen and other discounts are offered.

### Tioga Motel
$ • 906 Richmond Rd., Williamsburg
• (757) 229-4531

This newly remodeled family-owned motel has 26 rooms with parking at the door, an outdoor pool, cable TV, in-room coffee and efficiencies. All rooms have double beds. Senior citizen discounts are offered.

### Travelodge–Historic Area
$$$ • 120 Bypass Rd., Williamsburg
• (757) 229-2000, (800) 544-7774

Guests in these 152 hotel rooms start the day with the free continental breakfast. Free coffee all day, an outdoor heated pool, a small game room, nonsmoking rooms, laundry facilities and provisions for the handicapped are among the features provided. As if this weren't enough to bring you here, know, too, that staff is particularly courteous and helpful, or so we're told

by some Insiders. Senior citizen and other discounts also are offered. Children younger than 18 stay for free. Accommodations include a king-size bed or two double beds.

### Villager Lodge
$$$$ • 1413 Richmond Rd., Williamsburg • (757) 229-3400

Nothing fancy here, just 44 clean, efficient rooms in a highly convenient area, close to shopping, touring, the college, the Historic Area and many family restaurants. Amenities include an outdoor pool for guests to enjoy in warm weather. Pets are welcome but will cost you a $5 fee.

### White Lion Motel
$$$ • 912 Capitol Landing Rd., Williamsburg • (757) 229-3931, (800) 368-1055

Some of the 38 rooms at this motel have kitchenettes. It's a 10-minute walk to the eastern boundary of the Historic Area and about the same in driving time to Busch Gardens and Water Country USA. The outlet shopping and the Williamsburg Pottery Factory west of the city are a 15-minute drive, probably most quickly traveled to by I-64 West. AAA and senior citizen discounts are offered. There is an outdoor pool, children younger than 12 stay for free, and facilities are available for the physically disabled. Pets can be accommodated, but a $25 nonrefundable charge applies.

## Williamsburg Center Hotel
**$$$-$$$$ • 600 Bypass Rd., Williamsburg • (757) 220-2800, (800) 492-2855**

You'll enjoy the indoor heated pool or the game room after your day of traveling or touring, and the Jacuzzi and sauna will relax you for an evening of rest or entertainment. There is a free continental breakfast, and other dining options are a short drive away. The 141-room hotel is a five-minute drive from the Historic Area, Busch Gardens and Water Country USA and 10 minutes from the outlet shopping and the Williamsburg Pottery Factory west of the city. Rooms for the physically disabled are available. Small pets (15 pounds or less) are allowed. Senior citizen and other discounts apply, and children younger than 17 stay for free.

## Williamsburg Courtyard by Marriott
**$$$$$ • 470 McLaws Cir., Busch Corporate Ctr., Williamsburg • (757) 221-0700, (800) 321-2211**

You can enjoy the indoor/outdoor pool here after playing at Busch Gardens or touring the Historic Area, each a short drive away. The restaurant is convenient and good, and a visit to the lounge in the evening is a pleasant way to end your day. Courtyard's 151 rooms are popular for individuals conducting business with Anheuser-Busch or with any of the companies in the growing Busch Corporate Park, which surrounds the facility. If you are visiting for the Michelob Golf Classic, this choice is desirable, particularly for its proximity to Kingsmill and amenities. Rooms for the physically disabled, meeting rooms, nearby dining and shopping and quick access to I-64 are special attractions here. Senior citizen and other discounts are offered, and if your children are younger than 17, they stay for free.

## The Williamsburg Hospitality House
**$$$$$ • 415 Richmond Rd., Williamsburg • (757) 229-4020, (800) 932-9192**

This stately hotel with 295 rooms is directly opposite William and Mary's football stadium and Alumni House, which makes it popular with visiting parents and team fans as well as those visiting the area attractions. Inside, all is quiet elegance and deeply polished woodwork. You'll enjoy efficient attention to your needs. It is a two-block walk to Merchants Square and a 10-minute drive to Busch Gardens and Water Country USA to the east or to the outlets and the Williamsburg Pottery Factory to the west. Rooms accommodating the physically disabled as well as babysitting, a gift shop, golf and tennis privileges and an outdoor swimming pool are offered. Meetings of up to 750 people can be accommodated, and free parking is provided in the attached garage. The restaurant's atmosphere is refined, traditional and comfortable (see Papillon's and Christopher's Tavern in our Restaurants chapter), and the lounge is popular with students and townsfolk alike. Senior citizen and other discounts are offered (based on availability), and children younger than 18 stay for free.

## Williamsburg Marriott
**$$$$$ • 50 Kingsmill Rd., Williamsburg • (757) 220-2500, (800) 228-9290**

If Busch Gardens is your destination, you couldn't get closer. There are many amenities at your disposal. Racquetball, indoor and outdoor swimming, a health club, saunas and a Jacuzzi all cater to your workout needs, and a fine restaurant and lounge with live entertainment are featured here. Tennis privileges, meeting rooms and rooms for the physically disabled are also offered. The hotel has 284 rooms, some of which are suites. There is an excellent restaurant, J.W.'s, which lives up to Marriott's reputation for fine food, and Pitchers is a friendly, entertaining lounge. If you are visiting for the Michelob Golf Classic, this is a very convenient lodging. Children younger than 18 stay for free; senior citizen and other discounts are offered.

## Williamsburg Motor Court
**$$ • 2200 Richmond Rd., Williamsburg**
**• (757) 229-3191**

This 29-room motel is only open seasonally. It is 1.5 miles from the restored area and offers cable TV and a swimming pool. Pets are allowed here.

## Williamsburg Travel Inn
**$$$ • 1800 Richmond Rd.**
**• (757) 229-2781, (800) 362-6046**

Toward the western edge of the city and a short drive to all the area attractions, this lodging offers 77 large rooms with individual balconies or patios, two double beds, a swimming pool and nearby tennis courts. Many dining choices, including the adjacent Denny's, are within walking distance. Rooms are provided for physically disabled individuals and for nonsmokers. Senior citizen and other discounts are offered.

If you lodge with Williamsburg residents, you are continuing a tradition dating back more than 200 years.

# Bed & Breakfasts and Guest Homes

If your preference is for intimacy and you would like an up-close sampling of home life in Williamsburg, our bed and breakfasts and private guest homes give you the opportunity to enjoy the Southern hospitality for which the city is famous.

When the restoration of Colonial Williamsburg began in the 1920s, so did the need to provide quarters for an increasing number of visitors. Those were the days before the automobile enabled tourists to stay well out from the center and commute in; before that newfangled idea, the motel, became ubiquitous. You'll still find a couple of those early motor courts nicely renovated if a nostalgic setting appeals to you.

The response in our community was to do what folks in the 'Burg always have done: Open our doors to visitors and offer them hospitality. You soon will find that in Virginia there is a history to everything, and it's certainly true in this case. If you lodge with Williamsburg residents, you are continuing a tradition dating back more than 200 years, when, during "publick times" twice each year, the legal and governmental business of the colony took place, and the city was as crowded with visitors as you're likely to find it today.

Your hosts will not require you to sleep three or more to a bed and to bring your linen - and your meals - as was customary in Colonial times. Rather, you will find privacy in clean, comfortable and gracious settings where you can make yourself at home. These houses date from the Colonial Revival of the 1920s onward. No private Colonial-era homes in Williamsburg outside the Historic Area offer public accommodations. The City of Williamsburg's Architectural Review Board in 1993 did designate six of the houses as "historically significant" in helping define the city's character and representing architectural styles and cultural periods form the city's past: Applewood, Colonial Capital, Holland's Lodge, Homestay and Williamsburg Manor. The West Williamsburg Heights Architecture Preservation District includes some of the listings, and you may wish to discuss the architectural importance of the area with your hosts. Each of the residences listed below offers charm unique to its hosts and history, with special collections or furnishings for you to enjoy. What could be more "inside" than a short stroll home after a day in the Historic Area?

While many of these homes are on or adjacent to Jamestown and Richmond roads, originating at the west end of Merchants Square, several others are tucked away on quiet, little neighborhood lanes. Some are in the beautiful countryside around the city and in adjoining James City and Charles City counties. With the exception of perhaps two or three, all are within walking distance of the Historic Area. Discuss this with your hosts when you make your reservations.

Most of the homes take their own reservations. But many of the bed and breakfast owners also have joined the Williamsburg Hotel-Motel Association, which offers a toll-free number (800) 446-9244 for bed-and-breakfast reservations. In addition, a few also use Benson House of

Williamsburg in Richmond. This service also makes reservations for other bed and breakfasts in Virginia, including some in Richmond, Petersburg, Bowling Green and the Northern Neck on the Chesapeake Bay. If you are planning to stop at several Virginia locations, you may find them most helpful in matching your requirements with area offerings. Their numbers are (804) 648-7560 and (804) 353-6900.

We hope our descriptions here help you find the right match for your requirements, but you can't go wrong staying in any of the listed residences. Indeed, you may find yourself competing for space with regularly returning guests at the one you choose.

## Price Guidelines

The dollar signs in each entry indicate a range of rates for double occupancy (two persons) per night. Please be aware that, during peak season (generally any time other than January, February and March), rates may vary from those indicated. Also, some establishments offer lower rates for single occupancy, and some may require a minimum two-night reservation on select weekends. Please confirm your rate with your hosts at the time you book your visit.

| $ | Less than $45 |
|---|---|
| $$ | $45 to $60 |
| $$$ | $61 to $75 |
| $$$$ | $76 to $100 |
| $$$$$ | More than $100 |

Most establishments accept Visa and MasterCard. We've noted where this is not the case. If you plan to use another credit card, a personal check or traveler's checks, we suggest you check with the inn when you make your reservation. Handicapped accessibility can be tricky at bed and breakfasts. We recommend you discuss any special needs with your host ahead of time.

## A Primrose Cottage

$$$$-$$$$$ • 706 Richmond Rd. • 229-6421, (800) 522-1901, (888) 800-1705

This home is an attractive choice for European visitors: Owner Inge Curtis welcomes guests with warm hospitality and charm. A cozy, two-storied building, Primrose Cottage has a collection of antique furnishings including original paintings. Queen- and king-size beds, with down comforters, and private baths are available. All rooms have TVs, and an adjacent sitting room has a telephone. A harpsichord is available for those guests who play. Central air conditioning and heating keep the accommodations comfortable.

Inge bakes every morning, and the aroma from her kitchen is the best wake-up call you could want - apple pancakes, bread pudding, souffles, quiche and scones. The house is approximately a 10-minute walk from Merchants Square and features off-street parking and a quiet atmosphere. Primrose Cottage is a nonsmoking home, and pets cannot be accommodated.

## Alice Person House

$$$$ • 616 Richmond Rd. • 220-9263, (800) 370-9428/Access Code 41

Even George Washington couldn't book accommodations such as these in Williamsburg, because 18th-century accommodations simply didn't offer such understated elegance.

Innkeepers Jean and Harry Matthews are as inviting as their charming Colonial-Revival home, which is located within easy walking distance of the College of William and Mary and the city's Historic Area. The Matthewses also have perfect personalities for operating a bed and breakfast establishment - they're gregarious, articulate and knowledgeable about the city and its environs. Add to that their Southern charm and, well, your stay here is destined to be memorable.

Built in 1929, the lovely house is reminiscent of early 20th-century Williamsburg accommodations replete with high ceilings and spacious rooms, furnished with antiques and oriental rugs galore. It is located on one of the city's main streets, once lined with stately old homes and venerable old

*A candle in the window is an old Virginia tradition, and a promise of warm hospitality*

## Welcome to

### Candlewick
BED & BREAKFAST

Canopied Beds ~ Private Baths ~ Candlelight Breakfast
Homemade Baked Goodies ~ Free Bicycles

*800 Jamestown Rd., Williamsburg, Va.*
*800-418-4949*
*www.ontheline.com/cibb*

trees. The house features a formal parlor with fireplace on the first floor, where guests are welcome to sit and read or otherwise spend quiet time. There also are two lovely guestrooms, each with private bath, cable TV and VCR.

The Capitol Room features a queen-size, four-poster bed, while the King Room offers just that: An extra-large, king-size, four-poster bed, as well as an antique chest-on-chest.

The bathrooms feature plush, white towels, while European linens are used on the beds. The result is accommodations with flair that are so inviting you just might miss time otherwise spent touring the old town.

Guests won't go hungry here, either. Enjoy a full breakfast of Southern family recipes that can include biscuits, quiche, crepes and waffles served with Virginia sausage and bacon, seasonal fresh fruits, yogurts, coffees and teas.

Off-street parking is available, but no pets and no smoking, please. Children aged 10 and older are welcome.

### Applewood Colonial
### Bed & Breakfast
**$$$$-$$$$$ • 605 Richmond Rd. • 229-0205, (800) 899-2753**

It doesn't take long to see where the name of this elegant home comes from: The owners' Colonial-era apple print collection in the parlor immediately provides a fascinating conversation starter and point of interest, bringing individual charm to a romantic setting. This theme is carried throughout the house and includes a Tiffany lead crystal apple as well as Nancy Thomas folk art renderings. The house, built by a Colonial Williamsburg craftsman, dates to 1929 and features Flemish bond brickwork, Colonial decor, fireplaces and canopy beds in the four guest rooms, queen-size beds and private baths. One of the suites offers a private, sunny breakfast room and a fireplace surrounded by bookcases. Guests enjoy a full breakfast, offering such treats as spinach pie, ham quiche, blueberry flan, eggs and meat by candlelight at an antique table in Applewood. Children can be accommodated in the summer. This is a nonsmoking house, and air conditioning is further assurance of your enjoyment. Applewood has had guests from all 50 states and 28 foreign countries. On select holiday and college-event weekends, a two- to three-night minimum stay is required.

### INSIDERS' TIP

**When you inquire about a bed and breakfast or guest home, our advice is to ask lots of questions! If you have particular desires regarding decor, air conditioning, type of breakfast, shower or bathtub availability and location, dietary needs, check-in or cancellation policies, provision for children or pets, or even the kind of bedding you will have, just ask. When phoning, you are likely to be speaking to one of the hosts, and the rapport you establish at this time may be an indicator of your satisfaction later.**

## Candlewick Bed and Breakfast
$$$$-$$$$$ • 800 Jamestown Rd. • 253-8693, (800) 418-4949

Mary Peters remodeled this 1946 frame house in the style of her 1840 Pennsylvania farmhouse, and the results are as charming as any in *Country Living*.

Candlewick offers bedrooms with king-, queen- and twin-size canopy beds and private baths, with beamed ceilings and chair rails adding to the decor. A full country breakfast is served from 8:30 to 9:30 AM, with homemade breads and muffins guaranteeing your pleasure, and, when you're not touring, the cozy Common Room welcomes you to read, play board games or simply relax and watch television. The home is across from the College of William and Mary and a short walk from the Historic Area. It offers off-street parking for the convenience of its guests, and the free use of bicycles for those who would like to ride through the Historic Area and environs. Candlewick is strictly a nonsmoking residence. Children older than 12 are welcome, but pets are not.

If you plan to arrive before or after the check-in time (4 to 7 PM), please call in advance. Candlewick requires a two-night reservation on selected holidays and all weekends. Single rates and off-season weeknight discounts during January and February are other attractive features at this charming home.

## The Cedars
$$$$$ • 616 Jamestown Rd. • 229-3591, (800) 296-3591

We are particularly taken with the front garden approach to this house, a pleasure to view from Jamestown Road or the front windows. Canopy or four-poster beds, most in queen or king size, ensure your comfortable rest at The Cedars, which is across from William and Mary and a short walk from Merchants Square. Antiques and 18th-century reproductions throughout the house convey an elegant feeling as well, fitting to the claim as "Williamsburg's oldest and largest guesthouse."

Varied accommodations are provided

at The Cedars. For complete privacy, cottage suites with working fireplaces are offered in a quaint separate Country Cottage. A two-room suite, the William and Mary, is in the main house. The George Washington suite provides a queen-size canopy bed in the bedroom and a day bed in a sitting room as well as a private bath. The William and Mary suite has two rooms joined by a bath and is furnished with a four-poster bed in one and twin beds in the other. The other six sleeping rooms all have private baths.

You are invited to brace yourself for a day of touring with a full breakfast featuring fresh-baked muffins, a hot entree and coffee, tea, juice and fruit. The formal Georgian parlor has a fireplace. The Cedars is a nonsmoking house. You'll find off-street parking in the rear.

## Colonial Capital Bed and Breakfast
$$$$-$$$$$ • 501 Richmond Rd. • 229-0233, (800) 776-0570

Three blocks from the Historic Area and opposite William and Mary's Alumni House and football stadium, Barbara and Phil Craig and their resident golden retriever, Ginny, have opened their three-story Colonial Revival home, built about 1926, to guests. A 1989 renovation left many original fixtures throughout the house. The

# Colonial Gardens
# Bed & Breakfast

*Relax in a quiet woodland setting with luxurious suites and rooms. Screened sunporch, in-room phones, private baths, AAA-3 diamond inn.*

1109 Jamestown Road
Williamsburg, VA
(800) 886- 9715
http:\\www.colonial-gardens.com

*Wil & Scottie Phillips*
*Innkeepers*

zoned central air conditioning is especially welcome in summer. There are antique furnishings and oriental rugs throughout the house, and courtesy phones you may attach to in-room jacks for private use (the number is 229-7430).

You'll find a pleasant setting for conversation, quiet games or VCR watching in the plantation parlor on the main floor, kept cozy by a wood-burning fireplace in winter. In-room phones have been added for the convenience of guests, as well as dedicated fax lines accessible to guests using this technology. During temperate weather, you can enjoy the outdoors on the deck, patio or screened side porch. Smoking areas outdoors and nonsmoking guest bedrooms and bathrooms are offered. In the afternoon, tea and wine are available for your refreshment and relaxation. Bicycles also are provided at no charge, including an old Western Flyer tandem (built for two), regarded by locals as "the friendliest bike in Williamsburg."

Any one of the five large guestrooms (each with private bath) will make you feel right at home. The Chesapeake features a pencil-post queen-sized bed handcrafted by Barbara's father and an unusual corner sink. The James has canopied, four-poster twin beds handcrafted from a single tree by master craftsman Fred Craver. The

third-floor Pamlico has windows on three sides and can be combined with the sitting room across the hall with its half-bath, TV with VCR and sleeping accommodations for two, making the entire floor a private suite. Terry robes are provided here for the private hall bath. The Potomac Room has an en suite bath and a private porch with rocking chairs and features a king-size bed with canopied half-tester. The York is a favored room for honeymoons (package plans available) and anniversaries with its queen-size, turned-post canopied high rope bed and en suite bath with original claw foot tub. All rooms have remote-controlled ceiling fans and "Cozy Canopy" beds that get nightly turndown with a pillow mint.

Breakfast is a decadent affair with French toast, Western omelets, souffles and a variety of casseroles.

Pickup from Newport News/ Williamsburg International Airport and Williamsburg Amtrak and Bus Station is available upon request. Children older than 8 years old are welcome. Single occupancy rates, approximately 20 percent lower, are available.

## Colonial Gardens Bed & Breakfast
$$$$-$$$$$ • 1109 Jamestown Rd. • 220-8087, (800) 886-9715

This home sits on a quiet 2 acres, close to the Historic Area and Merchants Square shopping, that conceal their proximity to the center of Williamsburg. Guests have remarked how well they've slept in the woodland stillness - what better inducement to restful sleep could there be after a day spent visiting the area's attractions?

The gardens are an ongoing project for hosts Scottie and Wilmot Phillips, who are always adding to the work done by previous owners. The North Carolina rhododendron garden is simply stunning in bloom. You will notice right off, however, that the Colonial Gardens name reflects the interior as well as the exterior: An abundance of fresh seasonal flowers fills the house constantly. The Phillips' combination of family heirloom antiques with treasures from 30 years of collecting completes the furnishings beautifully and sets off Wilmot's own selection from his original paintings, largely architectural in subject, which reflect the couple's travels. Noted in galleries and showings in New York, Atlanta and Hilton Head, his works are sought by collectors.

A combination of suites and guestrooms named for blooms in the garden will satisfy every guest. All have private baths. The Rhododendron Suite features a king-size bed, marble-topped Empire dresser and chest and a sitting area in a sunny alcove overlooking the garden for which it is named. The Azalea Suite provides a plantation rice-carved, canopied queen-size bed and a magnificent 19th-century ornate English dresser. Its sitting room holds comfortable chairs for relaxation. If you enjoy antiques, don't miss the early 19th-century painted New England cottage dresser in the Primrose Room.

Breakfast menus change to provide the best start for the day according to season and weather. The sunroom overlooking the landscaping is the favorite for breakfast in warm weather, but in winter months, the warmly decorated formal dining room is the place to start the day. In the afternoon, light refreshments will help you make the

transition into your evening of relaxation. An 1830s hunt board in the foyer displays the city's dinner offerings on its posted menus, but you may wish to ask your hosts for their suggestions to suit your appetite. The living room's game table and piano will provide you with an enjoyable evening's leisure.

Plan on placing a deposit of 50 percent when making your reservation, with the rest due upon arrival. A two-night minimum reservation is required for weekends and holidays. Colonial Gardens accepts children older than 12 but is unable to accept pets. It is a nonsmoking inn.

### Edgewood Plantation

**$$$$$ • 4800 John Tyler Memorial Hwy. (Rt. 5), Charles City Co. • (804) 829-2962, (800) 296-EDGE**

You will enjoy the historic plantation trail (Route 5 west from Williamsburg) that leads through forests past this superb Carpenter Gothic house, built in 1849, located a quarter-mile west of the entrance to Berkeley Plantation. In countryside filled with the formalities of Georgian and Colonial Revival architecture, this is a truly refreshing lodging for you to consider.

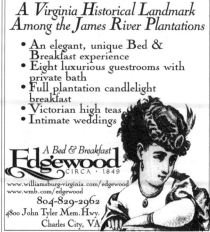

Photo: Colonial Williamsburg Foundation

The original Governor's Palace was destroyed by fire December 22, 1781.

On one bedroom window upstairs, Elizabeth "Lizzie" Rowland wrote her name with a diamond. Legend has it that she died of a broken heart waiting in vain for her lover to return from the Civil War. She reportedly still waits, watching from "Lizzie's Room."

Don't let the Edgewood ghost intimidate you, however. You will find comfort, relaxation and a good night's sleep in any one of the seven bedrooms or Prissy's Quarters, a cabin behind the main house. *Gone With the Wind* lovers will enjoy the third floor, with its sitting common area room, "Scarlett's Room" and "Melanie's Room." If Christmas is your favorite season, you will be amazed at the 17 Christmas trees at Edgewood. There is also a large collection of period clothing decorating the rooms.

Special features include king- and queen-size canopy beds, formal gardens, a swimming pool, a candlelight full breakfast, which varies from day to day. It may include fresh fruit, orange juice, crepes, quiche, croissants filled with fruit and cheese - or sometimes a country breakfast. Special features available upon request include Victorian teas and tours, luncheons and weddings. Smoking is allowed outside and in the kitchen only.

Williamsburg is a pleasant 25-minute drive to the east; Richmond and Petersburg are about the same distance to the west. If you're looking for a place to rest and collect special memories, this is one excellent option.

### Fox & Grape Bed & Breakfast
**$$$$ • 701 Monumental Ave. • 229-6914, (800) 292-3699**

Your hosts Pat, Bob and Virginia offer four guestrooms, each with a private bath. Two of the rooms have queen-size canopy beds. Breakfast can include pancakes, waffles or egg dishes and meats with fresh breads in a charming dining room decorated with handcrafted, regional decoys. You may also choose to enjoy your coffee on the spacious wraparound porch. The cup plate collection, Pat's counted cross-stitchery and Bob's stained-glass, walking sticks and folk art style Noah's arks are especially interesting conversation-openers. A minimum stay of two nights is required on weekends. The house is only five blocks north of the Capitol building in the city's Historic Area. Smoking is prohibited.

### Governor's Trace
**$$$$$ • 303 Capitol Landing Rd. • 229-7552, (800) 303-7552**

This Georgian brick house was built

during the restoration of Colonial Williamsburg and features all the same fine details including Flemish bond brick. This is the earliest of our listings to open specifically as a bed and breakfast rather than a guest home. Conveniently located in town, it is just steps from the eastern end of the Historic Area and is closest to the Capitol building and the taverns. This house occupies more than a half-acre of a former peanut plantation that extended the length of what is now Capitol Landing Road. Nearby, 13 of Blackbeard's pirates were hanged. *The Washington Post* has touted it as Williamsburg's "most romantic" bed and breakfast.

Today's visitors receive a much more cordial welcome than the pirates, however. Hosts Sue and Dick Lake are happy to tailor a touring itinerary to help you make the best use of your time. Shuttered windows, brass candlelight lanterns and a fireplace are featured in one room with a waist-high, four-poster king-size bed. Another room offers a private, screened porch, four-poster Colonial-style canopy bed, gingham, country florals and pastels against a background of family antiques. Private baths adjoin the rooms, which are air-conditioned.

One guestroom is reminiscent of *Gone With the Wind*'s Tara, according to some guests. Honeymooners love this room, which also can be combined with the adjacent room to turn the entire second floor into a suite for two couples traveling together. It offers a queen-size antique-brass bed. The morning light filtering through the plantation shutters brings the ivy-printed fabrics and some of Sue's favorite antique hummingbird prints to life, further enhancing the airy feel of the room. The bathroom, done in brass, features a large glass shower enclosure.

Governor's Trace serves breakfast in the rooms and provides cozy robes so guests need not "dress" for breakfast. A leisurely candlelight breakfast in your room might be just the perfect unusual touch to make your stay memorable. This is a non-smoking accommodation. It offers off-street parking. No pets are allowed.

### Hite's Bed and Breakfast

**$$$$ • no credit cards 704 Monumental Ave. • 229-4814**

We like the attractive Victorian decor of Faye and James Hite's Cape Cod home, just a seven-minute walk from Colonial Williamsburg. All rooms are large and nicely furnished with antiques and interesting collectibles, private baths, cable TV, phones, radios and coffee makers. A suite with a large sitting room is particularly inviting, and the claw-foot bathtub in the beautiful old bathroom will entice you to relax and refresh yourself. Robes, hair dryers and other nice touches ensure your convenience, and you can enjoy the old-fashioned yard swing while admiring the birds, squirrels and the goldfish pond. A beautiful old pump organ and hand-crank Victrola will entertain you in the parlor. A leisurely full breakfast, including stuffed croissants, eggs, juice, coffee, muffins, apple turnovers, sausage and different goodies every day, is served in the privacy of your room or in the dining room as you choose. Children older than 7 are accepted, but pets are not. This is a nonsmoking lodging.

## Holland's Lodge Bed and Breakfast
$$$-$$$$, no credit cards • 601 Richmond Rd. • 253-6476, (800) 253-8253

This home has a place in the area's history of hospitality with its claim as the first of our privately owned tourist homes in the city to offer accommodations to visitors. Members of the same Williamsburg family that greeted guests here in 1929 have seen the restoration of Williamsburg unfold and continue to offer congenial lodging in attractive, comfortable rooms. Margaret and Richard Holland's bed and breakfast is a 10-minute walk from the Historic Area and two blocks from William and Mary.

There are five guestrooms, with private and shared bath arrangements, and each room has individual remote-controlled temperature. Adjoining rooms can be made available, and two rooms with a bath between them can comprise another arrangement. The antiques, reproductions and other collectibles throughout the inn reinforce the Colonial mood of your visit. A full breakfast - bacon, ham or sausage, eggs, sweet baked goods, juice and fruits - is served to help you start the day on a pleasant note. Holland's Lodge has a no-smoking, no-alcohol and no-pet policy. Only children aged 10 and older, please.

## The Homestay Bed and Breakfast
$$$$-$$$$$• 517 Richmond Rd. • 229-7468, (800) 836-7468

Jim and Barbara Thomassen's lovely Colonial Revival home is adjacent to the College of William and Mary and only four blocks from the Historic Area. It is also a short drive away from Jamestown and Yorktown via the Colonial Parkway.

Three quiet guestrooms are available. The Victorian Room features an 1890 burled walnut Eastlake period double bed and washstand believed to have been made in or around Fredericksburg. The Country Room is decorated in an American country motif and can be configured either with a king-size bed or twin beds. The Garden Room is named for the wall mural painted as an English garden scene. The garden gate headboard of the king-size bed appears to lead you into this enticing scene. All rooms have private baths, and the Garden Room's bath features a skylight.

The entrance hall and formal dining room also contain walnut Eastlake period pieces. A full breakfast is served each morning that includes seasonal fresh fruit and a variety of home-baked breads and muffins. These are often served with herb spreads and jellies made from herbs grown in the hosts' garden. The hosts have a budding Pepsi memorabilia collection includ-

## INSIDERS' TIP

It's also important to ascertain if a residence is a comfortable walk to - and from - the Historic Area of Colonial Williamsburg. You did bring your walking shoes, didn't you? This detail may be particularly crucial since parking is sometimes difficult to find close to the Historic Area. It is also wise to ask if off-street parking is provided, if a deposit is required in advance and what manner of payment your hosts expect.

ing bottles from such far-off places as Russia, Spain and Morocco. You will also find their Noah's Ark collection a good conversation opener, since there is at least one in each room of the house.

Children 10 and older are welcome. The Homestay is a nonsmoking property, and pets are not accommodated. A minimum stay of two nights on weekends and special event dates is normally required.

## Indian Springs Bed and Breakfast

**$$$$-$$$$$ • 330 Indian Springs Rd. • 220-0726, (800) 262-9165**

Open since April 1992, this attractive home is just three blocks from Colonial Williamsburg in a quiet neighborhood setting. Kelly and Paul Supplee, your hosts, offer their hospitality to all ages. A special attraction is the Carriage House, which is a bi-level loft suite with a fireplace.

Accommodations are decorated in elegant yet inviting English-Country, American-Country and Queen Anne styles. There are private baths in all suites and private entrances overlooking a beautifully wooded ravine; the veranda facing this direction is a bird-watchers' haven. King feather beds and private sitting rooms in the suites, ceiling fans, dressing areas, built-in coolers and televisions are among the amenities, which also include individually controlled heat and air-conditioning.

Your morning meal is a two-course, full breakfast featuring a variety of fresh fruits, a cereal bar, freshly ground coffee and just-baked muffins. Depending upon your breakfast mood, you may have your choice of the formal dining room or the veranda and its woodland view. Your baggage may be held here before or after check-in and check-out times for your peace of mind while touring. Smoking is not permitted.

 **Alice Person House**

Enjoy luxury unknown to 18th century Williamsburg. Treat yourself to fine antiques, oriental rugs, and unique linens. As Virginia natives we learned Southern Hospitality first hand. Historical areas and the College of William & Mary are a short walk. We are here to serve you.

(757) 220-9263
(800) 370-9428 code 41
fax (757) 565-0693
616 Richmond Rd - Williamsburg VA 23185
www.alicepersonhouse

## Legacy of Williamsburg Bed and Breakfast Inn

**$$$$-$$$$$ • 930 Jamestown Rd. • 220-0524, (800) 962-4722**

This fine establishment was voted the best bed and breakfast in all the United States and Canada for 1997 by *Bed and Breakfasts, Inns and Guest Houses in the United States and Worldwide*. And it's no wonder. Located within a 10-minute walk of Merchants Square, it has re-created the feel of a Colonial tavern with random pine flooring, clapboard exterior and six fireplaces throughout, several in the guest accommodations. Beautiful oriental rugs add elegant color throughout. Each of the rooms offers a curtained canopy bed, private bath and cozy bathrobes, and each is named after a Colonial home.

Guests will enjoy the period antiques throughout the house and the pastimes offered as extras. An English billiard table and a dartboard invite friendly challenges,

## INSIDERS' TIP

**Keep in mind that, while bed and breakfasts generally offer your own key and access, a parlor or common room, breakfast area and telephone dedicated to guest use, guest homes generally provide only clean sleeping accommodations.**

and a candlelit Game Room transports you to the 18th century for games of the era or a nightcap by a warm fire. The Library offers books on American history, Colonial Williamsburg and 18th-century antiques for reading by the fire. The deck offers a quiet, wooded setting away from the hustle and bustle. Breakfast is served by the fireside in the Keeping Room or in the screened gazebo at treetop level. The host, a former restaurant owner, prides herself on her delicious breakfast specialties, such as Belgian waffles, amaretto French toast, gourmet omelets, quiche and muffins with pecans and apricots. The Legacy is a non-smoking bed and breakfast and accepts neither guests younger than 18 nor pets.

### Liberty Rose Bed and Breakfast
$$$$$ • 1022 Jamestown Rd. • 253-1260, (800) 545-1825

We're struck by the romantic interior design offered at the Liberty Rose, and if you are planning a honeymoon in Williamsburg, you might give this home special consideration. Since 1986, Sandra and Brad Hirz have completely renovated this 1920s house made from Jamestown brick and white clapboard. The house, on a hillside covered with beautiful old trees, is a mile from the Historic Area. Most recently the Hirzes have given additional charm to their backyard with new gardens, courtyards and old-fashioned "swings from the old oak trees."

The Hirzes' efforts have achieved high recognition: Liberty Rose is one of two Virginia bed and breakfast inns placed in the top-25 out of 13,000 inns in the country by *American Historic Inns*.

Inside you'll find English, Victorian, French Country and Colonial antiques - a mix of abundant conversation pieces and interesting knickknacks of all kinds. The rich fabrics and wallpapers contribute to the romantic mood. A grand piano and fireplace in the salon and gratis soft drinks at any time on the glassed-in breakfast porch are particularly inviting. Each guest room has its own name, and Rose Victoria, Magnolias Peach, Savannah Lace, Suite Williamsburg and Blossom - the last available for extra persons only - are accurate indicators of their charm. All rooms offer telephones, television, VCR, movies, lush bathrobes, bubble bath, a silk rose for the lady, a bowl of chocolates, alarm clocks and gold miniature flashlights. The ameni-

Photo: Colonial Williamsburg Foundation

Southern Hospitality is alive and well at area bed and breakfasts and guest homes.

ties seem never to end: Mention the famous chocolate chips, and you will find them outside your door for an evening's snack.

Suite Williamsburg offers a queen four-poster bed draped with vintage reproduction silks and velvets, a working fireplace, a sitting area, six windows and French doors into the lavish private bath.

If decorating is a hobby for you, consult your hosts as they are fountains of advice: They did all of the professional-quality sewing, papering, sawing, hanging, refinishing and final-touching that make this such a charming setting. One more thing: Be sure to ask each of the hosts about the home's name . . . then compare stories!

Breakfast here is not to be missed. It includes such delicacies as stuffed French toast with marmalade and cream cheese, fruit, juices and everything from apple-cinnamon pecan pancakes to eggs, toast and the like.

Liberty Rose cannot accept pets. It also is a nonsmoking lodging.

## Newport House
**$$$$$, no credit cards • 710 S. Henry St. • 229-1775**

If you came to immerse yourself in a Colonial atmosphere, this might be your choice. A five-minute walk from the Historic Area, the building is a reproduction from a 1756 design by Colonial architect Peter Harrison, whose buildings spanned the British empire from America to India and who was the architect of the Williamsburg Statehouse rebuilding in 1749. The building is furnished entirely with English and American period antiques and reproductions (even guests' blankets are historically authentic), and most of these furnishings are available for sale - to guests only.

Each bedroom has a private bathroom and contains two four-poster canopy beds (an extra-long queen and a single). Each is air-conditioned. A full breakfast in the morning usually includes dishes from authentic Colonial recipes and an interesting historical lecture by your host, John Fitzhugh Millar. He is a former museum director and captain of a historic full-rigged ship, as well as author and publisher of many books of history. Your hostess, Cathy Millar, is a registered nurse whose hobbies include gardening, beekeeping, needlework and making reproduction 18th-century clothing.

On Tuesdays at 8 PM you may participate in Colonial country dancing in the ballroom of the house. On some Thursdays Scottish country dancing is offered at the same hour. Beginners are welcome to join in or watch during both occasions. A harpsichord is available for guests' enjoyment, and with a few days' advance notice guests may rent Colonial clothing either for their entire stay or for dinner at one of the Colonial taverns. Newport House accepts no pets and is a nonsmoking house. With advance notice, it may be possible for your hosts to pick you up at Williamsburg's train/bus station or at the Newport News-Williamsburg International Airport.

Breakfast is based on 18th-century recipes and includes Rhode Island Johnny Cakes, a 1650s bread, scuppernong jelly, baked goodies and more.

Although credit cards cannot be used for payment, they can be used to hold a reservation.

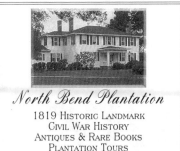

*North Bend Plantation*

1819 HISTORIC LANDMARK
CIVIL WAR HISTORY
ANTIQUES & RARE BOOKS
PLANTATION TOURS
FULL BREAKFASTS

*Located in James River Plantation country*
12220 WEYANOKE ROAD
CHARLES CITY, VA 23030

(804) 829-5176 • (800) 841-1479

## North Bend Plantation
**$$$$$ • 12200 Weyanoke Rd., Charles City Co. • (804) 829-5176**

One of the truly old bed and breakfast

structures in the area (built c. 1819 and enlarged in 1853), North Bend Plantation is on the National Register of Historic Landmarks and also is designated a Virginia Historic Landmark. Your hosts here are Ridgely and George Copland, the fifth generation of the family to own the home, which was built for Sarah Harrison, George's great, great aunt and sister of Benjamin Harrison, the ninth President of the United States.

The main house's Greek Revival design will meet your expectations of a plantation house and educate you concerning the changes in architecture on antebellum plantations. It is situated on 850 acres just east of Charles City Court House and 1 mile off Route 5 on Weyanoke Road, about a 25-minute drive west of Williamsburg in James River plantation country.

The Civil War (in these environs, you might better refer to it as The War Between the States) has close associations with this residence. In 1864, Union Gen. Phil Sheridan headquartered at North Bend, as you will see upon examining the plantation desk he used at that time. Union breastworks from the war still exist intact on the grounds. This is not Yankee territory, however: A direct ancestor of the owner fired the first shot at Fort Sumter in April 1861, the initial engagement of the conflict.

Possessions still treasured and displayed by the family are worth your interest: A fine collection of old and rare books, Colonial antiques from related early James River plantation families, and an antique doll collection are special features. Gentlemen no longer enjoy brandy and cigars after dinner here. As in many guest homes, smoking is limited to designated areas. In recompense, a fine swimming pool, a billiard room, croquet, horseshoes, volleyball and a full country breakfast - for once you may take this literally - more than make up for that restriction. Breakfast fills your plate with fresh fruit, juices, waffles, omelets, bacon, sausage and biscuits.

Accommodations include varying combinations of bed sizes and styles, and all rooms feature private baths. The Magnolia Room features a canopied queen-size rice bed and a shower. The Sheridan Room features a high queen tester bed (c. 1810-1840) that belonged to Edmund Ruffin, George Copland's great, great grandfather. The headboard was shot out in the Civil War. Gen. Sheridan's desk and a sitting area are in the room. The Federal Room features an iron and brass queen-size bed. The Rose Room has a queen-size canopy

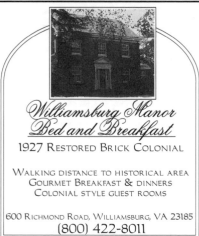

*Williamsburg Manor*
*Bed and Breakfast*

1927 Restored Brick Colonial

Walking distance to historical area
Gourmet Breakfast & dinners
Colonial style guest rooms

600 Richmond Road, Williamsburg, VA 23185
(800) 422-8011

acre Southall Plantation and today it is the oldest and best-preserved example of log architecture in Tidewater Virginia. The builder, Furnea Southhall, was the Sheriff of Charles City during the late 18th century. Edmund Archer Saunders, an extremely successful Richmond entrepreneur, owned Piney Grove until 1873 when it was sold to Confederate veteran Thomas Fletcher Harwood. Also on the property is Ladysmith, a modest Greek Revival plantation house built in 1857. Both houses have been meticulously restored to their original appearances and include every modern convenience for guests.

The four spacious guest rooms - each with a private bath, working fireplace, small refrigerator and coffee maker - are tastefully appointed with family heirlooms as well as antiques and artifacts that chronicle three centuries of habitation on the property. The rooms include one suite with a double bed in one room and a single twin in another, a second room containing a double bed and a twin bed and two other rooms with standard double beds.

Guests may enjoy the parlor library with its books of Virginia history; walks on the nature trail along Rippon's Run are also inviting, as are the gardens and pool. Mint juleps, hot toddies, Virginia vintages, Virginia sparkling cider and nightcaps of Virginia apple brandy await you no matter what the season. The weather does determine, however, whether guests' breakfasts will be serenaded by residents of the aviary or warmed by a roaring fire.

Piney Grove cannot accept pets. It is also a nonsmoking home. Children are welcome, however, and there are no age restrictions. Young guests will particularly enjoy the barnyard full of farm animals.

bed, a fireplace and a sitting area. The Maids Quarters connects to the Magnolia room and has a double bed. An upstairs sun porch (one of three) is available for guests' enjoyment.

Choice examples of Southern cooking in pleasant historic settings are available nearby at Indian Fields Tavern and at Berkeley Plantation's Coach House Tavern (see our Restaurants chapter); reservations for either can be made for you at North Bend, as guests will receive complimentary dessert at these restaurants. Children 6 and older are welcome, but pets are not. A two-night stay on holiday weekends is required. North Bend is available for weddings and receptions.

### Piney Grove at Southall's Plantation

**$$$$$, no credit cards • 16920 Southall Plantation Ln., Charles City Co. • (804) 829-2480**

A 12-mile drive west of Williamsburg on Route 5 and an additional 8 miles north of Route 5 on routes 623 and 615 is Southall's Plantation and Piney Grove. The Gordineers welcome discriminating travelers to their home, which is a Virginia Historic Landmark and is listed on the *National Register of Historic Places*.

The property was first occupied by the Chickahominy Indians. Piney Grove was built around 1800 on the prosperous 300-

### War Hill Inn

**$$$-$$$$$ • 4560 Longhill Rd. • 565-0248, (800) 743-0248**

Set on a bucolic working farm, this house was built in 1968 for hosts Shirley and Bill Lee under the guidance of a Colonial Williamsburg architect. The living room's paneling is made from trees cut on the property. Many other features are from old buildings from as far away as Pennsylvania Dutch country. Crickets, frogs, owls and Angus cattle are the closest neighbors, and it is easy, upon awakening, to imagine yourself having traveled 200 years back to a peaceful setting in the Colonial period. Among War Hill's attractions is a reproduction Colonial cottage available to guests, the Washington Cottage. It offers a canopy bed for a comfortable rest, a private bath and a whirlpool tub for your relaxation and enjoyment. Four other rooms all have private baths, antique furnishings and television. Inquire whether the accommodation you are considering has queen, double or single beds, as all are offered. Children are welcome here, and your entire party may enjoy "retiring to the country" after a day of touring. Smoking is not allowed in the house.

This accommodation is a bit (4 miles) out of the mainstream of Williamsburg life, in James City County, but don't let that daunt you. It's worth investigating.

### The White House on Washington Street
$$$-$$$$ • 111 Washington St. • 229-4495

In their home on a quiet street five minutes from the eastern end of the restored area, Stephen and Maria White offer two accommodations for visitors' enjoyment. The house is decorated in Southern eclectic, a nice alternative to the more formal 18th-century tradition, and this charming home features folk-art decor. The downstairs master suite has a queen bed, color TV with VCR, a small refrigerator, private bath and private entrance. Upstairs is a bedroom with a double bed and a bath shared with the owners. The sunroom breakfast is a brunch-style meal featuring Virginia specialties: Smithfield ham, Surry sausage and, in season, local seafood. Floral and herbal baths are available, and a smoking area is provided for guests' enjoyment, as is a fireplace in the living room. Breakfast in bed and picnic baskets can be ordered with advance notice. Children are welcome here, but pets cannot be accommodated.

### Williamsburg Manor Bed and Breakfast
$$$$-$$$$$ • 600 Richmond Rd. • 220-8011, (800) 422-8011

A five-minute walk from Merchants Square and steps away from the College of William and Mary is this lovely 1929 Georgian brick Colonial Revival manor house. Innkeeper Laura Reeves opened it to guests in 1992 and offers a wealth of experience and expertise to assure a wonderful stay.

Previously Director of Catering at Ford's Colony Country Club, Laura has decorated the house tastefully with fine antiques, reproductions and collectibles throughout, and the mood is gracious and warm, reflecting the traditions of Southern hospitality maintained by the hostess. She still operates the Catering Company of Williamsburg.

Five comfortable bedrooms - all with private baths, television and central air conditioning - are offered to guests. Four rooms offer queen-size four-poster beds, and one offers two twin beds. It will be difficult to remain in bed in the morning no matter how comfortable you are, knowing that your hostess will be serving you a culinary masterpiece for breakfast. She provides a lavish presentation of regional foods prepared to perfection, such as pear cobbler, individual quiches with shiitakes and oven-roasted tomatoes and asparagus, and

stone ground grits with chicken stock and heavy cream. In addition, Williamsburg Manor is the only bed and breakfast in Williamsburg that offers dinner. The multicourse, prix-fixe ($45 per person) menu changes nightly and features contemporary regional cuisine. Before or after dinner you will enjoy the lovely perennial and herb garden in the backyard.

Williamsburg Manor is available to cater weddings, private parties, anniversaries and other special occasions. It is a nonsmoking house where children are welcome and physically disabled individuals can be accommodated. Off-street parking is available to guests.

## Williamsburg Sampler Bed and Breakfast

**$$$$-$$$$$ • 922 Jamestown Rd. • 253-0398, (800) 722-1169**

Just steps across the street from the College of William and Mary and within a 10-minute walk of Merchants Square, this stately brick home in the style of an 18th-century plantation manor house is decorated throughout with antiques, books, a magnificent pewter collection, other Americana and - how did you guess? - a host of wonderful samplers that innkeepers Helen and Ike Sisane have collected and display for your enjoyment.

Excellence is a hallmark of the Sampler, and it has been widely recognized. In 1995 George Allen, the former governor of Virginia, officially recognized Williamsburg Sampler as the Inn of the Year in the Commonwealth of Virginia and said, "I call its significance to the attention of all our citizens." He also commented on their high recognition that year among travel organizations and magazines, saying, "You do Virginia proud!"

In 1995, Williamsburg Sampler was one of only two inns in Virginia to be rated in the top-25 of 13,000 inns by *American Historic Inns*. The home, once featured on CBS' T.V. show *This Morning*, boasts a wealth of authentic Colonial details, a lovely keeping room, a rich dining area, graceful wooden staircases, pegged hardwood planked floors and a reception foyer. A

welcome non-colonial touch, however, is central air conditioning.

The guestrooms offer a variety of accommodations, including two bedrooms or suites with fireplaces. Both king- and queen-size, rice-carved four-poster beds are available, and Thomasville furnishings, private bath and a comfortable sitting area with wing chairs or daybed are features of every guestroom. Television (tastefully concealed in the furnishings) is offered in each room, but for more convivial viewing, guests are invited to watch the set in the downstairs keeping room.

Breakfast at the Williamsburg Sampler has been rightfully dubbed the "Skip Lunch" breakfast. Fine china and pewter grace the large room where the hearty fireside meal - including fresh coffee and muffins and, frequently, "the best waffles in the USA" (a German guest's comment) - is sure to please. Be sure to ask Ike about the book he has in the works! Beautiful grounds at the rear invite a morning stroll or afternoon relaxation overlooked by a replica of Colonial Williamsburg's 18th-century Coke-Garrett Carriage House. Off-street parking is provided at this nonsmoking house. Children 13 and older are welcome. No pets, please.

Although credit cards cannot be used as payment, they can be used to hold a reservation.

## York River Inn Bed & Breakfast

$$$$$ • 209 Ambler St., Yorktown • 887-8800, (800) 884-7003

Discriminating visitors will enjoy the Colonial ambiance of the only Williamsburg-area bed and breakfast with a waterfront location. This charming lodge overlooks the York River and Coleman Bridge. The philosophy of innkeeper William W. Cole is that the inn "is more of a home with frequent guests than a small hotel," and he carries out that philosophy in every detail, from the warm greeting you receive to the elaborate breakfast. The inn provides cable television in each room, fresh flowers, plush bathrobes, fax services and other amenities for guests' enjoyment and comfort. Your host's experience in the museum field, including 19 years with Colonial Williamsburg and four as director of the Waterman's Museum, and his detailed knowledge of the area will help you spend your time here wisely and enjoyably.

The first floor public area has a panoramic view of the York River and Coleman Bridge, augmented by the deck at this level, which opens the view considerably. Virginia antiques from the innkeeper's family and his own collection of Virginia furnishings are features of the dining and living areas on this level. Time spent examining the maps of Virginia and particularly of Yorktown will give you a sense of the nationally important 17th- and 18th-century historical events that have marked the area.

Upstairs are three accommodations. The Presidents' Room on the second floor features an open deck overlooking the river. The queen-size bed and two comfortable lounge chairs are accented by the display of items associated with seven Virginia-born presidents. Facing the land on this floor, the Pocahontas Room also offers a queen-sized bed and other amenities. The items in this room, as might be expected, relate to Virginia's famous Native American princess. On the third floor, the Washington Room is the inn's largest. A Victorian bedroom suite, from the innkeeper's family, has a double bed and an elaborate marble-topped dresser. There are two seating areas, one overlooking the York River. The Jacuzzi is a special treat after a day of touring the area. You will find Yorktown's victorious general well honored in the decor of his namesake room.

This establishment claims to serve the largest and best breakfast of all the area bed and breakfasts. Goodies can include a clam casserole, three-cheese quiche, fresh honey-dew-pineapple-kiwi salad and pecan waffles with blueberry sauce.

A deposit of half the total is required when you reserve your room, the remainder due a week before your visit. This is a nonsmoking inn, and neither pets nor children can be accommodated.

To reach the inn from Route 17, turn onto Route 1001 (Mathews Street) and then immediately right onto Ambler Street. Proceed one block to the inn, which will be directly ahead of you.

# Private Guest Homes

Most of our guest homes do not accept credit cards but do take personal checks or cash. We have noted the exceptions in their entries.

## Bryant Guest Home

$-$$ • 702 College Terr. • 229-3320

This restored older guest home offers four rooms with private bath, private entrance and television. You'll find the rooms clean and well maintained, with either double or twin beds, and the hospitality inviting. Its location on College Terrace makes it extremely convenient to the college and Historic Area.

## Carter's Guest Home

$ • 903 Lafayette St. • 229-1117

This guest home, convenient to the Historic Area and to shopping, offers two rooms to guests; these rooms share a bath. One room has two twin beds, the other two double beds. Lafayette Street runs parallel and a block north of Richmond Road, and you have easy walking access from this residence to the Historic Area and to the bus and train connections to the city.

Cleanliness and friendly attention are the order of the day here.

## Drucilla King Guest Home
$ • 307 Cary St. • 229-7551

You will find three nice, clean rooms with a refrigerator, a private bath and private entrance. The beds are either double size or twins. Off-street parking is available here. The hospitality is inviting, and the location convenient: It is five blocks from the Historic Area and close to shopping. This is a nonsmoking guest home.

## The Elms
$ • 708 Richmond Rd. • 229-1551

One mile from the Historic Area you will find the gracious two-story Dutch Colonial home of Mr. and Mrs. E.J. Stinnett. You may choose double or twin beds in the four guestrooms - the twin room has a private bath, the others are semiprivate and all rooms are air-conditioned and have ceiling fans. It is a brief walk to Merchants Square.

## Forest Hill Guest Home
$ • 15 Forest Hill Dr. • 229-1444

Mr. and Mrs. Cliff Gauthier offer a first-floor, single room with king-size bed, cable TV, microwave and refrigerator, table for two, private bath and private entrance in a quiet, secluded wooded setting within walking distance of Colonial Williamsburg. Children cannot be accommodated.

## For Cant Hill
$$$$ • 4 Canterbury Ln. • 229-6623

Two guestrooms are available in the charming Colonial Revival home of Martha and Hugh Easler. In one room you will find a comfortable mahogany four-poster bed, and you'll enjoy the private bath, television and air conditioning. A second room provides the same amenities with twin beds. Guests can enjoy lovely Lake Matoaka from the house, which is a 15-minute walk to the Historic Area. As a courtesy to guests, Mrs. Easler will make dinner reservations of your choice. A large continental breakfast is provided.

## Goswick-Whittaker Guest Home
$ • 102 Thomas Nelson Ln. • 229-3920

Two miles from Colonial Williamsburg in the Skipwith Farms neighborhood, this ranch home offers two rooms with double beds, semiprivate bath and television for guests to enjoy, as well as central air conditioning. The home accepts children and is convenient for those visiting the Richmond Road outlets and the Historic Area.

## Holland's Sleepy Lodge
$ • 211 Harrison Ave. • 229-6321

Mrs. Holland's Dutch Colonial home has two guest rooms and a choice of queen or twin beds, as well as private bath. The name of the establishment is appropriate: You'll enjoy a good night's sleep in quiet, clean accommodations.

## Hughes Guest Home
$$ • 106 Newport Ave. • 229-3493

Across Newport Avenue from the Williamsburg Lodge, Mrs. Stuart Hughes offers three rooms for you to enjoy in her large, two-story home decorated with family antiques. One double-bed room features a private bath, and a suite with one double and two twin beds has a shared bath. It is a two-minute walk to the restored area.

## Johnson's Guest Home
$ • 101 Thomas Nelson Ln.          229-3909

Your hosts, Mr. and Mrs. Wallace Johnson, have opened their home to guests for more than a decade. Canopy beds grace two of their three guestrooms and twin beds are in the third. Private and semiprivate bath arrangements are offered, along with televisions. Combinations of rooms upstairs can be arranged for families or other groups.

## Lewis Guest Home
$ • 809 Lafayette St. • 229-6116

Mrs. Ruby C. Lewis' home offers two clean rooms to guests, each with a private bath and a double and single bed in each room. Window air conditioners are provided for guests' comfort. The location is convenient to the college, the Historic Area, the shopping centers on Richmond Road and rail and bus transportation. You'll find Mrs. Lewis' hospitality inviting and her dog, Brandy, a true host.

## Spiggle Guest Home
$$-$$$ • 720 College Terr. • 253-0202

Antiques grace this charming, centrally air-conditioned home, where four bedrooms are open to guests, each with a refrigerator, a television and a coffee maker. Queen, double and twin beds are available. Your hosts, Phil and Dottie Spiggle, offer more than 16 years' experience in accommodating visitors to the city. Their home is a 10-minute walk from Merchants Square and is in a lovely old shade-covered neighborhood at the edge of the college. On certain weekends higher rates may apply.

## Thompson Guest House
$ • 1007 Lafayette St. • 229-3455

Off-street parking and private baths are available for guests to use here. There are three rooms for guests, offering double or twin beds, and the location is convenient to shopping and the Historic Area.

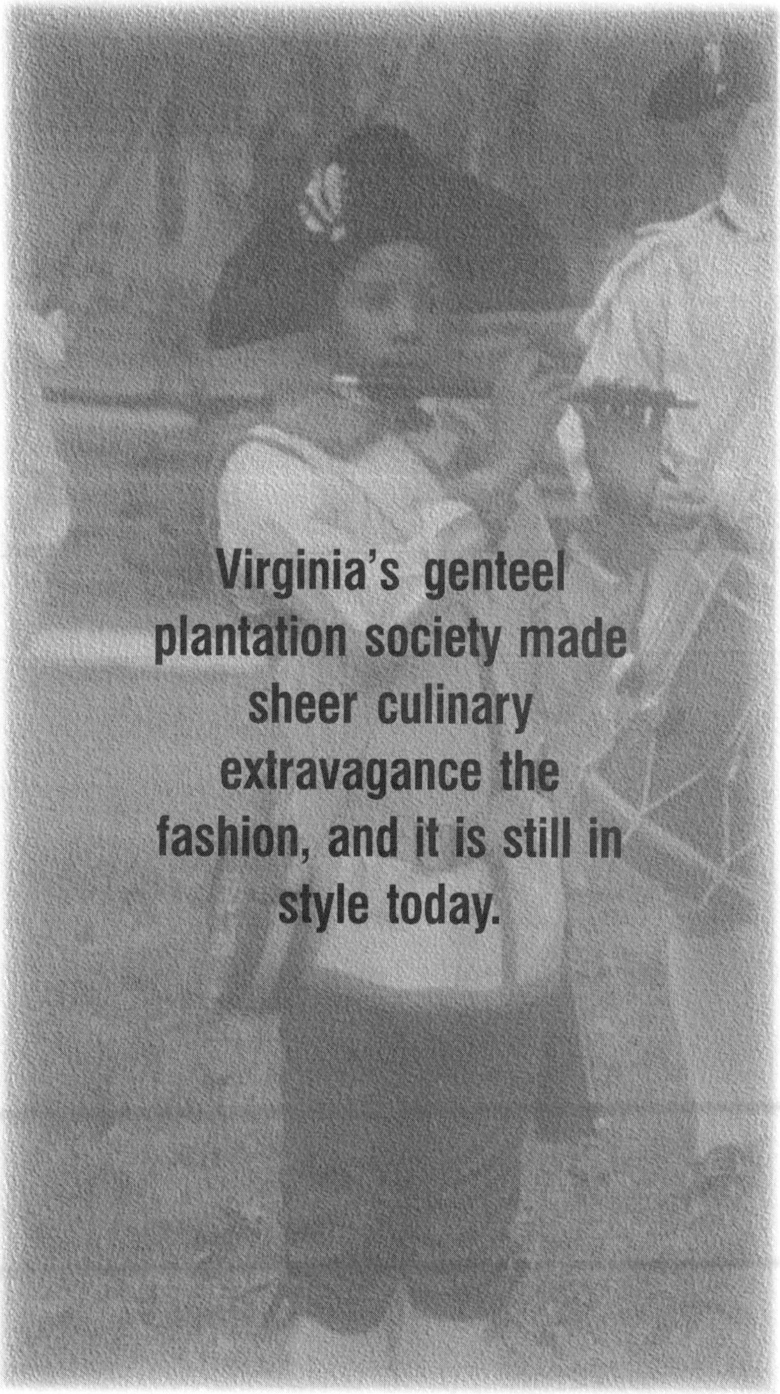

Virginia's genteel
plantation society made
sheer culinary
extravagance the
fashion, and it is still in
style today.

# Regional Cuisine and Wines

When you pull your chair up to a table in a Williamsburg eatery, bring a hearty appetite. Suffice it to say, this is the South. Where else could you delight in chicken, skillet fried to a golden brown, crab cakes chock-full of the sweetest backfin meat, freshly shelled black-eyed peas and butter beans accompanied by warm-from-the-oven corn bread? And don't forget the side dishes. Meals in Williamsburg often are served with melt-in-your-mouth buttermilk biscuits blanketing paper-thin slices of Virginia ham and big bowls of hearty Brunswick stew.

Since this is southern Virginia, more than likely you'll wash it all down with a gallon of sweetened iced tea, but if you have more "spirited" taste buds or just want to celebrate, order a bottle of Virginia wine. At last count, the Old Dominion had 49 wineries, including one in Williamsburg and another a couple hours' drive away. We profile both later is this chapter.

The Williamsburg area won't disappoint when it's time for dessert. For a true taste of the South, try a wedge of sweet potato or pecan pie. But if you're a certified chocoholic - and who isn't - stop off at Williamsburg's celebrated Trellis Restaurant, where the dessert menu includes sinful creations with names such as Chocolate Temptation, White Chocolate Balloon and Death by Chocolate.

## The Food

Williamsburg residents are born with an inherited cooking spoon in their mouths. After all, Virginia's tradition of hospitality began here in the Historic Triangle where early settlers cheerfully shared their victuals with neighbors and strangers alike. Once the more genteel plantation society was well established, sheer culinary extravagance became the standard. Of course, it was pretty easy finding good things to eat. Fish crowded Virginia's waterways, wild game roamed the forests, English vegetables and fruits flourished in the moderate climate, and pigs and other farm animals made themselves right at home here.

Settlers learned about a small miracle called corn from the Native Americans. Ground, it turned into a meal for bread; crushed, it gave them hominy, used to make grits. Distilled? Well, corn whiskey, ancestor to bourbon, was the happy result. The uses of corn were seemingly endless. Thirsty settlers even contrived to brew beer from green cornstalks. But mostly they made corn bread, hoecakes, ashcakes and pone, staples in the diet of poor and planter alike. The hominy they combined with Virginia-cured bacon.

In Colonial times, kitchens occupied separate buildings so the heat and smells of cooking wouldn't invade the house. Food preparation - slaughtering, plucking, skinning, skewering - was hard labor and largely the burden of slaves. Baking took place on the wide hearths of chimneys lined with hooks holding heavy iron cooking pots. Spits for roasting joints stood by the fire. While early fare was plain and plentiful, by the 18th century the colony was prosperous enough to support its share of feasts. Bounteous Williamsburg landladies and plantation housewives provided guests with "groaning boards": Early settlers' dining tables were literally boards set on trestles that "groaned" under the weight of the food that was heaped upon them.

Meals were lavish, dishes sometimes exotic, or so they seem to us today. Stuffed cockscombs, ragout of hogs feet and ears, and fricassee of rabbit are some of the recipes recorded in period cookbooks. Favorite foods of colonists included Virginia ham, roasts of all varieties, venison, meat pies, stews, oysters, crabmeat, jellies, tarts, fruits and cheeses.

Good food and pleasurable dining are as easy to come by in the Historic Triangle today. Browse through our Restaurants chapter for more suggestions on the best places to find the regional fare we describe, as well as your own favorite dishes. With all the fine food the region has to offer, we feel there are only two words left to say on the subject: Bon appetit!

# In a Stew

A number of regional specialties that evolved from the early bounty of Virginia's fields and rivers are proudly prepared and heartily consumed in the Historic Triangle today. Local restaurants serve Brunswick stew by the gallon. While the original version of this savory dish called for a couple of freshly shot squirrels and rabbits, contemporary recipes are a tad tamer. The meat you find in today's dishes typically is

chicken, with a little beef or ham tossed in for good measure. Onions, celery, corn, okra (if it's available), lots of tomatoes, potatoes, butter beans and generally whatever else is ripe in the garden are added, as are vinegar, sugar, salt and pepper, even ketchup. And to get it just right, this thick concoction must be simmered all day in a big iron pot. Don't even think of pushing those microwave buttons! By the way, you may have heard some apocryphal tales about the true origins of Brunswick stew. Brunswick County, North Carolina, claims it, along with several other East Coast Brunswicks. But we believe Virginia lore, which says intrepid hunters in the early 1700s created the dish in the Old Dominion's Brunswick County, relying on resourcefulness and whatever happened to cross their paths out in the wilds. In other words, squirrels and rabbits were all the game they bagged that day.

Frequently, you can find Brunswick stew on sale at any number of outdoor festivals or church bazaars. But to assure yourself of getting a stew of the highest quality, check out the Old Chickahominy House at 1211 Jamestown Road, 229-4689.

As we noted before, you'll probably see this regional specialty paired with another local delectable - ham biscuits. (An Insider who knows Southern cooking swears that the biscuits at the Old Chickahominy House are the best in the area.)

# Hamming It Up

We must note here that Virginia's most famous meat is ham, and you'd be missing something if you left town without sampling this treat. Its popularity dates back to Colonial times when hog and hominy were an essential part of the early settlers' diets. Ham was easy to preserve - an important quality in a time before refrigeration was invented. After slaughter, pig meat was smoked, dried, sugar-cured, even pickled. Virginia ham became so well known that it was soon being exported to the north and even abroad.

Before we go any further, let's clear up

the great Virginia/Smithfield/Williamsburg/ country ham confusion. On local menus you may see entrees prepared with Virginia ham, Smithfield ham, Williamsburg ham or sometimes simply country ham. While all of these pork products are similar in that they are salt-cured, there are some important differences among them. The one basic difference between Virginia hams and other cured hams is that Virginia hams are dry salt-cured before smoking. Technically, only hams cured in Smithfield, a small town across the James River and a little ways east from Williamsburg, can be called Smithfield hams. These hams, left in the skin and aged for up to a year, have a stronger, smokier taste than younger Virginia hams, sometimes known as Williamsburg or country hams. Smithfield hams are coated with pepper during the curing process, which enhances the hams' flavor. You may see these hams hanging in burlap sacks in local stores. They require overnight soaking before cooking, but don't make the mistake one Pennsylvania woman did upon her first encounter with a Smithfield ham. After years of preparing only the sugar-cured variety, she received a Smithfield ham from a generous son-in-law and proceeded to boil it hour after hour "to tone down the salty taste." The result: a stringy, inedible addition to the trash pile and a very dismayed son-in-law.

Once your Smithfield ham is prepared correctly (A knowledgeable Insider recommends soaking it for at least 24 hours, simmering it for about 20 minutes per pound, then baking it in a 350-degree oven for 20 to 25 minutes, basting frequently.), it should be consumed sparingly, thinly sliced. Typically, it is nestled in a buttermilk biscuit, but like its Italian sibling prosciutto, Smithfield ham works well as an appetizer, wrapped around melon for example.

# Get a 'Cue

It's obvious that pigs don't stand much of a chance in the Old Dominion. If it's not bacon or ham, it's barbecue, also known around here as Bar-B-Que. Make that a jumbo, please, but hold the cole slaw and hand over the hot sauce. Southerners don't have to be told how to eat their barbecue: that knowledge is instilled when they cut their first teeth. Non-Southerners probably won't notice or care about the finer distinctions between varieties of this pit-cooked, chopped-pork delight, but there are differences. Virginia barbecue tends to have a delicate, smoky flavor. The sauce adds a tang, not a kick. Down in the Carolinas, they make their barbecue with a stronger vinegar base, and you'll sometimes see references to pulled barbecue, which is more strip-like than chopped. We like our barbecue any which way and find that a little Texas Pete never hurt either a Virginia or a Carolina pig.

## Where To Find It

Here in the Tidewater area of Virginia, there's plenty of debate over who makes the best barbecue. We've listed a few of our favorite barbecue restaurants so you can try them all and cast your vote.

### Bodine's Hickory Smoked Bar-B-Que
754 J. Clyde Morris Blvd., Newport News • 596-7427

Specialties of the house include chopped pork barbecue slow-cooked over hickory wood. Complete platters are available. Bodine's is a favorite of the restaurant critics at the *Daily Press* newspaper.

### County Grill & Smokehouse

**INSIDERS' TIP**

In 1835, the Virginia wine industry received a big boost from viticulturist Dr. D.N. Norton, a Richmonder who developed the first "non-foxy" American wine grape. This fruit was used to produce a claret praised by connoisseurs, a feat that encouraged many Virginians to try their luck at grape growing.

1215-A George Washington Memorial Hwy., York Co. • 591-0600

A literal hangout for barbecue lovers, County Grill has beef and pork varieties available in sandwiches and platters. Tables are decked out in butcher paper and equipped with half a dozen different barbecue sauces. You can wash it all down with one of the microbrews you'll find on tap. A favorite of *Daily Press* readers for two years in a row.

www.insiders.com
See this and many other **Insiders' Guide** destinations online.
Visit us today!

## Pierce's Pitt Bar-B-Que
447 E. Rochambeau Dr., Williamsburg • 565-2955

A trip to Pierce's is mandatory for all barbecue lovers who come to Williamsburg. Be prepared for a big crowd and long lines, as Pierce's has become something of an institution in town. Pierce's is the unequivocal favorite of locals.

## Queen Anne Dairy Snack
7127 Merrimac Tr. (Rt. 143), Williamsburg • 229-3051

If you're in the mood for takeout, pick up a pint of this popular Carolina-style barbecue to take home with you. (Barbecue sandwiches also are available if you prefer your food more ready to eat.)

## Rocky Mount Bar B-Q House
10113 Jefferson Ave., Newport News • 596-0243

In the restaurant business, longevity pretty much says it all. Rocky Mount has been cooking North Carolina-style 'cue for more than 40 years. Tuesday is a great day to bring the kids - they get to munch out for free. One child per paying adult, please.

# Salute To Seafood

Of all our regional specialties, seafood is the undisputed king. Virginia's rivers were so full of fish in Colonial days that tales have come down about giant crabs, fish that literally jumped into boats and 12-foot-long sturgeon. Herring, shad and shad roe, mussels, oysters, clams and crab were some of the seafood most pleasing to early

Virginians' palates. Sadly, civilization and development have brought some decline from past abundance. Sturgeon are hard to find now, and oyster beds are disappearing. But area fishermen still reel in plenty of blues, croakers, shad, spot, pike, bass, crappie and other varieties of freshwater and saltwater fish.

On local piers you're likely to see weekend anglers patiently filling their buckets with crabs. Virginia's most common crab is the blue crab, or *Callinectes sapidus*, which translates as "savory, beautiful swimmer." This ornery-looking creature lives two or three years and periodically molts, shucking off its exoskeleton. For a short stretch of time after molting, the blue crab is soft and vulnerable, but a new, hard shell quickly forms. Commercial crabbers harvest this tender prey to sell as soft-shell crab, considered a delicacy locally but apt to make the non-initiate ask, "You mean I'm supposed to eat it legs and all?" Hard crabs are harvested too, of course, and come in a variety of stages and forms. Stopping off at area fishing docks you may overhear talk about peelers, jimmies, sooks, sponge crabs, busters and doublers

While commercial fishermen work from their boats, dropping large baited crab pots made of specially treated steel wire into area waterways, there is a simpler way to catch a crustacean dinner. Adults and children like to tie chicken necks or fish heads to kite string, grab a dip net and head for the shallows. The trick to this method of crabbing is to gently lure a nibbling crab close enough to net him from underneath. Crabs are smart enough to be frightened by abrupt movements or a sudden play of shadows on the water, such as a body blocking the sun. But they're not smart enough to stop coming back for more, so don't give up. (Crabs often turn up when you're not expecting them and, believe it or not, some fishermen don't want them. One Insider, trying to fill up her cooler with spot and croaker on a hot July day of pier fishing, kept on pulling in tenacious crustaceans, too few to eat, but enough to quickly deplete her bloodworm supply.) You also can buy small crab pots for use from piers in local sporting goods stores. Crabbing is a time-honored way to spend a leisurely morning in eastern Virginia.

## Cooking Up Crab

This quirky crustacean, so important to the culture and economy of the Hampton Roads area, has captured the imagination of cooks and consumers, spawning an endless variety of recipes from the humble crab cake to Crab Imperial. Backfin crabmeat is considered the tastiest and is often served simply – sauteed with butter or chilled with mayonnaise. You'll also see crabmeat served chilled, as a stuffing for avocados, tomatoes or mushrooms. Heated, it combines with shrimp, lobster and other seafood for a variety of baked dishes and casseroles.

Local cooks spar to create the best crab cakes, with feuds developing over whether cornmeal, cracker crumbs or bread and eggs provide the most suitable base. Deviled crab comes in several varieties, too - some swear by horseradish, some by chili powder. You may even see something called a crab burger on area menus. And backyard crab feasts, where determined partygoers stand around tables covered with newspaper and pick at hard crabs from a bushel basket, are a common summer's evening occurrence around the area.

As we mentioned before, soft-shell crab is prized locally but no longer is it only fried and stuffed in a bun or sauteed with butter and lemon. Marcel Desaulniers, chef and co-owner of the Trellis Restaurant on Duke of Gloucester Street, 229-8610, includes several innovative dishes made with soft-shell crabs in his Trellis Cookbook. Grilled soft-shell crab with cucumbers, dill-butter sauce, shiitake mushrooms and country ham is one such offering, but even more imaginative is Desaulniers' recipe for marinated soft-shell crabs, using vinegar, dry white wine and jalapenos.

By the way, fresh soft-shell-crab season runs roughly from May to early fall. If you see the dish offered at other times of the year, you're probably getting a frozen product, which is not recommended.

Crab bisques, soups and gumbos (both hot and chilled) are perennial favorites around here as well. Hampton crab bisque is made with cream, Tabasco and sherry. Crab soups are sometimes based on fish stock, sometimes tomato broth. She-crab soup, which combines sauterne or sherry with whipping cream, butter and lots of crab, including the roe, is just too good to miss. Unfortunately, this succulent soup is infrequently seen on menus. We wonder if this is because all of it is consumed in restaurant kitchens.

Some popular local eateries that serve up delicious crab cakes and other crab dishes are noted here. For a more complete listing turn to our Restaurants Chapter.

### Welcome South
**8558 Richmond Rd., Toano • 566-8255**

While this restaurant has wonderful barbecue and fried chicken, we recommend it here for its crab cakes. Believe us when we tell you they are grilled to perfection!

### The Dining Room at Ford's Colony Country Club
**240 Ford's Colony Dr., Williamsburg • 258-4100**

This extremely posh restaurant serves outstanding seafood. Although menu selections may vary, Ford's Colony has featured such delights as crab cakes topped

**INSIDERS' TIP**

If your vacationing pursuit of happiness includes a thirst for a fine Virginia wine, you're in luck. The Virginia Wine Marketing Program has put together a festival and tour guide for Virginia wineries. To receive a free copy, call (800) 828-4637.

with shiitake mushrooms and a delicious bisque that pairs roasted red peppers and crabmeat.

## Indian Fields Tavern
9220 John Tyler Memorial Hwy., Charles City Co.
• (804) 829-5004

For a Sunday brunch with regional flair, check out the crab cakes Harrison at this historic tavern. This dish features two crab cakes served over grilled Smithfield ham and toasted Sally Lunn bread topped off with hollandaise sauce. The brunch menu also features crab cakes Chesapeake, a dish that closely resembles eggs Benedict, with crab cakes served in the place of the traditional Canadian bacon. Dinner fare - served seven evenings a week - includes both the crab cakes Harrison and an excellent surf and turf, featuring filet mignon and (what else) crab cakes.

## The Regency Room
The Williamsburg Inn, Frances St. • 228-2141

This elegant dining room not only offers memorable surroundings (note the white tablecloths, polished silver and fresh flowers), the food is superb. Sample a crab cake in a mustard-dill sauce as an appetizer or order the signature dish, Crabmeat Randolph, crab served on a bed of Virginia country ham. If you like your crab au naturel, we recommend the fresh shellfish appetizer, a platter of oysters, clams, shrimp and crab, all beautifully presented.

## Happy As A Clam

Although crab is king in the Williamsburg area, brother clam has muscled his way in for a share of the limelight. Most people eat these shellfish raw or steamed, but if you're a soup lover, you might want to try Chesapeake Bay clam chowder. Unlike the New England version, with its creamy base, or the Manhattan recipe, which calls for a to-

mato broth, this savory chowder has a clear base made with clam stock to which onions, celery, potatoes and a variety of herbs have been added. Bacon is sometimes thrown in for added flavor.

# Vive le Vin!

What comes to mind when you think of wine? The Bordeaux region of France? California's Napa Valley? Perhaps the Finger Lakes area in upstate New York? How about the Virginia countryside? At last count, there were 49 vineyards in the Old Dominion, four of them new within the last couple of years. That's a huge increase from 1979, when there were perhaps only a half-dozen. The business of growing grapes has been going so well in this southeastern state that *Wine Spectator* magazine singled out Virginia as "the most accomplished of America's emerging wine regions." Indeed, the Commonwealth is making something of a name for itself in circles where the grape is served and celebrated. In 1993, Virginia wines were served to former Soviet Premier Mikhail Gorbachev at a 200th birthday bash for Thomas Jefferson. The following year, Old Dominion wines reaped awards and medals at the San Francisco Fair National Wine Competition, the San Diego National Wine Competition and INTERVIN International Wine Competition.

Several factors contribute to the flowering of this most pleasant of industries: Virginia's moderate climate, American consumers' increasing interest in wine, enactment of laws providing incentives for wineries and state funding of marketing and promotional programs. Today Virginia wines are served, consumed, praised and awarded around the world. Ronald Reagan gave a bottle of Virginia Seyval to Gorbachev (the gentleman certainly seems

---

**INSIDERS' TIP**

If you're looking for a wine to quaff with one of Virginia's varieties of seafood, here's a word of advice. With boiled shrimp, try a dry white; with oysters, champagne or a Chablis; and with cold crab, pop the cork on a chilled bottle of Riesling.

Photo: The Williamsburg Winery, Ltd.

The Williamsburg Winery has been growing the grape since the 17th century.

to appreciate fine wine) at the 1988 Moscow Summit. Locally, the Williamsburg Winery Ltd., set on more than 300 acres of farmland close to the James River, has garnered a number of awards, including the 1989 Governor's Cup for the best Virginia wine. In 1993, 1995 and 1997, the winery also earned a critic's choice award from *Wine Spectator* magazine. Each year, this coveted award is bestowed on 200 wineries throughout the world.

Times weren't always so good for growers of the grape in the Old Dominion. Early colonists used hardy native American grapes such as the scuppernong to produce wines at Jamestown and other Colo-

nial outposts. But these wines had a strong, "foxy" flavor European settlers found unpleasant. Some brought cuttings from French, Italian and German vineyards in an attempt to create more palatable vintages. Thomas Jefferson summoned a wine expert from Italy, Philip Mazzeo, to advise him on the vineyards near Monticello. The Italian was enthusiastic about Virginia's potential as a wine-producing region, and soon Jefferson was experimenting with European varietals on his estate. Until the 1850s, the Charlottesville area was known for its excellent claret. Unfortunately, cold winters, insects and diseases destroyed most early vineyards. Civil War battles also

## INSIDERS' TIP

Don't leave town without sampling Virginia's peanuts. After all, more than 30 percent of the 93,000 acres of peanuts planted in the state are in nearby Suffolk and Isle of Wight counties. Two of the best places in Williamsburg to sample this treat is The Peanut Shop of Williamsburg, 229-3908 or (800) 637-3268, on Merchants Square, or The Whitley Peanut Factory, 229-4056, at 1351 Richmond Road. You might also want to check out the Surrey House Restaurant, 294-3389 or (800) 200-4977, on Route 31 in Surry. Here you can begin your dinner with a cup of creamy Southern peanut soup, then top off your meal with a peanut-topped ice cream sundae or a slice of peanut-raisin pie, which the staff claims is world famous.

extensively damaged them. Meanwhile, California vintners had captured the domestic wine production market. In the 1920s, prohibition delivered the crowning blow to what little wine industry remained in Virginia.

California is still the best-known wine-producing region in the United States, but Virginia can once again boast of its own fruit of the vine, with grapes for wine now grown on more than 1,400 acres around the state. The climate of the Old Dominion seems especially well suited to cultivation of the Chardonnay and Cabernet Sauvignon varietals as well as hardier hybrids. But throughout Virginia you also will find Rieslings and Gewürztraminers, Vionier and pinot noir, Merlot and pinot grigio, Barbera and Chenin Blanc.

An agreeable by-product to all this viticultural enterprise is the vineyard tour. While most Virginia vineyards cluster around Charlottesville, Culpeper, the Middleburg-Leesburg area and the Shenandoah River Valley, visitors to Williamsburg now have the option of touring two area vineyards.

Readers interested in finding out more about wineries in the state might want to pick up a copy of *The Insiders' Guide to Virginia's Blue Ridge*. Included in this book is a chapter detailing the numerous Blue Ridge wineries.

As one of the expressions we have heard over the years advises: Life is too short to drink bad wine. We heartily concur.

## The Williamsburg Winery & Gabriel Archer Tavern
**5800 Wessex Hundred • 229-0999**

The closest and largest vineyard (The Williamsburg Winery produces 46,000 cases a year) got off, or perhaps we should say in, the ground when the first vines were planted in 1985. Two years later, the first wines were bottled. Today more than 50 acres are in cultivation, and Williamsburg wines are sold in the United States from Vermont to Georgia and as far west as Hawaii. The winery also is only one of a handful in the Old Dominion that exports its product. Wines with the Willliamsburg label can now be found in Belgium, France and Holland. Indeed, growth has been so healthy that, in 1996, the Virginia Chamber of Commerce listed The Williamsburg Winery as one of the 50 fastest-growing businesses in the state. Also in 1996, owner and founder Patrick Duffeler was selected as First Virginia Entrepreneur of the Year in

Photo: Northern Neck Travel Council

Ingleside Plantation Winery offers free tours and tastings.

an annual program sponsored by Ernst & Young.

## Tours and Tastings

To get an Insiders' peek at this popular winery, you can enjoy a guided tour that begins in the retail store and leads to the 18th-century-style brick building that holds a banquet room, underground cellars, a bottling room, warehousing space and offices. Tour guides explain the winemaking process and point out interesting objects associated with the winery, including pictures of a 17th-century skeleton found here during a dig and Duffeler's collection of more than 300 18th-century wine bottles dating as far back as 1710. Duffeler (who was born in Brussels, Belgium, and organized car races and consulted for a large cosmetics company before becoming a vintner) takes an approach to viticulture that combines traditional winemaking methods with modern technology. Currently the winery makes a number of different varietals aged in the 600-plus French and American oak barrels you'll see lined up in the temperature-controlled cellar where the woody aroma of fermentation greets guests. Stainless steel fermenters also are used here, mostly in the creation of blends.

By Virginia law, varietals - wines named after the grape from which they are produced - must contain at least 75 percent of that particular grape, such as the Chardonnay, Merlot, Cabernet Sauvignon or Riesling. However, The Williamsburg Winery uses 100 percent varietal grape in its Chardonnays, including the John Adlum regular bottling; the Acte 12 Chardonnay, named for the Virginia House of Burgesses 1619 act calling for the planting of vines by settlers; and a Vintage Reserve Chardonnay, entirely barrel-fermented. An altogether different bottling, the Gabriel Archer Reserve, is a Bordeaux-style blend of Cabernet Franc, Cabernet Sauvignon and Merlot. The winery also makes a Cabernet Sauvignon, a Merlot and Merlot reserve and James River White, a blend of Chardonnay and Seyval. Other blends include the Governor's White, a mix of Riesling and Vidal grape, and Plantation Blush, made from Riesling and Seyval. In 1996 the company released three new labels made at its Dominion Wine Cellars, a former wine cooperative in Culpeper that was purchased by The Williamsburg Winery a few years back. These include a Riesling, Late Harvest Vidal and Filipo Mazzei Reserve, a Cabernet Sauvignon and Nebiolo mix. The winery also plans to release a number of fortified dessert wines under the Dominion label.

After your tour, you will be invited to participate in a tasting, which will include samples of some of the wines mentioned above.

Once your palate has been thoroughly tempted, you can browse through the retail store, which sells winery products, international wines, replicas of 18th-century wine bottles that were handblown in the traditional manner by artisans who work at Jamestown Glassblowing House, fancy corkscrews and other accessories for the wine connoisseur. The winery also offers a collection of authentic salt-glazed pottery - coasters, pitchers, wine cups and coolers - designed with a grape motif by Duffeler. Prices for a bottle of wine begin around $7. Discounts are offered on orders of six or more bottles, and shipping is also available. Credit cards are accepted.

If it's time for lunch, you're in luck. The

## INSIDERS' TIP

Open since 1995, the Prince Michel de Virginia Wineshop in Patriot Plaza, 3044 Richmond Road, carries a variety of wines bottled at the Prince Michel vineyard in Leon, south of Culpeper. For $2, you can sample 10 different wines, and you can take home a bottle of whatever strikes your fancy. Prices start at $7.95. The wine shop is open from 10 AM to 9 PM Monday through Saturday and from noon to 6 PM on Sunday. Call 565-0814.

Gabriel Archer Tavern, which opened in 1996 and is named for an explorer who is believed to have chosen a landing site somewhere on the winery property, serves cheese and pate platters, smoked meats, specialty breads and wines by the glass, complete with a vineyard view "right in the Merlot," as winery vice president Rob Bickford describes it. The tavern is open from 11:30 AM to 4:30 PM seven days a week.

Or, if you'd like to reserve space for a private dinner or wine tasting, The Williamsburg Winery makes its facilities available after 6:30 PM every day year round. Relying on the expertise of local caterers, the winery can accommodate 25 to 125 people for just about any private function.

### Special Events

Throughout the year, the winery hosts a number of festivals and special events. Each spring, The Williamsburg Winery Run includes tours and tastings and raises funds to benefit a selected charity. In September, the Williamsburg Scottish Festival brings the sight of kilts and the sound of bagpipes to the vineyards. Throughout the year, musical events featuring such celebrated groups as the Virginia Opera and the Virginia Symphony are offered. For more information on upcoming events, contact the winery.

### Getting There

To reach the winery from Interstate 64, take Exit 57A, follow Route 199, and take a left turn onto Brookwood Lane. Turn left again on Lake Powell Road and you'll soon see the winery sign. From Williamsburg, follow Route 31 toward Jamestown. Turn left on Route 199 and take the next right onto Brookwood Lane. At Lake Powell Road, turn left and follow the signs. (The state's highway sign for vineyards, a cluster of grapes, will help guide you to the winery, too.) Hours of operation for tours are Monday through Saturday 11:30 AM to 4:30 PM and Sunday from noon to 5:30 PM. The wine shop is open the entire time. Winery tours are not available from mid-January through mid-February, although the shop remains open during that time. The tour and tasting cost $5 per person, which includes samples of wine, cheese and crackers and a souvenir glass with the vineyard's logo on it.

### Ingleside Plantation Winery
Rt. 638, Oak Grove • (804) 224-8687

Directions to Ingleside Plantation Winery in Oak Grove on Virginia's Northern Neck may seem a bit complicated to Williamsburg visitors. The winery can be reached by traveling Interstate 95 north of Richmond to Route 3, then south on Route 638 until you see the entrance signs; or by taking Route 17 across the York River, up to Route 360 and across the Rappahannock River, north on Route 3 to Route 638.

From May to October, a third alternative is to drive via Route 17, which you pick up south of Williamsburg on I-64, to Tappahannock. Once there, look for the signs for the Rappahannock River Cruise, which is right on Route 17, Tappahannock's main drag. The cruise offers a winery tour, wine tasting and lunch, catered by the

---

### INSIDERS' TIP

**Microbreweries are all the rage these days, and at last Williamsburg has one to call its own. Beers made locally by the Williamsburg Brewing Co. include a standard pale ale and a porter as well as seasonal brews such as its effervescent summer wheat. These microbrews are on tap at many local restaurants including Berret's and Second Street in Williamsburg. Beer also can be purchased at the brewery, located at 189-B Ewell Road. Tours are available. For more information, call 253-1577.**

Mount Holly Steamship Inn and served at the winery. The cruise runs from 10 AM to 4 PM every day except Monday and reservations are required. The cruise alone costs $18.50 for adults, with children 13 and younger half price. The cost of the lunch is $9.95 for adults and $7.95 for children. Call (804) 453-2628 for cruise information.

Enough preamble. Let's assume you're a dedicated wine aficionado and you've arrived at Ingleside Plantation Vineyards. What you'll find here are 50 acres of vineyards owned by the Flemer family and a winery facility overseen by winemaker Stephen Rigby. The roots of the winery go back to 1960, when the Flemers started with an experimental vineyard of French-American hybrids before turning to commercial winemaking in 1980. Ingleside's prize-winning wines are turned out in a former dairy barn, using methods embraced by small European chateau wineries. The winery's courtyard, which has been spruced up within the last five years or so, enhances the European ambiance.

Using state-of-the-art equipment, Ingleside produces a delicate, dry Chardonnay, a Cabernet Sauvignon and a Cabernet Sauvignon reserve, a claret, their Chesapeake Blanc, which is a mix of Seyval, Chardonnay and Sauvignon Blanc, and a number of innovative blends, such as the Chesapeake Blush, made with Vidal and Cabernet grapes. Two semisweet wines include Pope's Creek White, a blend of Seyval and Vidal grapes, and Virginia Rose, a dessert wine made with a blend of French hybrids. October Harvest Vidal, is a slightly sweet dessert wine with intense apricot flavors, while relatively new red wines include a Merlot and the medium-bodied spicy red Cabernet Franc. Ingleside is one of the few Virginia wineries to make a sparkling wine; champagne-making is labor intensive, and the availability of Virginia Brut changes from year to year.

Tours and tastings are free to the public and are conducted Monday through Saturday from 10 AM to 4:30 PM and Sundays noon to 4:30 PM (the winery closes at 5 PM daily.) In the retail store and gift shop you'll find Ingleside wines with prices ranging from $8 to $65, books about area history, gourmet foods and Virginia arts and crafts. The winery also hosts a series of special events each year, including barrel tastings, jazz concerts and a Christmas open house. A Northern Neck Seafood Extravaganza, introduced in 1994, brings a festival atmosphere to the winery each September. For a cover charge of about $15, patrons enjoy a tour and tasting and sample seafood from participating restaurants while listening to live entertainment. After nibbling tidbits from all the vendors, guests can purchase the meal that best suits their fancy. Of course, you'll also have the chance to quaff wines deemed suitable for the seafood of your choice. Reservations are required for this and other Ingleside events.

From traditional Southern fare like grits and hushpuppies to fine cuisine that will please the most discriminating palate, Williamsburg is a feast you must experience.

# Restaurants

As with every other aspect of life in Williamsburg, fine dining has a long history in this city. Today the tradition is continued in an astonishing assortment of restaurants and eateries throughout Williamsburg and the surrounding area. We would like to recommend each establishment where we have had a good meal, but then there wouldn't be room for anything else in this volume. Instead, the listings are our favorite representatives of the variety available to visitors and townsfolk.

The entries begin with the Colonial Williamsburg dining options, followed by an alphabetical listing of neighborhood haunts, favorite delis, out-of-the-mainstream locations and nationally acclaimed dining rooms. We also list other establishments offering some unique items of cuisine or special values we feel you ought to consider during your stay. Unless they are particularly good or offer something of special note, however, we do not list chain restaurants. Neither do we list hotel or motel dining rooms unless we know that Insiders seek them out or that visitors recommend them for a particular reason.

You'll find an extended article on food in our chapter on Regional Cuisine and Wines, but it's in order now to mention what you're likely to find in many of our restaurants. You non-Southerners are in for a treat as you discover regional favorites like spoonbread, crab cakes and grits (they're not just for breakfast, y'all). Hushpuppies are omnipresent companions to seafood in this area, usually appearing on your table in a heaping basket shortly after you order and often included in the price of your meal. As you try different restaurants you'll discover that area chefs make their particular hushpuppies a point of pride.

Another regional custom, surprising to many visitors, is that iced tea is the drink of choice to accompany all Southern meals. Those folks in Boston may have thrown their tea into the harbor, but Southern Colonials and their progeny love their tea and maintain that sugar, not salt, is the best companion for the Oriental leaf - and plenty of it! Remember to ask for your tea unsweetened if that is your preference.

You'll also notice that we mention Sunday brunch quite often in our listings. It sometimes seems that no one cooks the big Sunday meal at home anymore - and why should they with all of the delectable brunches available locally? You'll be standing in line with many of our townsfolk no matter which brunch you select.

One more thing frequently asked about: Often you'll see "ABC on/off" as part of a Virginia restaurant's advertising. The Commonwealth's Alcoholic Beverage Control (ABC) regulations require this designation for establishments serving beer, wine or spirits for consumption on or off the premises. Liquor stores are commonly referred to in Virginia as ABC stores.

With visitors and tourists comprising the majority of diners, casual dress is appropriate. Where there are exceptions, we indicate such.

Nearly all restaurants in this chapter offer diners a nonsmoking section. Those that do not, or those establishments that do not permit any smoking, are so noted.

Hours vary seasonally and on special weekends, so we note only particular deviations from what you might expect, and we recommend that you call your chosen establishment to be sure of its current hours of operation. And since the area is host to literally millions of visitors, you can find lines at most restaurants during peak dining hours in-season. Off-season dining is far more leisurely and you rarely, if ever, encounter lines at local eateries.

## Price Guidelines

Area restaurants almost universally accept major credit cards, so we note only exceptions to that standard. If you're not using Visa or MasterCard, we suggest you inquire in advance whether your American Express, Discover or Diners Club card will be accepted.

The following code indicates the average price of two entrees only - no appetizers, no dessert, no drinks, no tax or gratuity. Keep in mind that, as wholesale food prices fluctuate, so do corresponding menu prices. Also remember that rates may be higher in season (generally from mid-March to November and again during the winter holidays).

| | |
|---|---|
| $ | Less than $20 |
| $$ | $20 to $35 |
| $$$ | $36 to $50 |
| $$$$ | More than $50 |

Finally, enjoy yourself! That's the whole point of your stay here, isn't it? Good eating.

# Colonial Williamsburg Restaurants

A centralized reservation service, 229-2141 or (800) TAVERNS, makes it simple to assure a seating at any of the Colonial Williamsburg taverns, the Williamsburg Lodge, the Williamsburg Inn, Cascades or the Golden Horseshoe Clubhouse Grill. We strongly suggest you make use of this service, particularly when making dinner plans. Call for information on what options are available at the time you have selected, and a helpful representative will be happy to accommodate your party. If you have overlooked making a reservation for din-

ner and are feeling lucky, walk-ins at each site are welcomed if seating is still available. At all the taverns in the Historic Area, you will find a costumed host or hostess who will place your name on a list for the first available table. Each restaurant has its own particular charm, so consider all of the options before making your selection. Smoking is not permitted in any of the taverns.

### The Bay Room and The Lodge Coffee Shop
$$ • S. England St. • 229-2141 or (800) TAVERNS

Fine breakfasts, lunches and dinners are available in The Bay Room every day of the week, but two meals are worthy of special acclaim. Williamsburg Insiders return again and again to the brunch on Sundays that offers made-to-order omelets and a buffet with fine breads, pastries, fruits and hot dishes. Every Friday and Saturday evening, the Chesapeake Bay Seafood Feast offers a bounty of fresh seafood consistently favored by residents of the area. We recommend reservations for all Bay Room dinners, but especially for these two meals.

The coffee shop provides quick, excellent meals also. The setting, menu and price are scaled down somewhat from the Bay Room, and the mood is less formal. But the food is well prepared, well served and tasty. You must at least consider the desserts.

### Cascades
$$$ • Visitor Center Complex, Rt. 132 • 229-2141 or (800) TAVERNS

You may start your day here with the famous Hunt Breakfast buffet, offering a full range of choices from fruit waffles to fried chicken. Lunch and dinner are equally enticing, with prime rib, steaks, poultry and seafood to savor as you enjoy a beautiful view of a stream cascading down the hillside across from the dining room. Sunday brunch and the Bay Country Buffet on Sunday evenings are very popular with locals. Reservations are in order.

## Chowning's Tavern

$$$ • Duke of Gloucester St. • 229-2141 or (800) TAVERNS

Chowning's Tavern is a perennial favorite with visitors to the city, both for its ideal location - right in the center of the Historic Area - and for the 18th-century ambiance the reconstructed building provides. The furnishings are simple and rustic, and the pewter table service and costumed staff contribute to the impression that you truly have gone back 200 years to take your refreshment. You cannot make reservations here, so plan ahead and arrive in enough time to await your turn to be seated.

The menu is a blend of food found in English pubs and standard American favorites. At lunch a selection of sandwiches includes pulled-pork barbecue and other Virginia favorites on large sandwich rolls. If a bowl of stew is more to your liking, the house special Brunswick stew is always a favorite. At dinner, the stew remains on the menu along with barbecued beef ribs or pork back ribs, broiled deviled crabs, roast duckling and Chowning's Special Dinner (plantation vegetable soup, salad with chutney dressing, sauteed backfin crabmeat with ham and deep-dish apple pie with cheddar cheese). New favorites include Brighton chicken wings and Bubble and Squeak, fried puffs of mashed potatoes and cabbage.

After 10 PM, Chowning's staid propriety is put aside - in Colonial fashion - for the Gambols, rowdy 18th-century entertainment provided by costumed balladeers, magicians, minstrels and various other rogues and rascally sots - oops, sorts. Board games are provided, Virginia peanuts and various Colonial "liquid refreshments" accompany light snacks, and soon the crowd is singing along to tunes that frequently reflect a side of Colonial life not mentioned in the history books.

## Christiana Campbell's Tavern

$$$ • Waller St. • 229-2141 or (800) TAVERNS

George Washington favored meals at this establishment opposite the eastern end of the Capitol building. An enjoyable midday meal is Mrs. Campbell's brunch, providing a selection of omelets, waffles and skillet-fried chicken. At dinner, enjoy regional seafood favorites or such other standard fare as steaks cooked to order. Parking in the rear makes access convenient, and the authentic Colonial ambiance and strolling musicians contribute to a memorable time. Make reservations to assure a convenient seating, and in season don't be surprised to find a brief wait. If this should come to pass, fret not. Sitting on the wide porch is a pleasant prelude to your meal.

## Golden Horseshoe Club House Grille

$ • S. England St. • 229-2141 or (800) TAVERNS

A block from the Powder Magazine and across from the Williamsburg Lodge is the clubhouse for Colonial Williamsburg's fine golf course. One grill faces the famous Golden Horseshoe fairways; the other overlooks the Green Golf Course. Light lunches are available from 11 AM until 4 PM daily, dinners from 5 to 8 PM Wednesday through Sunday (seasonally). At lunch you are likely to see city business and professional people enjoying the excellent sandwiches, soups and salads, always up to the standard for which Colonial Williamsburg is noted. This place also is known locally for serving the best hamburger in town. The seasonal dinner offerings are just as high in quality, and children's menus are available. We recommend reservations for dinner.

## King's Arms Tavern

$$$ • Duke of Gloucester St. • 229-2141 or (800) TAVERNS

---

In its decor and its menu, this restaurant reflects the refined tastes of the Colonial gentry who dined here. Fried chicken, Virginia ham, filet mignon stuffed with oysters, peanut soup and Sally Lunn bread are house specialties, and we recommend the Colonial Game Pie for an unusual and authentic taste of early Virginia fare.

### Shields Tavern
$$ • Duke of Gloucester St. • 229-2141 or (800) TAVERNS

Operated by James Shields in the 1740s for a clientele of planters and the well to do, this tavern is the most recent one to be reconstructed. It has been carefully appointed to serve visitors authentic Colonial Virginia foods in a setting antedating the other taverns by 25 years. Foods based on recipes of the 1750s are available on the bill of fare: chicken roasted on a spit, crayfish soup, greengage plum ice cream (yum!) and other unusual items provide an education on the dining habits of the early 18th century. Liquid refreshments are equally unusual. Syllabub is a period drink of cream, white wine, sherry, sugar and lemon that separates into a meringue-like topping with the wine and sherry at the bottom of the glass. Bumbo is a 1740s-style mixture of rum, sugar and water. The Shields Sampler may be the best choice for your first taste of Colonial cooking: Indian corn pudding, chicken fricassee, carrot puffs and meat pasties. Don't overlook the peanut soup. Breakfast, lunch and dinner are available. In an attempt to cater to more modern taste buds, the tavern has added a few low-fat and vegetarian dishes, including a grilled polenta, a toasted corn meal pudding served with sauteed vegetables in a tomato sauce.

In the summer, Shields Tavern offers a special "dinner theater" four nights a week: two hours of period entertainments during your dining. Although it's a bit higher in price than a regular meal ($19.95 per person in 1998, $12.95 for children),it is very popular, so make your reservations when you decide to come to Williamsburg, not after you are here.

### The Williamsburg Inn Regency Dining Room
$$$$ • Francis St. • 229-2141 or (800) TAVERNS

Perhaps the finest restaurant in the Tidewater area, The Regency Dining Room is consistently recognized with fine dining awards - and with good reason. Executive Chef Hans Schadler and his staff offer a rare and pleasant experience with classic continental dishes and regional specialties. Elegant appointments surround you while an attentive service staff works unobtrusively to provide your requirements. Breakfast, lunch and dinner seatings are available. Gentlemen are required to wear a jacket and tie. Dinner reservations are the only way to assure seating at your preferred time.

### Woodlands Grill
$ • Visitor Center Complex, Rt. 132 • 229-2141 or (800) TAVERNS

Travelers arriving at the Visitor Center and wanting to make the most efficient use of their touring time might consider this option, serving a wide variety of simple foods at reasonable prices. Its cafeteria service is quick and efficient, and diners are just steps away from tickets, information and bus transportation for the Historic Area.

# Additional Favorites

### A Good Place To Eat
$, no credit cards • Merchants Square • 229-4370

This is a popular place for tourists to get a quick, simple breakfast or lunch. Hot and cold sandwiches, soups, ice cream and frozen yogurt are served at fast-food counters, and muffins and pastries from the bakery counter are popular items. Although there is ample seating indoors, Insiders like to sit outside in the sidewalk cafe area and watch the scene passing by on Merchants Square.

### A Taste of Olde England
$ • 322 Second St. • 229-6660

This British-owned and -operated restaurant and pub prides itself on serving authentic British cuisine, soups and desserts. Among the lunch and dinner entrees is the Chicken, Ham and Leek Pie - fresh chicken breast, ham and fresh leeks in a silky cream sauce baked in a homemade pastry and served in an earthenware crock. Or try the Lancashire Hot Pot - slow-roasted beef and caramelized onions simmered in rich beef broth and baked under slices of golden-browned potatoes. If that isn't tempting enough, try the Leominster - marinated chicken breast in a baguette with fresh herb mayonnaise, roasted peppers, caramelized onions and Edam cheese. A children's menu is available. For visitors hoping for a liquid taste of "olde" England, the pub offers a large selection of lagers, ales and wines. Come as you are to this charming eatery. Reservations are not required, especially if you plan to dine before 7 PM.

### Aberdeen Barn
$$ • 1601 Richmond Rd. •
229-6661

Known for its aged steaks, prime rib, lamb chops, seafood and combinations, this restaurant opens nightly for dinner. The decor is rustic, subdued and candlelit. The kids' menu makes everyone in the family happy. We recommend that you make reservations.

### Anastasia's
$$-$$$ • 7816 Richmond Rd., Toano • 566-0043

This restored farmhouse in Toano offers an intimate atmosphere for lunch and dinner guests, who can indulge in innovative Southern cuisine. The cuisine, prepared with a European touch, includes such delights as Cognac Pork Tenderloin flavored with a sauce of Cognac, shallots and lemons; and Anastasia's Chicken - a pounded chicken breast stuffed with spinach and mozzarella cheese served with a light wine sauce. The menu also offers quail, roast rack of lamb, crab bisque, fried calamari and Smithfield ham. Lunch is served Tuesday through Friday, and dinner is offered

Tuesday through Sunday. A Sunday brunch is also offered. The restaurant doesn't permit smoking. Seating is limited to 32. Is it any wonder reservations are strongly recommended?

### The Bagel Bakery & Yogurt Shop
$ No credit cards • Colony Square Shopping Center, Jamestown Road • 220-2777

If you're looking for a freshly prepared, tasty and inexpensive lunch with optional indoor or outdoor seating, check this place out. Seventeen varieties of bagels, all baked fresh all day and with a plethora of toppings to choose from, are available along with a menu of soups and daily specials. Choose from eight cream cheeses, salmon spread and everything from a BLT on a bagel to a pizza or veggie bagel, mesquite grilled chicken, hummus, tuna melt - you get the idea. Also available: Day-old bagels and freshly sliced and toasted bagel chips, fountain and bottled waters, teas and other beverages. Lots of choice for vegetarians here. Open 7 AM-6 PM Monday-Friday; 8 AM-6 PM Saturday; 8 AM-3 PM Sunday.

### Beethoven's Inn
$, no credit cards • Town and Country Plaza, 467 Merrimac Tr. • 229-7069

Look carefully to find this small restaurant, a very popular spot with townsfolk for lunches, deli purchases and light evening fare. Pass through the deli to the separate seating area in the rear, and prepare yourself for excellent New York-style deli food and dinners. Don't expect to eat quickly here. They pride themselves on not rushing. Classical music plays softly in the background to set the mood. You can't beat Beethoven's for the fresh-each-evening French onion soup and the house cheesecake, each worth a trip in itself. Beer and wine are available.

### Belgian Waffles
$, no credit cards • 7243 Pocahontas Tr. • 229-6018

In the tradition of the Williamsburg area's numerous pancake houses, this longtime establishment serves a fine selection of old standbys - silver-dollar-sized buttermilk pancakes, flapjacks, superb French toast, omelets and Colonial breakfasts. The restaurant serves breakfast and lunch daily in season.

### Berret's Restaurant & Raw Bar
$$$ • Merchants Square • 253-1847

Berret's location on Merchants Square can't be beat. In fine weather, the raw bar is popular with young professionals as well as with tourists and college students. In addition to the usual raw-bar fare, it offers grilled steaks, chicken and fish. Inside you'll find tasty, fresh Chesapeake Bay seafood and a wide selection of other choices served in a pleasant, modern atmosphere. The seafood chowders and fresh soups of the day are always wonderful. Ask for the specials of the day, as they are usually based on what is available locally. Smoking is not permitted.

### Big Apple Bagels
$ • 1222 Richmond Rd. • 253-8456

Bagel aficionados, listen up! The city's newest nosh stop is this charming, informal eatery, which features about three dozen different flavored bagels, all baked fresh daily. This locally-owned and -operated restaurant offers an innovative, varied menu with something for everyone. Especially good - and unique - is the Enchilada Bagelata. But more traditional fare includes bagels with anything from roast beef and turkey to Nova Scotia salmon, corned beef, pastrami, salami and more. Want to sample a variety? Try the Bit O' Bagel: A platter of bit-sized bits of bagels with three types of cream cheese on the side. Also offered are a variety of coffees and juices. Gift baskets also available. Open 6 AM to 7 PM daily. Conveniently located adjacent to Williamsburg Shopping Center.

### Bones
$$ • Four Points By Sheraton, 351 York St. • 564-7109

This restaurant features Black Angus prime rib, BBQ baby back ribs, spit-fired rotisserie chicken and a wide selection of fresh seafood. The atmosphere is relaxed, and the experience is worth savoring. Live entertainment is offered some evenings.

### Candle Factory Restaurant
$ • 7521 Richmond Rd. • 564-0803

In spite of its location away from the city, this restaurant draws residents who drive out for its good and plentiful family-style meals. It's not fancy, and it's not expensive, but it is good food. Specialties include freshly made soups, prime rib, barbecued pork ribs and scallops. Visitors to the shops attached to the Candle Factory consistently rate the restaurant here as excellent. The only drawback is that you must eat early: The restaurant closes at 8 PM. Groups larger than four may have a short wait unless they make reservations in advance.

### Captain George's Seafood Restaurant
$$$ • 5363 Richmond Rd. • 565-2323

Don't be startled by the tall ship splitting this restaurant. It's your landmark from the highway. The all-you-can-eat buffet inside is a sight to see and a challenge to even the hungriest members of your party: Dozens of baked, broiled and fried seafood dishes are complemented by separate complete salad and dessert bars. The full menu also offers Australian rock lobster tails and seafood shish kebab. Landlubbers can select from beef and fowl dishes. A children's menu is also offered, and there are banquet rooms for large parties. With seating for 2,000 at a time, this is the largest restaurant in the city. The line moves quickly, so don't anticipate a long wait. Dinner is served daily. The restaurant opens at noon on Sunday.

### Cary Street Bistro & Tavern
$$-$$$ • 500 Jamestown Rd. • 229-2297

Williamsburg's newest restaurant is located directly across the street from Phi Beta Kappa Memorial Hall. Here you'll find an upbeat, albeit casual, atmosphere, attractive to townsfolk of all ages as well as to the built-in student clientele that frequents this new eatery and tavern. Open for lunch (11 AM to 3 PM) and dinner (5 to 10 PM) daily, the menu is varied and imaginative, yet those who have a hunger for such standbys as burgers, fries and the like can find something to please them. The lunch menu offers soups, salads, sandwiches and burgers, of course. At dinner, however, things get downright interesting - and mouth-watering. Select from a variety of fresh seafood entrees - crab cakes, tuna with lime salsa, broiled flounder stuffed (and we do mean STUFFED) with crabmeat, chicken, duck, steaks, pastas and plenty more. Veggies and the starch of the day accompany entrees. Tempted to overindulge on entrees? Think twice. The dessert menu is as varied as the entree list. And while we could name each luscious option, the specialty of the house tells it all. It's a rich, dense chocolate pie with a sinful mocha chocolate crust - sweet, tart and tangy all at the same time. Yum! The menu lists a couple of kids' entrees, but better yet, they can order anything from the regular menu and pay half-price for a half-portion. Don't miss this place, even if you have to fast for a day or two in advance to enjoy it without guilt. A full bar with a large selection of beers, ales and wines is available until 10 PM. Reservations are taken but not usually necessary.

## Cattle Baron of Williamsburg
$-$$, Major credit card accepted • 6678 Richmond Rd. • 565-2800

Located at the entrance to the Williamsburg Pottery Factory, this restaurant offers the option of full-service menu dining or a quick and inexpensive buffet. The steak menu offers several cuts, all cooked to order. But the real bonus here is the daily buffet ($7.99 adults/50 cents per year for children aged 10 and under) that offers everything from fish, chicken, ham, roast beef and ribs to a variety of potatoes and veggies, plus dessert and salad bars. Lunch 11 AM-4 PM Serves dinner 4 PM till 10 PM. It's clean and convenient, especially if you're tired from touring or shopping as you are invited to show up "come as you are" casual.

## Charly's
$$, no credit cards • Williamsburg-Jamestown Airport, 100 Marclay Rd. • 258-0034

Here's a unique and excellent restaurant you might not find unless you fly directly into Williamsburg. It's well worth seeking out even if you arrive by land. Chef Charly Graff offers an excellent menu of fine meals for lunch. Homemade breads and desserts, a chef's salad piled with meats, fresh homemade soups and other salads are very tempting and complement the careful preparation of the main courses. We particularly recommend the seafood bisque and the French onion soup, crusted with cheese and topped with croutons from the homemade bread. The menu is varied and satisfying, with the most unusual ambiance in the area: The restaurant and its patio have a clear view of the runway, and it's fascinating to watch the takeoffs and landings while dining. Charly's offers a room with a runway view that accommodates 50 to 100 people for catered dinners, luncheons and parties and offers to-go meals and delivery service. On Sunday, a $9.95 delicious prime rib special is a great bargain. The restaurant is open 11 AM until 3 PM.

## The Cheese Shop Cafe
$ • Merchants Square • 220-0298

If you stop a local resident on Merchants Square at noon to inquire where you can get a reasonably priced, outstanding sandwich, chances are that he or she will direct you to The Cheese Shop, which has entrances both from Prince George Street and from the Merchants Square parking lot. Its fine reputation for super sandwiches was built on an outstanding freshly sliced roast beef special, served on fresh-baked French bread with a secret house dressing. Deceptively priced at $3.75, this sandwich is a meal. The cafe menu also offers fresh salads, quiche of the day and an array of sandwiches including smoked turkey, piquant barbecue, an assortment of cheeses, baked ham, liverwurst, Nova Scotia salmon and more. Assorted beverages, both alcoholic and soft, are available as is a mouth-watering selection of desserts. Place your order, and they'll call you when it's ready, usually within minutes, except at peak lunch hours (noon to 1:30 PM Monday through Friday). Then step outside and eat under gaily-colored umbrellas in the flower-encircled outdoor cafe, or take your order to enjoy on one of the Merchants Square benches. Don't forget to offer the crumbs to the birds there. They've grown used to them.

## Chez Trinh
**$$ • 157 Monticello Ave. • 253-1888**

Gourmet chef Craig Claiborne has described Vietnamese cuisine as "among the most outstanding on earth," and here's a fine opportunity to test his judgment. In the Williamsburg Shopping Center near Peebles and out of the mainstream of traffic, this restaurant might be a well-kept secret if it weren't for the high recommendation of Insiders. It's a cuisine distinct from the familiar Chinese. Taking from the best of classic Oriental and French food preparation techniques, Vietnamese dishes have their own distinctive appearance, flavors and delights, and the kitchen staff is skilled in presenting them at their finest for lunch and dinner. For a good introduction, we recommend the fixed-price banquet menu for a minimum of six guests, featuring the most popular house specialties, such as steamed shrimp with herbs. If you're in a rush, Chez Trinh offers take-out meals.

## Christina's Kitchen
**$, no credit cards • The Village Shops at Kingsmill, 1915 Pocahontas Tr. • 220-0887**

A few white cafe tables and chairs invite customers to take a light repast at this German-style bake shop, known primarily for its outstanding pastries. Christina is perhaps the best baker in town, presenting an array of baked goods, pies and pastries sure to delight all comers. In addition, she offers a catering service capable of everything from hors d'oeuvres to sumptuous desserts. It is best to drop in and order whatever has been plucked most recently from the baking ovens and enjoy your selection over a cup of coffee or tea. The restaurant is open daily.

## Coach House Tavern
**$$$ • Berkeley Plantation, Rt. 5, Charles City Co. • (804) 829-6003**

Here's something "very Virginian" - an outstanding restaurant in a restored outbuilding on the plantation where the first 10 presidents of the United States dined with the Harrisons. Coach House offers delicious, creative lunches to travelers on Route 5, to those touring the James River plantation country and to its loyal following of people who travel from Richmond, Williamsburg and even farther, knowing they'll be pleased with their meals. Entrees vary seasonally, but include fresh finfish, crab, oysters, steaks, poultry, pastas, salads, homemade soups and more. A candlelit dinner with a view of the English gardens on a moonlit night, served by a staff in period costume, will be a memory to treasure for a lifetime. Dinner reservations are a must.

## The Coffeehouse
**$, no credit cards • Williamsburg Shopping Ctr., Rt. 5 at Rt. 199 • 229-9791**

This bright addition to the restaurant scene features more than 40 varieties of coffee and 11 varieties of loose tea. Regional and estate coffee beans from the Americas, Africa, Southeast Asia and the Pacific are roasted on the premises, assuring coffee lovers the freshest, most tasteful brews. Espresso, espresso macchiato, cappuccino, cafe mocha, cafe latte and cafe au lait, along with a selection of teas, top the excellent variety of hot and cold beverages you may enjoy; Italian sodas and cream sodas are alternatives. Your

---

**INSIDERS' TIP**

Cappuccino is appearing on more menus in the area. For a real treat in the blistering summer heat, try yours over ice at one of the coffeehouses.

Outdoor seating at Historic Area restaurants is a treat for visitors as well as residents.

beverage selection can be complemented with the perfect baked treat from an extensive list of French pastries baked on premises and other home-baked cakes, cheesecakes, muffins and other delights. We're particularly partial to the New Orleans Pecan Bar, but you'd better check both display cases before making your choice. On Mondays and Thursdays, The Coffeehouse offers authentic fresh-baked French breads after 1:30 PM, and, on Friday afternoons, beignets are the featured treat, three for a dollar. The indulging doesn't stop there, however. Chocolate lovers are delighted to find that The Coffeehouse offers handmade Harbor Sweets chocolates from Massachusetts and Lake Champlain chocolates from Vermont, as well as chocolate-covered espresso beans. Of course all coffees and teas are prepared for you to enjoy on the premises or at home.

## College Delly & Pizza Restaurant
**$, no credit cards • 336 Richmond Rd. • 229-6627**

Across from the college and two blocks from Merchants Square, this restaurant is a longtime favorite with students, townsfolk and tourists looking for a good deli meal or pizza accompanied by a selection from the wide assortment of beverages in the wall cooler. Reading the sandwich ingredients from the menu will certainly fire up your appetite, and the freshly made Italian and Greek dishes (especially the souvlaki and shish kebab) are delicious and filling. Insiders are particularly fond of the Hot Holly: roast beef, cheese, turkey, bacon, lettuce, tomato and pickle on a toasted roll. The College Delly offers limited delivery service in the evenings until 1 AM, and the hungry nightowls among us find the hours to our liking: The restaurant is open until 2 AM.

## The Colonial Restaurant
**$ • 100 Page St. at Penniman • 253-5852**

You can find traditional Southern cooking at this restaurant whether you come for breakfast, lunch or dinner. The fried chicken is worth writing home about (we just had to use that phrase somewhere in a book for visitors, now didn't we?), and the steaks, seafood and Italian dishes are delicious and carefully prepared. This is a casual, family restaurant, established in 1955, and local business people and college faculty have made it a regular informal clubhouse at lunch. Smoking is not permitted.

## The Corner Pocket
**$ • Williamsburg Crossing Shopping Ctr., 5251 John Tyler Hwy. • 220-0808**

Here's an alternative to humdrum eating. The Corner Pocket is Williamsburg's upscale billiards club, but Insiders also know that it offers excellent sandwiches and light entrees for lunch and dinner, with daily specials. If you're going to the nearby movies, this will be a great before- or after-movie choice for a bite. Save your movie ticket stub: It can get you a discount on your meal at the right time. Not your typical pool hall by any means, The Corner Pocket requires proper attire, and children younger than 18 must be accompanied by an adult. On Wicked Wednesdays, pool is half-price from 4 to 7 PM, and Insiders take advantage of this for a light dinner and some early evening entertainment, often combining it with a movie. Check out whether there is live entertainment on the menu while you're in town. This establishment likes the blues and imports some of America's finest blues performers. The Corner Pocket is open until 1 AM.

## Country Harvest Buffet
**$ • 1425 Richmond Rd. • 229-2698**

This dining room offers an all-you-can-eat country buffet of roast beef, ham, turkey, chicken, meat loaf, vegetables and dessert. It's not fancy, but the food is fresh and bountiful. It is popular with families because it offers something for everyone. It's even more popular with children because of the enormous dessert bar. Senior citizen discounts are available from 3 to 5 PM.

## Courtyard Cafe
**$-$$ • Williamsburg Crossing Shopping Ctr., 5251 John Tyler Hwy. • 253-2233**

This cafe with a relaxed atmosphere has a small dining room that is often packed - evidence that the food and service are excellent. While casual in demeanor, the restaurant serves very fine grilled and baked entrees, with fresh fish, meats and pastas as well as burgers, a creative children's menu and super desserts from the Carrot Tree Kitchen, a popular local bake shop. Note that it is a favorite of those coming or going to the seven movie theaters around the corner. Open for lunch and dinner Monday through Saturday, it is usually busiest just before and after the evening movies. Insiders know not to leave without inquiring what freshly baked goodies are on the dessert list for the day.

## Cracker Barrel Old Country Store
**$ • 200 Bypass Rd. • 220-3384**

Anyone who has traveled in the southern United States is familiar with this chain of restaurants. The Cracker Barrel features an extensive, ever-changing seasonal menu of authentic country fare - from BBQ ribs and grilled steaks to country fried steak and chicken and dumplings. Vegetarians will delight in the sumptuous though very low-priced vegetable platter special that allows you to select from nearly a dozen vegetables and side dishes. Especially good are the hashbrown cheese casse-

---

**INSIDERS' TIP**

Watch for the Chamber of Commerce's A Taste of Williamsburg, an early spring event showcasing exquisite offerings from the area's top restaurants. It's an evening of spectacular eating. Order tickets immediately, 220-6511; they go fast!

role, whole baby carrots and real mashed potatoes. Note that this is one of the most popular stops in town, and it's often crowded. Just about any time of year you must plan to wait as long as 30 minutes, but it is worth the wait. Be sure to sign in with the hostess upon arrival. An inviting front porch is outfitted with many rocking chairs so you can relax and wait your turn. Too chilly to sit and rock? Browse through the charming country store until your party is called.

### The Dining Room at Ford's Colony
$$$$ • 240 Ford's Colony Dr. • 258-4100

Excellence is the standard here, and it starts with the careful attention of the valet parking staff. Contemporary American creations and innovative variations on classic American and European dishes are carefully prepared for discerning diners, with the menu changing seasonally. The extensive wine list (more than 1,000 items) has been honored with an award by The Wine Spectator magazine. The quiet, formal elegance of the room is matched by the equally quiet, efficient service of the staff. The chef works magic with just about everything he prepares, but his variations on salmon are among the best. Ask what he's prepared for the salmon dish of the day when you're there. Reservations are in order. The restaurant is closed Mondays.

### Doraldo's
$-$$ Major credit cards accepted • 1915 Pocahontas Trail, Village Shops at Kingsmill • 220-0795

Cozy and casual, this new Italian restaurant offers a traditional menu and serves up tasty, authentic cuisine. Chef Aldo and his wife, Dora, offer an extensive menu featuring a combination of Northern and Southern Italian dishes - including veal, fish, eggplant, chicken, seafood, beef and a glorious array of pastas and, of course, pizzas. The food is so good, in fact, that the small dining room fills up fast. And since food is prepared to order, plan to sit and relax. Open 11AM-3PM for lunch; 5-10 PM for dinner.

### Dynasty Restaurant
$$ • 1621 Richmond Rd. • 220-8888

Readers and critics of the Daily Press's annual restaurant survey consider this among the very best Oriental restaurants in Tidewater, and with good reason. The design of this restaurant, modeled on the ancestral mainland Chinese home of the host Liu family, makes it one of the most pleasing and most unusual buildings in the city. It is an elegant setting for delicious, authentic cuisine. Popular Chinese favorites are very finely prepared here, but there are also unusual, award-winning dishes created under the supervision of Grace Liu, an acknowledged gourmet chef and instructor in Chinese cuisine. If you're unfamiliar with Chinese cuisine, one of the Liu's, who are always on the premises, will gladly make a recommendation based on fresh, seasonally available ingredients. You won't be disappointed. The bar can provide your favorite cocktail or exotic Pacific-theme drink. Families are welcome, and the mood is casual and friendly. Carry out and delivery are available.

### Fireside Steak House & Seafood
$$ • 1995 Richmond Rd. • 229-3310

Westerners and Midwesterners visiting the East Coast might long for the fine beef they are accustomed to at home. If this applies to you, Fireside specializes in what you're longing for: steaks and other cuts from aged Western beef cooked just as you like them. Fresh seafood dishes and other favorites are also on the menu and equally tempting. Dress is casual here, in keeping with the family orientation, and take-out orders are welcome. Open daily, the Fireside also serves lunch on Sunday.

### Gabriel Archer Tavern at the Williamsburg Winery
$ Major credit cards accepted • 5800 Wessex Hundred • 229-0999

If you're looking for a quiet, inexpensive lunch in a wholly pleasant setting where a glass of wine is proffered along with made-to-order entrees, drive out to the Williamsburg Winery. This place is, indeed, special. The menu is limited - smoked salmon, selected pates, Italian prosciutto, sliced tenderloin, a wonderful fresh mozzarella and roasted red peppers sandwich on basil focaccia, and the like - but it is tastefully, carefully prepared and nicely served. But you're getting more than just a good meal for the money. You'll dine in a quiet setting amid grape orchards. Gentle breezes keep you cool on the veranda, or you can opt for the air-conditioned dining room. Both are wonderful in their own right. The service is attentive but low-key - and since this place is a little off the beaten track, it's rarely noisy or busy. It is tops among Insiders in the Know. Along with your meal, enjoy a glass of Governor's White, John Adlum Chardonnay. Other wines are offered as well. Top off your meal with a tour of the winery and a visit to the gift shop across the lane from the tavern. Open 11AM to 4:30PM daily.

## The Gazebo House of Pancakes and Waffles

$, no credit cards • 409 Bypass Rd. • 220-0883

This bright, airy restaurant is convenient to all lodgings on Bypass Road and is popular for both breakfast and lunch. There are 21 pancake and waffle dishes, complete Virginia country breakfasts offered all day and a variety of specials and fresh sandwiches available at lunchtime, when area business people join tourists to relax while enjoying the indoor garden environment. In season, The Gazebo also serves dinner. We suggest you call ahead to check on daily specials.

## The George Washington Inn Dining Room

$-$$ • 500 Merrimac Tr. • 220-1410

The nightly smorgasbord here is very popular with townsfolk and guests of the hotel. This is especially true on Sunday, when the famous $9.95 buffet brunch defies us even to sample all of the offerings from steamship round of beef, carved as requested, to fresh fruit dishes and a variety of pastry desserts. The nightly seasonal smorgasbord is served 4:30 to 9PM, and the Sunday brunch is presented from 9:30

AM until 2 PM. Unless you want to take a chance, we recommend getting on the seating list early. Reservations are in order.

## Gidi Gourmet

$ No credit cards • 6532 Richmond Rd. • 565-0300

The Gidi Gourmet is aptly named, as we've never tasted anything here that wasn't absolutely delicious! You must carry out your order as there is no place to sit, but trust us, it's worth the inconvenience. Eat in the car if you must . . . but don't miss this place. It serves up a tasty variety of soups, salads, grilled and hot sandwiches, cold sandwiches - all on a variety of fresh breads and rolls. This place offers a wide variety of fresh homemade salads, including those for vegetarians, some with meats, fruits, potatoes and pastas - as many as 25 selections per day - that are sold by the pound. But don't overindulge on your entree as you'll want to save room for dessert. Trust us again. Just don't fail to give this place a try. You won't be disappointed. Open daily except Sunday from 10 AM until 4 PM. In a rush? Call ahead, and your order will be ready when you arrive.

## Giorgio's Pizza Shoppe

$-$$, No credit cards • Colony Square Shopping Ctr., 1303 Jamestown Rd. • 229-0300

Under new ownership, you're in for a treat at this little place. Italian-style pizza is made fresh to order. While the decor - typical pizza parlor - is nothing to write home about, it offers casual, friendly service and comfortable booths and tasty food. Especially good: the Sicilian pizza and lamb stew. Yes, lamb stew. The chef is creative, adventuresome and uses only locally available, seasonal meats, veggies and seafoods. In addition to super pizza, the menu features assorted Italian and American subs and salads. Open 11 AM-10 PM Monday-Saturday. Too tired to wander out? They'll deliver anything on the menu to your door upon request. They also offer beer (including some unusual micro-brewery selections) and wine on and off the premises.

## Giuseppe's Italian Cafe
**$-$$ • Ewell Station Shopping Ctr., 5601 Richmond Rd. • 565-1977**

The enticing aroma of delicately blended olive oil and fresh garlic tells you immediately that this is real Italian food at its finest. We love it! Chef Daniel Kennedy and host Joe Scordo offer a pleasing blend of carefully prepared fine food, a comfortable, upbeat dining room and friendly service in their trattoria, with al fresco dining in season. An unusual and varied menu with a wide variety of prices offers such treats as crab-stuffed ravioli appetizers, several vegetarian entrees, an outstanding lentil and sausage soup and contemporary versions of old Italian standby desserts such as spumoni and cannoli. Everything is made to order, yet the small kitchen churns out meals quickly, so there's no waiting between courses. Because of the fine quality of the food, this is an extremely popular restaurant with Insiders for both lunch and dinner. Giuseppe's only takes reservations for parties of six or more.

## Green Leafe Cafe
**$ • 765 Scotland St. • 220-3405**

This is where the College of William and Mary students and other Generation Xers congregate. In addition to its proximity to the college campus, it offers a menu that can fill the bill whether you're looking for something simple (burgers and the like) to something a little more exotic (some super Greek and American specialties). Also check out the homemade desserts. The bar offers cocktails and bottled and draft beer. Live entertainment sometimes makes the evenings even more pleasant. Note that this place can be crowded, lively and loud, but the food is good, and the atmosphere is fun. The cafe serves food until about midnight; the bar is open until everyone is happy or 2 AM, whichever comes first.

## The Grille at Ford's Colony
**$ • 240 Ford's Colony Dr. • 258-4100**

Bistro fare - pastas, entrees and traditional grill items - is the specialty of this alternative to the more formal Dining Room at Ford's Colony. The Grille serves lunch and dinner in an intimate atmosphere. The menu is varied and the food is excellent. The grilled salmon is particularly wonderful. Note that this establishment is closed Mondays.

## Hayashi Japanese Restaurant
**$$ • 5601 Richmond Rd. • 253-0282**

Growing in popularity among locals, Hayashi offers traditional Japanese cuisine as well as a full sushi bar. The decor is understated, and the atmosphere makes for an enjoyable, serene and memorable repast. Lunch is served Monday through Friday, while dinner is served nightly.

## IHOP
**$ • 1412 Richmond Rd. • 229-9628**

Yeah, yeah. We know we're not supposed to list chain restaurants. But this International House of Pancakes is the only restaurant in Williamsburg that remains open 24 hours a day. Breakfast is served anytime. Lunch and dinner also are served. A children's menu is offered. IHOP is big enough to accommodate large groups and banquets. A word of caution: The entrance is at a busy intersection along Richmond Road. Be very careful turning in and out of this establishment.

## Indian Fields Tavern
**$$ • Rt. 5, Charles City Co. • (804) 829-5004**

Halfway between Williamsburg and Richmond is this superb restaurant in a remodeled, late 19th-century farmhouse. You can dine inside or outside, in favorable weather. The menu is varied, and specials are offered daily. It is open daily for lunch and dinner and on Sunday for brunch. We

---

**INSIDERS' TIP**

**In season, try soft-shell crabs lightly sauteed. There are few things tastier!**

strongly recommend reservations for dinner. It is a superb stop when you're touring the Route 5 plantations, as it is just minutes from Sherwood Forest, Berkeley, Shirley and Evelynton.

## James River Pie
**$ No credit cards • 1804 Jamestown Rd • 229-7775**

Everything about this restaurant is a little unusual - beginning with the name. But it aptly describes the place that offers primarily two things: pizza and pecan pies. The difference: They may be the best pizzas and pecan pie you've eaten in years. Chef Charly Graff (who also operates Charly's at the Williamsburg Jamestown Airport) does what he does best at this simple location, a stone's throw from the Jamestown Ferry. Pizza options include traditional red or white sauce pizzas with a variety of toppings, or Charly's house specialties: including a Greek option with feta, black olives, pepperoncini and mozzarella; a Mississippi River Pie with seafood marinara, shrimp, mushrooms, andouille sausage and mozzarella; the River Crab Pie with jumbo lump crabmeat, a white sauce and mozzarella; or the Maui River Pie with ham, pineapple, spring onions and cheese. Not in the mood for pizza? Choose from a cup or bowl of seafood bisque or chili, or enjoy a prime rib sandwich or southside BBQ. But, save room for a slice of the chef's legendary pecan pie. It may be the best in Southeast Virginia. The hours are quirky, so it's best to call ahead, though they're usually there 11:30 AM-2:30 PM and 5-9:30 PM Tuesday-Sunday. Closed Monday.

## J.M. Randall's
**$$ • 4854 4-16 Longhill Rd. • 259-0406**

Combine your favorite grill fare and specials with the music offered here, and you've got a hit. Especially popular among locals who frequent the small eatery, it's known for good home cooking and fun. Acoustic, progressive, blues, jazz - you'll find it all live, and the place swings until 2 AM seven days a week. Sunday brunch features NFL football on five screens, and

the same screens get another workout for Monday night football. The restaurant is open for lunch and dinner.

## The Jefferson Inn
**$$ • 1453 Richmond Rd. • 229-2296**

Since 1956, this restaurant has been delighting patrons with delicious steaks, fresh seafood and other choices from the wide variety on the menu. The charming English country decor invites a leisurely meal with cocktails and a selection from the wine list. We recommend reservations - and dessert - here.

## Jimmy's Pizza-Pasta Restaurant
**$ • 7201 Richmond Rd. • 565-1465**

Locals pack this place on weekends and often on weeknights, testimony to the fact that the pizza is authentic and the pastas are made to order. This small eatery is known for super pizzas (any style) with standard toppings, as well as pasta dishes sure to delight. Also on the menu are eggplant, chicken and veal Parmesan, served with salad, garlic bread and pasta on the side.

## Kingsmill Restaurants
**$-$$$ • 100 Golf Club Rd. • 253-3900**

There are several options here to suit your mood or your needs, and each of them affords wonderful views of the James River. The Bray Room, on the main level of the Conference Center, offers a menu of special selections each evening as well as wonderful fresh seafood, veal or beef. A wine list capable of pleasing the finest palate is available, as are delicious desserts. A beautiful view of the James River is the backdrop. This room is a very popular location with townsfolk for its Sunday buffet brunch of unusually fine selections. We think it's the best in town. The Bray Room is closed Sunday evenings.

The Kingsmill Cafe in the Golf Clubhouse offers breakfast, lunch and dinner. It is closed Monday evenings.

The Peyton Grille at the Sports Club serves light lunches and dinners.

For drinks in a casual setting, Moody's Tavern on the top level of the Conference Center specializes in Anheuser-Busch prod-

Photo: Busch Gardens

Dining at Busch Gardens becomes a part of the experience.

ucts and cocktails. We recommend reservations for dinner or the Sunday brunch. Smoking is not permitted in any of the Kingsmill Restaurants.

## The Kitchen At Powhatan Plantation
$$$ • 3601 Ironbound Rd. • 220-1200

If you're in the mood for a special night out and a superb dining experience in an atmosphere unlike any other in the area, this is the place to go. Located in a small outbuilding in the shadow of the restored, 18th-century Powhatan Plantation house, this restaurant is quaint but exquisite. Enjoy a limited but excellent menu featuring fresh seafood, wild game and regional favorites in a Colonial setting. An extensive wine list and excellent desserts and specials are offered nightly. The dining room is very small, so reservations are a must. The Kitchen is closed Mondays.

## La Tolteca Mexican Restaurante
$ • 5351 Richmond Rd. • 253-2939
$ • 135 Second St. • 259-0598

This popular, locally run Mexican restaurant now has two locations, one on either side of town. Both offer tasty, authentic Mexican food. Homemade tamales, chile rellenos, chalupas, chimichangas, enchiladas and burritos are among the dishes prepared fresh each day. An imported beer or cocktail might set your meal off just right, and there are eight of the former from which to choose. A vegetarian menu also is available. Is it any wonder why Insiders like these places? Both restaurants are small, so don't be surprised to find a line at the Richmond Road location. Hint: You'll rarely encounter that problem at the Second Street restaurant.

## Le Yaca
$$$ • The Village Shops at Kingsmill, 1915 Pocahontas Tr. • 220-3616

This is one of the area's finest restaurants, offering creative French cuisine in a country French atmosphere. All lunch and dinner, selections are sure to please even the most critical palate, and the proper wine to accompany each meal is available on the extensive wine list. A lovely, unusual buffet is offered at noon, but don't rush through it. There's always a choice of two homemade soups and an array of delicious salads and cold entrees such as couscous with herbs, cubed lamb and potatoes, marinated green beans or other veggies and so on. This is not your typical buffet - but then this is far from your typical restaurant. Whether you opt for lunch or dinner, do not miss the delicious onion soup: This is the onion soup you've always imagined existed somewhere in this country. The rest of your meal is sure to be equally outstanding. As you can expect, the wine list, like the food served here, is exquisite. We strongly suggest reservations.

## Lightfoot Pancake and Steak House
$ • Rt. 60 W. • 565-1105

Enjoy a filling breakfast, lunch or dinner at this popular pancake and steak eatery. The breakfast menu features a typical selection of pancakes, waffles, omelets and special Southern breakfasts. The lunch menu includes everything from three-egg omelets and super sandwiches to daily specials. Dinner is the time for soups, salads and assorted entrees, but the restaurant is especially popular for its grilled steaks.

## The Lobster House
$$$ • 1425 Richmond Rd. • 229-7771

Of course, the featured selection here is live Maine lobsters, cooked however you wish. Broiled fresh seafood from the area's waters, mesquite-grilled steaks, broiled chicken and many other items are also on the dinner menu.

## Mama Mia's Pizza & Delicatessen
$, no credit cards • 521 Prince George St. • 253-2225

Dine in or carry out from this deli, located a block from Merchants Square. The selection of food includes pizza, stromboli, gyros and souvlaki as well as steaks and seafood. A good selection of beer and wine is provided. Limited delivery is offered. The deli does not have a nonsmoking section.

## Mama Steve's House of Pancakes
$, no credit cards • 1509 Richmond Rd. • 229-7613

A landmark along Richmond Road, this restaurant offers breakfast and lunch every day of the week in a casual, inviting atmosphere. Parking is plentiful, and the Historic Area and the outlets are just minutes away.

## Manhattan Bagel
$ All major credit cards • 1437 Richmond Rd • 259-9221

If you're in the mood for authentic New York bagels, this is the place. Diners can select from among 23 different flavored bagels, baked continuously throughout the day, which are offered along with myriad accompaniments. Most popular selections include their deli sandwiches, featuring fine Boar's Head brand meats and cheeses. Also available are gourmet coffees, espresso and cappuccino included. Jumbo gourmet muffins, cinnamon rolls, pastries other sweets featured as well. The atmosphere is casual yet inviting, and this place is always impeccably clean. Open 6:30 AM-6 PM Monday-Friday; 6:30 AM-3 PM Saturday; 7 AM-3 PM Sunday.

## Maple Tree Pancakes & Waffles
$ No credit cards • 1665 Richmond Rd • 220-3544

What is it about being on the road that makes you crave a hardy breakfast - especially pancakes and waffles? In a town where there are more than your usual selection of pancake houses, this tidy little restaurant holds its own nicely. The menu offers an extensive selection of pancakes and waffles - from small silver dollar pancakes to jumbo flapjacks, and a mouth-watering selection of waffles - fancy or plain. Someone in your group not in the mood? There's also a selection of other breakfast fare - available from opening till mid-day closing- including assorted egg dishes, sausage, ham, bacon and corned beef hash as well as cereals and more. Open daily 7 AM until about 2 PM.

## Marino's Italian Cuisine
$$ • 1338 Richmond Rd. • 253-1844

There is an all-you-can-eat buffet with veal Parmigiana, spaghetti and salads, here. Diners can also select from a full menu of dishes including steaks and seafood. A children's menu is available. The restaurant also opens for lunch on Sunday.

## Martha's Plantation Breakfast
$ • 516 Merrimac Tr. • 220-1604

Adjacent to the George Washington Inn, this popular breakfast and lunch spot is known for generous portions, quick service and low prices. The daily breakfast menu is exhaustive and offers just about anything you could want from something simple (scrambled eggs and bacon) to something more exotic (eggs Benedict with Smithfield ham). Lunch offers as much selection in addition to daily specials that, for many people, serve as the large meal of the day. Note that while this large dining room fills fast (the good word is out), any line will move quickly. It is well worth the wait.

## Milano's Italian Family Restaurant
$$ • 1635 Richmond Rd. • 220-2527

The all-you-can-eat spaghetti, soup and salad bar is only one attraction at this restaurant. Your host directly prepares all meals, and the service staff is equally attentive to guaranteeing your satisfaction. The sauces here are delicious, and the offerings include northern Italian dishes that are hard to find in this area. A children's menu is available.

## Mr. Liu's Chinese Restaurant & Lounge

**$$ • The Village Shops at Kingsmill, 1915 Pocahontas Tr. • 253-0990**

In the Village Shops at Kingsmill, between the Historic Area and Busch Gardens, this restaurant is popular with tourists and townsfolk alike. Rick Liu and his staff present excellent Hunan, Szechwan, Mandarin and Cantonese cuisine in a quiet, modern setting accented by beautiful examples of Chinese art. The preparation and presentation of every dish, whether traditional or a house specialty, are attended to with great care. The daily luncheon specials draw folks from the offices nearby as well as residents of Kingsmill, and the restaurant is an ideal place to sample a cocktail or selection from the wine list, then to relax and enjoy an evening of good service and good food. If you are in a hurry or would prefer to take your meals with you, carry out orders are welcome. There is also limited delivery service available.

## Mongolian BBQ Restaurant

**$$ • Kingsgate Greene Shopping Ctr., 122 Waller Mill Rd. • 220-1118**

Here's one kind of barbecue that's news, even in the South! This restaurant is unique in the area. After enjoying one of the wonderful soups, move to the curved buffet line and select the ingredients for a fresh salad. We recommend the peanut dressing. After your salad, return to the buffet and fill a bowl with Chinese noodles and selections from the fresh-cut vegetables, then choose from a variety of meats, from chicken to lamb, and top it off with your selections from a variety of sauces and herbed oils - the unique secret of the restaurant. At that point, the show begins. Hand your bowl to the cook behind the curved buffet and watch as he sizzles it, walking slowly in a circle around the huge round grill and stirring your meal with what have to be the world's largest chopsticks. Every dish is different, and you may return to the buffet as often as you wish. There is a tasty dessert section at the buffet if you have any room left. The meal is prix fixe, with a lower charge for children.

## Morrison's Cafeteria

**$ • 1851 Richmond Rd. • 253-0292**

The finest in Southern buffet-style dining is found at Morrison's. You'll have to exert some control at the beginning of the line or else you may end up with everything from soup to nuts when you reach the cashier. Morning offerings run the gamut from pancakes, waffles and hot or cold cereals to eggs any style, juices and fruits galore, bacon, sausage, gravies and more. Fresh breads and biscuits round out the selection. The midday and evening offerings begin with an array of salads (congealed, green leaf, shrimp and more) and oh, what desserts! Next come the entrees, usually consisting of several seafood options, roast beef, fried and baked chicken, veal, spaghetti and more. In addition, an array of cooked vegetables is offered - broccoli, green beans, black-eyed peas, okra, cabbage, fried eggplant, stewed tomatoes, corn and others. Beverages range from iced tea and coffee to soft drinks and fruit juices. And the price can't be beat anywhere in town. Don't let the long line deter you. It moves fast.

## National Pancake House

**$ • Festival Marketplace at Kingsmill, 264 McLaws Cir. • 220-9433**

This restaurant features homemade Belgian waffles, pancakes, country fresh eggs and healthy alternatives, as well as a soup

---

### INSIDERS' TIP

Indulge yourself with a relaxing seafood outing: Take the Colonial Parkway to Yorktown and stop at Nick's Seafood Pavilion for broiled crabmeat a la Pavilion, seafood shish-kebab or lobster tails and a slice of rum cream pie.

and sandwich lunch menu. It is open through lunch only.

## Nawab Indian Cuisine
$$ Major credit cards accepted • 204 Monticello Ave. • 565-3200

The dining room is small, but crisp, white linens, ceiling fans and nicely attired, attentive waiters set the stage for this excellent East Indian restaurant, a newcomer to the local scene. The extensive menu offers something to please everyone - from the seasoned diner to those who are tasting Indian cuisine for the first time. The menu is so extensive that making a choice is the most difficult thing you'll face here. In addition to appetizers, soups and salads, the menu offers a variety of tandoori specialties - all cooked in a clay pit oven fueled by charcoal - including chicken, lamb, beef, shrimp and fish options. As you would expect, there are curries galore - with the temperature adjusted to your preference. Indian staples, such as raita, mango chutney, and specialty breads including naan, roti and pratha are featured. First timers might want to order the Nawab Special: A sampler of Indian foods that includes soup, tandoori chicken, lamb kabob, a choice of lamb, beef or chicken curry, vegetable korma, basmati rice and naan bread. Vegetarians will delight in the Vegetable Thali - a sampler of the best in Indian vegetarian cuisine. Remember, however, that when you order anything, specify if you want it prepared mild, medium, hot or Indian hot. There is a difference!

## New England Grill
$$ • 6925 Richmond Rd. • 220-2910

One of the area's newest eateries, this good restaurant is located in an old fried chicken restaurant location. But don't be put off by the exterior decor, as a massive makeover has brought the interior of this informal little family eatery into its own. Besides, once you open the menu, you'll forget where you are. The offerings are extensive and reasonably priced, featuring mouth-watering concoctions sure to tantalize the most discriminating or picky diner. Some regular menu items include Italian

Zuppa de Pesce (lobster, shrimp, clams, calamari and scungilli in marinara sauce over linguine), Caribbean Coconut Shrimp with Mango Chutney and Brazilian Rock Lobster Tails with Oyster Bar Sauce. Need we say more? You can come as you are, and no reservations are needed. . . yet. We predict the popularity of this place will force the owners to require reservations at some point in the near future.

## New York Deli
$, no credit cards • 6572 Richmond Rd., Lightfoot • 564-9258

The name of this popular deli should pay tribute to the delicious Greek food available here. Yes, you can get the standard New York deli fare: good corned beef and Swiss on rye, piled high roast beef, pastrami, kosher dills, smoked turkey and ham, cole slaw, assorted beverages and more - but try some of the Greek specialties if you want a taste treat. If you're lucky, Kiki will have made some of her fresh rice pudding. If your timing is really good, it will still be warm. This place is informal, but the food is something special. It doesn't offer a nonsmoking section, however.

## Old Chickahominy House
$ • 1211 Jamestown Rd. • 229-4689

This restaurant is extremely popular with locals, who keep it hopping during off season. But any other time of the year, the place is packed with visitors who remember a good thing and return again and again. Located on Jamestown Road a few blocks west of the Historic Area, this traditional Virginia plantation house is decorated in the style of a Colonial tavern, but the real attraction is the reasonably priced and excellent breakfasts and lunches. They include fresh chicken and dumplings, our favorite version of the traditional Virginia ham biscuit, and Brunswick stew. Miss Melinda's Special is a sampler plate we recommend to first-time guests. We strongly recommend that you save room for a slice of one of the delicious, home-made pies. They all are special, and making a choice is difficult. However, if you can force yourself to turn down the coconut pie or a slice of the delicious semisweet-chocolate pie, try the buttermilk - it is excellent and not commonly found in this area. We're getting hungry just writing about it. Upon arriving, be sure your name is added to the seating list, then enjoy examining the antiques and other items for sale in the shop. Tired? Have a seat on the large front porch and watch the passing parade. The restaurant is open for breakfast and lunch only – but, don't leave town without sampling it.

### Old Mill House Of Pancakes & Waffles

$ • 2005 Richmond Rd. • 229-3613

Open for breakfast and lunch daily, this restaurant presents 16 varieties of pancakes and waffles in an airy, cheerful atmosphere. There are also breakfast and lunch menus offering a large selection of other foods. The Plantation Breakfast is a must for hearty eaters, and the daily (except Saturday) luncheon specials are popular with townsfolk. Smoking is not permitted.

### Padow's Hams & Deli

$ • Williamsburg Shopping Ctr., 1258 Richmond Rd. • 220-4267

This is a great place to go for delicious made-to-order deli sandwiches - more than 40 varieties of them. The deli, which is open until 8 PM, also offers fresh soups and salads and a good selection of desserts. The friendly folks at Padow's will be glad to box your favorite sandwich, drink and other side orders if you are on the go. If you want to take a little more home with you, Padow's offers whole Smithfield hams, smoked turkeys, Virginia peanuts and gift baskets.

### Papillon: A Bistro

$$ • Williamsburg Hospitality House, 415 Richmond Rd. • 229-4020

The comfortable decor in this room provides a relaxed but somehow elegant setting in which to enjoy a meal Tuesday through Saturday. This is an upscale but comfortable restaurant with an excellent menu for breakfast and dinner. Christopher's Tavern, open daily, is located in the same building. It is famous for its burgers and business lunches.

### Paul's Deli Restaurant & Pizza

$ • 761 Scotland St. • 229-8976

Fresh "New England-style" pizza is this deli's featured dish, but you will also find Greek and Italian dishes on the menu. A large selection of imported and domestic beers and wines is available to complement your choice or to help you cheer as you follow the action on the large-screen television. Just off Richmond Road across from William and Mary's football stadium, this is a popular spot with students. It's open for lunch and dinner daily until 2 AM, and delivery to area lodgings is available.

### The Peddler Steak House

$$ • 3048 Richmond Rd. • 565-2904

This is beef lovers' heaven! A server wheels a cart laden with a slab of beef to your table for you to inspect and select your dinner portion. Then it is grilled precisely to your order over hickory charcoal. Meanwhile you can indulge yourself at the fine salad bar (which offers just about anything you could wish for) or with cocktails or wine. Prime rib is the specialty of the house, but other options include filet mignon, broiled teriyaki chicken, shrimp and surf and turf. Children are welcomed with their own menu.

### Peking Restaurant

$ • Kingsgate Greene Shopping Ctr., 122 Waller Mill Rd. • 229-2288
$ • Ewell Station Shopping Ctr., 5601-12 Richmond Rd. • 565-1212

These two establishments have quickly gained popularity with townsfolk and visitors alike, particularly for the Sunday brunch. In both locations, the Diau family offers diners a modern, bright and tasteful atmosphere decorated with beautiful Chinese art. Equally appealing are the fine Peking, Hunan and Szechwan meals. We especially like General Tso's Chicken, lightly breaded and glazed, but fresh ingredients, large portions and beautiful presentation are hallmarks of every dish. Both locations offer a daily lunch and dinner buffet. The wait staff is efficient, extremely helpful in recommending new alternatives, and very attentive throughout your meal. A nice alternative to the popular wines and Pacific-theme drinks is an order of sake, served warm in the traditional container with cups. On Sunday an extremely popular buffet brunch is offered at the Kingsgate Greene location from noon to 2:30 PM.

## Pierce's Pitt Bar-B-Que
$ • Rochambeau Dr. • 565-2955

Here's a true bit of local history: When highway construction on Interstate 64 restricted access to the restaurant, Pierce's barbecue fans parked their semis, cars and vans on the new highway's shoulders in order to get their "cue." The highway department put up a fence. No problem. What's a little ol' fence to a determined barbecue connoisseur? It was knocked down and scrambled over more than once by folks determined to get to Pierce's. Finally people have accepted that, to get to the restaurant, it's best to use the Lightfoot exit and follow Rochambeau Drive. The restaurant is a little more than a mile on your right. You are almost certain to have a short wait in line, but the pulled-pork barbecue made right on the premises (you can follow your nose to Pierce's on a clear day), onion rings and other selections are worth the wait. Indoor seating was added years ago, but the orange paint remains and somehow is perfectly in keeping with the whole experience. Just ask beachgoers and other travelers from all over the state who make the pilgrimage regularly. We'll even risk some friends' wrath by quietly admitting that your local hostess' barbecue was catered by, or carried out from, Pierce's.

## Pizzeria Uno Chicago Bar & Grill
$-$$ Major credit cards accepted • 205 Bypass Rd. • 220-5454

A taste of Yankee pizza right here in southeastern Virginia: that's what this restaurant is all about. The extensive, entertaining menu features authentic, hit-and-run traditional Chicago-style deep-dish pizzas with a variety of toppings. Also offered

are sumptuous appetizers, ample entrees and tempting desserts - and that's just for starters. The menu also offers a variety of fresh salads, sandwiches, burgers and pastas. Perennial favorites include Baked Chicken Spinoccoli, chicken fajitas, and cooked-to-order sirloin tips. Full bar on premises. Open 11AM-11PM Monday-Thursday; 11AM-Midnight Saturday and 11 AM-10 PM Sunday.

## The Polo Club Restaurant and Tavern
$$ • Colony Square Shopping Ctr., 1303 Jamestown Rd. • 220-1122

This restaurant is a very popular place with local folk at lunch and dinner. The tavern area is sufficiently separate from the dining areas to keep the moods distinct for those wanting a quiet meal. Later in the evening, the place becomes crowded and more boisterous as young professionals are joined by college students. The drinks are good, the food varied and always very tasty. Our favorite burger creations in the city are here, but other options on the menu and the daily specials frequently tempt us as well. A kids' menu is sensitive to their limited taste preferences, and the portions are scaled to their appetites.

## The Prime Rib House
$$ • 1433 Richmond Rd. • 229-6823

This restaurant is noted, of course, for its tender cuts of prime rib, but other specialties include Chateaubriand, rack of lamb, veal, chicken, quail, lobsters, shrimp and Eastern shore seafood. Various combinations can be ordered.

## Prince George Espresso & Roastery
$ • 433 Prince George St. • 220-6670

This is a wonderful addition to the Merchants Square area: an indoor cafe with the warm smell of freshly ground rich coffees and a delightful array of light meals. Fresh baked breads and gourmet pastries complement a variety of hot and cold sandwiches, each with a fresh twist in its creation. Prince George offers a variety of salads and soups, changing seasonally.

Photo: Busch Gardens

Tempting? Try some dessert at Busch Gardens.

Seating is on two levels: The downstairs Undergrounds is the main seating area, but you may enjoy pastries and coffee with a window view on the ground floor. The specialty, of course, is coffees, with daily special blends and great tasting pure bean selections guaranteed to remind you why you love the brew. An equally impressive assortment is available for those who prefer tea. The specialty drinks made with espresso, Torani Syrups, Ghirardelli chocolate or ice cream, or combinations thereof, are wonderfully inviting as a daytime refresher or as an evening treat. All espresso drinks are available decaffeinated. The items on the menu at Prince George Espresso and Roastery are guaranteed to revitalize weary shoppers or reward them for finding everything on their lists. With its offerings of jazz and acoustic entertainments, this is an excellent non-bar alternative for an evening's outing. We wholeheartedly agree with their motto: "Life's too short to drink bad coffee."

### Queen Anne Dairy Snack

$, no credit cards • 7127 Merrimac Tr. • 229-3051

Pulling up to this establishment is a retro visit to the 1950s era of walk-up window service. Though the building has seen a better day and only has a couple of old outside picnic tables and benches on which to sit, don't be put off. This little place serves some of the best fried shrimp, fried chicken, barbecue and burgers in this part of Virginia. To top it off, order one of their old-fashioned shakes, sundaes or malts. (All together now: I scream, you scream...) You can spend a lot of time making your selection from the variety posted in the window. The price is right, and if you're in the mood for a touch of tasty nostalgia, this is the place to visit.

### Sal's by Victor Italian Restaurant
$ • Williamsburg Shopping Ctr., 1242 Richmond Rd.
220-2641

This in-town location has been a popular eatery for residents and students for years. It has undergone an expansion and a bright new remodeling, and the menu has been expanded to include delicious new dishes. This may just be the best pizza in town - probably because a native-born Italian makes it. Running the kitchen is Chef Vittorio Minichiello, who hosts his guests with friendly warmth and enthusiasm. One sign of the authenticity of the cuisine is the home-made cannolis (pastry desserts), which are a delicious way to end your lunch or dinner - if you saved room. The veal dishes here are particularly delicious. The fresh pastas are unbeatable, and the espresso creations are outstanding. Be sure to check the chalkboard or ask your server about daily dinner specials, because they often are too good to pass up. FYI: Sal's delivers.

### Sal's Piccolo Forno Ristorante Italiano
$ • 835 Capitol Landing Rd. • 221-0443

This restaurant, not affiliated with the other Sal's restaurants, offers more cooking "like mama used to make" - if mama was a fine Italian cook! Excellent hot and cold appetizers and "the largest sandwiches in town" complement a wide selection of pastas and pizzas. Pastas and breads are fired in the brick hearth, which imports a special, smoky flavor that is unmistakable. If the place isn't busy, the chef often is willing to whip up something you desire but don't see on the menu. Children

are welcome. Gregarious owner Anna Liguria is usually on hand to welcome her guests. This location is a quarter-mile from the Historic Area and the Information Center.

### The Seafare Of Williamsburg
$$$ • 1632 Richmond Rd. • 229-0099

The seafood here is very well-prepared, as you would expect. For dry-land diners, options include milk-fed veal, prime beef dishes and tableside gourmet preparations. A wine steward will help you select a vintage to enjoy with your meal, and cocktails also are available. You might select one of the flambe desserts to top off a pleasant dinner. Seafare also is open for lunch on Sunday and dinner daily until 11 PM.

### Seasons Cafe
$$ • Merchants Square • 259-0018

Seasons has captured a loyal audience of Insiders since its opening in the old post office on Merchants Square in December 1993. The restaurant seats 350, with nearly one-third on an awning-covered patio outside. But the restaurant is divided into several rooms and small areas to provide a sense of intimacy. The theme is most definitely Southern (check out the plantation mural), but the cuisine is varied and delicious: contemporary burgers, linguine with spicy peanut sauce, fresh swordfish and Mexican-modeled chicken fajitas are favorites. We recommend you don't overlook the salad bar with its creative seafood and other salads, and the grilled sandwiches on sourdough bread. The smoked barbecued ribs are national award winners, and the tiramisu dessert is scrumptious. The same menu is offered all day, with lunch specials and a Sunday brunch for variety. For $10.95, the brunch is a bargain, with seafood Newburg, beef Burgundy and breakfast items such as flavored waffles. Flavored cappuccinos from the bar will round out an enjoyable meal.

### Second Street Restaurant and Tavern
$ • 140 Second St. • 220-2286

The sports center at this favorite local

hangout, with its seven television screens, is popular throughout the year but especially during football season. The mood is very casual, and when the college is in session, you may have to wait for a seat. Don't let the exuberance of the crowd daunt you - you'll soon be in a party mood yourself. A menu of steaks, seafood, munchies, sandwiches, salads and soups complements the full range of beverage offerings. This is not an adults-only establishment: A children's menu is provided. The grill is open and munchies are available for lunch and dinner until 1:15 AM; the bar is open until 2 AM daily. On Sundays the brunch is very popular.

## Shoney's Restaurant
$ • 1611 Richmond Rd. • 229-2170

Serving breakfast, lunch and dinner, this restaurant is very popular with tourists and townsfolk for its convenient location and its good, family-style dining. There is a full menu of choices including steaks, seafood, sandwiches and soups. A morning breakfast bar becomes a salad bar for later meals. Strawberry pie is a house specialty and a great way to finish your meal.

## Sportsman's Grille
$$ • Marketplace Shopping Ctr., 240 McLaws Cir. • 221-8002

With menu headings such as Starting Line-up, American All-Stars and Spring Training, you know you're in a sportsman's paradise at this restaurant. That's no simple pita sandwich, it's a Catcher's Mitt. Breadsticks are Louisville Sluggers, and the kid selections are teamed under Little League. Pasta dishes, salads, barbecue and pot roast complement the standard grill fare. For dinner, The Main Event offers entrees with salad or soup and daily entree and dessert specials. Insiders are particularly fond of the Birdie Chicken Salad, which pairs chunks of boneless, skinless white meat chicken with chopped pecans and zesty chutney on a bed of greens with thin, crunchy slices of garlic toast on top. Yum! And you don't have to be a sportsman to appreciate the cozy, inviting decor and friendly service. We love this place!

## That Seafood Place
$$ • 1647 Richmond Rd. • 220-3011

Guests enjoy every aspect of lunch and dinner at this locally-owned and -operated restaurant with its fresh Virginia seafood entrees and the outstanding variety on its "sardine can" salad bar. The hosts and service staff are very attentive, and the food is carefully prepared. A special children's menu is provided, and a private dining room is available. We suggest reservations for dinner.

## The Jewish Mother
$ Major credit cards accepted • 2021 Richmond Rd. • 565-0085

Casual and fun, especially for the kids, who are invited to scribble, draw or wax poetic on the walls in this unusual restaurant, which also features lives music most evenings. The menu - as the name suggests - is heavily Yiddish. Borscht, chopped chicken livers, pastrami, corned beef and the like are staples . . . but just the beginning. Sandwiches are piled high; side orders are voluminous and tasty. The menu is extensive and offers appetizers, soups, sandwiches, salads, hot and cold entrees and nightly specials. The breads and desserts are downright dangerous: fresh baked and upsized. A full bar is available, and the atmosphere gets loud after 9 PM when the live acts or deejay get into full swing. The children's menu is tailored to their tastes, and the prices are right on the money. This locally-owned and -operated restaurant is one of several in Southeastern Virginia. Its long-standing reputation isn't compromised here. Open 11 AM-2 AM Monday-Saturday. Closes earlier on Sundays.

## The Trellis
$$$ • Merchants Square • 229-8610

Ah, The Trellis! Please excuse us, but it's hard for Insiders to be casual when attempting to inform visitors about this nationally acclaimed restaurant. To dine here, whether for lunch or for dinner, is to experience a unique and wonderful combination of elegant but understated atmosphere, efficient and pampering service and, well, the menu. It's unforgettable, that menu.

A seasonal selection of noted Executive Chef Marcel Desaulniers' creations features mesquite-grilled fare and regional items such as Chesapeake Bay seafood and Smithfield ham prepared with gourmet accents such as shiitake mushrooms, fine sauces and unusual relishes. The soups and salads are equally fresh, creative and appealing. The menu is re-created each season, and the featured dinners and daily chef's selections are always unique. Listening to the service staff preview them at your table is an effective appetizer in itself. The perfect wine to complement your dinner is certain to be on the extensive list of European and American vintages. If you are not familiar with Virginia's - and particularly Williamsburg's - wines, the staff can advise you in making a selection (and you can also read about them in our Regional Cuisine and Wines chapter). You might wish to complete your dinner with something sweet: The desserts are as unique as the other dishes, and a love affair with one or another is entirely possible. You might think twice about ordering something called Death by Chocolate, but from experience we'd respond "O Death, where is thy sting?" about a dessert more immortal than mortal. If you're not prepared for such a glorious demise, other tasty pastry specials are available, as are homemade ice creams, sorbets and fresh fruits. Chocolate lovers may wish to obtain Chef Desaulniers' books *Death by Chocolate*, *Desserts to Die For*, *An Alphabet of Sweets*, *The Trellis Cookbook* or *Cooking With the Burgermeisters* as gifts or enticements for the cooks at home.

The various rooms in The Trellis have their own charms. Al fresco dining allows guests to view the passing parade on Duke of Gloucester Street. Inside rooms include a cafe with a popular, well-stocked bar and a limited menu (this is the least formal room). The intimate Vault Room has a glass-walled view of the wine selections. In the Grill Room you can enjoy watching dishes cooked to perfection over open flames. The more formal Garden Room is the most expansive

and provides windows overlooking Merchants Square. We suggest that you make reservations early to assure the seating time and room you desire. Attire is nice casual and beyond. The Trellis also offers take-out service for sandwiches, salads and desserts.

## The Veranda Room
**$$ • Fort Magruder Inn & Conference Ctr., Rt. 60 E. • 220-2250**

The Sunday brunch here is particularly popular with area residents who come to enjoy the delicious offerings and beautiful setting while listening to soft piano music. The dining room has views of the beautifully landscaped hotel grounds and offers a delicious variety of selections on its menu for breakfast, lunch and dinner. Special favorites appear on a children's menu. From 5 to 7 PM weekdays, the Sunset Dining special is a choice we recommend. Smoking is not permitted.

## Top's China Restaurant
**$-$$, All major credit cards accepted • 1203 Richmond Rd. and 5751 John Tyler Hwy. • 221-0069, 220-6868**

If you enjoy diverse Chinese cuisine, you ought to plan a lunch or dinner trip to the sumptuous buffet offered at the Richmond Road location. Too tired to dress up and venture out? Call in a take-out order to the Williamsburg Crossing Shopping Center location (220-6868), which offers a full menu of options. But back to the buffet: more than 200 items, including steamed King Crab legs at dinner and Mongolian BBQ anytime, along with dozens of appetizers, entrees, soups and desserts from which to choose. The food is good, the service is attentive and the place is always clean. Lunch ($5.25 adults/$3.50 children 9 and younger; under 2 free) is served 11 AM to 3 PM Monday-Friday; dinner ($8.95 adults/$5.50 children 9 and younger; under 2 free) is served 3-10 PM Monday-Friday. The buffet is offered all day Saturday (11 AM-11PM) and Sunday (Noon-10 PM). The price of a meal includes free beverage of choice and ice cream and cake.

## Vic Zodda's 1776 Restaurant
**$$ • Bypass Rd. • 220-1776**

In the Holiday Inn 1776, this fine eating establishment is popular with locals and visitors. Vic Zodda's offers a fine breakfast buffet every morning and a fine lunch. For dinner, you can choose from a varied dinner menu featuring Italian fare, seafood and steaks, or you may opt for the buffet. The Sunday night Surf & Turf Buffet is especially good and features crab legs, shrimp, roast beef, BBQ ribs, fried chicken and more - all you can eat!

## Welcome South Restaurant
**$ • 8558 Richmond Rd., Rt. 60 at the Rt. 30 intersection • 566-8255**

When we visit this restaurant 9 miles west of Williamsburg, and we do so often, we see right many of our townsfolk at the tables here, all having found or heard that it's worth the effort to enjoy these delicious meals. The kitchen specializes in "affordable Southern cooking with a light gourmet touch," and that includes entrees cooked over charcoal and smoked with mesquite and hickory. The chef makes an unusual and delicious meal of every dish he offers, from steak and chicken to seafood, with wonderful pasta creations and tasty variations on side dishes. This is home cookin' like mama only dreamed of! The atmosphere is very informal, the service is friendly, attentive and helpful, and the food is worth the drive. Oh, and you'd better save room for one of the generous helpings of homemade desserts offered with the requisite gourmet spin: Our favorite is the chocolate pecan pie. We also recommend the Tasty Breakfast Buffet on Sunday. The restaurant serves lunch and dinner. On weekend nights, make reservations if you want to avoid a wait; seatings are in demand. Welcome South is closed Monday and Tuesday.

## The Whaling Company
**$$ • 494 McLaws Cir. • 229-0275**

You can catch a glimpse of this restaurant from Route 60 E. on the way to Busch Gardens. It offers fresh seafood prepared in an incredible variety of ways. Fine beef, chicken and other dinners are satisfying alternative selections. Early bird discounts and a children's menu help make the establishment popular. We recommend reservations for dinner.

## The Whitehall Restaurant
**$$ • 1325 Jamestown Rd. • 229-4677**

This upscale restaurant, which opened in June 1997, features Italian cuisine along with other European specialties. The focus here is on delicious veal and chicken dishes, fine wines and delectable desserts - all served in an atmosphere conducive to memorable dining. Owner Karen Moor prides herself on her restaurant's elegant but laid-back atmosphere and adventuresome yet classic cuisine. Soups of the day vary from the classic fish soup to the more contemporary crab and spinach. Specialties of the house are Wienerschnitzel and Flounder Whitehall, which combines sweet flounder filet with prawns and fresh spinach in a pink sauce, all surrounded by real mashed potatoes. Pasta lovers must try the Trenette Pasta, topped with Pesto Genovese made daily on premises with homegrown basil. Finish your repast with any one of the fine desserts listed on the menu: a special tiramisu, chocolate raspberry torte, Italian cheesecake or creme caramel. The extensive wine list includes appellations from Italy, France, California and Virginia. With the exception of one small room, no smoking is allowed. Attire is nice casual and beyond. Reservations are not necessary during the week but are a must on weekends. This is a fine addition to the local restaurant scene.

## Williamsburg Coffee & Tea
**$ • Williamsburg Crossing Shopping Ctr., 5251-27 John Tyler Hwy. • 565-1400**

This place started out as a retail store carrying a voluminous selection of coffees and more than 200 teas and appropriate coffee and tea preparation paraphernalia. Then, proprietors Todd and Carol Arnette added a few baked goods for people buying a cup to drink on the premises. The next thing you know, there are a dozen or so tables, a solicitous wait staff, and - voila!

- a popular new eatery is born. Warm and cozy, it is only open for breakfast, lunch and mid-morning or mid-afternoon relaxation, but the menu is surprisingly adventuresome and the freshly prepared food and freshly baked bread are delicious. Breakfasts include a choice of egg options and standard sides such as bacon, ham, homefries, bagels with cream cheese and an assortment of cereals, and specials such as biscuits and gravy, Quiche Lorraine, pancakes or waffles. Lunch includes big sandwiches on fresh bread, a selection of hearty soups (our favorite is the Seafood Chowder) and big salads. But the real draw, as expected, is the coffee, cappuccino, espresso and teas - the latter served steaming hot in charming, individual stoneware teapots. Looking for a place to cool off or warm up before heading out to do more shopping or sightseeing? Bring your guidebook, map and tired feet here for a refreshing pick-me-up.

### The Williamsburg Drug Company Lunch Counter

$, no credit cards • Merchants Square • 229-6109

Few real luncheonette counters, like those popular in the 1930s and '40s, still exist. Except here, that is, where you can still walk up and take a seat on a swivel top stool at the counter and order anything from a quick burger or hot dog to a real New York-style egg cream. They hand-dip the ice cream here, and coffee, sodas and Cokes just taste better than usual. Looking for a bite of food in a time warp? Try out this tasty little place. The counter is open for breakfast and lunch.

### Yorkshire Inn Restaurant

$$ • 700 York St. • 229-9790

This was Williamsburg's first nonsmoking restaurant. It's a great place for fine beef, succulent seafood and fine, attentive service in a smoke-free environment. Prime beef and fresh seafood are favorites on the dinner menu, with beef shish kebab the house specialty. Insiders know, however, that the seafood shish kebab is equally delicious but requires a mammoth appetite. Opened and operated by a local family, this establishment has a large local and repeat visitor following, despite its understated location and ambiance. Excellent cocktails and fine wines and beers are available. Banquets can be accommodated, and there is a children's menu. Reservations are in order.

### Yukon Steak Company

$$-$$$ • 1735 Richmond Rd. • 229-1501

The Alaskan hunting-lodge theme of this new steak house is novel in Williamsburg, and the menu is as expansive as the dining room. Bring your appetite any evening for dinner and expect to be treated like you just won the Iditarod by a wait staff obviously trained to keep customers happy. That's not too hard, though. The menu keeps you busy once you're seated, and the selection offers something to everyone's liking. Open hearth cooking adds zest to Alaska Salmon, a variety of steaks (you can order from Pittsburgh rare to as well done as you please), chicken, baby back ribs, burgers and more. But everyone is talking about Yukon's prime rib, offered in 8-, 12- and whopping 16-ounce cuts. The menu also features a rich and creamy Alaskan Salmon Chowder, Alaskan King Crab Legs and a savory entree entitled The Arctic Trawler - shrimp or salmon over linguine with fresh basil, tomatoes, garlic and olive oil. The dessert menu, while limited to three items, is enticing, especially the Mile High Mudslide Pie. The Cub's Grub Menu is especially for kids. But the beer, wine and saloon specials list is just for thirsty adults. The festive atmosphere, reminiscent of the excitement of Gold Rush days, is contagious. This is a fun place to dine with family and friends. But they don't take reservations, so don't be surprised if you have a slight wait upon arrival. It's worth it.

Williamsburg has an abundance of jazz clubs and offers a variety of unusual twilight diversions - from candlelit walking tours to rowdy dinner theaters to 18th-century style concerts.

# Nightlife

What do Bruce Hornsby, Jimmy Buffett, Linda Lavin, Glenn Close and a host of other nationally known entertainers have in common? You might have guessed that we were going to say "Williamsburg," but maybe you don't know why Fact is, they've all performed here and return with some regularity.

This small, quaint town, with its 18th-century buildings and centuries-old traditions, has in the recent past played host to scores of famous people, including actors, rock stars, comedians and other notables. Visitors to the greater Williamsburg area are fortunate in that there is something to appeal to just about everyone when it comes to nightlife.

While you still can find DJs who spin loud, throbbing dance music, in recent years the local bar scene has become decidedly more low-key. Rock 'n' roll and country have taken a backseat to the soulful sounds of jazz and blues, and taverns that offer a quiet, restful place to sip microbrews and enjoy friendly conversations have elbowed out glitzier nightclubs. Fewer nightspots have live music, but those that do choose their acts carefully and make sure their patrons are properly entertained. There also are growing numbers of sports bars and a variety of unusual twilight diversions - from candlelit walking tours to rowdy dinner theaters to 18th-century style concerts - right in the heart of Colonial Williamsburg.

If you're in the mood to quaff a few, keep in mind that Virginia's legal age to buy, possess or consume alcohol is 21, and that a picture identification is required as proof of age. If do you choose to imbibe, it's always best to designate a nondrinking member of your party as chauffeur for the evening.

Because Williamsburg is a college town, there's always something happening at Phi Beta Kappa Hall on the William and Mary campus. To find out what's on the agenda at the hall - where entertainment runs the gamut from folk music to formal recitals - you can call 221-2655 and listen to the list of voice mail options. Or better yet, drop by during your tour of the Colonial capital: Upcoming events are posted in the lobby.

If you're in the mood for a bit of Broadway or an evening of opera and have the whole night to spare, you might want to plan an evening in Norfolk, about an hour's drive east on Interstate 64. Or, if you're looking for big-name musical acts, check out the schedules at the coliseums in Hampton and Richmond, Scope in Norfolk or the new Virginia Beach amphitheater. We give you all the information you need to map out your itinerary in our out-of-town nightspots section near the end of this chapter. For ticket information and availability, call the numbers listed or contact TicketMaster at 872-8100.

The best way to find out what's happening in and around Williamsburg is to check the *Virginia Gazette* (published in town on Wednesdays and Saturdays), the *Newport News Daily Press* (particularly Friday's Ticket and Sunday's Arts sections), *Williamsburg Magazine* (a free monthly publication you can pick up just about anywhere) and *Colonial Guide* (a seasonal publication available free at numerous locations around the greater Williamsburg area). *The Richmond Times-Dispatch* (published each morning) lists happenings and entertainments in the greater Richmond area. To find out what a particular evening's offerings include in and around the Historic Area, consult listings at the Colonial Williamsburg Visitor Center.

Considering the volatile nature of nightspots, whose popularity waxes and wanes with the lunar cycle, don't be afraid to ask residents their opinions on what's available to do any given evening. Chances are you'll learn about the brightest and best that Williamsburg has to offer from those who speak from personal experience.

Oh, by the way, Bruce Hornsby, Glenn Close and Linda Lavin have other, more personal connections to Williamsburg: Bruce is a native son, and Glenn and Linda are graduates of the College of William and Mary, where they studied acting early in their careers.

While we're confident you won't have any trouble finding a suitable venue for passing an enjoyable, memorable evening in Williamsburg, we offer the following list of possible options for an evening out. Happy hunting!

# Munchies, Music and Mayhem

What follows is a list of what we would consider to be typical nightspots. They offer music - either by band, DJ or jukebox, big-screen TVs to catch the game, libations and a bite to eat well into the evening. Stop by and give in to those late-night cravings.

### Bones Sports Pub & Rotisserie
Four Points Hotel and Suites by ITT Sheraton, 351 York St. • 229-4100

If the words "play ball" are music to your ears, check out this revamped sports bar. Open seven nights a week, Bones offers 18 televisions - including one big screen - so you can tune into any sporting event that strikes your fancy. (Lacrosse, anyone?) You also can test your expertise in the interactive trivia contest or fine-tune your hand-eye coordination in one of the dart lanes. There is occasional live music at Bones. Dinner is served from 5 to 11 PM, with light munchies available until the 2 AM close. Attire for the evening is casual.

### Copper Top Lounge
Holiday Inn Patriot, 3032 Richmond Rd. • 565-2600

On weekends, stop in at the Copper Top and enjoy the wide variety of music performed by the local band Natural Blend. Late-night hunger pangs can be sated by an assortment of homemade pizzas, buffalo wings, chicken tenders, potato skins and other finger foods. Some changes are under way at the lounge that may include expanding the number of brews on tap and the nights when live entertainment takes the stage, so call ahead to see what's happening before you head out.

### Green Leafe Cafe
Scotland St. at Richmond Rd. • 220-3405

Open since 1974, this is - without question - the most enduring nightspot in town. (It even says so on the restaurant's matchbook cover, which the owner assured us he pulled directly from this guide!) The Green Leafe is especially popular with locals, as well as with students from the College of William and Mary, which is located across Richmond Road. Good food, diverse conversations and occasional loud music characterize this rather Spartan hang out. Solid wood chairs and tables - impervious to the generations of partiers who have frequented this place - are crowded together, though not uncomfortable. This place rocks until all hours and offers an excellent selection of wines, brews and spirits. At last count, the selection included 100 varieties of bottled American microbrews, a 20-tap draft system (with frequent rotations among selections), 15 single malt Scotches and five single-barrel bourbons. The Green Leafe also offers a large selection of fine cigars, including sought-after stogies from Honduras and Mexico. Join the long line of locals who have helped close the place down night after night (365 times a year), either in the roomy front area or in the more intimate bar in the rear.

### J.B.'s Lounge
Fort Magruder Inn, Rt. 60 • 220-2250

This is a place where you can kick back, watch a baseball game, shoot a round of pool and listen to tunes on the jukebox any night of the week. The attire is casual, the bar is full and sandwiches and light snacks are available until closing at 1 AM.

## J.M. Randalls Restaurant & Tavern
Old Towne Square, 4854 Longhill Rd. • 259-0406

Since opening in 1995, this nightspot has developed quite a reputation for its blues and jazz offerings. As one local musician says: "They're real professionals, and they have the best music room in town." Open until 2 AM seven days a week, J.M. Randalls features local and national talent on Friday and Saturday nights, with Wednesday and Thursday night jam sessions that give aspiring musicians a chance to play with the pros. Big-screen football is a popular Sunday and Monday night option. Salads, sandwiches and moderately priced dinners (one local favorite - honey molasses barbecue ribs) round out the menu.

## The Library Tavern
1330 Richmond Rd. • 229-1012

Open since 1992, this popular nightspot is actually a family-owned restaurant serving pizzas, subs and salads every day of the week until 2 AM. But there's always something else going on to entertain the locals and visitors who flock here. The Library offers special ladies' and gentlemen's evenings, occasional DJs and live music, and an ongoing satellite trivia contest in which you use a computer keyboard and television screen to match wits with anyone and everyone across the country. When the weather is nice, enjoy the outdoor patio seating. And, if you're suffering from a touch of crowd overload, The Library delivers - just make sure you're within a 2-mile radius and plan to order at least $10 worth of food.

## Paul's Deli
761 Scotland St. • 229-8976

A popular destination of the college crowd, Paul's frequently offers a variety of progressive, alternative and acoustical music on occasional Friday and Saturday nights. Call ahead to find out who's on the agenda when you're in town. For those who like a little armchair (or barstool) quarterbacking, nine television screens will take you to the action. This lively spot is open until 2 AM.

## Rockin' Robin
1402 Richmond Rd. • 253-8818

Do you hanker for some good old doo-wop mixed in with your contemporary musical sounds? Get ready, Freddy! Open till the wee hours, here's a rockin' place that features a DJ spinning favorites of the 1950s all the way up through the '90s. And you're always welcome to challenge the DJ to spin your favorite. The decor is appropriate, with old 45 rpm platters featured, and the waitresses in tennis shorts and T-shirts will take you back to the more carefree days of your life.

This hotspot caught on quickly with locals of all ages. Your hosts, Ron and Judy Gee, will probably be mingling, assuring that you have a good time. Dancing is encouraged: In fact, lessons for popular country-line dances are offered every Wednesday, beginning at 8 PM. Rockin' Robin serves dinner entrees from 4 to 9 PM (9:30 PM in the summer). Appetizers and finger food are available nightly until 1 AM closing, but you must be 21 to get in after 9 PM.

## Second Street Restaurant & Tavern
140 2nd St. • 220-2286

There's enough happening in this popular watering hole to keep even the most

---

## INSIDERS' TIP

Join an evening Lanthorn Tour, a guided walk through the candlelit streets and into the workplaces of Colonial Williamsburg. Tours cost $10 ($7.50 for Patriot's Pass holders) and are offered nightly, but hours change depending upon the season. For information call 220-7645.

kinetic partier happy for an entire evening. This is, without a doubt, one of the most popular and perennial after-hours haunts in the Williamsburg area. With the bar open until 2 AM daily and the late-night grill cookin' until 45 minutes before closing, this is a good place to go after taking in a show or concert. A sports center features more than a half-dozen TV screens, offering hard-core sports fans an optimum vantage point from any of the numerous tables in the place.

**www.insiders.com**

See this and many other **Insiders' Guide** destinations online.

**Visit us today!**

those proper folks in the staid paintings were wont to behave at their leisure!

Ale and beer - including Chowning's own label - are available, and there's an assortment of Colonial spirits, beverages and light menu fare. Guests are welcome to join in the fun or to relax and take in the entertainments. Casual clothing is fine here after the dinner hour.

## Let the Games Begin

These two establishments are a bit of a twist on the traditional nightspot. The owners will still feed you and offer you a drink, but they may also ask you to take your turn in a game or two.

### Chowning's Tavern
**100 E. Duke of Gloucester St. • 229-2141**

This authentic Colonial Virginia alehouse, in the heart of the city's Historic Area, comes rambunctiously alive each evening at 9 PM when the "gambols," Colonial tavern games, begin. You'll be seated at big wooden tables side by side with visitors from across the country as you listen to impromptu serenades by costumed troubadours (be prepared: some are designed to bring a blush to the cheek of the fair maid or shy gentleman) and participate in 18th-century board games. The mood is extremely lively, accurately reflecting our forefathers' enthusiasm for the bawdy side of life. You may rethink your understanding of American history when you see how

### The Corner Pocket
**Williamsburg Crossing Shopping Center, Rt. 5 at Rt. 199 • 220-0808**

Here's something completely unique in Williamsburg: an upscale billiard parlor! This may be the perfect alternative to the usual choices for a date, for an early start on a trip to the cinemas a few doors away or for a stop after the show.

It's not your stereotypical pool hall: an 18-years-or-older policy (unless accompanied by a parent) and a dress code are enforced (among other things, that means, gentlemen, your shirts must have collars). There are eight 8-foot tables and three 9-foot tables (Ventana brass pool tables). If you take a break from shooting pool, you can enjoy the large murals, the televisions or the conversation about the armadillos. No, you're not seeing things, and yes, we said armadillos. Don't ask us, we'll just shrug; ask Lynn Allison, the manager and owner.

The Corner Pocket offers a daily menu of light meals featuring soups and unusual, creative entrees. From November through March, they serve lunch and dinner on Friday, Saturday and Sunday. At other times of the year, the restaurant opens for dinner daily at 4 PM. Popular menu items include

---

**INSIDERS' TIP**

Norfolk's Chrysler Hall hosts Broadway musicals every spring and fall. Recent and upcoming performances include *Grease, Chicago, Phantom of the Opera, Les Miserables, Miss Saigon* and *Peter Pan*. Shows are staged Tuesday through Sunday evenings. Matinees are offered on Saturday and Sunday. For more information, call 622-0288.

Get to know the more mischievous side of your forebears nightly at Chownings Tavern.

jambalaya, chicken burritos, a weekly pasta special and a rotating selection of microbrewery beers. Lynn also has begun experimenting occasionally with live music. Once a month during the summer, she brings in a national blues act. Tickets for these evenings, which follow no predetermined schedule but are publicized in the *Virginia Gazette*, start at $10 and can go higher depending upon the act. "The music is very special," says Lynn. "We've had some unbelievable nights here."

Rates for billiards are by the hour and have remained unchanged since The Corner Pocket opened in 1992. They also depend on the size of the party. For one person during the day, the charge is $3 per hour; for four people at night, it is $12 per hour. It's worth it, readers!

## Prince George Espresso & Roastery
**433 Prince George St. • 220-6670**

After shopping or taking in a movie in Merchants Square, stop in at this popular coffeehouse for a cappuccino, latte or flavored (hot or cold) coffee drink. And, if you need a little something to tide you over until morning, you're in luck. Prince George offers everything from muffins, bagels and biscotti to chocolate fudge cake and potato and mushroom knishes. The coffeehouse is open until 10 PM weeknights and 11 PM on weekends.

## Williamsburg Bowl
**5544 Old Towne Rd. • 565-3311**

If bowling is your bag, don your funkiest shirt - you know, the one with somebody else's initials that you picked up for a buck at a yard sale - and head to this popular alley for a round of "Extreme Bowling." This weekend program, which runs from 10 PM to 1 AM Fridays and Saturdays, gives up to six people the chance to rent a lane for two hours for $29.95, a price that includes a tub of popcorn, a pitcher of soft drinks, shoe rentals and a free movie pass for every two people. Or, if you choose, you can bowl on your own at other times. The alley is open until 11 PM Sundays, Mondays, Wednesdays and Thursdays; until midnight on Tuesdays; and until 1 AM Fridays and Saturdays. Cost per game is $2.75 for each person. Shoe rentals are $2.25.

# Lend Me Your Ears

The fun doesn't stop in Williamsburg when the sun goes down. There are plenty of tours, concerts and performances reserved especially for after hours.

## Summer Breeze Concert Series
### Merchants Square • 221-0614, 259-3200

A unique and thoroughly enjoyable entry on the entertainment scene and an excellent early-evening option is the Summer Breeze Concert Series held Wednesday evenings during the summer. Performances by artists from throughout Virginia are held in front of the Christmas Shop in Merchants Square and feature a variety of music from big band and contemporary to traditional jazz, acoustic and Dixieland music. While most concerts start at 6:15 PM, occasionally that changes, so call ahead or check schedules posted around town before you show up. Attendees are invited to bring folding chairs and blankets to the performances. This is a joint effort of the Merchants Square Association, the City of Williamsburg, James City County and WHRV, the local National Public Radio station. To find out who's playing on any given Wednesday, simply call ahead.

## Williamsburg Regional Library
### 515 Scotland St., Williamsburg • 229-7645
### 7770 Croaker Rd., Norge • 259-7729

If you think of a library as a place where the noise level never rises above a whisper, you're in for a surprise. At the regional library (which actually includes both the Williamsburg Library at 515 Scotland Street and the new James City County Library at 7770 Croaker Road in Norge), the evening agenda is crammed full of entertaining sights and sounds. Although the lineup varies, jazz concerts and classes, story readings for adults and classic movies are part of the typical early evening agenda. Many events are free; a few require tickets. Your best bet is to call ahead to see what's up while you're in town.

## The Music Theatre of Williamsburg
### Richmond Rd. • 564-0200,
### (888) 687-4220

With the recent metamorphosis of the Old Dominion Opry into The Music Theatre of Williamsburg, foot-stomping country has given way to a musical revue. The theater, in new digs on Richmond Road next to the Williamsburg Soap & Candle Company, offers a two-hour medley of big band, Broadway and good time rock 'n' roll music, including big hits of the '50s and '60s. Rest assured, there's something here for the music lover in everyone. Shows start at 8 PM each evening. Matinees can be staged for groups of 40 or more. Currently, tickets cost $18 for adults, $12 for ages 12 to 20 and children under 12 are free. Discounts are offered for military personnel and AAA and AARP members. An old-fashioned Christmas special and New Year's Eve extravaganza are offered annually. Reservations are required. We suggest you check the location of the theater when you call for tickets.

## Rosie Rumpe's Regal Dumpe
### Ramada Inn Central Williamsburg, 5351 Richmond Rd. • 565-4443

This three-hour dinner theater is billed as "Music, Magic & Medieval Mayhem at King Henry VIII's Favorite Tavern." Introduced in the spring of 1997, it's actually a lively (and somewhat bawdy) combination of acting, revelry and singing set in a 16th-century London pub run by Rosie, of course. There's plenty of audience participation with a variety of "saucy serving wenches, minstrels and court fools" (as well as Rosie and good old Henry himself). Oh, did we forget to mention all this is merely a side dish to the five-course meal served at your table? Served and consumed as part of the show, the meal includes soup and salad, a choice of entrees (prime rib, half a baked chicken and a cod fillet with shrimp Gouda sauce were on the start-up menu), all the potatoes, vegetables and homemade bread you can eat, nonalcoholic beverages and dessert—the English berry trifle is just grand. Appetizers and bar drinks may be purchased separately.

If you're in need of multiple belly laughs (and a very full belly), call and make a reservation. The cost is $34.95 per person. Shows typically are offered on Fridays and

Saturdays beginning at 7:30 PM. Additional shows may be staged during the summer months. "We like to say it's the most fun you've ever had . . . sitting down," says owner, director and actor George Hafenstab. "Of course, we're going to embarrass you, but it's not done maliciously. We've found people love to play along."

# At the Movies

In the past few years, movie options for residents have quadrupled. Not only have several multiplex theaters opened, but the Williamsburg Theatre on Merchants Square has left the mainstream to feature more foreign and arts pictures, much to the pleasure of area film lovers. Since the video revolution, which has allowed us to turn our living rooms into private viewing palaces, new movie rental stores seem to have popped up each week. Since they don't always last, we've listed below only the movie theaters in the area.

### Carmike Cinema 4
Monticello Shopping Center, 218 Monticello Ave.
• 229-6333

This small, four-screen theater is located on Monticello Avenue across from the Williamsburg Community Hospital. Films feature stereo surround sound. Ticket prices are $6.25 for adults and $4.25 for senior citizens and children younger than 12. All tickets for shows starting before 5:30 PM are $4.25.

### Kiln Creek 14
100 Regal Wy. (off Victory Blvd.), Newport News
• 989-5200

Located about 20 minutes from Williamsburg east on I-64 (Exit 256B), this 14-screen theater is one of our favorite places to take in a recently released flick. The lobby not only offers all the standard fare - popcorn, candy and soda - there also is table seating, a movie screen that offers previews and a coffee bar where you can gulp down an eye-opening cappuccino or espresso before the lights go down. Tickets for evening shows are $6 for adults and $4 for children younger than 12 and seniors 60 and older. All tickets for shows that start before 6 PM are $4. If you want to find out what's playing at any time, simply call the above number. An extensive recording even gives you playing times and a reminder that children aren't allowed in R-rated flicks without a parent accompanying them!

### Patrick Henry 7
Patrick Henry Mall, Jefferson Ave., Newport News
• 249-4117

A 15- to 20-minute hop from Williamsburg east on I-64 to Exit 255A, this seven-screen theater is adjacent to the Patio Food Court just inside the back entrance to Patrick Henry Mall. This theater continues to be our choice when we want to grab a quick bite to eat and do a little shopping before taking in a movie. As for ticket prices, the Patrick Henry 7 offers a number of options. On weekends, shows aired before noon cost $3, matinees are $3.75, and a special twilight engagement is $3. Tickets for evening films are $5.75 for adults and $3.75 for children ages 2 to 13 and senior citizens. If you want to guarantee getting a ticket for a new release or popular flick, you can call the theater's credit card line at 249-5456 and charge your tickets up to three days in advance. There's a 50-cent handling charge per ticket, but it's better than arriving at the box office only to be told the next showing is sold out!

### Williamsburg Crossing
**Rt. 5 and Rt. 199 • 253-2299**

Current movies are offered in eight auditoriums, all with stereo surround sound. Tickets are $4.25 for children and seniors and $6.25 for adults. All tickets for shows that start before 5:30 PM are $4.25.

### The Williamsburg Theatre
**428 Duke of Gloucester St. • 229-1475**

This chandelier-lit, 538-seat theater, with its maroon velvet curtain and "Colonial art deco" look, appears essentially as it did when it opened in 1933. Movies shown here run the gamut - from classics and foreign flicks to independent releases and brief second runs of commercial favorites, just to keep patrons guessing. To give you an idea of this theater's range, recent shows have included *Anna Karenina*, *Trainspotting* and Peter Fonda's *Ulee's Gold*. Shows are scheduled during the evenings, with a Sunday matinee. Midnight shows are offered occasionally. Tickets cost $3.50 for children, $4.50 for students and senior citizens and $5.50 for adults.

## Alternative Action

For those who prefer the great outdoors once night falls, Colonial Williamsburg of-fers a number of (historic and sometimes haunted) evening tours. So put on your walking shoes and check these out.

### Colonial Williamsburg Evening Tours
**Historic Area • 220-7645**

Special one-hour programs are offered every evening in Colonial Williamsburg. Themes range from Colonial dancing at the Capitol to storytelling at the Play Booth Theater to "Science, Conjuration and Humbug," a sampler of 18th-century itinerant entertainments at the Courthouse. Tours typically require a $10 ticket or $7.50 for holders of a Patriot's Pass. For a complete rundown of what's happening during your visit, call the number above or check listings in your *Colonial Williamsburg Visitor's Companion*, a weekly publication available at the Visitor Center.

### The Ghosts of Williamsburg Night Tours
**Historic Area • 565-4821**

When can the past make you gasp? At 8 PM every night of the week (and again at 8:45 PM June through August), if you choose to participate in a "ghosts" tour offered by a local tour company. Based on the book by L.B. Taylor, Jr., the 1¬hour tour introduces you to legendary ghosts of the Colonial capital. It actually is great fun and a nice alternative to the club scene. About 75,000 people take the spooky trek each year. Cost of the tour is $7; free for children 6 and younger. Group rates are available, and reservations are required.

## Out-Of-Town Nightspots

# Hampton

## Hampton Coliseum
1000 Coliseum Dr. • 838-4203

You never know what you'll find going on inside the Coliseum, easily visible as you head east on I-64, about 30 to 40 minutes from Williamsburg. One week, Vince Gill is in town. The next it's Gladys Knight or jazz great B.B. King. And, if you come in February, you can catch clowns, big cats and trapeze artists in the "Greatest Show on Earth." To find out what's happening for the dates you plan to be in town, call the box office.

# Norfolk

## Chrysler Hall
Charlotte St. and St. Paul's Blvd. • 622-0288

There's always something happening here - from the mesmerizing sounds of the Virginia Symphony to a full slate of Broadway musicals to nationally known musical acts. A sure bet for children is the Virginia Symphony Family Series, which offers a series of concerts, most staged at the Chrysler, as a way to introduce youngsters to the joys of classical music.

## Harrison Opera House
160 E. Virginia Beach Blvd. • 627-9545, 623-1223

The Harrison is home to the Norfolk-based Virginia Opera, which was formed in 1975 and performs regular series in Norfolk, Richmond and northern Virginia. Recent and upcoming Norfolk operas *include Madame Butterfly*, *The Elixir of Love*, *The Tender Land*, *Il Trovatore* and *H.M.S. Pinafore*. The opera house formerly was the Center Theater, which underwent a total restoration in 1993.

# Richmond

## Classic Amphitheatre on Strawberry Hill
600 E. Laburnum Ave. • (804) 228-3213

Located at the State Fairgrounds, this state-of-the-art outdoor amphitheater draws top-name entertainers to Richmond. Performers who had the chance to shine in 1997 included Alan Jackson, Leann Rimes, Indigo Girls, the Dave Matthews Band and Bela Fleck & the Flecktones.

## Flood Zone
11 S. 18th St. • (804) 643-8601

A haven for alternative music, the Flood Zone also is the place to go for blues, reggae, punk, blue grass, rock, African and even classical music. Tickets typically run $8 to $10. Call ahead to see what's happening.

## Richmond Coliseum
601 E. Leigh St. • (804) 262-8100

This is the place in Richmond to catch major sporting events and a variety of shows. Both the Richmond Rage, the local professional women's basketball team, and the Richmond Renegades, an ice hockey team, play home games here. In February 1998, the circus brought its death-defying acts to the Coliseum, and in March 1998 the Harlem Globetrotters did a little dunking here.

# Virginia Beach

## Virginia Beach Amphitheater
Dam Neck and Princess Anne Roads • 368-3000

It may be a bit of a drive (about 1 and a half hours on a good day), but this dazzling 20,000-seat amphitheater draws the really big acts to Hampton Roads. New in 1996, the outdoor arena's first year brought Jimmy Buffet, The Eagles, James Taylor and Sting to town. Ticket prices - either lawn or reserved seating - vary depending upon the act but average about $20. The facility is operated by Cellar Door Productions of Virginia Inc. Refreshments are available at every show. Parking is $2. To purchase tickets by phone, call TicketMaster at 872-8100 or 671-8100.

Charming Merchants Square, dating to 1935, is designed to appear similar to a late 18th-century village and contains a variety of shops, upscale clothiers, fine-food merchants and places to eat.

# Shopping

The variety of shops and stores in Williamsburg and the immediate vicinity is large enough for us justly to claim that, if you're shopping for something in particular, you'll find it. In reviewing the available shopping in a way that's useful, we'll work from the Colonial center of the city outward, disregarding restaurant, hotel and motel gift shops unless we know of some special item to be had inside. In general, you'll find specialty shops offering unique fine-quality items grouped in the heart of the city as well as in shopping centers scattered at the periphery.

If you're looking for manufacturers' outlet stores, shop your way westward on Richmond Road, where individual brand-name stores give way to multiple-outlet centers and finally to the famous Williamsburg Pottery Factory and its attached brand-name outlets. (See the Attractions chapter for more on the Pottery.)

We caution you against thinking that all the finest shops are in the center of the city. Exquisite items and specialty purchases can be found in the small private concerns scattered in shopping centers and among the large outlets, taking advantage of their high visibility and traffic. These shops cater to the visitors who come to the city, but their existence depends upon the return clientele of Insiders they develop over the years by offering quality, dependability and good, friendly service. Tidewater residents and shoppers from as far away as Washington, D.C., make regular visits to Williamsburg for special-occasion shopping throughout the year and especially at Christmas, taking advantage of the shipping service provided by most of the shops.

Don't take for granted, either, that "outlet" means "inexpensive." There are hundreds of bargains to be had, true, but only dedicated "shopping artists" (and you know who you are!) will uncover the real finds combining high quality with low price. Of course, that's what makes shopping so much fun: the thrill of the hunt, the tension of competition, the joy of discovery and the bragging rights when the trophies are brought home for display. OK, we'll buy it if you tell us that it's not the money one spends, but the money one saves that provides the satisfaction. Sure.

From our own experience and from what we observe through the windows of automobiles departing the area, there's an awful lot of shopping satisfaction happening in Williamsburg.

## The Historic Area

Along Duke of Gloucester Street are several shops where Colonial men and women made their purchases. Some are designed for the sale of items crafted on the premises by the artists and crafters you can observe hard at work: Sign of the Golden Ball and The Geddy Silversmith Shop offer a variety of large and small metalcraft items, including ladies', gentlemen's and children's fine jewelry in silver and gold keepsakes that can be engraved to order. McKenzie's Apothecary vends candy, spices, tobacco and herbs. The Post Office carries handmade papers, leather-bound books, maps, marbled paper, prints and cartoons. The Raleigh Tavern Bakery (just follow your nose) provides oatmeal and ginger cookies, breads, apple "pasties" and refreshing cider. M. Dubois' Grocer's Shop offers Smithfield hams, jams, relishes and other Colonial fare. General merchandise shops include Prentis Store, Tarpley's Store and Greenbow Store, carrying pottery, hats, games, toys, baskets, candles, pipes, handwoven linens, leather and wooden crafts, jewelry and many more items. These shops are open year round and are the places to find the perfect memento of your visit or the unique gift for a special occasion. You can obtain other information about shopping in Colonial Williamsburg shops by calling 229-1000. Also, see our chapter on Colonial Williamsburg.

# The City's Center: Merchants Square and Environs

Merchants Square centers on a block of Duke of Gloucester Street closed to traffic. For visitors, it's really the city's "shopping center." This charming area, dating to 1935, is designed to appear similar to a late 18th-century village, and it contains a variety of shops, upscale clothiers, fine-food merchants and places to eat. Ample parking is provided in lots in the center of each block and on streets at the periphery. Neatly trimmed plantings, brick sidewalks, comfortable cafes and wooden benches add to the pleasant, relaxed charm. The locations are leased to independent merchants by the Colonial Williamsburg Foundation, which operates two businesses of its own on the square.

A Good Place To Eat's fast service provides sandwiches, salads, bakery goods and ice cream at breakfast, lunch and dinner. Be sure to get in the line appropriate for your selection. You may eat inside, but Insiders prefer to watch the activity on Merchants Square from the outdoor cafe.

The Bacova Guild Ltd. sells various household accents in its new shop, including decorative fiberglass mailboxes, scatter rugs, kitchen rugs, towels, doormats and other accessories.

The familiar 31 flavors, waffle cones and soft drinks are available at Baskin-Robbins Ice Cream and Frozen Yogurt when you're ready for a treat. Sugar-free and 97 percent fat-free ice cream provides nice alternatives.

The Beecroft & Bull Ltd. offers fine traditional clothing and furnishings for gentlemen shoppers.

Berret's Seafood Restaurant & Raw Bar serves fresh regional seafood for lunch and dinner, and the raw bar outside moves indoors when the cool season arrives (see the Restaurants chapter).

Top designer fashions and other quality clothing for ladies are the specialties at Binn's Of Williamsburg.

The Campus Shop offers gifts and apparel focused on the College of William and Mary. At the Carousel, clothing and accessories for infants through preteens are the specialties. One-of-a-kind outfits, handsmocked dresses and clothing lines of small manufacturers are featured as well as baby shower registry.

Casey's Of Williamsburg is a well-stocked department store carrying traditional men's and ladies' apparel and shoes as well as cosmetics, gifts and gourmet items.

The Cheese Shop has cheeses, wines, picnics and specialty foods galore. At lunch time, Insiders like to buy one of the wonderful sandwiches from the takeout counter, select one of the many unusual beverages in the shop and enjoy both while seated on one of Merchants Square's many benches. (See our Restaurants chapter.)

It's the happiest of seasons year round in The Christmas Shop, which offers unusual Christmas ornaments and decorations.

Classic Cravats specializes in quality neckwear at affordable prices, including long ties, bow ties, pocket handkerchiefs, silk squares and men's jewelry and accessories.

Inside the College Shop, you'll find small souvenirs of your stay in Williamsburg as well as gifts, stationery and greeting cards. Colonial One-Hour Photo provides one-hour color processing and printing, same-day enlarging services and an extensive selection of frames, albums and photo greeting cards. The quality is top-notch. Colonial One-Hour Portrait Studio's specialty is professional family and commercial portraits. Proofs are ready for your selection in one hour.

The Colonial Williamsburg-owned Craft House sells authorized Williamsburg reproductions, including furniture, glassware, accessories and other items whose prototypes are on display in the Historic Area.

You'll find the finest in leather clothing, sportswear, footwear and accessories at D.M. Williams. If you want to take a little of Colonial Williamsburg home with you, stop by Everything Williamsburg. You'll find sweatshirts and other CW-labeled apparel, jewelry, exclusive Colonial Williamsburg tavern china and accessories and delicious specialty food products such as cider, jellies and sauces.

Goodwin Weavers offers fine woven throws and bedding. It features the Bob Timberlake collection of North Carolina Americana, bedding, prints, accessories and cards. Also included are woven throws and bedding from the Williamsburg Reproductions Program and merchandise from Perry Ellis, Emmanuel Ungaro and Norman Rockwell. And don't miss the Henry Street Chocolatier. It's a European-style chocolate shop featuring premium chocolates, imported and domestic. It also serves pastries and cappuccino to enjoy at small tables. Gift wrapping is available.

The J. Fenton Gallery focuses on fine American crafts. The emphasis is on unusual individual pieces by contemporary artists, many from Virginia. The selection includes stained-glass fireplace screens, fountains, kaleidoscopes, pottery, hand-painted clothing, puzzle boxes and jew-

elry. At Laura Ashley, the designs for which the label is famous are offered with emphasis on romantic ladies' and girls' fashions and home furnishings.

The Peanut Shop Of Williamsburg sells crunchy homestyle peanuts prepared in a variety of ways as well as Virginia hams and bacon and selected gifts. The Porcelain Collector offers fine porcelain, china, crystal, tableware and other gifts. The resident master jeweler at The Precious Gem specializes in stunning handcrafted items of gold and rare gems, designed by a resident goldsmith.

You will enjoy the Prince George Espresso Bar and Roastery for its fresh-brewed fine coffees and teas, espresso, cappuccino, sandwiches and specialty nonalcoholic dessert drinks. Fresh-roasted whole and ground coffees, coffee accessories, sandwiches and pastries to go and a selection of gifts are attractions. The Undergrounds here is an excellent alternative to the bar scene for an enjoyable evening (see our listing in the Restaurants chapter).

Antique and new quilts, high-quality regional handcrafts, fabrics and quilting supplies are for sale at Quilts Unlimited. You'll also find a selection of fine jewelry, clothing, toys and Virginia handicrafts.

R. Bryant Ltd. offers traditional men's and boys' clothing with a flair for fresh designs in classic items.

If it's been a while since you were last in Williamsburg, you may remember this as Scribner's, but the wide selection of books and the excellent service remain the same now that it's called Rizzoli Bookstore. Don't miss the belles letters and children's books upstairs or the discounted selections in the rear of the store.

Scotland House Ltd. displays imported ladies' and gentlemen's apparel, tartan, heraldry and gifts. At the Shirley Pewter Shop, pewter gifts, many of them made by hand in Williamsburg, are available, and engraving is done on the premises. Squires is the newest addition to the square. It offers a variety of types of music on compact disk and tape.

Individuals interested in folk art, furniture and gifts will enjoy shopping at Sign of the Rooster, owned and operated by Colonial Williamsburg.

The Silver Vault Ltd. offers a variety of treasures in silver and crystal, including unusual jewelry and accessories. The range of foreign and domestic toys at The Toymaker Of Williamsburg is amazing. Observe the crowd at the windows: The items on display captivate as many adults as children. The Toymaker sells Steiff, Brio, Galt, Playmobil and many other namebrand items for children of all ages.

The Trellis Restaurant and Cafe serves award-winning contemporary American cooking in the dining rooms at lunch and dinner. There is also a cafe bar offering light fare and refreshments (see our Restaurants chapter).

The full-service pharmacy, Williamsburg Drug Company Inc., offers Caswell-Massey and Ultima II products, fine tobaccos, film, newspapers and souvenirs. Wander to the back and you'll discover a number of Insiders at the soda fountain. (If you enjoy New York-style egg creams, this is the place to savor one.)

Only the most self-disciplined can come away from Wythe Candies and Gourmet Shop without at least one of its sweets or specialty foods. The homemade fudge is always excellent, but look around carefully: You'll find candies and gourmet foods you won't find elsewhere.

New to this shopping area in 1997, folk artist Nancy Thomas, who operates a gallery out of Yorktown, opened a shop a door or so down from The Christmas Shop, around the corner from The Trellis. Be sure to stop by, say hello and peruse the variety of high quality folk art that has made Nancy a national and international sensation. For more details, see our entry in the Jamestown and Yorktown chapter.

www.insiders.com

See this and many other **Insiders' Guide** destinations online.

**Visit us today!**

# More Downtown Shopping

Within two blocks to the north and west of Merchants Square are other shops offering unique wares and services. Not affiliated with the Square's merchants, these stores are equally worth investigating.

### Band Box Music & Video
**517 Prince George St. • 229-8882**

The darling of the collegiate set, this shop offers tunes, flicks and more. Its owners assure that the very latest music and specialty selections are available here. If your musical tastes are eclectic, you'll have a fascinating time checking out the stock.

**INSIDERS' TIP**

**For a restful interlude on a sunny day, get a Cheese Shop sandwich and soft drink to eat on a bench at Merchants Square. Then feed the crumbs to the small birds who gather for a handout.**

A good selection of videos also is offered for rental.

## The Book House
421-A Prince George St. • 229-3603

Here you'll find a nice selection of used, out-of-print books and antiques.

## The Flower Cupboard
205 N. Boundary St. • 220-0057

This florist specializes in beautiful 18th-century arrangements, like those seen throughout the Historic Area, but they can also box up a dozen roses with the best of them.

## Peacock Hill Antiques
445 Prince George St. • 220-0429

This unique antique shop offers an excellent collection of American, Oriental and European antiques as well as a separate showroom of new and unique graphics.

## Massey's Camera Shop
447 Prince George St. • 229-3181

A full-service camera store, Massey's has an assortment of equipment and supplies as well as fine-quality developing services.

## Parlett's Card and Gift Boutique
421 Prince George St. • 229-7878

This long-established boutique sells traditional and creative greeting cards for every occasion, wrapping paper and ribbon, local crafts, Colonial-style pierced-tin lanterns and many unusual gifts.

## Prince George Graphics
437 Prince George St. • 229-7644

Beautiful prints, graphics and posters from Prince George Graphics grace many of Williamsburg's homes, and the custom framing done in the shop is of the highest quality.

## Twentieth Century Gallery
219 N. Boundary St. • 229-4949

As might be deduced from the name, the gallery displays contemporary crafts and art pieces. Frequent shows feature new artists' works. In a city devoted to its past, this is a refreshing place to shop. Gallery openings are an occasion for the city's art lovers to meet, socialize and enjoy the featured artists' works.

## Webster's Incredible Gifts
443 Prince George St. • 253-8816

Webster's is the place to go if you're looking for just the right unusual gift or accent item. This little shop offers a great selection of high-quality items, often whimsical and certain to please.

# Along Jamestown Road

## Sports & Balloons In Store
1204 Jamestown Rd. • 229-8662

If you're looking for sports "stuff," look here first. This tiny, almost invisible little store offers fine athletic footwear, sporting clothes and accessories, swimsuits, team supplies, trophies, plaques and team printing. The store also delivers helium-filled balloons for special occasions. Parking is in the rear.

## Shirley Metalcraft
1205 Jamestown Rd. • 229-1378

Looking for many of the same wonderful, handcrafted wares sold at Shirley Pewter Shop on Merchants Square, but don't want to hassle with the parking? This shop is where the items are made! You'll see pewter and other fine materials worked into lovely objects to be treasured as keepsakes or as gifts. The Shirley mark is noted

**INSIDERS' TIP**

Williamsburg hosts often serve their punch in Jefferson cups from Shirley Pewter.

nationally for fine craftsmanship and elegant, creative design.

## Old Chickahominy House Restaurant & Antiques
### 1211 Jamestown Rd. • 229-4689

We love this place! The eatery part is covered in our Restaurants chapter, but the gift shop is worth investigating on its own merits. Antique furniture, 18th-century clocks, Dresden china, prints and oils, a Christmas shop with antique ornaments and other gift items all are available in several quaint showrooms. The outside appearance belies the size of this establishment. Don't plan a quick visit or you'll be sorry.

## Bookpress Ltd.
### 1304 Jamestown Rd. • 229-1260

A bibliophile's dream, Bookpress Ltd. offers antiquarian books, old prints and maps. The staff is also helpful in locating and obtaining rare books. In a college town like Williamsburg, items related to the college are popular with students, alumni and visitors alike. This is another shop where you'll kick yourself if you don't plan ahead and leave ample time to browse and enjoy.

## Colony Square Shopping Center
### 1303 Jamestown Rd. • no phone

Located just west of Route 199, this strip center draws most of its traffic from townsfolk and students because it is the most convenient center for Jamestown Road area neighborhoods. The busiest tenants are Eckerd Drug (where you'll also find a JCPenney Catalog Center), The Fresh Market and the Polo Club Restaurant and Tavern (see Restaurants). Williamsburg Jewelers designs and creates exquisite items on the premises and offers excellent gifts and collectibles. Morrison's Florist provides FTD service and charming arrangements as well as special sales on cut roses. Colonial Paint and Hardware is open Sundays to support weekend projects. Book Exchange of Williamsburg has more than 35,000 used paperbacks at half the cover price. You'll also find Hair Dimensions, Giorgio's Pizza Shoppe (see Restaurants), Quality Gifts & Glass and Kinks, Quirks and Caffeine. But our favorite stop here is the Bagel Bakery & Yogurt Shop. Try their veggie burger. It's the best in town.

## Vernon Wooten Studio & Gallery
### 1315 Jamestown Rd., Ste. 204 • 253-1953

This small but important studio is open by appointment only. It's worth making that appointment, however, to view Wooten's originals in oil, watercolor and acrylic. Framed and unframed limited editions of his prints are available. Limited editions are collectors' items.

## Carrot Tree Kitchen
### 1782 Jamestown Rd. • 229-0957

Talk about mouth-watering! This wholesale bakery was operated out of Debi Helseth's kitchen, but at last it found a site open to the public as part of the Carrot Tree Lodging. The carrot cake is popular with many Insiders, but our favorite is the coconut cake. You'll have to try them both and all the others as well. We bet you'll return. In addition to bakery goodies, Carrot Tree has a gift shop offering herbs, oils and antiques.

## TK Oriental Arts
### 1654 Jamestown Rd. • 229-7720

A showroom full of Eastern items awaits you at TK's. You'll want to visit often since new pieces come in all the time. They don't just house and sell their collection - restoration of antiques and fine items is their specialty. TK's has another store on Prince George Street.

Die-hard shoppers can mix consumerism with history at the millinery in Colonial Williamsburg.

# On Route 5

## Williamsburg Crossing Shopping Center

**5251 John Tyler Hwy. • no phone**

Williamsburg Crossing, as locals refer to this center, has become the main shopping point for the southern and eastern parts of the city. Along the frontage are Old Point National Bank, Taco Bell and Burger King, but the anchor store is Food Lion grocery, with its deli and bakery. At the other end of the center is the seven-screen Carmike Cinemas, the city's newest and largest movie house. Other tenants are Berkeley Pharmacy, Berkeley Cleaners (with dry cleaning, shoe repair and tuxedo-rental services), Hair Essentials, The Perfect Gift (offering glassware and jewelry), The Coffeehouse, Colonial Barber & Beauty Shop, The Comic Cubicle, The Corner Pocket (billiards and light food fare), Courtyard Cafe, Dairy Queen, Williamsburg Coffee & Tea, Little Caesar's Pizza, Mail Boxes Etc., Nottingham's Hallmark Cards, Papa John's Pizza carry out, Laney's Diamonds & Jewelry, Royal Gardens Florist, School Crossing (children's art and educational supplies), Subway deli sandwiches, Video Update, Walls Alive (offering interior decorating items and services), Timbleberry Shoppe (an unusual gift shop that carries everything from antique-style signs to tin angels to home-brewed potpourri), Nail Uptown, The Framery, Kyu Tailor, Blind's Galore (specializing in all kinds of window treatments),

Top's China Restaurant, Colonial Computers and Photo Center.

## Trevillian Furniture and Interiors
3301 Venture Ln. • 229-9505

If you're looking for home furnishings and accessories, check this place out. It offers fine furnishings and interior decorating services as well as a popular moving and transport service (they are especially skilled with antiques and prized items).

## Five Forks Shopping Center
4490 John Tyler Hwy. • no phone

This is a small center serving the developments that have sprung up around it. Amory Music is where local musicians go for supplies, scores and instruments. Marilyn's Beauty Salon, Williamsburg Hardware & Supply, Marine Supply, and Husky Wholesale Appliance complete the roster of current tenants.

# On Bypass Road

## Bassett's Classic Christmas Shop
207 Bypass Rd. • 229-7648

Fans of the holiday season find Bassett's an excellent store to hunt for ornaments, trees, Madame Alexander dolls and other fine gift items.

## Cracker Barrel Old Country Store
200 Bypass Rd. • 220-3384

Attached to a restaurant familiar to travelers in the South, the gift shop here offers an eclectic assortment of items from clothing and candles to candies, all in keeping with the establishment's country (and the emphasis is on mountain country) theme. Can't make up your mind about an item? Have a bite to eat, then decide.

## Southern States Cooperative
112 Bypass Rd. • 229-3427

Located across from Kingsgate Greene Shopping Center, also known as the Kmart Shopping Center by locals, is a well-established garden shop, nursery and farm supply store - a must stop for gardeners who need yard care, hardware and nursery items.

## Kingsgate Greene Shopping Center
120 Waller Mill Rd. • no phone

Kmart is the most visible store you see from the street, but there are other noteworthy shops here as well. In the center of the "L" are two restaurants, Peking Chinese restaurant and Mongolian Beef BBQ, both of which are extremely popular with Insiders and are featured in our Restaurants chapter. Other occupants of the center include a Revco drugstore, Video Update, Domino's Pizza, The Hair Cuttery, Feathered Nest pet shop, The Chamber Ballet Company, which offers a dancers' boutique, GTE Mobilnet and York River Wood Furniture Gallery.

# On Route 60 E.

## Festival Marketplace
264 McLaws Cir. • no phone

Located just east of the Route 199 intersection, this small strip center houses Postal Services Unlimited for parcel delivery and wrapping needs, The Hair Shop, and the popular National Pancake restaurant.

## Marketplace at Kingsmill
240 McLaws Circle • no phone

This busy little strip center is abuzz with a variety of retail shops, service businesses and one particularly popular restaurant. Here you'll find Sir Speedy Printing, Shear Creations, Kingsmill Food Mart (a deli and wine shop), Hometown Rentals (offering furniture, TVs and appliances), Ashley Jewelry, Swan Cleaner, Marketplace Texaco (which has a quick and cheap car wash) and the ever-popular Sportsman's Grill restaurant.

### The Village Shops At Kingsmill
1915 Pocahontas Tr. • 220-0085

The charming and varied shopping center gives the impression of a small village whose narrow lanes are lined with shops and services. Its feeling is European rather than American Colonial, more in keeping with nearby Busch Gardens than with Colonial Williamsburg. The items for sale are first-quality, and there are many one-of-a-kind selections. Insiders shop at the Pottery Wine & Cheese for the low prices on those items and the variety of gourmet foods on display. Major interest is being generated by America's Railroads on Parade, perhaps the largest layout of model railroads in the country open to the public (profiled in our Kidstuff chapter, but a delight for all ages). Other tenants include A Logo For You, which will put your company logo on T-shirts; American Harvest, which sells furniture and accessories; Baggs of Thrift Avenue; Cattails boutique; Charisma Florist and Gift Shop; Gallery Images Photography; J.L. McCandlish Antiques; Marie's Books; Haus Tirol/The Stitching Well needlework shop; Jeanne Reed Interiors; Kingsmill Art Studio; Kingsmill Jewelers; The Lemon Twist ladies' clothing; Lightfoot Manor Shoppe, which sells fine gifts such as brass, tobacco jars and glassware; Michelle's Potpourri; Oriental Textile Arts; The Personal Touch beauty services; The Perfect Edge; Q Tailor Shop; Silent Sparrow Framing; The Trimble Collection of European and Asian art; Two in a Zoo, offering art, antiques and stuffed animals; The Antiques Shop; The Golf Shoppe; Williamsburg Bridal Services, which provides planning services as well as sells new and used gowns, shoes and jewelry; and *Great Entertainer Magazine*.

For dining, there are Christina's Kitchen, Mr. Liu's Chinese Restaurant and Le Yaca French Restaurant.

### Fort Cherokee Trading Post
8758 Pocahontas Tr. • no phone

You don't have to be Native American to visit the trading post, and the totem poles and wigwam in front of the establishment make it easy to spot. Inside you will find Native American art and crafts created by artists of various tribes throughout the nation. We especially like the pottery offered here, but the staff is extremely helpful in advising you on some of the more unusual items such as drums and pipes. The clothing for sale is worth examining as well, and feet tired from walking through the area attractions might find genuine moccasins a welcome relief.

# On Merrimac Trail

### Williamsburg Farm Fresh Shopping Center
455 Merrimac Tr. • no phone

The anchor here is the huge Farm Fresh Super Store, which is open all night. In addition, there is a variety of stores in its two adjacent sections. These include Domino's Pizza, Cutting Edge Hair Care Center, Harvell's Decorating Center, Town & Country Dry Cleaning, Sherwin-Williams Paint Center, Safelite Auto Glass, Beethoven's Inn, Regina Shop (custom framing) and Heilig-Meyers Furniture.

# On Richmond Road

## Within The City

### Master Craftsmen
255 Richmond Rd. • 253-2993

This fine artisan's shop offers high quality, handcrafted jewelry, handspun pewter and a variety of beautiful keepsakes in silver and gold. They also provide engraving services.

## Williamsburg Shopping Center
157 Monticello Ave. • no phone

This was the first modern shopping center in the city, replacing the old shopping heart of town (where the specialty shops of Merchants Square are now located). Together with the adjacent Monticello Shopping Center, it is the heart of commerce for the residents of Williamsburg and students at the College of William and Mary. The anchor stores are Peebles Department Store, carrying fine clothing, jewelry, accessories and household items, Roses Department Store, with a full line of merchandise, and the recently remodeled and expanded Food Lion grocery store. Also located here are Ace Peninsula Hardware, CVS Drug Store and the Piece Goods Home Center. Also you'll find a variety of dining options: Chez Trinh (Vietnamese cuisine), Sal's Italian Restaurant & Pizza by Victor and the Subway Station. Music lovers of all kinds favor Echoes Tapes & Compact Discs for its huge and varied inventory tailored to the wide - and often arcane - range of tastes represented in the city. Kinko's Copy Center is open 24 hours and offers copying, printing, publishing and other business support services. Blue Ridge Mountain Sports provides complete outfitting for outdoor adventurers. Other retail tenants include Nottingham Hallmark, More Than Mail, A&N athletic supplies and clothing for men and women, Ski and Surf Quest clothing and outfitters, Fashion Bug and Fashion Bug Plus ladies' clothiers, and Sam's Camera Shop.

## Monticello Shopping Center
218 Monticello Ave. • no phone

Located one block off Richmond Road, the four screens at Carmike Cinema 4 are a popular attraction. This shopping center faces Williamsburg Shopping Center across Monticello Avenue. Other tenants are the Children's Hospital of the King's Daughters Thrift Shop, Nawab Indian restaurant, Ladda's Tailor Shop, Pet World, Pizza Hut Carry Out and The Barber and Beauty Shop of Williamsburg.

## Auto Parts and Supply Inc.
225 Monticello Ave. • 229-3580

Adjacent to the Carmike Cinemas at Monticello Shopping Center sits this small but helpful auto parts supply store. If they don't have what you're looking for, they'll gladly order it for you - and at a reasonable price.

## Williamsburg Professional Pharmacy
1302 Mount Vernon Dr. • 229-3560

This long-standing drugstore is conveniently located across Monticello Avenue from Williamsburg Community Hospital. Full pharmacy and drug services are available.

## The Williamsburg Chocolatier Ltd.
120 Tewning Rd., Ste. D • 253-1474

Making chocolates has been a family business here for more than 10 years. The sauces, pound cakes, fudge, truffles, cheesecakes and candies are out of this world. We particularly like the fanciful chocolate lollypops

## Whitley's Virginia Peanuts and Peanut Factory
1351 Richmond Rd. • 229-4056

You'll find delicious "home-cooked" Virginia peanuts, Virginia hams, gift baskets and other goods from the Commonwealth, all available for mail-order shipping - and we bet you'll take at least one can of peanuts out the door with you.

## Edwards' Virginia Ham Shoppe Of Williamsburg
1814 Richmond Rd. • 220-6618

This mouth-watering little shop sells Surry hickory-smoked hams and bacon direct from the family smokehouse, plus a variety of Virginian specialty foods, including jellies, jams, flours, cake and pie mixes, craft items and more. They'll wrap and ship, too, at your request.

## The Christmas Mouse
1991 Richmond Rd. • 221-0357

Chock-full of goodies for everyone's favorite season, The Christmas Mouse is open all year. Through their windows you'll see dozens of trees lighted and decorated with unique items. Inside you'll find more things associated with the holidays than you ever imagined were possible.

## Attic Collections
**2229 Richmond Rd. • 229-0032**

This minimall in a single building includes several individual shops. Don't let the size of the building fool you. More than 4,000 square feet of treasures reside here, including the useful and the whimsical, the elegant and the amusing. The largest items are furniture pieces, but there is glassware from the 18th century forward (including depression glassware), buttons, marbles, books, postcards, prints, paintings, posters, lamps, kitchenware, toys, vintage clothing, accessories and jewelry. Attic Collections closes Tuesday and Wednesday. Upstairs, you'll find Forget-Me-Nots and Sugar and Spice, which carry consignment clothing for adults and children, respectively.

# Along Route 60 W.

## Patriot's Plaza Outlets
**3044 Richmond Rd. • no phone**

The first of the outlet malls you'll find as you shop your way westward, this plaza offers a variety of goods. Crawford House Ethan Allen furniture gallery sells the finest in quality furniture, furnishings and accessories; Gorham Factory Outlet has seconds, discontinued patterns and limited edition crystal, china, sterling and silverplate. Prince Michel Wineshop offers Virginia wines as well as hors d'oeuvres and unusual imported gifts. West Point Pepperrell Mill Store is "bedquarters" for bed and bath fashions, and The Lenox

Shop offers outstanding prices on crystal. Villeroy and Boch Factory Outlet Store displays discontinued crystal and dinnerware and factory seconds, and Dansk Factory Outlet carries that maker's tableware. Ben & Jerry's Ice Cream, American Tourister, Ralph Lauren Home Collection and Leather Loft are also tenants whose products and prices are worth investigating.

## Carolina Furniture
**5421 Richmond Rd. • 565-3000**

This shop, with its large selection of furniture in varied styles and price ranges, is known for high quality and excellent service. Don't miss their scratch and dent and remnant room in the little building to the left of the main store. You buy it, and they'll ship it anywhere you want.

## Carolina Carpets
**5425 Richmond Rd. • 565-3006**

A sister store to Carolina Furniture, Carpets is the Williamsburg outlet for Karastan goods, offered at discounts of 40-60 percent. Broadloom carpeting and one-of-a-kind Oriental rugs also are discounted, another reason to stop in. Countrywide shipping service makes this store convenient to your home.

## Williamsburg Brass, Lighting and Textiles
**5425 Richmond Rd. • 565-3535**

This wonderful store features Virginia Metalcrafters and Baldwin Brass products along with period lighting fixtures, wallpaper and fabrics you can select to create a Williamsburg feeling to your decor.

## The Pennsylvania House Collector's Gallery
**5425 Richmond Rd. • 565-3535**

Specializing in comfortable solid cherry,

---

**INSIDERS' TIP**

You'll be able to brag about buying the "bargain du jour" from the annual Skid Row sale at the Williamsburg Pottery Factory, usually held in January or February.

oak, maple or pine furniture, The Pennsylvania House offers at least 40 percent off the suggested list price.

## Ewell Station Shopping Center
**5609 Richmond Rd. • 565-4526**

This well-maintained shopping center mainly serves residents in the western end of the area and saves them the drive into town for basic services. Visitors and townsfolk enjoy Peking, with its fine cuisine. Giuseppe's Italian Cafe is an extremely popular trattoria, providing delicious and creative dishes. Among other tenants are Food Lion, Rite Aid Pharmacy, Swan Cleaners, The Hair Shop, Little Caesar's Pizza, Prime Time Video, Subway and Thoughtful Occasions Gifts (offering cards, wrapping paper and a wide variety of gifts for men and women), and Hayashi Japanese Restaurant.

## Berkeley Commons Outlet Center
**5699 Richmond Rd. • 565-0702**

Top of the line in designer and fine namebrands is represented in the recently expanded outlets mall, which forms a large "U" shape facing Richmond Road. There are great savings ranging from 20 to 70 percent on items in these shops. Tenants include 9 West, Adolfo II, Anne Klein, American Eagle Outfitters, American Tourister, Bass Shoes, Geoffrey Beene, Big Dog Sportswear, Book Cellar, BOSE, Brass Factory, Britches, Brooks Brothers, Anne Klein, Cambridge Dry Goods, Capezio, Carole Little, Carter's Childrens Wear, Coach Leather, Cole-Haan, Collections, The Cosmetic Company Store, Crabtree & Evelyn, Designer Jewelry & Fashion, Eddie Bauer, Etienne Aigner, Famous Brands Housewares, Fragrance Outlet, Gant, Group USA, Guess?, Haggar Clothing Company, Harry & David, Harve Benard, Heritage Lace, He-Ro Group, Hickory

Hams, Izod, J. Crew Factory Store, JH Collectibles, J. Christopher, Jos. A. Bank Clothiers, Jones of NY, Jordache, Kasper ASL, Kitchen Collection, Le Creuset, La Chine, Lillian Vernon, Liz Claiborne, Lladro, Lucia...That's Me!, Maidenform, Maidenform Woman, Members Only, Mikasa, Movado, Music For A Song, NAP Womens Sleepwear, Naturalizer, Nike, NordicTrack, Olga Warner's, Orvis, OshKosh B'Gosh, Pelican Cafe, Perfumania, Pewtarex, Reebok/Rockport, Rocky Mountain Chocolate Factory, RooMakers, Royal Doulton, Seiko, Socks Galore, Starter Sportswear, Stone Mountain Handbags, Sunglass Hut, Tanner Factory Store, Timberland, Tommy Hilfiger Mens & Boys Apparel, Van Heusen, Joan Vass U.S.A., Waterford/Wedgwood, and Welcome Home.

# In Lightfoot

## Piano-Organ Outlet
**6315 Richmond Rd. • 564-9592**

This is a bit away from the other shopping areas, but very visible on the north side of the highway. The keyboard selection in this store is extensive, and prices are very reasonable.

## Williamsburg Outlet Mall
**6401 Richmond Rd. • 565-3378**

There are more than 60 factory outlet stores and plenty of benches for tired shoppers' companions in Williamsburg's only enclosed mall. The one-story structure is arranged in a cross shape, with food courts in the center and the long portion extending away from the highway frontage. The shops offer from 20 to 70 percent off regular retail prices.

Clothing and accessory stores in the mall include Arrow, Barbizon Fine Lingerie,

---

**INSIDERS' TIP**

**Christmas shoppers should look for the annual Williamsburg Craft and Folk Art Show in early October at**

Bass Factory Outlet, BonWorth, Bruce Alan Bags, Etc., Bugle Boy, Candles, Etc., Casual Male Big & Tall, Champion/Hanes Activewear, Claire's Boutiques, Diamonds Unlimited, Dress Barn, Dress Barn Woman, Executive Neckwear, Famous Footwear, Frugal Frank's, Gant, Genuine Kids, Gold Toe, Hamilton Luggage, Hit Or Miss, IZOD, Jockey, L'eggs/Hanes/Bali, Leslie Fay, Levi's Outlet By Designs, London Fog, Mercantile, New Concept Gifts, Rack Room, Rue 21, S&K Famous Brand Menswear, SBX, Silver Stream, Sports Stop, Sunshades, Swank, Today's Child and Totes/Sunglass World.

Other specialty shops are Avon at the Mall, Candles, Etc., Everything's A Dollar, Famous Brands Housewares, Kiddie Koncepts, Linens N' Things, Prestige Fragrance & Cosmetics, Publisher's Warehouse, Solid Brass of Williamsburg Inc., Southwest Accents, The Paper Factory, Toy Liquidators and Welcome Home.

A variety of food is provided by All American, Cafe Au Lait, Pizza Deli Express, Puttin' On The Dog, Rocky Mountain Chocolate Factory and We "R" Nuts.

## Williamsburg Pavilion Shops
### 6580 Richmond Rd. • no phone

This strip center has an eclectic set of offerings. Tenants are Fabrics Unique, Guild Hall of Williamsburg (which sells fine furniture and accessories), Lamplighter Shoppe, 360 The Cellular Store, A&N, Things Unique, Oriental Rug Mart, Electrolux Sales & Service and Special Somethings.

## The Gallery Shops at Lightfoot
### 6580 Richmond Rd. • no phone

Our favorite shop here is A Touch of Earth, Williamsburg's oldest American crafts gallery, offering highly prized American craftwork by fine artists in many media as well as the owners' own beautiful pottery. (Be sure to take a "Gloom Chaser" home!) Also represented here are Boyers Diamond and Gold outlet (featuring custom designs and wholesale prices on finest quality items), N.Y. Deli, Williamsburg Fine Arts (offering art by local artists, supplies, fram-

ing and lessons), The "new kid in the strip" is Ardsen Offset Printing, where you can get everything from a single copy of a letter made to an entire book printed and everything in between.

## Williamsburg Pottery Factory
### Route 60 W., Lightfoot • 564-3326

A shopping mecca that it is featured in its own section in the Attractions chapter of this book, the Pottery is in a class by itself. There are 32 buildings, with two more under construction, and 8,000 parking spots waiting for shoppers at this monumental business, less a factory than a bazaar with an international array of goods displayed along miles of shelves. Five million visitors a year shop at this area landmark, coming in bus caravans from all over. Don't miss this "shop 'til you drop" experience. For more details, flip to the Attractions chapter.

## Pottery Factory Outlets
### Route 60 W. • 564-3326

Located on Route 60 W. on the grounds of the Williamsburg Pottery Factory, these outlets include a Banister Shoes, Black & Decker Outlet, Cabin Creek Furniture and Gifts, Christopher's Leather Shop, Westport Ltd., The Emporium, Fieldcrest Cannon, Finishing Touch, Glass Elite, Hanover Brass (and Elvis Shop), IZOD Factory Store, King Neptune's Treasures, The Last Out baseball and other collectors' cards, Oneida Silversmiths, Peanut Shack, Pecan Factory, Pepperidge Farm, Pfaltzgraff Pottery, Prestige Fragrance and Cosmetics, Regal Kitchenware, Rolane Factory Outlet, S & K Crazy Price Warehouse, Totes, Van Heusen men's and women's apparel, Wallet Works and Boot Hill Western. See the Pottery section of the Attractions chapter for more details.

## The Colonial Town Plaza
### 6965 Richmond Rd. • no phone

This strip center is a collection of several buildings including Williamsburg House of Crafts' six showrooms of folk art, country furniture, flags and other handcrafted items, Out on a Limb's ultrasuede and facile fashions, and T-shirt City's garb for kids big and small. You'll also find Chestnutt Bay furnishings and James City True Value Hardware, Han's Tailor & Alterations, The Williamsburg Brass Shop, New England Grill and Fish Market, Barefoot Floor Covering and GCI Appliance.

# In Norge

### The Williamsburg Wicker and Rattan Shoppe
7422 Richmond Rd. • 565-3620

A charming Victorian house shop features many fine lines of wicker and rattan, including Henry Link, Lane Venture, Lloyd Flanders and Ficks Reed. Shipping is provided.

### Williamsburg Doll Factory
7441 Richmond Rd. • 564-9703

You can watch production of Lady Anne Porcelain Dolls during your visit here. The Doll Factory also offers doll houses galore, doll supplies of all kinds, fine stuffed animals and, of course, a huge selection with just the right doll to join your family.

### Corning Revere Factory Store
7461 Richmond Rd. • 564-0369

This is the place for outstanding savings on Corning, Visions, Corelle and Revere items. If you want something for your kitchen, or a gift for an excellent cook or hostess, it'll be here.

### Norge Shoppes
7405 Richmond Rd. • 564-7623

The major draw to this tiny strip center is Norge Station. What kid (regardless of age) doesn't love trains? Here you'll find N, HO, O and Gauge 1 items and operating layouts for the model railroader. In addition, there is a large selection of cars,

military models, kits and NASCAR collectibles. The sale table is one to keep your eye on while you're in town. This just may be where Dad and the kids get their revenge for waiting outside all those clothing outlets while Mom shopped.

### Williamsburg Soap & Candle Company
7521 Richmond Rd. • 564-3354

You can observe soap and candles being made at this strip shopping center. The specialty stores around the "factory" offer a complete shopping experience. Christmas House is full of novelties for the holiday season. Barney's Country Store has a variety of country-living items. Emporium has a selection of international gifts and greeting cards. Candy & Snack Shop serves great fudge, ice cream and sweets. The Tapestry Outlet provides quilts, fabrics, needlework supplies and quilting accessories. The Candle Shop has hundreds of unique candles and soaps crafted on site. Candle Factory Restaurant is popular with locals for breakfast, lunch and dinner.

# In Toano

### Charlie's Antiques and Repairs
7766 Richmond Rd. • 566-8300

Called "the largest in the area," this unique shop offers a selection of American and imported antiques and reproduction furniture, much of which is handcarved solid mahogany. The continental antiques are unusual in an area so replete with English items. Shipping and wholesale and retail prices are offered.

### Toano Toy Works
8003 Richmond Rd. • 566-0171

All the toys made here are wooden,

andthe selection is overwhelming. These are keepsake items certain to be prized through the years. Noah's arks, rocking and stick horses, games, cars, trains and boats are among the many creative items you'll find displayed. These unique treasures make excellent gifts for youngsters, particularly of preschool age.

### The Farm House
**7787 Richmond Rd. • 566-8344**

You can't miss this store - there's a selection of items sitting out front along the highway. Inside is an assortment of furniture for house, porch and garden at extremely attractive prices. Clean out the trunk - you must transport what you purchase.

### Basketville Of Williamsburg Inc.
**7761 Richmond Rd. • 566-8420**

A tisket, a tasket . . . If you've lost your Easter basket, make a trip to this sprawling shop that sells several hundred kinds of baskets from around the world, along with wicker furniture and sundry other items.

The stories of Powhatan and his daughter Pocahontas, the Indian princess who married Englishman John Rolfe and went to live in London, are part of the region's historic lore.

# Native American Culture

Long before European settlers arrived to conquer their New World, Virginia was an old world to quite a different kind of civilization - that of the Native Americans. Nomadic hunters occupied the region from as early as 10,000 B.C. After 5000 B.C., Woodland Indians established more permanent settlements and began cultivating the land. When European settlers came, they found Algonquian Indians, thought to have arrived around A.D. 1000, living in longhouses, hunting, fishing and growing crops, notably corn. Some 32 different tribes, ruled by Chief Powhatan, inhabited the area in the early 1600s.

By 1700, the number of Native Americans had dwindled to 15 percent of what it had been 100 years earlier. European diseases were responsible for much of this decline, and, as the Virginia Colony flourished and settlers continued to arrive, Native Americans were deprived of more and more of their ancestral land.

The history of 17th-century Native Americans is prevalent in the culture of the Historic Triangle today. The stories of Powhatan (whose real name was Wahunsonacock) and his daughter Pocahontas, the Indian princess who married Englishman John Rolfe and went to live in London, are part of the region's historic lore. Place names derived from the Indians are omnipresent; there are Powhatan and Pocahontas parkways, motels, condominiums and stores. While the Algonquian language, never written, has vanished, a number of Algonquian words - squash, succotash, opossum, toma-

hawk - are now part of everyday American English.

Artifacts uncovered during archaeological digs in the Historic Triangle have provided a mother lode of information about the lives of Virginia's first inhabitants. A dig at Governor's Land at Two Rivers, for instance, produced new data about the Pasbehegh Indians, whose village was the first to be destroyed by Jamestown settlers. Finds at the site, which may date back to 1500, include ceramics and a burial pit containing copper beads. At Jamestown Island and Jamestown Settlement, there are statues, displays and living history programs that focus on the role of Native Americans in the settlement of the New World.

But what about the descendants of these tribes of yore who met, traded with, sometimes massacred and ultimately were overpowered by the European settlers? In Virginia, eight different tribes dating back at least 200 years are recognized by the state. Census data from 1990 shows that about 16,000 people living in the Old Dominion call themselves Native Americans, and that several remnant tribes of the Powhatan Confederacy live within an hour or so of Williamsburg. Until very recently, the lives of Virginia's contemporary Native Americans often seemed obscured by our fascination with history and by stereotypes, not to mention Hollywood myth. While Virginia's Native Americans, including those living on reservations, are largely assimilated into mainstream society, the preservation of heritage is of vital importance to them. The Virginia Indian Heritage Festival, held each June at Jamestown Settlement, brings together Virginia's tribes with tribes from throughout the country for a day of celebrating Native American tradition and customs. To learn more about this event, take a look at the Annual Events chapter. The information we've listed below about the region's Native Americans and their programs, events and ongoing traditions is proof that their culture is alive and thriving here today. The phone numbers listed at the beginning of each entry are where you can call to learn more about the tribe and are not necessarily the phone numbers for the chief.

# Tribes

## Mattaponi Reservation
Off Rt. 30 at Rt. 626, King William Co. • (804) 769-2194
Chief Webster "Little Eagle" Custalow

The name Mattaponi is an Anglicized version of the original Mattapanient, which may mean "landing place." Some 75 Mattaponi Tribe Indians live on a 125-acre reservation established in 1658 north of the Pamunkey River. These residents are the descendants of Indians who once served and worshipped the Great Spirit, their god of the heavens, sun, moon and stars. Today the members of this tribe are Southern Baptists who have made their church a center of their community's activities. In the 17th century, Powhatan and his successor, Opechaneough, are said to have visited here. Today the tribe is self-governed by a chief and council. A pottery now occupies the old reservation schoolhouse; potters fashion both traditional and nontraditional objects, using clays from the riverbanks and from commercial sources. The Wahunsunakah Drum Group, which performs traditional Native American drumming, operates out of the reservation.

## Upper Mattaponi
Off Rt. 30, northwestern King William Co. • (804) 769-4767
Chief Edmund S. Adams

The Upper Mattaponi Indians, an urban, nonreservation group who trace their origins to both the Mattaponi and Pamunkey reservations, reside in northwestern King William County. The tribe is developing a new cultural village across from its house of worship, the Indian View Baptist Church.

## Pamunkey Reservation
Off Rt. 30, King William Co. • (804) 843-4792
Chief William P. "Swift Water" Miles

While the Pamunkey were once the most powerful people in the Powhatan Confederacy, today fewer than 100 live on their reservation in King William County. The Great Chief Powhatan and his daughter Pocahontas once lived among the Pamunkey empire of 10,000 people. Indeed Chief Powhatan governed territory that spread from Washington, D.C., to North Carolina. The reservation in King William County is now on the Virginia Historical Landmarks Register. Pamunkey women founded a potter's guild in the 1930s, and today they're dedicated to preserving the traditional coil-and-pinch method of making pots, using clay collected from the banks of the Pamunkey River. Etched bowls, vases, jugs, pipes and other handcrafted items are sold at the reservation. The reservation is about 40 minutes from Williamsburg, off Route 30 to secondary Route 633.

## INSIDERS' TIP

If you want to take home some Native American pottery, drums, pipes or clothing, stop in at the Fort Cherokee Trading Post, 8758 Pocahontas Trail (Route 60 E.). The trading post, which has no phone, carries wonderful examples of the arts and crafts fashioned by members of various tribes from across the country.

Photo: Colonial National Historic Park

Pocahontas supplied the Jamestown colonists with food and warned Capt. John Smith of danger from the Indians.

## Chickahominy

Charles City Co. • (804) 829-9452
Chief Arthur Leonard "Lone Wolf" Adkins

The name Chickahominy means "crushed corn people." Close to 1,000 Chickahominy Indians live in the United States, with the largest concentration in Charles City County. The Chickahominy have never been reservation Indians; at the core of their active community are the Samaria Baptist Church and Charles City Primary School.

While the Chickahominy are largely as-similated into mainstream American soci-ety, tribe members maintain strong ties with each other and work at passing on Native American traditions. The fourth Saturday of every September, the Chickahominy Indian Fall Festival and Powwow is held on the tribal grounds, with activities including traditional dances and handmade jewelry exhibitions. Many of the traditional dances are performed by the Chickahominy Redman Dancers, a troupe that also is fea-tured at the Thanksgiving at Berkeley Plan-tation celebration in November and at

Jamestown Settlement's Virginia Indian Heritage Festival in June. For more on either of these events, turn to our chapter on Annual Events.

## Eastern Chickahominy
New Kent Co. • (804) 966-2719
Chief Marvin "Strong Oak" Bradby

About 150 members of this division of the Chickahominy tribe became residents of New Kent County, 25 miles east of Richmond, in 1925. This relatively new organization carries on the responsibility of educating and administering to the religious needs of members. The Eastern Chickahominy church is Tsena Commocko Baptist in New Kent.

## Other Tribes

There are several other Indian tribes that are recognized by the Commonwealth of Virginia. They include the 500 members of the Monacan, (804) 929-7571, in Amherst County, the westernmost of the state's eight recognized tribes; the Nansemond, 487-5853, whose 300 members live throughout the cities of South Hampton Roads; and the 700 members of the United Rappahannock, (804) 769-0260, who live in King and Queen County.

# Museums

## Hampton University Museum
## American Indian Collection
Huntington Building, Frissell Ave. • 727-5308

More than 1,600 objects of art and artifacts from 93 tribes constitute the large American Indian collection at Hampton University Museum. The collection became available for public viewing in October 1998, when its move to the Huntington Building from the now-closed Academy Building of 1881 was completed. Established in 1868, most of the collection was gathered between that year and 1923 by faculty, friends of the school and Native American students sent by the federal government to receive an education at Hampton University. Most artifacts are from Plains Indians, but some pieces of contemporary Pamunkey pottery are also part of the collection. The Huntington Building opened in the spring of 1997, and collections gradually are being relocated to the expanded facility. By the way, the museum's central collection of 19th- and 20th-century African-American paintings, sculptures and prints is one of the country's best. Museum hours are 8 AM to 5 PM Monday through Friday and noon to 4 PM on weekends. Admission is free. To reach the museum from Williamsburg, take I-64 E. to Exit 267 in Hampton and follow the signs.

## Jamestown Settlement
Rt. 31 and Colonial Pkwy., Jamestown • 229-1607

At this popular museum, explored thoroughly in our Jamestown and Yorktown Chapter, the Powhatan Indian Gallery is devoted to the tribe that inhabited coastal Virginia when the English arrived in 1607. Visitors to the gallery are greeted by life-size figures of a Native American family and can listen to a recording of a dialect of

---

**INSIDERS' TIP**

A popular Native American dish served at all the powwows is fried bread — a round piece of deep-fried dough topped with honey or powdered sugar, similar to funnel cakes or elephant ears. For those with an underactive sweet tooth, fry bread can be seasoned with ground beef, cheese and vegetables to create a variation on the Mexican taco.

Algonkin, the language of the Powhatans. Detailed exhibits examine the life, religion, social structure, government, trade and food of the tribe. An outdoor Powhatan Indian Village - complete with costumed interpreters - gives kids and grown-ups alike a taste of life as it was lived by the original Americans. Admission to the settlement is $13.25 for adults and $6.50 for children ages 6 to 12.

## Mattaponi Indian Museum and Minnie Ha Ha Educational Trading Post
On Rt. 2 off of Rt. 30, 12 miles west of West Point, King William Co. • (804) 769-2194

The Mattaponi Indian Museum, built here in 1954, features tribal artifacts, including a stone necklace worn by Pocahontas and the tomahawk used by Opechaneough in the battles of 1622 and 1644. Some ancient artifacts on display date back to 5000 B.C. Classes in Mattaponi history, beadwork, cooking, Indian medicine, crafts, dance and lore are taught at the nearby trading post. The museum is open on Saturdays and Sundays from 2 to 5 PM or by arrangement. Admission is $1. Arrangements must be made in advance for classes at the trading post. The fee for each program participant is $2.50.

## Mariners' Museum
100 Museum Dr. (Exit 258A off I-64), Newport News • 596-2222

The Chesapeake Bay Gallery of this world-renowned museum, described in detail in our Newport News and Hampton chapter, features a dugout canoe from 1630, one of the few Indian vessels ever discovered.

## Pamunkey Indian Museum
Off Rt. 30 and Rt. 133, King William Co. • (804) 843-4792

On the Pamunkey reservation is the Pamunkey Indian Museum, designed to resemble traditional longhouse Indian dwellings, with displays of artifacts, replicas of stone tools and the ongoing tradition of pottery making in the centuries-old manner of the Pamunkey women. Many of the pieces made at the museum can be purchased in the gift shop. Museum hours are 10 AM to 4 PM Tuesday through Saturday and 1 to 4 PM on Sundays. Admission is $2.50 for adults, $1.75 for seniors and $1.25 for children.

Williamsburg residents have long been familiar with stories about ghosts said to inhabit some of the town's historic buildings, but one of the legends to make the news most recently concerns a cemetery, a grave desecration, mysterious manuscripts and secret tunnels.

# Myths and Legends

Everyone likes a good ghost story. There's nothing like a well-told tale of terror - or simply one of legendary proportion - to get the heart pounding and the pulse beating a little faster. Williamsburg, it seems, has more than its share of spooky specters and appalling apparitions. The tales that follow about the Colonial capital and its environs aren't exactly backed up by years of historical research, but they sure are fun to recount. So sit back and enjoy. Perhaps before you leave our historic city you'll have one to add to our list. If so, don't hesitate to share it. Unlike some things that go bump in the night, we don't bite.

The author who perhaps has best chronicled the area's ghosts is L.B. "Bob" Taylor, Jr., of Williamsburg, who for the past 14 years has written numerous books on the subject. (See our close-up "Virginia's Ghostwriter.") Some of the tales in his regional volume *The Ghosts of Williamsburg* are summarized below.

## The Strange Saga of Aunt Pratt

The elegant Shirley Plantation, a Colonial mansion halfway between Williamsburg and Richmond, is noted for its fine collection of family portraits. One of those paintings is of Aunt Pratt, reportedly a late 17th-century resident of the plantation, although little is known about her life. For a number of years after Aunt Pratt died, her portrait occupied a suitable place in a downstairs bedroom until it was banished to the attic. It

seems Aunt Pratt, despite being dearly departed, as they say, did not approve of her portrait being moved. Residents and guests at the mansion reported hearing a rocking chair in the attic, but those who summoned up the courage to climb the stairs to the attic never discovered the source of the sound. Eventually, the rocking became so disturbing that the house's occupants retrieved the portrait and returned it to the bedroom wall. Once that was a *fait accompli*, the strange rocking sounds never were heard again. The tale of Aunt Pratt's portrait doesn't end there. But that's a story we'll save for another time . . . .

## The Triple Ghosts of Westover

In his book, Taylor recounts the tales of three ghosts that reportedly haunt Westover Plantation in Charles City County. There's the benevolent spirit of Evelyn Byrd, a beautiful young woman who made a pact with close friend Anne Carter Harrison that whoever should die first would return to visit in a way that would not frighten anyone. As legend has it, Evelyn died of a broken heart after her father forbade her to see the suitor she loved. Anne, of course, was the first to see Evelyn's spirit, but as years passed, others reported seeing an ethereal figure dressed in white in rooms throughout the house and floating over the lawn.

Another spirit that haunts Westover is

thought to be the ghost of Elizabeth Carter Byrd, wife of Evelyn's brother, William Byrd III. William apparently was a gambler and a womanizer, and Elizabeth's life with him was miserable. Reportedly, at the urging of her much-hated mother-in-law, Elizabeth tried to search for evidence of her husband's infidelities in the drawer of a huge chest in an upstairs bedroom. As she tried in vain to reach the top drawers, the chest toppled over and crushed her to death. Ever since that day, servants at Westover have told of hearing high-pitched calls for help coming from that bedroom. Although most surmise that the cries are from Elizabeth, another theory says it is the disturbed voice of the mother-in-law, who regretted the role she played in Elizabeth's death.

The third and final Westover ghost is that of William Byrd III himself who, just six months after Elizabeth was buried, married a Philadelphia woman. Although the couple was happy together, William, true to form, eventually squandered the family fortune and took his own life in his favorite room of the house. More than 150 years later, a guest spent the night in the room and reported that, at the stroke of midnight, the door opened, a crash resounded through the house and a shadowy presence seemed to glide through the room, turning the atmosphere into the chill of death. The apparition, said the visitor, was the spitting image of the portrait of William Byrd III that hangs at Westover.

# The Mother-in-law Tree

This Jamestown legend concerns the mother-in-law tree that grew between two tombs by Jamestown Church. The tale begins when Sarah Harrison broke off her engagement to one young suitor and married James Blair, 18th-century cofounder of the College of William and Mary. James had quite a few years on Sarah, and her mother, disapproving of the match, tried to have their marriage annulled. As the legend goes, Sarah's mother was struck by lightning and killed before she accomplished her plan. Sarah, who was shunned by her family, later died and was buried in a separate area from the rest of her family in the Jamestown Church cemetery. Upon his death, Blair was buried at her side. Soon, however, a sycamore tree sprouted between the couple's graves, breaking the tombstones and pushing Sarah's grave over toward the family plot, away from her husband. So, it is said that the mother-in-law ended up having the last word after all.

# William and Mary's President's House

Poor James Blair just can't rest in peace. He also happened to be the first inhabitant of the College of William and Mary's President's House, which is said to be haunted. This House is the setting of a number of strange phenomena. For a long time, a certain bedroom closet door in the house wouldn't stay shut. No one could figure out why. Then, workmen making repairs in a ceiling crawl space found a skeleton embedded in the wall. (No, it wasn't Blair's mother-in-law.) Once the skeleton was removed, the closet door stopped popping open. But the ghost purportedly occupying the house can't be so easily expelled. Footsteps, supposedly those of a French soldier who died in the house during the Revolutionary War, can be heard mounting and descending an upper staircase. A number of the college's past presidents have reported visits from the spirited fellow.

# The Brafferton Building

Perhaps the French soldier's ghost is trying to get out of the President's House to head over to the Brafferton building across the college yard, where the spirits of Native American boys who once attended the old Indian school are said to still be in residence. Then again, if he's looking for a little female company, he need only cross the street to Colonial Williamsburg, where several lady specters preside over the spirit set.

# Peyton Randolph House

In the Peyton Randolph House on Nicholson Street, a hand-wringing woman wearing 18th-century nightclothes has appeared to a number of overnight guests. This ghost is always described as anguished and has contributed to the building's reputation as a house of sorrow.

# Wythe House

The Wythe House behind Bruton Parish Church is said to be haunted by a beautiful woman in ballroom attire who sometimes runs upstairs. Legend identifies this hurried phantom as Lady Anne Skipwith who once fled a palace ball in a fit of jealousy over her husband's attention to another woman.

# Tales of Ruth Hankins

Many past and present residents of the Williamsburg area have their own haunting tales to tell. In 1984, Ruth Hankins, whose husband was a member of an old James City County family, shared her ghostly recollections for a local oral history project. In one of her reminisces, Mrs. Hankins, who was 86 at the time, described the origins of the "witch doors" that were part of many early Williamsburg and Jamestown houses. These heavy, wide doors carried the image of a cross and a section shaped like an open Bible. Every house was supposed to have at least one, according to Mrs. Hankins, and its purpose was to ward off witches and evil spirits. As long as the witch door was closed, no evil apparition could enter the room behind you.

In another of her tales - one a little closer to home - Mrs. Hankins spoke about the ghost that took up residence with her family. It first made its presence known when her sons were young. The family was gathered in one room, where the children were doing their homework. Suddenly, a yellow pencil rose into the air and began scribbling on a sideboard, before falling to the ground. Mrs. Hankins and her children ran to see what was etched in the dust on the sideboard but found nothing.

Another time, Mrs. Hankins was working in her house when she heard a voice say, "Good afternoon." Without thinking, she said "Well, it isn't afternoon yet. I haven't had my lunch," before realizing that there wasn't another soul anywhere nearby. A fairly rational woman, she was ready to explain the voice away as a product of her imagination, until she glanced over at her little dog, who looked petrified and was staring bug-eyed into space. For a long while after the incident, Mrs. Hankins noted, her dog avoided the area from which the ghostly voice had emanated.

**www.insiders.com**
See this and many other **Insiders' Guide** destinations online.
**Visit us today!**

## Carter's Grove

In a downstairs parlor at Carter's Grove plantation, George Washington proposed marriage to Mary Cary, and Thomas Jefferson proposed to Rebecca Burwell, though both women refused the offers. In the room where the refusals took place, a ghost has been rumored to appear, reportedly tearing up flowers that had been left in the room. Legend implies that the ghost is one, or both, of the women who later came to regret the decision not to marry her famous suitor. Then again, perhaps the rejected suitors are to blame for the shredded blossoms.

Another Carter's Grove legend, that of Colonel Banastre Tarleton's charge on horseback up the entry staircase during the Revolutionary War, is widely disputed. Some still hold, however, that the indentations on the banister are from Tarleton's saber.

# The Legend of Bruton Parish Vault

Williamsburg residents have long been familiar with stories about ghosts said to inhabit some of the town's historic buildings, but one of the legends to make the news most recently concerns a cemetery, a grave desecration, mysterious manuscripts and secret tunnels. Some locals call it much ado about nothing, but we call it the Legend of Bruton Parish Vault.

It all began, according to believers, in the 17th century when Nathaniel Bacon came to the New World to flee the persecution of King Charles. The legend goes that Bacon brought with him precious documents: a Utopian blueprint for a peaceful world in the 21st century, original versions of the King James Bible and Book of Saint Peter and manuscripts proving that Sir Francis Bacon, his father, authored Shakespeare's plays and sonnets with a little help from a few friends. These priceless pages were first buried at Jamestown. Then, in 1674, through tunnels from the George Wythe House, Geddy Foundry and William and Mary's Wren Building, a large vault containing the documents, along with gold chalices, was conveyed in secret to a spot beneath Bruton Parish Church property. At some later date, presumably, an original draft of the U.S. Constitution was slipped into the vault.

Time passed and the vault slumbered until 1938, when Marie Bauer Hall of Los Angeles decoded a book written by George Withers in 1635. It's not clear how Withers knew where the vault was buried before it

# Virginia's Ghosts

There is probably no one who knows more about Virginia's ghosts than Williamsburg author L.B. "Bob" Taylor, Jr. For the past 14 years, Taylor has researched and chronicled hundreds of terrible and traumatic ghost tales from throughout the Old Dominion. His eerie narrations include everything from the "Mad Escapades of the Powhatan Poltergeist" to the "Green-Eyed 'Monster' of Richmond."

Taylor, 64, became interested in ghosts after a chance assignment from Simon & Schuster to do a book on haunted houses. "In doing the research, I came across so much material I couldn't use in the book," he said. He decided to put the stories to good use and pen his own manuscript on Virginia's specters. Nine more books have followed. Topics include a second volume on the ghosts of Virginia and regional books on the ghosts of Williamsburg, Richmond, Tidewater, Fredericksburg, Charlottesville and Lynchburg (Taylor's hometown). One of his most recent books, Civil War Ghosts of Virginia, was released in October 1995, just in time for Halloween. A third statewide book came out in 1996, and Taylor currently is hard at work on Ghosts of Virginia, Volume IV.

Taylor's research demands considerable legwork. "I do a lot of digging in

— continued on next page

Photo: L.B. Taylor Jr.

L.B. Taylor writes about Virginia's ghosts.

archives, old county histories and, for the Civil War book, magazines dating back to the early 1900s," he noted. Taylor also tries, whenever possible, to interview folks who have had firsthand encounters with Old Dominion ghosts. He gives a number of talks throughout the area on the subject of ghosts, he said and afterwards, "people come up to me and tell me their stories." After following up on those leads and checking out the tips he gets via cards and letters from throughout the state, he soon has enough material to begin a new book.

The author admitted that a ghost has never visited him, although it's an experience he said he would welcome. As for believing in apparitions? Until he began writing about ghosts, he said, he never really thought that much about them. "But I've talked to so many people who are so sincere in their encounters that I tend to believe there's something there," said Taylor.

To obtain a copy of Taylor's most recent book, Ghosts of Virginia, Volume III, ask around at local bookstores. Or, if you'd like an autographed copy of any of his books, you can write the author at 108 Elizabeth Meriwether St., Williamsburg VA 23185.

You might glimpse the ghost of a Colonial American during your stay in Williamsburg.

---

was indeed, supposedly, buried, but symbols in his book led Bauer to the Williamsburg churchyard in search of Utopia. Since the tunnels allegedly had been filled with cement by the Colonial Williamsburg Foundation, Bauer obtained permission from church officials to dig in the cemetery. Nine feet down, past foundations of the original church, she hit a coffin with brass tacks, and church officials stopped her.

Bauer continued to believe in the existence of the vault, however, and founded an organization called Veritat, who pressured the church to allow excavation. Limited authorized testing of the site with radar in 1985 and '86 brought inconclusive results, rekindling interest in the vault theory.

Was it really there, or was it all a midsummer night's dream?

Enter Marsha Middleton of Santa Fe, who calls herself a New Age Christian Mystic and believes that she was Saint Peter in a previous incarnation. In 1991, Middleton, along with her group Ministry of the Children, conducted two illegal midnight digs in the churchyard. She, her husband and a third conspirator were charged with trespassing and vandalism. To flee or not to flee, that was the question for the Francis Bacon fugitives. They fled back to more mystic-friendly New Mexico to avoid facing charges. But all that under-cloak-of-darkness activity brought the national spotlight to focus on Bruton Parish. In January 1992, The Wall Street Journal poked gentle fun

---

**INSIDERS' TIP**

**To purchase tickets or to find out more information on any of the attractions in the Williamsburg area, stop in at the Williamsburg Attraction Center at Berkeley Commons Outlet Center on Richmond Road. The center opened in February 1997 to offer one-stop shopping for tickets to just about anything and everything in and around the Historic Triangle. The office is open 10 AM to 9 PM Monday through Saturday and 10 AM to 6 PM Sunday. Call 253-1058.**

at the whole undertaking in a front-page article, further upsetting church leaders.

The comedy of errors was far from over. Under continued pressure from the Veritat vigilantes and other interested groups to allow excavation, Bruton Parish caved in during the summer of 1992. No, the church didn't fall down, but the vestry agreed to let Colonial Williamsburg archaeologists investigate. In August, they dug a 20-by-20-foot site, uncovering mud, water, graves and pieces of bone from a corpse apparently damaged during the earlier digs. Alas, poor Yorick.

A geologist from the College of William and Mary undertook further tests, drilling holes some 20-feet deep around the site with a hand auger. He, too, found mud, but no sign of disturbed earth, no elusive vault. Church officials are satisfied they've proved beyond the shadow of a doubt that nothing unusual is buried in their cemetery. What do Bauer, Middleton and others believe? They may think the Virginia Shakespeare Festival should be renamed the Virginia Bacon Festival, but they apparently - at least for the time being - have decided to let sleeping artifacts lie.

# Yorktown

Yorktown has its own ghostly apparitions. A British soldier who was killed during the last days of the Revolutionary War is said to sometimes make his presence known in the historic Nelson House. And the Moore House, a property restored and operated by the National Park Service, is believed by many to contain a young ghost, Augustine Moore, Jr., who also may have been killed during the Revolutionary War. This particular spirit doesn't make appearances, but leaves impressions on bedcovers and a chair where he likes to sit, or so employees have claimed.

# Jamestown Pocahontas and John Smith

Perhaps the oldest and most famous area legend surrounds Pocahontas, who was an adolescent at the time English settlers arrived in Jamestown. The story goes that Captain John Smith had ventured too far into Indian territory and was taken prisoner. The Indian Chief Powhatan was ready to have the captive beheaded when his favorite daughter, Pocahontas, threw herself on the Englishman's body, pleading for his life. Powhatan, a doting father, acquiesced, and a grateful and relieved John Smith was allowed to return to Jamestown. (A much romanticized version of this legend, as anyone with small children knows by now, was made into the 1995 Walt Disney movie *Pocahontas*.)

Reconstructed with a meticulous eye for authenticity, Colonial Williamsburg offers 173 acres of 18th-century history along with a full slate of lectures, concerts, theatrical performances and militia exhibits all year long.

# Colonial Williamsburg

Is there anywhere else in America where you can listen to a traveling actor and a politician (both wearing wigs, mind you) discuss the Boston Tea Party and its possible effects on the colony of Virginia as though the controversial event happened weeks, rather than a couple centuries, ago? Or get to participate in the trial of an 18th-century witch — and help decide her fate? Or pause in your pleasant stroll down a dusty street as the local Fife and Drum Corps marches out of the past, making a musical memory on its way from the Capitol to the Palace Green?

There's probably nowhere else in America where the past comes alive in the present as it does in Williamsburg. Reconstructed with a meticulous eye for authenticity, Colonial Williamsburg offers 173 acres of 18th-century history along with a full slate of lectures, concerts, theatrical performances and militia exhibits all year long. Throughout the historic area, costumed interpreters toil at their trades like their kinsmen of yore. In Colonial taverns, balladeers serenade their audiences with the bawdy tales that were popular with previous generations while learned gentlemen of the time discuss the political issues that were at the forefront of everyone's mind.

With 88 original structures, 50 major reconstructions, 40 exhibition buildings and 90 acres of gardens and greens, Williamsburg isn't a city you can see in a day — or even two. It's a place to be savored, so make sure you allow enough time to listen to an evening reveille, dance in the candlelit House of Burgesses, even treat your own American Girl to a tour that follows the life of Felicity Merriman, a fictional 9-year-old growing up in Williamsburg in 1774 who is patterned after one of the American Girls Collection of dolls. The memories you'll come away with are unlikely to be duplicated anywhere else. To start you on your trip to another era, we begin with a comprehensive look back at how it all began.

## Historical Overview

### Promising Beginnings

Williamsburg served as Virginia's capital from 1699 to 1780 and, during that time, grew from a small settlement to a thriving, sophisticated urban center, symmetrically designed to reflect the city's prominent role. By mid-18th century, the population was nearing 2,000; slaves accounted for roughly half of that number. When courts convened, Williamsburg's population more than doubled, with citizens from the far reaches of the vast Virginia Colony arriving to participate in the fairs, festivities and fancy dress balls of Publick Times.

American ideals of democracy and liberty took root here in the 1700s, as colonists began to question, and finally repudiate, British rule. Patrick Henry inveighed against taxation without representation in the House of Burgesses. The First Continental Congress was called from Williamsburg in 1774. The Declaration of Rights, soon to become the foundation for the first 10 amendments to the Constitution, was penned here by George Mason. Thousands of Continental Army soldiers were billeted in Williamsburg, which bustled with revolutionary fervor. In 1780, however, Thomas Jefferson's campaign to move the capital to Richmond succeeded, and Williamsburg, no longer the heart of social, political and economic life in Virginia, entered an era of sleepy decline. Population lagged, and businesses were forced to close. While it continued to function as county seat, 19th-century Williamsburg was mostly a market town for area farmers.

The College of William and Mary and the Public Hospital remained the only institutions of much size or importance. Some public buildings fell into neglect and burned (the Palace in 1781), but most of the 18th-century homes and structures continued to be used simply because there was little reason to build anew. While interim uses were at times less than noble (Prentis Store survived in the early 20th century as a gas station; the Magazine once served as a stable), the structures were saved from destruction.

## Two Men and a Dream

Williamsburg might still be a sedate spot on the map if not for the actions of two men who conceived of a grander future for the once-great city. The Rev. W.A.R. Goodwin, rector of Bruton Parish Church, dreamed of restoring the heritage of Virginia's Colonial capital. He was successful in raising enough money to restore his own church, but in 1908 left Williamsburg to become rector of a Rochester, New York, church. In 1923, however, he returned as professor of religion at the College of William and Mary. As luck would have it, the college chose Goodwin as its representative at a 1924 Phi Beta Kappa dinner in New York. Also attending the dinner was John D. Rockefeller, Jr., philanthropic heir to the Standard Oil fortune.

This meeting led to the Rockefellers' 1926 visit to Williamsburg, during which negotiations for the restoration of certain 18th-century buildings began. Planning was carried out in a highly secretive manner. Measurements of buildings were taken under cover of dark. Rockefeller insisted on signing documents pseudonymously as "Mr. David." Town residents felt understandably apprehensive and mystified as they watched their rector buying

up land. Rumors spread, and real estate values took off. Soon it was necessary to reveal to Williamsburg citizens the nature of the restoration plan. Initially, not all were pleased; some balked at the idea of their town being "sold." Others were skeptical about the practicality of such a scheme. As the restoration process began, however, the economic benefits of the project became clear. Tenancy agreements allowed most previous residents of 18th-century buildings to occupy their homes for life.

## A Reconstruction Frenzy

Though Rockefeller at first intended to subsidize the restoration of a small number of structures, his enthusiasm and ambitions grew as research turned up more and more pertinent data. Drawings, maps and records culled from libraries and museums in Europe and America revealed a trove of historical details. Teams of architects, led by William Graves Perry, worked to authentically restore original 18th-century sites and to reconstruct others on original foundations. Hundreds of more modern buildings were razed or removed. Eighteenth-century building and brick-making techniques were painstakingly researched so that a restored or reconstructed building would resemble the original as closely as possible.

The success of Goodwin's and Rockefeller's grand vision is well-documented today. About a million visitors tour Colonial Williamsburg (Or CW, as Insiders like to say) each year. They step out of their 20th-century lives into an authentic, engrossing 18th-century world. The Historic Area contains hundreds of restored public buildings, residences, outbuildings, dependencies, shops and hostelries, plus acres of formal and informal gardens, pastures and lanes.

While in one sense the restoration Goodwin and Rockefeller envisioned is complete, the Colonial Williamsburg Foundation continues to pursue its vision — or perhaps we should say revision — of the past. In recent years, Colonial Williamsburg has redirected its focus somewhat. Previously, restoration efforts and programs at Colonial Williamsburg concentrated on the lives of an elite group — Colonial governors, revolutionary leaders, and prominent citizens. Today in the Historic Area and its museums, you will find more space given to the 18th-century community as a whole. Slaves, indentured servants, women, tradespeople, the typical family of the period and other "middling" folk are increasingly featured in interpretive programs that more accurately reflect the complexities of 18th-century history.

One program, for instance, explores the paradoxical issue of freedom in a society that fought to win its independence from the British Crown while practicing and condoning slavery. Colonial Williamsburg also has used grant monies to improve and more fully assimilate interpretation of the 18th-century African-American experience into its presentations. The role religion played in the daily lives of colonists is being more fully explored and interpreted for the benefit of visitors through lectures, tours and concerts. Each year, month-long observations of black history, women's history, music and religion are observed with special programming. Re-enactments and re-creations of historical events — from a day of fasting, humiliation and prayer in response to the Boston Tea Party to a Market Square military encampment that portrays the British occupation of the City of Williamsburg by soldiers under the command of Lord Cornwallis — occur on a regular basis throughout the Historic Area.

The best way to find out what's on tap when you're in town is to consult your *Colonial Williamsburg Visitor's Companion*, a publication that is updated weekly and contains a map and information on sites, special programs, lodging, shopping and dining within Colonial Williamsburg.

Perhaps the biggest physical change in recent years in the Historic Area is the relocation of the Armistead House from Duke of Gloucester Street to the 300 block of South Henry Street. Until November 1995, the house was the sole Victorian frame house left amid its older brethren along the restored street. Built in 1890 by Cary Peyton Armistead, the house was maintained as a family residence until 1984. Then, the Association for the Preservation of Virginia Antiquities operated it as a museum until 1993. The museum was finally closed because of declining attendance. Now, with the house relocated and restored to its original color (a creamy peach), Colonial Williamsburg most likely will rebuild an 18th-century coffeehouse or tavern on this prime site next door to the Capitol after it finishes its in-depth archaeological studies.

Another, more recent, change that has a significant impact on CW research is the opening of the $37.2 million Bruton Heights School Education Center. Just outside the Historic Area, the center includes new facilities for the John D. Rockefeller, Jr., Library, with its collection of 65,000 books, 43,000 manuscripts, 12,000 rare books and 50,000 architectural drawings; the DeWitt Wallace Collections and Conservation Building, which houses up to 20,000 reserve objects from CW's fine and decorative arts collection; an audio-video production area; and other departments that previously had been scattered in various locations throughout Colonial Williamsburg. "Now, at last, we have a campus for the people who conceive and develop our programs," noted CW President Robert C. Wilburn when the facility officially opened in April 1997.

As a way to acknowledge and offer more services to CW contributors, The Colonial Williamsburg Foundation has opened the St. George Tucker House Donor Reception Center on Nicholson Street next to the Palace Green. This hospitality center is open daily from 9:30 AM to 4:30 PM for annual donors of $100 or more. Volunteers staff the center, which offers VIPs light refreshments and special assistance with reservations and visit plans. Each year more than 50,000 donors support Colonial Williamsburg's educational mission.

**INSIDERS' TIP**

If you forget to pick up the weekly *Visitor's Companion* before you leave the Visitor Center, don't panic. You can always grab a copy on the bus that takes you to the Historic Area. Pocket-size dining guides for the Colonial taverns also are available on the buses.

Photo: Colonial Williamsburg Foundation

The Governor's Palace and Gardens are two of Colonial Williamsburg's most popular and beautiful attractions.

From a historical standpoint, the Tucker House was the site of the first Christmas tree in Williamsburg and was owned by the Tucker family for more than 200 years until 1993. The $1.1 million renovation was funded by — what else? — donations.

## Change Is in the Air

In recent years, the winds of change have begun blowing a little more forcefully down the dusty streets of Williamsburg. The bid for tourists' time — and money — is a competitive business, and The Colonial Williamsburg Foundation has grown increasingly concerned in recent years over stagnant attendance figures. In the 1980s annual ticket sales regularly hit the $1.2 million mark, but for the last six or seven years have been stuck around $950,000 or so. A few months of serious discussion in 1997 focused on the possibility of closing the streets of the Historic Area to all but paying customers in an attempt to increase revenues. After a multitude of complaints from the public, countless letters to the editors of local newspapers and several meetings with city officials, the foundation withdrew the idea on the eve of the nation's July 4th birthday.

Even with the option of strolling through the city free of charge, your visit to Williamsburg would be in no way complete if you failed to take advantage of the opportunity to enter the one-of-a-kind structures in the Colonial capital and literally watch history unfold before you. In other words, if you want to truly do Williamsburg, a ticket is a must.

## Help Make History

During your stroll through Colonial times, we urge you to get involved in what is happening all around you. The teaching of history is a primary goal in Colonial Williamsburg, and folks here do it as well as most classroom teachers. To engage visitors as fully as possible, Colonial Williamsburg offers a variety of lively, hands-on learning presentations. Audience-interactive programs such as the trials of the Virginia Witch and other courtroom dramas allow visitors to enjoy a living history experience. Children and parents will find programs that deal with family issues — and possibly have the chance to help Grandma Geddy (mother of eight) with the laundry — at the Geddy House, home of a working-class, 18th-century family. You also will have the opportunity to meet many of the other women of Williamsburg — from Grissell Hay, a widow and "Gentlewoman of Note," to Venus, daughter of Old Paris, one of the Carter's Grove slaves. Other notable "persons of the past" are George Wythe, a gentleman and scholar, and Lewis Tyler, enforcer and practitioner of the law.

Martha Washington, who became part of the Colonial cast in 1995, has proved to be a perennial favorite as she sips tea with Sunday guests in the Williamsburg Inn. Portrayed as a 28-year-old during her first two years in Williamburg, Martha finally has caught up in age to her historical brethren. In June 1997, a more "mature" interpreter took over the role and transformed our original First Lady into the 43-year-old wife of a newly elected member of the House of Burgesses.

And, in response to visitors' requests, CW has recruited more children and youth volunteers to portray characters in the Historic Area during the summer months when they are out of school. Most of the youngsters are in costume — whether they're doing their lessons, sewing a sampler or studying religion — and they are responsible for only two four-hour shifts a week.

## A Continuing Commitment

Colonial Williamsburg's commitment to authenticity remains strong. Historians, archaeologists and researchers continue to uncover documents and artifacts that reveal new aspects of the past and make possible more exact interpretations of history. As we mentioned earlier, excavation work has been ongoing at the former site of the Armistead House and will continue for several years. In the first year or so of digging, researchers unearthed evidence of the porch to a coffeehouse from the 1760s and uncovered more than 15,000 artifacts, including broken wine glasses and bottles, smoking pipes and tavern mugs. These continuous and painstaking efforts ensure that America's heritage will continue to be preserved and enriched for future generations. It is this sense of ongoing discovery that makes history seem alive here and motivates visitors to keep returning across the miles and centuries to a place called Williamsburg.

# Getting Started

## Visitor Center

The Visitor Center, on Visitor Center Drive (132-Y), should be the starting point for any tour of Colonial Williamsburg. Follow the green-and-white directional signs placed around town, and park for free in one of the center's 2,000 parking spaces. Tickets are on sale here, and sightseeing information, maps, guidebooks and Colonial Currency, which can be used as actual money throughout the Historic Area, also are available. Reservations for

**INSIDERS' TIP**

Colonial Williamsburg and the College of William and Mary have teamed up with seven other Virginia historical sites for a cooperative travel and tour program that celebrates the life and accomplishments of Thomas Jefferson. Other sites on the tour include Barboursville Vineyards, Monticello, Natural Bridge, Thomas Jefferson's Poplar Forest, Tuckahoe Plantation, The University of Virginia and the Virginia State Capitol. Passports are available that provide admission to all of these sites. In 1999, they are $57 for adults and $25 for children ages 6 through 12. At Colonial Williamsburg, the passport is good for two consecutive days of admission to all exhibition buildings, trade shops, history walks and Colonial Williamsburg museums. Tickets may be purchased at Colonial Williamsburg or by calling (888) 293-1776.

special tours and presentations, for meals in Colonial Williamsburg's several taverns and restaurants and for lodging at its hotel facilities can be arranged here as well. The Visitor Center Bookstore is well-stocked with titles relating to Colonial history, including sections on antiques, archaeology, crafts, gardening, decorative arts and biography. Other sections hold books detailing the roles of African Americans, Indians and women in Colonial life. Souvenirs and gifts as well as postcards, film and camera accessories also are for sale. The Visitor Center is open from 8:30 AM to 8 PM daily during the summer, although hours are shortened during the fall and winter months. You may want to call ahead before showing up. Any and all questions you have about visiting Colonial Williamsburg attractions can be answered here, or by calling (757) 229-1000 or (800) 246-2099.

## Tickets

Visitors will need a ticket to enter exhibition buildings, historic trade shops or to ride the buses provided by Colonial Williamsburg. Tickets can be purchased at the Visitor Center, the Merchants Square Information Center on S. Henry Street or at the Lumber House ticket office on Duke of Gloucester Street in the restored area. For general admission, which includes entry to the more than 30 homes, historic trade shops and public buildings in the Historic Area, plus use of the Colonial Williamsburg buses and a viewing of *Williamsburg — The Story of a Patriot*, you can choose one of three options: a Patriot's Pass, a two-day Colonist's Pass or a one-day Basic Admission Ticket.

In 1999, a Patriot's Pass costs $33 for adults and $19 for children ages 6 to 12. This pass is good for all major exhibits, museums and tours, including Carter's Grove. It also en-

www.insiders.com
See this and many other **Insiders' Guide** destinations online.
**Visit us today!**

titles the bearer to a 25 percent discount on evening programs (except for those in December). Valid for a full year, this ticket allows for unlimited exploration of Colonial Williamsburg and free parking at the Visitors Center. This is an excellent option for folks living close enough to come to Williamsburg several times a year.

The Basic Admission Ticket is good for one day and costs $25 for adults and $15 for children ages 6 to 12. It gets you into the Abby Aldrich Rockefeller Folk Art Center, the DeWitt Wallace Gallery and all of the exhibits in the Historic Area except the Governor's Palace. Before buying this ticket, make sure you don't want to visit the exhibits not covered, or you may end up adding on single admission tickets and losing money.

The $29 Colonist's Pass gives you more bang for your buck. For $29 for adults and $17 for children ages 6 to 12, visitors not only get a second day (both days must be consecutive) to check out the many sights of the Colonial Williamsburg Historic Area, but also get to visit the Governor's Palace, undoubtedly the most impressive single structure on the tour.

Listed below are the prices of separate tickets to several Colonial Williamsburg museums and exhibits.

### Museums Ticket
**$10 for adults, $6.50 for children**

This ticket combines admission to the Wallace Gallery, the Folk Art Center and Bassett Hall.

### Governor's Palace
**$17 for both adults and children**

This ticket includes use of the Colonial Williamsburg bus system and admission to the introductory film shown at the Visitor Center.

## INSIDERS' TIP

**When the skies are clear, visitors can enjoy carriage and wagon rides through the Historic Area. Tickets can be purchased at any ticket sales location. Rides are on a first-come, first-served basis.**

## Carter's Grove
**$15 for adults, $9 for children ages 6 to 12**
This ticket only covers admission to Carter's Grove.

## Annual Museums Ticket
**$17 for adults and $10 for children**
An annual museums ticket includes entry to the Wallace Gallery, the Folk Art Center and Bassett Hall for a full year from the date of purchase.

## Good Neighbor's Pass
**Free to residents**
Newcomers to the area should know that Williamsburg, James City County and York County Bruton District residents can ask for a free Good Neighbor's Pass to Colonial Williamsburg. This pass, introduced in April 1993, provides admission to the Governor's Palace, the DeWitt Wallace Gallery, Carter's Grove, Abby Aldrich Rockefeller Folk Art Center and all Historic Area buildings, plus news and information about special events and programs mailed directly to your home as well as free parking at the Visitor Center. The Good Neighbor's Pass also entitles holders to a 25 percent discount for regular price evening programs (except for those in December) and a 40 percent discount on up to 10 admission tickets each year, a treat when guests come to town. You'll need proof of residency to obtain this pass, and you will automatically be sent a renewal sticker each year. There is a small replacement charge for lost cards. The passes are available at the Visitor Center guest services desk. Call (757) 220-7562 for more information.

## Revolutionary Fun Family Package
**Average price for a family of four for three nights is $629, for four nights, $699**
If you want to plan your entire Historic Triangle experience with a single phone call and then just show up on your prearranged dates, this is the way to go. The Revolutionary Fun Family Package, initially introduced as a "5-4-1 ticket" in 1994, includes lodging and a combination admission ticket to Busch Gardens, Colonial Williamsburg, Jamestown Settlement, Water Country USA and the Yorktown Victory Center. With this ticket you have unlimited visits to all five participating attractions during the package stay. Lodging is in one of the four official hotels of Colonial Williamsburg: Governor's Inn, Williamsburg Woodlands, Williamsburg Lodge or the Williamsburg Inn. (For more information on these properties, turn to our chapter on Accommodations.) To request a brochure or find out more about the family package, call (800) 441-3254.

# Hours of Operation

Colonial Williamsburg is open every day of the year, including all holidays. The Visitor Center, where your tour should begin, is open from 8:30 AM to 8 PM daily during the summer, with reduced hours during other seasons. Buildings in the Historic Area typically are open from 9 AM to 5 PM. During the summer, some buildings remain open until 6 or 7 PM.

# Transportation

A fleet of gray-and-white Colonial Williamsburg buses circulates through and around the Historic Area, stopping at major points of interest. They carry visitors to and from the Visitor Center continuously from 8:50 AM to 10 PM, and ticket holders may board at any stop. Special assistance and shuttle bus service is available to visitors with disabilities. If you need this service, inquire at the Visitor Center, Lumber House ticket office or Merchant Square Information Station. As we mentioned in our Getting Around chapter, cars are more bother than they're worth when touring the Historic Area. Parking around the Historic Area is limited, and the streets are closed to vehicles, typically from 8 AM to 9 PM. Parking at the Visitor Center is $6 for ticketholders, $12 per day without a ticket and free for those with a Patriot's Pass or a Good Neighbor's Pass. You can rent bikes and strollers at the Williamsburg Lodge if the weather is nice. Strollers rent for $7.50 a day. Bikes can be rented by the hour for $5, for a half-day (four hours) for $12, or for a full day for $19.95.

# Historic Area Attractions

While it's impossible to absorb everything Colonial Williamsburg has to offer in a day or two, some visitors can't stay much longer. Even a short visit will be memorable if you take the time to plan your tour in advance. When you arrive in Williamsburg, ask hotel personnel or staff at the Colonial Williamsburg Visitor Center for a copy of the weekly updated *Visitor's Companion*, a daily calendar and schedule that gives operating hours for Historic Area buildings, restaurants, tours and events. This publication, without which we personally wouldn't step foot in Williamsburg, can help you decide on an agenda for each day.

Below, we highlight the major buildings and exhibits you won't want to miss, no matter how brief your stay. We recommend the escorted half-hour introductory tour Colonial Williamsburg offers as orientation for a leisurely self-touring vacation, or just as a pleasant — if short — excursion into the world of 18th-century Williamsburg. You also will want to read through the *Official Colonial Williamsburg Guidebook and Map* (available at the Visitor Center), an excellent introduction to the diverse and sometimes complex experiences in store for you as you travel back in time. While we mention which buildings and exhibits require special reservations, it's always best to check at the Visitor Center the day you plan to tour a specific site, as hours of operation vary, and buildings occasionally are closed to the public.

## The Buildings

### Governor's Palace

Set on 10 acres of restored gardens, this elegant mansion housed a series of Royal Governors and the Commonwealth of Virginia's first two governors, Patrick Henry and Thomas Jefferson. The original construction began in 1706 and took 17 years to complete; alterations and redecoration continued until the December 22, 1781, fire that left only the Palace foundation. At the north end of the Palace Green, the reconstructed mansion, with its entrance hall, parlor, ballroom, dining rooms, bed chambers, waiting areas and even

a wine cellar, is opulently furnished from an inventory of more than 12,000 items dating to the period of Lord Dunmore, Virginia's last royal governor. Lord Dunmore and his family lived in Governor's Palace in the early 1770s.

Children delight in trying to count the muskets mounted in a circle on the entrance hall ceiling. (We know how many are up there, but it's more fun if you guess before asking your guide.) Check out the incredible crown moldings and wall coverings (that's leather on the walls in the upstairs meeting room), and don't miss all the interesting details throughout the Palace. The chairs in Lady Dunmore's upstairs bed chamber are made to simulate bamboo, there really were Venetian blinds on the windows, and the small statues lining the dining room mantel are the actual figurines representing the costumed characters from the masquerade ball commemorating King George III's 21st birthday.

During the 18th century, the Governor's Palace was the scene of many get-togethers of early America's well-to-do. Dances, for example, were held about every three months in the Palace ballroom, each typically lasting up to 18 hours, since- many visitors had journeyed three or more days on horseback to reach Williamsburg, and it would have been exceedingly impolite to send them home too soon.

On the Palace grounds you will find a stable and carriage house, a kitchen, scullery, laundry and a hexagonal "bagnio" or bathhouse, a real frill in Colonial times. Take the time to stroll through the formal gardens, similar to early 18th-century English gardens, which lead to informal terraces and a fish pond. The palace is one of Colonial Williamsburg's most popular attractions, drawing 650,000 visitors annually.

### Capitol

Prior to the Revolutionary War, the House of Burgesses and a 12-member council met in this ornate structure at the east end of Duke of Gloucester Street. Once war began, and until 1780 when the capital was moved to Richmond, it housed state government. Foundations were laid in 1701 for the H-shaped building, designed with two wings to hold the bicameral legislative bodies that made up Colonial government. Like the Palace, the original

Photo: Colonial Williamsburg

Visitors assume the roles of witness, defendant and jurors during Order in The Court.

Capitol building suffered fire damage, burning in 1747. Its replacement, neglected after the capital moved to Richmond in 1780, eventually burned also. What you see today is a reconstruction of the first Capitol, about which more architectural evidence was found. Here, you can tour the House of Burgesses, Council Chambers and General Courtroom and join in a number of special evening programs. These include *Dance, Our Dearest Diversion*; *Cry Witch*, a court trial re-enactment that encourages audience participation; and a concert of spirited tunes from the 18th century.

## Public Gaol

Behind the Capitol on Nicholson Street is the Public Gaol (pronounced jail), with partially original walls and wholly authentic grimness. Shackles that were excavated while the gaol was under restoration are on display. Take a look in the small, dank cells hung with leg irons, and consider spending a winter night in such a place with only a thin blanket for cover. Among the 18th-century inhabitants of these cells were Blackbeard's pirate crew, runaway slaves, Indians, insolvent debtors and, occasionally, mentally ill persons. During the Revolution, British captives, accused spies and Tory sympathizers were cordially allowed to use the gaol facilities. Part of the gaol has been

refurbished to reflect its other function — home to the gaol keeper and his family. Furnishings are representative of those owned by a typical family of the period.

## Raleigh Tavern

Revolutionary heroes like Patrick Henry and Thomas Jefferson gathered to discuss politics and reach important conclusions in this famous Duke of Gloucester Street tavern, the first of Colonial Williamsburg's reconstructed buildings to open for public viewing. Built around 1717, the Tavern was the axis around which 18th-century Virginia society, business and politics revolved. George Washington dined here often and mentions the tavern in his diary. The Phi Beta Kappa Society was founded here as well. The tavern burned in 1859, but original foundations and drawings aided architects in the 1930s reconstruction. We're particularly impressed by the billiard table: Its 6-foot by 12-foot dimensions required that a room large enough to hold it be added onto the tavern. Behind the Tavern is the Bake Shop where visitors line up for gingerbread, Shrewsbury cakes, sweet potato muffins and other home baked goodies. The tavern is on Duke of Gloucester Street near the Capitol.

## Magazine and Guardhouse

Across Duke of Gloucester from the popular Chowning's Tavern is the octagonal Magazine, which was built in 1715 to store arms for the protection of the colony and for trade with the Indians, and a Guardhouse, reconstructed in 1949. The Magazine played an important role during the French and Indian War (1754-63), when it became evident that the wooden stockade surrounding it served as woefully inadequate protection from enemies. In 1755, Peyton Randolph, Carter Burwell, John Chiswell, Benjamin Waller and James Power were named as directors to hire workmen to build both a brick wall around the Magazine and a Guardhouse to protect this valuable weaponry storehouse. Although no one knows who actually erected the first Guardhouse and what it looked like, the original structure most likely consisted of a room for the officers, another for the men and a piazza or porch for the sentry. It is believed that the reconstructed Guardhouse, following that formula, closely resembles the original.

Perhaps the biggest conflict surrounding the Magazine occurred before dawn on April 21, 1775, when British soldiers removed 15 half-barrels of gunpowder from the storehouse, stirring a protest from Williamsburg's angry citizenry and fanning the fires that led to Revolution. (Other arms and ammunition stored in the Magazine at the time included shot, flints and military equipment such as tents.) After the Revolution, the Magazine housed a market, meetinghouse, dance school and livery stable. Humble as they seem, these interim uses probably saved the original building from abandonment and destruction.

## Wythe House

Together with outbuildings and gardens, this spacious original building affords an understanding of gracious living in 18th-century Williamsburg. The house, featuring two great chimneys and large central halls, was used as George Washington's headquarters before the Battle of Yorktown. Owner George Wythe was the nation's first law professor and an influential teacher of Thomas Jefferson. During the last few years, the environmental and security systems were upgraded at the Wythe House, and a $750,000 redecorating project was completed in 1995. The changes involved replacing marble fireplace mantels with more authentic ones of red sandstone and installing custom handprinted wallpaper after painstaking analysis revealed that the Wythe House most likely was wallpapered during Wythe's lifetime (1726-1806).

Behind the house you'll find symmetrical gardens, a tree box topiary and an arbor of shady hornbeam. In reconstructed outbuildings, including a stable, smokehouse, laundry, kitchen and lumber house, interpreters periodically demonstrate domestic activities such as cooking a batch of apple fritters over the kitchen's open hearth.

## Bruton Parish Church

On Duke of Gloucester Street west of the Palace Green, Bruton Parish Church is one of America's oldest Episcopal churches, in use since 1715. While Bruton Parish is owned not by Colonial Williamsburg but by congregation members, the public is welcome to tour the church from 9 AM to 5 PM Monday through Saturday and Sundays from 1 to 5 PM. The church was fully restored in 1940. Walls and windows are original. The stone baptismal font, according to legend, was brought from an earlier Jamestown church. The churchyard holds many 18th-century graves. Buried inside the church is Francis Fauquier, one of Virginia's royal governors. An evening organ recital frequently is presented at the church. For more on the Bruton Parish Church, turn to our chapter on Attractions. And be sure and check out the Tale of Bruton Parish Vault in our chapter on Myths and Legends of the Historic Triangle.

## Historic Meals

A visit to Williamsburg, no matter how short, should include at least one meal in one of the popular restored taverns. All Colonial Williamsburg taverns are furnished with an 18th-century flair, but each offers a different adventure in dining. Once you read the descriptions below and choose the tavern that tickles your fancy, reservations can be made by calling (757) 229-2141 or by stopping in at the Visitor Center, where you also can find out about hours and seasonal openings.

Take a look, too, at our Restaurants chapter for more information about tavern dining and entertainment. Recipes from the tavern kitchens as well as from other Colonial Williamsburg restaurants have been published in two books available at the Visitor Center bookstore: *Favorite Meals from Williamsburg: A Menu Cookbook* has more than 200 recipes from Colonial Williamsburg chefs; *The Williamsburg Cookbook* contains 185 recipes, traditional and contemporary, culled from the taverns and other restaurants in Colonial Williamsburg.

## Chowning's Tavern

The public that frequented Chowning's Tavern on Duke of Gloucester Street were locals — farmers who sold produce at market, people with business at the courthouse and bystanders with a little time to kill. Chowning's resembles an alehouse and offers traditional English pub fare. Try shepherd's pie, Cornish pasties, fish and chips and the ever-popular Brunswick stew. There are a number of beers on tap, including Chowning's own brand of ale.

## King's Arms Tavern

In its original incarnation, the King's Arms Tavern, also on Duke of Gloucester Street, catered to Virginia's gentry. Today, the menu features recipes from English cookbooks of the 17th and 18th centuries. Choose from a variety of Colonial favorites including peanut soup, potted salmon, game pie and roast prime rib of beef. Complement your meal with a selection from the extensive wine list and, for dessert, pucker up for a bite of sour cherry trifle.

## Christiana Campbell's Tavern

Christiana Campbell's Tavern on Waller Street, where Washington also dined, specializes in fresh seafood, offering foods from all 13 original colonies. Specialties include New England clam chowder and codfish cakes, Maryland crab cakes and oyster fritters and fish muddle from the Carolinas. Christiana Campbell's is open for dinner only.

## Shields Tavern

The fourth and newest tavern operated by Colonial Williamsburg, Shields Tavern on Duke of Gloucester Street, served lower gentry in the middle 1700s. The menu here is inspired by early American cookbooks. Surprisingly, this includes many modern dishes, including gazpacho, polenta and fried chicken and macaroni and cheese. Or, if you prefer, there's always the grill of wild boar sausage and quail and syllabub with fresh berries.

# Trade Shops and Demonstrations

Scattered throughout the Historic Area are costumed craftspeople, journeymen and apprentices practicing the various old trades that were part of life in the 18th century. At the Printing Office on Duke of Gloucester Street, visitors can see newspapers printed on an 18th-century press, learn about bookbinding and watch periodic demonstrations of typesetting, papermaking and decorating. At the James Anderson Blacksmith Shop, seven reconstructed forges operate, and smithing techniques are demonstrated. Silversmiths craft

## INSIDERS' TIP

**Colonial Williamsburg's outdoor Christmas decorations are considered quite unusual as they are made of natural materials that would have been available during the 18th century. These typically include boxwood and pine wreaths adorned with fresh pineapples, oranges, pomegranates, apples, nuts, pine cones, holly and the like. In addition, more than 200 plain white pine wreaths and 900 yards of white pine roping are used to put the finishing touches on doorways, windows, columns and railings.**

mote spoons — decoratively perforated and good for straining tea — at The Golden Ball, where you can also buy gold and silver jewelry. The Margaret Hunter Shop re-creates the atmosphere and activity of an 18th-century milliner's, with hats, gloves, purses, shoes and embroidery pieces on the shelves.

Next door to the King's Arms Tavern, a wigmaker uses goat, horse and human hair to conjure up a few curls. Out on North England Street, you can visit Robertson's Windmill, where wind-driven sails power stones that grind corn. Nearby, coopers shape and assemble staves to form casks, piggins and other wooden containers. In addition, harness and saddle makers, shoemakers, cabinetmakers, brass founders, gunsmiths, wheelwrights, carpenters, cooks and basket makers go about their business in Historic Area sites.

## Mercantile Shops

While some of the historic trade shops sell crafted items, several operating mercantile shops accurately re-create 18th-century business premises, offering wares and services representative of Colonial times. Finest among these is Prentis Store, an original building dating from 1740 that features reproductions of 18th-century wares. Tarpley's Store sells pottery, baskets, candles and soaps, while the Greenhow Store's inventory includes candy, three-cornered hats and fifes. These stores, along with the Mary Dickinson Store, which sells jewelry, toiletries and women's accessories, and the M. Dubois Grocer, where you can pick up a bottle of tavern sparkling cider, can all be visited on Duke of Gloucester Street. At the Colonial Post Office you'll find an extensive collection of 18th-century prints and maps as well as postcards that can be hand-canceled using the original 18th-century Williamsburg postmark.

## Other Buildings and Exhibits

If you aren't pressed for time, you may want to explore more restored or reconstructed sites in the Historic Area, and there are a few we'd like to particularly recommend.

## James Geddy House and Foundry

The James Geddy House and Foundry, on Duke of Gloucester Street just across the Palace Green from Bruton Parish Church, was home to a family of artisans that worked in bronze, brass, pewter and silver. Visitors to the house can learn about the life of an 18th-century tradesman and his children by helping out at the foundry or assisting Grandma Geddy (mother of eight) with the laundry.

## Brush-Everard House

The Brush-Everard House on the Palace Green is known for its carved woodwork. The yard is paved with original bricks found during excavation, and the smokehouse and kitchen are original restored structures. The Brush-Everard House was one of three buildings included in a recent $2.5 million renovation project that included adding state-of-the-art air conditioning and heating, fire detectors, security systems and computerized humidity and temperature controls. While the restoration work was going on, historians had a rare opportunity to explore much of the building and readjust their thinking about its history. The house was built by John Brush then occupied by Henry Cary, who extensively renovated it between 1730 and 1740. Thomas Everard moved in around 1770 and added wallpaper in the dining room and chamber. The Colonial Williamsburg tour focuses on the life of Everard, an immigrant and public official, and the lives of his family and slaves.

## Wetherburn's Tavern

Wetherburn's Tavern, an original building, was carefully refurnished using information gleaned from a detailed inventory left of Henry Wetherburn's estate and from artifacts uncovered during excavation at the site. Tours spotlight the lives of Wetherburn's family and slaves. The house is on Duke of Gloucester Street next to Tarpley's Store. With its cupola, weather vane and round-headed windows, the Courthouse is visible up and down Duke of

Gloucester Street. A series of special programs allows visitors to experience the day-to-day functioning of early American jurisprudence. Costumed interpreters and guides lead visitors through participatory scenes, such as trials and impromptu dialogues. Interesting furnishings include the chief magistrate's throne-like chair and cloth-bound docket books used by Colonial clerks and sheriffs.

# Beyond the Historic Area

Visitors lucky enough to have more than a few days to spend in the area, those on return trips and those with special interests can enhance their appreciation of 18th-century history, arts and related phenomena by visiting some of the properties operated by Colonial Williamsburg outside the Historic Area. Entry to some of these attractions comes with general admission tickets, but we've noted where an additional ticket is required.

## Bassett Hall
**Off Francis St. • (757) 229-1000**

Bassett Hall is the two-story, 18th-century frame house that was the Williamsburg home of John D. Rockefeller, Jr., and his wife, Abby Aldrich Rockefeller. While earlier tours of the home focused on Mrs. Rockefeller's folk art collection, visitors now learn about the Rockefellers themselves and their contribution to the creation of Colonial Williamsburg. The house is set on a 585-acre tract of woodlands, and the property includes a teahouse and three original outbuildings: a smokehouse, kitchen and dairy. The tour consists of three elements: a 10-minute video shown in the reception area of Bassett Hall, an audio-tour through the house and onto the grounds with reminiscences and observations by people who knew the Rockefellers, and the chance to explore replantings of Bassett Hall's seasonal gardens and surrounding grounds. For more information about touring Bassett Hall, consult your *Visitor's Companion* or the staff at the Visitor Center, or call the previously listed number. Admission to Bassett Hall is included in the purchase of a Patriot's Pass, Colonist's Pass or Basic Admission Ticket, and tour reserva-

tions are required. The hall is closed on Wednesdays.

## Abby Aldrich Rockefeller Folk Art Center
**S. England St., across from Williamsburg Lodge • (757) 220-7698**

This facility reopened in the spring of 1992 following a three-year expansion and refurbishment. The addition tripled the space available for exhibits, allowing more of the museum's extensive and renowned collection of American folk art dating from the 1730s to be displayed at one time. The Folk Art Center now includes 18 galleries in 19,000 square feet of exhibition space. The public can view scores of imaginative works by untutored artists and craftspeople, including quilts, pottery, tinware, painted furniture, wind toys, ship carvings, needlework, oils and watercolors. You'll see scrimshaw on a porpoise's jaw, learn that whirligigs often served satirical purposes, and you'll probably find yourself chuckling a good bit. Folk art is serious business for scholars, curators and critics, though, and better facilities for research also have been included in the new center's design.

Among the changing exhibits here are "The Kingdoms of Edward Hicks," a retrospective on the arts that runs from November 30, 1998, through March 1999. "Holiday Magic: Classic Toy Trains from the Carstens Collection," a colorful exhibit of toy trains and accessories, runs Nov. 6, 1999, through Feb. 13, 2000.

The museum is open from 10 AM to 6 PM daily. Admission is included in any of Colonial Williamsburg's three ticket options. For program information, call the above number.

## Public Hospital
**Corner of Francis and S. Henry Sts. • (757) 229-1000**

The somber building at the corner of Francis and South Henry streets is a reconstruction of the first public institution for the mentally ill to be built in Colonial America. Opened in 1773 and known as the Hospital for Lunaticks, this facility first treated its inmates more as prisoners than patients, as the early small cells indicate. Nineteenth-century scientific and medical advances improved methods of treatment, which the hospital's interpretive exhibits chronicle, but also on display are a number of devices used to treat patients, some of which resemble implements of torture. The hospital is open from 10 AM to 6 PM daily.

## DeWitt Wallace Decorative Arts Gallery
**Corner of Francis and S. Henry Sts.**
• **(757) 220-7724**

Adjacent to the Public Hospital is a fascinating museum devoted to British and American decorative arts from 1600 through 1830. The contemporary two-tiered building, completed in 1985, features exhibits of metal, ceramics, glass, prints, textiles, costumes and other decorative objects from Colonial Williamsburg's permanent collections. The collection of Virginia furniture is the largest of its type in the world, and the collection of English pottery is more vast than any on this side of the Atlantic. The museum features 12 galleries and 26,000 square feet of exhibition space, where more than 8,000 objects and works of art are on display. Among the finest pieces are a full-length portrait of George III, painted by English artist Allan Ramsay; a burl walnut and guilt Tompion Clock, which is among a handful of the most important pieces of English furniture in the United States; and a 1735 mahogany tea table, which had been owned by the Galt family for more than 200 years.

Changing exhibits include: "Am I Not a Man and a Brother: Abolition and Anti-Slavery in the Early Chesapeake," which explores the pre-1835 abolitionist and anti-slavery movements in the Chesapeake. Feb. 6, 1999-January 2000. "1699: When Virginia was the Wild West!" mounted in conjunction with the 300th Celebration of the founding of the City of Williamsburg. It rounds up some of the rarest 17th-centuy decorative arts objects from what was then the western frontier, plus more than 300 extraordinary archaeological artifacts excavated from early African, English and Native American settlements on both sides of the Chesapeake Bay. May 1, 1999-mid-February 2000. And, "Revealing Fashions," focusing on pattern, construction methods and fit of clothing from 1750-1790 based on 25 original garments in the Colonial Williamsburg costume collection. Dec. 4, 1999-September 2000.

It would be easy to spend the better part of a day browsing through the illuminating museum or lingering in the comforting natural light of the museum's glass roofed courtyards. Fortunately, a cafe on the gallery's lower level serves lunch, tea and light refreshments. A gift shop selling reproductions and decorative arts journals is also on the premises. The museum is open from 10 AM to 6 PM. Admission is included in any Colonial Williamsburg ticket. Call the number above for information on tours and exhibits.

## Carter's Grove, Wolstenholme Towne and the Winthrop Rockefeller Archaeology Museum
**U.S. Route 60, 8 miles east of Historic Area**
• **(757) 220-7453**

On the James River, 8 miles southeast of Williamsburg, is Carter's Grove, a beautiful 750-acre tract of land with a richly complex history. Tours begin at the modern but unobtrusive Reception Center, a lodge-like building surrounded by woodlands. Visitors can purchase tickets here and watch a 14-minute film titled *A Thing Called Time* that serves as an introduction to the 400 years of events — some glamorous, some deadly — Carter's Grove has witnessed. Take the time to walk through the Reception Center exhibit, where you'll learn more about plantation society, tobacco cultivation and the Native Americans who first inhabited the region. You'll see artifacts and photographs related to the mansion's many stages of life. The Burwell family Bible on display here is especially interesting.

Area residents may prefer to visit the mansion and slave quarters one day and return later to see the museum and town site, as a complete tour of the several attractions can prove exhausting. Visitors who have only one day to spend can choose their own route after exiting the Reception Center; some prefer to tour the Carter's Grove mansion before heading down to the slave quarter, the Winthrop Rockefeller Archaeology Museum and Wolstenholme Towne site. To give your visit a more linear order, you might want to begin with the slave quarter, just across the pedestrian bridge from the Reception Center, then proceed to the museum and town site. From the reconstructed John Boys residence down by the bluffs of the James, you can return via a reconstructed 18th-century garden to the mansion.

If it sounds like you might need a rest somewhere, you're right — a visit to the museum, town site and mansion entails a good bit of walking. The Colonial Williamsburg folks have placed comfortable benches at numerous strategic locations inside the museum and around the grounds. If you do tour the slave quarter, museum and Wolstenholme Towne site first, you can stop for drinks and snacks at the Stable Bake Shop adjacent to the mansion before proceeding there.

## The Slave Quarter

But let's go back to our linear visit, which begins at a slave quarter built on its original 18th-century site. Ironically, the quarter was uncovered by accident, when archaeologists looking for remnants of plantation outbuildings came upon a series of pits that slaves had dug for storing food under their dwellings, similar to those common in Africa. Gar-

dens, corn cribs and chicken compounds have been re-created here, along with three rustic domiciles that would have housed 24 slaves. Inside the dirt-floor dwellings are objects typical of those owned by slaves — gourd utensils, chipped crockery, straw pallets as well as garden tools and the occasional fiddle. Throughout the day, costumed interpreters go about their everyday chores — sewing, gardening and cooking — to give visitors a more accurate feel for the time. There also are periodic interactive presentations, which strive to involve visitors in the experiences of 18th-century Africans and African Virginians on the plantation. To help enhance historic accuracy and add more credibility to their portrayals, six members of CW's department of African-American interpretations and presentations traveled to Africa in 1996, where for two weeks they met with the people of Senegal and Ghana and immersed themselves in African culture.

## Winthrop Rockefeller Archaeological Museum

Signs will point you next to the Winthrop Rockefeller Archaeological Museum, opened

The Junior Fife and Drum Corps marches down Duke of Gloucestor Street on Saturday afternoons.

Photo: Colonial Williamsburg Foundation

in June 1991. Two tales are told in the 7,000-square-foot underground facility. First is the tale of ill-fated Wolstenholme Towne and the English colonists who lived there from 1619-22, when Powhatan Indians virtually destroyed the settlement. Second is the story of the rediscovery and excavation of Wolstenholme Towne by Colonial Williamsburg archaeologists in the 1970s. Hundreds of artifacts are displayed here, but history is not allowed to sit mute and remote behind glass. Archaeologist Ivor Noel Hume's audiotaped voice explicates the history of the Wolstenholme settlement and the excavation of the vanished town site. Audiovisual displays, reconstructive paintings, photographs from the excavation itself and interactive opportunities, such as the diver's mask through which visitors can watch the excavation of a shipwreck, make for a dynamic museum experience.

Walking from exhibit to exhibit, visitors learn the history of the Martin's Hundred settlers who erected Wolstenholme in 1619. At least 57 of the town's inhabitants were killed, and others were taken captive on March 22, 1622, when once friendly Powhatan Indians staged a regional uprising. Many questions remain about this massacre: How many exactly survived? What became of those the Indians took as captives? When was the fort burned? New settlers from England eventually did arrive at Wolstenholme to bolster the population, but the town never fully recuperated. Contagion and starvation left scarcely 30 occupants by 1625. Gradually, the settlement disappeared from view, grown over and forgotten.

## Wolstenholme Towne

While up to half of the Wolstenholme site may have been lost already to shore erosion, it's almost certain that much more of our early history remains buried in the many fields of Carter's Grove. Whether future excavation will uncover answers to the mysteries of Wolstenholme or just more enigma, only time will tell. Down the slope from the underground museum's tunnel-like exit is the partially reconstructed Wolstenholme site, including palisades, buildings and fences. More audiotapes of Noel Hume's voice play in barrel stations around the site, offering historical insight and further detailing the excavation process.

After trekking past the four main reconstructions — domestic unit, fort, compound and barn — you can either continue to the John Boys home site and follow a path to the spacious garden below the mansion or bypass the John Boys site and head straight back to either mansion or Reception Center. Allow two hours or more for this first part of your visit. Tours of the mansion begin at the Stable Bake Shop, where drinks and snacks are on sale. Benches and shaded tables make this a convenient spot to take a break.

## Carter's Grove Mansion

On a bluff overlooking the river stands this lovely brick mansion, which visitors usually tour next. Built in the 1750s by Carter Burwell, grandson of Robert "King" Carter, Colonial Virginia's wealthiest planter, the plantation house was considered sophisticated in design and was elegantly furnished for the entertainment of Virginia aristocracy. The interior woodwork of soft Virginia pine is especially remarkable, as are the mahogany balustrade of the staircase, the fluted ionic pilasters on the wall and the intricate cornice work. The "Grove Farm" passed out of Carter family hands in 1838, however, after which a succession of owners made changes to the original Georgian structure, adding a Victorian veranda and painting over pine paneling. Then, in 1928, Archibald McCrea bought the property and a full-scale renovation of the mansion began. The result of the wealthy McCrea's "restoration" of Carter's Grove was a grand Colonial Revival style plantation manor, often called America's most beautiful house. The McCreas' restoration raised the roof, connected dependencies and added modern plumbing but hid the toilets. The restoration revealed more about the romantic view of the past held by members of 1930s high society than about actual Colonial history and Colonial Williamsburg, to whom the mansion was deeded in 1969.

The restoration initially sought to restore Carter's Grove as an authentic 18th-century plantation. Plans changed, however, and today visitors tour a Carter's Grove mansion that largely reflects the McCreas' Revivalist tastes. This was done partially in deference to the interest in historic preservation in America that Colonial Revival enthusiasts like the McCreas helped spark. The mansion tour takes approximately 45 minutes. Interpreters talk about the McCreas' lifestyle, with its studied appreciation of 18th-century traditions. Visitors can view the fine carved woodwork of the entry and mahogany staircase as well as pilasters and cornices created by English master artisan Richard Baylis in the 1750s. Furnishings reflect the mansion's mixed uses and ancestry — chintz sofas in drawing rooms and an assortment of 1940s objects juxtapose a spinning wheel and flatirons in the kitchen. If it happens to be Garden Day at the mansion, you'll be treated to the sight of artfully arranged displays of flowers through the house.

After a tour of the house, visitors often take in the river vista once again and explore the garden, where 18th-century ornamental plants and fruits and vegetables are grown. (Carter's Grove also is profiled in the Attractions chapter.) Count on spending some time at the Carter's Grove/Winthrop/Wolstenholme Towne site with its diversity of intriguing exhibits. The Reception Center has vending machines for snacks and drinks, and a boxed picnic lunch is available for purchase.

Tickets for the tour are available at any ticket sales location. A single admission ticket currently costs $15 for adults, $10 for children ages 6 to 12. Carter's Grove is open from 9 AM to 5 PM daily except Mondays and is closed January through early March and for a few days after Thanksgiving to decorate for the holidays. November and December hours are 9 AM to 4 PM. Motorists can come by way of U.S. Route 60 and return on the more scenic 8-mile country road that begins at Carter's Grove and ends at S. England Street in the Historic Area. Call (757) 220-7453 for more information.

# Seasonal Programs and Special Tours

No matter what time of year you come to Colonial Williamsburg, you'll find an array of special tours and programs available. Although the programs are constantly changed and updated, here are a few examples of what you may come across.

# Family Programs

If you think a historical site is not a place to take children — and still have a good time — think again. Colonial Williamsburg offers a number of special programs designed to enrich every family's exploration of the past. While there are literally dozens of programs designed specifically for family enjoyment and participation, we have highlighted a few we're sure you will enjoy. Although there are some exceptions, the majority of family programs are offered beginning in mid-June and continuing through the summer. Since activities not only vary from day to day, but also from hour to hour, check that indispensable *Visitor's Companion* for specific times and locations.

## Family Life Adventures

These activities take place at buildings throughout the Historic Area. At the Benjamin Powell site, children can engage in normal household tasks using objects straight from the 18th century. At the Wythe House, they can congregate in the backyard and learn to make stitch books, watercolor paintings, put together old-fashioned puzzles or be instructed in the fine art of writing. At the Governor's Palace, the activities are decidedly more genteel: Parents are encouraged to join their youngsters in a game of lawn bowling, hoops, pickup sticks, tops or checkers.

## You Are There

In Colonial Williamsburg, adults aren't the only ones who get to have all the fun. Several interpretive programs engage children, from re-enactments of county and city court sessions to military encampments, where your child can experience 18th-century military life through marching, musket drills and observing a cannon firing.

## African-American History

A number of programs are designed to help your child understand the life of 18th-century slaves. An outdoor walking tour, for instance, helps them explore the domestic slave's experience and the relationships formed with others in the community, while a visit to school mistress Ann Wager and her students illustrates the importance of education for both free and enslaved children.

## Neat Things To See and Do

As your family strolls through Colonial Williamsburg, attentive youngsters will be rewarded with the unusual sights, sounds and opportunities afforded by the Historic Area. Where else would they get to help brick makers knead clay to mold into bricks, watch cooks stir up batches of 18th-century victuals, chat with Thomas Jefferson or Benjamin Powell about events of the day or form a bucket-brigade on an 18th-century fire engine? For the animal lover in the group, there's also the rare opportunity to glimpse winged and furry creatures they may never see elsewhere — the English Leicester longwool sheep, Red Devon milking cattle and American Cream draft horses that were part of the landscape in the 1700s.

## Felicity in Williamsburg

In this popular tour, patterned after the life of Felicity Merriman, one of the characters from the popular American Girls Collection, your daughter can don her finest dress and walk in the footsteps of a child growing up in Williamsburg in 1774. For a day, she can easily imagine herself as the spunky, strong-willed 9-year-old, as she and a group of new-found friends walk with their costumed guide exploring houses and stores that were part of Felicity's era. As the tour unfolds, your guide will knowledgeably weave Felicity's adventures into an actual lesson about 18th-century history. Young ladies also enjoy afternoon tea with Miss Manderly, Felicity's teacher, and learn to curtsey, dance, sew and properly serve and sip tea.

The Felicity tour is offered as a complete vacation package for two adults and two children, which includes two nights' accommodations, two breakfasts, dinner in a Colonial Williamsburg tavern, four tickets for the tour and four Patriot's Passes. In 1999, rates started at $522 but may vary depending on the season and your choice of hotel. Day tickets for the tour also can be purchased in advance for $55 for adults and $41 for each child 12 and younger (and include a Patriot's Pass). While the two-night tour is available daily through the summer and on weekends in the spring, fall and early winter, day packages are available on a limited basis. Children must be accompanied by an adult for the tour and lessons, which aren't appropriate for girls younger than 5. For information or reservations, call (800) 404-3371.

# Evening Tours and Events

Below are some of the programs offered after hours in Colonial Williamsburg. Currently, these programs require a separate $10 ticket or a $7.50 fee with a Patriot's Pass. Evening tours, which are here year round, begin at the Lumber House ticket office on Duke of Gloucester Street, across from Bruton Parish Church. To join a tour, buy a ticket at any ticket sales location and head to the site of the program about 10 or 15 minutes before the fun is scheduled to start. Most programs last about an hour. Check your *Visitor's Companion* for specific dates and times during the week you are visiting. As we noted above, programming changes frequently, so selections may be different during the time you are in town.

## Lanthorn Tour

Take a walk down the streets of yesteryear and stop into four of Williamsburg's candlelit trade shops to see how journeymen and craftsmen actually produced goods during Colonial days.

## Legends of the Past

This evening walk through the Historic Area gives you the opportunity to listen to and view re-enactments of some of the stories and legends that intrigued the colonists.

## Palace and Capitol Concerts

Check out the sounds of yesteryear during these evenings of musical celebration. At the Palace, you can listen to a chamber music concert from the Age of Enlightenment. A separate concert in the Capitol features spirited songs and tunes from the 18th century.

## Dance, Our Dearest Diversion

Oh, how those colonists must have liked music. In fact, dance was the passion of Colonial Virginians. Listen in, and you may find your feet tapping in time to the music. Go ahead! Join the fine ladies and gentlemen of the period in their evening of merriment at the Capitol.

## Science, Conjuration and Humbug

For your amusement, stroll over to the Courthouse and watch 18th-century entertainment in action. This evening program features folks with names like Wondrous Wisdom, Marvelous Magic, Precocious Puppets and many others.

## Jumpin' the Broom

Spend the evening hours at Carter's Grove and watch this re-creation of a slave wedding. Listen in while Esther and Manuell share their hopes and dreams and pledge their love for one another before the community. Please be aware that this program deals frankly with interracial relationships and contains some subject matter that is not suitable for young children.

# Military Demonstrations

Several programs illustrating military life in the 18th century can be viewed during a visit to Colonial Williamsburg.

## The Fife and Drum Corps

The Fife and Drum Corps takes regular marches down Duke of Gloucester Street from April to October, while the young boys and teens in the Junior Fife and Drum Corps make the march Saturday afternoons throughout much of the year. On various dates (which are always noted in your *Visitor's Companion*), visitors can enjoy the 18th-century ceremony of reveille at 9 AM at Market Square Green. At 5 PM, the corps does its retreat, a time when pickets are posted, flags lowered and the soldiers relieved of their daily duties.

## Military Encampment

The Military Encampment, where you can learn about Colonial military life by going to Revolutionary War boot camp and assisting costumed soldiers with routine tasks, is held daily during the summer and is included in the cost of a basic admission ticket.

## The Military by Night

"The Military by Night" is a candlelight tour during which soldiers of the Virginia State Garrison Regiment (founded in 1777) transport visitors back to the days of the War of Independence for discussions of camp life and battlefield maneuvers. A separate ticket, which can be purchased at any of the ticket offices, is needed for this program.

## Interpretive Programs

Many of Colonial Williamsburg's activities allow visitors to learn about 18th-century life while also being entertained. The foundation's interpretive programs are among the most enjoyable of these, and several new re-enactments have been added to the roster in recent years. Separate tickets are required for each of these events and may be purchased at the Visitor Center, the Lumber House or the Merchants Square Information Station. For specific dates and times for any program listed below, call Guest Services at (757) 220-7645.

## Cry Witch

One of the most enduring of Colonial Williamsburg's programs, this is a highly enjoyable presentation of an early 18th-century witch trial. Audience members may pose questions to witnesses and play the role of jury in the strange case of Grace Sherwood, accused of causing neighbors' crops to fail, bewitching folks and turning herself into a cat. The location of this program sometimes varies, but it is typically held at the Capitol.

## Cross or Crown

Our third president truly was a man of many talents. This program guides you through Thomas Jefferson's experiences as he changed from Virginia aristocrat to a defender of the rights of the common man. The man himself will explain what is unfolding through dramatic scenes that culminate in a debate on freedom of religion. Hone up your debating skills, you may be asked to participate. The program is held at the Capitol.

## Conflict or Compromise: A Revolutionary Debate

This program takes you back to the eve of Revolution as it explores the colonists' three positions on independence — patriot, loyalist or undecided. You'll have the chance to defend one of these viewpoints in open debate before a vote is taken as to "whether these Colonies should be free and independent states." The program is held in the Hall of the House of Burgesses at the Capitol.

# African-American Heritage

In recent years, Colonial Williamsburg has begun to examine more fully the experiences of African Americans brought to the Virginia Colony in the 18th century. The foundation's black history department was created in 1982, and in its early years included only one tour and a few music programs. But in 1988, the Department of African-American Interpretation and Presentations was founded and, for the last nine years or so, this creative and ambitious group has put together dramatic interpretations depicting everything from runaway slaves to the relationship of Thomas Jefferson to his personal servant. After all, half the population of Williamsburg in this time period was made up of slaves and free blacks. To more accurately reflect the population of the time, a number of tours and programs dealing with these inhabitants' lives are now offered throughout the year.

Although it is not being offered at this time, one African-American program that focused national attention on Colonial Williamsburg was a controversial slave auction staged in October 1994. The program, which brought a crowd of thousands to Duke of Gloucester Street, recounted the selling of a pregnant slave and her husband to different masters as well as the sale of two other slaves along with land and farm equipment during an auction to settle estates and debts. It was the first such re-creation for the Colonial Williamsburg Foundation, and it brought protests from the NAACP and the Southern Christian Leadership Conference, a vote of acceptance from Jesse Jackson, front-page headlines in local newspapers and praise and criticism from across the country. When all was said and done, however, the program, which emotionally depicted the horrors of slavery, made the point it had set out to make in the first place. Whether the slave auction will ever be revived is still a matter of discussion.

Here we have listed some of the tours, re-enactments and other special events that currently are being offered in the Historic Area. Keep in mind that, because of frequent scheduling changes, all of the programs listed below may not be offered at the time of your visit. To obtain specific dates and times, your best bet is to consult your *Visitor's Companion*.

## The Other Half Tour

This 60-minute walking expedition provides an overview of African-American experiences with special focus on the middle passage, slave trade, education, religion and music. Tours begin at the Greenhow Lumber House ticket office, where you can also make reservations. Check at the Visitor Center or in the *Visitor's Companion* for a daily schedule.

## Affairs of the Heart

During this program, a repeated sellout, you get to closely examine a gentry marriage and how it affects the household of both the groom and his intended. It is here that you will meet William, who has a child by his slave Rachel, as he ponders his decision to marry and carry on his family's name. The performance, which requires a separate ticket, is held at the Wythe House. For specific dates and times, check your *Visitor's Companion*. One added note: Visitors are cautioned that Affairs of the Heart deals frankly with racial relationships of the era and contains subject matter that may not be suitable for young children.

# Remember Me

Step back in time and spend an evening with Old Paris, as he recalls Africa and his enslavement. You will also watch and understand the spiritual and cultural ties and customs that helped Old Paris — and those like him — survive slavery. The program is offered in the Hennage Auditorium of the DeWitt Wallace Arts Gallery, and admission is included in a Patriot's Pass or Museums ticket.

## Trying to Git Some Mother Wit

Join three elderly African-American women as they share advice on surviving slavery, outsmarting the Master, love and romance and curing whatever ails you. This program is offered in the Hennage Auditorium of the Dewitt Wallace Decorative Arts Gallery, and admission is included in a Patriot's Pass or Museums ticket.

## Neither Seen Nor Heard: Life Under the Master's Roof

Held several times a week at the Brush-Everard House, this program explores the urban and domestic slave's experiences and the relationships they formed with others in the community.

## Musical Traditions of African Americans

During the summer you can enjoy a 45-minute program of Musical Traditions of African-Americans that features traditional hymns, polyrhythms and dances that reflect the survival of African culture. And, in early December at Carter's Grove, where a slave quarter has been excavated and restored to reveal much about the lives of the African Americans who toiled on the 18th-century plantation, you can join residents as they celebrate the season with soulful music, dance and family reunions. See our section on Carter's Grove for more information about the re-created slave quarter.

# Annual Events

There are a number of celebrations that take place in the restored area throughout the year. Perhaps the most well-known — and certainly the most spectacular — is the Grand Illumination, which marks the beginning of the Christmas holiday season in Colonial Williamsburg. This decades-old tradition attracts thousands of revelers to the Historic Area the first Sunday of December to hear the cannon sound, see the thousands of candles that illuminate the windows in public buildings and view the colorful explosion of fireworks. Other annual events include a February Antiques Forum, in its 50th year in 1998; a Garden Symposium each April; and a fall History Forum. For a complete and detailed rundown of these events and other yearly festivals and celebrations, please turn to our chapter on Annual Events.

Many of the annual events that occur in Colonial Williamsburg are organized by the newly formed Williamsburg Institute. Founded to provide unique educational opportunities to area visitors, Institute programs range from one-day workshops to multiday seminars whose topics include architecture, 18th-century life, historic trades, culinary arts and health and fitness. (You can sign up for everything from candy making and country dancing to silver production and West African cooking.) Most classes are taught by Colonial Williamsburg historians, tradespeople and others, all considered experts in their respective fields. For more information about Institute programs, call (800) 603-0948.

# Attractions

There's so much to see and do in the Williamsburg area, it's hard for visitors to decide what not to include on their itineraries the first — or even second — time around. After you've strolled through the Colonial Williamsburg Historic Area, seen the beginnings of American civilization as we know it at Jamestown and relived the Revolution that took place on the Yorktown Battlefield, there still is a multitude of historic treasures to tour. These include the James River Plantations, along Historic Route 5; the College of William and Mary, which celebrated its 300th birthday in 1993; and a number of Williamsburg churches that date back as far as 1715.

The other attractions profiled in this chapter are of the decidedly modern sort — the high-flying thrills at Busch Gardens, the wet and wild tube rides at Water Country USA and the downright euphoric feeling shopaholics get as they enter the sprawling Williamsburg Pottery complex just off U.S. Route 60.

We admit that stretching your time and budget to make room for all Williamsburg has to offer is difficult. Our best advice is to plan ahead, choosing the activities best suited to your interests. But we also think good vacations should allow room for a little spontaneity. So be flexible, be outrageous, try something completely new. And most of all, make sure you mean it when you mail off those postcards that proclaim to friends back home: "Having a great time in Williamsburg!"

## James River Plantations

While Virginia's Historic Triangle offers visitors plenty to see and do, it also provides easy access to myriad attractions just a short drive outside the immediate Williamsburg area. Of particular interest to history and architecture buffs are the historic James River plantations in James City and Charles City counties. For many whose vision of Southern plantations has been shaped by *Gone With the Wind*, these structures will be a surprise. Predating the era of Greek Revival columns and other such adornments, the refined Georgian architecture of the buildings, executed in rich red brick or in white wood, is understated and takes its elegance from simplicity and tasteful detail. These were among the first mansions in the country, and their history is, in a sense, ours. These magnificent estates are located along the James River because that was the area's main artery when they were built. Luckily, many are open to the public. In cases where the houses are not open, visitors usually are welcome to tour the grounds. The trip on Va. Route 5 from Williamsburg to Richmond to visit the plantations is gorgeous, passing through thick, overarching forests and wide-open farmlands. It was Colonial Virginia's premier land route and remains an Insiders' favorite route west, especially in autumn.

Of particular note, a block ticket is now available for guests to tour the gardens and grounds of four Charles City County plantations. For $9, guests can tour the gardens and grounds at Piney Grove, Westover, North Bend and Edgewood. For information on this combo ticket, call (804) 829-2480. A group tour option, including interior house tours for these plantations, also is offered. The price is $36 per person for groups of 20 or more. For details, call the above referenced number.

### Belle Aire Plantation
**11800 John Tyler Hwy. (Va. Rt. 5), Charles City Co. • (804) 829-2431**

Just off Virginia's scenic byway, Route 5, east of the Charles City County courthouse complex, this charming and deceptively large mid-17th-century frame house — the only one known to still stand in the Commonwealth — was built around 1650. While it was open to the public for many years, unfortunately today it is not, though the owners do open their doors to group tours of 20 or more, provided they make reservations and it is convenient for the family. An admission of $7 per person is charged, with a $100 minimum. (Belle Aire also is open during Historic Garden Week, near the end of April each year.) Although the grounds, too, are closed to the public, you can enjoy a brief stop along the side of Route 5 and peer down the short drive to the house, which can be seen from the roadway, less than a quarter-mile west from the more formal, signed entrance. If you pull to the edge of the road and step out, you can enjoy the beauty of this fine home from a short distance.

## Berkeley Plantation
**Va. Rt. 5, Charles City Co. • (804) 829-6018**

This was the site of the first official Thanksgiving in North America, celebrated by English settlers on December 4, 1619. It is on Route 5, halfway between Williamsburg and Richmond. Berkeley is one of Virginia's most historic plantations, as it was the birthplace of Benjamin Harrison, a signer of the Declaration of Independence, and his third son, William Henry Harrison, who was the ninth president of the United States. The plantation was patented in 1618, and the stately Georgian mansion, overlooking the James River, was built in 1726 of brick fired on the site. It is said to be the oldest three-story brick house in Virginia and the first with a pediment roof. The handsome Adam woodwork and double arches in the Great Rooms were installed by Benjamin Harrison VI in 1790 at the direction of Thomas Jefferson. The rooms in the house are furnished with period antiques. As you approach the site along Route 5 in Charles City County, you'll have to follow a sharp curve onto a side road that leads to the plantation drive.

Two tidbits of Berkeley history deserve particular attention. "Taps" was composed here by USA Gen. Daniel Butterfield in 1862 during the Civil War while Union troops encamped on the site. And the first bourbon whiskey in America was distilled here in 1621.

The plantation is open daily from 8 AM to 5 PM. Tickets cost $8.50 for adults and $4 for children ages 6 to 12 for a garden and house tour and $5 for adults and $2.50 for children for a tour of the gardens only.

## Carter's Grove Plantation
**U.S. Rt. 60 E., James City Co. • (757) 220-7453**

Owned and operated by The Colonial Williamsburg Foundation, this 18th-century plantation and mansion is off Route 60 about 7 miles southeast of Williamsburg in James City County. The fine Georgian mansion was built by Carter Burwell and completed in 1755. It measures 200 feet in length along its riverfront. Burwell died less than six months after the house was completed, and ownership passed to his young son, Nathaniel. The house and its furnishings from the 17th, 18th, 19th and 20th centuries can be seen today much the way they were when the house was occupied by Mr. and Mrs. Archibald M. McCrea, who purchased the property in 1928. It was during their ownership that the house was modified and enlarged.

Also on the property is the Wolstenholme Towne site, a settlement established by English settlers in 1619 and was annihilated by the Indian Massacre of 1622. Partial restoration of the town site is interpreted by numerous "talking barrel" stations. An archaeology museum housing many of the artifacts unearthed on the site, reconstructed slave quarters and a reception center are within the Carter's Grove complex. Tickets to tour the mansion and grounds cost $17 for adults and $10 for children. Hours vary seasonally, so call ahead for information on dates and times the mansion is open. For more on Carter's Grove, see our Colonial Williamsburg chapter.

## Edgewood Plantation
**4800 John Tyler Hwy. (Va. Rt. 5), Charles City Co. • (804) 829-2962**

You will enjoy the section of the historic plantation trail (Route 5 west from Williamsburg) that leads through forests past this superb Gothic Revival house (c. 1849) in Charles City County. With only a minimum of imagination, you might envision Edgar Allan Poe passing in a carriage in the other direction. (Indeed, the house is reputed to have a ghost in residence!) In a countryside filled with the formalities of Georgian and Colonial Revival architecture, this is a truly refreshing structure. Today the plantation is operated as a delightful bed and breakfast inn, which we have profiled in our Bed and Breakfasts chapter. Even if you choose not to go in, you will see it clearly from the highway.

Edgewood arranges tours by appointment, with luncheon and candlelight tours the most popular. Our choice is a tour and High Victorian tea, available for groups of 10 or more, during which visitors don special period hats provided by your hostess and enjoy delicate cucumber, crab salad and tomato basil sandwiches as well as homemade scones with clotted cream, pound cake and a variety of other desserts in the plantation's beautiful tearoom. Cost of the luncheon tour or afternoon tea tour is $25 per person. At Christmas, the 17 or so trees in the house for the Victorian Christmas are dazzling. For standard tours without lunch or tea, the cost is $7, which includes a peek at the home's first and second floors and an adjacent tavern. During the Christmas season, the tour costs $10.

### Evelynton Plantation
**6701 John Tyler Hwy. (Va. Rt. 5), Charles City Co. • (804) 829-5075, (800) 473-5075**

This exquisite plantation has been home to the Ruffin family since 1847. The family patriarch, Edmund Ruffin, is said to have fired the first shot of the Civil War at Fort Sumter. Along Historic Route 5 just east of Westover Church in Charles City County, it is about a 30-minute drive west of Williamsburg. The mansion is situated at the end of a long drive lined with stately trees. The original house was burned during the Civil War, but in the 1930s noted architect Duncan Lee, who oversaw restoration of Carter's Grove in James City County, was commissioned to design a Geor-

gian Revival manor house atop the original foundation. Constructed of 250-year-old brick, the house is an excellent example of Georgian Revival architecture, featuring fine detailing inside and out.

This house, like the original, is named for a daughter of William Byrd II, the founder of Richmond. It is furnished with American, English and European antiques, many of them family heirlooms.

The house, gardens and grounds are open from 9 AM to 5 PM daily except Thanksgiving and Christmas. They are closed Tuesday, Wednesday and Thursday in January and February. Admission is $7.50 for adults and $3.50 for children ages 6 to 12. Seniors and military personnel pay $6.50. AAA members pay $6, and students pay $5.50. For a grounds-only tour, the cost is $3.50. A fine gift shop is on the property.

### Piney Grove at Southall's Plantation
**16920 Southall Plantation Ln., Charles City Co. • (804) 829-2480**

Piney Grove was built around the year 1800 on the 300-acre Southall's Plantation, a property that was first occupied by the Chickahominy Indians and survives as the oldest and best preserved example of log architecture in southeastern Virginia. In recent years, Piney Grove, 8 miles north of Route 5 on Route 623 (which eventually becomes Route 615), has served the public as a beautifully appointed bed and breakfast inn. In 1994 the owners introduced a self-guided tour of the plantation grounds, which takes visitors along a splendid nature trail that begins beneath a century-old cedar, meanders around a swimming hole and past a gazebo and then winds along the edge of a ravine where the trail is canopied by beech, hickory and white oak trees. A short path leads down into the ravine to Piney Springs, where constantly flowing water eventually funnels into the Chickahominy River. Past the ravine, the trail

---

**INSIDERS' TIP**

A $25.50 plantations block ticket that provides admission to Shirley, Berkeley, Evelynton and Sherwood Forest is available at any of the plantations.

skirts a horse corral and pasture, offering a scenic view of Piney Grove, as well as a view of Moss Side Barn, once part of the Southall's Plantation. The trail ends at Glebe Lane, originally called "The Old Main Road from Barret's Ferry to Charles City Court House."

Cost of the grounds tour, which is offered daily from 9 AM to 5 PM, is $3 per person. House tours can be arranged by appointment for $10. To find out more about Piney Grove's operations as a bed and breakfast inn, consult our Bed and Breakfasts chapter.

## Sherwood Forest Plantation

**14501 John Tyler Hwy. (Rt. 5), Charles City Co. • (804) 829-5377**

Without a doubt, this is one of the loveliest homesteads in this part of Virginia. Sherwood Forest Plantation was the home of President John Tyler. It is about a 20-minute drive west of Williamsburg. Considered the longest frame house in America, it measures 300 feet along its front facade. Built c. 1730, the original structure was altered and renovated by President Tyler in 1844. The house today looks very much like it did when Tyler retired here from the White House in 1845. He brought with him his new bride, Julia Gardiner of Gardiner's Island, New York. Since then, the plantation has been continuously occupied by members of the Tyler family and has been a working plantation for more than 240 years.

The house features a private ballroom 68 feet in length and is furnished with an extensive collection of 18th- and 19th-century family heirlooms. President Tyler's china, porcelain, silver, mirrors, tables, chairs and other furnishings are still in use here. In the library are the books of Governor Tyler (President Tyler's father), John Tyler and his son, Dr. Lyon Gardiner Tyler, who served as president of the College of William and Mary. The house, outbuildings and grounds are open daily, except Thanksgiving and Christmas, from 9 AM until 5 PM. Admission is $8.50 for adults and $5.50 for students in kindergarten through college. Senior citizen, military and AAA discounts are offered. Children younger than age 6 are admitted free. A gift shop in one of the outbuildings sells everything from postcards to elegant glassware. Refreshments are available.

## Shirley Plantation

**501 Shirley Plantation Rd., Charles City Co. • (804) 829-5121, (800) 232-1613**

This fine plantation, off Route 5 on the banks of the James River about 35 miles from Williamsburg, is perhaps the most famous of Virginia's plantations. Designated a National Historic Landmark, Shirley was founded in 1613 and granted to Edward Hill in 1660. The present mansion house was begun in 1723 by the third Edward Hill, a member of the House of Burgesses in the Virginia Colony, for his daughter Elizabeth, who married John Carter, son of King Carter. It was finished in 1738 and is largely in its original state.

The house is a recognized architectural treasure. Its famous walnut-railed staircase rises three stories without visible means of support and is the only one of its kind in America. The mansion is filled with family portraits, furniture, crested silver and other family heirlooms. George Washington, Thomas Jefferson, John Tyler, Teddy Roosevelt and John Rockefeller were all guests at Shirley. Robert E. Lee's mother, Anne Hill Carter, was married to "Light Horse" Harry Lee in the parlor.

The house opens daily, except Thanksgiving and Christmas, at 9 AM, and the last tour of the day begins promptly at 4:30 PM. The grounds remain open until 6 PM. Admission is $8.50 for adults, $5.50 for ages 13 to 21 and $4.50 for children ages 6 to 12. Seniors 60 and older pay $7.50, and children younger than 6 get in free.

## Westover Plantation

**7000 Westover Rd., Charles City Co. • (804) 829-2882**

During the Colonial period, this exquisite plantation was the property of William Byrd, who owned extensive properties that stretched for many miles in each direction. Off Route 5 in Charles City County, it is adjacent to Berkeley Plantation. Situated on the banks of the James River, this palatial Early Georgian house is sometimes described as the most elegant Georgian structure in the United States. The plantation features an outstanding Georgian boxwood garden and 150-year-old giant tulip poplars. William Byrd's tomb is also on the property. The gardens and grounds are open to visitors from 9 AM to 6 PM daily except Saturday, when the house is open 9 AM to 1 PM. Special group tours can be arranged by appointment of the first floor of the plantation house. The grounds tour is $2 for adults, 50¢ for children ages 6 to 16 and free for those younger than 6. For groups of 12 or more, a $1 fee is charged. The group home tour costs $8 per person and is by appointment only. The plantation house also is open for five days during the Garden Club of Virginia's Historic Garden Week, held in late April each year.

# College of William and Mary

The next entry on our list of historic attractions brings us back to Williamsburg, where you will find numerous noteworthy sites on the gracious campus of the College of William and Mary, which in 1993 celebrated the 300th anniversary of its February 19, 1693, chartering in England.

The college campus is at the western end of Duke of Gloucester Street between Jamestown and Richmond roads. Directly across from the end of Merchants Square, you'll find a visitors center in the first floor of the Sir Christopher Wren Building, where you can obtain information to help you conduct a self-guided walking tour of the campus. These tours are permitted on weekdays only. For information, contact public information at (757) 221-2630.

As you approach the Wren Building, you'll notice the brick wall surrounding the triangular College Yard, which also holds two other pre-Revolutionary War structures: the President's House and Brafferton, formerly an Indian School.

While the college was chartered by the Crown in 1693 in response to a 1691 petition from Virginia's General Assembly, bricks weren't laid for the Wren Building (originally known as "The College") until two years later, making it the oldest academic building in continuous use in the United States.

Indeed, the building actually was the guest of honor for a major birthday bash in August 1995, complete with yellow and green balloons, cake and a passionate speech by Pulitzer Prize-winning historian David McCullough on the significance of historic buildings to modern America.

But the mood pervading the Wren wasn't always so celebratory. For several years, the building served as temporary headquarters to Virginia's Colonial government. Then, in 1705 and again in 1859, fires destroyed portions of the building, which was twice rebuilt by using the remaining foundation and walls. Alas, in 1862, Federal soldiers set the building afire again. Despite such damage, the original exterior walls survived to be restored during the 1920s and '30s, and the Wren Building visitors see today has the appearance of the pre-1859 fire structure. Today, the Wren houses William and Mary's Philosophy Department. Visitors to the building also will see early classrooms, the 1732 chapel — under which noted Virginians such as Sir John Randolph and Lord Botetourt are buried — and Great Hall, where the Burgesses assembled.

North of the Wren Building in the College Yard is the President's House, built in the early 1730s. Besides serving as a home to such famous college presidents as James Madison and James Blair, it also housed British General Cornwallis before his Yorktown surrender to Revolutionary forces led by Washington. The building is still in use as a residence for College of William and Mary presidents.

The third and smallest structure facing the

Photo: Sherwood Forest Plantation

Descendants of President John Tyler have occupied the Sherwood Forest Plantation since 1842.

College Yard is the Brafferton, now used for offices, but originally an Indian school. The Brafferton was built in 1723 with funds provided by an English scientist determined to bring Christianity to area Indian youths, who already were forced to attend a training school in Williamsburg. Apparently, the young boys were not at all happy about living in town, learning English or wearing uniforms, and they longed for their villages and tribes. Legend has it that the spirits of these homesick lads still inhabit the Brafferton — footsteps, moaning, even drumbeats are said to be audible at times in the building. Another William and Mary myth holds that one of these Indian students can sometimes be seen running quick as the wind across campus at night, as if trying to regain his freedom.

Don't worry — you probably won't encounter such ghosts while visiting the William and Mary campus. You can stroll in the Sunken Garden west of the Wren Building or through shady Crim Dell with its footpaths and small pond. Other buildings worth noting on campus include Phi Beta Kappa Memorial Hall, Earl Greg Swem Library and the Muscarelle Museum of Art. Visitors are welcome at the Muscarelle, whose collections and programs are described in the Museums and Galleries section of The Arts chapter.

Although you're surrounded by history as you stroll on the William and Mary campus, not all the buildings can lay claim to 200 or 300 years. Tercentenary Hall, named to commemorate the college's 300th anniversary in 1993, was dedicated during homecoming festivities in October 1995. The four-story, Georgian-style structure houses the college's applied science program as well as classroom space for geology, physics and computer science programs.

The Bookstore, (757) 221-2480, run by Barnes and Noble on Jamestown Road, is open to the public and sells more than textbooks. A wide variety of books is on sale here — contemporary fiction titles, children's books and reference works, for example. The Bookstore also stocks stationery, greeting cards, art supplies and a variety of clothing items inscribed with the College of William and Mary logo. Hours of operation are Monday through Friday 8 AM to 7 PM, Saturday from 10 AM to 6 PM and Sunday noon to 5 PM.

There are a number of cultural events at the college that both students and locals may attend year round. These are listed in detail in our chapter on The Arts. New Williamsburg residents who want to know more about educational opportunities at the college — a state-supported, four-year university with a prestigious reputation — should turn to our chapter on Education and Child Care.

# Historic Churches

## Bruton Parish Church
### Duke of Gloucester St., Williamsburg
• (757) 229-2891

On Duke of Gloucester Street west of the Palace Green, Bruton Parish Church, in use since 1715, is one of America's oldest Episcopal churches. The church's history is rich: Its architectural features include the 1769 Tower; high box pews dedicated to Presidents Washington, Jefferson, Monroe and Tyler, all of whom worshipped here; and a bronze lectern donated by Theodore Roosevelt. Fully restored in 1940, the church also boasts original walls and windows and a stone baptismal font said to have come from an earlier Jamestown church. The churchyard holds many 18th-century graves. Church tours are offered from 9 AM to 5 PM Monday to Saturday and Sundays from noon to 5 PM. No admission is charged for church tours, but donations are welcome. The Bruton Parish Book & Gift Shop, (757) 220-1489, also is on Duke of Gloucester Street next to Casey's Department Store. Open 10 AM to 5 PM Monday through Saturday and 1 to 5 PM Sunday, it stocks not only religious books but also jewelry, stuffed animals and other gifts.

## Hickory Neck Church
### 8300 Richmond Rd., Toano • (757) 566-0276

The Virginia landscape is dotted with small brick churches dating to the Colonial period, many associated with plantations, others with small communities that vanished in the ensuing years. One worship site of historic interest is Hickory Neck Church on the western side of Toano. The edifice was built about 1740 and continues to be the worship place of an active Episcopal parish. On April 21, 1781, it housed militia opposing the British army. Later that year, the militiamen fought in the siege of Yorktown. Standing with your back to busy Route 60, it is still possible here to glimpse a vista without 20th-century encroachments. If you're interested in attending worship services, they are held at 8 AM and 10 AM on Sundays.

Although there are no official tours, the church is always open. "We're a small country church of 125 families," says Jim Kellett, who has been rector for 10 years. "A procession at our church takes about a half-second."

## The First Baptist Church
### 727 W. Scotland St., Williamsburg • (757) 229-1952

Another church of historic note is The First Baptist Church. One of the earliest Baptist congregations in the country, it is more importantly one of the first African-American churches in America, organized in 1776. Blacks had been allowed to worship in Bruton Parish Church, where they were seated in the North Gallery. Because they were not included in the worship service, they left the parish and built Brush Harbor on the Greensprings plantation west of town, where they worshipped early in the morning, late at night and sometimes in secret. This site was remote from the city, so they built a second Brush Harbor at Raccoon Chase, nearer Williamsburg, and sought spiritual fellowship there. A resident of Williamsburg, Jesse Coles, heard of these communities and made his carriage house available to blacks in the city. The group that met there organized in 1776 as The First Baptist Church. The church applied for admission into the Dover Association in 1791 and was accepted two years later. For just more than a century, the congregation worshipped in a brick church building built in 1855 on Nassau Street, but that's now gone. In 1956 the congregation moved into its present structure at 727 W. Scotland Street. In the lower level of this church is a fascinating display tracing the history of this important congregation; furnishings of the earlier church are used in various parts of the current edifice.

# Thrills, Chills and a Shopper's Paradise

We may learn from the past, but we live in the here and now. While our earlier entries in this chapter focused on historic attractions, the information we provide here gives you all you need for a thoroughly modern good time. In this section we'll look at the lighter side of Williamsburg — the side that brings you Busch Gardens, Water Country USA and the Williamsburg Pottery Factory.

### Busch Gardens
**U.S. Rt. 60, 3 miles east of Williamsburg • (757) 253-3350, (800) 343-7946**

Busch Gardens Williamsburg will be 24 years old in 1999, yet its appeal remains ageless. No wonder; the diversions seem endless. Within Busch Gardens are over 30 rousing rides, including a number of gravity-defying roller coasters; Escape from Pompeii, a fiery boat ride through replicas of ancient Italian ruins; Questor, the park's high-tech flight simulator adventure; nine 17th-century European theme villages where you'll find musical shows, feats of magic and street entertainers; strapping Clydesdale horses and miniature animal breeds; resident and visiting craftspeople; and German oompah bands and a singing Burgermeister.

The park's many eateries offer a variety of international temptations for your taste buds — everything from barbecue and bratwurst to biscotti and Black Forest torte can be purchased and consumed within Busch Gardens' confines. (To get an idea of how ravenous park visitors can get, consider that more than 700,000 hamburger buns and 350,000 pizza crusts are created annually in the in-house bakery at Das Festhaus in the German village.)

While resident potters, woodcutters, glass blowers and blacksmiths show off their talents at the park on a regular schedule, a variety of European artisans trek across the Atlantic each season to demonstrate their well-honed Old World skills. You can watch a master painter from Germany work magic on a stein or an Italian artist brush a new face on a Venetian mask. In the past, the park has hosted a David Winter Cottage master painter from Italy and an M.I. Hummel figurine master artist from Germany. And, to top it all off, the park was voted "Most Beautiful Theme Park" by the National Amusement Park Historical Association for five consecutive years. While beauty is in the eye of the beholder, cleanliness is easy to assess. And we give Busch

Gardens an A+ in that department. The grounds are practically litter-free, and it's our experience that restrooms are as clean at 5 PM as they were when we first arrived that morning.

## Full of Surprises

Busch Gardens has so much to offer that there's always something new, even for repeat visitors. The 1997 season brought Alpengeist, which, at 195 feet tall with speeds of 67 mph, is billed as "the world's tallest, fastest, most twisted inverted roller coaster." The year before, the smaller "Wild Izzy" roller coaster got off the ground, its name a tribute to the 1996 Summer Olympics. (It since has been redubbed Wilde Maus.) One year earlier, Escape from Pompeii debuted its fiery special effects and wild, wet conclusion. In 1994, the park introduced Land of the Dragons, a children's adventureland built around a three-story tree house and a central character named Dumphrey. This enchanting area features special rides for the pint-sized, a theater and a wading pond with stepping stones and geysers that actually erupt.

Kids will beg moms and dads to let them return again and again, for there's plenty more for the pint-sized crowd, from the carnival atmosphere with jugglers, puppets and street characters to watching Grandpa ride the Big Bad Wolf roller coaster for the umpteenth time. For their part, adults enjoy the shows, the variety of fine foods, the looks of wonder on the children's faces and the rides. Area residents cite the park's well-maintained grounds, courteous employees and overall cleanliness as a drawing factor. Since its 1975 entry on the Williamsburg scene, Busch Gardens has been one of Virginia's most popular tourist attractions, partly because of the constant addition of new rides, musical revues and theme villages. In fact, each year Busch Gardens plays host to more than 2 million guests, often 25,000 to 30,000 in a single day.

The entertainment park, a not-so-small world of its own, occupies 3,600 acres of woodlands bordering the James River just 3 miles east of Williamsburg. Many visitors to Colonial Williamsburg, Jamestown and the other history-rich attractions in the area find that a trip to Busch Gardens provides a timely change of pace — a day or two of sheer, unadulterated vacation fun.

Because the assortment of amusements here can at first seem confusing, we've divided helpful information on Busch Gardens into four sections: Getting Inside, Getting Around Inside, Rides and Countries, and Entertainment and Dining. All you have to do is get in the car and go for it.

## Getting Inside

Busch Gardens is open on weekends from April to mid-May and during Easter week from 10 AM until 10 PM on Saturday and 10 AM until 7 PM on Friday and Sunday. From mid-May to early September, the park is open daily. Peak season (summer) hours are generally 10 AM to 10 PM Sunday through Friday and 10 AM to midnight on Saturdays. The park also is open 10 AM to 7 PM weekends in late March and on weekends and some weekdays in the early fall, closing for the season the last weekend in October. It's best to call ahead for closing times, as a new schedule is made each year and is always subject to change.

To drive to the park from Williamsburg, follow Route 60 about 3 miles east of town, and you'll see the vast parking facilities on your right. Busch Gardens can accommodate 7,000 vehicles and charges $6 per car, $9 for oversized vehicles and $4 for motorcycles. Buses park free. One note of caution: During the summer months, the parking lots tend to fill up, leaving late-arrivals to find their own alternatives. We recommend you plan to reach the park early so you won't face this problem or the morning traffic backups that often occur on routes 60 and 199 during peak season. Whatever you do, don't park along the shoulder of Route 60, as police routinely ticket and tow cars that are illegally parked there.

On to the ticket booths. Expect to pay about $31.50 for adults, $24.50 for ages 3 to 6, and $28.35 for military ($22.05 for ages 3 to

6) and seniors 55 and older. Ticket holders are entitled to unlimited rides, the park's regular show lineup, in-park transportation and other entertainments, but small fees may be charged for arcade games and certain special events. For $41.95, or $33.95 for children ages 3 to 6, visitors can buy two-day tickets. Discount twilight tickets, (good after 5 PM when closing time is 10 PM or after 3 PM for 7 PM closings), run about $24.95 and $17.95 for children ages 3 to 6.

If you're also planning to wade over to Water Country USA, your best bet is to buy a three-day pass for $47.95 that enables you to move between the two parks as often as you wish (within 14 days of the time of purchase). Area residents or those in town for the summer can purchase season passes to Busch Gardens, currently selling for $99.95 or $79.95 for children ages 3 to 6 (if purchased by mid-May). Combination season passes to Busch Gardens and Water Country USA, special group rates, military passes and senior discounts also are available. For more information, inquire at the gate or call ahead, and be aware that rates change every year or so.

## Getting Around Inside

Tree-lined wooden walkways and arched bridges link the various villages and areas in the park, but the Aeronaut Skyride can take you from England to France to Germany on a 3,000-foot triangular route. Sit back in the aerial cable cars and enjoy panoramic views of the park and surrounding woods. Busch Gardens' futuristic Eagle One monorail takes visitors from Hastings village to the Anheuser-Busch Hospitality Center. In addition, two steam locomotives, replicas of European trains, chug along on a winding track around the attractions, crossing the Rhine on a trestle bridge and stopping in Heatherdowns, New France and Festa Italia.

Even with the in-park transportation op-

**INSIDERS' TIP**

More than 32 million gallons of water and 44,000 gallons of chlorine are used at Water Country USA annually. In spring, the park uses artesian wells to help fill the pools, which are heated with propane in the fall and when temperatures dip in the summer.

tions, a tour of Busch Gardens can require a good deal of self-locomotion. Wear good walking shoes (we can't stress this enough), bring strollers for infants and toddlers and perhaps hats or visors on hot, sunny days. Strollers and wheelchairs can be rented near the ticket booths, but the numbers are limited. Single strollers rent for $6, and double strollers are $12 for the day. Manual wheelchairs rent for $9, and electric wheelchairs are $30 for the day.

# England/Scotland

## Banbury Cross

This English theme village is home to a Big-Ben-like clock tower and a replica of Shakespeare's Globe Theatre where shows are staged daily. Try English pastry at the Muffin Man, and visit Her Majesty's Fancy for English soaps and porcelain gifts. Have your likeness sketched by a sidewalk artist, research your family coat of arms at the Heraldry and don't miss the Globe's Haunts of the Olde Country, a 3-D movie filmed on location at haunted castles in Scotland and Ireland. A 60-by-28-foot screen image and special effects such as cold air, mist and fog make this a supernatural experience.

## Heatherdowns

Move on to Heatherdowns, a Scottish Village easily spotted by the Loch Ness Monster. "Nessie," one of the largest, daredevilest steel roller-coaster rides in the world, transports you into two minutes of pleasurable terror. You'll drop 114 feet, reach speeds of 60 mph, double loop upside down, shoot over the quiet waters of the Rhine and through a dark cavern before the monster lets you loose.

Once you've recovered from Nessie, you can have your picture taken with the Anheuser-Busch Clydesdales, shop for a kilt in Tweedside Gifts or climb aboard the Balmoral Castle and Die Hochbeinigin steam locomotives, which make the main stops on their circular course here.

## Hastings

Back in England, cross the drawbridge back in time into this medieval village. Visitors can partake in games of yore such as crossbow, Jacob's ladder and slingshot at Threadneedle Fair; watch a free-flight demonstration by exotic birds and raptors at the Feathered Folles Theatre; visit the bald eagles in Eagle Canyon; enter a computer-animated show called The Enchanted Laboratory; or visit the arcades and Wizard Works magic shop. The bold and brave can help search for the magic crystal aboard Questor, Busch Gardens' fantasy ship adventure with flight simulator and special effects. Don't forget to visit the Magic Lantern Theatre for the new cruise-ship-style song and dance revue, *Rockin' The Boat*.

# France

## Aquitaine

Next it's Vive la France in Aquitaine, a quaint village reminiscent of Provence. Delicious food, a French preoccupation, is available here in the sidewalk cafe and Le Grande Gourmet European dessert shop, where French singers Lizbet and Louis-Louis serenade guests. To stimulate digestion, hop in one of the replica racing cars on the Le Mans Raceway and maneuver through a track of tunnels and bridges or shop for environmentally themed sportswear at La Belle Maison. If you're ready to sit for a spell, check out the Royal Palace Theatre, with its 5,200 seats and special events ranging from a dazzling outdoor ice show to a Russian tumbling act to a laser-light show against the backdrop of a summer evening sky.

## New France

The French-Canadian trappers' village you walk to next features homespun fun and crafts displays. Rustic log cabins and country music provide the background for a potter, blacksmith and woodcarver demonstrating their trades. Smoked meats and barbecue are offered in New France's restaurant, hand-thrown pots and bowls are on sale in the Caribou Pottery Shop, and you can have a tintype photograph taken of your family or group decked out in old-fashioned regalia in the photo studio. (One of these Insiders did this years ago when our older daughter was an infant, and she still has the photo of Mom and Dad as

Get a new perspective aboard The Alpengeist at Busch Gardens.

gunslingers cradling a babe in arms on her bedroom wall). A pair of country music shows at the Canadian Palladium round out the entertainment, but the main attraction still is Le Scoot, a log flume ride with a 50-foot drop. On a hot summer day, it is truly a treat. Timberrrr!

## Germany

### Oktoberfest

Next stop Germany, where the Drachen Fire roller coaster features first-of-its-kind elements guaranteed to make you wish you had skipped lunch — a camel hump, a corkscrew and a bat wing. Drachen Fire is a mere 150 feet high with 3,550 feet of twisting, plunging, torturous track. The Big Bad Wolf lumbers in Deutschland, too — you can't miss him as he perches over Oktoberfest's Bavarian village. The Wolf, a suspended roller coaster, is 5 acres big and bad and lunges over Bavaria at 48 miles per hour. The finale to this ride is an 80-foot dive toward the Rhine. After you test your wits against these two metal monsters, stop off at the 2,000-seat Das Festhaus to recuperate. Here you'll find German food, beer, stage performances, folk dancing and serenading by the Burgermeister, who has been with the park since its beginning. Beyond the Festhaus is a rides and games area featuring a wave swing, Der Autobahn bumper cars and Der Red Baron, an airplane ride for kids.

### Rhinefeld

If you have young children along, you will not want to miss picturesque Rhinefeld, where you can take a scenic riverboat cruise down the Rhine while listening to an oompah band. Here, there are miniature versions of adult rides and an antique carousel that dates to 1819. Rhinefeld is also home to the place that our kids loved best — Land of the Dragons. This delightful adventureland features a three-story-tall tree house inhabited by Dumphrey and his dragon playmates and several rides of the rather gentle sort. While the tree house is a great place to climb, our favorite feature is the shallow wading pond with waterfalls and erupting geysers. After hours of walking, you may want to cool your tired feet here. But be advised: As a safety precaution, no one is allowed to walk barefoot through the pool (something we found out the hard way). Also in Rhinefeld are gift stores, where you can shop for beer steins, M.I. Hummel figurines and imported German chocolates.

Another new Rhinefeld attraction is Wilde Maus, which debuted as Wild Izzy in honor of the 1996 Centennial Olympic Games and was renamed a year later. This single-car roller coaster simulates the motion of a mouse through a maze and, at 46 feet tall with top speeds of 22 mph, is the smallest (but not necessarily the "gentlest") of Busch Garden's coasters.

## Alpengeist

Oh, but what is that lurking on the outskirts of Rhinefeld and Oktoberfest? Could it be some new beast stalking the hamlets of Busch Gardens, taking visitors by surprise? It's Alpengeist, and the wild, twisted ride it offers isn't for the faint of heart. This 195-foot inverted roller coaster doesn't really have a home in any particular European country. (There's some scuttlebutt about the beginnings of Switzerland, but that hadn't been confirmed at this writing.) To begin the upside-down adventure of their lives, riders climb aboard a ski lift like no other ski lift on earth and head out into a heart-stopping blizzard of fright. Thrills include a half-dozen inversions from the Cobra Roll to the Flat Spin to the High-Speed Spiral, which we could describe here but which really needs to be felt for the full effect. There's even an amazing 170-foot vertical drop that happens so fast you're down before you even knew you were up. The Alpengeist spans Rhinefeld, Oktoberfest, Aquitaine and New France and drifts over the scenic Rhine much of the time. Brrrrr! We get chills just thinking about it.

## Apollo's Chariot

Apollo's Chariot, new in Spring 1999, boasts nine, pulse-quickening drops, the first of which plunges passengers down 210-feet of steel track. Riders experience weightlessness as they race up and down a series of camelback humps at 75 mph. Another unique element of this new coaster is the seating. Passengers are elevated above the car's frame, which creates a "free-flight" feeling. Busch claims the ride plummets passengers

more than any other coaster in the world. In any case, with its 4,882-foot length track, Apollo's Chariot offers a relatively long ride with a total drop of 825 feet. Need we say more?

# Italy

## San Marco

From Germany, a long footbridge leads across the Rhine into the Italian village of San Marco, complete with red-tiled roofs, porticos and a tiered piazza. Relax under leafy trellises and enjoy a slice of spicy Italian life. Save some room for pasta because it's available in abundance at the open-air restaurant. San Marco is the place to watch *Funiculi, Funicula*, a modern Italian opera, and jitterbug fans can sway to the sounds of swing when the Starlight Orchestra takes the stage. Capodimonte porcelain can be purchased here as well.

Next to the San Marco piazza you'll see Da Vinci's Garden of Inventions, a rides area built as a kind of accolade to Leonardo Da Vinci, the 15th-century artist, genius and inventor. Da Vinci's Cradle, The Flying Machine and The Battering Ram as well as special rides for children are located here. Don't be misled by the gentle look of the Cradle, which starts to rock slowly but soon takes off on a spin, round and round in a 360-degree circle until riders beg for the bough to break.

## Festa Italia

If Da Vinci's Cradle makes you ready for more thrills, walk over to Festa Italia and climb on the Turkish Delight, a teacup spin, or aboard the Sea Dragon, which offers high-speed, circular excitement. Festa Italia, where an Italian street carnival is re-created, also features Roman Rapids, a raft expedition that sends riders swirling past ruins, through fog and down the rapids for a wet and wild time. Watch out for the leaky aqueduct, and don't carry on anything that won't survive a good dousing.

The Italian village is home to Escape from Pompeii, a 3½-minute ride that transports the daring through 75-foot-tall Roman ruins, where they are blasted with the sounds of Mount Vesuvius erupting amid fiery explosions. The action doesn't stop there. Statues and beams tumble around riders, who can feel the heat of the volcanic flames on their faces. It's all over when the door to the ruins opens, and riders plunge 50 feet into a pool of water. No sweat!

# Entertainment and Dining

Busch Gardens provides diverse entertainments for park guests, from ice shows, laser displays and black-light puppeteers in the Royal Palace Theatre to *Rockin' The Boat*, a larger-than-life musical production in Hastings Village that combines a Broadway medley with the soothing sounds of a Caribbean cruise. And, in the spring of 1998, the park introduced the 15-minute movie *Pirates 4-D*, a high-tech offering that includes special effects within the cinema to create an unusual experience for moviegoers. Set aboard a pirate ship, the musical slapstick comedy stars Leslie Nielsen, Monty Python's Eric Idle and Adam Wylie of Picket Fences. The movie will be shown in the park's Globe Theatre. Sure to please all ages, these shows are presented daily (or nightly) and feature internationally famous acts as well as performers chosen from Busch Gardens' annual audition tour. Check ticket booths for schedule information.

The park also sends its costumed street characters out to perform at various locations around the park. Sit down a spell with Beatrice Bloom, royal botanist, biochemist and butterfly lover of Buckingham Palace, and listen to her daily readings for children in the Royal Preserve Petting Zoo. Gossip about Harriet Hartshorn and Harvey Hoosler, two truly tasteless American tourists who find themselves lost in Europe. Let the child in you delight in the misadventures of Dumphrey the Dragon, a favorite of both the young and young-at-heart. Savor the sounds of the gracious Burgermeister, as he sings a song or two while stepping lively to a German polka.

In addition, European artisans visit Busch Gardens each season to demonstrate their art, sign their work and give visitors an opportunity to learn more about historic trades.

The Hospitality Center, which you reach by taking the Eagle One monorail, offers a slightly different form of entertainment for Busch Gardens visitors. Here you can learn about Anheuser-Busch's many enterprises, including its brewery and resort community, Kingsmill on the James. You can take a self-

Slip and slide down the Malibu Pipeline at Water Country USA.

guided tour of the brewery, and those 21 or older can sample beers. Foot-long hot dogs, club sandwiches, pizza, French fries, salad and desserts also are on sale at the Hospitality Center.

To provide authentic and delicious foods in the park's many restaurants, Busch Gardens sends its chefs to Europe to research and receive special training. You will taste the results of these trips when you sample such fare as the desserts at Aquitaine's Le Grand Gourmet, cannelloni a la Stella in Italy, or spicy wursts and Black Forest torte in the German area.

The largest Busch Gardens restaurant is Das Festhaus, a 2,000-seat festival hall that serves authentic German cuisine, but there are 20 or so places to grab a bite to eat throughout the park. In the mood for ice cream? Head to the London Dairy in England. Kids want pizza? Then La Cucina in Festa Italia is a must for your group. But no matter what your taste buds are craving — from smoked beef brisket to corn dogs and French fries — we guarantee you'll find it somewhere in Busch Gardens.

If you packed a lunch, leave that picnic basket in the car. No outside food is allowed inside the park, although there are picnic tables scattered throughout the grassy areas of the parking lots. Be sure to get your hand stamped as you leave the park.

Groups of 40 or more can arrange for catered picnics in the Black Forest Picnic Village next to Das Festhaus. Reservations are required.

## Water Country USA
**Va. Rt. 199, 3 miles east of Williamsburg • (757) 253-3350, (800) 343-SWIM**

Water, water everywhere — let's drop into the drink. We may have taken a little poetic license with that one, but Water Country has a genuine license to thrill. If you don't mind getting wet (you're going to if you come here), check out this combination of waterfalls, waves and flumes, and get ready to make a big splash.

Opened in 1984 and purchased by Anheuser-Busch in 1992, Water Country USA sits on 40 acres of wooded land 3 miles east of Colonial Williamsburg. The largest water

theme park in Virginia, Water Country now offers more than a dozen water rides as well as a pool, sunbathing, live shows, a variety of restaurants, arcades and, of course, bathhouse facilities. (The park recently received approval from government officials to add 37 acres of attractions to its existing facility. At this writing, the whens, whats and wheres of the expansion had not been released.)

The theme at Water Country is 1950s and '60s cool. The park is landscaped with palms, ornamental grasses, pines and bold, bright flowers like hibiscus, hot pink geraniums and blazing yellow marigolds. Bare feet abound, but we prefer to wear swim shoes or waterproof sandals for protection from hot pavement and stubbed toes. If you do don shoes and don't want to wear them on some of the rides, there are "sneaker keepers" at the base of many attractions. Some strollers — shaped like dolphins, of course, are available near the main concession area. They can be rented for $7, which includes a $2 refundable deposit.

This family-friendly place boasts rides suited to all ages and all levels of swimming ability. All pools and rides are temperature-controlled, especially helpful for early season splashing. And while thrills are the main business of this attraction, relaxation hasn't been forgotten. Beach bums can catch a wave at Surfers' Bay, then grab a few rays on the four-tiered sun deck. Parents can sit on deck chairs while the kids splash around in the supervised play area. All ages appreciate Project Duck, a show in which the park's mascot teaches kids and teens all about protecting the environment.

Visitors will be pleased to know Water Country USA has been rated among America's safest theme parks by Barclay & Associates, an independent risk-management firm.

## Getting Inside

Water Country USA is open Memorial Day through Labor Day and on some weekends in May and September. From mid-June through August hours generally are 10 AM to 8 PM, although the park typically closes at 6 PM earlier in the season and at 7 PM in late August and early September. On hot summer days we like to start early to get in as much water action as we can before the park gets really packed.

To reach the park from I-64, take Exit 57B to Route 199 and head east. From Route 60 or Highway 143, take Route 199 E. You'll pass over I-64 and see the park entrance a quarter-mile on the right. Parking costs $5 per car, $8 per oversized vehicle and $3 per motorcycle. To get into the park, expect to pay about $25, or $18.95 for children ages 3 to 6. Seniors 55 and older pay $22.90, and children 2 and younger enter free. If you're only interested in an afternoon cool-down, arrive at 3 PM or later and pay only $16.50. Another option to consider is the three-day ticket that gets you into both Busch Gardens and Water Country USA for any three days within a two-week period at a discounted rate of $51.95. Real water lovers can buy season passes through the park's sales department. Cost is $89.95 or $69.95 for children 3 to 6, and discounted prices for active duty military are available. Combo season passes to both Water Country USA and Busch Gardens Williamsburg are $119.95 for adults and $99.95 for children aged 3 to 6. (Note: The park allows you to apply your one-day admission price to the purchase of a season pass, if you buy it before leaving the grounds.) Groups of 15 or more are offered special rates if they make advance reservations.

Lockers are available; rentals cost $7, which includes a $1 deposit. Unless you or a member of your group decides to sit the day out, we suggest you rent one. Since the lockers are centrally located, they're a good, safe place to keep funds (paper money, after all, isn't waterproof), as well as a dry set of clothes for when the frolicking is over. If you must carry cash with you, your best bet is to bring along or purchase one of those plastic cylinders that hangs from a cord around the neck. Need a little more persuading? We know of at least one thrillseeker who is out 26 bucks because he kept his money in a sandwich bag stashed in his pocket. If you're like us and can't get by without sunglasses, they, too, should be worn on some type of head-hugging cord. We remember one visit where we stood around for a half-hour while a park diver searched the bottom of one pool for a new pair of expensive sunglasses. Yes, they belonged to one of us, but we're not saying whom. One last word of advice: Take towels with you, and park them on lawn chairs at

Surfers' Bay or one of the children's play areas. That way you'll have a home base to return to when you just want to sit awhile or test the waters in the wave pool.

The park has a fairly large supply of free life vests for nonswimmers and small children. Because you can find them on racks throughout the park, many people pick them up and drop them off as needed. We have found that after 2 PM it's hard to locate one of the smaller children's vests — it might be a good idea to hold onto one for your entire visit.

# Water Attractions

Now that you've stashed your valuables and suited up, it's time for the main event. What follows are individual descriptions of each of the water rides and play areas.

### Surfers' Bay

This is Virginia's largest wave pool, though it seems more like an ocean with its 650,000 gallons of water. Periods of mechanically produced 4-foot waves alternate with times of smooth surf for relaxation. Want to really chill out? Stretch out in one of more than 1,000 lounge chairs on the wood sundeck surrounding the bay. Or, if you're looking for a little shelter from the elements, head for one of the bright canopied cabanas found poolside. Grab your seats early as they go fast.

### Aquazoid

If you like special effects, you'll love this ride. Named for a 1950s mutant movie monster, Aquazoid's big black tubes have enough space for a family of four to pile in together and zip through curtains of water into a pitch dark tunnel before splashing through yet another curtain of water at the speed of 11 feet per second. On your journey, your senses will be assaulted by beams of light and howling sound effects as you escape from the Aquazoid's lair and plunge 78 feet into a splash pool.

### Big Daddy Falls

Get the whole family together and climb into a humongous inner tube for a wet and wild river-rafting adventure. This water ride splashes through twists and turns, slips into a dark tunnel, then plunges into a slow-moving river alive with waterfalls before racing around the bend to a final splashdown. (The first time we tried this ride we thought the waterfall effect was a little overdone until we realized it had started to rain buckets as we slid through the tunnel.)

## H2O UFO

The park's newest and largest interactive children's play area has a sci-fi theme and features a fun combination of slides and spray jets. There's even a fairly long, scaled down water slide for kids (and their parents) who aren't quite ready to take a walk on the wilder side. Park your gear on one of the many lawn chairs and make a splash.

## Cow-A-Bunga

This expanded children's play area features a 4,500-square-foot heated pool, an interactive speedboat with a water skiing cow (what "udder" silliness), a curving water flume, a short but slick triple slide and several fountains. There is plenty of deck seating for parents who want to watch the action from the sidelines.

## Kids' Kingdom

Kids 12 and younger delight in this shallow play pool full of animal slides, huge floats and inner tubes. Parents can sit on the surrounding sundeck and snap pictures to their hearts' content while their gleeful offspring slide down a pelican's pouch or a whale's open mouth. For drier fun, there's a children's obstacle course enhanced by bubbles and balls. Other Kids' Kingdom features are Minnow Matinee, an outdoor theater that hosts magic and juggling routines, and Guppy Games, a child-oriented arcade.

## Adventure Isle

Another of Water Country's four pool areas, Adventure Isle's main event is a zany water obstacle course featuring agility ladders, rings and inner tube walks. Waterfalls, a children's waterslide and several adult rides are here. The two enclosed tubular slides — Peppermint Twist and Lemon Drop — are popular with the more adventurous. But more on those rides later.

## Malibu Pipeline

Opened in 1993, the Malibu Pipeline is a twisting, two-person tube ride through enclosed double flumes, complete with strobe lighting, waterfalls and a splash pool at the bottom. The dark-as-night flumes made this one of our favorite rides, and our 5-year-old deemed it "wild, wild, wild."

## Wild Thang

Take another walk on the wild side — with a companion — on this popular 500-foot-long double inner tube ride past jungle scenes, under waterfalls and through tunnels before splashing down.

## Peppermint Twist

This is one of Water Country USA's most breathtaking rides. You'll plunge into a pool after spinning down a tangle of curving tubes. Fast and fun!

## Lemon Drop

Next door to the Peppermint Twist is this short but, dare we say it, awesome adventure. Two hydrochutes, one curved, one straight, rocket the rider down and drop him about 4 feet over the pool below. Maybe the fact that one Insider has nicknamed this ride "The Splat" gives you an idea of what we're talking about. Be prepared to make water contact with a major splash.

## Double Rampage

Grab your surf 'boggan, and speed down 75 feet of steep, slick Teflon slide. Then shoot across the long landing pool, and try to catch your breath. This is one of the shortest and perhaps the scariest rides in the park. One Insider was ready to climb back down after catching the view from the top until her young daughter took the plunge and shamed her into trying it for herself.

Comments made by riders (and would-be riders) at the Double Rampage: "My heart was just thumping . . . I can't do this, and no one is going to make me . . . I'm scared, but I'm going (out of the mouth of the 5-year-old) . . . You mean I'm supposed to lean forward? . . . That's a wild drop . . . Aaaaaaaaaaaaaaaaaaaa!"

Photo: Busch Gardens Williamsburg

After a thrilling escape from ancient Pompeii, this boatload of adventure seekers splashes down at dockside.

### Jet Scream

Everybody loves flume rides, and Water Country USA's is one of the longest and most exciting in the nation. Start 50 feet off the ground and streak down one of four twisting water slides at 25 miles per hour into a splash-down pool.

### Atomic Breakers

Meant to resemble a white-water river trip, this inner tube ride takes you through churning rapids as well as tranquil pools, all connected by cascading waterfalls.

### Rambling River

This ride is engineered to provide soothing relaxation for the whole family. Float your tube down the lazy river that surrounds Adventure Isle.

## Entertainment and Dining

Caban-A-Rama Theatre is the site for daily shows. In 1997, Sports Spectacular, a combination high-dive and gymnastics show, brought some of the world's best athletes to the park. The dives made from an 85-foot tower into a small, 11-foot-deep pool were truly breathtaking. Schedules are posted at the theater's entrance.

Water Country USA's eateries sell burgers, hot dogs, smoked sausages, chicken, pizza, pretzels, subs, fries, funnel cakes, ice cream, lemonade, sports drinks and beer (which must be consumed in a single enclosed area). Snack bars are situated around the park and open for business as crowds dictate. Guests can eat purchased meals at shaded outdoor tables, and a catering facility may be reserved in advance for groups of 20 or more. Groups also can make reservations for educational seminars on water safety. Our Insiders' tip, since prices for park fare are a bit steep and service can be slow, is to bring a picnic. You'll have to eat it at tables on grassy areas in the parking lot, as no food or beverages may be brought into the park itself. But the tables are on grassy median strips and most are shaded by umbrellas, so it's both a cheap and pleasant alternative. There's also a shaded pavilion for picnicking off to the right of the park entrance if you prefer. Make sure to have your hand stamped at the gate so you can get back in.

Swimwear, gifts, souvenirs, sunglasses and sunscreen are for sale at on-site surf and gift shops.

### Safety Features

Water Country USA has an excellent reputation as a safe, fun place to enjoy water without hitting the beach. The park employs more than 80 certified lifeguards and stations supervisors at each ride and attraction. Lifeguards are trained in CPR, first aid and accident prevention, and they participate in ongoing training programs and drills.

A first-aid station is open during all operating hours, walks are treated with salt to prevent falls, pool depths are clearly marked, and individual safety rules are posted at each ride. Children younger than 8 must always be in the company of a parent or other adult. This combination of rules and features at Water Country USA set the standards for safety among the nation's water parks. Precisely because the park is so safety-conscious, visitors can truly relax and enjoy a wet and wild adventure.

### Williamsburg Pottery Factory
**U.S. Rt. 60, Lightfoot (or Exit 234A off I-64) • (757) 564-3326**

Imagine a building the size of eight football fields filled from floor to ceiling with fine crystal, plants, dried and silk flowers, baskets, microwave ovenware, folk art, woodwork, lamps, home accessories, glassware, pottery and more — all on sale at wholesale prices or less. What you've envisioned is just one of more than a dozen such buildings that make up the Williamsburg Pottery Factory, a 1-million-square-foot retail complex that must be seen to be believed.

Just 5 miles west of Williamsburg on Route 60 in Lightfoot, the Pottery draws upward of 3 million customers annually, and as such it qualifies as one of the Williamsburg area's greatest attractions. It is Virginia's largest retail operation under single ownership at a single location, and it is unique in other ways as well.

Photo: Busch Gardens Williamsburg

Busch Gardens' roller coasters, musical revues and rides have been entertaining visitors since 1975.

The Pottery is open seven days a week and is closed only one day a year: Christmas. Hours, however, vary from season to season, so we suggest you call ahead to check the hours if you're planning to head to Lightfoot early or want to go later in the day. Generally, it is open 8 AM to dusk from mid-March through December and 9 AM to 6 PM January through mid-March.

## Getting There

It takes about 10 minutes to drive from downtown Williamsburg to the Pottery via Route 60. An alternate route is to take I-64 to the Lightfoot Exit and follow Route 199 where you will see signs directing you to the Pottery entrance.

## Pottery Background

The Pottery is the ultimate American success story. Started in 1938 as a roadside stand where local potter James E. Maloney could sell his saltglaze pottery made in 18th-century tradition, the Pottery evolved from a one-man operation to one of the largest bargain centers on the East Coast. The roadside stand has grown into a multisectioned retail complex. Its offerings have expanded and multiplied, and the Pottery is unlike anything you've seen or experienced.

The Pottery makes a lot of what it sells to avoid middlemen's profits. Small factories on the premises make cement gardenware, wood items, lamps, custom frames, trophies and plaques, etched glass, painted plasterware, floral arrangements and other decorative items. You can also purchase unusual items here you won't find anywhere else. If the spirit moves you, there are Elvis Presley coffee mugs, black squid ink pasta, life-size statues of bulldogs, even a planter shaped like a man with a cactus growing out of his pants. Get the picture?

Simple buildings and a constant din create a carnival atmosphere as shoppers grab for, pore over and wander amid aisle after aisle of assorted goods. While you'll find piles of junk or junque (as your tastes dictate), there's no denying this place offers some of the best buys on first-quality goods as well. The Pottery is almost always crowded (except first thing in the morning — a good time to do your serious shopping), and it's not unusual to arrive and find 25 or more buses lined up at the entrance (they're actually chartered from as far away as North Carolina, New York, New Jersey and Pennsylvania). Fear not, there's plenty inside for everyone, and the stock is seemingly endless and constantly being replenished by the scores of workers who help keep the place humming.

Whether you're in a buying mood or not, a trip to the Pottery is a must while you're in the Williamsburg area. We must warn you that few visitors escape without succumbing to the urge to spend, and with good reason.

The Pottery is not fancy. Wear casual clothes and comfortable shoes. Be sure to block out several hours at least, and a full day if possible, to do the place justice. Remember that there are 34 buildings on the property. (Two structures — an 8,000-square-foot production building and a 16,000-square-foot display building, both for cement items such as birdbaths, fountains, statues and flower pots — were added in 1996.) If you're willing to trek through miles of aisles, bargains do abound.

## The Shops

The Pottery complex is split into two parts, bisected neatly by the CSX railroad tracks. On one side is the Pottery, with its ceramic factory, the Solar Shops, greenhouses, Buildings 21, 22 and 23, plus production and warehouse facilities. On the other side is a bevy of factory outlet stores, about 25 or so, plus Pottery production areas for cement gardenware and terrastone, a brass foundry and a Western shop.

If you plan to spend the day, you'll want to grab a shopping cart as soon as you can. This will come in handy once you accumulate an armload of packages. There are maps of the area available at the entrance gate. While it is always fun wandering around, discovering all the Pottery has to offer, the map is a useful timesaver. If you don't find one readily available, ask a security guard where you might pick one up.

To maximize your time, we suggest you arrive as early in the day as possible. The Pottery has a restaurant, a cafe and a snack bar on the premises where you can eat breakfast, lunch and a light dinner, if necessary.

The Solar Shops, so named because of the energy-efficient heating and lighting system installed when this building was constructed, are housed under a single, albeit gigantic, roof. Here you will find a great variety of household and decorating items, silk flowers, lamps, picture frames (a custom framing service is provided), mirrors, wooden accessories, imported crystal, baskets, prints, folk art, Oriental art, fine china, collector dolls, ribbon, Mexican imports and more. Fine gold jewelry is sold here at about half the retail price.

Building 21, the second-largest building on the site, is where you will find a fresh bakery, gourmet foods, wine and spirits, kitchenware, a cheese shop, brass, candles, cushions, Oriental carpets and furniture, clocks, ceramics, linens and other decorator items.

If you're in the market for nursery plants, trees, shrubs, flowering plants, vegetable seedlings, herbs or decorative bushes, stop by the greenhouse or the landscape nursery near the 550-space Pottery Campground. Fine local, regional, exotic and tropical plants in all shapes and sizes are sold. The Pottery grows many plants from seedlings and imports still more in bulk. All are sold at rock-bottom prices. In addition, you'll find bargains on gardening tools, accessories and plant-care items. The shop

---

**INSIDERS' TIP**

**Of particular interest to history and architecture buffs are the historic James River plantations in James City and Charles City counties.**

even sells Christmas trees in season from its tree farm in the Virginia mountains.

Bargains from around the world are commonplace at the Pottery. At any one time you can spy goods from around the United States, the Orient, the Caribbean, South America, Europe, India and elsewhere. Goods are purchased and sold in volume with substantial savings passed on to the customer. Another key to the Pottery's success is its low overhead: Your purchases will be wrapped in newspaper and bound with masking tape, an inelegant but inexpensive system.

Of special interest is the "Skid Row" sale of selected merchandise held each January and February. Here goods are sold for 50 to 90 percent off the regular price.

Another draw is the Pottery Outlet Shops, where you'll find a variety of items sold directly by the manufacturers at cost or slightly higher. These shops are open according to the Pottery's operating hours.

You could easily spend an entire morning in these shops alone; again, wise planning of your time is a must. Included among the outlets are shops offering sleepwear, outerwear and sportswear for men, women and children, hardware and small appliances, linens, sweaters, cosmetics, perfume, shoes galore, needlework accessories and supplies, designer clothing, candy, ice cream and nuts. See our Shopping chapter for more details.

Although more than 8,000 parking spaces are provided, parking can be difficult on busy days. We suggest that when you find a parking spot, stay there and walk from place to place. Parking is free, and lots are on all sides of the complex. We do warn you to observe strictly any no parking signs.

Visa and MasterCard are accepted for purchases. Personal checks (even from out of state) are welcomed if accompanied by a picture identification card and a major credit card. Checks must be approved at one of the Pottery's information desks prior to checkout.

Jamestown was the Virginia colony's first capital.

# Jamestown and Yorktown

A visit to the Historic Triangle is, as the very name of the area suggests, a journey back in time. While Colonial Williamsburg, with its painstaking restoration of life in the 18th century, typically is the focal point for visitors' explorations into the past, it was Jamestown where English colonists first struggled to establish themselves in this part of the New World. The colonists' early years on American soil are brought to life and made meaningful through re-enactments, interpretations and displays. In Yorktown, the National Park Service has preserved and restored a Revolutionary War battlefields. It also stages re-creations of Colonial life in all its charm and adversity.

But even when it comes to re-creating history, time doesn't stand still. In the past year, archaeologists at Jamestown literally have dug up conclusive evidence as to the location of James Fort, the original colony fortification of 1607. In fact, continuing excavations at the original site of Jamestown, which are being conducted by the Association for the Preservation of Antiquities, have been called "the most exciting breakthrough in 17th-century archaeology in decades," by Dr. Thomas E. Davidson, curator for the Jamestown-Yorktown Foundation, which administers Jamestown Settlement. You can learn more about archeological work at Jamestown in this chapter's close-up "Dig This."

Yorktown, too, is a work in progress. In May 1997, a newly built farmhouse opened at the Yorktown Victory Center. The 16-by-20-foot house was designed to show visitors to the area exactly the type of dwelling the typical Virginia planter of the period inhabited: a small, plain, even crude house with no formal entryway or individual rooms. New county ad-ministration buildings, including an eye-grabbing courthouse, have spruced up Ballard Street near the Yorktown waterfront, while work has started on a riverwalk that, when completed, will connect the Victory Center to Water Street. And talks are ongoing about transforming the former courthouse building into a cultural arts center to provide more diverse entertainment for both visitors and locals alike.

But these are just a few examples of how Jamestown and Yorktown — two of the Historic Triangle's crown jewels — continue to reinvent themselves while making strides to enhance the authenticity of each and every visitor's journey back in time. Read on and learn all the details in this tale of two towns that once were — and still remain — such an integral part of our American heritage.

## Jamestown

### History

Imagine leaving your home and country with little more than what few possessions you could carry in a small chest. Imagine boarding a vessel powered only by breezes (or gales for the more unfortunate) to cross the boisterous Atlantic Ocean. Imagine months at sea with no privacy, little fresh food, no heat or comfort of any kind, all in order to reach a land said to be inhabited by fierce native tribes where previous attempts at settlement have ended in disaster. Who would undertake such a journey? But imagine, too, dreaming of a fertile and bounteous land. Imagine dreaming of being free — from debt, from lack of opportunity, from city squalor, from whatever mistakes or burdens were part of your past. Imagine holding in your mind simultaneously the alternating hopes and forebodings of such an enterprise, and you can begin to fathom the experience of the Jamestown settlers.

In December of 1606, three wooden ships sailed from London for the New World. Southerly winds blew the 105 adventuresome members of the expedition to the Caribbean, where one of them died. Here they obtained fresh provisions before voyaging again, this time up North America's eastern coast. Some four months and 6,000 miles after their departure from England they found a swampy wilderness on the banks of the James River and pronounced it fit for settlement. Thus began the long and fascinating story of our country's beginnings.

The early years were difficult ones for the settlers of Jamestown, the New World's first permanent English-speaking colony. The climate proved hot and humid, the land marshy and mosquito-ridden. Several of the colonists' attempts at industry, including glass making, failed to create a solid economy. And the large native population of Indians, ruled by Powhatan, was understandably distrustful of these invaders from across the seas. The winter of 1609-10, known as the "starving time," was especially terrible for the colony. Only about 90 gaunt members of the colony still were alive when supplies and reinforcements finally arrived. Indeed, more than half of the colonists who came to Virginia in the colony's first seven years died. Ultimately, tobacco cultivation succeeded where all else had failed, ensuring survival. More and more settlers arrived, attracted by cash-crop opportunities as well as the desire for a better life than that afforded by the rigidly hierarchical societies of Europe. Soon the Virginia Colony was flourishing; plantation society took firm root in its rich, sandy soils and lush woodlands.

Jamestown was the Virginia colony's first capital. It remained a thriving community until 1699 when, after the burning of the State House, the seat of government was moved inland to Williamsburg for reasons involving health problems caused by insects in this lowlying marsh and location. No longer a vital political and economic hub, by 1750 Jamestown ceased to exist as an actual community. Fortunately, much of the Jamestown story has been restored to us. Some genuine remnants of the famous settlement survive, including the bell tower of the church the colonists built and foundations of their simple homes. Archaeological discoveries (the highly acclaimed Jamestown Rediscovery Project, an ongoing archaeological dig, began in 1994), scholarly research and a number of organizations' dedication to understanding our nation's past have combined to produce the Jamestown historic experience today.

For purposes of this guide, we have divided our entry on Jamestown into two parts: historic Jamestown, coadministered by the National Park Service and the Association for the Preservation of Virginia Antiquities, and the delightful adventure of Jamestown Settlement, operated by Virginia's Jamestown-Yorktown Foundation. While these two attractions operate separately, they are but a mile apart and can be easily visited in the course of the same day. This excursion back in time is well-worth taking, and it's a large part of what makes the Historic Triangle such a popular tourist destination.

# Getting There

To get to Jamestown from Interstate 64, take Exit 242A, Va. Route 199. Va. Route 199 W. brings you to the Colonial Parkway, where signs will lead you to Jamestown. If you're coming from Williamsburg, simply take Jamestown Road and follow signs from there. Visitors arriving from the south on Va. Route 31 will cross the James River on the Jamestown Ferry, a pleasant excursion we profile in our chapter on Daytrips. Jamestown Settlement lies at the intersection of Route 31 and the Colonial Parkway, just up from the Jamestown Ferry docks.

# Attractions

### Jamestown/Jamestown Island
**Western end of Colonial Pkwy. • (757) 229-1733**

At Jamestown, a National Park Service

employee will collect your admission fee at the park entrance (see prices that follow). Drive past the entrance to the reconstructed Glasshouse on your right and head straight to the larger main parking area, where a wooden pedestrian bridge through shady woods takes you to the spacious visitors center. Here, you can view a 15-minute orientation film, join scheduled tours led by park rangers, pick up self-guiding leaflets if you prefer to go at your own pace and view changing exhibits as well as an extensive collection of 17th-century Jamestown artifacts. Guided tours for groups are available, on a reservation basis, in spring, winter and fall. Take note: Refreshments are not sold in the visitors center, and only drinks are available from vending machines in the parking lot for the reconstructed Glasshouse.

River tides have washed away part of the early town site, but on your walking tour of Jamestown you can explore the 1639 Church Tower, the sole 17th-century structure still standing, and view ruins of the original settlement made visible by archaeological exploration. These include foundations of some of the early statehouses and ruins of the original glass furnaces built in 1608. Near the Church Tower along the James River waterfront is the Jamestown Rediscovery archaeological excavation site, where you can watch researchers sift through the remains of the James Fort, once believed lost forever. You'll also see statues of John Smith and Pocahontas as well as the Dale House, which sits near the seawall, just beyond the Confederate earthwork. The Dale House serves as an archaeological lab. In its visitors' gallery many of the recently uncovered artifacts of the Jamestown Rediscovery project are on display. Along the way, explanatory markers help those on self-guided tours understand the rich, multi-layered history of the site.

After you've toured the town site, take one of the loop drives around Jamestown Island. These 3- and 5-mile self-guided automobile tours through a wilderness of pine and swamp will bring you close to the vision early colonists must have beheld when they set foot in America — a natural environment at once beautiful and frightening. Herds of deer still roam the forested ridges of the island, sometimes coming close to the ruins under cover of dusk. Muskrats hide in the Jamestown marshes; you might glimpse one paddling leisurely through the swamp. A profusion of waterfowl, including osprey, heron and mallards, make seasonal stops. Roll down your windows, listen to the music of songbirds, feel the stillness all around you. We guarantee you'll feel an almost otherworldly peace in this place that, as one Insider likes to say, does not belong to us but to all of those who walked the land before us. If time permits — and you should make sure it does — you can pull over to read the markers inscribed with interesting historical and botanical data.

The next logical stop is at the reconstructed Glasshouse, where costumed craftspeople demonstrate 400-year-old techniques, making glassware much like that created and used by settlers. While hard woods such as hickory and oak fueled the kilns in 1608, today natural gas heats the fiery furnace. No matter. The products, which register a red-hot 2,000 degrees when first pulled from the heat, are lovely. Clear and green goblets, bell jars, flasks, wineglasses, pitchers and the like can be purchased here. A display case also shows off some of the glassblowers' after-hours work — the vases and such they make to perfect their skills long after you and I have gone home.

You may want to return to the visitors center for souvenirs before leaving. Reproductions

**INSIDERS' TIP**

**Want a bird's-eye view of the Historic Triangle? Aerial tours are available of Jamestown Island, Williamsburg and the James River plantations. All flights originate at the Williamsburg-Jamestown Airport and average 30 to 50 minutes. The cost ranges from $30 to $45 per person, depending upon the tour you select. For information, call (757) 253-8185.**

of Colonial stoneware, glassware made at the Glasshouse, a vast selection of books, videotapes, toys, games and other keepsakes are for sale in the gift shop.

Admission to Jamestown Island is $5 per adult, age 17 or older, and covers re-entry for up to a week. Children 16 and younger are admitted free. A Golden Age pass for visitors 62 and older is available for $10. The pass, good for life, is valid at all national parks. Educational groups are admitted free of charge, but advance notice of at least one month is required. Audiocassette tapes are available for the town site and loop drive and may be rented for $2.

Jamestown is open every day of the year except Christmas, but hours vary seasonally, so call ahead before planning a visit. Parking is always free.

## Interpretive Programs

To truly get a feel for the place and the era, children may participate in a number of special programs. These include the Young Settler program during the summer months and Colonial Junior Ranger programs, where children 12 and younger can learn about Jamestown while enjoying a series of activities with their families. The Junior Ranger program, which is designed for family groups only, provides each child with a chance to earn a patch and a certificate. Other interpretive programs are offered seasonally, including Old Town tours that explore the struggles of the earliest settlers and living history programs that provide first-person accounts of the harsh life at Jamestown. Pre-registration is not required. Most programs are either free with admission or cost $1.50 per child.

## Jamestown Settlement
**Va. Rt. 31 and Colonial Pkwy. • (757) 229-1607**

Known as Jamestown Festival Park until 1990, Jamestown Settlement is operated by the Jamestown-Yorktown Foundation of the Commonwealth of Virginia. The settlement blends an indoor theater and museum exhib-

its with an outdoor living history program that re-creates both the early colonists' experiences and Native American habitats and customs. Here you'll also have a chance to board replicas of the ships that brought the English settlers to the New World in 1607.

Start off your visit, after purchasing a ticket in the entrance lobby, by watching the 20-minute film, *Jamestown: The Beginning*, in the comfortable 100-seat theater of the museum building. Narrated by an actor playing the role of colonist John Laydon, this docudrama familiarizes visitors with the origins of the Jamestown Colony and also serves as introduction to museum exhibits. It is shown every 30 minutes.

## English Gallery

Three distinct galleries make up the indoor portion of Jamestown Settlement. In the English Gallery, you can examine artifacts, three-dimensional dioramas, reproductions and graphics that explain British motivations for exploring and settling the New World. The role of the British Crown in colonization and the founding of the Virginia Company, which sponsored Jamestown, are highlighted, as is the crucial role played by new navigational and shipbuilding techniques that made long ocean voyages feasible. There are replicas of the clothing worn by both the commoners and the well-to-do of the time and an explanation of the role wool production played in the economy of England. (In fact, British dependence on wool led to the common expression of the day that "England is a country where sheep eat men.")

## Powhatan Indian Gallery

An imposing brass statue of Chief Powhatan, who ruled 32 Algonquian tribes in coastal Virginia, stands in the museum lobby. These tribes are now referred to simply as the Powhatans, about whom you'll learn more in the second exhibit gallery, the Powhatan Indian Gallery. Inside the gallery you'll see the life-size figures of a Powhatan Indian man, woman and child, plus a full-size replica of

Powhatan's mantle, or ceremonial cloak. Displays of originals and reproductions of tools, weapons, fishing and farming implements, along with scenes of everyday life offer a perspective on Native American culture during the period. Did you know, for instance, that Powhatan women built the houses for their tribe or that Indian babies were bathed daily in cold streams to make them hearty? Be sure to listen to the recording of an Algonquian dialect. You also can touch treated samples of deerskin the Powhatans used as clothing.

## Jamestown Gallery

The Jamestown Gallery completes the triad, depicting the growth of the settlement from its earliest rugged days to the bustling period when it served as the political and economic cornerstone of the sizable Virginia Colony. Tribulations endured by the first settlers are described here, and the story of Captain John Smith is told. Also detailed are the roles played by tobacco, by Africans first brought to Jamestown in 1619 and by the church. Miniature replicas of the types of homes settlers built also are part of this gallery.

Jamestown Settlement's indoor exhibits are fascinating, but your most vivid memories probably will come from the outdoor re-creations of 17th-century life. These offer a unique hands-on journey into our country's past. Not only do authentically costumed interpreters re-enact the chores and amusements of daily life in Colonial Virginia, they also encourage visitors to take a turn at many of these activities. Children especially like this aspect of Jamestown Settlement.

## Powhatan Indian Village

In the Powhatan Indian Village, a short walk from the museum exit, you'll see several Native American houses (the British called them longhouses but the Algonquian word is "yahekan") made of sapling frames covered with reed mats. These Native American dwellings were re-created from archaeological evidence and the eyewitness drawings of a New World explorer. Walk around the ceremonial "dance face circle" made up of seven carved wooden poles created by an Indian artist and her husband. It is easy to get the feel for this place as you watch a historical interpreter costumed as a Powhatan Indian making tools from bone, while another works to grow food or prepare a meal. Children can get a taste of Native American life in Colonial times as they carry wood in for the fire, grind corn or play a game of cob darts, pitching dried corn ears through a hanging vine hoop.

## Three Ships

Follow the path down from the Indian village to the pier where full-sized replica ships, the *Susan Constant*, the *Godspeed* and the *Discovery*, float in a recess of the James River. The *Susan Constant*, a replica that was actually built here at the settlement from 1989 to 1991, is brightly painted and fully rigged. It replaces an earlier replica built before the discovery of evidence that the original *Susan Constant*, probably built in 1605, had a 120-ton cargo capacity. Exploration of shipwrecked vessels of similar make and period also provided clues as to the appearance and construction of this remarkable craft. Go on board the 116-foot-long replica and imagine calling it home for nearly five months. Remember, including crew there were probably 143 men and boys aboard the three ships that reached Jamestown in 1607. You can climb down to the 'tween deck, where passengers were quartered, for an idea of just how cramped conditions were. When we remarked on the small size of the deck, one of the interpreters told us conditions were even worse than we imagined: During the voyage from England, the deck probably was loaded with cargo waist

---

**INSIDERS' TIP**

**If you really like to plan ahead, mark your calendars for a return visit to Jamestown during the year 2007, when the Historic Area will pull out all the stops for its 400th birthday bash.**

Photo: Jamestown-Yorktown Foundation

The *Susan Constant, Godspeed* and *Discovery* await visitors at Jamestown Settlement.

high, then covered with mattresses, where most of the passengers spent many idle hours lolling about in utter boredom!

Take note that the *Susan Constant, Godspeed* and *Discovery* are functioning ships, and sometimes one of them sails off from Jamestown Settlement to participate in a maritime event. But visitors always have access to at least one of the ship replicas. Costumed crew members interpret life at sea, unfurling sails, dropping anchor, posting colors and letting hardy souls try their hand at navigating or nautical knot tying. Children learn the role of 17th-century ship's boys and may be asked to ring the ship's bell, brandish a sword (very carefully) or read directions on the compass.

## James Fort

When you're ready to stand on solid ground again, debark and head up to James Fort. Enter these stockade walls, and you'll experience the rough-and-ready life of early settlers — thatched roof, wattle-and-daub huts with rudimentary furnishings, the smell of wood smoke, the ceaseless worry and toil of survival. Inspect a cannon, try on armor, help a colonist tend the garden. Children delight in knocking down the wooden pins of a primitive bowling game, playing quoits (ring toss) or watching the periodic muster of the militia.

Sometimes, kids get to watch stew or potage being made and are asked to toss potato peels and onion scraps out the window to the chickens that roam the grounds freely. Male settlers may be engaged in the industries of Virginia, such as lumber manufacture or blacksmithing, while the women are often cooking or splitting wood. During the winter of 1995, a 50-foot barracks was erected within the fort confines, the only building on the premises with a clapboard roof.

You may be amazed by what the re-enactors tell you. We learned, for example, that, while men couldn't marry until 19, girls of 13 were permitted to wed; that two or three entire families lived in a small 10-by-12-foot house; and that the punishment for failure to attend one of the two daily church services was no food for the day.

In addition to regular exhibits and activities, Jamestown Settlement sponsors a number of special programs throughout the year. These include a public lecture series; children's programs, always featuring hands-on learning activities; an Indian Heritage Festival in June that brings together members of Virginia's eight recognized tribes for a one-day powwow; a November Foods and Feasts presentation that demonstrates how the early colonists prepared and preserved food and traditional English Christmas festivities. (For more complete discussions, see our Annual Events chapter.) For information on special programs, call (757) 229-1607.

## Restaurant and Gift Shops

After touring Jamestown Settlement, or if you need a break before plunging back into the 17th century, you can relax and eat a snack at the cafe, which serves a variety of sandwiches, salads and munchies. The restaurant is open from 10 AM to 5 PM daily but may be closed in January and the first half of February. There are also snack and drink machines. The settlement runs two gift shops, where you can purchase everything from reproductions of 17th-century glassware and pottery to a variety of souvenirs, trinkets and toys. The museum shops recently have expanded their selections of publications, reproductions, jewelry and gift items. If you have fallen in love with the settlement, you may want to pick up the 32-page *Jamestown Settlement: A Pictorial Guide*, which features dozens of color illustrations of the area.

Jamestown Settlement is open from 9 AM to 5 PM daily, except for Christmas and New Year's Day. Obviously, you don't want to go on a rainy day, unless you are interested only in the museum exhibits. Keep in mind that extreme heat and humidity may interfere with the pleasures of touring Jamestown Settlement during the height of summer, though river breezes help make all but the hottest of days tolerable. And try to allow two to three hours for a thorough exploration.

You may want to start planning a return trip for 2007, when the settlement will celebrate the 400th anniversary of America's first permanent English colony. Indeed, the countdown already has begun, and special observances will be planned. Lest you think this historic event is not a big deal, consider that a Celebration 2007 Steering Committee has developed a special logo, and a commemorative license plate is in the works.

Admission to Jamestown Settlement is $10.25 for adults, $5 for children ages 6 to 12. It's possible to purchase a combination ticket for both the settlement and the Yorktown Victory Center, also run by the Jamestown-Yorktown Foundation. That ticket costs $14 for adults and $6.75 for children ages 6 to 12. Residents of York and James City counties and Williamsburg are entitled to free entry.

### Jamestown Explorer
**Jamestown Yacht Basin • (757) 259-0400**

If you would like to experience Jamestown from the water — just like the original colonists did — sign up for the Jamestown Explorer cruise. Introduced in 1996 by Recreational Concepts of Norfolk, this 1½-hour narrated cruise winds through the creeks and marshes around Jamestown Island, eventually venturing onto the James River. The view is breathtaking, and Mother Nature usually obliges with a few treats of her own: Deer, eagles, osprey and heron just about always make an appearance. The trip out — a combination of nature, folklore and history — will take you past the replicas of the three ships anchored at the Jamestown Settlement, the point where the first settlers were believed to have come ashore and the site of the Jamestown Rediscovery project. On the way back, you'll be able to pull up a dredge that might contain a few clams and some small fish and hoist a crabpot. Binoculars are on board if you'd like a closer look at anything and everything. The Jamestown Explorer leaves the docks, weather permitting, April through October. The cost is $12.50 for adults, $10 for seniors and $8 for children ages 4 to 12. Children younger than 4 ride for free. Reservations are not required. Departure times are 11 AM and 1 and 3 PM daily. Also available are kayaks, which are rented for $30 for a half-day and $50 for a full day. Minors must obtain a signed release form in order to rent the kayaks. The yacht basin is directly behind the Jamestown Settlement parking lot just off the Colonial Parkway.

# Yorktown

## History

There are scores — maybe hundreds — of American towns dozing gracefully along wide rivers, awakened occasionally by the passing of some historic event, then retreating into the quiet thread of their own affairs. At first impression, Yorktown appears to be merely another one of these, and, in a sense, it is. Very few dates in its 300 plus years of existence are marked by anything of importance to outsiders. In fact, there's just one: October 19, 1781.

The small scale of this village on the bluffs overlooking the wide York River belies both its age and its importance. The history books tell another story. They tell it, of course, with all the proper names, dates, facts and numbers. For us Insiders, however, and for the others who have walked its streets and fields in many seasons, there is something else here, something still alive and profoundly significant. Spend just a few quiet minutes overlooking the battlefield on an October evening, or at dusk on a hot summer day after the sightseers have departed, and you might sense that the spirit of the place is capable of overwhelming you.

The decisive victory of the long war for American independence from Britain was won here. The major British force in the colonies surrendered here. And, what had been rebellious colonies until then were, in fact and by their own will, freed here to seek their destiny on their own terms — or, rather, to seek our destiny on our own terms.

Compared to the battlefields of our own era, the place where the British empire's rebellious children came of age is compact, reflecting a combat situation of classic simplicity. The British under Lord Cornwallis were backed against the edge of the bluff and on the waterfront below it. The American and French forces surrounded them in an explosive arc of continuous cannon and musket fire. After the Comte de Grasse sealed the mouth of the Chesapeake Bay with the French fleet in the Battle of the Virginia Capes, the British were cut off from reinforcement or retreat and faced inevitable defeat. . In brief, fierce, hand-to-hand combat, the Americans and French captured the outlying British defenses — the redoubts — and the war ended.

The most significant moment must have come when the British troops filed out of the city, flags furled, to turn in their weapons at the Allied encampment while the humiliating tune, "The World Turned Upside Down" was sounded by their own fifes and drums. Lord Cornwallis, pleading illness, had sent his representative, General O'Hara, to surrender his sword as acknowledgment of defeat. Disdaining the Colonials, this proud British commander approached General Rochambeau, leader of the French troops on the Allied side, and attempted to offer him the sword. Rochambeau, with grace but firmness, refused. He indicated instead that the sword rightfully should be handed over to the other commander present, General George Washington. Washington, acknowledging O'Hara's inferior rank, in turn directed that the sword be handed to his second-in-command, Major-General Benjamin Lincoln.

In that moment, with those gestures, the two greatest empires of the time — for whom this war had been merely one remote episode in their extensive and long-running quarrels — acknowledged that a new entity had come into its own. The American states, united in their desperate bid for independence, were, from then on, to be full and respected players on the field of history.

How wonderful it is that, more than 200 years later, we can stand on that spot in the profound peace and beauty of Surrender Field and ponder all that led to that moment and all that has proceeded from it. In many ways, tiny Yorktown is both cradle and monument to events of immense significance.

# Getting There

Although there are several ways to approach Yorktown, our usual preference and recommendation is via the Colonial Parkway, the backbone of the Colonial National Historical Park, as it stretches 23 miles from Jamestown Island to the Yorktown Visitor Center. At the change of seasons in the spring and fall, this ride is spectacular, with scattered dogwood and redbud trees brightening the bare woods in the earlier season and a bright riot of oak and other foliage in the autumn. The modern world doesn't intrude on the parkway, thanks to careful landscaping and the maintenance of a greenbelt along its length. It also is closed to trucks and commercial vehicles. There is abundant wildlife visible along the route. Turnouts on both sides of the three-lane roadway provide a stopping place to read markers, some accompanied by paintings, indicating the historic significance of each place and giving visitors a feeling of the rich and varied life of the Colonial planters and their descendants. For traveling breaks or for enjoying your own cooking, there are quiet, lovely picnic areas with restrooms, but the views of the James and York rivers from the parkway are outstanding, and the pullouts are popular places to rest and reflect. Near the Yorktown end of the parkway, you can pull over and watch the ships as they are armed at the piers of Yorktown Naval Weapons Station, which extends much of the length of the York River between Williamsburg and Yorktown. As its name suggests, this installation is where ordnance used by the Atlantic Fleet is maintained and stored.

In recent years extensive repairs have been made to the Colonial Parkway, including the installation of guardrails, all aimed at providing a safer, more pleasant experience for travelers. Our advice: Take your time and enjoy the ride, but keep an eye out for bikers and joggers, who enjoy exercising along the scenic parkway.

An alternative — but not nearly as picturesque — route to Yorktown is to travel east from Williamsburg on I-64, exiting at the Naval Weapons Station in Lee Hall, then turning left onto Va. Route 143, traveling to the first stoplight and there turning left again onto Va. Route 238. Proceeding on this road will bring you to the Yorktown waterfront.

## The Town

In August 1991, Yorktown celebrated its 300th anniversary, but, of course, the history of the area goes back even further than that. The original settlers along this stretch of the York River were the Kiskiack Indians, who called the water the Pamunkey. Captain John Smith explored the area in 1607, but it was nearly 20 years before any large numbers of English settlers began to cultivate the rich land. The town itself was founded in 1691 by the "Act for Ports and Towns" passed by the Virginia General Assembly for the transport of the colony's lucrative tobacco crop to Europe via England. This was also, in part, an attempt to force urban growth in the colony and cen-

tralize the water traffic among the numerous plantations spreading up the Chesapeake Bay. Taking advantage of the deep channel of the York, British ships could pull far enough upriver for shelter from the storms of the Atlantic Ocean and the Chesapeake Bay. The network of creeks that crisscrosses the Virginia Peninsula allowed access from the James River side as well.

The town takes its name from surrounding York County and the York River, which were so called around 1643 to honor the Duke of York, later King James II. Fifty acres of land on the plantation of Benjamin Read — including a wharf, ferry, store and well — were set aside for a county seat which, it was intended, would grow and prosper in commerce. Sheltered by the bluff, with a wide beach to hold the storehouses and other businesses of the sea trade, the site became busy and flourished throughout the Colonial period.

The oldest house in the town is the Sessions House, built in 1692 by Thomas Sessions and a survivor of the siege of 1781 and later the Civil War. A courthouse has stood on the same site since 1697, and a new church for York Parish was built in the same year. After their construction, the town's growth accelerated. By the mid-18th century, as many as 50 large trading ships would be in the vicinity of Yorktown at any given time, and the town had grown relatively prosperous.

In the latter half of the 1700s, however, the tobacco trade had shifted to the inland Piedmont region, and the shipping patterns shifted accordingly. A slow process of decline began, and by 1776, the port was less important in Commonwealth affairs. The Battle of Yorktown hastened the decline of the community. The intense barrage of cannon fire from the allied siege line and the fighting during the battle destroyed more than half of the town, and it never fully recovered.

## Historic Buildings

Structures dating to the Colonial period attest to the wealth citizens gained from Yorktown's prominence. Some of the most notable are listed here.

## Customhouse
**Main St., Yorktown • (757) 890-2806**

Reputed to have been built by Richard Ambler in 1721 as his "large brick storehouse" and used by him while he served as customs collector, this sturdy monument to Yorktown commerce is administered by the Comte de Grasse Chapter of the Daughters of the American Revolution and believed to be the oldest customhouse in the United States. It is open infrequently, and hours are seasonal, so it's best to call ahead for an appointment.

## Grace Episcopal Church
**Church St., Yorktown • (757) 898-9315**

In Colonial times, this church was known as the York-Hampton Church. It was damaged several times by war and fire, but the original walls have been standing since 1697 and have been incorporated into a number of reconstructions. It remains the place of worship for an active Episcopal parish. A book shop on-site offers theological and devotional literature, selected gifts and cards. The church is open for viewing from 9 AM to 5 PM Monday through Saturday. The bookshop is open from 11 AM to 2 PM Tuesday through Saturday. Sunday services are held at 8 AM, 9:15 AM and 11:15 AM.

## The Nelson House
**Main St., Yorktown • (757) 898-3400**

With its Georgian design, glazed Flemish bond brickwork and lovely formal gardens, The Nelson House was home to one of the wealthiest of the town's families. The most notable scion of the Nelson family was Thomas Nelson Jr., a governor of Virginia, commander of the Virginia militia and signer of the Declaration of Independence. It was this home that Cornwallis used as headquarters during the siege, and Colonial cannonballs still are lodged in the wall facing the American siege line. Legend has it that Thomas Nelson, Jr., himself gave the order to fire those cannons, even though it might have meant the destruction of his home and possibly his fortune, an act putting literal force behind his pledge in the Declaration of Independence. The Nelson House is open daily spring through fall.

## Poor Potter House
**Read St., Yorktown • (757) 898-3400**

The site of the largest-known pottery factory in Colonial America tells the story of how this industry flourished in Yorktown during the early 1700s. A shop on the premises offers reproductions from the period, including bird bottles, leech jars, milkpans and other unusual items. Hours are seasonal, so call ahead before you visit.

## Drum House
**Main St., Yorktown • (757) 898-9418**

This free museum is operated by and is headquarters for the Fifes and Drums of York Town, a volunteer group that recreates the music that led men into battle and directed their movements on the field. The museum is open on weekends throughout the year and daily in the summer. Call ahead for hours of operation.

## Archer Cottage
**Water St., Yorktown • (757) 890-0916**

This former waterfront tavern, originally built in the early 1700s and reconstructed after an 1814 fire, probably played a key role in Yorktown's early days as a bustling, hard-drinking port. Decorated from the Revolutionary War period, it now serves as the home of the recently established Yorktown Foundation, a nonprofit group that promotes the revitalization of Yorktown. The cottage is open to the public on weekends, but call ahead for hours. An archaeological dig is in progress near the cottage.

## The Augustine Moore House
**Moore House Rd., near the Coast Guard Station, Yorktown • (757) 898-3400**

This is the historic home where the terms of surrender were drawn in 1781. It has been restored and furnished to its 18th-century appearance. A living history program tells the interesting story of the arguments that took place during the negotiations. The house is open from spring through fall. For specific dates and times, contact the National Park service at the above number.

# Dig This

Digging in the dirt isn't just child's play. On Jamestown Island, a very adult type of excavation is going on. Started in April 1994, the Jamestown Rediscovery project is an exhaustive - and occasionally exhausting - attempt to unearth 400 years of early American history. The project is being conducted on acreage near historic Jamestown Church, property owned for more than 100 years by the Association for the Preservation of Virginia Antiquities (APVA), and is scheduled to continue at least through the year 2004.

Although they expected to labor long and hard before uncovering anything of historic significance, archaeologists hit paydirt just two years into the project. On the heels of early discoveries of 17th-century knife fragments, musket balls, pieces of rusted iron, shards of broken pottery and 16th-century coins, researchers found what they were looking for - the long-lost remains of the original James Fort built in 1607 as part of the earliest permanent English settlement in the New World. For more than 100 years, scholars had believed that the elusive fort had washed away into the nearby river. Thanks to the painstaking efforts of scientists in Jamestown, they - and the rest of the world - now know that just isn't so.

By revealing history, the Jamestown Rediscovery project has made history. In September 1996, representatives of national media descended on the island for Virginia Gov. George Allen's unprecedented announcement. Locally, the *Daily Press* newspaper ranked the discovery first among a listing of the year's top cultural events.

But there was even more good news to savor. The day before the public learned about James Fort, archaeologists at the site made another major discovery - an intact skull and skeleton found in the remains of a coffin. Because of the condition of the teeth and bones, the skeleton is believed to be the remains of a young male - no older than 18 or 19 - who died in the earliest months of the Jamestown colony. Researchers are using computer technology and have teamed up with a forensic artist to reconstruct the colonist's features.

The skeleton is perhaps the most dramatic of the more than 220,000 artifacts researchers uncovered in the project's first three years. Many of these artifacts are on display at the APVA Archaeological Lab (also known as the Dale House), which is open daily to Jamestown Island visitors.

The public also can watch the work in progress during visits to Jamestown. Conceived as a public dig, the project already has attracted tens of thousands of people to Jamestown Island since 1994. To accommodate such intense outside interest, plans are in the works to build an observation platform to give visitors a better view of

Photo: Cheryl Cease

The Jamestown Rediscovery project has unearthed evidence of the original James Fort.

— continued on next page

the excavations. "Education is one of the most important goals of this project," notes Bill Kelso, director of archaeology for the project. "And we have a lot of things for people to see."

For a more in-depth exploration of the dig, pick up a copy of *Jamestown Rediscovery III*, the third in a series of annual reports about the project. The 59-page booklet can be purchased at the Jamestown Visitor Center for $6.95. It includes illustrations of numerous artifacts, the excavation site as well as period maps and discussions of the latest findings.

As the first statewide preservation group in the nation, the APVA has a great deal of information to share with the public. The organization owns at least two dozen historic properties throughout Virginia, from the Cape Henry Lighthouse in Virginia Beach to Bacon's Castle in Surry County. Through APVA efforts, these and other significant Old Dominion landmarks have been preserved, restored and interpreted for future generations. For more information on the APVA and its work, call (804) 648-1889 or write APVA, 204 W. Franklin Street, Richmond VA 23220.

## Other Points of Interest

The Dudley Digges House is an original restored town house dating to the early 1700s. Digges, a lawyer, served as a council member for the state of Virginia during the Revolutionary era. The house is on Main Street but is not open to the public.

The original restored home of Captain John Ballard can be seen on Nelson Street. The prosperous merchant and sea captain lived here from 1727 to 1744. The house is not open to the public, but interpretive signs located outside explain the home's significance.

The Swan Tavern Group on Main Street is a reconstruction of the tavern and dependencies built in 1722 on the site. Although it survived the siege of 1781, it was ruined during the Civil War. Today it is an antique shop presenting a faithful reproduction of a period tavern.

### Celebrations

Although there is little evidence remaining, the Civil War brought renewed activity to the town. During the Peninsula Campaign of that conflict, Yorktown was one anchor of the Confederate defenses crossing the Peninsula to block Union progress toward Williamsburg; the fortifications of the Revolutionary War were renovated for that purpose.

Each year Yorktown observes two major celebrations related to its military history. Independence Day is celebrated with the rest of the nation, and crowds of people gather in and about the town to enjoy the traditional Fourth of July parade and the individual observations, entertainments and celebrations at the museums, homes and centers. The day culminates in a spectacular fireworks display on the York River, visible for miles around. On October 19, Yorktown again pulls out all the stops with exhibits, re-enactments of military life, "tall ship" visits, naval re-enactments, music and other celebrations as Virginians and visitors celebrate with appropriate enthusiasm Washington's — and the United States' — victory.

During Labor Day weekend in 1997, the Yorktown Foundation hosted its first Celebrate Yorktown Festival, a decidedly grown-up event that brought 35 wineries, chefs from gourmet restaurants, antique dealers from all over the country, 15 different bands, and a number of artists to the Yorktown waterfront for two days of a more genteel sort of event. (For more on yearly events in and around Yorktown, turn to our Annual Events chapter.)

## Yorktown Today

As the town's fourth century unfolds, work

continues on revitalizing Yorktown to honor its age and history. During the summer of 1994, Yorktown Beach on the York River was restored, and two specially engineered breakwaters were built out from the shoreline to preserve the beach from future erosion. Beginning in 1995, the refurbished beach was open from Memorial Day to Labor Day with public restrooms and changing facilities. The Yorktown Foundation, a group created to promote the historic town, was established in 1993 and incorporated in 1995. The goals of the nonprofit organization include commemorating the history of Yorktown while helping to preserve its historic buildings and educating the public about the significance of the town. As we noted above, the Foundation sponsored its first Celebrate Yorktown Festival in August 1997, featuring artists, performers, gourmet foods and a number of Virginia wineries.

An extensive riverwalk, a 4,000-foot path curving from the Yorktown Victory Center to National Park Service property at the eastern end of Water Street, is under construction and should be completed in 2002. Granite curbs, cobblestone gutters, brick walks, streetlights and information kiosks tell the story of this historic riverport.

# Attractions

## Yorktown Visitor Center
**Eastern end of Colonial Pkwy., Yorktown • (757) 898-3400**

The centerpiece of the National Park Service's presentation and interpretation of the Yorktown Battlefield is here. We encourage visitors to make this their first stop before exploring the area because the 16-minute orientation film (shown every half-hour) and other information and exhibits bring to life the events that transpired in and around Yorktown in October 1781. George Washington's original field tents are a popular display, and youngsters of any age will enjoy a special children's exhibit of dioramas depicting soldier life from a young boy's point of view. Guided 30-minute walking tours of the battlefield and Yorktown are offered seasonally. Or, if you prefer, you can pick up a free map of the park at the center, which will help direct you on a 7- or 9-mile self-guided auto tour that winds through the siege lines and encampment areas of the 1781 battle. There is also a great bargain in the

Photo: Jamestown-Yorktown Foundation

Children can dress in 18th-century-style clothing in the children's discovery room of the Yorktown Victory Center.

recorded tour of the battlefield that can be rented with its own cassette player for just $2. The battlefield is open to pedestrian access from the visitors center, and a one-way road travels from the British fortifications through the Allies' lines to the Moore House and Surrender Field, then back into town. It's a fascinating drive, and there are opportunities to get out of the car and inspect the earthworks (but please do not climb or walk on them) and vistas. Admission to the center, the battlefields and the historic houses is $4 for adults 17 and older. Children 16 and younger are admitted free. The center is open daily from 8:30 AM to 5 PM (6 PM in the summer). The Moore and Nelson houses are open seasonally, so call ahead if you'd like to make visits to these historic homes part of your itinerary. During the spring, fall and winter, group reservations are accepted for guided walking tours. Please provide a 30-day notice.

## Yorktown Victory Center
**Old Va. Rt. 238, Yorktown • (757) 887-1776**

The history of the Revolutionary War and its culmination in the battle at Yorktown are told through a time line, thematic exhibits and living history interpretations at the center. The center, erected by the Commonwealth of Virginia in honor of the battle of Yorktown, is administered by the Jamestown-Yorktown Foundation, an agency of the Commonwealth.

The events that led to the revolution are chronicled along the "Road to Revolution," an open-air exhibit walkway that traces events leading to American independence. A time line, together with quotes and illustrations, explores the shifts in the relationship between Britain and the colonists from 1750 through 1776. This time line links four exhibit pavilions that focus on the events and issues that eventually culminated in the Revolutionary War.

Indoor galleries begin with "Witnesses to Revolution," which tells the stories of 10 people whose lives were greatly influenced by the American Revolution. The next exhibit, "Converging on Yorktown," uses artifacts, maps, weapons and documents relating to the Yorktown campaign to convey how Yorktown became the setting for the battle that won American independence. In this gallery, visitors can view *A Time of Revolution*, an 18-minute film shown every half-hour in the 200-seat Richard S. Reynolds Foundation Theater. The film, set in a nighttime encampment during the Siege of Yorktown, dramatizes recollections of soldiers and their officers. The next gallery, "Yorktown's Sunken Fleet" recounts the fascinating epic of British ships lost during the siege of 1781 with a number of artifacts recovered during underwater excavations. The re-created bow of the British supply ship Betsy serves as the exhibit's centerpiece.

In the Mathews Gallery, the exhibit, "A Soldier's Lot: Military Life and Medicine in the Revolutionary Era," relates the experiences of ordinary soldiers using military items, while "The Unfinished Revolution" recounts the steps that led to adopting the U.S. Constitution and Bill of Rights. "A Children's Kaleidoscope" offers youngsters a chance to try on history by donning 18th-century-style clothing or checking out the tent of a Continental Army private.

The center also boasts an outdoor re-creation of a Continental Army camp that gives visitors a real feel for how soldiers lived and how war was fought in the 1700s. Military drills and musket and cannon firing are demonstrated, and would-be surgeons wield their medical knives as they would have on the Revolutionary battlefields. Be advised that visitors often are drafted into service and may be called upon to fire a musket or serve on a cannon crew.

Of special interest is the outdoor, year-round re-enactment of life on a typical 18th-century Tidewater farm. The setting for the re-enactment includes a tobacco barn, log kitchen, crop fields and a vegetable and herb garden. In May 1997, a typical wood-framed, one-story house joined the agrarian landscape. Interpreters present farming methods, gardening, candle making, flax and wool preparation and 18th-century games, often involving visitors in the activities. Most intriguing to visitors is the fact that these interpreters do everything the way it was done in the 1700s — from starting fires with flint and stone to using pails rather than hoses to water gardens to chopping wood on the stump of a tree. Interpreters also use monthly journals kept by Yorktown's early farmers as a reference for growing crops, while the pottery pieces employed in the kitchen are authentic re-creations of the era. In fact, about 90 percent of the products used in demonstrations throughout the year are produced at the farm. Outside purchases include only seeds, supplemental food, some additional flax, animal feed and a few spices.

In early 1995, the Yorktown Victory Center completed a major expansion and renovation that had begun two years earlier. The $3.86 million renovation of the main exhibit building included the design and fabrication of new exhibits to broaden the museum's theme to include the formation of a new government after the Revolution and to interpret the war from varied points of view.

A changing exhibition at The Victory Center is "The Washingtons of Colonial Virginia." Marking the 200th anniversary of the death of George Washington, the exhibit focuses on his ancestors in Virginia and their role in the history of the colony. Although not equal in wealth or social status to Virginia's greatest planter families, the Washingtons played a part in colonial government and significant historical events such as Bacon's Rebellion. This exhibit lasts from June 4, 1999, to February 28, 2000.

A special lecture, "George Washington and the Virginia Frontier, 1748-1758," will be presented by Shenandoah University history professor Dr. Warren Hofstra at 7:30 PM on June 22.

The Victory Center is open daily from 9 AM to 5 PM, except Christmas and New Year's Day. For everyone except residents of Williamsburg and James City and York coun-

ties, an admission fee is charged. The fee is $7.25 for adults and $3.50 for children ages 6 through 12. The best deal is to purchase the combination ticket — $14 for adults and $6.75 for children — also entitling you to enter Jamestown Settlement, which re-creates the life of the first English colony in the New World. Although you must tour the site when you purchase your ticket that day, your ticket for the other attraction is good for a year from the date of purchase.

## U.S. Coast Guard Reserve Training Center

**Route 238, Yorktown • 898-3500**

Located on a small peninsula near the mouth of the York River, the Reserve Training Center site is rich in history, with the original village of Yorke located nearby in the early 1600s. In 1691, the port of Yorktown was chartered a few miles upriver. But Yorktown's moment in history, of course, was to occur on Sept. 28, 1781, when an army of Colonial and French soldiers set out from Williamsburg to lay siege to the British army that had fortified the seaport hamlet. Twenty-one days later, Washington defeated British General Cornwallis and his regiments. The surrender of the British to American forces was signed in the Moore House, located just outside the entrance to the Reserve Training Center.

This site was first used for training when the U.S. Navy established its Mine Warfare School here in 1940. The Coast Guard took possession of the site in July 1959.

Annually, the training center offers more than 100 courses to more than 6,000 U.S. Coast Guard active duty, reserve, civilian and auxiliary personnel, employees of numerous state and federal agencies, and members of allied nations. Additionally, teams from Yorktown provide training to coast guards and navies all over the world, visiting more than 50 countries a year. In February 1996, the Performance Technology Center was established under the Training Center command to better identify and implement the most appropriate solution to Coast Guard performance problems. The center provides computer-based training, job aids, videos, correspondence courses and distant learning as well as traditional resident training.

The schools located at the training center have grown from the original Officer Candidate and Marine Safety Schools to 17 schools, including the Contingency Preparedness School,, Marine Science Technician School, Inspection and Investigation Schools and others. The training center also is responsible for producing and maintaining correspondence courses and examinations for 50 nonresident courses offered.

Visitors are allowed on the center grounds for informal, self-guided driving tours between the hours of 9 AM and 5 PM daily. You must present a picture identification at the gate upon arrival.

## Victory Monument
**Historic Main St., Yorktown • (757) 898-3400**

On October 29, 1781, a resolution of the Continental Congress made a call for a Yorktown Monument to the Alliance and Victory. It was to be a century, however, before the cornerstone was laid on October 18, 1881. The monument is the record of the centennial celebration that took place in the town that year. The stirring inscriptions around its base are worth investigating, and there is a convenient parking lot across the street so you may walk over to do so. The monument has been struck by lightning several times, causing damage to the very top of the figure of Victory, so don't be surprised at the lightning rod added to prevent additional damage. For information, contact the Park Service at the number above.

## The Watermen's Museum
**309 Water St., Yorktown • (757) 887-2641**

Right on the York River, The Watermen's Museum preserves and interprets the long history of Tidewater Virginians' working relationship with the water and its bounties. The museum features an excellent and growing collection of artifacts, literature, exhibits and photographs depicting crabbers, oyster harvesters and clammers at work on the Chesapeake Bay and its tributaries from the original Native American fishermen down to the present. On the grounds, you can see a deadrise workboat,

a 100-year-old log canoe and other traditional equipment once so common on our waters. Programs, seminars, activities and special events are available to the public throughout the museum's season, which runs from early April through mid-December.

The main building of the museum is a 1935 Colonial Revival house; a masterpiece of engineering that was floated 3 miles across the York River from its original site in Gloucester County in 1987. The house now is a handsome and fitting tribute to the generations of men and women in the area who gained their livelihood from the water. A later expansion added a second building overlooking the York River, designed for additional exhibits, public lectures and educational programming. A renovated Carriage House, which also was brought from Gloucester to Yorktown and features an expansive dock overlooking the York River, can be rented for wedding receptions, private parties and meetings.

At $3 for adults and $1 for students, admission to The Watermen's Museum is a bargain. Groups may make arrangements to visit any time — even during the off-season — by calling in advance. Discounted rates are offered for group tours. The museum is open to the general public from early April through mid-December. Hours are 10 AM to 4 PM Tuesday through Saturday and 1 to 4 PM Sunday. Please also see our Shopping section below for information on the museum's outstanding gift shop.

## York River Cruises
**Watermen's Museum Dock, 309 Water St., Yorktown • (757) 879-8276, (804) 693-8276, (804) 642-5096**

From Memorial Day through October, weather permitting, you can head to the Watermen's Museum Dock and climb aboard the Miss Yorktown for either a day-long fishing excursion or an evening river cruise. The boat is piloted by Captain David Laurier. Fishing trips begin at 8 AM and run to 2 or 4 PM, depending upon which run you choose. The exception is Thursday, which offers a half-day fishing trip from 8 AM to noon. Depending on the season, the weather and a number of other variables, you can expect to catch just about

Photo: Jamestown-Yorktown Foundation

Young visitors prepare for battle at Jamestown Settlement's re-created fort.

anything the York River has to offer such as flounder, croaker and gray trout. Cost is $30 for the eight-hour excursion, $25 for the six-hour trip and $20 for the four-hour outing on Thursdays. (Children younger than 12 pay half-price.) Tackle and squid are included in the cost, bloodworms are available for purchase, and a license is not required.

Friday, Saturday and Sunday evening river cruises are about 1½-hours long, and reservations are required. The narrated cruise takes you past the sights and sounds of Yorktown while you learn about its military bases, its role during times of war and the history of the community. Cost of the river cruise is $10 for adults and $5 for children ages 6 to 12. This seasonal excursion requires a minimum number of guests before it leaves the dock, so inquire ahead of time to make sure the boat is running.

# Restaurants

### The River Room
**$ • Duke of York Motor Hotel, 508 Water St., Yorktown • (757) 898-5270**

This small, clean restaurant looks across the parking lot at Yorktown Beach and the York River beyond. It serves breakfast and lunch (sandwiches, seafood and pasta) year round at reasonable prices.

### Nick's Seafood Pavilion
**$$ • Water St., Yorktown • (757) 887-5269**

This restaurant is practically a historic site itself. Undergoing several enlargements since its founding in the 1940s, Nick's is named after the late founder, a patriot dedicated to hon-

# Price Guidelines

**$Dinner for two less than $20**
**$$Dinner for two between $20 and $35**

Credit cards are accepted at these restaurants unless we have noted otherwise.

oring the importance of the town. Today it is managed by the Yorktown Education Foundation.

The restaurant is truly chock-full of amazing items. There are huge crystal chandeliers and ballroom mirrors dating to the era of lavish style in hotels and restaurants; they are kept company by huge paintings and numerous allegorical statues throughout the dining rooms, culminating in the fountain pool of the Nile Room.

The service is equally lavish and reminiscent of a grander style than is practiced in most restaurants today. Greek-costumed waitstaff give professional attention throughout the meal, and busboys in uniform scurry through the dining rooms bearing huge trays. The house salad is a bargain, with fresh vegetables in a wonderful dressing, and every kind of seafood imaginable is available — broiled, skewered, baked or fried to order, or served in a salad. We recommend the seafood shish kabob or the crabmeat à la Pavilion, but the other items on the menu are equally wonderful. There are non-seafood delicacies here as well. You can sample everything from whole pheasant in casserole and broiled quail Grecian style to French lamb chops and a variety of pasta dishes. A slice of rum cream pie or a baked Alaska will make a wonderful end to the meal if you still have room, and the coffee is among the best on the Peninsula.

On any given night, dress ranges from highly informal to very formal. No reservations are accepted, but the waiting line moves fast. The restaurant is open for lunch and dinner.

## Water Street Landing
**$$ • 524 Water St., Yorktown • (757) 886-5890**

A new addition to the Yorktown culinary scene, this eatery overlooking the York River serves lunch and dinner Tuesday through Sunday. A more casual lunch menu features specialty sandwiches, homemade pizzas, salads and a quiche, lasagna and soup of the day. Dinner offers a variety of entrees, from steaks and chicken to pasta and whatever seafood is available fresh that day. Among the changing items on the menu are crabcake sandwiches, Water Street shrimp over pasta in a white wine sauce, poached Atlantic salmon with a creamy dill sauce and a variety of clam and oyster dishes.

## Yorktown Pub
**$, no credit cards • 540 Water St., Yorktown • (757) 886-9964**

This popular beachfront restaurant doubles as watering hole and social center for area folks, tourists and the many military people stationed nearby. As a good beach pub should be, it's very casual, with plenty of jeans in evidence, knotty pine walls and worn wooden booths. A good assortment of food comprises the menu, with raw or steamed clams and oysters, steamed shrimp and other finger foods, salads and soups and entrees such as steak, scallops and soft-shell crabs. Deli sandwiches and pub specialty sandwiches are also available, with late-night snacks served until 1 AM.

# Accommodations

Credit cards are accepted at these lodging facilities unless otherwise noted.

## Duke of York Motor Hotel
**508 Water St., Yorktown • (757) 898-3232**

This three-story motel is the only one you'll find with rooms facing the beautiful York River. There's a nice swimming pool in the cool courtyard on the side away from the river. Connecting rooms can be provided upon advance request. In July, the rate for a basic double is $71 (off-season it's $60), very reasonable considering that you have a water view, beach access, all of the Yorktown history to explore and the beautiful Colonial Parkway with its scenic 20-minute drive to Williamsburg and

Jamestown. Breakfast and lunch are served in the hotel's River Room, mentioned in our previous section on restaurants.

## Yorktown Motor Lodge
**8829 George Washington Hwy. • (757) 898-5451**

On U.S. Route 17, the main highway leading into Yorktown, this 42-room motel was remodeled in 1994. You will find pleasantly furnished rooms complete with a microwave and refrigerator. Outside, there's a pool for cooling off after a summer's day of sightseeing. Rates are reasonable (about $45 for double occupancy in summer), and AAA and AARP discounts are offered.

## Marl Inn
**220 Church St., Yorktown • (757) 898-3859**

This bed and breakfast, which opened in September 1996, has two rooms with double beds and private baths and two full suites, each with a kitchenette, living room, bedroom and bath. Innkeeper Eugene Marlin (hence, the name of the inn) built the Colonial-style two-story house in 1977, then added three rooms before opening his inn. Marl Inn serves a "continental plus" breakfast, featuring quiche, cereals, fresh fruit, coffee and tea. Complimentary bicycles are available for guests. Nightly rates are $95 for the rooms and $120 for suites. (See our Bed and Breakfasts chapter for more details.)

# Shopping

## Nancy Thomas Gallery
**145 Ballard St., Yorktown • (757) 898-0738**

A master folk artist with a national reputation (Whoopi Goldberg once commissioned a set of 12 monthly plaques) and a presence in museums and films (her work can be seen in Jessica Lange's apartment in *Tootsie*), Nancy Thomas calls Yorktown her home. This fascinating shop is where you will find her nationally acclaimed works on display: paintings, wood plaques and sculptures, freestanding whimsical animals, angels, trees, wreaths, Christmas decorations and a variety of textiles

and ceramics. In addition, she showcases the work of a number of national artists who display and sell their work in the gallery. You will find their beautiful work in textiles, pottery, painting and other media. The gallery also carries primitive antiques and a line of custom upholstered furniture created by a California artist. A second Nancy Thomas Gallery opened in Williamsburg's Merchants Square in 1997. Hours at the Yorktown store are Monday through Saturday from 10 AM to 5 PM and Sunday from 1 to 5 PM.

## On the Hill Cultural Arts Center
**121 Alexander Hamilton Blvd., Yorktown • (757) 898-3076**

Sponsored by the Yorktown Arts Foundation, this arts gallery offers exhibits of more than 60 regional artists working in a variety of media. The gallery was started back in 1976, when a contingent of art-minded people each tossed 10 bucks in a hat to start the ball rolling. For more than two decades, the center has helped thousands of visitors become familiar with the engaging work of local artists. It offers changing monthly exhibits and provides workshops and classes to children in York County schools. Hours are Tuesday through Saturday from 11 AM to 5 PM and Sunday from noon to 5 PM.

## Gallery on the Green
**Main St., Yorktown • (757) 989-0191**

Also operated by the Yorktown Arts Foundation, this gallery, which features the work of local artists, offers fine arts and crafts. Look for outdoor exhibits during the summer. Hours are Tuesday through Saturday 11 AM to 4 PM and Sunday noon to 3 PM.

## Period Designs
**401 Main St., Yorktown • (757) 886-9482**

Stop in and check out the wide variety of reproductions of 17th- and 18th-century decorative arts. This shop carries fine floor coverings, ceramics and furniture as well as items in tin, brass, leather, iron and glass. Its framing service is museum quality. Hours are Tuesday through Saturday 10 AM to 5 PM and Sunday 1 to 5 PM.

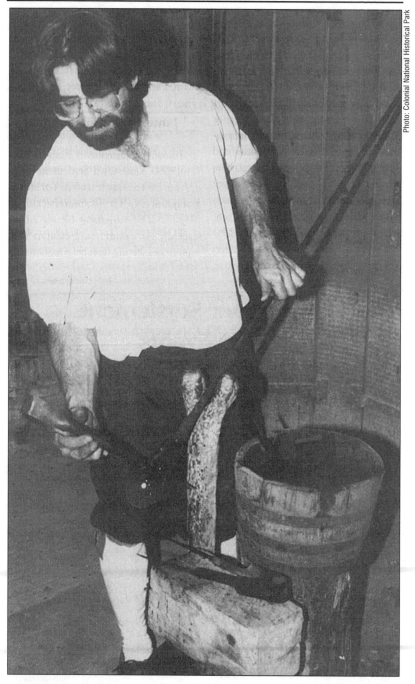

A skilled craftsman demonstrates the art of glassblowing at the Jamestown Glasshouse

## Swan Tavern Antiques
**300 Main St., Yorktown • (757) 898-3033**

This fine shop, housed in a charming re-created structure, offers one of the finest collections of antiques in the area. The collection concentrates on 18th-century English items and oak furniture, candlesticks, prints and accessories. The items are of the highest quality, and each is a prize find. Hours are Tuesday through Saturday from 10 AM to 5 PM. It's open noon to 5 PM Sunday.

## The Watermen's Museum Gift Shop
**309 Water St., Yorktown • (757) 888-2623**

This excellent shop on the museum's grounds offers a variety of interesting and unusual items, showcasing local artists and artisans and featuring items related to the water. You will find many pieces in here to be cherished as high-quality souvenirs or as gifts for those to whom Yorktown and the Chesapeake Bay are important. The work of a local artist, craftsperson or author is featured each month.

## The Yorktown Shoppe
**402 Main St., Yorktown • (757) 898-2984**

In this small shop you will find a number of items appropriate to the setting and period to which Yorktown is a monument. There are fine carvings and paintings, replica and whimsical houses, pierced lanterns, Colonial history dolls, Old World Santas, special clothes, a variety of wrought-iron items and the extremely popular Old World balance toys, in which a figure balances on a horizontal bar. Hours are 10 AM to 5 PM Monday through Saturday and 1 to 5 PM every other Sunday.

Kidsburg is a perfect place where little ones can burn off some energy in a fun, unique setting that challenges their minds and bodies.

# Kidstuff

"There's nothing to do in this place!" It's the perennial cry of young people in the area. You'd think the name of the city was Williamsbored. They have a pretty good case, though. Since most of the emphasis here is on history and shopping, there are few places for young people to go for plain old fun with their peers. Teenagers especially have major cause to complain. School dances, parties at homes, the movies and heading for the Peninsula's malls traditionally have been about the only options for them.

Happily, the situation is improving for youngsters and teens. Kidsburg, a community-developed children's playground, opened about five years ago at Mid-County Park on Ironbound Road near Route 5. And the James City County-Williamsburg Community Center, formerly the local recreation center, has been expanded and renovated and now offers a drug-free, alcohol-free gathering place off Longhill Road for local teens.

If you have a bored young person in your house or traveling with you, you ought to check out these places and see if there isn't something to do after all. With a little advance planning, creative options abound.

Let's begin with the major options. Flip back a few pages and check out our detailed sections on Busch Gardens and Water Country USA in the Attractions chapter. If you arrive here and your kids haven't begged you to take them to Busch Gardens or Water Country USA, they must have had their noses buried in their schoolbooks deeper than you thought. Few kids arrive in the area without scoping out information on tickets and hours for these two immensely popular theme parks, both owned and operated by Busch Entertainment Corp.

One is for landlubbers, while the other, as its name suggests, is a super place to spend a hot, sultry summer day. Kids love these parks and can spend hours - even whole days - safely entertained within.

Colonial Williamsburg offers a variety of activities for kids. The Powell House re-creates the daily life of a Colonial family, and participants learn how they might have lived in the 18th century by performing tasks as well as observing. Colonial games are played at several locations in the Historic Area, and kids can try their skill at trundling the hoop, stilt walking, jumping rope, lawn bowling, nine pins, leap frog, blind man's bluff and other games. At Robertson's Windmill, visiting children help with seasonal farm chores. During the summer, hands-on activities include doing laundry, making soap or dipping candles. Those more inclined to dirtying clothes rather than washing them will enjoy the Carpenter's Yard, where young helpers can tread clay in the pit in preparation for brickmaking. For more details about what the Historic Area has to offer, see our chapter on Colonial Williamsburg, check the information offered by the Visitor Center or call 229-1000 to inquire about a given day's activities.

The Jamestown-Yorktown Foundation offers summer history activities for children at Jamestown Settlement and the Yorktown Victory Center. Programs change annually and vary according to age group, but children ages 4 through 16 can always find something of interest amid the array of entertaining, educational programs offered daily. One of the more popular programs in summer 1997 was "Consider the Source," a five-day, hands-on program that dealt with navigation, archaeology and generally why settlers came to Jamestown. Programs are held at both Jamestown and the Yorktown Victory Center. Advance registration usually is required. For detailed information about programs and registration, call 253-4939.

Those are the biggies - the ones that have made this area. What follows is a list of attractions that don't get the same kind of spotlight, but by no means pale in comparison.

# Amusement Parks and Minigolf

## Go-Karts Plus
**6910 Richmond Rd. • (757) 564-7600**

If you've shopped all day at the Pottery and the kids are demanding something a little more exciting, try Go-Karts Plus. This thrills and spills park, located a softball's throw west of the Williamsburg Pottery Factory on Route 60, features bumper boats, miniature golf, rides and video games. And it must rate high with kids and teens because the place is always packed.

Admission and parking, which is ample, are free. Rides are paid for with tickets purchased at a counter. You'll pay $1.25 per ticket and use one to five tickets per ride. Discount books, good for the season or as long as you're in town, can help reduce the cost of the rides. There's a $20 value pack that includes 20 tickets. Summer hours are 11 AM to roughly 11 PM. Spring and fall hours vary according to the weather, so call in advance to avoid disappointing the troops.

## Kidsburg
**Mid County Park, 3793 Ironbound Rd.**
**• (757) 229-1232**

Kidsburg is the best deal of all when it comes to finding a place where little ones can burn off some energy and let loose without fear of breaking something in the motel room.

For years to come, many Insiders will drive by Mid County Park and smile with pride as they think, "I helped build that!" They sure did. A lot of them. A whole lot of them. In fact, in May 1994, well more than 1,000 volunteers pitched in and turned an empty grassy site into a play environment unlike any that local kids had experienced before. It was certainly unlike most the builders had ever conceived, let alone raised. They built a challenge to children's minds and physical skills.

The committee worked closely with James City County officials and Learning Structures, a professional firm that meets with local planners around the country and designs one-of-a-kind playgrounds to match local needs. They held a series of public hearings to get community input for the design of the playground and to address concerns about safety, access, level of challenge and other issues.

Today, you'll see the structure swarming with kids enjoying the mock-ups of the Jamestown Settlement's ship *Susan Constant*, the James Fort Tot Lot, the George P. Coleman Memorial Bridge and two theaters.

## Mini-Golf America
**1901 Richmond Rd. • (757) 229-7200**

Mini-Golf America is another place packed with kids all season. This compact and attractive, yet somewhat challenging, miniature golf course, is nestled next door to Wendy's. If you drive by too fast you might miss it, so observe the speed limit and have the future golfers in the backseat keep an eye out.

Summer hours at this one-course attraction are from 1 to around 10:30 PM. September and October hours depend on the weather but generally run weekdays from 5 to 8 or 9 PM, Saturdays and Sundays from 1 to 8 or 9 PM. If in doubt and to check it out, call the above number.

# Planes, Trains, Etc.

## Jamestown Explorer
**Jamestown Yacht Basin, 2080 Jamestown Rd. • (757) 259-0400**

If your youngster is adventuresome and has had his or her fill of theme parks, they may enjoy cruising around historic Jamestown Island on the Jamestown Explorer, a flat-bottom boat that meanders around the old island so passengers can view native flora and fauna. The 90-minute cruise is different each time you sail, so don't be afraid to take a repeat ride after you've done it once. The boat leaves from Jamestown Yacht Basin at 11 AM and 1 and 3 PM daily, weather permitting. Advance reservations are not required. It's a good idea to call and see if the boat will sail at the time you prefer before you make the trek to Jamestown. Tickets are $12.50 for adults, $8 for kids and $10 for senior citizens.

## Williamsburg-Jamestown Airport
**100 Marclay Rd. • (757) 253-8185**

Photo: Colonial Williamsburg

The Felicity in Williamsburg program allows girls 5 to 12 to walk in the footsteps of American Girls Collection's Felicity Merriman and learn to sew, dance and curtsey.

If time allows and you're game, you can treat your youngsters to a different view of greater Williamsburg. Even teens will get excited at the prospect of taking a Historic Air Tour, offered at the Williamsburg-Jamestown Airport. Several different tours are offered. The Peninsula Tour runs 35 minutes and $35 per person. The James River Tour heads towards Richmond, lasts 55 minutes and costs $45 per person. The Hampton Roads Tour covers Norfolk and everywhere in between, lasts 55 minutes and is $45 per person. The plane holds three passengers. It's a good idea to make reservations a day or two in advance.

### America's Railroads on Parade
**The Village Shops at Kingsmill,**
**1915 Pocahontas Tr. • (757) 220-8725**

A viewing treat for kids of all ages is the spectacular exhibit, "America's Railroads on Parade," in the Village Shops at Kingsmill. The exhibit features more than 4,000 square feet of multilevel model train layouts, including classic and collectible trains, porcelain buildings and a hands-on model railroading exhibit. The layouts are chock-full of non-railroad miniatures that add to the authenticity of the exhibit by re-creating scenes from the late 1930s through the 1950s, such as New York's World's Fair. There are so many things to see in the miniature worlds re-created here that several return visits are in order. In addition to the exhibit, the site offers limited edition train-inspired art and a variety of gifts. There is a charge to view the exhibit. Hours are seasonal, so call the previously listed number before visiting.

### Peninsula Model Railroad Club
**Lee Hall C&O Station, 17426 Warwick**
**Blvd., Newport News • (757) 722-7905**

For those would-be engineers whose in-

---

**INSIDERS' TIP**

Williamsburg-James City County Schools and the James City County-Williamsburg Recreation Center have instructions for phone calls to the North Pole during the week or so before Christmas. Kids younger than 7 can speak with Santa, Mrs. Claus or an elf by calling 229-5676.

terest is more hands-on, the Peninsula Model Railroad Club meets at 8 PM every Thursday at the Lee Hall C&O Station. It's right on Route 60 east of Williamsburg. The club runs 13 model trains and one trolley in the old station and opens to the public for demonstrations several times during the year. Call 722-7905 for information.

# The Great Outdoors

**www.insiders.com**

See this and many other **Insiders' Guide** destinations online.

**Visit us today!**

## Little Creek Reservoir Park
**180 Lake View Dr. • (757) 566-1702**

If your child likes to fish and wants to try his luck at another fishing hole, consider taking a morning or afternoon to do just that at Little Creek Reservoir Park. Bring your own rod and cast your line off the 91-foot boat dock or the 104-foot fishing pier. There is no charge for fishing off the pier. Or, rent a johnboat for $8 and troll out to fish in deeper waters. A Virginia fishing license is required for persons older than 16. However, the park does not sell licenses.

Don't forget to bring a lunch (just in case your morning of fishing only rewards you with a story about the one that got away). There are grills where you can heat up your grub, and picnic tables where you can enjoy your spread. The park is located about 15 minutes west of Williamsburg and is open 7 AM until sunset during the week and 6 AM to sunset on weekends, March through November. On winter weekends it is open from 7 AM to 5 PM.

## Waller Mill Park
**Airport Rd. • (757) 220-6178**

Spend a day outside enjoying nature and getting some exercise at Waller Mill Park, one of the best kept secrets in the area. Here families can rent pedal boats and canoes or sim-

ply go fishing or hiking as they please. A freshwater fishing license is required for anyone older than 16 and can be purchased at the park. Virginia residents can purchase a five-day license for $5.50, while a nonresident will pay $6.50. Senior citizens 65 and older pay $1.50. The park offers a fitness trail and a hiking trail. Also, the Dogwood Bike Trail is a rugged, 4.5-mile loop that offers a challenging ride for bicyclists. Pack a picnic lunch and plan to enjoy a repast under one of four large picnic shelters. Ball fields and playground equipment also are located here, so kids of all ages can play hard or simply relax as they prefer. It's a lot of country just a few miles from the city's restored area. Call the above number for details.

## Yorktown Waterfront
**Water St. • no phone**

On a warm, sunny day, what child doesn't enjoy a trip to the beach? And a trip to the small, yet inviting, Yorktown waterfront offers a wonderful change of pace for traveling families. The beach stretches about 2 miles along the York River. A large picnic area is located east of the beach, so carrying lunch is an option. Several restaurants within walking distance also are open during the day should hunger strike. Public restrooms are available at the west end of the beach and are open from early morning until after supper. Several trees can offer escape from the midday sun and a boardwalk, really a sidewalk, can take you from one end of the beach to the other. Lifeguards are on duty from Memorial Day to Labor Day.

Kids find it fascinating to watch locals fish and crab from the pier at the east end of the beach, which is before you get to the picnic area. The pier once led to an underwater cofferdam where divers investigated remains of

## INSIDERS' TIP

**Headhunters Headquarters, 7852 Richmond Road, sells fishing licenses. The store is located about a half-mile from Waller Mill Park. Everyone older than 16 must have a license to fish.**

H20 UFO is Water Country USA's newest and largest interactive kids area.

Revolutionary War era ships sunk off the shore. Diving is no longer done there, but the pier remains for fishing use only. Now people tie chicken legs to crab pots and slowly lower them into the water to the river bottom. Inevitably, a short while later, they hoist the wire baskets to find wiggling crabs eating the bait.

The pier, difficult to miss, is located across Water Street from Cornwallis' Cave, another attraction sure to interest your young ones. Punch the button on the cave wall, and you hear the story of the role the cave played during the Siege of Yorktown during the American Revolution.

# Camps, Concerts and Classes

## James City County Library
**7770 Croaker Rd. • (757) 259-3200**

A little farther up the road, the James City County Library, west of Norge, offers yet another series of free options for children of all ages.

The library, also a part of the Williamsburg Regional system, offers a summer reading program, as well as special kids programs throughout the week. Puppets, crafts, story times, special videos and even a program about snakes, including a visit by one of the creatures, are part of the wide array of interesting activities offered. For more information, call the number above.

## James City County Parks and Recreation
**5301 Longhill Rd. • (757) 220-4700**

James City County Parks and Recreation offers myriad programs for young residents. Summer playgrounds have fun things to do for toddlers, while Total Rec camps for 5- to 14-year-olds offer full-day programs including field trips, swimming, reading, sports, games, arts and crafts and special events. Specialty camps for children ages 5 to 16 focus on specific themes that are studied with a hands-on approach. Registration opens in the spring, and slots fill early. For information on other recreation and sports programs, check out our

Photo: Busch Gardens Williamsburg

Busch Gardens' Land of The Dragons offers more than an acre of activities and fun for younger guests.

Parks and Recreation chapter, or call the number listed above.

## Muscarelle Museum of Art
**Jamestown Rd.** • **(757) 221-2703**

Each year, the Muscarelle Museum of Art offers eight classes in the Gallery Studio summer session, with students in preschool through 10th grade eligible to participate. Each class uses art on display in the museum as inspiration for its activities. The museum offers two other similar sessions during the year. Call for current information on this program and details about scholarships that might apply.

## The Williamsburg Regional Library
**515 Scotland St.** • **(757) 229-7646**

When the lights are on and it's open for business, The Williamsburg Regional Library provides services for children from birth through high school. Note, however, that the facility closes each Friday. Plan your trip here accordingly.

Programming at the library is designed to promote the love of reading and to increase language skills among children. It includes story time for preschoolers and early elementary school children, author visits, children's theater groups, professional storytellers, puppet theaters, workshops and arts and crafts. And best of all, it's usually free.

## The Williamsburg Symphonia
**312 Waller Mill Rd.** • **(757) 229-9857**

The Williamsburg Symphonia offers eight youth concerts annually in addition to its regular subscription series. Reservations are on a first-come, first-served basis. Information on the concerts can be obtained from the Symphonia at the above number.

Throughout the academic year, the College of William and Mary offers outstanding talent both from within its ranks and from among the best performers throughout the world.

# The Arts

If you have a passion for - or even a friendly interest in - the creative arts, the Historic Triangle offers plenty to see, hear and do. There are several museums and galleries in the area that display the visual arts. From fall through late spring, cultural events provide ample entertainment in the performing arts, and special shows and festivals feature both the visual and performing arts throughout the year. A recent and very popular addition to the arts scene is First Night, an alcohol-free New Year's Eve Celebration of the Arts, with performances staged at several venues in the heart of the city. For information on this and other yearly events, we recommend you read our Annual Events chapter.

## Venues

Two Williamsburg venues are the sites of the majority of the fine performances produced in the city. Phi Beta Kappa Memorial Hall, facing Jamestown Road on the campus of the College of William and Mary, two blocks west of Merchants Square, has the larger theater and hosts many of the major performances on the arts calendar. The Williamsburg Regional Library has a smaller theater and hosts small symphonic and dramatic events as well as a variety of other performances by classical and popular artists.

### Phi Beta Kappa Memorial Hall
**College of William and Mary, Jamestown Rd. • (757) 221-2655, box office 221-2674**
This hall is venue for a variety of performances, lectures and forums of the highest quality, with the College of William and Mary the most frequent sponsor. The college's theater department - whose graduates include Glenn Close and Linda Lavin - offers a high-quality season of performances here during the academic year, and the music and dance departments provide concerts of equally fine

caliber. The William and Mary Concert Series held in the hall is a subscription series of performances by nationally and internationally acclaimed performers and groups presenting symphonies, ballet, chamber music, theater and solo performances. Ticket sales are publicized in the fall. Think ahead - tickets go very quickly.

### Williamsburg Regional Library Art Center
**515 Scotland St. • (757) 229-7326**
The library has done an extraordinary job of becoming, in effect, the community's cultural center and intellectual focus. In the Art Center's lobby there are small ongoing exhibits by visual artists working in a variety of media. The auditorium provides venue for lectures, debates, forums and performances of all kinds, from symphonies, chamber concerts and choral presentations to high-school-band rock 'n' roll. The Art Center's emphasis is on providing enriching, educational programming for the community. The library is open Monday through Thursday and Saturday from 10 AM to 6 PM. It is closed Friday and Sunday. Events held here are typically free, but occasionally an event organized by an outside group will charge a minimal fee.

## Performing Arts

### Music

Symphonic, operatic and recital performances by touring professionals and virtuoso students from the College of William and Mary's music department are presented throughout the year at Phi Beta Kappa Memorial Hall. Williamsburg also is home to several professional and skilled amateur musical groups, each presenting a varied program throughout the season. The venues differ depending upon the performance. The best way to get timely information is to monitor the *Virginia Gazette*'s arts and performance sections.

## Capriole
**P.O. Box 558, Williamsburg VA 23187-0558 • (757) 220-1248**

This vocal and instrumental ensemble specializes in Baroque and Renaissance chamber music and dance. Throughout the year, Capriole offers community outreach performances for schools, civic groups and retirement communities and workshops on early music and dance. The season ends in February. For ticket information and times, please call the number listed above.

## Williamsburg Symphonia
**312 Waller Mill Rd. • (757) 229-9857**

The Williamsburg Symphonia offers four concerts by subscription and is noted throughout the region for the excellence of its programs. Maestro Ruben Vartanyan directs the professional chamber orchestra, and a number of outstanding solo artists perform with the ensemble for specific programs. Most performances are at Phi Beta Kappa Memorial Hall, but some occur elsewhere in the area. The Williamsburg Symphonia is helping to cultivate new generations of music lovers with its annual programs that open classical music performances to students in all area schools.

## Williamsburg Choral Guild
**P.O. Box 440, Williamsburg VA 23187-0440 • (757) 220-1808**

Formed in 1975, the Williamsburg Choral Guild offers concerts in the fall and spring under the direction of Genevieve McGiffert. The group is known for its gala Christmas holiday season concert and its equally grand spring event, usually held at a local church. Call the number listed for information about auditions, concert dates and tickets.

## Williamsburg Women's Chorus
**P.O. Box 685, Williamsburg VA 23187-0685 • (757) 220-1537**

The Williamsburg Women's Chorus is an all-volunteer group of 40 women who come together to sing in a variety of musical styles. Since 1992, the group has been under the direction of Cindy Freeman. They rehearse at the Williamsburg United Methodist Church Thursday mornings from 9:30 to 11:30 AM. The chorus performs throughout the greater Williamsburg area. Auditions are required of aspiring new members.

## Summer Breeze
**Merchants Square • (757) 259-3224, 259-3200**

A popular and informal arts offering is the Summer Breeze Jazz on the Square that features performances of America's original art form on Wednesday nights during the summer. Attendees are invited to bring folding chairs and blankets for these outdoor performances on Merchants Square from 6:15 to 7:30 PM. A temporary stage is set up in front of the Christmas Shop, and the whole spectrum of music, from folk to jazz to Big Band sounds, delights listeners. Summer Breeze Jazz on the Square is a joint effort of the Merchants Square Association, the City of Williamsburg and James City County.

## College of William and Mary
**Phi Beta Kappa Memorial Hall, Jamestown Rd. • (757) 221-2655, box office 221-2674**

Throughout the academic year, the college offers outstanding talent both from within its ranks and from among the best performers throughout the world. The varied offerings are most frequently offered at Phi Beta Kappa Memorial Hall, but occasionally performances are at other venues. It's best to check the *Virginia Gazette*'s arts and performance listings or call the numbers given above to obtain accurate details on particular performances.

## INSIDERS' TIP

**The Chamber Ballet Company's annual Christmas season performance of *The Nutcracker* is so popular that the company has had to add performances from year to year. Call 229-1717 for information and an early choice of tickets.**

Photo: Colonial Williamsburg

The DeWitt Wallace Decorative Arts Gallery displays pieces of Colonial Williamsburg's permanent collection.

Ticket prices vary widely depending on whether the performance involves students, local talent, a touring company or professionals, but they typically run between $10 and $29.

During the academic year, the first-class William and Mary Concert Series hosts nationally and internationally renowned performing groups, which over the years have included the New York City Opera National Company, the Alvin Ailey American Dance Theater, Jazz at Lincoln Center and a variety of other performers from around the world. This is a subscription series, but seats are sometimes available. To get information on these seats for a particular performance, call the number listed.

The William and Mary Chamber Orchestra holds outstanding performances of popular as well as rarely performed chamber works. For the schedule of their concerts, call 221-1086. The William and Mary Choir and Chorus give concerts in the fall and spring semesters, and The Botetourt Chamber Singers, an ensemble from the choir, gives concerts throughout the region.

The Jazz Ensemble, directed by Laura Rexroth, is a 21-piece big band that plays at college functions, conventions and the annual An Occasion for the Arts (see our Annual Events chapter). The Concert Band, founded in 1929, joins wind, brass and percussion instruments to play selections from 400 years of music.

The Ewell Concert Series, offering "Music at the Muscarelle," is noted for both the excellence and the intimacy of its performances at the Muscarelle Museum next door to Phi Beta Kappa Memorial Hall.

The Sinfonicron Light Opera Company, a student company, offers its single production in the spring, typically a Gilbert and Sullivan light operetta.

## Colonial Williamsburg
### Various locations • (757) 229-1000

Throughout the restored area, Colonial Williamsburg entertainers provide a variety of musical diversions on an almost nightly basis. You'll find more information in our Nightlife chapter, but, if your taste runs to music in a historical context, you might want to give special consideration to the following offerings. The number listed is the general information number for Colonial Williamsburg that can provide you with current information on performances, times and venues. The *Colonial Williamsburg Visitor's Companion*, available throughout the Historic Area and at the Colonial Williamsburg Visitor Center, also is an invaluable aid in identifying and selecting fine arts offerings.

A popular entertainment is to hear a chamber concert or see costumed dancers perform 18th-century dances during special programs in the candlelit hall of the Governor's Palace. Throughout the restored area, wandering minstrels regale guests with songs that were familiar to 18th-century inhabitants of the Colonial capital city. Troubadours, magicians and other entertainers also delight visitors at nightly gambols in select Historic Area taverns. From time to time, special performances by soloists, chamber groups and other Colonial Williamsburg artists are offered. The area is alive with the sound of music (sorry, just couldn't resist), so be sure to check with the Visitor's Center or scan a copy of the *Visitor's Companion*.

www.insiders.com

See this and many other **Insiders' Guide** destinations online.

Visit us today!

## Theater

Williamsburg enjoys Shakespeare's plays annually in a summer festival honoring the Bard. There are also very high quality classic and contemporary plays available throughout the year, compliments of the Williamsburg Players, who perform in their playhouse on Hubbard Lane. Another excellent season is offered by The William and Mary Theatre.

### The Virginia Shakespeare Festival
**Phi Beta Kappa Memorial Hall, Jamestown Rd. • (757) 221-2655, box office 221-2674**

This series has developed an enduring audience over the years. Sponsored each July by William and Mary's Theatre Department, the festival season of at least two plays offers a variety of the Bard's works. The plays are performed alternately so that those in town for

only a short period can attend a performance of each. The nightly curtain is at 8 PM, and there are also Sunday matinees. See our Annual Events chapter for more details about this summer tradition.

### The Williamsburg Players
**200 Hubbard Ln. • (757) 229-1679, reservations 229-0431**

From September through June, the Williamsburg Players produce plays of extraordinary quality in its cozy playhouse. The season usually consists of five plays, mixing little-known and more famous works, with emphasis on modern and contemporary authors. The casts are all volunteers, but the Players draw upon more than 30 years of experience, so don't let that put you off at all. Their staging and performances, thanks to their willingness to risk breaking conventions to advance their art, consistently receive the highest reviews and accolades. There are only 115 seats in the theater, and tickets go fast. General admission is $7, senior citizens and students pay $6, and children younger than 12 are $3. We recommend the season tickets as a guarantee of seating. As a patron, you'll have the added enjoyment of an opening-night reception.

### William and Mary's Department of Speech and Theatre
**Phi Beta Kappa Memorial Hall, Jamestown Rd. • (757) 221-2655, box office 221-2674, theater information 221-2660**

The college's students stage four plays during the academic year. Season subscribers may see all four shows for the price of three. Matinees are at 2 PM, and evening curtain is at 8 PM. In addition, plays performed, written and directed by students are presented

---

**INSIDERS' TIP**

Community members can get on the William and Mary Cultural Events Calendar mailing list. For information about this or general information about college-sponsored arts happenings, call 221-4000, the college's general information number.

in the Premiere Theater. The department usually stages one or two performances per semester. Tickets are around $7.

## Colonial Williamsburg's Company of Colonial Performers

**P.O. Drawer C, Williamsburg, VA 23187**
**• (757) 229-1000**

This company presents delightful comedies and farces of the Colonial era in repertory each season in the auditorium of the Williamsburg Lodge. Often bawdy, delightfully and authentically overacted, these works feature a lot of "playing to the audience," and the result is great 18<sup>th</sup>-century style fun for everyone. Admission is $10 but only $7.50 for holders of a Patriot's Pass.

## Dance

Fine dance performances are available in Williamsburg. The local dance companies listed below have entertained many enthralled audiences with excellent productions.

## Eastern Virginia School of the Performing Arts

**Village Shops at Kingsmill, 1915 Pocahontas Tr. • (757) 229-8535**

The school's curriculum under the direction of Sandra Balestracci assures the very highest quality instruction and performance in ballet, modern dance, jazz, tap, musical theater song and dance, ballroom and creative fitness (the last for boys only). Young dancers ages 3 to 6 also benefit from the school's special, creative pre-ballet and tap instruction designed for those ages. Two programs are offered to students: The Conservatory Program features intense study in a graded curriculum for those seeking intensive training, and the General Division offers study within a less-restricted framework. Call for a schedule of the

resident professional performing company's recitals.

## The Chamber Ballet Company

**Kingsgate Greene, 120-D Waller Mill Rd.**
**• (757) 229-1717**

Since 1968, The Chamber Ballet Company has offered professional training for all ages. The curriculum provides expert and experienced instruction to assure students the finest development of their skill in ballet, offering classes in creative dance, tap, jazz, floor gymnastics, character and ballet. Two productions are staged during the year and are very popular in the community. *The Nutcracker* at Christmastime is a tradition that's more than 15 years old, and another performance is staged during the year. Call the number listed above for information on upcoming recitals.

# Visual Arts

## Museums

## Abby Aldrich Rockefeller Folk Art Center

**307 S. England St. • (757) 220-7698**

Reopened in 1992 after a major expansion that tripled its exhibition space, this wonderful museum's holdings include an impressive array of 19th- and early 20th-century folk art. There are folk paintings and carvings, weather vanes, handmade toys and dollhouses, quilts, coverlets and counterpanes, earthenware, furniture, tinware, signboards and numerous other practical and whimsical items. Admission to the center is included in the price of your Colonial Williamsburg ticket. Admission without a Colonial Williamsburg ticket is $10 per adult and includes entrance to this center as well as the Dewitt mentioned below. See our chapter on Colonial Williamsburg for additional information.

## DeWitt Wallace Decorative Arts Gallery
**Public Hospital, Francis St. • (757) 220-7724**

It is difficult for visitors who have been in this gallery to reconcile its size and scope with the structure one sees from Francis Street in the Historic Area. Although the entrance is through the lobby of the reconstructed Public Hospital, this fascinating museum is housed mostly underground. It displays prized pieces of Colonial Williamsburg's permanent collection - furniture, textiles, maps, prints, paintings, metals and ceramics dating from the 1600s to about 1830 - in exhibits designed to instruct viewers in the aesthetics and tastes of the Colonial period. Perhaps the largest collection and premier interpreter of objects from the households of early America, the gallery mounts special exhibits for several years at a time to allow large numbers of visitors to view them. Thorough research precedes each showing, and the results are presented in understandable and memorable ways. The overall effect on gallery visitors is an understanding of each object in the context of its function, design and use.

An $10 admission fee is charged for those not holding passes to Colonial Williamsburg and is paid at the entrance. The gallery is open daily from 10 AM to 6 PM. There is a cafe onsite, and the entire museum is accessible to the handicapped. Read our chapter on Colonial Williamsburg for more information.

## Joseph and Margaret Muscarelle Museum Of Art
**Jamestown Rd. • (757) 221-2700**

In the evening, this museum, just west of Phi Beta Kappa Memorial Hall on the William and Mary campus, is easy to spot. Multiple columns of color are lighted along one exterior wall, and the effect is quite startling when viewed from Jamestown Road for the first time. The museum, designed by famed local architect Carlton Abbott, offers lectures, films and tours, but the holdings are the major draw. The permanent collection includes works by European Old Masters as well as modern works, and a special holding is the collection of Colonial-period portraits of Virginians. The museum is open daily, 10 AM to 4:45 PM Monday through Friday, noon to 4 PM Saturday and Sunday. Be sure to obtain a permit from the museum entitling you to reserved parking in the lot in front of the building. Parking spaces are at a premium on campus, and you risk having your vehicle towed otherwise.

## The Watermen's Museum
**309 Water St., Yorktown • (757) 887-2641**

Virginia's watermen, generations of them, are the focus of this small but lively museum located on Yorktown's waterfront. Five galleries and a variety of outdoor exhibits chronicle the story of generations of Virginians whose livelihood stemmed from the waters of the Chesapeake Bay and its tributaries. Here visitors see ship models, paintings, photographs, artifacts and tools in permanent and rotating exhibits on this ancient trade.

The museum hopes to preserve the heritage of the watermen, to interpret their culture and their contributions to the region in an effort to provide and support educational opportunities and preserve and enhance the environment of the fragile bay. All generations are represented, from the original Native American fishermen to today's working men and women. On the grounds you can see some of the work boats and other traditional equipment once so common on our waters. The museum provides a variety of programs, seminars, activities and special events to the public.

A nominal admission fee is charged, $2.50

---

## INSIDERS' TIP

The Twentieth Century Gallery mounts a popular month-long Christmas crafts show each holiday season. Among the objects offered for sale are handcrafted items in a variety of media such as pottery, glass and jewelry.

for adults and 50 cents for children. Groups or individuals may make arrangements to visit any time by calling in advance. The museum is open April through mid-December. Hours are Tuesday through Saturday 10 AM to 4 PM and Sunday from 1 to 4 PM. The museum is closed Mondays. The Watermen's Museum Gift Shop features works by more than 40 local artists and crafters with unusual original works that will be cherished by those who appreciate folk art.

# Galleries

## Andrews Gallery
**Jamestown Rd. • (757) 221-2531**

This exhibition gallery for the Department of Fine Arts at the College of William and Mary is behind the Phi Beta Kappa Memorial Hall. Periodic exhibits of traveling shows and of faculty and student art make the gallery an interesting window on the art scene. Hours are from 9 AM to 5 PM Monday through Friday.

## Gallery On The Green
**307 Main St., Yorktown • (757) 989-0191**

Adding to Yorktown's reputation for quaint little shops and galleries is On The Green, operated by the Yorktown Arts Foundation, founder of On The Hill, the granddaddy of fine crafts gallery in York County. Here, you will find an eclectic array of artisan's work in media ranging from paintings and pottery to jewelry, glass and wood. Hours are 10 AM to 5 PM Tuesday through Saturday, and noon to 5 PM Sunday.

## Nancy Thomas Gallery
**145 Ballard St., Yorktown • (757) 898-3665**

A master folk artist with a national reputation and a presence in museums (and in films - her work can be seen in Jessica Lange's apartment in *Tootsie*), Nancy Thomas calls Yorktown home. This fascinating shop is where you will find her works on display: paintings and sculptures, freestanding whimsical animals, angels, trees, wreaths, Christmas decorations and much more. You are likely also to find Ms. Thomas herself displaying a new item or ready to discuss any of the wonderful things you might find interesting. In addition, she sponsors the work of other local artists who exhibit in the gallery. You will find their beautiful work in pottery, painting and other media presented. Hours are Monday through Saturday from 10 AM to 5 PM and Sunday from 1 to 5 PM. See our Shopping entry in the Jamestown and Yorktown chapter for more information. Note, too, that Ms. Thomas recently opened her second gallery, located on Merchants Square, adjacent to the city's Historic Area.

## On The Hill Cultural Arts Center
**121 Alexander Hamilton Blvd., Yorktown • (757) 898-3076**

Operated by the Yorktown Arts Foundation, this creative arts cooperative gallery offers exhibits of the work of contemporary area artists working in a large variety of media. There are daily demonstrations at the center, which also offers art workshops. Hours are Tuesday through Saturday from 11 AM to 5 PM and Sunday from noon to 5 PM.

## A Touch Of Earth
**The Gallery Shops in Lightfoot, 6580 Richmond Rd. • (757) 565-0425**

Owned and operated by Lianne Lurie and Paul Pittman, this gallery, the oldest in the area, area, features fine decorative and functional crafts by more than 90 contemporary American artists. With a concentration on unusual

Photo: Colonial Williamsburg

Acres of formal and informal gardens decorate Colonial Williamsburg.

works appealing to many senses, the selections include wind chimes in both clay and metal, glassworks, jewelry, lamps, musical instruments, kaleidoscopes, candle holders and textiles - many of them signed one-of-a-kinds. Monthly shows at the gallery feature the work of individual artists, and the gallery also sponsors frequent demonstrations by artisans. The basic collection of lovely free form and wheel-thrown stoneware and fine porcelain is the work of the owners and includes the unique Gloom Chasers, intricately decorated and pierced stoneware lanterns. It is open from 10 AM to 5 PM Monday through Saturday, 11 AM to 5 PM Sunday and by appointment.

## Twentieth Century Gallery
**219 N. Boundary St. • (757) 229-4949**

As the name indicates, the focus of this gallery is work by contemporary artists, both regional and national. Shows featuring all media change on a regular basis, with an annual Christmas crafts show and spring crafts exhibition. The Gallery, an affiliate of the Virginia Museum of Fine Arts in Richmond, displays traveling exhibits of that museum. Hours are from 11 AM to 5 PM Tuesday through Saturday and from noon to 5 PM on Sunday.

From the ever-popular performances of Shakespeare's plays to the rousing sounds of Scottish bagpipes to the exquisite lights of Christmas, the Williamsburg area gives you a diverse menu of events and activities from which to choose.

# Annual Events

Before you decide when you want to make the trek to Williamsburg, you might want to take a gander at just what's going on. While the summer guarantees plenty of fun at area theme parks and you can pretty much count on Colonial Williamsburg keeping you busy year round, you might consider planning your vacation around a special event. The local festival season doesn't really kick in until April, but from then on, your choice of fun activities pretty much runs the gamut. From the ever-popular performances of Shakespeare's plays to the rousing sounds of Scottish bagpipes to the exquisite lights of Christmas, the Williamsburg area gives you a diverse menu of events and activities from which to choose.

Below, we've listed the major - and a few more low-key but fun- celebrations that take place in and around the Williamsburg area. For those of you willing to drive a little farther for a good time, we've also included some of our favorite celebrations that take place in other pockets of Hampton Roads. Our annual events and festivals are listed month by month to make your vacation planning a little easier. The prices we provide are subject to change, but they should give you a solid ballpark figure to use when tallying up that vacation budget. We noted where events in the Colonial Williamsburg Historic Area are included in your ticket purchase. Prices for tickets to the Colonial area vary, but, as a rule, a basic one-day pass costs about $25 for adults and $15 for children ages 6 through 12. Two-day and year-round tickets also are available. For more information, turn to our chapter on Colonial Williamsburg. But, before you do, take the time to read through our listings and highlight any and all that strike your fancy.

## January

**Wildlife Arts Festival**

**Omni Newport News, 1000 Omni Blvd., Oyster Point Park, Newport News 757-595-1500**

The Virginia Living Museum sponsors this annual tribute to our native surroundings. More than 50 artists display and sell a wide range of wildlife art - from stained glass and jewelry to oils, watercolors and one-of-a-kind photography. Live animal shows and exhibits are part of the fun. Admission is $3 for adults; children 12 and younger are free.

## February

**Antiques Forum**
**Williamsburg Lodge Conference Center, S. England St. (800) 603-0948**

In early February, the Antiques Forum comes to Colonial Williamsburg, bringing collectors and experts who share their knowledge in seminars, attend lectures given by Colonial Williamsburg's curators, take special tours and socialize. The forum brings together scholars, collectors and antique buffs to reexamine past judgments about American decorative arts. The week-long event tentatively costs $500, which includes all lectures, tours, special programming, opening receptions and five days of continental breakfasts, coffees and afternoon teas. Register well in advance: Reservations are taken in August and September. In 1998, the Antiques Forum marked its 50th anniversary with a special seminar on Mark Catesby, an 18th-century watercolorist.

## March

**Colonial Williamsburg Learning Weekends**
**Hennage Auditorium, DeWitt Wallace Gallery, S. Henry and Francis streets**

**(800) 603-0948**

Sponsored by the Williamsburg Institute, a subsidiary of the Colonial Williamsburg Foundation, each year's annual Learning Weekend zeroes in on a specific historical theme. Held for four days in early March, this event explores different aspects of 18th-century history. Past topics include 18th-century food and transportation, archeology and architectural restoration. The cost is about $250 per person.

## Williamsburg Film Festival
**Comfort Inn - King George, 706 Bypass Rd., Williamsburg • (757) 566-1855**

Here's something new for movie buffs. Begun in 1997 by the Mid-Atlantic Film Buffs Inc., this two-day festival in early March features showings of old movies and television shows. The first festival brought character actor Gene Evans, television actor Dale Berry and Willie Phelps of the Phelps Brothers to Williamsburg. Peter Boone, son of Richard Boone, displayed a collection of his father's movie memorabilia. Expect similar guests and exhibits from future festivals. Daily admission is $15 per person. For more information, call the above number or write Cindy Peery, P.O. Box 127, Toano VA 23168.

## Annual Antique Show and Sale
**Walsingham Academy, 1100 Jamestown Rd., Williamsburg • (757) 229-2642**

Each year for three days in mid-March, dealers converge on this Williamsburg school with their vast and unusual collections of antique jewelry, collectibles and furniture. Live and silent auctions are part of the fun. Come cast your bid for that can't-live-without-it wicker chaise or cameo brooch and get a little footloose at the Saturday night dance. Daily admission is about $5 per person.

## St. Patrick's Day Parade
**Granby St., Ocean View section of Norfolk • (757) 587-3548**

This particular wearin'-of-the-green event may not take place in Williamsburg, but if you're in the mood to celebrate your Irish heritage or simply wish to get caught up in the revelry, check out Norfolk's St. Patrick's Day Parade and Festivities. The parade, held the

Saturday closest to St. Paddy's Day, is the area's oldest and largest. (And, no, we don't know if they serve green beer.) The route begins at Northside Middle School on Granby Street (about 45 minutes from Williamsburg on I-64 East on a good day) and winds up on W. Government Avenue. You don't have to pay to watch the parade, but food concessions and rides are available at points near or along the route. Knights of Columbus Council 3548 is the sponsor.

# April

## Occasional Downtown Doo Dah Parade
**Main St., Norfolk • (757) 441-2345**

Wacky, zany, even downright silly. That's probably the best way to describe this relatively new Norfolk tradition that takes place the Friday closest to April Fool's Day. Normally staid businessmen and women don trash cans, wooden barrels, frilly tutus or whatever else suits their fancy and converge en masse at noon on Norfolk's Main Street for this good-time free-for-all. Best of all, the laughs don't cost a cent - and that's no joke!

## William and Mary Writers' Festival
**University Center, College of William and Mary • (757) 221-3909**

The William and Mary Writers' Festival, an annual event since 1977, takes place the first week in April with afternoon and evening readings by well-known and emerging writers. This well-attended three-day festival is jointly sponsored by the College Lectures Committee, the English Department and the Virginia Commission for the Arts. Internationally known English poet Stephen Spender, prolific author George Plimpton and Mexican novelist Carlos Fuentes have read from their works in previous years. Closer to home, poets Dave Smith and Amy Clampitt and fiction writers Ann Beattie, Larry McMurtry and Bobbie Ann Mason have been honored guests. Although most readings are held at the University Center, campus locations occasionally vary, so call ahead for specific information. Readings are free and open to the public and are followed by wine and cheese receptions.

## Gloucester Daffodil Festival
**Main St., Gloucester (804) 664-6492**

Considered the opening event in the busy Hampton Roads festival season, the Gloucester gala celebrates, what else, but spring's harbinger, the sunny daffodil. Held on a single Saturday in early April, this free festival features food, arts and crafts, bus tours, children's events, games and historic displays. To get to Gloucester, follow Route 17 north from Yorktown over the Coleman Bridge. Expect to pay a parking fee of about $1.

## Garden Symposium
**Hennage Auditorium, DeWitt Wallace Gallery, S. Henry and Francis streets (800) 603-0948**

Colonial Williamsburg's four-day crash course on cultivating a green thumb, held in mid- to late April, marked its 50th year in 1996. If you want to know how to make your garden grow, join more than 200 horticulturists and gardening enthusiasts for a host of lectures, tours and master classes. The theme for 1998, when the symposium will coincide with Virginia's Historic Garden Week, is "The Style and Grace of American Native Plants." Cost typically runs about $300 per person.

## Historic Garden Week
**Various locations (804) 644-7776**

Sponsored by garden clubs throughout Virginia, this special week celebrating nature's beauty (and the decorating skills of a number of homeowners) is held the last full week in April. On Tuesday of that week, the Williamsburg Garden Club sponsors its garden week tour of both the gardens and interiors of five homes in the Williamsburg area. In addition, a walking garden tour of portions of the Colonial Williamsburg gardens is offered. Block tickets that cover entrance to all five houses and the walking garden tour are $15. Individual tickets for each house and/or the garden are $5. Tickets may be purchased the day before the event at either the Colonial Williamsburg Visitor Center or the Williamsburg

Photo: Colonial Williamsburg Foundation

Fourth of July celebrations are almost as numerous as the sparks from a fireworks display.

Lodge or at the door of any of the houses the day of the event. Since the chairperson of the local event changes annually, your best bet for more information is to contact the Historic Garden Week Headquarters at the above number or write them at 12 E. Franklin Street, Richmond VA 23219.

## Virginia Waterfront International Arts Festival

**Locations vary throughout Hampton Roads • (757) 664-6492**

Introduced in 1997 as a way to provide locals and tourists with a more varied cultural menu, the inaugural festival started in late April and ran through mid-May. Modeled on the Charleston, South Carolina, Spoleto Festival, the local lineup includes dance, theater and a range of music, with more than two dozen performers and companies from as far away as Chile and Germany. The 18-day 1997 program included a Multicultural Festival, Circus Flora, stage performances of *Oklahoma* and *A Prairie Home Companion* with Garrison Keillor. Although most events are held at sites throughout Norfolk, several are staged in Williamsburg or elsewhere on the Peninsula. Ticket prices for individual events range from $9 to $50 with package deals available.

# May

## Greek Festival

**Annunciation Greek Orthodox Cathedral, 7720 Granby St., Norfolk • (757) 440-0500**

If you like Greek food - and don't mind rubbing elbows with tons of others who like Greek food just as much or even more - Norfolk's annual Greek Festival is the place for you to be the first weekend in May. Held from Thursday through Sunday, this event has grown by leaps and bounds in the past decade or so. Highlights include live Greek music and dancing, lamb feast dinners and an a la carte menu of an array of Greek delicacies. Food is served cafeteria style and the lines are long, but all the camaraderie and good cheer make the wait seem brief. Festival events are free; food items are priced individually.

And the festival is easy to find: Just follow I-64 to Exit 276, which dumps you right onto Granby Street. The goings-on will be about a mile down the road on your left.

## Jamestown Landing Day

**Jamestown Settlement, Rt. 31, Jamestown • (757) 253-4838**

Held in Jamestown Settlement one weekend in early May, Jamestown Landing Day commemorates the anniversary of the 1607 founding of America's first permanent English colony with a number of activities that show the effects of contact between English settlers and native Powhatans. Participation in events is covered by the price of admission to the Jamestown Settlement museum: $9.75 for adults, $4.75 for children 6 through 12.

## American Heritage Festival

**Yorktown Victory Center, Rt. 238, Yorktown • (757) 253-4838**

Experience the rich and diverse cultural heritage of your American ancestors through entertainment, crafts and interpretations of early lifestyles and occupations. The festival typically is held during a weekend in mid-May. Admission is $6.75 for adults and $3.25 for children ages 6 through 12 and includes entrance to Victory Center exhibits.

## Yorktown Civil War Weekend

**Varied locations throughout Yorktown • (757) 898-3400**

Special interpretive programs, tactical demonstrations, Union and Confederate encampments and a Confederate field hospital interpret the role Yorktown played during the Peninsula Campaign. Cost is $4 for adults 17 and older. Children younger than 17 are admitted free.

## Pungo Strawberry Festival

**Pungo section of Princess Anne Rd., Virginia Beach • (757) 721-6001**

This festival may be a little off the beaten path - from Williamsburg it's about a 1 and 1/2-hour drive - but it's so unusual we thought it should be included. As its name suggests, this event celebrates the splendid strawberry. Usually held the last weekend in May, the festival offers craftspeople, carnival rides, children's games and strawberries - and strawberry dishes - galore. Entrance to the festival is free, but a $5 parking fee is charged.

To get to the festival, take I-64 East to Route 44, the Norfolk-Virginia Beach Expressway. At the Birdneck Road Exit, turn right and follow to General Booth Boulevard. Turn right on General Booth, which eventually changes to Princess Anne and follow until the intersection of Indian River Road. Look for festival signs along the way.

# June

## Harborfest
**Town Point Park, Waterside Dr., Norfolk**
**• (757) 441-2345**

Norfolk's humongous waterfront bash is more than 20 years old. Considered the premier waterfront celebration on the East Coast, this free, weekend-long event features music, food and entertainment, including sailboat races, water shows, games for the children and a whole range of local and national performers. Harborfest typically is held the first weekend in June in Town Point Park and along the Norfolk waterfront. It attracts about a quarter-million people annually, so the place is a zoo. Many Insiders won't miss it, while others wouldn't be caught dead in downtown Norfolk that weekend. It's your call, but if you truly love a party and can handle a mob scene, check it out. To get to downtown Norfolk, take I-64 East to 264 and follow the Waterside Drive exit. Parking is available in several area garages and averages about $4 a day. And one final teaser if you're deciding which day to go: The fireworks on Saturday night are spectacular!

## Virginia Indian Heritage Festival
**Jamestown Settlement, Rt. 31, Jamestown**
**757-253-4838**

This one-day powwow, held mid-June in Jamestown, brings together Native Americans from throughout the country for eight hours of traditional Indian dancing, drumming, music,

crafts and food. Educational programs and children's activities are also part of the festivities. Admission, which includes entrance to Jamestown Settlement museums, is $9.75 for adults, $4.75 for children ages 6 through 12. The festival is cosponsored by the Virginia Council on Indians.

## Bayou Boogaloo & Cajun Food Festival
**Town Point Park, Waterside Dr., Norfolk**
**• (757) 441-2345**

If you like your food spicy and your entertainment hot, hot, hot, head over to Norfolk's Town Point Park for the Bayou Boogaloo & Cajun Food Festival. Held each year over a weekend in mid-June, the festival combines Cajun and Zydeco music with such activities as Cajun Critter Races, pepper-eating challenges and Cajun cooking demonstrations. The event is free, but bring along plenty of cash for beverages.

## Hampton Jazz Festival
**Hampton Coliseum, Exit 263B off I-64**
**• (757) 838-4203**

If you like jazz, you'll love this popular Hampton festival. How much will you love it? Let me count the ways: 1) Aretha Franklin; 2) Isaac Hayes; 3) Stevie Wonder; 4) B.B. King; 5) Barry White; 6) Kenny G; 7) Luther Vandross; 8) Gladys Knight; 9) Patti LaBelle; 10) George Benson. Not all in the same weekend, of course, but there's usually a couple of major headliners performing each year. The festival typically is held in late June at the Hampton Coliseum. Cost for each concert is about $35. To find out more, call after April 1.

# July

## Independence Day Celebration
**Main St., Yorktown 757-890-3300**

Family-oriented festivities are the order of the day at the Fourth of July celebration at Yorktown. Activities include a foot race, parade, arts and crafts, musical entertainment and, of course, a magnificent display of fireworks. The free celebration is sponsored by the Yorktown Fourth of July Committee.

## Annual Independence Day Ice Cream Social
**Wren Building Courtyard, College of William and Mary • (757) 259-6079**

It's July and the operative word is hot. Enjoy a refreshing double dip at this annual July 4th event, sponsored by the Williamsburg Community Hospital Auxiliary. Held from 5:30 to 8 PM (to help you cool off and settle in before the fireworks), the event offers more than just ice cream. There are hot dogs, homemade cakes, drinks and entertainment. Even better, 500 chairs are set out on the courtyard lawn so your tired feet can get a much-needed rest. You are welcome to bring your own chairs or a blanket if you prefer. The sitting part is free; food items are priced individually. OK, all together now: I scream, you scream . . . .

## Independence Day Festivities
**Colonial Williamsburg Historic Area • (800) 246-2099**

The day typically begins with a 10 AM march to Bruton Parish Church by the Colonial Williamsburg Fifes and Drums Corps. There, the corps sets up a military altar with flags and drums and prayers for peace are

offered. At noon, the Declaration of Independence is read at the steps of the Courthouse. The day ends with a salute on Palace Green by the corps at 8:45 PM, followed by a fireworks display. Admission is included in your ticket to the restored area, which costs about $25 for adults and $15 for children ages 6 through 12.

## Fourth at the Fort
**Waller Field at Fort Monroe, Hampton • (757) 727-3151, 737-3302**

Celebrate Independence Day on an active Army post with the Continental Army Band, food, children's activities and a fireworks display. The setting can't be beat: Fort Monroe overlooks the Chesapeake Bay. Admission is free.

## Colonial Children's Fair
**Yorktown Victory Center, Rt. 238, Yorktown • (757) 253-4838**

This weekend of fun is for the whole family - but children are the guests of honor. Kids have a chance to play the games enjoyed by their forefathers and foremothers when they were just wee lads and lasses in knickers and

### INSIDERS' TIP

Each year, the Williamsburg Institute sponsors the Williamsburg Inn's Wine and Food Classic weekends, which offer fine food and wine based on a distinct culinary theme. The dates for these special weekends vary throughout the year, but each one includes culinary demonstrations, wine tastings and workshops, topped off by a gourmet dinner in the Williamsburg Inn's Regency Dining Room. The 1999 gourmet weekends themes are: in January, "A Weekend of Things Scottish;" in February, "A Culinary Tour of Asia;" and in July, "Fine Food and Exceptional Wines with Kevin Zraly," which will be held July 9-11. Included in this weekend are two cooking demonstrations by restaurateur Zraly of Windows on the World, wine tastings and lively commentary. The program also includes behind-the-scenes tours of colonial kitchens and the wine cellar at the Governor's Palace. The weekend climaxes with a gala black-tie dinner in the Williamsburg Inn's award-winning Regency Room. Packages for this event are $245-$285 per person.

Package rates for all other gourmet weekends begin at $190-285 per person. Package rates include lodging in a Colonial Williamsburg property. For reservations and information, call (800) 603-0948 or write the Williamsburg Institute, Wine and Food Classic, P.O. Box 1776 Williamsburg, VA 23187.

Photo: Kingsmill Resort

The Michelob Championship of Kingsmill draws PGATour professionals to the area every year.

pinafores. Pie-eating contests, hoop rolling races and stilt-walking are all part of the adventure. Admission is $6.75 for adults, $3.25 for children ages 6 through 12, which includes entrance to Victory Center exhibits.

### Virginia Shakespeare Festival
**Phi Beta Kappa Memorial Hall, College of William and Mary • (757) 261-2674**

The Virginia Shakespeare Festival has been a highlight of the Williamsburg summer since its inception in 1978. Performances typically are held throughout July in the 750-seat Phi Beta Kappa Memorial Hall on the campus of William and Mary. Professional directors work with an acting staff of student interns and professional performers. Recent performances include *Richard III*, *The Merry Wives of Windsor*, *Twelfth Night* and *Hamlet*. Curtain is at 8 PM Tuesday through Saturday and 2 PM Sunday. For tickets, which go on sale in June and are about $12 per play, call the box office at the number above.

# August

### James City County Fair
**Upper County Park, 180 Leisure Rd., Toano • (757) 566-1367**

In its 20th year in 1997, this free event has been growing like gangbusters. The two-day fair, held on a Friday and Saturday in early August, features rides, exhibits, crafts and foods, including barbecue, gumbo, fish sandwiches and the omnipresent hot dogs and hamburgers. To keep the fair's local flavor firmly intact, anyone selling goods must live or work in James City County, Williamsburg or the Bruton District of York County.

### Hampton Cup Regatta
**Mill Creek, Hampton • (757) 727-1102**

If you're an armchair speed freak, head to Hampton in early August for the oldest and largest inboard hydroplane powerboat race in the United States. The summer national championships, which are sanctioned by the American Powerboat Association, include 11 classes of boats (including the Grand Prix hydroplanes, billed as the fastest piston-powered craft in the world) and speeds that top 170 miles per hour. There's also live entertainment and food. The races, which run for three days at Fort Monroe's Mill Creek, are in their 73rd year in 1999. Admission is free, but get there early to grab a prime viewing spot, as race sponsors expect about 160,000 thrill seekers to show up.

# September

## Celebrate Yorktown Festival
**Yorktown Waterfront • 890-0916**

This decidedly adult festival, held the weekend before the Labor Day holiday, definitely has the art-loving adult crowd in mind. Introduced in 1997, the festival features samples and displays from 35 Virginia wineries, foods from gourmet restaurants throughout the area, an antique fest, a juried art show and 15 different bands. Tickets cost $15 and cover the cost of wine tastings; food is sold separately.

## Bay Days
**Downtown Hampton • (757) 727-6122, 727-1102**

During the second weekend of each September, the city of Hampton celebrates the heritage of the Chesapeake Bay with its three-day Bay Days bash. Admission to the Bay Days site is free, but parking - whether in city lots or private makeshift lots set up for the occasion - averages $5. (Satellite parking and shuttle service is available at the Hampton Coliseum lot just off Exit 263B of I-64.) Featuring everything from hands-on Bay education activities for the kids to a teen entertainment area to rides, crafts, food and a juried art show, Bay Days has something for everyone. Continuous entertainment is staged at various locations throughout the celebration, which takes place along the Hampton waterfront and in the closed-off streets and parking lots of downtown. The Saturday night explosion of fireworks is a must-see. The festival concludes Sunday evening with a headline performer. In 1996, the featured artist was country star Patty Loveless.

## Poquoson Seafood Festival
**Poquoson Municipal Park, 830 Poquoson Ave., Poquoson • (757) 868-3580**

If you're in the area in mid-September and in the mood for seafood and the type of fun that's part of small-town living, head down I-64 for the three-day Poquoson Seafood Festival. The fun is free (there's a $3 or so parking fee) and features music, fireworks, dance exhibitions, and, of course, plenty of succulent seafood. Started in 1981, the event is a tribute to the working watermen of Hampton Roads and has become a tradition in the region. To get to Poquoson, which is a bit off the beaten path, take I-64 East to Exit 256 to Route 171 and follow signs for shuttle parking. Or, if you think you'll get lucky and find a parking place at the festival site, follow Route 171 for about 5 or 6 miles then turn left onto Wythe Creek Road. Turn right on Hudgins Road, bearing right onto Poquoson Avenue, then left on Municipal Drive. Enjoy!

## Williamsburg Scottish Festival
**Williamsburg Winery Ltd., Lake Powell Rd. • (757) 564-0130**

This popular annual event, in its 22nd year in 1999, typically takes place on winery grounds from 9 AM to 5 PM on the fourth Saturday in September. Festival-goers can watch or participate in Scottish games, Highland dancing and athletic events, witness a parade of the clans and a war-cry rally and, of course, listen to the bagpipes skirl. Individual drumming, piping and band competitions also are held, with cash prizes, but participants must pre-register. Children's activities include games of nine pins, quoits, shuttlecock, palm ball tennis and goff, a Colonial version of golf. Border collies demonstrate their sheep-herding skills, and Scottish crafts and imports - books, jewelry, weaving, woolens - are on display. An honored guest from Scotland is always in attendance and more than 65 Scottish clans, societies and vendors take part in this large gathering. Performances by demonstration bands (the Scottish Transport Regiment Pipes and Drums and the Canadian Air Command Pipes and Drums are two recent participants) are among the highlights of the day's events. Visitors can sample Scottish cuisine - everything from pasties and bridies, a meat-filled popover, to shortbread and Scottish candy - or fill up on barbecue and fish and chips. Scottish soft drinks and beer are sold. Tickets to the day of festival games cost about $8 for adults, $4 for children ages 6 to 12.

# October

## An Occasion for the Arts
**Merchants Square, Williamsburg**
• **(757) 220-1736**

October in Williamsburg means An Occasion for the Arts, with outdoor exhibits and entertainment on Duke of Gloucester Street and Merchants Square. Held the first Sunday in October, this free autumn salute to visual and performing artists boasts the oldest juried invitational art show in Virginia, limited to 100 artists and craftspeople. The juror typically is a respected area arts professional. In addition to the art show, a variety of entertainers - magicians, musicians, dancers, mimes - are on hand, performing on 11 different stages. The art show starts at 10 AM. Entertainment begins at noon, with most performances lasting from 30 minutes to an hour. Food and beverages, including hot dogs, barbecue, ice cream, cookies, beer, wine and soft drinks, are on sale. As a finale, a professional band or musical group gives a 5:30 PM concert on the festival grounds. (The 1997 performance was staged in the jazz tent in Merchants Square.) This concert, dubbed "the Capper" by organizers, lasts about an hour.

First held in 1969, An Occasion for the Arts now draws between 20,000 and 30,000 people over the course of a single day. Artists and participants may park in designated lots a few blocks away. Visitors are encouraged to park on the William and Mary campus just off South Boundary Street, although other campus parking is usually available. The juried show, which has a May deadline, is not limited to Virginia residents; artists wishing to participate can get on the mailing list for an application by writing to: An Occasion for the Arts, P.O. Box 363, Williamsburg, Virginia 23187. For more information, contact Suzanne Scudder at the number above.

## Newport News Fall Festival
**Newport News Park, Jefferson Ave.**
• **(757) 926-8451**

Somehow, the sun always manages to shine for this two-day festival held in the wooded environs of Newport News Park. This free, early October event features crafts galore (we've purchased many one-of-a-kind Christmas gifts here). And, for a crafts festival, it's a fairly kid-friendly environment. There's always a children's area with stage shows and hands-on crafts. Our children are endlessly fascinated by the sheep-shearing, candle-making and fabric-weaving demonstrations. The event draws huge crowds, warranting two bits of advice: Arrive early because on-site parking (which costs about $4) can be an extended ordeal; and, eat early, as lines tend to get really long, leaving you ravenous by the time you get a chance to dig into your pit-cooked steak sandwich and butterfly fries.

## Michelob Championship of Kingsmill
**Kingsmill Golf Club, James City Co.**
• **(757) 253-3985**

Previously played in the blistering heat of

---

**INSIDERS' TIP**

If you love an old-fashioned parade, check out the Williamsburg Area Chamber of Commerce-sponsored Christmas procession, held the first Saturday in December each year. The parade, which attracts more than 100 participating groups, moves along Duke of Gloucester Street to Richmond Road to Brooks Street. The day after the event is the Sunday of the Grand Illumination. Call 229-6511 closer to the event for the specific time.

July, this week-long, big-name golf tournament was switched to early October in 1997. Each year, the classic draws a number of PGA Tour professionals to the Williamsburg area to compete for more than $1 million in prize money. Daily and weekly grounds and clubhouse tickets are available as well as several package deals. Tickets start at $10 and go as high as $2,500 for an "Executive Package," so your best bet is to call the above number for more information. Discounts are available for those who order early. For more information, turn to our chapter on Golf.

## Yorktown Victory Day Celebration
**Yorktown Victory Center, Rt. 238, Yorktown • (757) 253-4838**

On October 19, 1781, British General Cornwallis and his forces surrendered to the Americans at Yorktown; the American Revolution was essentially over, though the signing of treaties came later. This momentous day is commemorated each year with a daylong celebration of parades, fanfare and re-enactments. An encampment of revolutionary War re-enactors presents tactical demonstrations at both the Victory Center and on the Yorktown Battlefield. Admission is $6.75 for adults and $3.25 for children ages 6 through 12 and includes entrance to Center exhibits.

## Publick Times
**Colonial Williamsburg Historic Area**
**(800) 246-2099**

This late October gala of lively entertainment simulates the exciting times in 18th-century Williamsburg when General Court was in session and the population of politicians, socializers and swells was at its peak. Colonial Williamsburg stages dances, auctions, horse races, magic shows, military reviews and much more to re-create the fair and market atmo-

Photo: Colonial Williamsburg Foundation

Christmas in Colonial Williamsburg inspires wreaths, tree lightings and The Grand Illumination.

sphere of Publick Times. Some 500 military re-enactors camp out in the Historic Area, contributing to the general merriment and fantasy of the weekend. Reveille sounds in the morning, the Fifes and Drums hold a parade and the Royal Governor reviews the militia troops. Colonial gallows have been reconstructed and used during Publick Times for mock hangings. Activities are continuous from morning until dark. Schedules of events may be obtained at the Visitor Center or by calling in advance. Admission is included in a ticket to the Historic Area, which runs about $25 for adults and $15 for children ages 6 through 12.

# November

## History Forum
**Hennage Auditorium, DeWitt Wallace Gallery, S. Henry and Francis streets • (800) 603-0948**

Since 1987, Colonial Williamsburg has sponsored a yearly history forum during which participants discuss and examine crucial aspects of American history. Recent themes include "First Amendment/Second Thoughts: Hindsight on Freedom of the Press and America's Earliest Communications Revolution" and "The American Family That Never Was." Registration space for the three-day gathering is limited. It includes special tours, evening tours, passes to the Historic Area and some meals. Cost of the program is about $250.

## Food & Feasts in the 17th Century
**Jamestown Settlement, Rt. 31, Jamestown • (757) 253-4838**

This three-day event, held in late November, illustrates how the Powhatan Indians and Jamestown's earliest colonists prepared and preserved foods nearly 400 years ago, including the processing of a whole hog. The festival typically draws about 5,500 visitors over the three days. Admission is included with the purchase of a museum admission ticket; $9.75 for adults, $4.75 for children ages 6 through 12.

## Thanksgiving at Berkeley Plantation
**Off Rt. 5, Charles City Co. (804) 272-3226**

In early December 1619, a company of Englishmen arrived to settle a grant of Virginia land known as Berkeley Hundred. Their sponsor had instructed that the day of their arrival be "a day of Thanksgiving," so the settlers celebrated and gave thanks, more than a year before the pilgrims who landed at Plymouth, Massachusetts, in 1620 first did. A re-enactment of the first Virginia Thanksgiving has taken place the first Sunday in November since 1958 at Berkeley Plantation in Charles City County. As many as 5,000 people have attended in recent years; some years a paddleboat even brings a group of participants down the James River from Richmond. Besides the re-enactment of the landing, there are vendors selling hot drinks and food (everything from french-fried sweet potatoes to Brunswick stew) and puppet and magic shows and games for the children. But the day's main event is a traditional Thanksgiving feast, featuring all the foods we have come to love and expect (turkey, stuffing, sweet potatoes and a big wedge of pie for dessert) when we gather around the table on this special day. On the day of the celebration, gates open at 9 AM, when visitors are encouraged to tour the mansion and plantation grounds; activities begin at 10 AM and continue until 4 PM. Tickets for the feast cost about $25 for adults and $15 for children ages 5 to 12. Advance registration is required. Call the previously listed number or write Virginia Thanksgiving Festival, P.O. Box 5132, Richmond, Virginia 23220 for more information.

# December

## Williamsburg's Grand Illumination
**Colonial Williamsburg Historic Area (800) 246-2099**

On the first Sunday in December, Colonial Williamsburg kicks off the Christmas season by lighting candles in hundreds of windows in Historic Area buildings. Cressets and bonfires also illuminate the evening. Locals come in droves, and visitors love this splendid and energetic yuletide event, which includes a performance by the Fife and Drum Corps, the firing of the cannon on the town green, dancing, caroling and carousing at four stages scattered throughout the restored area and fireworks displays at three locations - the Governor's Palace, the Capitol and the Magazine.

Candlelight tours are held and 18th-century plays and concerts are performed; tickets are required for some events. Outdoor activities start at 4:45 PM and are free to the public. Arrive early to avoid parking hassles and bring a flashlight. When it comes to holiday programs, the Grand Illumination is merely the star atop the tree, so to speak. Throughout this magnificent season, the Historic Area is adorned in holiday finery and bustles with candlelit concerts, decorating workshops, 18th-century plays, yuletide banquets and numerous other programs. Carolers sing on the steps of the Courthouse at twilight during the season, while exhibits and holiday programs at the Abby Aldrich Rockefeller Folk Art Center, 220-7698, and the DeWitt Wallace Gallery, 220-7724, draw visitors indoors where it's warm.

## Newport News Festival of Lights
**Newport News Park, Jefferson Ave. • (757) 247-8451**

Remember when you were little and your parents would pile you in the car and drive up and down neighborhood streets to look at all the splendid and not-so-splendid Christmas lights? Whether they were terrific or tacky, as we recall, they all served to spark a little holiday magic. Since 1993, Newport News has re-created and magnified that magic about a million times with its annual Festival of Lights. Two miles of lighted scenes dazzle folks driving through Newport News Park. The festival became even more dazzling in 1996 with the addition of close to 50,000 new lights. Cost is $6 per vehicle Sunday through Thursday, $7 on Fridays and Saturdays.

## Yorktown Tree Lighting Festivities
**Historic Main St., Yorktown • (757) 890-3300**

One evening in early December, area families are invited to hold aloft candles and walk down Main Street to participate in the annual holiday tree lighting fun. There's caroling and background music by the Yorktown Fife and Drum Corps. Light refreshments are served.

## A Yorktown Christmas
**Yorktown Victory Center, Rt. 238, Yorktown • (757) 253-4838**

This event, which typically runs for about two weeks in early December at Yorktown Victory Center, allows you to take part in a variety of 18th-century Virginia holiday activities in the re-created farm and Continental Army encampment. Costumed interpreters prepare traditional Christmas fare and tell stories of the holiday season. An annual tree lighting is scheduled, during which 13 evergreens - representing the 13 original colonies - are illuminated. Cost is included in the Center admission price of $6.75 for adults and $3.25 for children ages 6 through 12. Admission to the tree lighting ceremony, held one evening during the two-week event, is free.

## Community Christmas Tree Lighting
**MarketSquareGreen,ColonialWilliamsburg • (800) 246-2099**

On Christmas Eve each year, Williamsburg residents gather for a special celebration of this physically cold, yet spiritually warm, season. A huge tree stationed at Market Square Green near the Magazine is festooned with white lights, a tradition that dates to 1935. Members of the community circle around, holding lighted candles and singing carols. A short speech is delivered, and the festivities begin, including a presentation of the story of the area's first tree, which was decorated by a German professor living in the St. George Tucker House. The annual lighting is cosponsored by Colonial Williamsburg and the Williamsburg Kiwanis. There is no charge to participate.

## A Jamestown Christmas
**Jamestown Settlement, Rt. 31, Jamestown • (757) 253-4838**

Typically held from just before Christmas to year's end, this tradition envelops visitors to the Jamestown Settlement with 17th-century Yuletide traditions. Join the Lord of Misrule in games and entertainment. Admission is included in a ticket to the Settlement, which costs $9.75 for adults, $4.75 for children ages 6 though 12.

## Festival of Lights
**301 Monticello Ave., Williamsburg**
• **(757) 259-6079**

Sponsored by the Williamsburg Community Hospital Auxiliary, this Christmas tree lighting is held on the grounds of the hospital in early December. The lights, purchased in honor or memory of loved ones as an auxiliary fund-raiser, are switched on at 5:30 PM by the mayor.

## First Night of Williamsburg
**Various locations • (757) 258-5153**

This alcohol-free New Year's Eve celebration of the performing arts, introduced in 1993, is an event for the entire family. The First Night concept originated in Boston in 1976 and since has spread to more than 120 cities in the United States, Canada and Australia. The local celebration is held from 6 PM to midnight in downtown Williamsburg, on the campus of the College of William and Mary and in locations bordering the Historic Area. More than 200 artists perform, including actors, dancers, singers, musicians, jugglers, puppeteers, storytellers and clowns. Other events include an animation festival, an exhibition of paintings and a fireworks display. While guests can easily reach the First Night grounds on foot, complimentary buses also travel a circuit around the area and connect to ample satellite parking. The celebration typically attracts a crowd of about 5,000. Food and beverages are available from churches and businesses located along the site. The fete is open to anyone - from ages 2 to 102 - but participants must wear commemorative buttons, which cost $7 before the event and $10 on December 31. Children 5 and younger are free. Buttons are available from many of the local merchants beginning in early December or can be purchased at advance prices by writing First Night of Williamsburg, P.O. Box 1382, Williamsburg VA 23187.

Once you drop anchor in Norfolk, you will wish you'd reserved an entire day to take in all this seafaring city has to offer.

# Daytrips

We admit it: You have to devote a big chunk of time to get to really know Williamsburg and the surrounding Historic Triangle. But don't let time constraints dissuade you from checking out the neighboring countryside. After all, a change of scenery perks up the body, soul and mind as it broadens your perspective on the Old Dominion and helps you satisfy that old demon, wanderlust. What we've outlined below are some of our favorite daytrips, places you can go by simply hopping behind the wheel and heeding our directions. Whether you ferry across the James River, grab some R and R on Tangier or Smith islands, stroll along the historic streets of downtown Smithfield, wander amid the Civil War battlefields of Richmond or splash in the surf of Virginia Beach, you get to call the shots. You are, in a sense, master of your fate, captain of your dear old daytripping soul. All of these Insider favorites are worth a good eight to 12 hours of your time and most (with the exception of the islands) take well under two hours of driving time. (We can't guarantee traffic.) So what are you waiting for? Adventure beckons. Grab that Virginia map, or go mapless if you're feeling really spontaneous. And, remember: area codes vary depending upon where you're heading. In Richmond, it's 804, on Smith Island 410, and for the rest of our daytrips, it's 757, just like Williamsburg. (No need to memorize the codes, however. We note when a different one is required.) Got all that straight? Then let's start exploring!

## Jamestown-Scotland Ferry
### End of Jamestown Rd.  (800) 823-3779

The mercury hovers at 95 degrees and your tired dogs cower at the thought of making contact with sizzling pavement. What you would rather do is relax and luxuriate in a cool breeze, preferably with someone else in the driver's seat. Why not cruise to Scotland, tour the rural landscape, and savor some of the best authentic regional cooking available? No, we're not crazy; just check your map (if you didn't leave it back in your hotel room). It's entirely possible to schedule a free, fresh-air cruise to Scotland, something both locals and visitors do regularly aboard the Jamestown Ferry.

While the ferry isn't your destination, it's a wonderful and scenic means to an end, so we've given it a separate write-up in our Daytrips chapter. This state-run service, the last of a once-thriving ferry commerce in Hampton Roads, crosses the James River from Jamestown to Scotland Wharf in Surry County in Southside (many contend that the South doesn't really begin until one is securely below the James). For a large number of residents, this scenic ride is a twice-daily commute, either to the Surry Nuclear Power plant across the river or to jobs on the Peninsula. For many others, especially on weekends in good weather, it's a favorite daytrip. Until July 1997, a trip aboard the ferry cost $4 each way. The toll was dropped as a result of legislation passed by the General Assembly, giving new meaning to the phrase "a free ride." (For years, Surry officials have claimed the toll thwarted the county's efforts to bring in tourists.)

You can reach the ferry by traveling either Jamestown Road or the Colonial Parkway to its southernmost end, near Jamestown Settlement. We prefer the parkway route, which is less direct but much more scenic, offering beautiful views of the expanse of water you are about to cross. If you haven't done so already, you might also want to visit Jamestown Island first: there, you'll see landmarks you'll view later from the ferry. Be sure to note the ferry schedule posted on a large sign on the right side of Jamestown Road as you approach its end, and plan your trip to allow time for a convenient return trip. From early in the day until evening, two ferries run every 30 minutes. From 8:30 PM until 5 AM, only one boat is used, but it still departs on the half-hour.

While on the concrete dock waiting to board, you'll notice the three restored ships of Jamestown Settlement to your left: the *Susan Constant*, the *Godspeed* and the *Discovery* to your left. You don't get a better waterside view of all three ships than this, and your wait might be a prime opportunity to pull out the camera. The trip takes a little less than 20 minutes from castoff to docking and offers beautiful views, especially on clear autumn days or during late-summer sunsets.

Once you have boarded one of the ferries of the fleet, you may leave your vehicle (being careful, of course, not to ding your neighbors' car doors) and enjoy the view from the railing or from bow or stern. There is a small cabin upstairs with water fountains and restrooms as well as good views, but there is no seating on most of the ferries.

The unique experience of riding a ferry is periodically threatened with extinction by studies that call for a replacement bridge spanning the river, either here or upstream. Each year, approximately 625,000 vehicles use the ferry service.

# Surry County

Once you're across the James and docked at Scotland Wharf, you'll drive off into Surry County. Many Insiders choose to go directly down Route 31 to the Surrey House (yes, that's the spelling) or Edwards' Ham for delicious Southern cooking. Others prefer exploring Smith's Fort Plantation, traveling to Bacon's Castle, or going to Chippokes Plantation State Park and Chippokes Farm and Forestry Museum. Whatever your choice, you'll find that a voyage across the James is a trip into the quiet, rural southern landscape of Surry County that is the only memory of what the Peninsula used to be. Miles of farmland and two-lane highways separate small, historic communities. Weathered tobacco barns, more tall than wide, occasionally are visible in fields where prized Virginia peanuts are now the major crop. It's a world away from generic fast-food restaurants, hotel chains and the sometimes frantic pace of an established tourism industry. In Southside, life is savored.

# Attractions

## Smith's Fort Plantation
### Rt. 10 • (757) 294-3872

You may be surprised to note that the Smith in the name of this historic plantation is none other than Captain John Smith, who built a fort on high land at nearby Gray's Creek in 1609 as protection for Jamestown, directly across the river. The land has other famous connections as well, having been part of Chief Powhatan's wedding gifts to Pocahontas and John Rolfe. The building on the site is a fine example of a Georgian brick manor house with its typical one-and-a-half stories and central entrance. It can be toured Tuesday through Saturday from 10 AM to 4 PM and Sundays from noon to 4 PM. Admission is $4 for adults, $3 for AAA members and seniors, $2 for college students and $1 for children ages 3 and up. The manor is open on weekends only during March and November, for one week only in December and is closed during January and February.

## Bacon's Castle
### Rt. 10 • (757) 357-5976

Williamsburg may have a palace, but Surry has its own castle - Bacon's Castle on Route 10. You might think you heard all about the Virginia colonists' rebellion as you toured Williamsburg, but did you know that, 100 years before the Revolution, another rebellion occurred? In 1676, Nathaniel Bacon began the colony's first act of insurrection against Gov. William Berkeley's harsh rule. The struggle spread to Surry County, and, on September 18, Bacon's commander, William Rookings, captured this building, home to Major Arthur Allen, in a siege.

For about four months, the county was under Rooking's control. Major Allen built the house in 1665, and now, more than 330 years later, it is the oldest documented brick house in English North America. Architecturally, it is of extreme interest. Unlike its surviving, typically Georgian, contemporaries, the building has curving Flemish gables and triple chimneystacks. Its front and rear facades also are unusual in that they are broken midpoint by an entrance-and-porch tower in front and a corresponding stair tower in back. This gives the building a cruciform shape, the first house in the colony so designed. A formal garden has been excavated and restored, and the whole estate has a sense of antiquity and a peace that contrasts with its most famous historical event. The house is closed Mondays, and open 10 AM to 4 PM Tuesday through Saturday and noon to 4 PM Sunday. It operates on the same seasonal schedule as Smith's Fort. Admission is $5 for adults, $1 for children ages 6 to 18 and $2 for college students. Senior tickets for anyone age 65 and older are $3, and group tours can be arranged by appointment. A $6 adult ticket that provides entrance to both Bacon's Castle and Smith's Fort Plantation can be purchased at either site.

### Chippokes Plantation State Park
#### Rt. 634 off of Rt. 10 E.• (757) 294-3625

The 1854 Manor House at Chippokes Plantation State Park might be a welcome change from the Georgian architecture on which this part of Virginia prides itself. Formal gardens surround the house and contain one of the largest collections of crepe myrtles on the East Coast. This plantation, named after a Native American chief friendly to the settlers, has been continuously farmed for more than 370 years, which makes the model farm and the adjacent Farm and Forestry Museum a fitting part of the state park. There are biking and hiking trails, picnic shelters, a swimming pool and fishing. Some folks on the Peninsula are unaware of the fine public swimming pool here, but Insiders know that a daytrip to swim here is well worth the effort. The park is the site of the Steam and Gas Engine Show in June and the Pork, Peanut and Pine Festival in July,

both of which draw huge crowds from all around the region for a weekend of good food, entertainment, educational experiences and fun. In the summer, the manor is open Wednesday through Saturday from 1 to 5 PM. (It is closed during the winter and open some spring and fall weekends.) Admission is $3 for adults and $1.50 for children ages 6 to 12. Also in the summer, the museum is open Wednesday through Sunday from 10 AM to 6 PM. From early April to late May, the museum is open on weekends only. Admission is $2 for adults and $1 for children ages 6 to 12. Both the museum and manor house are open for group tours by special request. Since seasonal hours may vary, call ahead for an exact schedule for the time you plan to visit.

### S. Wallace Edwards & Sons
#### 11381 Rolfe Hwy. (Rt. 31) • (757) 294-3121, (800) 222-4267

If you like ham, plan to stop in at S. Wallace Edwards & Sons, just down the street from the Surrey House and the source of the ham served at the restaurant. For three generations, the Edwards family has been creating some of the finest hams you can find anywhere in Virginia, and the very popular tour of their smokehouse offers a fascinating glimpse into how the curing process, taught to the settlers by the Native Americans, has become a modern art. Each of the hams, selected for its high quality, is hand rubbed with a special dry cure then aged perfectly. A notable mahogany color is achieved with days of exposure to hickory smoke and supervised aging. While some long-cut hams are aged for a year, the company's most popular hams are ones that have aged between four and six months.

Edwards' hams have a wide following. The

---

**INSIDERS' TIP**

Horseracing fans can trot up I-64 to Colonial Downs, a racetrack in New Kent County. The track opened for an inaugural 30-day meet September 1, 1997. Thoroughbred racing season is from September 5 to October 10. General admission is $5 for adults, which includes parking, a program and a selection sheet. Children younger than 12 are admitted free. Races typically run Friday through Tuesday. To reach Colonial Downs take I-64 W. to Exit 214. Turn left and the racetrack will be on your left. For more information call (804) 966-7223.

company receives orders from mail-order merchandisers like Williams-Sonoma, Harry & David, Winterthur and Neiman-Marcus - especially during the busy holiday months. Every September, those same hams capture blue ribbons at the state fair in Richmond. Surry's most famous pork products have even earned a stamp of approval from none other than celebrated chef and cookbook author Julia Child.

If you wish to take the free tour of the ham-processing operation, we suggest you call ahead for the schedule. (Tours typically are scheduled between 9:30 AM and 4:30 PM daily.) We also recommend that you spend some time in the retail shop: Your taste buds will demand it, and you won't regret purchasing a ham as an unusual and appreciated gift or culinary remembrance of your visit. The price of a ham starts at about $28. If you can't make it to Surry, check out Edwards' Virginia Ham Shoppe of Williamsburg, 220-6618. Located at 1814 Richmond Road, it's open seven days a week.

## Restaurants

### Surrey House Restaurant
**Rt. 31 • 294-3389, (800) 200-4977**
Somehow it wouldn't seem right if you left Surry County without stopping in at the Surrey House Restaurant, a favorite destination for Williamsburg residents, especially on a sunny Sunday after church. Established in 1954, the Surrey House specializes in ham, seafood, pork and poultry dishes as well as other regional fare - it's Southern cooking at its best! We recommend that you begin your meal with peanut soup, a creamy delicacy full of chunky bits of world-famous Virginia peanuts. As a main dish, the Surrey House Surf and Turf is typically Virginian, featuring a combination of ham and crab cakes. Other regional dishes include delicious hamhocks, great Southern fried chicken and homemade desserts. For the latter, we prefer the peanut raisin pie, a proudly served local variation on the South's ubiquitous pecan pie. It's delicious.

This restaurant has a waiting list on weekends and holidays, so we recommend reservations.

### Village Diner
**Rt. 10, a quarter-mile past blinking light**
**• (757) 294-3633**
This family eatery, which bills itself as "home of the sweet potato cake," serves up home-cooked steaks, seafood, hamburgers and sandwiches and grinders galore at affordable prices. Kids eat free on Friday nights when adults purchase the beef or seafood special. This truly is good old-fashioned home-style cooking. The diner opens at 7:30 AM for breakfast. Midday, try one of the special lunch plates. Village Diner is closed on Sundays.

## Smithfield

While you're over on Southside, you might want to head to Smithfield in Isle of Wight County, the true home of the world-famous Smithfield ham. While ham has placed Smithfield on the map in recent years, the town actually grew up around the trade and commerce that flourished on the Pagan River. Its rich past provides Smithfield with much to tempt the daytripper. The city's charming downtown is a National Historic District, and the restored pre-Revolutionary War homes that line Main Street are a delight to behold. In recent years, a downtown improvement project has added new brick sidewalks, old-fashioned street lamps and attractive landscaping.

While Smithfield isn't exactly next door to Williamsburg, it's just down Route 10 from Bacon's Castle and Chippokes Plantation. Take the ferry to Scotland Wharf, then follow Route 31 to Route 10 in Surry County, where you'll turn left. Drive down Route 10 for another 18 miles or so until you come to a stoplight. Turn left, and you'll be on Smithfield's Main Street. If you hit the ferry at the right time, the whole trip should take about 50 minutes. (One word of advice: As you approach Smithfield on Route 10 disregard the signs that direct you to the Smithfield business district. This is a roundabout route that takes you past the area's meatpacking plants. Following our directions, you'll reach downtown much more quickly).

## Isle of Wight County Tourism Bureau
**Corner of Main and Mason Sts. • ( 7 5 7 ) 357-5182, (800) 365-9339**

To start your visit, stop by the old Isle of Wight Courthouse and pick up brochures and a walking map from the county tourism bureau. The courthouse was built in 1750 and is owned by the Association for the Preservation of Virginia Antiquities. If you follow the walking tour guide, you'll stroll past dozens of gorgeous old houses, actually a blend of 18th-century Colonial, Federal, Georgian and Victorian period houses sitting side by side. There are 65 structures on the tour - and they really are within comfortable walking distance of one another - including the Oak Grove Academy at 204 Grace Street, which was built in 1836 as Oak Grove Academy for Young Ladies. You'll also see the Keitz-Mannion House at 344 S. Church Street, which was erected in 1876 as the Methodist parsonage and was originally located across the street from where it now stands. Other points of interest are Smithfield Academy, 205 S. Mason Street, once a private school for young men, and Christ Episcopal Church, 111 S. Church Street, which was built in 1830. Its bell was said to have been tendered to the Confederate Ordnance Department in 1862 during the Civil War.

## Isle of Wight County Museum
**103 Main St. • (757) 357-7459**

This museum, housed in a former bank built in 1913, offers archaeological displays that highlight county history. It features imported marble and tile and an impressive Tiffany-style dome skylight. Exhibits include Civil War displays, a narrated slide presentation on Isle of Wight County's past and present and a country store, complete with old post office boxes, a potbellied stove, a checkerboard and old pharmacy and hardware supplies. Other exhibits focus on Smithfield's famous meatpacking industry and archaeological digs that have been conducted throughout the county. The museum is open Tuesday through Saturday from 10 AM to 4 PM and Sunday from 1 to 5 PM. Admission is free.

## Saint Luke's Church
**14477 Benns Church Blvd. (Rt. 10) • (757) 357-3367**

As you leave town and head about 2 miles east on Route 10, you'll come to Saint Luke's Church. Built in 1632 and nicknamed "Old Brick," this Episcopal church is the country's only original Gothic church and the oldest church of English foundation in America. The church features its original traceried windows, stepped gables and a rare mid-17th century communion table. Since 1957, St. Luke's has been home to the oldest intact English organ in America. Constructed circa 1630, the organ recently had its beautifully painted doors restored. This National Shrine is open Tuesday through Saturday from 9:30 AM to 4 PM and from 1 to 4 PM on Sunday. The shrine is closed during January; admission is free.

## Fort Boykin Historic Park
**7410 Fort Boykin Tr. (Rt. 673) • (757) 357-2291**

Out in the country along the banks of the James River sits Fort Boykin Historic Park, which was created in 1623 to protect the settlers from Indians and raiding Spaniards. The fort, shaped in a seven-point star, has been involved in every major military campaign fought on American soil and still retains earthworks dating to the Civil War. According

---

**INSIDERS' TIP**

On Smith Island there are no sidewalks, beaches, convenience stores, boat rentals, movie theaters, liquor stores, bars, fast-food chains, boutiques, amusement parks, laundromats or taxi cabs. The islanders you meet will enjoy answering your questions - except for when they're busy in boats or sheds unloading, sorting and packing their catch.

to legend, the guns of Fort Boykin sunk two British men-of-war in 1813. A gazebo overlooks the river, and a picnic area is available. The fort is a tad off the beaten path, so your best bet is to pick up a brochure and map at Smithfield's Tourism Bureau. The fort is open for self-guided tours daily, 8 AM to dark. Admission is free.

# Restaurants

## C.W. Cowling's
**1278 Smithfield Plaza • (757) 357-0044**

Located in a shopping center just east of downtown, Cowling's has everything for lunch and dinner from Cajun specialties and seafood pasta dishes to fajitas, steaks, chicken and ribs. A variety of burgers and sandwiches - from catfish to chili cheese dogs - round out the menu. A kid's menu has a number of options - all for less than $3 - and desserts include such temptations as fried apple pie and a chocolate peanut butter pie topped with whipped butter frosting.

## Ken's Bar-B-Q
**Rt. 258 • (757) 357-5601**

Ken's is a popular and friendly roadside restaurant that serves up some truly authentic Carolina-style barbecue and ribs. The pit-cooked steaks are a good choice and come in a variety of sizes. Portions are huge and prices reasonable (an average entree is less than $10). Ken's is open for lunch and dinner daily and serves up breakfast on Saturday and Sunday. You'll have to bring cash, because credit cards aren't accepted.

## Smithfield Confectionery & Ice Cream Parlor
**208 Main St. • (757) 357-6616**

A family-run business since 1982, this old-fashioned ice cream shop sells subs, deli sandwiches, salads and, of course, ice cream dishes. Belly up to the traditional soda fountain counter and please your palate with a banana split or triple scoop of chocolate chip mint. The parlor is open for lunch and dinner seven days a week.

## Smithfield Gourmet Bakery and Cafe
**218 Main St. • (757) 357-0045**

Since the spring of 1993, this delightful little eatery has served up tasty and unusual sandwiches to an adoring public. All breads are Smithfield Gourmet recipes, baked fresh daily. Cold pasta dishes and salads also are served. A variety of fresh-baked items - cookies, pies, cinnamon rolls, muffins and a cake of the day - are available. The most expensive entree is around $6.

## The Smithfield Inn
**112 Main St. • (757) 357-1752**

This elegant dining spot in the heart of downtown Smithfield was built in 1752. Fine food - seafood, pork, lamb, beef and chicken - is served in an atmosphere of candlelight, flock wallpaper and crisp linens. While your average entree runs more than $15, there's a less expensive tavern menu available. Lunch is served Tuesday through Sunday, dinner Wednesday through Saturday. The restaurant is closed Mondays. Reservations are advised.

## Smithfield Station
**415 S. Church St. • (757) 357-7700**

A popular destination for boaters, Smithfield Station is one of our favorite haunts. It sits at the foot of a small bridge overlooking

---

**INSIDERS' TIP**

Each year about 27 million vehicles travel through the Hampton Roads Bridge-Tunnel, the main artery connecting Norfolk to the Virginia Peninsula. That's a daily average of close to 75,000 cars, trucks and buses (closer to 100,000 on summer days). If you're planning a daytrip to Norfolk or Virginia Beach, try scheduling your visit to avoid prime traveling times - evening rush hour, summer weekends and holidays. And make sure you have plenty of gas in that tank!

Photo: Richmond Convention and Visitors Bureau

Shockoe Slip's former warehouses in Richmond now operate as eateries and boutiques.

the Pagan River. The restaurant serves seafood, pork, pasta and daily specials for lunch and dinner. We especially like the house salad, which is prepared with a slightly sweet Italian-style dressing and baby shrimp. The fried flounder also comes highly recommended. After dining, stroll out on the deck that surrounds the restaurant and connects it to the marina or mosey along the boardwalk. A raw bar and grill on the boardwalk serves crabs and other seafood delicacies for a more casual meal. Concerts frequently are staged on the boardwalk during summer weekends, and the river walk also is the site of an occasional art show. The raw bar is open May through September. (We'll let you in on a little secret: Aside from the ambiance, which is wonderful, Smithfield

Station holds a special place in the heart of one of this guide's authors, who became engaged at the restaurant and returned every Valentine's Day for dinner until she had her second child - then she switched to having brunch there on Mother's Day.) Smithfield Station also has a marina, complete with a bathhouse, swimming pool and picnic gazebo, and 17 waterfront rooms, including two suites in an adjacent lighthouse built a few years back.

## Tangier Island

An excursion to fancifully named Tangier Island makes for an enjoyable daytrip from Williamsburg. It was Captain John Smith who chartered this remote island in 1607, naming it for the Moroccan region he thought it resembled. Twenty miles from the mainland and only 1 mile wide by 3.5 miles long, Tangier Island actually is part of Accomack County on the Eastern Shore.

During the Revolutionary War, the British used Tangier as a base for raiding American ships. Pirates also frequented the island, finding it a great hideaway from enemies. After the war, the island's population began to swell as more and more people settled down for the long haul and began working the Bay. Today, Tangier Island is home to some 700 inhabitants, most of whom rely on the Chesapeake Bay for a living. You'll hear the accents of 17th-century Elizabethan English here, as isolated residents have retained some of their ancestors' ways of speaking.

The cruise to Tangier Island leaves from the town of Reedville in Virginia's Northern Neck. To get to Reedville from Williamsburg, take the Colonial Parkway east to Yorktown. From there, take Route 17 across the York River and north to Saluda. Follow Route 33 to Route 3, which will bring you to Kilmarnock. From here, follow Route 200 north to Route 360, which leads to Reedville and signs for the cruise. The rest of your journey will be by water. The cruise ship *Chesapeake Breeze* leaves Reedville for Tangier Island at 10 AM from May though October 15 and returns to Reedville at 3:30 PM. The trip across the Chesapeake Bay to the island takes about 1 1/2 hours. You can stand on the upper open deck or the enclosed lower deck to watch the menhaden fishing boats and occasional pleasure craft go by, or relax in the *Chesapeake Breeze*'s air-conditioned lounge. Cold drinks and refreshments are available at the snack bar. Tickets cost $18.50 for adults and $9.25 for children. Kids 3 and younger ride free. Reservations are required. For schedules and further information, call Tangier and Rappahannock Cruises at (804) 453-2628.

As you approach the dock via the water, take the time to look around you. You will see dozens of crab farms, neat little sheds rising above the water on stilts. In small wooden pens inside these farms, crabbers horde their catch until the crustaceans have moulted and can be sold as softshell crabs. The work is tedious, as the pens must be checked every

three hours around the clock throughout the entire season. A missed "peeler," as the softshells are called, turns into a quick meal for fellow captives.

Once on the island, you will have several hours to sightsee, take a golf cart or bike tour (at last count there were five cars here) and grab lunch before it's time for departure. The island's pathways lead past charming white frame houses, and you'll probably notice only one school, which serves 170 youngsters from kindergarten through high school.

## Restaurants

### Hilda Crockett's Chesapeake House
• **(757) 891-2331**

When you start hunting down a place for lunch, you'll find your choices are limited. But, as long as you like seafood, you can't go wrong trying out Hilda's, which serves lunch family-style with crab cakes, clam fritters, Virginia ham, vegetables, potato salad, cole slaw, applesauce, homemade rolls, pound cake and endless refills of iced tea. Cost of your meal - served from 11:30 AM to 6 PM - is $11.75 for adults and $5.75 for children 8 and younger.

### Fisherman's Corner
• **(757) 891-2571**

If you prefer to select your lunch or dinner from a menu, stop in Fisherman's Corner for seafood, steaks, sandwiches and hamburgers. The restaurant is open from 11 AM to 7 PM seven days a week, and, while credit cards are not accepted, personal checks with proper ID, are.

# Smith Island

Smith Island in the Chesapeake Bay is actually a chain of marshy islands with a fascinating history. Pirates once hid their boats in the tricky waters surrounding this archipelago, waiting to raid passing ships. Dissenters from the Jamestown colony settled here, eventually forming the three villages of Ewell, Rhodes Point and Tylerton. Today, Ewell, the island's largest town, is sometimes referred to as its capital. Here, commercial fishermen catch hard and softshell crabs and send them to the mainland to serve markets throughout the world. Life for these islanders is often harsh but is guided by a strong religious faith. Joshua Thomas established the Methodist church here and on several other Chesapeake Bay islands during the late 1800s; it continues to be the only organized religion on the island today.

If you're interested in a daytrip to Smith Island, which is Maryland's only inhabited offshore island, contact the Somerset County Tourism Office, (800) 521-9189, and ask for a copy of the brochure describing the island. The pamphlet includes a detailed self-guided walking tour of Ewell, along with maps, historical information and important tips on island etiquette. For example, the island is dry, meaning islanders don't appreciate public consumption of alcohol. An alternative is to wait until your visit and stop in the Smith Island Center, (410) 425-3351, a combination visitors' center and heritage museum, which opened in 1996. At the center, you can watch a 20-minute film featuring the people of Smith Island and view a number of exhibits on the history, environment, watermen, women and church. Admission to the center, which is open from noon to 4 PM daily May through October, is $2 for adults, with children 12 and younger free.

Cruises to Smith Island leave from the Chesapeake Bay/Smith Island KOA Campground in the Smith's Point area of Reedville. To reach the KOA from Williamsburg, take the Colonial Parkway east to Yorktown. Follow U.S. Highway 17 north to Saluda, then Virginia Highway 33 to Virginia Highway 3 and Kilmarnock. From here, follow Virginia Highway 200 north to U.S. Highway 360, which leads to Virginia Highway 652. Go east on Va. 652 until it becomes Virginia Highway 644, then turn north-

east on Virginia Highway 650. It sounds complicated, but signs for the Smith Island Cruise provide adequate directions. The drive takes about an hour and 45 minutes.

The cruise, aboard the *Captain Evans*, leaves the dock at 10 AM and pulls in at Ewell around 11:30 AM, allowing visitors several hours to roam at will and grab lunch before departing around 2 PM or so. Current round-trip rates for the Smith Island cruise are $19.50 for adults and $9.75 for children 3 to 12. Children younger than 3 ride free. The 1999 group rate for 25 adults or more, including cruise, family-style luncheon at Bayside Inn and narrated island bus tour, is $27.50 per person. If you decide to spend the night in one of the campground's six air-conditioned cabins, you'll have access to a swimming pool and pavilion, a new bathhouse with private showers and a number of planned weekend activities, including hayrides, lollipop hunts and crab races for the kids. Cabin rental rates start at $33.95 for two people. For more information about the cruise or the campground, call (804) 453-3430.

Once you arrive, the main attraction, of course, is the island itself. The leisurely pace of life here is a welcome change from the hustle and bustle of mainland existence. This is a place where you can put your feet up on a back porch railing and enjoy the soft breezes off the Chesapeake Bay. If it's spring, you might catch the fragrance of blossoming fig, pear, mimosa and pomegranate trees, which grow in all of the island's towns.

Once you're rested, there is plenty to do and see. A walking tour of Ewell will take you past Cape Cod-style homes, rustic country stores and the sunken remains of the Island Belle I, one of the earliest island ferries. Goat Island, across Levering Creek, is home to a herd of about 20 formerly domestic goats. Natives rely on the goats' migration to the

---

**INSIDERS' TIP**

The Olden Days Festival in Smithfield, which typically is held throughout downtown over the Memorial Day weekend, is a delightful way to step back in time and enjoy carriage rides, antique sales, crafts, music and even a children's dress-up parade. Our kids especially enjoyed the opportunity to wield an honest-to-goodness firehose and douse pretend flames. For information call (800) 365-9339.

water's edge to obtain salt from the marsh grasses as a sign that rain or snow is imminent. Other attractions include Pitchcroft, the island's first settlement, and the wooden keel remains of the 60-foot bugeye sailboat *C.S. Tyler*, built for islander Willie A. Evans.

You can also tour, by foot or bicycle, Rhodes Point, the island's center for boat repair. This small town originally was called Rogue's Point because of the pirates who frequented the area. Here, you'll see boats being made and repaired and see the ruins of some of the earlier vessels that plied their trade on the Bay.

During your visit, you also may notice how friendly everyone seems. Islanders in cars and trucks honk their horns and wave to greet every vehicle and pedestrian they meet. This hospitality also is extended to a hefty population of stray cats, which seem to be everywhere, but look especially well fed and comfortable despite their rather nomadic existence.

## Restaurants

### Bayside Inn
• **(410) 452-2771**

Located on Ewell's Harbor, this charming restaurant dishes up family-style meals. A typical menu includes crab soup, crab cakes, baked ham, clam fritters, baked corn pudding, stewed tomatoes, macaroni salad, cole slaw, homemade rolls, iced tea and homemade pie. The meal costs $11.95 for adults, half price for children 6 to 12 and $1 for kids younger than 6. A separate sandwich menu also is available.

### Harbor Side Restaurant
• **(410) 425-2201**

Open only on Sundays for both lunch and dinner, Harbor Side offers hungry customers the same type of family-style meal as Bayside (listed above) - the menu is almost identical - for $11.95 for adults and half price for kids 12 and younger.

### Ruke's Seafood Deck
• **(410) 425-2311**

This very casual eatery is open seven days a week in the summer for lunch and dinner. (It does close between 5 and 6 PM daily to regroup, so plan accordingly.) Choose from crab cakes, soft-shelled crabs and a few other sandwiches. Your meal will be served on a screened-in deck. Payment policy is cash only.

# Richmond

The Old Dominion's capital certainly is worth a day of your time, particularly if you are a Civil or Revolutionary war buff or someone who enjoys the beauty of a large Southern city. The architecture here is splendid to behold. Trees and parks are everywhere, and an abundance of street festivals, outdoor concerts, garden and flower shows and cultural events can keep you busy throughout the year. Although Richmond is well known for its significant role in the unfolding of American history, you may not know that the city was the site of America's first hospital, built in 1611. Richmond was where military "aircraft" (tethered balloons actually) first were used for aerial reconnaissance during the Civil War. Richmond was home to the first electric streetcar in 1888, and it was where Dupont produced its first cellophane in 1930. And, the first beer packaged in tin-plated steel cans (Krueger Ale of Newark) was test-marketed here in 1935. But there's much, much more to the Old Dominion's capital than this.

Richmond truly is an inspired city, architecturally speaking, and no place illustrates this better than the famed Fan district. Named for the layout of its streets, which fan out toward the western part of town, the Fan is an interesting, diverse community of town houses and single-family structures, some restored, some marginally renovated. Shops and restaurants abound here as well as some unusual art galleries. The Fan is bordered by Monument Avenue to the north, Main Street on the south, Laurel Street on the east and the Boulevard on the west. Another slice of Richmond life is Shockoe Slip, a quaint, riverside area of downtown Richmond that bustles with restaurants and unusual boutiques. Between 12th and 14th streets on E. Cary Street, Shockoe Slip is the cobblestone warehouse district of old Richmond, with many structures dating back a century or more. We suggest the best way to discover all this magnificent city has to offer is to experience it up-close and personal.

The quickest way to reach Richmond from Williamsburg is to head west on Interstate 64 and keep going for about 50 miles. As you approach the city, take the Fifth Street exit to Broad Street and begin your city tour at that point. If you'd rather meander a bit and take the scenic route (which is what we advise), hop on historic Route 5 and wander along this two-lane road through James City and Charles City counties. The speed limit on this road is lower than on the interstate, so the drive will take you a bit longer, but you'll wind past stately old homes and historic plantations. In fact, this old road, which at points is shaded by overhanging trees, is reminiscent of byways familiar to travelers from an earlier era. Route 5 eventually will intersect with Broad Street and you can proceed from there.

These are just a few of our capital-city favorites. For a more complete treatment of the area, pick up a copy of *The Insiders' Guide to Richmond*.

**Metro Richmond Convention and Visitors Bureau**
550 E. Marshall St., Richmond VA 23219
• (800) 370-9004 or 782-2777
**Metro Richmond Visitor Center**
1710 Robin Hood Rd., Exit 78 off I-64
•(804) 358-5511

Before you arrive, you may want to orient yourself to Richmond's wonderful museums, historic neighborhoods and excellent restaurants. If so, call ahead or write to the visitors bureau and ask for brochures, a map and information on key points of interest. Or, if you prefer to wait until you actually arrive in town (what a free spirit!), stop in at the Metro Richmond Visitor Center off I-64 for literature and assistance. One item you should be sure to ask for is a pocket-sized map of city trolley routes. Two separate routes - a red one and a blue one - will take you to within two blocks of most restaurants, shops, museums, theaters and hotels. The trolley runs from 11 AM to 11 PM weekdays and Saturdays, making stops every 10 to 15 minutes from 11 AM to 8:30 PM and every 25 minutes after 8:30 PM. The fare each time you board is 25 cents. For more information, call (804) 358-GRTC.

## Attractions

**Richmond National Battlefield Park Visitor Center
(Chimborazo Visitor Center)**
3215 Broad St. • (804) 226-1981

The Science Museum of Virginia in Richmond is housed in a former railroad station.

Located at the site of the largest Southern hospital during the Civil War, this is the perfect first stop for military enthusiasts. The center, which is free and open daily, has exhibits, a film and knowledgeable employees to guide you toward the city's numerous battlefields. The National Battlefield Park contains 10 park units that offer one-of-a-kind insights into this tragic period of American history. Make sure you ask about the battle sites, cemeteries and markers east of downtown Richmond in Chesterfield, Hanover and Henrico counties. Specific Civil War sites from 1862 include the Chickahominy Bluff, Beaver Dam Creek, Gaines Mill and Malvern Hill. The 1864 sites include Cold Harbor and Fort Harrison. The center is open daily from 9 AM to 5 PM. All activities are free.

## Museum and White House of the Confederacy
**12th and E. Clay Sts. • (804) 649-1861**

For more on the War Between the States, schedule a visit to this museum and house, home of Confederate President Jefferson Davis from 1861-1865. These two places house the world's most comprehensive collection of Confederate artifacts, including more than 500 flags, Robert E. Lee's Appomattox sword and the plumed hat of J.E.B. Stuart, the Confederacy's most famous cavalryman. One of the newest exhibits at the museum is "A Woman's War: Southern Women Civil War and the Confederate Legacy." Continuing indefinitely, this exhibit includes more than 200 objects drawn from public and private collections, including drawings, paintings, engravings, historical documents, newspapers, textiles and flags. Among the highlights of the collection are a Gen. Beauregard doll, named after Confederate leader P.G.T. Beauregard, one of many military-style dolls made for Southern children during the Civil War, and *The Burial of Latane*, an 1864 William D. Washington painting that commemorated the sacrifice of Southern women as well as the valor of a fallen Confederate soldier. Both the museum and the White House are open from 10 AM to 5 PM Monday through Saturday and noon to 5 PM Sunday. Tickets to both the museum and house are $8 for adults, $7 for senior citizens

and $5 for children 7 and older. Children younger than 7 are admitted free.

## Agecroft Hall
**4305 Sulgrave Rd. • (804) 353-4241**

Originally built in England more than 500 years ago, Agecroft Hall was moved to Richmond and reconstructed brick by brick in the 1920s. Situated on 23 acres overlooking the James River, it is a wonderful example of pre-Elizabethan architecture. It is open Tuesday through Saturday from 10 AM to 4 PM and Sunday 12:30 to 5 PM. Admission is $4.50 for adults, $4 for seniors and $2.50 for students. A tour of just the gardens is half price, and group discounts are available for 10 or more.

## Edgar Allen Poe Museum
**1914 E. Main St. • (757) 648-5523**

The Poe museum, which actually occupies five small buildings, pays tribute to the life and career of the famous writer, a native son of Richmond who was born in 1809 and died just 40 years later. At the center of the museum is Richmond's oldest structure, the Old Stone House, built circa 1737. Behind the Old Stone House lies the Enchanted Garden, awash in the color of the flowers and plants favored by Poe during his lifetime. The museum documents Poe's accomplishments with pictures, relics and, of course, verse. A museum shop sells books, prints, post cards and T-shirts. The museum is open Tuesday through Saturday from 10 AM to 4 PM and Sundays and Mondays from 1 to 4 PM. It is closed Christmas Day. Admission is $5 for adults, $4 for senior citizens and $3 for students.

## Richmond Children's Museum
**740 N. Sixth St. • (804) 788-4949**

If you have youngsters along, you'll want to spend a couple of hours at this popular kids' hangout, where classes, workshops and hands-on exhibits introduce children to the arts, nature and the world at large. The museum opened in 1981 to provide Central Virginia with an inviting place for entire families. Exhibits are geared toward youngsters ages 2 to 12 and include the Children's Bank, where kids learn about economics, international currency and mathematics; the WRCM-TV studio, where the younger set can try out their on-air skills in front of working cameras; a Computer Station for testing high-tech knowledge and solving puzzles; and, The Cave, which offers a look inside a 40-foot replica of a real Virginia limestone cave. There's also an art studio, performing stage and a KidShop that sells a variety of interactive toys, games and trinkets from around the world. The museum is open from 9 AM to 5 PM Monday through Friday during summer months and 9 AM to 1 PM on weekdays September through May. The same hours are observed Saturdays and Sundays year round: 10 AM to 5 PM Saturdays and 1 to 5 PM Sundays. Admission is $3 for children ages 2 to 12, $4 for adults.

## Science Museum of Virginia
### 2500 W. Broad St. • (804) 367-1083

Another popular destination for the young and young-at-heart is Richmond's science museum, which offers hands-on fun in everything from aerospace and astronomy to chemistry, crystals and computers. Housed in the old Broad Street Train Station, the museum contains more than 250 exhibits as well as an IMAX theater. The museum is open Monday through Saturday from 9:30 AM to 5 PM and Sunday noon to 5 PM. From Memorial Day to Labor Day, the museum closes at 9 PM Fridays and Saturdays. Admission is $5.50 for the museum, $4 for the film only and $8.50 for a combination ticket for anyone 13 to 59. For seniors 60 and older, the cost is $5 for the museum, $4 for the film and $8 for both, and, for children ages 4 to 12, the cost is $4.50 for the exhibits, $4 for the film and $7.50 for both.

## The Valentine Museum
### 1015 E. Clay St. • (804) 649-0711

The Valentine collects, preserves and interprets the life and history of Richmond through its changing exhibits and innovative programming. Founded in 1892, the Valentine maintains the South's largest collections of costumes and textiles as well as extensive holdings in photos, documents, industrial artifacts and decorative arts. The exhibit "Shared Spaces, Separate Lives," for instance, explores the lives of both Richmond's slaves and free residents before the Civil War. The Valentine also offers a garden cafe and a museum shop that sells everything from gifts, books and jewelry to unusual children's items. The museum is open daily from 10 AM to 5 PM. Admission is $5 for adults, $4 for students and seniors, $3 for ages 7 to 12, and free for children 6 and younger.

## Virginia Museum of Fine Arts
### 2800 Grove Ave. • (804) 367-0844

This is one Richmond attraction you shouldn't miss. This first-rate museum showcases 5,000 years of mankind's artistic achievements. The museum's gallery holds the largest public collection of Faberge eggs outside Russia, as well as outstanding collections of art nouveau, art deco, India art, contemporary impressionists and British sporting art. Artists you will see represented on the museum's walls include Monet, Renoir, Degas, Picasso and Warhol. Here you also will find treasures from ancient Egypt, Greece and Rome as well as an abundance of Medieval and Renaissance art. There is an on-site gift shop and two cafes, one located in the museum's Sculpture Garden. Museum galleries are open from Tuesday through Sunday 11 AM to 5 PM and until 8 PM on Thursdays. Admission is free except for occasional special exhibitions.

## Paramount's Kings Dominion
### I-95 north of Richmond • (804) 876-5000

It's not exactly in Richmond, and we wouldn't advise planning a daytrip that included both an amusement park and a major city, but if you have a whole day to spare and are in search of an amusement park, this is a good one. Located 23 miles north of Richmond on I-95 near Ashland, King's Dominion, which opens daily June through August and on weekends during much of the spring and fall, offers more than 100 rides and attractions. In 1997, the park premiered KidZville, an area

## INSIDERS' TIP

**The fiercely independent residents of Tangier Island had no electricity, indoor plumbing or telephone service until the 1950s.**

that lets kids play, build, slide, climb and dig to their heart's delight. The indoor roller coaster, The Outer Limits: Flight of Fear, catapults you to 54 mph in four exhilarating seconds before hurtling you into a universe of inversions, twists and startling sensations. And that's just the beginning. There also are rides with names like Grizzly, Anaconda, Shockwave and Days of Thunder. And, for really hot days, bring along your swimsuit and take the plunge into Hurricane Reef, a 6-acre water park that's included in your admission fee. Of particular delight to the younger set is Splat City, 3 acres of Gak vats and Green Slime where messy scenes modeled after Nickelodeon TV episodes unfold.

To get to the park from Williamsburg, take I-64 West to 295 West to I-95 North. Get off at Exit 98. Admission to the park was $33.95 for anyone 7 and older, $24.99 for children ages 3 to 6, and $28.99 for seniors 55 and older in 1999.

# Restaurants

Deciding where to eat is a delicious quandary in Richmond. Whether you're in the Fan District, Carytown, Shockoe Bottom or near Virginia Commonwealth University, you'll find plenty of places that serve great food. We hit a few of the high points here.

### Crab Louie's
**13500 Block Midlothian Tnpk. • (804) 275-2722**

A variety destination for locals since 1981, Crab Louie's is the perfect place for a luncheon or dinner celebration. Located in the historic Sycamore House, this seafood restaurant serves great she-crab chowder, crab cakes and homemade breads and relishes. With old wooden floors and a decor featuring antiques, Crab Louie's is a step back in time.

### Joe's Inn
**205 N. Shields Ave. • (804) 355-2282**

What can you say about a restaurant that has been around since 1952? Joe's Inn, a perennial favorite with locals, serves up generous portions of a variety of American and Italian food. The dress code is casual, the atmosphere is friendly and, with most dishes run-

ning less than $10, the price is right. Drop in anytime. Joe's serves breakfast, lunch and dinner.

### The Frog and the Redneck
**1423 E. Cary St. • (804) 648-3764**

Voted Richmond's favorite restaurant in a fall 1996 survey done by the Greater Metro Richmond Area Restaurant Guide, this 6-year-old restaurant already has developed a national reputation for its neon atmosphere and changed-daily cuisine. Recent offerings include fresh tuna with aged Parmesan butter sauce, fresh mussel in a basil, tomato and garlic broth and roasted leg of lamb with rosemary sauce. Don't forget to order some vino from the exceptional wine list. The restaurant only serves dinner. It's closed on Sunday. For more on The Frog and the Redneck, turn to our close-up in the Restaurants chapter.

### Texas-Wisconsin Border Cafe
**1501 W. Main St. • (804) 355-2907**

If casual dining is more your cup of tea, grab some Tex-Mex cuisine or a fiery bowl of chili in this funky eatery. How casual is it? The last time we dropped in was after a weekend camping trip, and we felt right at home. Most entrees are less than $10. Stop in for lunch or dinner daily or for their Saturday or Sunday brunch.

### The Tobacco Company
**1202 E. Cary St. • (804) 782-9431**

This historic restaurant, located in a former tobacco warehouse in Shockoe Slip, has been serving up great prime rib, seafood and daily chef specials since 1977. Lunch and dinner is served every day. They also serve a Sunday brunch. The downstairs club is one of the most happening nightspots in town. Reservations are accepted but not necessary.

# Norfolk

On the eastern edge of Hampton Roads in the world's largest natural harbor, Norfolk has been a sailors' city for more than 200 years. Norfolk Naval Base is the world's largest navy base, and the numerous posts and bases that support it have been temporary home to thousands of men and women from around the nation over the years, particularly during World War II. While Uncle Sam has always played a key role in the city's economy and demographics, Norfolk also serves as the region's financial hub: Within a two-block radius of downtown Norfolk are the Hampton Roads headquarters for all of the state's major banks. But, business often takes a back seat to culture, as Norfolk also is home to the area's four dominant arts organizations: the Virginia Stage Company, the Virginia Symphony, the Virginia Opera and the Chrysler Museum. (See our Nightlife chapter for more information.)

During the past 15 years or so, the city has undergone a Renaissance of sorts, transforming a decaying waterfront into an attractive gathering spot with the addition of the Waterside festival marketplace and new hotels, parks and office buildings.

Although Williamsburg residents tend to turn toward Richmond for employment and for large-city conveniences, many residents commute to Norfolk for jobs, and still others make the trip for an evening out.

The approach to Norfolk from the Historic Triangle is stunning by any criteria: I-64 moves out over the mouth of Hampton Roads on a bridge-tunnel that affords a breathtaking view of the harbor and the Navy base on the far shore. To get downtown once you've crossed the water, follow I-64 to I-264 W., then take I-264 until it becomes Waterside Drive. The Waterside Festival Marketplace will be on your left, and parking will be to your right. If you're feeling adventuresome or just want to see a little more of Norfolk, an alternate - and more direct - route is to take the Granby Street exit from I-64, then follow Granby Street (a six-lane highway for much of the drive) through the neighborhoods of Norfolk until Monticello Avenue splits off to the right. Follow Monticello downtown. Several downtown garages offer public parking. Cost runs 50 cents for the first hour, 75 cents for the second hour, then a

dollar for every successive hour up to an $8 daily maximum.

The drive takes about an hour from Williamsburg, longer if traffic is backed up at the tunnel - and it frequently is during rush hour, on summer weekends and on holidays. Signs along the interstate refer travelers to a radio band for traffic advisories well before the tunnel, and an alternate route to Southside via the James River Bridge is marked with checkered attachments to highway signs. Interstate 664, which also spans the James River via a tunnel and a bridge, is a scenic - though somewhat roundabout - route into Norfolk.

There are special times of year when a trip to Norfolk has added interest. In late April through early May, the Virginia Waterfront International Arts Festival brings world-class music, dance, theater and visual arts to the Norfolk waterfront; the late-April International Azalea Festival is staged amid the blossoms at Norfolk Botanical Gardens; and, during the first weekend in June, you can join a crowd of thousands for Norfolk's annual Harborfest celebration, which brings music, food and entertainment to the downtown waterfront for three days of fun in the sun.

Before venturing south to Norfolk, you may want to pick up a copy of *The Insiders' Guide to Virginia's Chesapeake Bay* for more detailed listings of restaurants, accommodations and attractions.

## Norfolk Convention & Visitors Bureau
**236 E. Plume St. • (800) 368-3097**

This is the best place to stop in during weekday business hours for brochures and pamphlets. Or call the number above and ask to have a visitor's guide sent to you. The bureau also operates a Visitor Information Center just off I-64. Take Exit 273, the second exit after you come east through the Hampton Roads Bridge-Tunnel. The center offers bro-

### INSIDERS' TIP

The first ferry from Scotland to Jamestown debarked in 1925. The service was operated by A.F. Jester, grandfather to well-known Surry businessman S. Wallace Edwards, Jr. The state of Virginia purchased the ferry system in 1947. Today, annual operating costs for the ferry total about $7 million.

chures and a hotel reservation service; staff members there can answer all your questions.

# Attractions

Once you drop anchor in Norfolk, you will wish you'd reserved an entire day to take in all this seafaring city has to offer. Many of the city's attractions are in the heart of downtown, but along its western fringe is an area known as Ghent, the place where the downtown crowd likes to hang out. It's no wonder. Colley Avenue, the main corridor in Ghent, is home to many small specialty shops, some very good restaurants, and a bona fide old-fashioned movie house. Another Norfolk neighborhood is Ocean View, with 7.5 miles of public beaches bordering the Chesapeake Bay. Especially popular from the turn of the century to the 1950s, Ocean View's three city beaches offer a place to swim, sun and picnic. Ocean View is one of the first areas of Norfolk you'll come to after crossing the Hampton Roads Bridge-Tunnel; an exit is marked for it on the interstate.

## The Chrysler Museum
**245 W. Olney Rd. • (757) 664-6200**

If you appreciate visual arts, this is the cream of the crop in Hampton Roads. The Chrysler is considered one of the top 20 art museums in the country. Its collection contains more than 30,000 pieces from all time periods. Holdings include works by Renoir, Matisse and Gauguin, and its art library is the largest in the southeastern United States. The Chrysler also is known for its 8,000-piece glass collection, which includes the works of Tiffany, Lalique and other masters, its superb collection of 19th-century sculpture and its well-recognized collection of photographs. Changing exhibits are excellent: In 1996, a gorgeous display of original illustrations from children's literature drew masses of young people, while the 1997 "Rembrandt and the Golden Age," on loan from the National Gallery of Art, entranced visitors with its two acclaimed portraits by Rembrandt and a dozen other important works from the mid-1600s.

If you get the munchies while browsing, the Chrysler has its own elegant cafe that serves lunch. Chrysler hours are 10 AM to 4

PM Tuesday through Saturday (5 PM in summer) and 1 to 5 PM Sunday. An admission fee of $4 for adults and $2 for seniors and children is charged.

## d'art Center
**125 College Pl. • (757) 625-4211**

Wander through this cooperative center and enjoy the creations of the 30 or so artists who sometimes will work their magic before your very eyes. You'll see painters, sculptors and jewelry makers in their studios and can negotiate with most of the artists to purchase what catches your fancy. The center has been open since the late 1980s.

Hours are 10 AM to 6 PM Tuesday through Saturday and from 1 to 5 PM on Sunday. Admission is free.

## Douglas MacArthur Memorial
**MacArthur Sq. • (757) 441-2965**

For those intrigued by our nation's military history, the Douglas MacArthur Memorial honors the life and times of Gen. MacArthur. The controversial general is entombed here, and his signature corncob pipe and the documents that ended the war with Japan are on display in the galleries. A 25-minute film featuring newsreel footage of MacArthur is shown in the memorial's theater, and the gift shop even displays the general's shiny 1950 Chrysler Crown Imperial limousine. In 1994, several new exhibits were added, including one on segregated military forces and another on female prisoners of war during World War II. No admission is charged for any of the exhibits, but donations are requested. The museum is open from 10 AM to 5 PM Monday through Saturday and 11 AM to 5 PM Sunday.

## Harbor Park
**150 Park Ave., Downtown Waterfront • (757) 622-2222**

Just a baseball throw from Waterside is Harbor Park, home base for the Norfolk Tides, a Triple A farm team of the New York Mets. Designed by the same firm that built the Baltimore Orioles Park at Camden Yards, Harbor Park was selected as the minor league's best stadium in 1995 by the publication Baseball America. Catch the boys of summer in action from early April through Labor Day. Tickets cost $7 for box seats, $5.50 for an adult re-served seat and $4.50 for a child's reserved seat. Tickets can be purchased at the park, or you can order them through TicketMaster by calling 872-8100.

## Historic Ghent
**Colley Ave. and 21st St. • (757) 664-6620**

About a mile from downtown, this intrigu-ing neighborhood is a mix of cafes, boutiques and a bona fide old-fashioned movie house called the Naro, 625-6276. This is where the folks who work downtown like to mix and mingle on any given evening! Join the crowds and enjoy a little people watching while you sip espresso in an outdoor cafe!

## Nauticus
**One Waterside Dr., Downtown Waterfront • (757) 664-1000, (800) 664-1080**

Norfolk's newest museum is the National Maritime Center, more commonly called Nauticus. This $52 million attraction opened in the spring of 1994 on the western edge of the downtown waterfront, adjacent to Town Point Park. It is designed to have equal ap-peal for both adults and children with a mix of theaters, hands-on displays and interactive exhibits about the world's oceans, marine tech-nology, the weather, shipbuilding and the U.S. Navy. A big kid pleaser is Virtual Adventures, a computer-generated, interactive experience that takes participants on a simulated deep-sea voyage in search of the Loch Ness Mon-ster. If you just want to drop in for a bite to eat at The Galley Restaurant or for a peek into the Banana Pier Gift Shop, you can enter the museum's ground floor for free. Access to the Hampton Roads Naval Museum, which moved from the Norfolk Naval Base to Nauticus and is operated by the U.S. Navy, is also free. The city of Norfolk took over operation of the facil-ity in January 1997 and currently is rethinking its approach to exhibits. There may be changes in store in the not-too-distant future. Currently, the museum is open daily 10 AM to 5 PM throughout the summer but is closed on Mon-days October through April. On off-season Sundays, Nauticus is open from noon to 5 PM. Admission is $7.50 for adults, $5 for chil-dren ages 6 to 17 and $6.50 for senior citi-zens, Triple A members and military person-nel.

## Norfolk Botanical Gardens
**Azalea Garden and Airport Rds. • (757) 441-5830**

The great outdoors in all its splendor beck-ons at the Norfolk Botanical Garden near the Norfolk International Airport. This 155-acre garden began in 1938 as a Work Project Ad-ministration grant. Today, it boasts more than 12 miles of pathways and thousands of trees, shrubs and flowering plants arranged in both formal and natural gardens. There are more than 20 themed gardens, including the 3.5-acre bicentennial rose garden, healing and herb gardens and the fragrance garden for the visually impaired. We think the best time to go is in spring when the more than 250,000 azaleas are so spectacular they take your breath away, but there's something blooming just about any time of year. (Even during the winter months you can enjoy camellias, witch hazel, wintersweet and colorful berries.) Newer gardens include a perennial garden, wildflower meadow and a renovated Japanese garden. There's even a "surprise" garden with chang-ing blooms that always offer a hint of color and something new for visitors. One of the best ways to view the gardens during the warm-weather months is by a 30-minute boat or tram ride. The gardens are open from 9 AM to 7 PM mid-April through mid-October, and until 5 PM the rest of the year. The visitor cen-ter closes at 5 PM year-round. Admission is $3.50 for adults, $2.50 for seniors and $1.50 for youth ages 6 to 18. Children 5 and younger are admitted free. Tickets for the boat and tram rides are sold separately and cost $2.50 each or $4 for a combination ticket.

## Norfolk Naval Base
**Norfolk • (757) 444-7637**

Another place to satisfy the military buff is the Norfolk Naval Base, the world's largest navy base. The base encompasses thousands of acres and includes some of the buildings from the 1907 Jamestown Exposition. It is home port to more than 100 ships of the At-lantic Fleet. A guided tour is offered through Tidewater Regional Transit, 642-6300, with tick-ets available at the Naval Base Tour Office at

9070 Hampton Boulevard. From March through December, a tour bus also departs daily from Waterside. Cost for the 45-minute tour is $5 for adults, $2.50 for children ages 3 to 11 and for seniors older than 60. Once you've handed over your ticket, you'll be whisked past the piers where you can get an up-close look at the mammoth aircraft carriers and submarines. The tour also goes by the air station, heliport and Marine security battalion. Tours are offered beginning at 9 AM daily. On weekends, several ships are open for visitation from 1 to 4:30 PM., the part of the trip the younger set seems to enjoy the most. Be advised that the wait to tour ships can get long, so bring along a snack.

## Virginia Zoological Park
**3500 Granby St. • (757) 441-2706**

If you like to take a walk on the wild side - and if you have small children along - a stop at the Virginia Zoo is a must. Situated on 55 acres along the Lafayette River, the zoo is small but certainly charming. It is home to some 350 animals, including reptiles, nocturnal animals, rare Siberian tigers, primates, llamas, rhinos and a pair of elephants who like to toss around tires and douse each other with water. A few years back, the zoo was singled out for praise by Attorney General Janet Reno for making its facility more accessible to persons with disabilities. The zoo is in the early stages of a 10-year, $15 million improvement plan that calls for a Dismal Swamp walkway around the duck pond, a butterfly house, Asian and Australian exhibit areas, a new entry and educational complex and an African Okavango River Delta exhibit that will bring lions, zebras, giraffes and warthogs to Norfolk. The African exhibit is the first one planned to be completed in the fall of 1999. Special children's programs are offered year-round. Zoo hours are 10 AM to 5 PM daily. Admission is $3.50 for anyone older than 11; $1.75 for children ages 2 to 11 and $1 for seniors 62 and older.

## Waterside Festival Marketplace
**333 Waterside Dr. on the Elizabeth River**
**• (757) 627-3300**

No trip to Norfolk is complete without a visit to Waterside, the city's festival marketplace overlooking the Elizabeth River. In fact, sometimes this is the only destination visitors have in mind when they come to Norfolk. The marketplace is a colorful mix of shops, restaurants and entertainment, and, in recent years, it has become the focal point for Norfolk's public celebrations and civic occasions. It is constructed of steel and glass on two levels and is connected to a parking garage across the street by a second-level walkway. Eateries are concentrated downstairs, while most of the shops and numerous kiosks are on the second level. Live entertainment occurs almost daily, and an attached marina makes the place convenient for pleasure sailors. From Waterside, it's an easy stroll to Nauticus, Harbor Park and other downtown attractions. The marketplace is open from 10 AM to 9 PM Monday through Saturday and noon to 6 PM Sundays, with extended hours for special events. Admission is free.

# Restaurants

While Norfolk has pretty much anything your heart - and palate - desires, we have a few favorite haunts we want to mention. If you're looking for a satisfying meal in appealing environs, you can't go wrong with any of the eateries listed here.

## Baker's Crust
**The Palace Shops, 330 W. 21st St. • (757) 625-3600**

Sandwiches, salads and homemade breads - we're talking more than 20 varieties from fat-free baguettes, boules, batards and country loaves to challah, brioche, fruit and nut and pan foccacia. The soup of the day will come served in a bread boule on request, and

---

**INSIDERS' TIP**

To find out what's on the agenda in Richmond, you can request a quarterly calendar of events. Just call (888) RICHMOND.

a complete repast of rotisserie roasted chicken is available. Most sandwiches, soups and salads run between $4 and $6, and breads run the gamut from $1.50 to $4.50. If you come at noon, be prepared to wait, as this is a very popular lunch destination for the local crowd.

### Bistro! • (757) 622-3210

This award-winning restaurant serves some of the most creative fare in town. Innovative creations by chef/owner Todd Jurich include crab cakes on black beans and rice with roasted red banana chutney, Tuscan-style roast leg of lamb and morel mushroom cappellini with garlic confit, sun-dried yellow tomatoes, veal glace and Jack cheese. Get the picture? It may sound strange but, believe us, it all tastes wonderful. A dinner for two - entrees only - will set you back about $35. Bistro! serves lunch and dinner Monday through Friday and dinner only on Saturday.

### Bobbywood
**7515 Granby St. • (757) 440-7515**

We love this place, where chef Bobby Huber is on stage in an open kitchen, concocting amazing soups, steaks, fresh fish and vegetable dishes. One of our favorites is the lightly fried potstickers, served with a lip-smacking sauce, but other popular creations have included onion-crusted salmon with spinach potato cakes and sage cream, grilled lump crab cakes with garlic grits and a signature pizza topped with roast garlic puree, wild mushrooms and four cheeses. Bobbywood is closed on Sunday. (We found this out the hard way when we were hankering for Mother's Day reservations.) Don't you make the same mistake. This restaurant is worth a visit, not only for the food, but for the fun and carefree atmosphere that keeps things hopping. Bobbywood is open for lunch and dinner Monday through Friday and dinner only on Saturday.

### Doumar's
**20th St. and Monticello Ave. • (757) 627-4163**

We couldn't decide if this was an attraction or a restaurant, but since you'd be hard-pressed to drop in and leave without eating, we've listed it here. What makes Doumar's so special? For one thing, it is one of the only remaining Hampton Roads eateries that still has carhops. For another, it has been at the same location since 1934. But, perhaps most interestingly, restaurant founder Abe Doumar invented the ice cream cone back in 1904 during the St. Louis Exposition. Doumar's serves up outstanding, inexpensive pork barbecue, burgers, fries and milk shakes in old-fashioned soda fountain glasses. And the limeade is superb. The restaurant is closed on Sundays; they're open for lunch and dinner the rest of the week. Doumar's does not accept credit cards.

### The Dumbwaiter
**117 Tazewell St. • (757) 623-3663**

You have to actually visit The Dumbwaiter to get the true flavor of this popular Norfolk restaurant; a description just won't do it justice. A lively setting provides a fanciful backdrop for the diverse assortment of dishes: grits, sweet potatoes, meat loaf and grilled chicken better than your own grandmother ever made on one hand, sauteed salmon, grilled tuna steak and smoked beef tenderloin on the other. Stop in at The Dumbwaiter for dinner Monday through Saturday or for lunch Monday through Friday. The restaurant is closed on Sundays.

### First Colony Coffee House
**2000 Colonial Ave. • (757) 622-0149**

If chilling out is a priority and the hour is still early, drop in at First Colony for a cup of java and a slice of fruit tart or cappuccino cheesecake in classy but casual environs. If you're alone, the copper-top bar decked out with reading lamps is the perfect place to down an espresso and catch up on the day's news. Although we prefer to stop in for a coffee break, First Colony also is open for lunch and dinner. Our advice: Try the white chili. All of the food is good, but it's probably one of the best meals on the menu.

# Virginia Beach

You say you're from western Ohio, Central Pennsylvania or some other landlocked region and the last time you saw the Atlantic Ocean was on a post card sent to you by a vacationing friend? Well, then by all means schedule a daytrip to Virginia Beach. After all, it isn't every day you get to dip your toes in the ocean, bury your spouse in the sand or sip a pina colada while watching the waves break.

A day at the beach also is the perfect addition to your itinerary if you have small children. In fact, it may be the only opportunity you have to stretch out in the sunshine as the kids frolic in the surf and sand. (Although we advise you to keep a very close eye on the little ones. The surf may, on occasion, appear gentle, but the ocean's undertow is unpredictable.)

The route to the beach is pretty direct. Simply hop on Interstate 64 and head east through the Hampton Roads Bridge-Tunnel until you hook up with Interstate 44, the Norfolk/Virginia Beach Expressway. (Take note: Renumbering the Expressway to I-264 to make it less confusing to motorists - I-264 heads to Norfolk from I-64 - is expected to take place in the next year or so.) Follow the expressway until it ends and head straight until you intersect with Atlantic Avenue. Turn right and you're cruising the beachfront. (The entire trip should take you about 1 and 1/2 hours.) You'll find there's plenty of parking spaces - both free and metered, depending on how close you are to the water - on side streets all up and down the beach, but they fill up fast. There's also paid parking in a number of municipal lots. Your best bet is to get to the beach early on a weekday so you can grab a prime spot for parking - and sunning.

Virginia Beach prides itself on being a family destination, and over the last several years has backed up its claims with a $94 million modernization of both the boardwalk and Atlantic Avenue that includes new landscaping, whimsical sculptures, attractive signs, street lights and a special bike-riding lane along the boardwalk. You didn't bring your bike? Not to worry. You can rent one right at the waterfront, complete with a child seat if you need it.

If you prefer to plan your visit around a special event, you're in luck. In mid-June, the city hosts its annual Boardwalk Art Show and Festival, which brings close to 400 artists to the oceanfront to display and sell the fruits of their creative endeavors. In mid- to late September, the Neptune Festival salutes summer's end with free musical entertainment, a world-famous sandcastle contest and a military air show. During the Christmas season, there's Holiday Lights at the Beach, a two-mile stretch of glittering lights and animated displays that transform the boardwalk into an altogether different sort of winter wonderland. Or, you can always take in a concert at the Virginia Beach Amphitheater. New in 1996, the outdoor complex brings big name entertainment to the "Beach" throughout the summer months. Headliners in 1997 included James Taylor, Jimmy Buffett, Bob Dylan and Elton John.

Of course, there's always the possibility that you may not want to do much more than turn over while you're at the beach. But, if you have a hankering to take in some of the sights, there are a number of places to visit along the waterfront.

# Attractions

## Atlantic Waterfowl Heritage Museum
**113 Atlantic Ave. • (757) 437-8432**

This new museum interprets the heritage of wildfowl - everything from ducks and geese to songbirds - through art exhibits, interactive displays and special demonstrations. The museum's five galleries feature artwork and decoy carvings, including some that date back

Photo: Norfolk Convention and Visitors Bureau

Norfolk's Waterside houses numerous shops and eateries and serves as the focal point for downtown celebrations.

to the turn of the century. Overlooking the ocean, the museum is located in the 1895 Dewitt Cottage, the last remaining oceanfront cottage from the late 19th century. The museum is open Tuesday through Saturday from 10 AM to 5 PM and noon to 5 PM Sunday. From October through February, the museum is closed on Mondays. Admission is free, although donations are accepted.

### Association for Research and Enlightenment (A.R.E.)
**67th St. and Atlantic Ave. • (757) 428-3588**

This intriguing attraction is the headquarters for the work of the late psychic Edgar Cayce, who resided in Virginia Beach and was best known for falling into a trance and diagnosing and prescribing cures for medical ailments. Each year, A.R.E. hosts thousands of international visitors and researchers who have an interest in Cayce's remarkable talents. There are free lectures, video and film presentation, ESP demonstrations and daily tours. There's even a meditation room overlooking the ocean and a bookstore with overflowing shelves. A.R.E. is open 9 AM to 8 PM Monday through Saturday and 11 AM to 8 PM on Sunday. Admission is free.

### Old Coast Guard Station
**Oceanfront on 24th St. • (757) 422-1587**

Housed in a former U.S. Life-Saving/Coast Guard Station built in 1903, this simple wooden structure is reminiscent of an earlier, simpler oceanfront era. Inside, two galleries give glimpses into the history of the people who risked their lives to save strangers during shipwrecks. A permanent display focuses on the impact of World Wars I and II on Virginia Beach.

The museum is open Tuesday through Saturday from 10 AM to 5 PM and Sunday noon to 5 PM. From Memorial Day to October 1 the museum also is open Mondays. Admission is $2.50 for adults; $1 for children 6 through 18, military personnel and seniors 60 and older.

## Old Cape Henry Lighthouse
**Fort Story, extreme north end of Atlantic Ave. • (757) 422-9421**

Construction of this lighthouse was authorized by George Washington and was completed in 1791 at a cost of $17,500. The edifice continued to guide mariners until it was replaced in 1881. The stone used in the structure came from the same Virginia quarry that supplied the White House, Capitol and Mount Vernon. Over the years, the edifice has become the official symbol of Virginia Beach. The lighthouse is open from 10 AM to 5 PM, beginning in mid-March and continuing through October. Admission is $2 for adults, $1 for students and senior citizens. Children 6 and younger and military in uniform are admitted free.

## Virginia Marine Science Museum
**717 General Booth Blvd. • (757) 437-4949**

An extremely popular destination for the entire family, the marine science museum completed a $35 million expansion in 1996. This fine facility - which continues to draw huge crowds throughout the year - now features three new buildings and dozens of exciting exhibits, from the Atlantic Ocean Pavilion, which showcases schooling fishes, sharks and other deep sea creatures in a 300,000-gallon aquarium, to the Family Channel IMAX 3-D Theater, one of only a handful in the country. Visit the Owls Creek Marsh Pavilion where you can view a live river habitat and outdoor marsh bird aviary. Dozens of hands-on exhibits give children the opportunity to tong for oysters or make a few waves. And, by all means, stop and pet the rays, which may look a tad odd but are as friendly as any well-loved puppy. The museum is open 9 AM to 5 PM daily and until 9 PM daily during the summer. Admission for the museum only is $7.95 for adults, $5.95 for children ages 4 through 12 and $6.95 for senior citizens. The IMAX theater costs $6.95 for adults, $5.95 for children, and a combination ticket is $11.95 for adults, $9.95 for children and $10.95 for senior citizens.

## First Landing/Seashore State Park
**Shore Dr. • (757) 481-4836**

This 2,770-acre sanctuary has more than 336 species of trees and plants, a self-guided nature trail and a visitors center with books for sale and exhibits. Nine trails, including one for handicapped visitors, cover 17 miles and are part of the National Scenic Trails System. A 5-mile bike trail connects to the city's bike trails. There also are places here to picnic, so if you're planning a visit, you might want to pack a lunch.

# Restaurants

All that splashing around in the ocean is sure to work up an appetite. While the "Beach," as locals call it, has a well-rounded selection of restaurants for your dining pleasure, we've singled out a handful sure to please.

## Le Chambord
**324 N. Great Neck Rd. • (757) 498-1234**

One of the most charming restaurants in the area, Le Chambord serves divine French cuisine like Chateaubriand Bearnaise or quail au jus. Meals are a little pricey - expect to pay $40 or $50 for entrees for two - but there's a companion bistro next door that sells more affordable American continental cuisines if your plastic has begun to lose a few of its numbers. Lunch is offered Monday through Saturday, and dinner is served nightly.

## Isle of Capri
**39th St. and Atlantic Ave. • (757) 428-1711**

If you're looking for a place to dine along the waterfront, you might want to pop into this restaurant in the Holiday Inn Sunspree Resort. Set six floors above the boardwalk, Isle of Capri offers great pizza and other wonderful Italian fare. It's open for dinner only.

## Pasta E Pani
**1069 Laskin Rd. • (757) 428-2299**

If you like Italian, you'll thoroughly enjoy this restaurant, whose name translates to pasta and bread. Both are homemade and delicious, making this restaurant a perennial favorite of Insiders who come here for lunch or dinner. A dinner for two should run about $25 to $30.

## The Jewish Mother
### 3108 Pacific Ave. • (757) 422-5430

Lunch and dinner are offered at this kid-friendly restaurant, a Virginia Beach landmark since 1975, serves up an incredible array of sandwiches, wonderful desserts and more than 90 different varieties of beer. Prices are reasonable.

## Three Ships Inn
### 3800 Shore Dr. • (757) 460-0055

This is the place for a romantic dinner for two. As soon as you are seated (if it's chilly, request a table beside the enormous fireplace), you'll be pampered by knowledgeable servers, ably describing dishes such as duck with black cherry sauce or brace of quail. While a visit to Three Ships might stretch your budget - expect to pay up to $50 for a meal for two - it's worth it. The restaurant is open for dinner only Tuesday through Sunday.

Many visitors enjoy biking through the Historic Area, especially on quiet and picturesque back streets where the illusion of a return to the past is most complete.

# Parks and Recreation

Bungee jumping, surfing and snow skiing may be the only forms of recreational activity unavailable (as of yet) to Historic Triangle residents. Whether you play as hard as you work or take a more laid-back approach to your free time, you'll have no trouble finding activities to suit you and organizations to support your favorite pastimes.

If you seek leisure activities, you can find just about anything you want. Your only problem may be choosing which park to explore, which league to join or where to go fishing.

It's through the parks and recreation departments of the local governments that most of the organized sports and recreation activities take place. The sports leagues for enthusiasts of all ages and skills are too numerous to list in this section; their organizers are volunteers, so the contacts change too frequently for a comprehensive listing of their phone numbers to be useful. Anyone interested in sports and recreation information should consult the comprehensive coverage in *The Virginia Gazette*'s sports section. The James City County Parks and Recreation's comprehensive seasonal publication is available at the JCC-Williamsburg Recreation Center and other sites, as are the listings of the Williamsburg Parks and Recreation publications.

For those of you hoping to hit the links during your stay, please turn to our golf chapter for information on area courses.

## Parks

## Departments

### James City County Division of Parks and Recreation
**5301 Longhill Rd. • (757) 259-3200**

This department oversees a wide range of recreation programs throughout the county including those at the James City-Williamsburg Community Center, the James River Community Center, Little Creek Reservoir, Mid County Park and Upper County Park. Office hours are 8 AM to 5 PM.

### Williamsburg Recreation Department
**202 Quarterpath Rd. • (757) 220-6170**

This department oversees a wide range of recreation programs as well as Quarterpath Park, Waller Mill Park and Kiwanis Park. The department's regular office hours are 8 AM to 5:30 PM, although someone is on duty whenever the recreation center is open.

## Locations and Activities

### Quarterpath Park
**202 Quarterpath Rd. • (757) 220-6170**

This park is home to some huge area sports leagues, and for good reason. Its facilities include free tennis and basketball courts, an outdoor pool that's open through Labor Day, three softball fields, a playground and indoor courts for basketball or volleyball. Morning aerobics classes are offered for a fee. The Williamsburg/James City County recreation and sports complex and offices are here as well. The center holds a 10-lane pool, whirlpool, saunas, fitness equipment and racquetball courts. Hours are Monday through Thursday 6 AM to 9 PM, Friday 9 AM to 8 PM, Saturday 9 AM to 6 PM and Sunday 1 to 6 PM. Guests may use the facilities for a small daily fee or purchase memberships for three months, six months or a year. For information call 220-6170 (Williamsburg residents) or 220-4700 (James City County residents).

## College Landing Park
**S. Henry St. • (757) 220-6170**

This small park, on the southern edge of town off S. Henry Street, is always open. It is built alongside a marsh and has picnic areas, a boat ramp and a quiet boardwalk. It is wheelchair accessible.

## Waller Mill Park
**Airport Rd. (Rt. 645) • (757) 220-6178**

On Route 645 west of Williamsburg, Waller Mill is the place to go for a picnic or a lazy paddle around the lake. Open from sunrise to sunset March to mid-December, Waller Mill offers shelters, tables, nature trails, jogging trails and fishing, plus canoe, rowboat and pedal-boat rental. Boats for fishing rent for $4 per licensed angler per day. Pedal-boats rent for $4 an hour; canoes and rowboats for pleasure are $3 per hour. For a nominal fee, you can launch your own fishing boat at the boat ramp. There's also a walking course for senior citizens.

## York River State Park
**5526 Riverview Rd. • (757) 566-3036**

The Virginia Department of Conservation and Recreation operates this large tract off I-64 and adjacent to the York River year round. Here you'll find excellent hiking trails, picnicking and fishing, including two-hour guided canoe trips on weekends April through October, good bird-watching and boat ramps. The 1.6-mile Taskinas Creek Trail gives hikers a fascinating look at a Chesapeake Bay estuary. The park is open from 8 AM to dusk. During the week, visitors enter the park for a $1 parking fee per car. They can then pay to rent boats and fish. On weekends, visitors pay $2 per adult and $1 for kids. This fee includes parking, boat rental and fishing.

## Upper County Park
**180 Leisure Rd., Toano**
**• (757) 566-1451**

This James City County facility is open from Memorial Day to Labor Day and boasts an outdoor pool, bathhouse, community room, picnic shelters and fitness course. Entrance to the park is free, although use of the pool is $3.50 per day for adults and $3 per day for kids younger than 18. Families can purchase season pool passes for $70. The park is open from 11 AM to 7:45 PM daily.

## Mid County Park
**3793 Ironbound Rd. • (757) 229-1232**

Fitness trails, soccer, softball and volleyball are a few of the recreational activities available at this James City County park, which is open daily from 9 AM to dusk. Located off Route 199, Mid County also offers picnic shelters and Kidsburg, an all-volunteer, community-built children's play area with portions modeled on area attractions. For more on Kidsburg, see our Kidstuff chapter.

## Kiwanis Municipal Park
**123 Longhill Rd. • (757) 229-9184**

Little League baseball fields, basketball courts and lighted tennis courts make this Longhill Road park one of the best places where locals can do their leisure-time thing without traveling far. Tennis classes are also available.

## New Quarter Park
**Lakeshead Dr. • (757) 890-3500**

Near the Queens Lake area of Williamsburg, this York County park is solely for group activities. Groups of 20 or more may use the park free of charge by making reservations. However, a $100 refundable deposit is required. Family reunions, company picnics, business meetings and the like can make use of the park's 545 acres to boat, hike, fish from piers and enjoy picnics in the pavilions.

## Yorktown Beach
### Rt. 17 and Water St., Yorktown

Yorktown Beach is open to the public year-round free of charge. Lifeguards are on duty daily during the summer months. Water lovers can swim, fish and boat here and even take a shower afterwards.

# Recreation Centers

## James City-Williamsburg Community Center
### 5301 Longhill Rd.    • (757) 220-4700

A favorite biking trip is the 23-mile Colonial Parkway, which provides a good variety of landscape and wonderful views without the heavy traffic of area streets and highways.

This large facility has just about anything a person could want in recreation. Among the offerings are: a gymnasium with two full basketball courts or four volleyball courts; a two-lane indoor suspended track; 25-meter-by-25-yard swimming pool with three lap lanes always available for lap swimming; locker rooms with showers and saunas; racquetball courts; whirlpool with capacity for 16 people; fitness room with free weights, two circuits of Cybex and 23 pieces of cardiovascular equipment; a teen area equipped with TV and games; a senior area with pool table and game table. The hours of operation are Monday through Thursday 6 AM to 9 PM; Friday, 6 AM to 8 PM; Saturday, 9 AM to 6 PM; and Sunday 1 to 6 PM. Annual access passes for residents are as follows: family, $320; adult, $160; youth (age 5 and older), $55; senior citizens, $125. All resident patrons without a monthly pass must purchase a $5 access pass to use the center. The pass must be shown each time the patron visits the center and pays the daily admission fee. The daily admission fee is $5 for adults and $2 for youth.

## James River Community Center
### 8901 Pocahontas Tr. • (757) 887-5810, TDD machine 259-3215

The center includes a gymnasium, racquet-ball court, fitness room, ping-pong and pool table, three tennis courts, basketball courts, a sand volleyball court, soccer field, softball field and a nature trail. The center is open Monday through Thursday from noon to 9 PM; Friday, noon to 8 PM; Saturday; 9 AM to 6 PM; and Sunday, 1 to 6 PM. Cost for a one-year resident access pass as of August 1997 is: adult, $30; family, $45; senior, $20; youth, $15.  An annual resident combination pass to James River Community Center and the James City-Williamsburg Community Center is $355 for families; $180 for adults; $135 for seniors; and $60 for youth. All resident patrons without a monthly access pass must purchase a $5 access pass to use the center. This pass must be shown each time the patron visits the center and pays the daily admission fee. The daily admission fee is $5 for adults and $2 for youth.

# Activities

## Biking

Many visitors enjoy biking through the Historic Area, especially on quiet and picturesque back streets where the illusion of a return to the past is most complete. Guests of Colonial Williamsburg hotels and inns or anyone who has a general admission ticket to the Historic Area can rent bikes for $5 per hour, $12 for four hours, or $19.95 for the day at the Williamsburg Lodge. Call 220-7690 for more information. Bikes are also available from the following private businesses.

## Bikesmith of Williamsburg
### 515 York St. • (757) 229-9858

Bikesmith sells, rents, services and repairs bicycles near the east end of the Historic Area. You'll pay $10.50 for four hours or $14.50 for eight hours to rent some wheels. Hours are seasonal and vary, so call ahead, especially if you're vacationing off-season.

## Bikes Unlimited
### 759 Scotland St. • (757) 229-4620

Near both the college and the west end of the Historic Area, this company offers complete biking services, including rentals ($10 per day). We suggest you call for current hours.

## Peninsula Biking Association
P.O. Box 12115, Newport News VA 23612
• (757) 875-1594

This 25-year-old touring association is open to area residents of all ages and skill categories. The PBA sponsors frequent short-distance rides and two long (more than 40 miles) rides a year. Meetings are held each month at area restaurants to discuss bike-related topics and to socialize. A monthly newsletter keeps members up-to-date on club activities. Dues are $12 a year.

# Bowling

## AMF Williamsburg Bowl
5544 Olde Towne Rd. • (757) 565-3311

Regular hours here are 9 AM to 11 PM Sunday through Thursday, 9 AM to 2 AM Friday, 9 AM to 1 AM Saturday. Colorful excitement is offered in the form of the Extreme Bowl Package. The fun begins at 11 PM Friday and continues until 2 AM Saturday and again 11 PM Saturday until 2 AM Sunday. During these events, regular lighting is turned off, the music is turned up and black lights provide special effect lighting on the pins, which glow in the dark. Three times a year Williamsburg Bowl hosts tournaments, which may make getting a lane difficult. The Virginia Women's Tournament takes place over several weeks in October and November. Colonial Virginia's Men's Tournament comes along during March and April. During the Colonial Virginia's Mixed Tournament in June, July and August, they really mix it up. Special rates are offered to children, senior citizens and groups. This is an excellent spot for a child's birthday party since they offer special packages.

# Fencing

## Williamsburg Fencing Club
AHEPA Hall, New Hope Rd. • (757) 229-2069

The Fencing Club meets at the American Hellenic Educational Progressive Association (AHEPA) Hall, just off Richmond Road. Fees are $15 per month and meetings are held from 7 to 9 PM Tuesday and Thursday. Membership includes use of the facility, equipment and instruction for beginners. To enroll, just show up.

www.insiders.com
See this and many other
**Insiders' Guide®**
destinations online.
**Visit us today!**

# Fishing and Hunting

Water surrounds the Historic Triangle - rivers, tributaries, lakes, ponds, wetlands, estuaries, and the Bay. A complete guide to area fishing would require a hefty volume. Here we offer merely some local fishin' holes and information about licenses. If you're a die-hard angler, check with the Department of Game and Inland Fisheries in Richmond, (804) 367-9369, for a copy of its annual state fishing guide and the facts on seasons and creel limits, etc. Or, look in local bait and tackle shops for the Department's pamphlets.

Saltwater fishing requires a license for anyone younger than 65. Freshwater fishing requires a license for those 16 and older. Licenses are valid for the calendar year during which they are bought and are available at local bait and tackle shops, marinas, sporting goods counters of larger stores and county circuit court clerks. For more information on fishing licenses or for boat licenses, contact

---

**INSIDERS' TIP**

A favorite biking trip is the 23-mile Colonial Parkway, which provides a good variety of landscape and wonderful views without the heavy traffic of area streets and highways.

the Department of Game and Inland Fisheries.

If hunting is your sport, you'll need a license, too. Hunters 16 and older who have previously had a license can purchase one valid in Virginia at most bait and tackle stores or at the Williamsburg Kmart for $12.50. If you've never had a hunting license before or are between the ages of 12 and 15, you must first take a Hunter Safety Course to obtain a Virginia hunting license. These courses are given by the state for free. Again, contact the Department of Game and Inland Fisheries.

### Waller Mill Park
**Airport Rd. (Rt. 645) • (757) 220-6178**

For freshwater fishing, try Waller Mill Park, which is one of the area's deepest lakes, known for large striped bass, crappie, largemouth bass, perch, pickerel and channel catfish. There is no charge to fish from the pier. The fee to rent a boat is $4 per day per person. That charge includes fishing privileges. The park is usually closed from mid-December to mid-February.

### Little Creek Reservoir
**180 Lakeview Dr., Toano • (757) 566-1702**

Little Creek Reservoir in Toano, covering 996 acres, has a boat ramp, a dock and a fishing pier. You can also fish from the shore. Crappie, largemouth bass, pickerel, bluegills and walleye can be hooked here. Little Creek is open daily March through November; December through February it opens weather permitting. Season passes are available. Boats can be rented for $8 per boat per day, and that includes fishing privileges. Children younger than 16 fish for free. Boats for pleasure riding can be rented for $3 per hour or $10 per hour with motor. This wonderful, practically secret lake is a bit hard to find for the new resident: from Route 60 in Toano, take Route 610 (Forge Road) 2 miles to the first left, which is Lakeview Drive.

### Lee Hall Reservoir
**Jefferson Ave. in Newport News Park
• (757) 886-7915**

If northern pike is your favorite catch, consider a trip to Lee Hall Reservoir, a 230-acre lake in northern Newport News (about a 30-minute drive east on Route 143). The reservoir is reputed to offer good largemouth bass fishing as well as perch, sunfish, crappie and the occasional northern pike. Pedal boats can be rented for $4.22 an hour; canoes and rowboats are $3.17 per hour.

# Health and Fitness Clubs

### Aerobics Plus
**Williamsburg Shopping Center, 147 Monticello Ave. • (757) 220-0556**

This coed club offers five workout rooms, locker rooms, saunas, free weights, bikes and more. It holds more than 50 fitness classes per week, including aqua sessions, and offers daily rates for visitors - $9 for a day pass. Aerobics Plus also offers free weights, shower facilities and childcare.

### Iron Bound Fitness Center
**1228 Richmond Rd. • (757) 229-5874**

This coed center, behind Williamsburg Shopping Center's Food Lion, features the usual weights and machines, a sauna, an outdoor pool, a Jacuzzi and a tanning bed. Guest rates are $5 a day or $20 a week. The center is open daily.

# Horseback Riding

### Carlton Farm
**3516 Mott Ln. • (757) 220-3553**

Carlton Farms offers lessons, boarding, training, summer camp and sales and has an indoor lighted arena. They specialize in hunter horses and have a special package for beginning riders. Instructors at the farm suggest that beginning riders have at least three private lessons to get used to being on a horse. Those lessons are $35 an hour. From there, the rider would be given group lessons at $25 an hour.

### Cedar Valley Farm
**804-A Lightfoot Rd. • (757) 565-2585**

Off Lightfoot Road, Cedar Valley Farm gives private lessons to groups or individuals in English riding. Summer camps are offered sometimes, and horse owners can obtain per-

The Plantation Course at Kingsmill was designed by Arnold Palmer.

mission to ride at the farm. Cedar Valley Farm also runs the William and Mary college riding program and show team.

## Jogging and Running

Joggers will find that many area parks offer some kind of fitness path. Waller Mill offers four trails - its mile-long trail is one of the best - and the trail at the James City County-Williamsburg Community Center is also very popular. But Insiders love running along the Colonial Parkway best of all.

### Waller Mill Park
**Airport Road, (Rt. 645) • (757) 220-6178**

This park offers a wide range of trails for the jogger, walker and bicyclists. All of them wind through a wooded setting. The mile-long Fitness Trail is especially popular because it features fitness stops along the way for different exercises. The other trails include the 1.5-mile Bayberry Nature Trail, the 3-mile Lookout Tower Trail and the 4.5-mile Dogwood Trail that is used by joggers and bicyclists.

### James City-Williamsburg Community Center
**5301 Longhill Rd. • (757) 220-4700**

The center includes a two-lane indoor suspended track. The inside lane is reserved for walking and is also accessible to wheelchairs and canes. The outside lane is reserved for joggers and speed walking. The facility also has two miles of walking and bicycling paths on the grounds.

### Colonial Road Runners
**• (757) 220-1439**

This club, which promotes running and walking in the area, sponsors monthly runs, interval workouts, training sessions and social activities. Races include the Williamsburg Winery Run, Ford's Colony 8K, William and Mary Homecoming Run, Governor's Landing Run and the Queen's Lake Run. New members are welcome. The group meets monthly for group runs and pot luck socials and weekly for workouts. Annual dues are $10 for adults and $6 for students.

## Tennis

### Public Courts

### Quarterpath Park
**202 Quarterpath Rd. • (757) 220-4700**

## Mid County Park

3793 Ironbound Rd. • (757) 229-1232

There are three asphalt surface courts at both Quarterpath Park and Mid County Park with no charge and a first-come, first-play basis.

## Kiwanis Municipal Park

123 Longhill Rd. • (757) 229-9184

Kiwanis Municipal Park has seven hard surface courts that are free during the day and $2 per hour after dark when the courts are lighted. Reservations can be made by calling 220-6176.

# Semiprivate Courts

## Kingsmill Tennis Club

931 Kingsmill Rd. • (757) 253-3945

The Kingsmill Tennis Club's 15 courts are free to guests of the resort and available at the rate of $26 per hour for clay courts and $18 an hour for hard courts to nonguests. For persons wanting a court in the morning, the club suggests making reservations a day or two in advance. Regular tennis shoes, not running shoes, must be worn.

## Williamsburg Inn

136 E. Frances St. • (757) 220-7794

Colonial Williamsburg provides its guests and the general public with access to tennis courts on the property of the Williamsburg Inn near Providence Hall. Memberships for area residents are available. Two hard and six clay courts can be rented at $18 per hour for singles or $24 per hour for doubles. Lessons are available for $40 an hour from the resident pro.

# Soccer

This sport is thriving here, with the number of youth soccer clubs on the increase.

## York County Division of Parks and Recreation

301 Goodwin Neck Rd. • (757) 890-3500

Boys and girls in kindergarten through 12th grade from York County, James City County or Williamsburg can participate in the Youth Soccer Program sponsored by York County Division of Parks and Recreation, 890-3500. There are spring and fall programs. Practices take place at area elementary and middle schools and county parks. Registration begins at the end of August. Fees are currently $20 for the first child, $15 for each additional child. Coach certification programs are also offered. A weather hotline at 890-3501 keeps participants informed of weather cancellations.

## James City County Division of Parks and Recreation Youth Soccer League

5249 Olde Towne Rd. • (757) 565-6920

James City County offers a youth soccer league in the spring and fall for boys and girls in grades 1 through 8. There also is a class for kids ages 3 to 5. Soccer camps are offered, including a half-day camp for children 4 to 11 years old, and a full-day camp for youth to age 18.

## Soccer Club of Williamsburg

• (757) 220-3794

The Williamsburg Soccer Club promotes the growth of soccer. It sponsors boys and girls travel teams for kids ages 10 to 19. House league teams are open to all children ages 4 to 9. The club's Annual Labor Day Tournament draws about 140 youth teams each year, with games played at the Recreation Center, area parks and schools, Fort Eustis and Anheuser-Busch. In 1992, teams from six states and Ontario, Canada, participated.

By far, the area's biggest golfing draw is the PGA Michelob Championship, held at Kingsmill each October.

# Golf

Williamsburg is fast becoming one of the premier golf destinations on the East Coast. In the last five years, 108 holes have been added to the mix. And if construction can keep pace with plans, the number of courses will grow from 15 to more than 20 over the next three to four years.

By far, the biggest draw is the PGA Michelob Championship at Kingsmill held each October. Prior to 1997, the event was held in July — and seemingly coincided with the hottest week of the year. The move to October has strengthened the field, which includes the likes of host pro Curtis Strange, Ryder Cup captain Lanny Wadkins, 1997 winner David Duval, two-time winner Mark McCumber, Davis Love III, and a host of other top names. The tourney carries a purse of $1.9 million with the winner walking away with $342,000. Off-site parking is free, with shuttle buses running every few minutes. Directional signs are posted on I-64, U.S. Route 60 and Va. Route 143. For ticket information, contact the Michelob Championship at 328 McLaws Circle, Williamsburg, VA 23185, or call (757) 253-3985.

Many of the courses cater heavily to the communities with which they are associated, as well as the growing local retired population and visitors looking for an alternative to touring or shopping. Insiders have become accustomed to the pricey greens fees, but they also know there are some good bargains out there. They also know to make tee times in advance. . In this chapter, we give you an overview of the courses, including greens fees, yardages (from the men's tees) and directions. Greens fees include cart unless otherwise noted. We've also tried to let you know when carts are a must for a particular course. Soft spikes are required at many of these courses, so be sure to ask when you call for tee times.

## The Courses

### The Colonial Golf Course
**8251 Diascund Rd., Lanexa • (757) 566-1600, (800) 566-6660**

In Lanexa, on Diascund Road (which is off U.S. Rt. 60, 7 miles west of the Williamsburg Pottery), the course opened in 1995. It is a daily-fee course, carved out of dense woods and wetlands, with several holes overlooking the Chickahominy River. This championship course plays to a par 72 and is 5881 yards long. Unique features include a three-hole practice course ($18, with cart and practice balls) and the Teaching Center and Golf Academy. Different rates apply for the various teaching and clinic packages, and reservations are appropriate. A round, with cart (a must), is $75.

### Colonial Williamsburg Golden Horseshoe Golf Course
**S. England St., Williamsburg • (757) 220-7696**

You can choose from three beautiful, challenging courses here. Robert Trent Jones designed the Gold Course, which opened in 1963. A multi-million dollar renovation was completed in 1998. Nationally renowned, the course features numerous elevation changes, tight fairways and plenty of water. Its signature hole, the par 3 16th, boasts the first island green ever built in America. Playing to a par of 71, the 6248-yard layout's five closing holes are a test for any golfer. The Golden Horseshoe — known locally as "the Shoe" — offers full clubhouse amenities, including a pro shop, locker rooms and a lounge.

The second course opened in 1991, and is just down the road from the Gold Course. The Rees Jones-designed Green Course is a 6244-yard, par 72 course where mounds abound and the par 5 18th hole requires a 200-yard carry off the tee. More wide open than its sister course, this design still offers a stiff test for hackers of all levels. Like the Gold Course, the Green features a first-class clubhouse, pro shop and restaurant.

After designing the Gold Course, the senior Jones took the time to create the nine-hole Spotswood Course. Its executive length design allows golfers to get around it in quick order, perfect for a late afternoon of fun.

Guests staying in Colonial Williamsburg hotels pay $95 to play the Gold or Green Courses; nonguests pay $125 for the Gold and $115 for the Green (cart included). Guests pay $30 for the Spotswood, nonguests pay $40 (carts not included). Carts rent for $20 per person, and club rental is available for $30. Lessons from the pro are $35 for 30 minutes or $25 from an assistant pro.

## Ford's Colony Country Club
**240 Ford's Colony Dr., Williamsburg • (757) 258-4130**

Thirty-six holes of world-class golf, designed by Dan Maples, are set on verdant hills with water, water everywhere at Ford's Colony. Here, you will find four nine-hole layouts that can be played in a number of combinations. Opened in 1991, the Gold nine plays 3113 yards. With undulating greens and water on seven holes, it is a real challenge. Other options are the Red nine (3074 yards), the White nine (3163 yards) and the Blue nine (3069 yards). Greens fees at Ford's Colony vary seasonally, so inquire about fees when calling for a tee time. Generally, fees run from $95 to $105, with discounts available during twilight time. You will need a cart. Lessons are available, and guests of the Manor House, an on-site luxury hotel, can purchase golf packages. The clubhouse facilities are first-rate, and, after your round, world-class dining awaits. Ford's Colony recently began construction of 18 more holes, scheduled to open in spring 1999.

## Kingsmill Golf Club
**100 Golf Club Rd., Williamsburg • (757) 253-3906**

The three courses at this golf club have something to satisfy every golfer. Kingsmill on the James, a planned community, and Kingsmill Resort surround the courses. But the wide, exceptionally well landscaped vistas and breathtaking views of the James River remove you from any sense of encroachment. Kingsmill is home to the PGA Michelob Championship. The River Course is the crown jewel. Designed by the legendary Pete Dye, the par 71, 5001-yard course is both challenging and scenic. Holes No. 4, 8, 10 and 16 are bears, but your reward is the par 3 No.17, which overlooks the historic James River. In recent years, changes to several holes have toughened up the layout.

The Plantation Course, par 72, is a 5503-yard Arnold Palmer design. Undulating greens make for a putting challenge, and a couple of the par 4s will test you off the tee. In 1993, the 18th hole was redesigned to feature a new fairway and green.

Lastly, there is the Woods Course, designed by Tom Clark and Kingsmill touring pro Curtis Strange. East of the other courses, this 6030-yard achievement looked like a course that had cured for 20 years on the day it opened. It features its own clubhouse with all the amenities you would expect at a world-class resort such as Kingsmill.

All three courses are open to the public. Greens fees vary depending on which course you play. For visitors, the cost is $125 ($100 for resort guests) for the River Course. The Plantation and Woods courses are $100 for visitors and $85 for resort guests. All fees include the mandatory cart. Lessons are $65 with a pro and $45 with an assistant pro. Visitors can reserve a tee time 24 hours in advance.

## Kiskiack Golf Club
**8104 Club Dr., 10 min. west of Williamsburg • (757) 566-2200, (800) 989-4728**

This John LaFoy-designed course opened in the fall of 1997. Created from woodlands and rolling terrain, Kiskiack is quickly becoming a favorite among local golfers. Ten minutes west of Williamsburg, at the Croaker Road exit on I-64, this 6405-yard, par 72 layout is a treat. The par 3 2nd hole, requiring a hefty carry over water, is easily the signature hole. Greens fees, including cart, are $65, and getting a tee time in advance is a must.

### The Legends at Stonehouse
**Va. Rt. 30, Williamsburg • (757) 566-1138, (888) 2 LEGENDS**

This new course has generated more comment than any other has in recent years. Located about 15 miles west of Williamsburg near Toano, Stonehouse is said to be one of the most beautiful mountain courses in the Mid-Atlantic region. It features beautiful, deep bunkering, awesome vistas and undulating, fast greens comparable to Cypress Point in Pebble Beach, California. Some greens sit atop cliffs, while others meander along spring-fed creeks. The par 71 design measures 6111 yards. Greens fees are $100, and lesson costs vary. We strongly recommend a cart. Call the toll-free number for tee times. The quickest route to the course is via I-64 west to Exit 227. The entrance is a half-mile north on the right.

### Newport News Golf Club at Deer Run
**Newport News Park, 901 Clubhouse Way, Newport News • (757) 886-7925**

Insider golfers looking for a lower-cost day on the links often take advantage of Deer Run. The par 72 courses offer 5863 yards on the Cardinal Course and 6324 yards on the Championship Course. Greens fees are lower than those in the immediate Williamsburg vicinity. Greens fees with cart run from $21 to $36. Lessons cost $40 per half-hour with a pro and $35 with an assistant pro. The course is an easy 15-minute drive east on I-64. Take the second Ft. Eustis exit, go straight through the light and take the second left.

### Royal New Kent
**Va. Rt. 155, Providence Forge • (804) 966-7023, (888) 2 LEGENDS**

The second Legends course to open in the Williamsburg area is an unusual one, said to be unlike any other on this side of the Atlantic. Instead, it has been compared to Ballybunion and Royal County Down in Scotland, two of the world's greatest courses. Among other things, it features stone walls, hidden greens and blind fairways, giving this course a particularly natural setting. This par 72 course is 6200 yards long. Greens fees run $105 with a cart, which we recommend. Soft spikes are required. Call ahead for tee times and golf packages. The course is about 30 minutes west of Williamsburg; follow I-64 to Exit 214 (Providence Forge). Take Va. Rt. 155 south 2.5 miles to the course entrance.

### Williamsburg National Golf Club
**3700 Centerville Rd., Williamsburg • (757) 258-9642, (800) 826-5732**

Club Development Associates of Pinehurst developed the Williamsburg National just east of Williamsburg near the intersection of Va. Route 5 and Centerville Road. Within the developing Greensprings neighborhood, this 6448-yard course is open to the public and offers 18 holes designed by Jack Nicklaus Associates. It's designed for both the low and high handicapper. For example, the 4th hole lets golfers play a shot over wetlands, but there is a safe area to the left for the high handicapper. The $64 fee includes cart, which you will definitely need. Lessons are $50 an hour, $30 a half-hour. A new 18-hole course should be completed by the fall of 1999.

# Golf Supply Shops

### Golf USA
**6588 Richmond Rd., Williamsburg • (757) 564-9782**

Williamsburg's newest golf shop, this place opened in 1998. Near the Williamsburg

---

**INSIDERS' TIP**

It's a good idea to reserve tee times at least a day in advance for courses in the Williamsburg area.

Photo: Kingsmill Resort

Kingsmill Golf Club offers three courses to the public.

Pottery in Lightfoot, Golf USA features a full line of golf items, computerized swing analysis and club regripping.

## Caddy Shack Golf Works
**118 Second St., Williamsburg • (757) 229-9786**

For golf supplies, you will want to check the pro shop at each course. In addition, we suggest you check out this simple, small yet good supply shop. Here, David Murray, known locally as "Dr. Golf," does excellent professional custom repairs and offers a wide range of golf items, including new and used clubs as well as handmade clubs.

## The Golf Shoppe
**The Village Shops at Kingsmill, 1915 Pocahontas Tr., Williamsburg • (757) 253-2881**

Golf shopping goes high-tech here. Computerized shaft selection is available as well as a full line of golfing supplies. For the serious golfer, artisans will craft custom equipment to suit your needs. It's well worth a visit.

## Williamsburg Golf Club Co.
**8225 Old Mill Ln., Williamsburg • (757) 566-4871**

The pickings are on the slim side, but we recommend you drop in for a look-see. These folks excel at making custom clubs as well as repairing those you already own.

The 200-mile-long estuary known as the Chesapeake Bay is the largest and most biologically productive estuary in North America, home to more than 2,700 species of plants and animals.

# The Environment

While the gentle waves of the Chesapeake Bay don't actually lap the shores of the Historic Triangle, this magnificent body of water directly affects the region's environment. For one thing, this narrow, wooded peninsula is bound by three rivers - the James, the York and the Chickahominy - all of which feed into the Chesapeake Bay. For another, the Peninsula encompasses miles of shoreline, extensive wetlands and thousands of acres of watershed. Consequently, one of the most unsettling environmental issues facing the region focuses on what is happening out there in the magnificent, 200-mile-long estuary known as the Chesapeake Bay.

## Some Bay Basics

Let's take a little time here to give you the lowdown on the Bay. It may surprise you to know that the Chesapeake Bay, formed 10,000 years ago, is the largest and most biologically productive estuary in North America, home to more than 2,700 species of plants and animals. While this long stretch of water averages 15 miles across, its depth averages a mere 28 feet. Other facts about the Bay, compiled by The Chesapeake Bay Foundation, are detailed below.

The Bay covers 2,500 square miles and holds 18 trillion gallons of water.

Flowing into the Bay are 49 rivers with 102 branches and tributaries. These can be navigated for 1,750 miles.

There are more than 15 million people living in the Bay's watershed, which includes Virginia, Maryland, West Virginia, Pennsylvania, Delaware and New York.

The Bay's blue-crab harvest annually represents more than half of our country's total catch.

The Bay is the winter home for about 500,000 Canada geese and 40,000 whistling swans.

The Bay has more than 8,000 miles of shoreline, but only 2 percent of it is accessible to the public. The rest is privately owned.

Amazingly, if you reduced the Chesapeake Bay to the scale of a football field, its average depth would equal three dimes. The bay's shallowness makes it vulnerable to pollution because ample water is not available to absorb toxins, nutrients and sediment.

Each new person in the Bay watershed generates about 50,000 pounds of waste each year.

## Trouble in Paradise

With the stage already set for trouble, the lifestyles, business practices and environmental nonchalance of most of the 20th century merely added insult to injury. As a result, the Bay, once renowned for its plentiful populations of oysters, crab, shad and other finfish, has watched as their numbers diminished dramatically and, in some cases, virtually disappeared from its waters. A number of other forms of marine life have also showed signs of decline. The causes have been multiple and complex: overharvesting by commercial fishermen, pollution, shellfish diseases and loss of crucial wetlands to development.

But years of vigilance are beginning to pay off. Bay watchers will be happy to hear of the numerous positive developments in the past decade. For example, biologists recently noted an increase in hickory-shad spawning in the upper Bay as well as improvements in the reproduction rates of white perch. And, while harvests of blue crabs, always a prolific symbol of the Bay's abundance, dropped for three consecutive years in the early '90s, the 1996 harvest was back up to the levels of earlier decades. In fact, results from a nine-year study, released in May 1997, suggest that there are no real problems with blue crab populations in the Bay, and that a record increase in the number of young crabs born in Hampton Roads' lower Bay occurred in 1996. But a separate study released a month later is contradictory. It concludes that heavy fishing and environmental factors have kept the crab population below historic levels. Some believe that crab populations are actually cyclical and that their numbers ebb and flow in a predictable, 12-year cycle.

Both environmental and governmental groups advise caution. The crab industry currently is an $88 million-a-year trade in Virginia, which puts enormous pressure on the Bay's crab population to produce. Even with the recent spate of good news, Virginia plans to continue restrictions imposed a few years back, including maintaining a cap on the number of crab pots commercial harvesters can drop into the water. A 1997 Bay-wide crab management plan stresses the need to improve water quality and protect underwater grass beds in which young crabs thrive. Regulatory groups haven't ruled out imposing additional restrictions in the future.

# Oyster Anxiety

The crab's compatriot, the tasty Bay oyster, hasn't fared quite as well. In fact, in recent years, the decline in the numbers of this shellfish has been dramatic. The harvest of market-sized oysters dropped from about 3.5 million bushels in the mid-1950s to less than 50,000 (and falling) in recent years. In 1994, there were signs of improvement: the market oyster harvest was more than triple the previous year's total, while the number of seed, or immature, oysters rose 62 percent. Still, conditions are grave and any improvements are slight, at best. And, marine scientists and watermen can't agree on whether the main reason behind the oyster's demise is disease, pollution or excessive harvests.

Researchers have been looking for ways to revive the Bay's ailing oyster population. One of the most recent - and promising - studies has been undertaken by the Virginia Institute of Marine Science at Gloucester Point, just across the York River from Yorktown. Marine scientists at VIMS have placed experimental Japanese oysters in a variety of habitats throughout the Bay to see how well they will grow in those foreign environments, and if they are immune to the diseases that have decimated native oyster populations. This same species of oyster already has been introduced in Europe, the Pacific Northwest and Chile. In 1998, VIMS scientists started testing a second species of Asian oysters in Bay waters.

VIMS doesn't restrict its aquatic research to oysters. Chartered in 1940 as an arm of the College of William and Mary, VIMS is the largest marine center in the nation focused on coastal ocean and estuarine research. Because of its groundbreaking work, the Institute is recognized internationally as a world leader in marine science. In the recent past, researchers have helped establish hard clam and softshell crab aquaculture in the state and have done considerable research on the bay scallop. Recently, VIMS announced it would create a new aquaculture genetics and breeding center to step up the pace of its seafood farming research.

While the fate of many types of shellfish remains iffy, one species of aquatic life that appears to be making a comeback is the striped bass, more commonly known as a rockfish to local anglers. Rockfish live all along the East Coast but primarily spawn in the Bay and were plentiful in area waters during the 1960s and early 1970s. Continued heavy fishing drove populations to all-time lows, and stringent restrictions were placed on rockfishing in the early 1980s. Indeed, in 1989 Virginia banned commercial striped bass fishing in order to replenish declining populations. Those efforts, perhaps aided by a cyclical resurgence of the species, have paid off. Rockfish are once again plentiful in the Bay and neighboring waters, and restrictions have been eased considerably.

# Water Woes and Wonders

While many species of fish and shellfish are suffering, the bodies of water that sustain them have their own set of problems.

The York River has low dissolved-oxygen counts, indicating large amounts of waste discharge and sluggish flushing action. Some shellfish grounds have been condemned in recent years as a consequence of these conditions. The James River has recuperated from Kepone (a highly toxic insecticide) contamination since the Kepone ban was established in the 1970s, but sewage overflows from Richmond plague the river, as do industrial discharges and agricultural runoff. Although the latter two problems have improved somewhat in recent years, shellfish grounds here, too, have been condemned in various areas due to contaminants.

But help is on its way in the form of two new important state bills. The Virginia Water Quality Improvement Act and the Water Quality Monitoring, Information and Restoration Act will establish and fund programs that address the amount of nutrients entering the Bay's tributaries and the impact of toxic chemicals on state waters, while accurately assessing the state's water quality.

One local body of water that teems with life is the Chickahominy River, which extends from western Henrico County, northwest of Richmond, to the James River just upstream of The Governor's Land at Two Rivers subdivision in James City County. Named after the Native American people who still live in the area, the word Chickahominy means "coarse pounded corn people." To this day, the Chickahominy remains one of the cleaner tributaries to the Chesapeake Bay, providing homes for herons, egrets and bald eagles in its marshes, swamps and surrounding land. Rare plant species such as swamp pink and yellow cowlily can be found in the middle and lower sections of the watershed, and even freshwater mussels, highly sensitive to any disturbances in the environment, make their home in Chickahominy tributaries. But an influx of development around the cities of Richmond and Williamsburg has raised concerns about the watershed's future. In an effort to prevent new problems from developing and old ones from escalating, a comprehensive effort is under way to document the watershed's resources and to learn more about how the health of its wetlands and waterways are related to the use of surrounding land.

# The Air We Breathe

Air quality in the Historic Triangle is affected not so much by industrial discharges as by automobile emissions and the area's proximity to the urban centers of Richmond and Hampton Roads. When it comes to cars, the

## INSIDERS' TIP

**Boaters who want to cruise the Chesapeake Bay should pick up a free copy of the Chesapeake Bay and Susquehanna River Public Access Guide. The guide, published jointly by the states of Maryland, Virginia, and Pennsylvania and the District of Columbia, lists more than 500 boat ramps, beaches and natural areas in the Bay region and is available at local tourist centers or by calling the Chesapeake Regional Information Service (CRIS) at (800) 662-2747.**

main culprit is nitrogen oxides, which, together with the hydrocarbons emitted by vehicles, combine with sunlight to produce ozone. It is this lower-atmosphere ozone that can cause respiratory problems in people.

To keep future highway plans from violating federal clean-air laws, the region may have to give up a few of its larger road projects and consider using cleaner fuels and stricter emissions testing. However, analyses indicate the region's road plans through the year 2010 are very close to meeting federal standards, and data from the last 15 years suggest that ozone levels continue to drop in the region. In fact, the U.S. Environmental Protection Agency announced in 1997 that the region had not violated federal smog standards for four years, an accomplishment that removed the region from a federal list of places with smog problems. All indications are that the region should be able to comply with current federal smog standards for the next decade through the continued use of cleaner-burning gasoline and compliance with new federal regulations on paints and other products. That doesn't mean the area is completely out from under a dark cloud, however, as there are rumblings that the federal government will tighten air pollution rules in the not-too-distant future.

# Friends of the Environment

While we tend to focus on the problems we have in taking care of our environment, the news on the local "green" front is getting better all the time. Throughout Williamsburg and the rest of the Peninsula, individuals and groups work together to make the area a better place in which to live. In 1990, Colonial Williamsburg established its Environmental Action Council, a group that celebrates Earth Day each year with a festival at its recycling center. Each Arbor Day, the Williamsburg Area Council of Garden Clubs recognizes numerous businesses and organizations that have made strides in beautifying their properties. Earth Day activities abound across the Peninsula every April. And, Virginians continue to show support for the environment through the purchase of "Friend of the Chesapeake" license plates, which sport a blue crab on a sea grass background. Each time a set of plates is purchased, a donation is deposited into a Chesapeake Bay restoration fund.

And to make environment-friendly habits easier to establish in the region, the Virginia Peninsulas Public Service Authority (VPPSA), the organization that oversees recycling in Williamsburg, York and James City County, expanded its recycling program in late 1996 to include mixed paper - a broad category that covers everything from cereal boxes and computer paper to magazines and telephone books. In May 1997, the VPPSA also began monthly collections of hazardous household chemicals to give residents an alternative to dumping them down the drain or stashing them in trash bins.

# Environmental Groups

Residents interested in trying to eliminate the region's environmental problems can begin by contacting a number of local, state and national organizations, including the following.

### Williamsburg Land Conservancy
P.O. Box 2000, Williamsburg VA 23187
• 565-0343

Founded in 1990 as the Historic Rivers Land Conservancy, this private, nonprofit land trust is dedicated to promoting the preservation, protection and enjoyment of local natural resources, primarily in the James and York River watersheds. To achieve this goal, the conservancy supports education about and scientific study of the area's ecology and encourages innovative methods of conservation and environmentally sound land use. The conservancy also strives to protect the environment through land acquisition, conservation easement and other management practices.

# Cleanup Crusader

Back in the 1980s, Robert Dean was a recreational boater who liked to motor on the Chesapeake Bay and its many tributaries. What he noticed on his pleasure trips soon appalled him.

"I saw the garbage everyone was throwing into the waterways," said Dean, who lives in Virginia Beach. "People are using the earth as a trash dump."

Dean got busy. In 1989, he organized the first Clean the Bay Day, an all-volunteer effort to get people out to pick up every can, bottle or plastic container they came across as they walked the shore. That year, about 2,000 people carted away 30 tons of trash from 52 miles of coastline - trash that not only was unsightly but also endangered marine wildlife, especially birds, sea turtles and fish.

After such an auspicious beginning, the cleanup effort continues to grow. In 1996, thousands of volunteers gathered more than 386,000 pounds of coastal debris - everything from microwave ovens to mopeds - from 202 miles of shoreline. On the Peninsula, coastal areas of the York, James and Chickahominy rivers and Buckroe and Grandview beaches in Hampton are cleaned. In recent years, cleanup efforts have been expanded into Pennsylvania, Maryland, Delaware and Washington, D.C., and to include underwater cleanup, done by volunteer scuba divers from the civilian and military community.

With assistance from the Center for Marine Conservation, which is based in Washington, D.C., but operates a field office in Hampton, the cleanup effort has become fairly streamlined. Volunteers are now given data cards listing the categories of items that most frequently turn up on the beaches, along with information on how the data card is used to compile an assessment of beach debris. "Since 1989, we've picked

— continued on next page

Photo: Hampton Conventions and Tourism

Grandview Nature Preserve in Hampton is one of the
beaches cleaned annually on Clean the Bay Day.

up more than 2 million pounds of debris," says Dean. "When you consider that 52 percent is plastic, it's an incredible volume because plastic is so lightweight."

Another big offender is cigarette butts. "If you look at our major highway intersections, you'll see hundreds of cigarette butts where people have dumped their ashtrays," says Dean. "When it rains, they get washed into our storm water and eventually reach the Bay." Contrary to what many people think, it takes six to seven years for a single cigarette filter to break down in the environment, he added.

As Clean the Bay efforts become more widespread, education has become a key component of the program. Research data, a public speakers' bureau and two videos directed at children and adults now are available. The Clean the Bay Day annual poster and T-shirt theme is reproduced as a Scout patch that can be earned by participating scouting groups. Still, despite the scope of the program, it relies almost exclusively on volunteer involvement. And, it seems as if there is no end in sight to the need for this extensive grassroots effort.

Unfortunately there has been little improvement in peoples' habits over the past eight years or so, notes Dean, an avid defender of the environment. "We haven't seen any dramatic changes at all," he laments. "When I started this project, I thought that, in four or five years, we wouldn't need it anymore. But if it weren't for all the volunteers who pick up garbage along the beaches and the streets, our cities would look like trash dumps."

Clean the Bay Day is held from 9 AM to noon on a Saturday in early to mid-June. For more information, call (800) SAVEBAY.

---

### The Alliance for the Chesapeake Bay
**530 E. Main St., Ste. 501, Richmond VA 23219 • (800) 662-2747**

This nonprofit environmental organization is a coalition of environmentalists, business people, governmental officials, scientists, farmers, sports enthusiasts and others who are working together to protect the Bay through habitat restoration projects, field trips, special clean-up days and educational programs aimed at improving stewardship of the Bay. Formed in 1971, the Alliance also provides the public with information and opportunities to become involved in Bay activities.

### Chickahominy Watershed Alliance
**530 E. Main St., Ste. 501, Richmond VA 23219 • (804) 775-0951**

As part of the Alliance for the Chesapeake Bay, this coalition of concerned citizens and environmental groups works to help maintain the high quality of the Chickahominy watershed and to preserve its multitude of natural resources. The Alliance sponsors field trips and educational meetings as well as restora-

tion projects and welcomes any and all volunteers to join its efforts.

### Center for Marine Conservation, Atlantic Regional Office
**306-A Buckroe Ave., Hampton VA 23664 • 851-6734**

Formed in 1972, this 120,000-member environmental group works to protect marine life in all its abundance and diversity. One of the largest nonprofit groups in the world dedicated solely to this effort, the center's agenda focuses on everything from pollution prevention to the creation of marine sanctuaries. The center also is recognized by the United Nations Environment Programme as one of its 500 Friends of the Environment.

### Chesapeake Bay Foundation
**1000 W. Plume Center, Norfolk VA 23510 • 622-1964**

With more than 83,000 members, the foundation is the largest nonprofit conservation group working to save the Bay. Each year, Foundation educators go out into the marshes and open waters in workboats and canoes to provide tens of thousands of students with in-the-field environmental education. A Foundation lands program works to manage growth and development in the Bay watershed.

## Chesapeake Bay National Estuarine Research Reserve in Virginia
**P.O. 1346, Gloucester Point VA 23062**
**• (804) 684-7135**

Managed by and operated out of the Virginia Institute of Marine Science, the reserve was started in 1991 as part of the U.S. Coastal Zone Management Act. Currently, there are 22 (soon to be 25) reserves nationally, all of which were formed to provide outdoor laboratories for research and education in support of coastal resource management. The best place to view the ongoing work of the reserve is at Taskinas Creek at the York River State Park on Riverview Road in Croaker. At the park, a trail winds through the edge of the marsh. Vigilant (and quiet) visitors can spy ospreys, bald eagles, fiddler crabs and other wildlife all along the trail.

## James River Association
**P.O. Box 110, Richmond VA 23218**
**• (804) 730-2898**

The 1,500 members of this group work together to promote conservation of the natural and historic resources of the James River watershed. The Association's goals include supporting creative land use policies through the watershed and educating the public so that it can better appreciate the resources of the James River. Its accomplishments include getting 25 miles of the James River designated as a Historic River, producing a complete inventory of natural and cultural resources along

the river and developing a Watershed Resources Management plan and videotape.

## People for the Ethical Treatment of Animals (PETA)
**501 Front St., Norfolk VA 23510**
**• 622-PETA**

Although this group has a different mission from the others we have discussed, it's mentioned here because it's large, often controversial and its U.S. headquarters are in Norfolk. Formed in 1980, PETA has more than a half-million members worldwide who are dedicated to establishing and protecting the rights of all animals. The PETA principle is basic: Animals are not ours to eat, wear, experiment on or use for entertainment. In addition to numerous campaigns against the use of animals in laboratory testing and in the fur industry, PETA staff members regularly speak to student groups across the country.

# Events

## Estuaries Day
**York River State Park, Riverview Rd., Croaker • 566-3036**

Another way to get acquainted with environmental groups and projects in the region is to participate in Estuaries Day, which is held the third Saturday in September as part of the three-day national CoastWeek program. Hosted by York River State Park, Estuaries Day offers guided hikes, educational cruises, canoe trips and games as part of the celebration of the fertile waterways where rivers meet the sea. Musical entertainment, catered food, environmental videos, a bird hike in the early morning hours and pontoon boat cruises are

---

### INSIDERS' TIP

**It may surprise you to know that everyone lives in a watershed - land where all precipitation with sediments and other materials flows to a waterway or a common outlet, such as a bay or the ocean. To do your part for the environment, you can prevent erosion by keeping vegetation in your yard, by using splash blocks and downspouts, by planting native trees and shrubs for wildlife habitat and to hold soil in place and by refraining from overfertilizing your lawn or garden.**

typical treats of the celebration. Other highlights of the day include fossil geology, net fishing, children's arts and crafts and a participatory performance about the Bay for children. All Estuaries Day events are free, although a $4 parking fee is charged. Reservations are required for many of the cruises and trips and are accepted by phone only. The event is cosponsored by the Virginia Department of Conservation and Recreation and the Chesapeake Bay National Estuarine Research Reserve in Virginia.

### Clean the Bay Day
**Various locations • (800) SAVEBAY**

On the annual Clean the Bay Day in early to mid-June, volunteers collect trash from beaches around Jamestown and Yorktown as well as the rest of Hampton Roads. The purpose of this one-day effort is not only to enlist the help of citizens to spruce up beaches and shorelines, but also to quantify and document the types of litter found. Check out the close-up in this chapter for more information on this grassroots cleanup effort.

### International Coastal Cleanup Day
**Various locations • 851-6734,**
**(800) CMC-BEACH**

Volunteers also arm themselves with trash bags the third Saturday in September and patrol area beaches on International Coastal Cleanup Day, organized by the Center for Marine Conservation in Washington, D.C., which operates a regional office in Hampton. The event began in Texas in 1986 and expanded its reach across the nation within two years. By the mid-1990s, volunteers in more than 70 countries were participating in the annual cleanup. Today, these volunteers use standardized data collection cards to record more than 80 specific debris items in numerous categories: plastic, foamed plastic, glass, rubber, metal, wood and cloth.

# Recycling

### Virginia Peninsulas Public Service Authority (VPPSA)
**Williamsburg • 220-6140**
**James City County • 253-6811**

Photo: Chesapeake Bay Foundation

A great blue heron patiently waits for breakfast to swim by.

**York County • 890-3780**

Residents of Williamsburg, James City County and York County are served by the Virginia Peninsulas Public Service Authority (VPPSA). Residents of each of these communities have curbside recycling as a weekly service. Residents may recycle newspaper, glass, aluminum, bimetal, No. 2 plastics, corrugated cardboard, brown grocery bags, steel paint cans (washed and without lids) and empty aerosol cans (no lids.) In November 1998, VPPSA added mixed paper - magazines, catalogs, telephone books, junk mail, computer paper, stationery, school paper, envelopes and single-layer cardboard - to the list of items it would recycle.

## Reynolds Aluminum Recycling Center

**2001 Pocahontas Tr., Williamsburg**
**• 220-2660**

This center is another option for Williamsburg residents interested in recycling aluminum, copper and brass. The center pays varying amounts for these items and accepts them between 9 AM and 4:30 PM, Monday through Saturday.

## Jolly Pond Convenience Center

**1204 Jolly Pond Rd., James City Co.**
**• 253-6811**

One of four recycling centers run by the county, Jolly Pond is the only location that accepts materials that are not included as part of the curbside recycling program. These items include antifreeze, used motor oil, automotive batteries and large appliances that do not require a cooling element. The center is open from 7 AM to 5 PM, seven days a week. The county also offers a detailed phone message on the various components of its recycling program when you call the number above.

The county also offers a detailed phone message on the various components of its recycling program when you call 253-6809.

## York County Recycling Center

**145 Goodwin Neck Rd., Grafton • 890-3780**

This drop-off facility accepts antifreeze, used oil, automotive batteries and scrap metals. It is open 8 AM to 4 PM, Monday through Saturday.

The City of Williamsburg retains the spirit and feel of a small, unique community safe from the problems, the mall-ing and the generic sameness of other areas.

# Neighborhoods and Real Estate

The City of Williamsburg retains the spirit and feel of a small, unique community safe from the problems, the mall-ing and the generic sameness of other areas, even as the population in our immediate vicinity grows and neighborhoods proliferate.

This sense of continuity in character can be attributed to several things, foremost of which may be our citizens' dedication to cherishing and cultivating the values that keep us here.

Of course, those values differ for every individual and group, but a few weeks' reading of the *Virginia Gazette*'s opinion sections or an afternoon of conversations with residents reveal a pride in our small-town climate, a commitment to our local institutions and neighborhoods, the pleasure of easy access to shopping and parking and the delight of socializing among familiar faces.

At the same time we congratulate ourselves (maybe a bit too smugly) on our small-town charm, we are thankful for the sophisticated touches that small towns usually don't afford. This includes cosmopolitan national and international visitors for whom we must provide a world-class experience; the active intellectual and cultural life of a nationally esteemed college; a "jewel" of a community library system (truly, the word doesn't suffice); unusual and edifying museums, galleries and public occasions; and a sense of the special history evident all around us.

We can't overlook the contributions of geography to our community's character. We began as Middle Plantation, and our location in the middle of the Virginia Peninsula has been a boon to our cohesiveness as a community. The York River to the north and the James River to the south have blocked growth in those directions while providing some of the most beautiful scenery we could desire. To the east, the federal properties of the Colonial National Historical Park with its Colonial Parkway, Fort Eustis, Naval Weapons Station, Cheatham Annex and Camp Peary form a band that effectively keeps us from being absorbed into the explosive growth of the cities on the lower part of the Peninsula. Only the beautiful woodlands and farmlands to the west of the city remain for growth, and among them are the new developments in James City County and western York County.

The Virginia Peninsula in general is a fairly transient area, with many military families coming and going on assignment and young businesses bringing in people who later move on to other locations. In addition, a growing population of retirees has come here from northern cities to seek the milder winters and coastal atmosphere. All of the development that has taken place to serve these people has been reflected in the Williamsburg area over the last two decades with an increase in the number of neighborhoods and in the population in James City County and western York County.

A vital real estate industry has cultivated that western advancement - for the most part with sense and sensibility, though the disappearance of groves and fields is marked with regret by many of us who have grown accustomed to enjoying the rural beauty so close to home. There's a lot of land on which to disperse as the Peninsula widens to the west, and the woods throughout the area often provide natural barriers between developments and more public areas. Indeed, unless you set out to count them, the number of neighborhoods scattered in Williamsburg and environs is only grasped by people in the business to know: real estate agents, government planners and the utility and service people who keep the neighborhoods functioning.

We counted more than 130 neighborhoods and condominium and apartment complexes in preparing for this chapter, and we are sure we overlooked some of the newer or smaller ones. Home prices range from about $69,000 to more than $2.5 million, with everything in between available. Generally the pricey homes are on the waterfront or in planned communities such as Kingsmill on the James, Ford's Colony and The Governor's Land at Two Rivers. The lower-cost homes are in the older neighborhoods and the small, new developments tucked along the roads of James City and York counties.

Of course, with 130-plus neighborhoods, there are far too many to consider here, so we present a sampling of them to give you an indication of the range of options available. If you are looking for a residence in the area, our Insiders' suggestion is that you check out the real estate sections of the local newspapers, drive around the back streets and roads of the area to see what appeals to you, then contact one of the many real estate agencies listed in this chapter for a closer look, other options and more specifics about your choices. Our best discoveries have been the accidental ones we just happened to drive past one day.

# Neighborhoods

## Adam's Hunt

This subdivision off Centerville Road, about midway between Route 60 and Longhill Road, features modest homes on good-sized lots in a heavily wooded, rolling terrain. The one and two story houses are in a mixture of styles. It is a good beginner neighborhood for people interested in getting into the single-family housing market for $100,000 to $130,000.

## Banbury Cross

About 5 miles west of Williamsburg, this lovely, sprawling neighborhood is accessible by Route 64, exiting at Route 646 north. Large lots, mostly an acre or more, are the rule here. Lots of natural woods with tall pines, oaks and mountain laurel make this an ideal setting for those interested in living near town but beyond the suburbs of Williamsburg. Homes are large, Colonial or transitional in style and range in price from $120,000 to about $250,000.

## Baron Woods

This Sasha Digges property proved so popular that lots sold about as fast as they could be subdivided. The charming neighborhood features modest homes on small lots with many tall trees. It's on Ironbound Road, just north of Route 5 at Five Forks. Here, homes sell between $100,000 and $120,000.

## Berkeley's Green

Proving to be one of the area's most popular subdivisions, Berkeley's Green is off Route 5 and Greensprings Road. Tucked discreetly behind a facade of tall oaks and pines, this neighborhood features several carefully executed home designs, Colonial as well as transitional, with prices ranging from $150,000 to $200,000.

## Birchwood Park

Birchwood is one of Williamsburg's established neighborhoods, located off Route 199. Its modest homes, many of them ranch-style, have landscaped yards and established gardens. It is especially accessible to shopping and schools, as well as Interstate 64. Houses sell for $100,000 to the high $120,000s.

## Canterbury Hills

Also an established, small neighborhood, this charming area boasts winding roads shaded by large, old trees, neatly tended yards and larger, well-maintained homes. Off Route 5 and very accessible to the Williamsburg Crossing Shopping Center, it is bounded by Indigo Park and Mill Creek Landing. Houses sell in the $150,000 range.

## Chanco's Grant

A few years ago, this neighborhood began as a two-street, starter-home subdivision with low-priced homes on small lots. It proved

Homes in the Williamsburg area range in style from Colonial to contemporary.

so vastly popular that it has developed by leaps and bounds to include an abundance of attractive Colonial-style homes on several well-tended streets. It is on Ironbound Road, midway between Route 5 and Jamestown Road, close to Clara Byrd Baker Elementary and convenient to shopping. Houses sell for $95,000 up to $115,000.

## Chickahominy Haven

What started out as a recreational community with small summer homes tucked away on the river from which it gets its name, Chickahominy Haven now boasts lots of year round residents who have built a mix of large and small transitional or contemporary homes interspersed among the summer cottages. It's a drive back through the James City County woods to get there, but take Forge Road off Route 60 W., keep bearing right and wind your way to the river. Prices vary depending on which side of the road a house sits on, but expect to pay $75,000 up to $190,000.

## The Coves

Off S. Henry Street, after it winds its way past the College of William and Mary's Marshall-Wythe School of Law, is this pristine little subdivision along two short lanes. Most homes here are masterpieces, custom-designed and meticulously maintained by their owners. Every once in a while, someone will put a lot up for sale in this extremely desirable location, but not very often - and they are pricey when they do come available. But its location - within walking distance of Colonial Williamsburg, Merchants Square, the college and more - is ideal. It also offers easy access via Route 199 to I-64. That's why homes sell for $275,000 to $400,000.

## Druid Hills

An established neighborhood off Jamestown Road, Druid Hills features a mix of large and small homes - two-story Colonials as well as contemporary ranches - on winding lanes shaded by old trees. Because of its proximity to the campus of the College of William and Mary, many professors, students and their families live here. Homes sell for between $119,000 and $145,000.

## Drummond's Field On The James

This one-of-a-kind, small but spacious subdivision centers on an equestrian complex with fields and stables. Located off Greensprings Road in the shadow of the Jamestown Ferry, it is bounded on the west by the James River and is a stone's throw from the Colonial Parkway. Expensive, large homes sit along the riverbank, while smaller, family-sized homes line the other streets. Unlike most upscale subdivisions in the area, trees here are relatively young since this neighborhood, as its name reveals, was, in its former life, a farmer's field. An attraction is the access to a small beach and a dock on the James. Prices range widely depending on location and size but go for anywhere from $250,000 to over $1 million.

## Fernbrook

Large, heavily wooded lots in James City County's new Fernbrook development off Greensprings Road will appeal to families seeking to locate within 10 minutes of the heart of Williamsburg. Colonial and transitional homes populate the area. There are 104 lots, with homes ranging in price from $185,000 to $275,000.

## Fieldcrest

This upscale neighborhood offers luxurious living in a country setting. Large, new homes line its wide streets. Old, stately trees shade Greensprings Road as it leaves Route 5 and leads to the entrance of this lovely subdivision. Homes are primarily transitional in style and usually brick. Prices range from $185,000 to $329,000.

## First Colony

About 5 miles west of Williamsburg on Route 5, this large, established neighborhood has a large lake stocked with fish, a boat dock and a private beach on the James River. It boasts an eclectic mix of homes, both large and small, ranging from sprawling, contemporary ranch homes to modest, formal Georgian colonials. Depending on location, homes sell from $120,000 to $350,000 and up.

## Ford's Colony

If you're looking for an elegant home in a gorgeous community replete with golf, lighted tennis courts and a restaurant boasting gourmet dining and one of the state's most extensive wine lists (turn to our Restaurants chapter for details about The Dining Room and The Grille), this expansive planned community is tailor-made for you. The homes are large and luxurious; the condominiums, townhomes and cluster homes are equally elegant. The two golf courses here are outstanding and will provide continual challenges (see our Golf chapter for more information). Ford's Colony is a gated community of 2,500 acres on Longhill Road, a couple of miles west of the Historic Area. Lots run in size from a third-acre to a half-acre and range from $40,000 to about $120,000, while homes go for $200,000 to $450,000.

## Fox Ridge

Still one of the most affordable subdivisions in the greater Williamsburg area, Fox Ridge is off Centerville Road between Longhill Road and Route 60. Charming, smaller homes are interspersed among tall trees, dogwoods and mountain laurel on rolling hills. Prices range from $100,000 to $130,000.

## Gatehouse Farms

Off Neck-O-Land and Lake Powell roads, this large subdivision is tucked away between Jamestown Road and the Colonial Parkway. It features large, contemporary homes on nicely landscaped lots. It is just moments away from the College of William and Mary campus or, in the opposite direction, the Jamestown Ferry. Homes sell here in the low $100,000s.

## The Governor's Land at Two Rivers

This is, without reservation, the most el-

**www.insiders.com**

See this and many other **Insiders' Guide**® destinations online.

**Visit us today!**

egant subdivision on the west side of James City County. Smaller than Kingsmill but no less impressive in its amenities and terrain, this developing subdivision offers large home sites, many along the river's edge. Off Route 5 at the confluence of the James and Chickahominy rivers, it offers the last riverfront acreage in the county. A professional golf course, beach facilities, nature trails, a swimming pool and tennis courts are in place, and the clubhouse offers all one could wish to complete the high quality of the neighborhood. Expect to pay at least $350,000 for a modest home here.

## Graylin Woods

Understated is the best description of this charming, elegant, albeit small subdivision off Route 5 between Route 199 and Five Forks. Large, stately homes on modest, lovely wooded lots and rolling hills give this elegant neighborhood charm and character. Prices range from $225,000 to about $350,000.

## Green Springs Plantation

Williamsburg's newest golfing community is an excellent option for anyone, but especially the golf enthusiast looking for an affordable home. Lots range in size from a third-acre to a half-acre, sometimes a bit larger. Prices run from $45,000 to $140,000 in the rolling, wooded hills adjacent to the new Williamsburg National Golf Club, an 18-hole championship golf masterpiece designed by Jack Nicklaus' Golden Bear Associates. In addition to the wonderful golfing, amenities include a full-size pool, tennis courts, a recreational center and two children's play areas. Homes are selling from $229,000 to $375,000.

## Heritage Landing

This elegant subdivision off Route 5 west of Five Forks features large brick and wood custom homes on large lots. Rolling hills, winding lanes and flowering trees and shrubs make this an exquisite venue just far enough out of town to make you feel like you're on vacation. Houses here go for between $180,000 and $250,000.

## Holly Hills of Williamsburg

Upper-end new property within the city limits is at a premium. Holly Hills on Jamestown Road is the newest (and perhaps one of the last) development to serve this market. It is nearly 300 acres of heavily wooded property just a mile from the Historic Area and the College of William and Mary. Homesites range in size from .40 to 2 acres. Strict architectural guidelines assure that the appearance and value of properties will remain high. Houses sell for between $300,000 and $400,000.

## Hunter's Creek

This family-oriented subdivision is small but attractive with its modest Colonial homes and well-tended gardens. Off Route 60 west of Williamsburg on the edge of Toano, it offers quick and easy access to I-64. Homes go for $115,000 to $130,000.

## Indigo Park

One of the Route 5 area's earlier developments, Indigo Park has endured as a charming neighborhood of well-maintained homes along rolling, winding lanes shaded by large, old trees. A family-oriented neighborhood with a private pool for residents, Indigo Park is within a five-minute drive of Williamsburg Crossing Shopping Center and schools, as well as Williamsburg's Historic Area and other shopping areas. Two-story ranch homes in brick or wood are a good buy at $100,000 to $130,000.

**INSIDERS' TIP**

Much of James City County's land tests positive for hydric soil, which is no big deal, provided the builder of your home has taken appropriate measures for "shrink-swell," the shifting of soil due to high water content. It's best to have a test done before you build or buy.

## Kingsmill On The James

One of Williamsburg's most prestigious neighborhoods, this multifaceted development of 2,900 acres includes everything from sprawling estates to tidy condos on the edge of its PGA golf course - and everything in between. Kingsmill residents enjoy several recreation areas, a world-class 18-hole golf course, several superb restaurants, an outstanding recreation and conference center, a private marina, dry-dock facilities and a riverside beach. Developed by the Anheuser-Busch Corporation, it also features a 24-hour private security force and limited-access entrances. Prices, which vary widely, range from about $250,000 to $500,000 and up for single-family homes.

## Kingspoint

This quiet neighborhood is tucked away at the foot of S. Henry Street just across Route 199. Bounded by the Colonial Parkway on one side and College Creek on the other, it is a wide, tree-covered peninsula. Kingspoint is noted for its graciousness and friendliness as well as its convenience to the heart of town on Henry Street and its quick access via Route 199 to other parts of James City County and the interstate. You'll find an eclectic mix of sizes, styles and ages from '60s to '90s. Expect to pay $175,000 to $500,000.

## Kingswood

Conveniently located off Jamestown Road, about halfway between Merchants Square and the Jamestown Ferry, this idyllic, quiet neighborhood is the choice for those seeking convenience and solitude. Well-tended yards and an assortment of older contemporary and traditional homes line the area's streets and lanes. The neighborhood has a private pool that is open for a fee each summer to guests from nearby developments as well. Homes sell for $150,000 to $200,000.

## Kristiansand

The Norwegian name pays tribute to the town of Norge, which is adjacent to this small subdivision. Off Route 60 W., it is just down the road from the Williamsburg Pottery Factory. It offers quick and easy access to Ewell Station Shopping Center and I-64 as well as local schools. Affordable homes begin at $85,000 and go up to about $130,000.

## Lake Toano

If you don't mind driving about 15 minutes west of Williamsburg along Route 60 W., you can find this subdivision situated in a heavily wooded area surrounding a quiet reservoir in the Toano area. Large and small homes, both contemporary and traditional, line the streets and cul-de-sacs that make up this country neighborhood. It is just minutes from the I-64 exit for Toano. Homes in this well-kept secret run from $150,000 to $225,000.

## Longhill Gate

Located on Longhill Road just before the entrance to Ford's Colony, these attached homes range in size from moderate to fairly large. Sidewalks, manicured landscapes and winding streets are indicative of the low-key family ambiance that sets the tone of this charming neighborhood. Homes sell for between $110,000 and $170,000.

## The Meadows

Looks are deceiving as you approach this small community of small to moderate sized homes, between Strawberry Plains and Ironbound roads. At the back edge of a wide-open field, the streets of this neighborhood dip and wind, curve and wander. Neatly kept yards and pristine houses characterize this subdivision, halfway between downtown Williamsburg and Jamestown via Sandy Point Road. Prices range from $110,000 to $140,000 in the older section and from $150,000 to $170,000 in the newer.

## Mill Creek Landing

Without a doubt, this elegant subdivision - with custom-built homes (nearly all of them brick) situated around a 7-acre fish-stocked pond - is one of the area's best-kept secrets. Limited in size, it is still under development. Off Route 5 and Stanley Drive, it offers a country setting less than 2 miles from Williamsburg's Historic Area, with easy access to schools, Williamsburg Crossing Shopping Center (which is within walking distance) and I-64. The 7-acre pond bottom is home to ducks, turtles, a stock of fish and at least two pairs of Canada geese who stop by on their winter migrations. Home prices range from $199,000 to $375,000.

## Mirror Lake Estates

About 15 minutes west of the Historic Area out Richmond Road, this inviting neighborhood features small, moderate and larger starter homes, all built within the last five to 10 years. It also may be reached via I-64, which is less than a mile from the entrance to this growing subdivision. Homes sell for $110,000 to $150,000.

## North Cove

Off Route 646 in York County, this large-lot subdivision features rolling hills, large homes, lots of trees and quick access to I-64. About 10 minutes west of Williamsburg, it is a charming setting that seems far removed from the bustle of downtown. It is also near York River State Park and a public boat ramp on the York River. You'll find homes in brick, cedar and stucco. Prices range widely, from $112,000 to $160,000.

## Piney Creek Estates

Currently under development by two of the area's most renowned builders, Ronald T. Curtis and Joel S. Sheppard, Piney Creek is a prime Williamsburg address. Clearly defined covenants assure high quality for all construction that takes place along the gaslit streets. It is within a mile of the James City County-Williamsburg Community Center and Kiwanis

Park, and it's a short drive from all area attractions and shopping. Its location within city limits means low city taxes. Transitional and Colonial homes in brick sell for around $225,000.

## Poplar Hall

About 8 miles east of downtown Williamsburg, this meandering neighborhood is tucked discreetly away from the traffic of Route 60 E., off of which it is located. A variety of sizes and styles characterizes this subdivision, which boasts both older and new homes. It is midway between two I-64 interchanges and is just minutes from Busch Gardens and the Anheuser-Busch brewery. You can buy a house here for between $85,000 and $100,000.

## Port Anne

One of the last subdivisions in the city where you can still purchase land and build a house, this neighborhood is for the discerning homeowner in search of an idyllic setting above College Creek. Large, custom-designed homes on smaller lots provide the perfect place to settle down in style. A clubhouse, tennis courts and pool are among other amenities. It also offers quick access to I-64 and is within biking and walking distance of the city's Historic Area. Lots sell for $60,000 to $100,000, while homes range from $300,000 to $600,000.

## Powhatan Crossing

One of the developing moderate-income neighborhoods in James City County, this small but charming subdivision is just east of Route 5 at Five Forks. It features affordable, small to moderate size affordable homes along a cozy lane that stretches into the woodlands. It offers easy access to downtown Williamsburg or I-64 via Route 5. Prices range from $125,000 to $150,000.

## Powhatan Secondary of Williamsburg

On the site of the early 17th-century Powhatan Plantation off Ironbound Road at Mid-County Park, this popular and growing subdivision offers choice homesites at reasonable prices. The attractive custom-built homes are a mix of contemporary and traditional styles, all meticulously maintained and landscaped. The community includes 45 acres of recreational land and lakes for homeowners to enjoy, wooded lots and a variety of floor plans from nine quality builders. Single family homes range from $180,000 to $225,000.

## Powhatan Shores

While most neighborhoods offer some attractive amenity to their homeowners, this charming family neighborhood has them all, especially for the boating enthusiast. Nearly every lot has private access via a creek to the James River. It is just a few minutes from the city's Historic Area and is close to Route 199 and I-64. Homes are priced from $185,000 to $260,000.

## Queens Lake

This stately, established neighborhood, bounded by Queens Creek and the Colonial Parkway, is one of the most prestigious neighborhoods in the greater Williamsburg area. Tennis courts, a pool, a recreation center, a marina and more are among the amenities. Some of the area's loveliest homes are situated on the rolling, wooded lanes of this charming subdivision. It offers country living just minutes from I-64, Colonial Williamsburg and area schools. Expect to pay from $200,000 to $750,000.

## Queenswood

Off Hubbard Lane, this family-oriented neighborhood features newer homes on moderate-size lots away from the activity of downtown Williamsburg and major roads. Ranches and two-story Colonials are the norm here, and meticulously landscaped and maintained homesites are typical. It is within minutes of Colonial Parkway, James York Plaza Shopping Center and Route 143, which leads to I-64. Prices range from $115,000 to $140,000.

## Richmond Hill

A new, small, high-end neighborhood in the city limits very close to the Historic Area, Richmond Hill has only 15 lots, and homes range in price from $400,000 to $500,000. All brick homes are Federal architectural designs similar to those on Richmond's Monument Avenue. Three golf courses, indoor tennis and the shopping and dining of Colonial Williamsburg are all within walking distance.

## Rolling Woods

Lovely mid-range homes with brick, vinyl and cedar exteriors tucked away under stately oaks and pines make this understated subdivision much sought after. Off Lake Powell Road in James City County, it offers seclusion just minutes from the congestion of downtown Williamsburg. It is near Route 199 and I-64. Prices range from $130,000 to $205,000.

## Seasons Trace

One of the most popular planned communities in the area is this neighborhood with its neatly maintained townhomes, condos, cluster homes and private homes. Off Longhill Road, adjacent to Lafayette High School and across the road from the Windsor Forest subdivision, Seasons Trace features winding lanes and a pond stocked with fish and populated with several ducks. Also offered are such amenities as a pool, tennis courts, a basketball court and dry-dock storage for boats and RVs. Single-family homes sell for about $130,000 to $159,000.

## Settler's Mill

Off Jamestown Road approximately halfway between Route 199 and Jamestown, Settler's Mill is turning out to be a very popular development in a wooded community with

---

**INSIDERS' TIP**

If you should decide to buy a lot and custom build a home rather than buy a resale, or perhaps buy a spec house that is ready and waiting, you might wish to check out local builders before signing on the dotted line. A call to the Peninsula Housing & Builders Association could ease your mind or save you money in the long run. Call 595-1600 and they'll be glad to assist you.

Some area neighborhoods offer residents waterfront property and 18-hole golf courses.

hardwoods, a lake, ponds and rolling hills. It is a joint venture of four of the most prestigious names in residential building and development in the area: Larry McCardle, Sterling Nichols, Joel Sheppard and Ron Curtis. The nicely detailed spec homes feature a variety of traditional and transitional styles. Prices range from $260,000 to $300,000.

## Skimino Hills

Developed in the late 1970s and early 1980s, this large subdivision is situated on gently rolling hills in western York County. Off I-64 at Route 646, it offers large lots with trees and lush growths of mountain laurel and dogwood. A mix of large and small contemporary and traditional homes lines its narrow streets. It's a great neighborhood for young families who can pay $99,000 to $169,000.

## Skipwith Farms

This was the city of Williamsburg's first real subdivision, built in the 1950s and '60s, and it features modest single- and two-story homes. If location directs choice, few options are more centrally located or offer easier access to shopping, recreation and area schools. It is off Richmond Road, less than 3 miles from the heart of the city's Historic Area. Prices run from $85,000 to $150,000.

## St. George's Hundred

One of the area's most popular, family-oriented neighborhoods, St. George's is off Route 5 about 5 miles west of Williamsburg. Charming homes, mostly Colonial style, line the streets. Established more than two decades ago, this neighborhood continues to grow. In addition to its easy access to area shopping and schools, it features a recreation area with picnic tables, basketball courts and a softball field for residents. Prices in this sprawling neighborhood range from $125,000 to $189,000.

## Vineyards Of Williamsburg

Off Neck-o-Land Road, this subdivision of large, stately homes is quickly becoming one of Williamsburg's most prestigious addresses. Larger houses are the rule, but there are a few areas offering smaller, exquisitely constructed dwellings. Most are tucked away discreetly among old shade trees. Breezes from the nearby James River and proximity to both Jamestown Road and the Colonial Parkway make this a much sought-after location. Houses begin at $375,000 and go way, way up.

## Westray Downs

Rolling hills, winding lanes and charming new homes characterize this relatively new neighborhood off Route 5 in James City County. Ranch-style homes, traditional two-story homes and some charming colonial-style homes add interest to the landscape. It is minutes from the county's Law Enforcement Center and Fire Station on Route 5 and offers quick, easy access to Williamsburg Crossing Shopping Center, Five Forks, the Jamestown Ferry and I-64 via Route 199. Home prices run from $140,000 to $170,000.

## Westmoreland

Off Olde Towne Road near its intersection with Long Hill Road, this small new development is offering homes in the $215,000 to $250,000 range. It currently has 15 single-family lots, on richly wooded property developed by the Hornsby family (relations of Bruce Hornsby). Convenient access to shopping and amenities on the Richmond Road side of town, a 10-minute drive to the Historic Area and convenient access to I-64 are strong advantages to this neighborhood.

## Windsor Forest

Before Ford's Colony joined the ranks, this was the most upscale subdivision on the northeast side of James City County. It is off Longhill Road, and large homes - some contemporary, most traditional colonial-style - are the norm here. Amenities include a community pool. Nearby are the county recreation center and lots of shopping. There is easy access to I-64 via Airport Road, and the city's Historic Area is just a few miles away. Prices run from $160,000 to $300,000.

## The Woods

This handsome, upscale subdivision is quickly establishing itself as one of distinction. Large, stately homes are situated on rolling hills amid lush woods and tall, old oaks and pines. Off Jamestown Road and within a brisk walking distance of the city's Historic Area, this fine subdivision offers easy access to just about everything, including Interstate 64 via Route 199. Expect to pay $275,000 to $350,000.

# Real Estate Companies

It stands to reason that there should be plenty of Realtors to bring housing seekers and sellers together, and there are. We have listed below a sample of some of the area Realtors with which we are most familiar.

## Abbitt Realty Company Inc.
**901 Richmond Rd. • (757) 253-7600**

Established in 1946, Abbitt Realty is a recognized leader in the Peninsula real estate market, with five offices in the area. A member of RELO, the nation's largest and oldest effective relocation network, Abbitt has reinforced its leadership with a full complement of associated divisions, enabling the company to integrate for each client all aspects of the real estate industry.

## Berkeley William E. Wood Realtors
**1326 Jamestown Rd.  229-0550**
**907 Richmond Rd. • (757) 253-0524**

Berkeley is one of the community's largest and longest-established companies, handling commercial, residential and land sales, and has a reputation for client satisfaction. Two convenient offices and linkage to the Better Homes & Gardens network are assets for potential clients to consider.

## Cale Realty Company
**107 Colony Square Shopping Ctr.**
**253-2950**
**212 Jones Mill Ln. • (757) 229-0441**

Established on the Virginia Peninsula in 1951, Cale Realty has developed a solid reputation throughout the community based on its commitment to performance, knowledge of the market, needs of the client, a promise of customer satisfaction and a bottom line of proven results. The office on Jones Mill Lane handles sales in the Holly Hills area.

## Jim and Pat Carter Real Estate
**1321 Jamestown Rd. • (757) 220-3700**

Carter Real Estate is noted for expert handling of large high-end and estate properties on both sides of the James River. Highly discriminating individuals looking for home or investment properties in or around Williamsburg will find this company's knowledge of the market and experience strong assets.

## GSH Real Estate,

## Williamsburg Office
**Busch Corporate Ctr., 264 McLaws Cir.**
**• (757) 253-2442**

GSH has a major presence in the Tidewater area and is heavily involved in commercial real estate and property management. The local office provides full and expert representation in commercial, residential and land transactions. They've been in business for more than 50 years.

## Hornsby Real Estate Co.
**4732 Longhill Rd. • (757) 565-0100**

This is a long-established (more than 45 years) and highly respected company handling commercial, residential and land transactions throughout the greater Williamsburg area. Currently, the firm is developing the upscale Westmoreland subdivision off Olde Towne Road. (See the Westmoreland listing under Neighborhoods in this chapter.)

## Kingsmill Realty Inc.
**100 Kingsmill Rd. • (757) 253-3933**

While other companies represent properties in Kingsmill, Kingsmill Realty is an obvious option for those seeking to own in the Kingsmill on the James planned community. On top of what's available as well as what's coming onto the market in all of Kingsmill's neighborhoods, the company's agents can help find clients the ideal location.

## Executive Homes Realty
**124 Quaker Meeting House Rd.**
**• (757) 565-1963, (800) 584-0861**

Executive Homes Realty handles properties in prestigious golf, waterfront and gated communities surrounding Historic Williamsburg. Their specialty is buyer representation while purchasing a homesite or an existing home as well as buyer representation during the construction of a new home.

## Prudential McCardle Realty
**1201 Jamestown Rd. • (757) 253-5686**
**811 Richmond Rd. • (757) 229-6151**
**3449 John Tyler Hwy. • (757) 220-9500**

An independent, locally owned company with more than 25 years of experience, McCardle is the largest real estate company in town, both in size and in volume of sales. The three convenient offices have approximately 50 full-time Realtors to assure customer service and satisfaction. McCardle belongs to RELO, a national and international network of independent companies that can assist those leaving for or moving from other parts of the country. McCardle handles commercial, residential (new and resale) and land transactions.

## William E. Wood and Associates Realtors
**1335 Richmond Rd. • (757) 229-0900**
**926-A J. Clyde Morris Blvd., Newport News**
**880-7579, (800) 866-3201**

This longtime player with more than 25 years in the local real estate market is a full-service agency handling commercial and residential sales and property management. The agency has 18 offices and leads the greater Peninsula area in volume and sales. It also is a major corporate relocation provider affiliated with nearly 85 percent of the nation's corporate relocation agencies. The local office specializes in the Williamsburg marketplace as well as New Kent County and Providence Forge.

**The Christopher Wren Association for Lifelong Learning, an innovative educational program at the College of William and Mary, welcomes any Williamsburg-area resident of retirement age who loves learning.**

# Retirement

The Historic Triangle has become a popular place to retire for a number of reasons. The climate is relatively mild. People retiring from military service in the Hampton Roads area are familiar with the amenities to be had, and they settle here. The cost of living is low in comparison to many other parts of the country, particularly Northeast urban centers. Recreational opportunities are numerous. Local healthcare is very good. And, as a college town, Williamsburg offers a broad spectrum of generally inexpensive cultural activities.

According to the most recent Donnelly Demographics survey, more than 14 percent of the population living in Williamsburg ZIP code areas is age 65 or older. Obviously, such a large population group has a need for special services and rightly deserves some special privileges. All residents are eligible for a Good Neighbors Pass from Colonial Williamsburg that entitles them to free admissions, bus service and shopping discounts in Colonial Williamsburg's properties. Each September, Senior Time, so dubbed because so many retirees travel to Colonial Williamsburg after students return to school in the fall, features discounts on admissions and special programs. For information call 229-1000.

Seniors also are eligible for discounts at most other area attractions, including Busch Gardens and Water Country USA. All residents of York County, James City County and Williamsburg are entitled to free admission to Jamestown Settlement and Yorktown Victory Center. Proof of address is required.

Additional courtesies abound. *Senior Times* monthly is a good place to look for current discount information. (See our Media chapter for more information.) Revco and Berkeley pharmacies offer senior discounts, as do all the local movie theaters and some area apartment complexes. Real bargain hunters will be pleased to know that the Williamsburg Pottery Factory offers a 10-percent discount to seniors every Wednesday.

Discounts are abundant for visiting seniors as well; you just have to do a little asking around. We suggest that when making reservations or inquiries at area hotels, restaurants and attractions, you always ask if there are reduced rates or special offerings for seniors. Some hotels, such as the Days Inn chain, offer price reductions to those older than 55. Holiday Inns will discount rooms for members of the AARP. Check also with the National Council of Senior Citizens, at 925 15th Street N.W., Washington, D.C., 20005, for news on low-cost travel options.

Whether you're here for a few days, or a few years, this area has a lot to offer. In this chapter, we profile the facilities, amenities and opportunities available locally to retirees.

## Services

### Meals on Wheels
**Williamsburg Baptist Church, 227 Richmond Rd.  •  (757) 229-9250**

Everyone gets into the act here! Seniors help serve other seniors who are either homebound or too elderly or infirm to cook for themselves on a regular basis. Operated out of an office in the Williamsburg Baptist Church, this volunteer group serves more than 80 senior citizens each day a free, nutritionally-balanced hot meal prepared by Williamsburg Community Hospital. Anyone wishing to write for more information can send their inquiry to Meals on Wheels, P.O. Box 709, Williamsburg VA 23187.

### Peninsula Agency on Aging
**739 Thimble Shoals Blvd., Suite 1006, Newport News**
**•  (757) 873-0541**

The central source of information on services for senior citizens throughout the entire area, this office provides services and programs covering needs such as housing, health, employment, income or financial aid, community services, adult day care, legal services, nutrition and meal programs, transportation, recreation, in-home support and social services. The staff will make an appropriate reference for the service closest to you that meets your needs.

### Riverside Adult Daycare Center
**1000 Old Denbigh Blvd., Newport News**
**• (757) 875-2033**

This organization provides a structured environment for seniors from 7:30 AM to 5:30 PM. While this group caters to seniors with physical limitations and mental disorders such as Alzheimer's Disease, the center is open to all interested seniors including those in good health. The center is located in upper Newport News, however, and no transportation is provided for people living in the Williamsburg area.

### Williamsburg Community Sentara Home Care Services
**1100 Professional Dr. • (757) 229-3232**

This service, provided through the local hospital, provides home nursing care, companions, sitters and social services for the elderly. The hospital offers case management for 24-hour care, whether or not the principal caregiver lives in the area. Medicare and other insurance are accepted.

# Publications

### Services for Citizens 55 and Older
**James City County Social Services Office,**
**5249 Olde Towne Rd. • (757) 259-3100**

James City County's older residents can pick up *Services for Citizens 55 and Older*, a free guide on local resources, that is provided by James City County Social Services. It contains information about recreation, medical emergencies, day care and support services. The office is open Monday through Friday from 8 AM to 5 PM.

### Assorted national, regional and local publications

**Williamsburg Regional Library**
**515 Scotland St. • (757) 220-9216**

Williamsburg Regional Library keeps on file a variety of published resources of interest to senior citizens. These free resources include publications especially for older Americans, such as those issued by AARP and other special senior-focus groups.

# Activities

Active seniors interested in participating in social, civic and special interest activities don't have to look very far. The College of William and Mary sponsors concert series, theater productions, exhibits and gallery talks, usually for a small admission fee or no charge at all. We describe some of these in our Arts chapter. Call 221-4000 for details. What follows is a list of some clubs and programs unique to the area.

### The Christopher Wren Association for Lifelong Learning
**College of William and Mary • (757) 221-1079**

No report on retired living in the Historic Triangle would be complete without mention of The Christopher Wren Association for Lifelong Learning, an innovative educational program at the College of William and Mary. Any Williamsburg-area resident of retirement age who loves learning is welcome to take part in this course of study. Don't worry, there are no grades or tests here, though intellectual challenge is amply present.

The association, founded by retired college professors Ruth and Frank Kernodle, is peer-run and peer-taught. By tapping the area reservoir of retired persons with expertise in an art, a field or a phenomenon who are willing to offer their services as teachers, the Kernodles have hit upon a formula for continued education that already is popular with area seniors. So far, courses have been offered on Japanese culture, U.S. foreign policy, opera, astronomy, the Chesapeake Bay, comparative religions and 20th-century Irish Poets, to name a few. For a $75 membership fee, lifelong learners can enroll in 12 weeks of classes. The Association also sponsors social events, brown-bag lunches, writing workshops and

Photo: Busch Gardens Williamsburg

Many area attractions offer discounts to senior citizens.

daytrips for its members. Another option, the associate membership, is designed for those interested in receiving the newsletter, attending the convocation and participating in trips, retreats or bag lunches, but not in taking classes. An associate membership is $25. For brochures and more information about The Christopher Wren Association, call the previously listed number.

### Fifty Plus
**P.O. Box BB, Williamsburg VA 23187 • (757) 229-1771**

This ecumenical program, sponsored by Williamsburg United Methodist Church, is open to all interested persons age 50 and older. The group undertakes church-related social and fundraising projects, travel programs and more.

### Retired and Senior Volunteer Program (RSVP)
**312 Waller Mill Rd. • (757) 220-2907**

This office recruits and places people age 55 and older who are interested in providing community service. The office usually is open 9 AM to 1 PM Monday through Friday, and seniors who want to check out their options are welcome to drop by. Volunteers give their time to more than 250 places such as Meals

on Wheels, nonprofit agencies, convalescent centers and hospitals in the area.

### Senior Citizens Bridge Club
**700 Conway Drive, #202 • (757) 229-5760**

Persons age 50 and older join this card-playing social group for $2 a year. In return, they can participate in various social activities that include luncheon at 11:15 AM the second and fourth Thursday of each month in the Holiday Inn Downtown. The meals are followed by (what else?) a round of bridge.

### Town and Gown Luncheon
**College of William and Mary • (757) 221-2640**

One popular activity is the Town and Gown luncheon and lecture series, sponsored by the College of William and Mary usually held in the Campus Center. This program attracts many area retirees, who gather when the college brings in speakers from near and far to give informal talks after a catered luncheon on topics of sometimes general, sometimes specialized, interest. Visitors not wishing to take part in the luncheon can listen to the speaker for no charge. Otherwise, there is a minimal fee ($2 to $3, depending on the speaker). Reservations in either case are necessary so that adequate seating may be provided.

# Residential Living

While many seniors choose to live in conventional, mixed-age neighborhoods, others prefer the more exclusive, secure or convenient atmosphere of the retirement community. Currently, Williamsburg can provide several such options for retirees in search of a community lifestyle.

## Chambrel at Williamsburg
**3800 Treyburn Dr.** • **(757) 220-1839**

Located directly opposite Williamsburg Community Hospital on Monticello Avenue is this attractive, well-maintained senior community, built on 52 acres in James City County. Active seniors can choose from a number of lifestyle options, including apartments or cottage homes. All units feature washers and dryers.

In addition, Brandon House at Chambrel offers assisted living, and York Manor, a special-care needs section of Chambrel, features an enriched-living program, with services tailored to the specific requirements of each category of resident.

Amenities at Chambrel include biweekly housekeeping service and weekly linen service, a common area with an elegant dining room, a library, a swimming pool, a fitness room and a whirlpool. Chambrel residents can take advantage of scheduled transportation, maid service, travel opportunities, social and cultural events, walking trails in natural woodlands, an on-site clinic, on-site banking services, a barbershop and a beauty salon. Shopping areas, Colonial Williamsburg, the College of William and Mary and golf courses are nearby. Chambrel charges residents a monthly fee determined by the category of their living

arrangement, with no admission charge or endowment required. We speak from very pleasant personal experience with Chambrel.

## Dominion Village
**4132 Longhill Rd.** • **(757) 258-3444**

Many seniors in need of long-term, assisted-living care opt for this facility, conveniently located about 5 miles from the city's Historic Area. It provides permanent and short-term residence options in private and semiprivate rooms. Located across from the entrance to the Ford's Colony subdivision, it is situated near shopping, bus lines and several area churches, making it extremely convenient to visiting family members and friends.

Dominion Village offers three levels of care, from minimal assistance and graduating to more extensive assistance with activities of daily living. They also offer a secure, positive atmosphere for residents with Alzheimer's Disease or dementia. The monthly rental fee covers nearly everything: three meals and an evening snack, around-the-clock nursing care, assistance with bathing, dressing and personal care as needed, medications monitored by the nursing staff, daily activities programs, weekly church services, housekeeping and linen services, cable TV and all utilities except telephone. Amenities include a dining room, living room, cozy sitting areas, an activity room for crafts, art, reading and conversation, an outdoor garden patio for cookouts and an emergency call system in each room. Fees are based on the level of care required and range from $1,100 per month for a semiprivate room for persons who are fairly independent to $2,900 per month for someone requiring intensive assisted living but who still prefers to live in a private suite.

**www.insiders.com**

See this and many other **Insiders' Guide**® destinations online.

**Visit us today!**

---

## Patriots Colony

**6000 Patriots Colony Dr. • (757) 220-9000, (800) 716-9000**

Retired military officers and their spouses can investigate this gated, full-service, continuing-care retirement community with 60 private villas and 90 apartment homes starting at $73,500. Located adjacent to the Greensprings Plantation National Historic Site on historic Route 5 west of Williamsburg, Patriots Colony offers 150 residences and a community center featuring fine dining, a fitness and wellness center and recreational areas. Other amenities include all utilities, weekly maid service, one meal per person per day, total interior and exterior building maintenance and a community greenhouse, pool and tennis courts. The community is open to retired officers of the seven uniformed services and retired senior federal civil service employees only.

## Williamsburg Genesis Eldercare

**1235 Mount Vernon Ave. • (757) 229-4121,**

This established facility, part of the Genesis Eldercare System, offers long-term and skilled respite care, varied activities, and physical, occupational, respiratory and speech therapies. Services and amenities include a dining program tailored to each resident's dietary needs, a dessert cart that circulates throughout the living area and an extensive volunteer program that brings in church groups, civic groups, students and local musical entertainment on a regular basis. This center offers an enclosed courtyard for those residents who wish to spend time out-of-doors in nice weather. The facility is located directly across the street from Williamsburg Community Hospital, which has, more than once, made a difference in an emergency. Rates range from $111 to $140 per day depending on accommodations and level of care.

## Williamsburg Landing

**5700 Williamsburg Landing Dr. • (757) 253-0303**

At this lovely, upscale community that must be seen to be believed, seniors can choose home or apartment living and can take advantage of health services that range from a minimal wellness program to licensed nursing-home care in a gated community with around-the-clock security service. Amenities include housekeeping service, all interior and exterior building maintenance, all appliances in each unit, all utilities except cable TV and phone, trash removal, one meal per day, shuttle bus service to doctor offices and access to local shopping and special events in town. The Landing also offers on-site banking, shopping, library, computer room, woodworking shop, billiards room, health spa, outdoor pool, tennis courts and more. Pets are welcome.

This long-term care facility, situated on 135 woodland acres next to College Creek, offers social, recreational and cultural activities such as concerts, tours, physical fitness classes and events in conjunction with the College of William and Mary. Outpatient clinic services, overseen by a director of outpatient services and a medical director, include services and care by physicians and registered nurses from 8 AM to 4:30 PM Monday through Friday. Many locals, upon retirement, sell their homes and move to the Landing to live out their senior years in style, comfort and convenience. There are 129 cluster homes (priced $208,000 to $303,000, 90 percent refundable at the time of resale) and 110 apartments (priced from $99,000 to $188,000, 90 percent refundable at the time of resale). The long-term care program is designed to offset the significant added costs you would have if you required long-term care in an assisted living facility or nursing home. Costs in the assisted living facility range from $60,000 to $99,000, 90 percent refundable at the time of resale. Those who need to move temporarily or permanently into The Pavilion, the nursing home facility, can choose private or semiprivate care at prices ranging from $118.80 to $151.50 per day.

The centerpiece of medical services is the expanded Williamsburg Community Hospital, which has the fierce loyalty of area citizens and provides high quality care for nearly all medical needs.

# Healthcare

Healthcare has come a long way since Colonial times, when doctors, trained in the medical practices of the times, tried to keep soldiers alive on the battlefields of the American Revolution. In fact, a revolution of sorts has taken place in the healthcare community of this area, where hospitals have expanded and simultaneously broadened local services and alternative healthcare options are growing in popularity.

The healthcare environment in the Williamsburg area is strong. The distance between hospitals on the lower and upper Peninsula and the need to serve a growing local population, a large retirement community and millions of visitors each year have made the community a good place for the development of medical facilities and practices.

The centerpiece of medical services is the expanded Williamsburg Community Hospital, which has the fierce loyalty of area citizens and provides high quality care for nearly all medical needs. A new oncology center, located directly across the street from the hospital, is a tangible sign of the commitment local medical community has made to better serve the community's needs.

The hospital's emergency room is among the best in the region. In addition, three professionally staffed urgent-care centers are strategically located around town.

Needs that can't be met in Williamsburg are provided at one of the Richmond, Newport News or Norfolk hospitals (including the Medical College of Virginia in Richmond, the Children's Hospital of the King's Daughters in Norfolk and Mary Immaculate, and Riverside Hospitals in Newport News). Emergency transport services include state-of-the-art ambulances and Nightingale helicopters, depending upon the urgency of care.

Numerous general practitioners and specialists have long-established practices in the immediate area and participate in the state medical network.

Dial 911 for medical emergencies in any Historic Triangle location. This number puts you in immediate touch with a trained professional who will take information about your location and the nature of your problem before dispatching the appropriate police, fire, rescue or ambulance services to assist you.

## Emergency Healthcare

Medical emergencies can be treated at several locations around Williamsburg. The most complete treatment is available at Williamsburg Community Hospital Emergency Care Center, of course, but minor and immediate-attention emergencies can be handled at the other care providers listed.

### Williamsburg Community Hospital
**301 Monticello Ave. general 259-6000, emergency • (757) 259-6005**

The city is justly proud of the role that Community plays in serving local patients as well as visitors to the Historic Area. A highly qualified staff of certified physicians and medical professionals gives careful attention to patients, and the Community Emergency Care Center provides excellent treatment 24 hours a day in all situations requiring immediate attention. The hospital also offers various outreach services. Patients needing quick, specialized attention available at other hospitals can be airlifted here by Nightingale helicopter service.

### Williamsburg Urgent Care
**Williamsburg Crossing Shopping Center, 5251 John Tyler Hwy. • (757) 220-8300**
**Ewell Station Shopping Center, 5601 Richmond Rd. • (757) 220-8300**

The number for both locations is the same to provide quick, efficient service. The first location is particularly convenient to the Jamestown Road side of town and the Route 5 corridor. The second location is convenient

# For Emergencies

In case of emergencies, dial 911. But in non-emergency cases, these mental health service numbers will put you in quick contact with persons appropriate to assist you.

**Williamsburg/James City County**
220-3200
**York County** 220-3200
**Eastern State Hospital** 253-5161

from Richmond Road and points west, including Norge, Lightfoot and Toano. Most x-ray and laboratory requirements can be handled on-site. Others are referred to Williamsburg Community Hospital. We've used their services often and have heard from readers who commend Urgent Care's staff and range of services. Hours at the Williamsburg Crossing location are 8 AM to 8 PM Monday through Saturday and 10 AM to 6 PM Sunday. At Ewell Station, the hours are 8 AM to 8 PM Monday through Friday and 10 AM to 8 PM Saturday. It's closed on Sunday. No appointment is needed. MasterCard, Visa and personal checks are accepted.

### First Med Of Williamsburg
**312 Second St. • (757) 229-4141**

On the side of the city closest to Busch Gardens and Water Country USA, this clinic offers a range of emergency and family medical services with x-ray and laboratory support. It is open 9 AM to 8 PM Monday through Friday and 9 AM to 5 PM Saturday. It's closed on Sunday. No appointment is necessary. MasterCard, Visa and personal checks are accepted.

# Mental and Therapeutic Healthcare

### Colonial Community Mental Health Center

**1657 Merrimac Tr. • (757) 220-3200**

This agency offers professional counseling 24 hours daily. Normal operating hours are from 8 AM to 5 PM Monday through Friday, but an answering service can put emergency callers in touch with professional counselors at all other times.

### Williamsburg Health Care and Rehabilitation Center
**1235 Mount Vernon Ave. • (757) 229-4121**

This center offers physical, occupational, respiratory and speech therapies as well as long-term comprehensive health and nursing care. The large staff demonstrates affection and concern for individual residents, and the social and entertainment programs are topnotch. The community takes an active interest in the center, with organizations volunteering a variety of services and activities.

# Referral Services

Williamsburg Community Hospital provides a Physician Referral Service at (757) 229-4636. The hospital also will advise on home health care at this number.

The three local jurisdictions' health departments can provide additional helpful information. In Williamsburg, call 253-2292; in James City County, 565-6860; in York County, 890-3900.

# Crisis and Support Groups

### AIDS: Peninsula AIDS Foundation
**326 Main St., Newport News • (757) 591-0971, (800) 377-1701**

This foundation provides a range of client services, including crisis intervention, emergency financial assistance, educational programs and support groups for people with HIV infection or AIDS and their friends and families.

### Williamsburg AIDS Network
**P.O. Box 1066, Williamsburg, VA 23187 • (757) 220-4606**

This local organization, funded in part by

Photo: Virginia Beach Convention and Tourism Bureau

Bikes offer hours of entertainment and exercise as well as the ability to explore nooks and crannies wherever you're visiting.

the Greater Williamsburg United Way, serves as a resource, referral and support group for persons with HIV infection or AIDS, as well as their families. The group provides comprehensive case management services and offers a bimonthly support group. Case management services include assistance in accessing medical care, medications, financial assistance and information and referral to other services in the area. In addition, the group provides HIV prevention education speakers for local schools, churches and community groups.

## Alcoholics Anonymous • (757) 595-1212

There are more than 150 AA meetings each week on the Peninsula, including more than 20 in greater Williamsburg. Meetings are held at 5:30 PM Monday through Friday at St. Martin's Episcopal Church on Jamestown Road in Williamsburg. But many more are scheduled throughout the city, James City and York counties. Call the 24-hour hotline number listed above for specific scheduled meetings and locations.

## Avalon, A Center for Women and Children
hotline • (757) 258-5051, office • (757) 258-5022

This shelter serves Williamsburg, James City County and York County. In addition to immediate shelter, it offers a 24-hour women's helpline, rape crisis intervention, legal and housing aid and support groups.

## Domestic Violence Hotline • (757) 723-7774

This hotline is run by the Virginia Peninsula Council on Domestic Violence. It is staffed around the clock.

## United Way Community Resource Service

## INSIDERS' TIP

Nightingale Air Ambulance service is available to fly patients out for emergency care at regional centers more advanced in treatment for certain disorders, such as head trauma or severe heart complications. The main heliport is across Mount Vernon Avenue from Williamsburg Community Hospital.

312 Waller Mill Rd., Ste. 100 • (757) 229-2222

This helpline is available 24 hours a day to refer those in need to appropriate agencies that provide for human needs such as child care, clothing, housing, medication, mental health services and other forms of assistance.

## Hospice Support Care of Williamsburg

312 Waller Mill Rd.
• (757) 253-1220

This agency provides professional and volunteer services to terminally ill patients at home or in a hospital or nursing home located in Williamsburg, James City or York counties. Time out for caregivers and patient care supplies and equipment also are available to those who need them. Bereavement support and cancer support programs and related consultation and referral services also are offered. The agency is supported by the Greater Williamsburg United Way, so there are no charges for goods or services provided by this group.

# Alternative Healthcare

At present, the alternative healthcare options locally include several types of services, from chiropractic care to acupuncture, massage therapy, meditation and variations on more traditional medical treatments.

Gaining in popularity and garnering growing support from the medical community at large, local chiropractors offer treatments in everything from lower back pain, disk problems, spinal curvatures, headaches and migraines to neck, shoulder and leg pain. The range of services provided by individual practitioners and chiropractic centers varies, so we urge you to call and ask questions before making an appointment. But among the chiropractic options in the Williamsburg area, traditional modalities have been enhanced to include laser and electro-acupuncture treatments as well.

Certified massage therapists have come a long way since the days their trade was associated with Navy towns and questionable business enterprises along New York's Times Square area. Area therapists must be licensed by the state and certified by the locality in which they practice. Treatments vary with the practitioner, so we suggest you call before arranging to meet with a massage therapist. But, if you decide you're interested, you'll find them willing to meet you upon appointment, either at their place of business or at your home or business. Several therapists have portable massage tables and massage chairs that enable them to bring the treatment to you. The price of such treatment varies widely, however, so we urge you to broach this subject at the time you query a therapist about services rendered.

Two alternative healthcare options locally deserve special mention: Physmed and Phoenix Rising Yoga Therapy.

Physmed, located at 1318 Jamestown Rd., 253-1900, is a physical medicine and wellness center that integrates several alternative care practices with an eye toward total well being. Physmed takes an integrated approach to healthcare, treating the whole person, not just

---

**INSIDERS' TIP**

**If you should end up in the emergency room or at one of the urgent care centers, and doctors determine you need to be transported by ambulance elsewhere for treatment, ask for the gamut of options open to you. There are several ambulance services, and the cost of transporting patients varies wildly. If you want the best price, have someone inquire about your options and ask about prices directly from the provider. Six months down the road, you'll be glad you did.**

an isolated symptom. The process includes consultation, examination, X-ray treatment, acute, corrective and maintenance care by a team of chiropractors in concert with a massage therapist and other practitioners. The center also provides counseling in nutrition, diet, ergonomic and lifestyle management to help facilitate each patient's overall good health.

Practitioner Quinn Sale, 229-2482, operating as a Phoenix Rising Yoga Therapist, has offered clients this unusual method of body-mind-spirit wellness maintenance since 1991. A trained psychotherapist and licensed professional counselor with more than 15 years experience, Sale combines the ancient wisdom of Yoga with nondirective dialogue techniques.

Through a sequence of carefully assisted Yoga postures and breathing tailored to each client's individual needs, this therapy provides the opportunity for release of habitual holding patterns from specific areas of the body. Yoga therapy is based on the idea that we all hold our histories in our bodies as well as our heads. Unlocking the body's armature can unblock pent-up feelings, fears and resistances, leaving the individual feeling more open, relaxed, balanced, emotionally stable and mentally clear. Most sessions are one-on-one, catered to the needs of the individual client. Sessions with couples and small groups also are offered. No previous experience with yoga is necessary.

A two-year community college and four-year colleges and universities with advanced graduate level programs in a variety of disciplines are all located within a 50-mile radius of Williamsburg.

# Education and Child Care

Williamsburg is very much a family-oriented community. Even our visitor attractions are designed to appeal to the whole family. Advanced business and industry, the military and the mild climate attract more new residents every year - mostly young families and retirees.

More families mean more youngsters moving into the area and lots of parents faced with meeting their children's needs at various stages of development. This chapter offers helpful, preliminary information about the options Williamsburg-area newcomers and residents have when looking for childcare or schools for their children. We begin this chapter with an overview of the public school system, followed by the private schools in the area. For those of you who are interested in furthering your education, we include a section of the colleges and universities nearby. The second half of the chapter is devoted to childcare, both for those who plan to live in this area and for those who just need a night away from the little ones while on vacation.

## Public Education

The Williamsburg-James City County School System is unified and serves the majority of students in the area from kindergarten through high school. The York County School system serves families in the northern and eastern portions of the Historic Triangle.

Jamestown High School, the Williamsburg-James City County School District's second high school, opened in the fall of 1997 on Route 5. And none too soon. Until the opening of the new facility, Lafayette High School on Longhill Road was bursting at the seams with a rapidly growing enrollment, something the entire district is experiencing. That facility recently underwent a major renovation. Currently, the district consists of Lafayette and Jamestown high schools; Berkeley, James Blair and Toano middle schools; six elementary schools; and the Eastern State Educational Program. Districting for middle schools in the Williamsburg-James City County system is determined by where the children attended elementary school so that groups stay together as they progress. Bright Beginnings, a preschool program based at Rawls Byrd Elementary School, is part of the school system's efforts to promote the achievement of at-risk children. Programs for gifted and talented children and one for profoundly handicapped preschoolers also are available.

Options for high school students include advanced-placement courses, vocational education, technology education, business, practical nursing and fine arts sequences. The school district's graduation rate is about 97 percent. Approximately 90 percent of its graduates go on to some form of higher education.

Elementary school hours are 9:10 AM to 3:40 PM. Middle school hours are 7:50 AM to 2:20 PM and high school hours are 7:40 AM to 2:40 PM.

For information on public school registration, Williamsburg and James City County residents should call 253-6762.

The York County School System has four high schools, three intermediate schools and 10 elementary schools. The newest facility is the Grafton high school/middle school complex. A boom in enrollment has been rather lopsided, with upper York County schools under-enrolled while other schools are crowded. Portable classrooms have been added at Tabb High School, Queens Lake Middle School and Bethel Manor Elementary School.

Residents of upper York County near Williamsburg enjoy a zoning plan designed to let children attend the schools that are closest to their homes. This plan routes students of Waller Mill and Magruder elementary schools to Queens Lake Middle School and Bruton High School. Both Bruton and Tabb high schools converted to a rotating block schedule in 1992, with students attending three 90-minute classes a day instead of the traditional six shorter class periods. For information about districts and registration, call 898-0300.

# Private Schools

## Walsingham Academy
### 1100 Jamestown Rd. • (757) 229-2642

If you prefer a private school experience for your child, Walsingham Academy merits serious consideration. Enrolling students of various faiths, this independent Catholic academy is coeducational and emphasizes a value-based, high-standard curriculum for students from preschool through high school. Enrollment is on the increase at the Lower School and is limited. We recommend application at the earliest possible time: for the Lower School, when they are a year or two out; for the Upper School, at the end of the year prior to the fall in which they wish to attend. The student/teacher ratio is 20 to 1. The school just built a multimillion-dollar sports facility and indoor gym complex for the Upper School. Most of Walsingham's graduates matriculate to excellent colleges and universities. For information on the Lower School (up to 7th grade), call

229-2642. The number for the Upper School (grades 8 to 12) is (757) 229-6026.

## Williamsburg Christian Academy
### 309 Waltz Farm Dr. • (757) 220-1978

Another private school option is Williamsburg Christian. Opened in 1978, this school focuses on Christian values and Biblical viewpoints. The Academy, which became an independent, interdenominational Christian school with no church affiliation in 1992, is located in the former Jamestown Academy adjacent to Skipwith Farms. Programs serve four-year-old preschoolers through 12th graders. The school boasts a 15 to 1 student/teacher ratio. Most students go on to college.

## Hampton Roads Academy
### 739 Academy Ln., Newport News
### • (757) 249-1489

Founded in 1959, Hampton Roads Academy, or HRA as it's referred to locally, has an enrollment of more than 470 students, more than 100 of whom commute 30 miles from the Greater Williamsburg area to attend school. The academy offers curriculum for students in grades 6 through 12. From its inception, HRA has stood for excellence in college preparatory education and has earned the designation as a "Blue Ribbon School" from the U.S. Department of Education. The school is fully accredited by the Virginia Association of Independent Schools. HRA appeals to a wide cross-section of students because of its broad-based athletics, arts and music programs, commitment to community service, small class size, active Honor Council and honor code and its reputation for sending 100 percent of its graduates to four-year colleges and universities. It offers bus service from Williamsburg. HRA just completed a $2 million wing that houses a new library, computer center and

---

**INSIDERS' TIP**

The local fire departments offer classes in CPR and basic babysitting skills for area teenagers. When you hire a sitter, inquire whether they have taken the course or if they are trained in emergency first aid and CPR.

classrooms. Six years ago, the school opened a new fine arts and science wing.

# School Closing Information

It doesn't snow often in the Historic Triangle, but when the white stuff even threatens to appear, nearly every family radio in the area - teachers' and administrators' as well - tunes in for information about school closings. There is no objective measurement to determine when schools will close. The decisive factor for most students is a judgment by the Williamsburg-James City County Schools superintendent as to whether roads are safe for bus travel and whether students at bus stops are at risk from the weather. The superintendent makes an informed decision: Virginia Department of Transportation (VDOT) workers test buses on rural roads between 2:30 and 4 AM; they then contact the highway department, the National Weather Service and state, county and city police offices for current local weather conditions and predictions. This information goes to the transportation director and the finance director of Williamsburg-James City County who recommend that the superintendent close the schools, open them late or go ahead with normal opening times. By 6 AM, the media is notified, and the information is included in frequent broadcast announcements. In addition, the Williamsburg-James City County Schools have established a hotline that offers, among other information, the latest on school closings. The hotline operates 24 hours a day. That number is 872-6535. Private schools generally follow the lead of the public schools but are listed school-by-school in the media reports. Colleges and universities announce their closings by name through the same media listed below for the school systems.

If snow develops during the day, schools may close early, occasionally even in the morning. Parents do well to monitor the weather and school closing information throughout the school day.

While the media generally carries comprehensive listings of closings, use the following lists to be sure of accurate, timely information for your school. Stations are listed for schools in the order in which they are notified.

Williamsburg-James City Schools announces closings through WDCK-FM 96.5, WTPG-AM 740, major television stations in Norfolk, Portsmouth and Richmond, WRVA-AM 1140, WHRO-FM 90.3 and WFOG-FM 93.

The York County School System's closings are announced by WTPG-AM 740, WNIS-AM 850, WRVA-AM 1140, WTJZ-AM 1270, WYCS-FM 91.5, WJQI-FM 94.9, WQSF-FM 96.5, WGH-FM 97.3, WNOR-FM 98.7, WXGM-FM 99.1, WCMS-FM 100.5, WWDE-FM 101.3 and all major television stations in Norfolk, Portsmouth and Richmond.

Walsingham Academy closings are covered by WTVR-TV Channel 6, WWDE-FM 101, WFOG-FM 93, WTJZ-AM 740, WQSF-FM 96.5, WRVA-AM 1140 and WRVG-FM 94.

Williamsburg Christian Academy announces its closings through WVEC-TV Channel 13, WQSF-FM 96.5, WFOG-FM 93 and The COAST 93.7 FM.

Hampton Roads Academy students should monitor WTAR-FM 95.7, WNOR-FM 98.7, WAFX-FM 106.9 and WWDE-FM 101.3.

# Colleges and Universities

A number of colleges and universities serve the Historic Triangle and surrounding communities. Whether high school graduates are seeking to further their education or older residents are looking to obtain advanced degrees, technical certifications or new spheres of knowledge, there's an institution of higher learning sure to offer a curriculum geared to each individual's particular interest.

A two-year community college and four-year colleges and universities with advanced graduate level programs in a variety of disciplines are all located within a 30-mile radius of Williamsburg.

### College of William and Mary
**PO Box 8795, Williamsburg VA 23187**
**• (757) 221-4000**

William and Mary, established in 1693, is a nationally recognized institution. The majority of undergraduates are resident students from elsewhere, but the number of local students is growing. While out-of-state visitors often assume William and Mary is a private school, it is actually a state-supported, four-year university with a prestigious reputation. Often referred to as a "public ivy," William and Mary offers its students the diverse resources of a large institution with the community atmosphere of a smaller school. In addition to a broad and thorough undergraduate liberal arts and sciences curriculum, the college offers graduate courses for master's degrees in many fields and Ph.D. level studies in several fields. The Marshall-Wythe School of Law awards the juris doctor degree; and, at the Virginia Institute of Marine Science at Gloucester Point (VIMS), both master's degree and Ph.D. programs are offered.

Most students live on campus, though a few commute. Most students matriculate here directly out of high school, so the student population is young.

Residents as well as visitors can take advantage of numerous cultural events and opportunities sponsored by the College of William and Mary (see our Arts chapter). Local citizens are offered special rates if they want to attend William and Mary's Alumni College, a four-day course offered each June to explore complex issues, such as modern technology. Call 221-1174 for details. The Christopher Wren Association, a lifelong learning program in which retirement-age citizens with a particular field of expertise share their knowledge with fellow retirement-age community members, has become a big hit at the university. This program is described in our Retirement chapter. Call 221-1079 for information.

The Wendy and Emery Reves Center for International Studies was established at the college to foster broader understanding of global issues at the university, across the nation and throughout the world. At William and Mary, the center supports and integrates international programs in the arts and sciences, professional schools and interdisciplinary programs. It coordinates six undergraduate degree programs in international relations and area studies, administers study abroad programs for William and Mary undergraduates and supports international studies on campus. The center also

promotes faculty research and sponsors lectures, colloquia, workshops and symposia on many issues of global concern.

Student-led tours of the college campus are available throughout the year. For information on tours call 221-4223. For other information about the college, see our Attractions chapter profile or call 221-4000.

## Christopher Newport University

**50 Shoe Ln., Newport News • (757) 594-7000**

Once part of the College of William and Mary, CNU split from W&M in the 1980s and since has developed an identity of its own. Located on a verdant, 110-acre campus about 25 miles southeast of Williamsburg in Newport News, this four-year institution offers a wide variety of undergraduate and graduate courses and degrees.

"We are a young university on the move that enjoys a growing reputation for really caring about students, great teaching, small classes and having Virginia's safest campus. At CNU we put our students first. We are proud to have a Student-First Faculty, Student-First Academics and Student-First Community," said CNU President Paul S. Trible, former U.S. Senator.

In short, CNU is a young college offering 50 undergraduate and graduate programs to 4,600 students in business, science, technology, education, government and the performing arts.

The Students-First Academic Program includes the Presidential Leadership Program, a minor in leadership studies; and the Presidential Scholars Program, a recognition program for students that provides annual scholarships ranging from $1,000 to $5,000.

CNU's stellar performing and fine arts program will soon be located in a new Center for the Arts, being designed by the world-renowned architectural firm of Pei Cobb Freed & Partners. The college's Sports, Wellness and Convocation Center, also scheduled for completion by 2000, will serve as a gathering place for sports, entertainment and civic events. CNU's intermural sports program in-

Photo: William K. Geiger

Educational opportunities abound in and around the Historic Triangle.

cludes NCAA Division III contests in 17 sports including a nine-time national championship women's track and perennial national ranked men's basketball team.

Christopher Newport University has many recent high school grads but also draws a contingent of older students who return to school after working for a few years. Most CNU students commute, though some live in dorms on campus.

## Thomas Nelson Community College
**99 Thomas Nelson Dr., Hampton**
**• (757) 825-2700**

Based in Hampton, but with the Historic Triangle Learning Center and classroom complex at the Busch Corporate Center, the college is part of the statewide community college system. It offers two-year associates degrees in strong university-parallel transfer courses, engineering and technical and occupational programs. Significantly lower tuition rates than those at four-year Virginia colleges and an emphasis on teaching over research make the college attractive to area residents. The student population ranges from recent high school grads to senior citizens wishing to take courses after retirement. Nationally recognized for its contributions to the economic development of the area, the college provides education, training and related services enhancing the business community's productivity, quality and competitiveness. The Williamsburg location offers transferable associate degrees in liberal arts, science and

business administration, as well as credits for training in computing and software. The Williamsburg site also offers academic, career and personal counseling and planning services. Both day and night classes are offered at this location. A permanent site in Williamsburg is being planned. The number listed above is for the college's main campus switchboard. The Historic Triangle Learning Center's main number is 253-4300. For a catalog or more information, call the admissions office at 825-2800.

## Hampton University
**Hampton VA 23668 • (757) 727-5000**

Privately supported Hampton University, formerly Hampton Institute, celebrated its 130th anniversary in 1998.

When it opened its doors on April 1, 1868, it was known as the Hampton Normal and Agricultural Institute, which had a few buildings on 120 acres of land, little equipment, two teachers (who earned $15 a month), 15 students and a dormitory retrofitted from a converted hospital barracks.

Today, Hampton University is the most popular black college in America. It boasts a student population of 5,600 (about the same size as the College of William and Mary), a $140 million endowment, the highest SAT scores of entering freshmen for any historically black college, state-of-the-art facilities, a distinguished faculty (including Effie Barry, the ex-wife of former D.C. mayor Marion Barry) and an innovative curriculum. It offers a variety of programs including especially strong

---

## INSIDERS' TIP

**Child Caring Connection, in cooperation with James City County Parks and Recreation, cosponsors a Play Day in the Park each summer in July at Kidsburg at Mid County Park, off Ironbound Road. A variety of fun and educational activities are designed especially with kids in mind. Events in the past have included face-painting, bubble-making, parachute games, clay molding, storytelling and more. Local arts groups have given live performances and the fire department usually brings a truck that children are allowed to climb aboard. For more information or specifics on date and time of the next Play Day in the Park, call 229-7940.**

ones in science, engineering, business (including an MBA degree), architecture and nursing.

Listed among famous graduates are Booker T. Washington (Class of 1875, who took what he learned here south where he founded Tuskegee Institute), Spencer Christian (Class of '70 and weatherman on ABC's *Good Morning America*), Ms. Frankie Freeman (Class of '37 and former U.S. Civil Rights Commissioner) and Vanessa D. Gilmore (Class of '77 and a federal judge in Texas).

# Childcare

The busy pace of family life, especially for those with two working parents and single-parent households, creates a need for safe, dependable child-care services. Yet, the search for such care can be an anxiety-ridden experience.

While word of mouth remains one of the best ways to find good childcare, newcomers may not be sure whose recommendations to trust. The majority of child-care centers are licensed by the state, and there are two ways to find out current information about providers

in whom you have an interest. Several options for finding local care providers are available as parents begin their search.

### *The Parents' Guide to Children's Services in Hampton Roads*
**New Health Enterprises, P.O. Box 3107, Lee Hall VA 23603• no phone**

This free guide offers information not only about day care but also about health services and retail products for children. It is published each summer, and you can pick it up at area schools and in retail outlets throughout the area.

### The National Association for the Education of Young Children • (800) 424-2460

This national organization, known for high standards, is another source of information on childcare. Guidelines from this group can be picked up locally at the Virginia Social Services Department, which can be reached by calling 594-7594.

### Child Caring Connection
**312 Waller Mill Rd., Ste. 500 • (757) 229-**

Colonial Williamsburg offers summer programs for children and families that delight as well as educate.

**7940**

This nonprofit organization is a resources and referral service funded primarily through the United Way. Here, parents are provided with assistance finding licensed, home-based care providers. A computerized directory of area day-care centers and information concerning all local child-care options, including nanny services, aids the search. In addition, the Connection maintains a resource library of books and videos pertaining to many aspects of parenting, including immunizations and healthcare. They offer support services to parents interested in shared care (when two mothers of two toddlers trade days off), an education program for people interested in starting up a home-based childcare business, bimonthly newsletters and more. The Child Caring Connection charges a fee based on income, beginning at $15 per year.

### Child Development Resources
**150 Point of Woods Rd., Norge • (757) 566-3300**

Parents of children with special needs or who might benefit from early evaluation and intervention can contact this nationally recognized organization, based in Norge, about 10 miles west of Williamsburg. Professionals here offer testing, information, advice, referrals and support for families with children who have special needs, particularly those faced with out-of-the-ordinary needs.

### AuPairCare - European Nanny Service
**1 Post St., 7th Fl., San Francisco CA 94104 • (800) 428-7247**

This service matches American families with European child-care providers between the ages of 18 and 25 who are interested in spending a year in the United States. The au pairs are screened and complete thorough applications. Host families choose the au pair who best matches their needs and personalities. Unlike an employee, the au pair functions much like a family member, sharing meals and social occasions, as well as helping with basic household chores. In exchange for room, board and weekly spending money, the au pair acts as a live-in, long-term caregiver, providing 45 hours per week of childcare. Local AuPairCare community counselors provide support to both the families and the au pair during the program's duration.

In the first year, the family pays $4,070 for the care itself, plus a $225 application/interview fee. The host family must provide room/board and $139 per week in wages for 45 hours of care by the au pair. For more information, call customer service at (415) 434-8788.

# Babysitting Services for Visitors

With so many families visiting the area, there are frequent inquiries about the babysitting services available to nonresidents. Maybe mom and dad want to celebrate a special occasion by dining alone or maybe they want to attend one of the many concerts, plays or other "grown-up" offerings in the area; maybe the children would like to play alone or with others their age. Maybe the generations just need a little break from each other. Whatever the case, there are babysitting options for visitors.

Area hotels and motels routinely used to offer sitting services for their guests, but this service is declining. Typically, we are told that "we could arrange for babysitting, but we'd need to know well in advance, and the guests would have to make their own arrangements with the sitters to whom we refer them." The key is advance planning.

If you would consider leaving your child with a sitting service or private individual, it is critical for you to have references, to know if the sitter is bonded, what First-Aid and medical training the sitter has and if the care will be provided in your lodging or elsewhere. You must be sure to give the sitter your evening's itinerary, including phone numbers. Be prepared to pay a premium if you are visiting. For an idea of what you might pay, note that residents pay from $1.50 to $4 per hour, occasionally more, for private sitters.

### Colonial Williamsburg
**P.O. Drawer C, Williamsburg VA 23187 • (800) HISTORY**

Colonial Williamsburg offers babysitting

services for guests staying in one of its hotels or inns. Babysitters listed with this service have been carefully screened and interviewed, and their services are used regularly by guests of the foundation. The number of sitters is limited, however, so it is wise to make arrangements well in advance, perhaps even at the time you make your lodging reservations. Once you're in Williamsburg, call 229-1000, the main switchboard, to make arrangements for a babysitter. The charge is $6 per hour for one child, with an additional $1 per hour for each additional child left in the sitter's care.

## Child Caring Connection
**312 Waller Mill Rd., Ste. 500 • (757) 229-7940**

Child Caring Connection, mentioned earlier in this chapter, keeps a list of College of William and Mary students who make themselves available as babysitters to earn money for school, books and extra spending money. Obviously, this particular service is dependent upon the college's academic calendar, though some babysitters listed live in town and are available year round. The fee for sitting is negotiable between the student and family seeking babysitting services.

Church building flourished during the 18th and early 19th centuries. Some of these beautiful old buildings are still in use and open for tours, such as Bruton Parish in Williamsburg.

# Worship

Early English settlers in Jamestown met solemnly each day to "have Prayer with a Psalme," a custom that mystified the local Indians. The Virginia Colony wasn't founded for wholly religious purposes, but religion was of primary importance in the lives of settlers, who claimed their new home for their church, the Church of England, as well as for their king. Everywhere they moved they built churches, nothing fancy at first, but more ambitiously conceived than their dwellings. By the time Jamestown was 3 years old, its church had two bells in the steeple, cedar pews and windows.

The Church of England dominated religious life in the Virginia Colony. Church attendance was mandatory in Colonial Virginia - twice a day every day of the week in some settlements. Delinquents spent the night in the guardhouse or were fined in pounds of tobacco. Keeping the Sabbath holy was a serious preoccupation for early courts: Pity poor Thomas Scully who, in 1624, was ordered to pay "5 pounds sterling in good tobacco" for "going a hunting" on a Sunday.

Witch trials didn't occur only in the New England colonies; Jamestown is where the first charge of witchcraft in British North America was recorded in 1626. Colonial Williamsburg now periodically presents an audience-interactive dramatization of the 1706 trial of a well-known Virginia witch accused of, among other things, shrinking herself and sailing to North Carolina on an eggshell. Other religious nonconformists in the colony, notably the Quakers, faced persecution, even banishment.

But as dissent fomented in England, diversity and a bit of tolerance spread to America. Presbyterian, Methodist and Baptist churches were founded here by the end of the Colonial era. Presbyterians organized in Williamsburg in 1765. Williamsburg Presbyterian Church at one time met on the Palace Green on a lot bought from the College of William and Mary in 1885. In 1930, during the restoration of the Palace Green area, that property was sold; the new edifice at 215 Richmond Road was completed in 1931. The church now serves a congregation in excess of 1,400.

During Colonial times, the Williamsburg Baptist Church, 227 Richmond Road, met in members' houses and in the Powder Magazine, which later was remodeled into a church and housed the congregation until Colonial Williamsburg's restoration began. Chartered in 1828, the church moved to the current building in 1935.

Church building flourished during the 18th and early 19th centuries. Some of these beautiful old buildings are still in use and open for tours, such as Bruton Parish in Williamsburg and Grace Episcopal in Yorktown. (For information about these and other historic churches, please turn to the Attractions and Jamestown and Yorktown chapters.)

As the Williamsburg area continues to grow and prosper, so does its religious community. Existing congregations have flourished, with membership filling edifices to capacity. Many long-standing churches locally have had to expand, and congregations have split their populations between two or more churches. For example, St. Bede Roman Catholic

## INSIDERS' TIP

**Tourists pour into area churches on Sundays. Insiders know to arrive earlier than usual in season to assure both parking and seating for services.**

English settlers celebrated the first Thanksgiving at Berkeley Plantation on December 4, 1619.

Photo: Berkeley Plantation

Church, which lists nearly 2,000 member families, has seen the emergence in recent years of St. Olaf, a new Catholic parish in upper James City County. While many of its congregants used to attend St. Bede, they now go to the more conveniently located little parish in Norge. And the original St. Bede, located on Richmond Road in the shadow of the College of William and Mary campus, is bulging to the seams and busy planning a new church off Ironbound Road near Mid-County Park.

At the same time, new and diverse congregations are opening with amazing regularity. Route 5 is quickly becoming a "church row" of sorts, with numerous new churches

**INSIDERS' TIP**

Local churches welcome guests — some even make a point to acknowledge them during services. Don't be surprised if you and your family are asked to raise your hand or stand up and be greeted. It's the congregation's way of letting visitors know how much they are appreciated.

sprouting up between the city and the county line at the confluence of the James and Chickahominy rivers.

Once tiny church communities, such as the Ascension of Our Lord Byzantine Catholic Church, are gaining members weekly. This church, located at 114 Palace Lane, off Bypass Road, holds several liturgies on Sunday and others during the week. And, once Catholics realized they fulfilled their Sunday obligations by attending masses here, the parish began to flourish. The liturgy is offered in English, with much of it sung, and it retains much of the pomp and circumstance lost in the Roman liturgy since Vatican II.

The Jewish community, once a tiny group, has grown tremendously in recent years, as has the Unitarian Universalist congregation, which a couple of years ago opened an exquisite and expanded edifice on Ironbound Road between Jamestown Road and John Tyler Highway.

What we have presented is not an exhaustive list of what Williamsburg has to offer in the realm of worship but simply a brief overview. We recommend that readers seeking information concerning worship services and times call the church they wish to attend for exact information. We also recommend that readers consult the *Virginia Gazette* on Saturdays for current listings of religious observances around the Historic Triangle.

Endview Plantation in northern Newport News is a $10 million Civil War interpretive center.

# Our Military Heritage

From the weapons of early Native American warriors to the stealth aircraft that stalk today's skies, the Hampton Roads area not only has witnessed the most advanced weaponry and military power of each age but also has been instrumental in their development. In addition, hundreds of thousands of American service men and women have been stationed at one or another of the major military installations in the area, many eventually retiring to local communities. The Air Force, Army, Coast Guard, Marines and Navy still are very much a part of the local fabric, while numerous sites and monuments have been erected to commemorate the battles waged on our lands.

The earliest contacts between Native Americans and Europeans occurred, of course, in the early 1600s in and around Jamestown. Today at Jamestown Settlement (see our chapter on Jamestown and Yorktown), exhibits detail the culture of the Native Americans and the earliest settlers. A re-created Powhatan Indian village portrays the daily life of the people who originally lived on the land. Costumed interpreters there and at James Fort demonstrate the weapons and battle tactics of both groups during the early 17th century. And, behind the scenes are the archaeologists and researchers whose discoveries continue to improve upon our understanding of this period.

## Digging Deeply into History

Recently, researchers dug up even more information about Jamestown's battle-scarred past. In September 1996, the region made international headlines when archaeologists working on the Jamestown Rediscovery Project on Jamestown Island unearthed conclusive evidence of the original fort erected in 1607. For more than two years, the team had searched for signs of this vanished military bastion, which most scholars thought had washed away into the James River decades ago. To date, the majority of the more than 150,000 artifacts uncovered - including an intact Cabasset helmet (an elongated metal helmet constructed of two parts joined together at a center seam) and breastplate, pieces of cut-up armor and matchlock muskets and dozens of other weaponry fragments - underscores the military mission of James Fort. Members of the excavation team spent the winter months sorting through and identifying artifacts. Work on the dig resumed this past spring. (For more on this fascinating archeological project see the close-up, "Dig This" in our Jamestown and Yorktown chapter.)

But don't think that Jamestown corners the market on interesting dirt. Carter's Grove Plantation, where the Wolstenholme Towne site was the scene in 1622 of a massacre that wiped out the inhabitants there and nearly destroyed the fledgling colony, has seen its share of exciting discoveries. Earlier excavations of this site, originally called Martin's Hundred plantation, uncovered the first two intact closed (face-covering) helmets found in North America. The Winthrop Rockefeller Archaeological Museum at Carter's Grove (see our Colonial Williamsburg chapter) is a treasure-trove for those interested in 17th-century military life. A film at the museum depicts the unearthing of those helmets and modern armorers making reproductions. The history of the settlement and the archaeological excavation that has uncovered and interpreted it is very well-depicted here in a series of fascinating exhibits.

# 18th-Century Military Culture

The military history of the next century is revealed in many exhibits throughout the area. The Powder Magazine at Colonial Williamsburg is the focal point of 18th-century military interpretations. It houses a large collection of weapons of the 1700s, with an emphasis on the muskets used by the Colonial militia. In Market Square at Colonial Williamsburg, period cannon are fired daily in demonstrations of the drill required to load, aim and discharge the pieces. The military uniforms of the era are worn by costumed interpreters and the members of the Colonial Fife and Drum Corps, who demonstrate the martial music of the period in frequent parades on Duke of Gloucester Street. In the central hallway of the Governor's Palace, the display of firearms serves as a reminder of the power that both protected and controlled the British colony.

The most elaborate interpretation of 18th-century military culture is found at Yorktown. (See our Jamestown and Yorktown chapter). The Yorktown Visitor Center displays uniforms, arms and accouterments of the military forces that engaged there, and it includes a full-size reconstruction of a quarterdeck of a man-of-war of the era. The Yorktown Battlefield provides an experience of the siege defenses of the period; interpretations in the center and mounted around the battlefield, particularly

along the driving tour, will help you envision what warfare was like for soldiers of the day. At the Yorktown Victory Center at the other end of the crescent of fortifications, outdoor living history presentations by costumed interpreters give visitors a memorable vision of the camp life of the common soldier in the 1700s. Inside the center are more exhibits that offer rich detail about the military experiences of the day.

# Entrenched in Civil War

Two 19th-century periods of military interest are represented within easy driving distance of the Historic Triangle. At Fort Monroe in Hampton, the moat-surrounded fortification that served as an important Union base for campaigns throughout the Civil War. The Casemate Museum at the fort offers a rich interpretation of the military history and lifestyle of the early 1800s and of Fort Monroe in particular (see our Newport News and Hampton chapter). The fort, which, by the way, is still an active Army post, played an important role in the Civil War, remaining in Union hands throughout the conflict and housing Jefferson Davis as a prisoner after the war. Nearby Fort Wool, accessible only by boat, dates to 1819 and was another Union stronghold throughout the Civil War. The first battle of ironclad warships took place offshore near Chesapeake Avenue in Hampton. Neither side emerged the victor, but the battle changed naval warfare forever; wooden fighting ships began to disappear from the world's navies and were replaced by better-armed metal successors. The battle engagement of the *Monitor* and *Merrimac* warships is honored by the name of the Monitor-Merrimac Bridge-Tunnel spanning the James River upstream from the site of the conflict.

In Newport News Park, just east of

Williamsburg on Route 143, Dam No. 1 and Confederate gun positions, as well as remaining Union trenches, are evidence of the Peninsula Campaign. The Visitor Center in the park interprets the action that took place there and offers literature on other sites nearby. At Lee's Mill, located along Route 60, just south of Fort Eustis in Newport News, the city has purchased six acres of Civil War earthworks and adjacent land for a small public park.

Also in Newport News, you'll find some ongoing restoration of Civil War sites. The most notable is the transformation of Endview Plantation in northern Newport News into a $10 million Civil War interpretive center. The plantation was built in 1720 on a road that led to Yorktown and is the second-oldest house still standing in what was formally Warwick County. The Virginia War Museum, located at the southern end of the city, has taken over the house and is hard at work recapturing its fascinating Civil War history. And, what a rich history it is.

During the war, Dr. Humphrey Harwood Curtis recruited local residents, including nine of his own family members, to form the Warwick Beauregards. A farewell party was staged on the front lawn of Endview, and the Beauregards reported for active duty with the 32nd Virginia Infantry. During this time, Endview also became an important campground for Confederate units, while the house was turned into a hospital during the Warwick-Yorktown siege. Later, during the Confederate retreat of May 3, 1862, the Union army occupied Endview and it, too, used the estate as a hospital. A couple of days later, Endview was visited briefly by Union Gen. George McClellan while he was on his way to the Battle of Williamsburg. Union and Confederate camps have been set up on the grounds of the historic plantation to make it easier for visitors to step back in time.

The Virginia War Museum also is restoring Lee Hall Mansion, located about a mile from Endview Plantation just off Route 143 on

Photo: Colonial Williamsburg Foundation

Costumed interpreters wage war at the Yorktown Victory Center's Revolutionary War Camp.

Yorktown Road. Built around the 1850s by a wealthy planter, the mansion was used as one of the headquarters for Confederate Gen. John Bankhead (J.B.) Magruder during the Peninsula campaign. The grounds are open to the public, and a preserved earthwork sits in front of the mansion, which opened for guided tours in the spring of 1998. (For more on the Virginia War Museum and its historic Endview Plantation, see our chapter on Newport News and Hampton).

The Civil War left other vestiges in the immediate area. On and near the grounds of the Fort Magruder Inn and Conference Center on York Street are remains of the fort, which was active in the defense of Williamsburg. Several Confederate defense works remain on the banks of the James River, testimonials to the attempts of the Confederacy to block Union passage upriver. Near Jones Mill Pond on the Colonial Parkway are remains dating to the Battle of Williamsburg in 1862. General Magruder reworked the defenses of the Battle of Yorktown as the northern anchor of defenses crossing the Peninsula to prevent McClellan's Union forces from advancing on Richmond.

The Confederate secondary line at Williamsburg stretched from Queens Creek on the York River to College Creek on the James River, with Fort Magruder at the center (remains of the outer fort still exist near the swimming pool of the motel there). Fourteen individual strongholds were located on the line, 12 of which still exist in varying states of preservation. The Confederate withdrawal westward through Williamsburg on May 4, 1862, led to the battles that raged along that line from May 4 through 6. All in all, 3,900 men of both sides - about one-tenth of the combatants - were casualties in the fighting at Williamsburg.

Union troops eventually occupied Williamsburg on May 6, and, for a while, it was the closest Union-held city to Richmond. Full of Union troops and spies from both sides, the city of Williamsburg remained under martial law until the end of the war. On September 9, 1862, a former James City County lawyer, Confederate General Weiss, attacked Williamsburg and drove the Union forces back to Fort Magruder with a charge down Duke of Gloucester Street. The victory was ephemeral, however, lasting only one day. That afternoon, a fire of unknown origin partially burned the Wren Building at the College of William and Mary. From that day on, Union troops remained in control, though the citizens chafed under their rule.

The campaign passed westward. McClellan headquartered at Berkeley Plantation in Charles City County and conferred there with President Lincoln about the Peninsula Campaign of 1862. McClellan's march up the Peninsula to Richmond was unexpectedly halted for 29 days along the Warwick River. Union Gen. Daniel Butterfield during that campaign composed the haunting melody of "Taps" at Berkeley.

Within daytrip distance are the Richmond and Petersburg battlefields as well as other sites significant to the Civil War, including several along Route 5 in Charles City County, just west of James City County. Historical markers alert motorists of their existence. In Richmond-about an hour west of Williamsburg on I-64 - the Capitol, White House and Museum of the Confederacy are great places to visit (see the Richmond entry in our Daytrips chapter). Battle Abbey, also in Richmond, houses a mammoth research library of records and relics of the war, and Monument Avenue, one of the most beautiful boulevards in the nation, honors the

---

## INSIDERS' TIP

**The North Atlantic Treaty Organization (NATO), headquartered in Norfolk, oversees defense of the entire Atlantic area. This area includes 12 million square miles from North America to Europe and Africa.**

Photo: Newport News Tourism and Development Office

Newport News Shipbuilding has been constructing warships since the Spanish-American War.

Confederacy's heroes with bronze statues at its major intersections.

The Siege Museum in Petersburg gives an extremely informative interpretation of the military actions that transpired in the area, and the exhibits put a human face on history. Farther to the west, Lexington is home to Virginia Military Institute and the tombs of generals Robert E. Lee and "Stonewall" Jackson, which are shrines for many Southerners and other admirers of those consummate tacticians. The battlefields at Manassas, Fredericksburg, Spotsylvania, New Market and Cold Harbor are also close enough daytrip options for visitors to the Historic Triangle who are interested in the Civil War. To simplify the process of planning your trip, consider picking up a copy of *The Insiders' Guide to Civil War Sites in the Eastern Theater*. It includes 21 tours, covering nearly the entire state of Virginia and portions of Maryland, Pennsylvania and West Virginia, as well as maps, personality sketches of figures that played key roles in the war and chapters on accommodations and restaurants.

## The 20th Century

Military matters in our own century have

**INSIDERS' TIP**

**The area has seen many U.S. military firsts. Among these are the first fort, James Fort (1607); America's first battleship, the USS Texas (1892); and America's first aircraft carrier, the USS Langley (1922).**

left their marks on the area as well. The coastal gunnery fortifications at Fort Monroe are testimony to the developments in armaments that bridged the old and new centuries. The Civil War, after all, was America's first modern industrialized war. During that time, this nation witnessed the first battle between ironclads, the launching of two gas balloons and the introduction of the first "coffee mill" gun, so called because of its rapid-fire technology. The Victory Arch in downtown Newport News and a Vietnam Memorial in Huntington Park outside the Virginia War Museum commemorate the millions of troops that sailed from here to France to fight in World War I as well as the citizens of the Commonwealth who risked and gave up their lives in Southeast Asia in the 1960s and '70s.

Newport News Shipbuilding in Newport News has been building America's mightiest warships since the Spanish-American War and continues that service today, producing carriers and submarines and overhauling or refitting older vessels. Hampton's Langley Air Force Base, home of the Combat Air Command, played a central role in the Gulf War, and stealth craft from the base can be observed in the skies over our area.

## Today's Military Muscle

And, despite Uncle Sam's downsizing and the privatization of many government functions, it seems you just can't take the military out of Hampton Roads. After all, more than 30 percent of our area's population is in some way connected to some branch of the service. Region wide, the Navy's presence remains particularly strong: Close to 100,000 active-duty sailors and Marines serve in the area together with more than 33,000 Navy civilians. Most of those, of course, are stationed at the

Norfolk Naval Base, the world's largest navy base.

And, reversing a nationwide trend of shrinking military installations, the Fort Eustis Army Base in Newport News has been selected as the site for a new regional transportation headquarters that should result in another 500 jobs by the turn of the century. Fort Eustis already is home to the Army Transportation Center and the 7th Transportation Group, factors that played a key role in the decision to consolidate the Eastern and Western Commands of the Military Traffic Management Command and relocate its headquarters to the Virginia Peninsula. Another coup for the military in Hampton Roads was a decision by the Navy to make the Oceana Naval Air Station in Virginia Beach the sole site of its F-14 Tomcat training program, which should bring another 5,330 personnel to the base by 1999.

If you are interested in exploring our military heritage in more depth, you will find the following major military installations, sites and museums discussed in the chapters on their various localities. Many of the installations have museums open to the public.

In Jamestown, Jamestown Settlement will offer a rich insight into the military life of the period. Turn to our chapter on Jamestown and Yorktown.

In Yorktown and York County, check out the National Park Service's Yorktown Visitor Center and Yorktown Battlefield, The Yorktown Victory Center, the Coast Guard Reserve Training Center, and the Naval Weapons Station. See our chapter on Jamestown and Yorktown.

In Newport News, look up the Virginia War Museum, Endview Plantation and Lee Hall Mansion, the Mariner's Museum, the Newport News Park Visitor Center and Fort Eustis' U.S. Army Transportation Museum. See our chapter on Newport News and Hampton for more information. In the same chapter, look for information on Hampton's attractions, such as Fort Monroe and its Casemate Museum, Langley Air Force Base and the Virginia Air and Space Center. Also, do not overlook the real trove of information and artifacts pertaining to American-Indian life in earlier centuries at the Hampton University Museum American Indian Collection. Hampton National Cemetery, near Hampton University, holds remains from the Civil War to the present, and the Hampton Veterans Administration Hospital continues to serve the medical needs of generations of veterans.

In our Daytrips chapter, check out the Norfolk section for information on the General Douglas MacArthur Memorial and the Norfolk Naval Station.

You will find information on the White House and Museum of the Confederacy and Richmond National Battlefield Park in the Richmond section of our Daytrips chapter and also in *The Insiders' Guide to Richmond*.

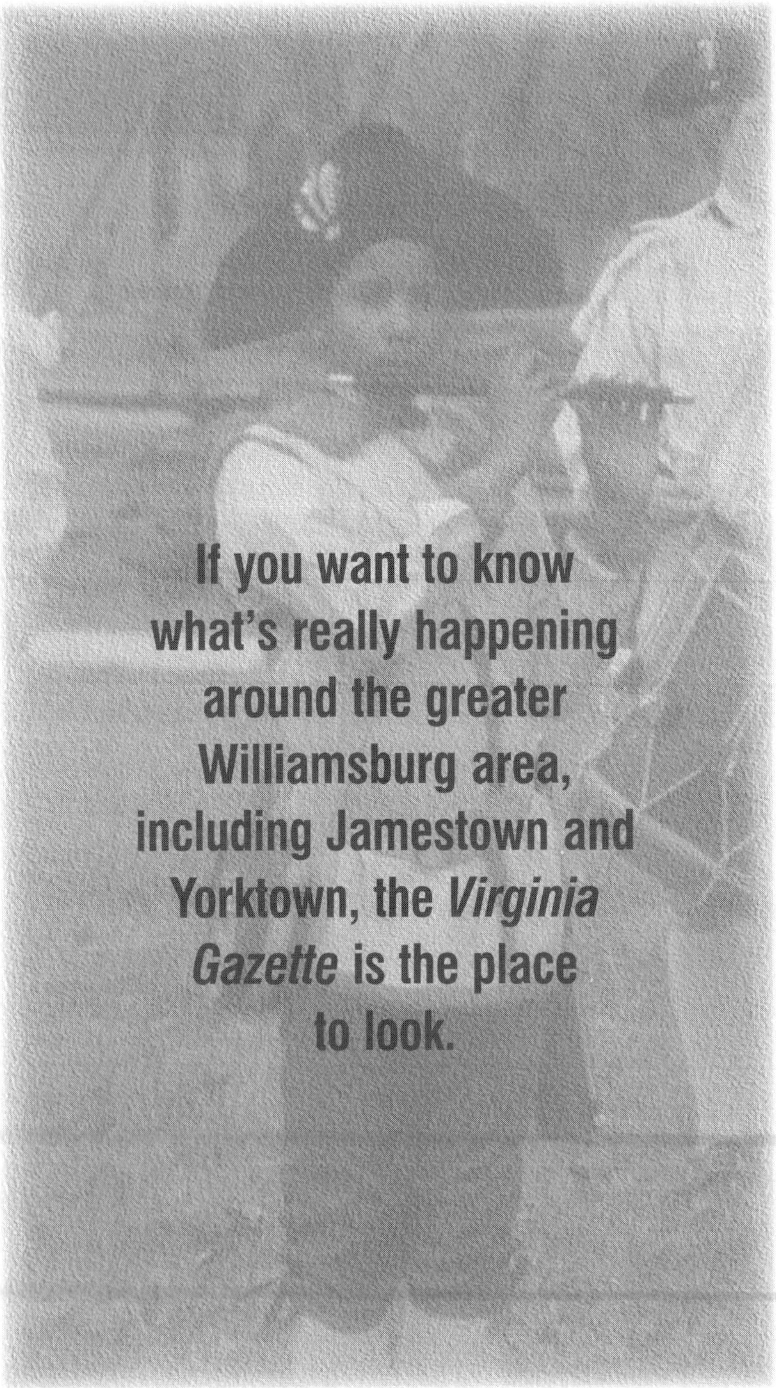

If you want to know
what's really happening
around the greater
Williamsburg area,
including Jamestown and
Yorktown, the *Virginia
Gazette* is the place
to look.

# Media

Williamsburg, Insiders will tell you, is unusual in that it has few media outlets of its own. Instead, it relies heavily on print and broadcast media, including daily newspapers and national television network affiliates, in the Richmond and Hampton Roads areas to supplement what is provided by locally operated media.

## Newspapers

### The Virginia Gazette
**216 Ironbound Rd., Williamsburg • (757) 220-1736**

If you want to know what's really happening around the greater Williamsburg area, including Jamestown and Yorktown, this is the place to look. The *Virginia Gazette*, a semiweekly newspaper, covers only local news - with a vengeance. First published in the colonial capital city in 1736, and with the exception of a few stops and starts during its early years, it is the oldest continuously published newspaper in the commonwealth. It hits the streets each Wednesday and Saturday.

The paper is regarded as a public forum where readers, including those from elsewhere in Virginia and around the country, comment freely and regularly on everything from local politics to their experiences as visitors. Circulation is 16,000.

It also is a gold mine for information on attractions, local restaurants, places to stay and what special events are on tap during your stay in the area. It's not a bad idea to get a short-term subscription prior to your visit, and the circulation department will gladly set it up for you if you call 220-1736 or 220-2224. After reading a few editions, you'll arrive well informed on what to expect and experience during your visit.

### York Town Crier

**4824 George Washington Memorial Hwy., Yorktown • (757) 898-7225**

If you're interested in learning more about historic Yorktown, you might want to pick up an edition of the *York Town Crier*, published weekly. It covers York County events, including updated information on Yorktown area attractions and serves as a useful tool when touring this restored riverside town and its battlefields. You'll also find some coverage on major issues affecting Williamsburg.

### The Daily Press
**7505 Warwick Blvd., Newport News • (757) 247-4800**

*The Daily Press* is owned by the Chicago Tribune Co. The newspaper has a news team assigned to the Williamsburg area to cover significant local issues and events as well as national and international news. *The Daily Press* also has 1-Line, a free 24-hour information telephone service that lets callers access the latest information on news, sports, weather and entertainment. That number, for touch-tone phone users, is 928-1111.

### The Richmond Times-Dispatch
**401 Duke of Gloucester St., Williamsburg • (757) 877-2334**

The Richmond paper, owned by Media General, is the state paper of record, and maintains a Williamsburg bureau that covers significant local issues as well as stories in Richmond and on the national and international scene. Look for information on area attractions, tourism-related issues and money-saving coupons as well. It also carries news of special events of interest to visitors, such as entertainment news, and reviews of local restaurants.

### The Virginian-Pilot
**150 W. Brambleton Ave., Norfolk • (757) 446-2000**

Owned by Landmark Communications Inc., the *Pilot* (as locals call it) is the largest daily newspaper in Virginia. News-wise, it covers all of Hampton Roads and offers a zoned North Carolina section that covers the northeastern portion of that state. There is no home delivery to Williamsburg or other parts of the Peninsula, but the *Pilot* can be purchased from boxes or at newsstands throughout the region. The *Pilot* also offers a free telephone information service for 24-hour updates to news, weather, sports and entertainment. To access the service, dial 640-5555 from a touchtone phone.

### The William and Mary News
**College of William and Mary, P.O. Box 8795, Williamsburg VA 23187 • (757) 221-2639**

If you want to know what's happening on the campus of the College of William and Mary, it is a good idea to pick up a copy of *The William & Mary News*, published every other Wednesday during the school year and once a month during the summer. Copies are available throughout the campus. *The William & Mary News* is aimed at faculty and staff as well as townspeople. You'll find a schedule of lectures, programs and concerts going on around campus.

### The Flat Hat
**College of William and Mary, P.O. Box 8795, Williamsburg VA 23187 • (757) 221-3281**

*The Flat Hat*, the college's student paper, is published each Friday during the regular academic year. It's a quintessential student newspaper, expounding on events useful and controversial from the student perspective. There's an itinerary of upcoming performances, lectures and programs, presented by faculty, students, national performing troupes and artists as well as by local organizations.

# Magazines

### Williamsburg Magazine
**216 Ironbound Rd.,**
**Williamsburg • (757) 220-1736**

For feature stories on the local scene, there's *Williamsburg Magazine*, published monthly by Chesapeake Publishing, which also puts out the *Virginia Gazette*. This lively, informative magazine includes close-ups on tourist attractions, people who are shakers and movers in the tourism industry, what's new and what's timely, as well as details on when attractions open and close, special events, operating hours and ticket prices. It is free, but it's also extremely popular. If you see one, grab it. They can be found at the entrances to many supermarkets and convenience stores, gas stations, restaurants, hotels and motels. They hit the streets right around the first of each month all year round.

### Williamsburg: Great Entertainer Magazine
**1915 Pocahontas Tr., Ste. E-3,**
**Williamsburg • (757) 229-8508**

Also helpful and readily available, especially in area hotels and motels, is *Williamsburg: Great Entertainer Magazine*, a free lavish, full-color magazine designed with visitors in mind. Published by the Williamsburg Area Hotel & Motel Association, it comes out seasonally, so the articles aren't as timely, but the photos are crisp, the information useful and the advertising especially helpful when you're looking for something specific.

# Radio Stations

There are three radio stations originating in Williamsburg, including the campus station for William and Mary. Residents also can pick up stations broadcast from quite a number of other cities, including Norfolk, Portsmouth, Virginia Beach, Hampton and Richmond. Below is a list of what you'll find when you scan the dial.

**Big Band**
WMBG 740 AM (Williamsburg)

**Country**
WCMS 100.5 FM (Norfolk)
WPEX 1490 AM (Norfolk)
WKHK 95.3 FM (Richmond)

**Easy Listening**
WFOG 92.9 FM (Norfolk)

**Eclectic**
WCWM 90.7 FM (College of William and Mary)

**Jazz**
WHOV 88.3 FM (Hampton University)
WNSB 91.1 FM (Norfolk)

**News, Talk, Popular Music**
WRVA 1140 AM (Richmond)

**NPR**
WHRO 90.3 FM (Norfolk)
WHRV 89.5 FM  (Richmond)

**Oldies**
WLEE 96.5 FM (Williamsburg)

**PBS**
WCVE 89.9 FM (Richmond)

**Rock**
WNOR 98.7 FM (Norfolk)
WAFX 106.9 FM (Norfolk)
WRXL 102.1 FM (Richmond)

# Television Stations

Williamsburg, James City County and upper York County residents pick up a variety of channels from Newport News, Portsmouth, Norfolk, Gloucester and Richmond. Most televisions are hooked to cable, and cable channels often are different from the channels assigned to different stations, but hotels and motels provide cable conversion charts to help you out. Also, the cable stations provide listings of their offerings on a cable channel, so flipping through the different channels can serve this up as well. Cox Communications is the sole cable provider for the Williamsburg area. For service in Williamsburg, call (757) 723-6046; James City County, (757) 229-7060; and York County, (757) 898-7140.

The Vacation Channel (TV4), an independent cable channel, is available in most hotels and motels in the Williamsburg area. The format is a continuous broadcast of available recreational activities, shopping and dining. If you miss the beginning of a broadcast, stick around and it'll begin anew every so often.

Listed below are some of the main channels in the area.

WTKR Channel 3 (CBS), Norfolk
WTVR Channel 6 (CBS), Richmond
WRIC Channel 8 (ABC), Richmond
WAVY Channel 10 (NBC), Portsmouth
WWBT Channel 12 (NBC), Richmond
WVEC Channel 13 (ABC), Norfolk
WHRO Channel 15 (PBS), Norfolk
WCVE Channel 23 (PBS), Richmond
WTVZ Channel 33 (Fox), Norfolk
WBH Channel 51 (Independent), Gloucester

Hampton prides itself on being a city of "firsts." Settled in 1610, it is the oldest continuous English-speaking settlement in America and it was the site of America's first Christmas.

# Newport News and Hampton

Interested in exploring a little more of southeastern Virginia while you're in the neighborhood? Then check out Newport News and Hampton, adjacent cities southeast of Williamsburg on Interstate 64 that truly are one of a kind. If the ocean depths fascinate you, you can submerge yourself in the sights at The Mariners' Museum in Newport News, one of the largest and most comprehensive maritime museums in the world. If you're more given to far-flung flights of fancy, the Hampton Roads Air and Space Center in Hampton is a must-see. But, even if you're a bona fide landlubber who likes to keep both feet planted firmly on Mother Earth, these two Virginia Peninsula cities offer a variety of cultural and recreational resources that are more than worth a detour south for a day or two.

In this chapter, we provide you with an overview of each city, thoroughly explore the region's main attractions, offer insights into recreation and direct you to the best places to dine and rest your weary head before venturing out for another day of sight-seeing. Because Hampton and Newport News are next-door neighbors - and you pretty much get to each city the same way - we've combined much of our information. For convenience and ease of planning, however, we've kept listings of the attractions, restaurants and accommodations in each city separate.

## Notes on Newport News

Newport News' somewhat curious name has an intriguing origin. It was Captain Christopher Newport who guided the Discovery and her two sister ships as they carried set-

tlers to Jamestown and the rest of the New World in 1607. After his initial voyage, the good captain continued to make the trek between England and America, carting supplies, additional colonists and word from home to the struggling Jamestown residents. To say the settlers awaited his arrival with great anticipation probably would have been the understatement of the 17th century.

Indeed, Captain Newport became quite beloved, and the sight of his boat in the lower reaches of the James was very good news to all those living in the rugged New World. So good, in fact, that Newport's name became linked with the idea of news from home forming the moniker for the city that eventually grew along these shores. Even so, Newport News wasn't much of a town until 1882, when Collis P. Huntington brought the C & O railroad to the body of water called Hampton Roads, a superb natural harbor formed at the joining of the James, York, Elizabeth and Nansemond rivers. (Today, the term Hampton Roads also is commonly used to refer to all of southeastern Virginia, embracing the Virginia Peninsula to the northwest and south Hampton Roads cities and counties across the James River. See our Getting Around chapter for a more detailed explanation.)

A few years later, Huntington created the Newport News Shipbuilding and Drydock Company, and the city's fortunes took off like a speedboat. Shipbuilding booms spurred by the world wars, along with the establishment of Fort Eustis and other military bases, spawned greater economic expansion. A former subsidiary of Tenneco Inc., the shipyard recently began steering its own course into the future as a separate, independent company with its own publicly traded stock and board of directors. Despite the changes and a long wave of layoffs caused by U.S. Department of Defense belt tightening, the yard still ranks as one of Virginia's largest private employers with approximately 18,000 workers.

A glance at a current map shows that Newport News - home to about 180,000 - is a long, narrow city, covering 69.2 square miles from the James City County line to the mouth of the James River. The city also boasts an amazing 30 miles of coastline, most of it along the James and Warwick rivers. With so much shore at its disposal, it's not surprising that Newport News has one of the finest natural harbors in the world. In fact, Newport News Marine Terminal - part of the successful Hampton Roads port system - is here. The port, which is in the midst of a $28.7 million upgrade, creates 6,244 jobs for a $166 million annual payroll and generates $45.1 million in taxes each year for the city of Newport News alone. With defense dollars disappearing, Newport News has relied on its port connections, a modernized airport and the Monitor-Merrimac Memorial Bridge-Tunnel spanning the James River to help bring in industry and carve out a more diverse economic base.

A number of international businesses have been attracted to Newport News and its sister municipalities on the Virginia Peninsula over the past decade, including Canon Virginia, a major manufacturer of copy machines. Bringing this Japanese company to the city was one of the biggest regional economic coups ever. An international newcomer is Muhlbauer Inc., the American arm of a German-based company. Muhlbauer, which has located in the brand new Jefferson Center Research and Development Park, makes high-speed machines for producing "smart cards," such as prepaid telephone cards and credit cards that contain computer chips. The Jefferson Research Park is growing up around the Thomas Jefferson National Accelerator Facility, a cutting-edge physics research lab that has made Newport News a familiar name in scientific circles. The new park also is home to the seven-story Applied Research Center, site of ongoing research and development by local colleges and universities.

But, as they say, progress has its price. Continued residential growth and the influx of new industry has further burdened the city's major highways, already hampered by having to serve the needs of a population spread out over this long, thin city. While work continues on widening I-64 and rebuilding the Jefferson Avenue interchange in upper Newport News, motorists - including vacationers - are advised to avoid this area during the late afternoon and early morning rush hours. (And don't expect relief anytime soon. The multi-million dollar project to eventually widen I-64 to eight lanes on the Peninsula likely will span the next decade.)

# Say Hello To Hampton

Neighboring Hampton prides itself on being a city of "firsts." Settled in 1610, it is the oldest continuous English-speaking settlement in America. Our nation's first free education has its roots in the city, which was also the site of America's first Christmas. And the list continues. The city also was the site of the nation's first formal trading post, first continuous Anglican Church, first national seafood festival and the first site for the National Advisory Committee for Aeronautics, the precursor of the National Aeronautics and Space Administration (NASA, for short).

Hampton's NASA Langley Research Center actually was established in 1917 to advance the nation's airplane research. Proponents of the center say the work done there in the 1930s on the design of advanced airplane wings gave the United States and its allies the advantage that made them World War II victors. It wasn't until the late 1950s and early 1960s that NASA established the Space Task Force and located its office at Langley. While engineers and scientists in that group worked on America's original manned space program, today Langley is moving more toward the aeronautics research of its younger days. Indeed, one of the projects NASA scientists continue to tinker with is the Waverider, an aircraft designed and equipped to catch up to its own shock wave and ride it - at five times the speed of sound. At that rate, the trip from New York to Los Angeles would take only 45 minutes! In theory it may sound great, but the reality is at least a decade away

- if NASA decides it wants to invest the time and money needed to get this ultimate speed machine off the ground. The NASA Langley Research Center also was singled out in July 1997 by Vice President Al Gore for its recent contributions to airline safety, including technology that visually updates pilots on weather patterns and a new system that offers pilots an electronic liquid-crystal display of any airport they are approaching, showing them locations of active runways, ground traffic and how close they are to the airport surface. The latter technology debuted in the summer of 1998 at Hartsfield-Atlanta International Airport.

Hampton may have been "first to the stars" as city promoters like to say, but it also boasts a rich - and rather bloody - seafaring history. It was here in 1718 that the freshly severed head of Blackbeard the pirate was stuck on a stick and left at the harbor entrance. And during the Civil War, the ironclads *Merrimac* and *Monitor* battled it out in the Hampton harbor, exchanging futile cannon fire over this Confederate stronghold.

Throughout the centuries, Hampton has proved itself a city of resolute spirit, having survived shelling during the Revolutionary War and twice enduring devastating fire - first during the War of 1812, and next during the Civil War, when Hampton citizens set fire to their homes rather than see it fall to Union forces. Today's Hampton is a vibrant and colorful city where commercial fishing, military installations and aeronautic enterprises, along with smaller businesses and industries, sustain a population of close to 139,000. A revitalized downtown area with dozens of attractions has at its nucleus the captivating Virginia Air and Space Center. In recent years, new shops and restaurants have opened, and a rejuvenated nightlife has blossomed. Downtown's Mill Point Park, which borders the Hampton River, is the site of numerous festivals and Queen's Way, a cobblestone downtown street, is the scene

of the popular Saturday night block parties, in their fifth season in 1999.

Queen's Way is also the setting - or at least the focal point - for Hampton's major annual bash known as Bay Days. This celebration, held the second weekend of September, pays homage to the bounty of the Chesapeake Bay with marine-life displays, water-conservation tips and educational materials and activities for both the young and old. But, Bay Days also is a festival, complete with all the celebratory trappings. Once you're there, you can't help but be hooked by the arts and crafts, the rides, the vast array of food and the live entertainment that runs continuously on a number of stages throughout the festival grounds.

Hampton also is home to Hampton University, the nation's largest historically black private university. Each June, the college, together with the city, sponsors the renowned Hampton Jazz Festival, which brings popular entertainers such as B.B. King, Aretha Franklin and Kenny G. and thousands of jazz fans to the city for three days of soulful sounds and rousing good times.

The southernmost city on the Peninsula has its own share of highway headaches. Fortunately for both locals and visitors alike, the biggest roadblock to an easy drive through the city is just about done. For the past several years, work to widen Mercury Boulevard - Hampton's main commercial artery - has caused traffic snarls, temper flare-ups and more than a few fender benders. With the work completed in 1997, motorists' misery is over and access to stores, restaurants and other businesses along the Mercury corridor has never been better.

## Getting Started

In planning your daytrip to the middle and lower Peninsula, there are a few logical places to start. We've listed these fonts of information here.

## Newport News Tourist Information Center

**13560 Jefferson Ave. (Exit 250B off I-64)**
**• (757) 886-7777, (888) 4WE-R-FUN**

As you motor down I-64 from Williamsburg, stop here for brochures, directions and general information about any city attraction.

## Newport News Tourism Development Office

**2400 Washington St. •**
**(757) 926-3561,**
**(800) 333-7787**

Another place to obtain a current visitor guide or other information is this downtown office. Your best bet is to call - rather than stop - here and ask to have what you need mailed to you.

## Hampton Visitor's Center

**Downtown Hampton waterfront**
**• (757) 727-1102, (800) 800-2202**

The Hampton center, built as part of downtown revitalization efforts, is set back off Settlers Landing Road, next door to the Radisson hotel. Stop here for reams of brochures on everything from restaurants and accommodations to walking tours and citywide attractions. This also is the place to purchase tickets for a Hampton waterfront cruise, which departs from docks right at the center.

Once you get your bearings, it's time to start exploring. For the sake of convenience, we've divided our listings under separate city headings, when appropriate. We've also included phone numbers so you can call ahead and organize your stops for optimum enjoyment. Although it once required a long-distance charge, folks now can call between Williamsburg and the lower Peninsula for free.

# Getting There

Both cities are a straight shot from Williamsburg east on I-64. The interstate runs through the northern half of Newport News before practically bisecting Hampton from end to end and crossing over and under the water to Norfolk via the Hampton Roads Bridge-Tunnel. While traffic congestion can be troublesome from 4 to 6 PM in the eastbound lanes, there's a chronic traffic problem westbound between the J. Clyde Morris Boulevard and Victory Boulevard exits, where three lanes bottleneck into two. We have to admit this area is almost always backed up, but it gets worse around rush hour, so plan your trip accordingly. If the interstate is clear, it should take you about 15 or 20 minutes to get to Newport News, 30 to 40 minutes for the trip to Hampton.

Seafaring tourists also can set sail for the lower Peninsula and tie up at the Downtown Hampton Public Piers outside the Radisson hotel. Showers, restrooms, dumpsters, telephones and pump-out facilities are available along the downtown waterfront. Keys to showers and restrooms may be obtained from the Hampton dockmaster for a one-time fee of $4 for the shower key and a $10 deposit (which is returned to you) for the restroom key. Pump-out service costs $5. For more information call 727-1276.

In Newport News, many of the attractions you'll be interested in are concentrated near the intersection of J. Clyde Morris and Warwick boulevards. To reach that part of the city, exit the interstate at J. Clyde Morris (Exit 258A), and follow the highway to its endpoint at Warwick. The quickest route to lower Newport News is to follow I-64 to I-664 South (Exit 264) and then take Exit 5. In Hampton, the main focus is downtown, also accessible by interstate exits that are clearly marked. But if your interests lie elsewhere or you're just the exploring type, you'll want to venture onto other highways and byways. Since both cities cover a decent amount of square mileage, your best bet is to contact your destination and get specific directions. Don't be shy when making your requests. Traffic can get to be a headache - particularly in Newport News where Jefferson Avenue and Warwick Boulevard are the major north-south arterials - and you'll want to know the best time to venture off the interstate into the hinterlands.

A two-hour harbor cruise leaves from Waterman's Wharf in Newport News and allows passengers to view both the Newport News Shipyard and the Norfolk Naval Base.

# Attractions

## Newport News

Nowhere is the old adage "geography is destiny" truer than in Newport News. The long, narrow shape of the city has given rise to some distinct neighborhoods with very different identities. One of the fastest growing is Denbigh, near the northern tip of the city. Home to the bustling Patrick Henry Mall, the new and expanding Yoder Farms Shopping Center, the Newport News-Williamsburg International Airport and some of the city's newest eateries, Denbigh has its own weekly newspaper, the Denbigh Gazette. An influx of young professionals in the '80s spurred construction with new housing developments and shopping centers shooting up practically overnight. All of this growth has created its own set of problems: Road construction hasn't kept pace with the population explosion, and traveling in Denbigh on Jefferson Avenue anywhere near rush hour can generate a major migraine. But once the 5 o'clock whistle is a distant memory, this is a great place to venture out for a night on the town.

Head toward the southern end of the city and you'll stumble upon Hilton Village, a charming enclave that contrasts nicely with the newness of Denbigh. Hilton, whose 500 English cottage-style homes were erected in 1918 to provide housing for shipyard employees, has evolved into one of the most desirable addresses on the Peninsula. The local elementary school is first-rate, and the shopping district, blessed with wide bricked sidewalks, beautiful landscaping and shade trees, offers everything from a coffee shop and ice cream parlor to a goldsmith and a furrier.

The downtown waterfront - in the southernmost part of the city - is home to Newport News Shipbuilding, one of the largest private employers in the state of Virginia, and the Newport News Marine Terminal of the Port of Hampton Roads. The Virginia Port Authority, the group that oversees the port, has future plans to develop a $7 million cruise passenger terminal and pier that could eventually draw 12 to 15 cruise ships (we're talking Carnival Cruise caliber) a year to Newport News. This two-level passenger terminal would include an assembly and catering area that would be able to handle a banquet for 300. It also will provide direct access to bus, taxi and limousine service.

### Fort Fun
**Huntington Park (off Warwick Blvd.)**
• **(757) 926-8451**
Head south on Warwick toward downtown

Newport News and, about a mile past Main Street, you'll come to another favorite kid spot. The 13,500-square-foot Fort Fun is a great place for kids to work off pent-up energy. This playground, on a bluff overlooking the James River, features a multilevel wooden structure that provides a maze, fun house, haunted castle, tightrope, bucking bronco, fire pole, sandbox, slides, swings, tunnels, balancing beams and much more.

The most amazing thing about Fort Fun is that it was built in only five days by some 1,500 community volunteers with more than $85,000 in donated materials and supplies. The playground, designed by Robert S. Leathers & Associates of Ithaca, New York, is wheelchair accessible, free and guaranteed to keep children happy for long periods of time, though parental supervision is advised. We suggest that if your children are very young, make sure there is one adult per child as it's easy to lose sight of the kids among the play equipment and crowds. While you're at it, take along a picnic lunch and some fishing poles and try out the children's fishing pier on nearby Lake Biggins.

## Harbor Cruise

**917 Jefferson Ave. (Exit 7 off I-664) • (757) 245-1533, (800) 362-3046**

Since so much of it borders water, one of the best ways to see Newport News is by boat. The Harbor Cruise, which runs April through October, explores the entire Hampton Roads harbor, from the Newport News Shipyard to the Norfolk Naval Base, where hulking aircraft carriers and supply vessels can be viewed up-close. The two-hour, narrated cruise has daily noon departures during the spring and fall. During the summer months, cruises are scheduled at 10 AM and 1 PM. The cruise costs $14.50 for adults and $7.50 for children ages 6 through 12. Children younger than 6 are free, and the rate for seniors is $13. Five-hour

harbor fishing cruises also are offered, as are October Fall Foliage Cruises along the James River. A spectacular eight-hour Intracoastal Waterway excursion, which costs about $44.50 and includes a continental breakfast, buffet luncheon and music, is part of the itinerary from May through October. Customized group tour packages are available for parties, reunions or receptions. For more information or to make reservations call the number above.

## Japanese Tea House

**Christopher Newport University, 50 Shoe Ln. • (757) 594-7331**

Another Newport News attraction is the Japanese Tea House, on the campus of Christopher Newport University, just off Warwick Boulevard. A gift from the *Asahi Shimbun* Newspaper and Nomura Securities to the State of Virginia, it is considered one of the most authentic teahouses outside Japan. The teahouse formerly was part of one of the most successful exhibits ever at the National Gallery of Art in Washington, D.C. CNU was selected to receive the teahouse by then-Gov. Gerald Baliles because of the university's extensive Japanese studies program. Admission is free (although donations are accepted), and group tours must be prearranged. Families and individuals can tour the teahouse by stopping first at the Student Center across the street. Each April and October a traditional Japanese tea ceremony is staged at the Tea House, complete with hostesses in kimonos, green tea and a light Japanese sweet. The tea is open to the public and costs $5 for adults, $4 for seniors and $3 for students. Call the above number for more information.

## Matthew Jones House

**Harrison Rd., Fort Eustis • (757) 895-5090, 878-4123**

While you're visiting Fort Eustis, stop by this restored Virginia Historic Landmark, which

---

### INSIDERS' TIP

**If you plan to go biking in Newport News, make sure you bring along your child's helmet. Since January 1, 1997, children ages 14 and younger must wear a helmet when riding or being carried on a bicycle on any street, sidewalk or bikepath throughout the city.**

originally was designed as an architectural museum house exposing three historic periods. The Matthew Jones House boasts 90 architectural features that are labeled as teaching points. A tour booklet keyed to the numbers helps you identify each feature. In-house collections highlight the history of Mulberry Island and the Jones and Webb families who lived there for a span of 275 years. The house is open weekend afternoons June through August and by arrangement for tours. Admission is free but donations are accepted.

## The Mariners' Museum
### 100 Museum Dr. (Exit 258A off I-64)
### • (757) 596-2222, (800) 581-7245

Once you're back on dry land, you might want to further explore the region's maritime history with a visit to this world-renowned museum, which boasts the nation's most extensive international marine collection. Founded in 1930, the museum has preserved and interpreted the culture of the sea for millions of visitors over the decades. Its collection contains more than 35,000 maritime treasures including ship models, scrimshaw, maritime paintings, decorative arts, carved figureheads, navigational instruments and working steam engines.

<Body text>In June 1997, the museum unveiled the National Maritime Museum Initiative, a cooperative venture with the New York-based South Street Seaport Museum, which has the largest privately maintained fleet of historic vessels. The alliance allows the two museums to exchange exhibits, share educational programs, link Web sites and offer reciprocal memberships.

The Mariners' Museum currently has a dozen permanent galleries, ranging from displays of miniature ships to a 26-foot antique boat. These galleries are described below.

### Age of Exploration

Using maps, ship models, charts and rare books, this gallery chronicles the scientific and technological changes in shipbuilding, ocean navigation and cartography from the 15th through the 18th centuries. The gallery tells its tale through 15 short videos and a hands-on library where visitors can examine reproductions of the books and navigational instruments used by early explorers.

### Antique Boats

Ship ahoy! Make that very old ship ahoy! In a gallery reminiscent of a 1930s' boat dealer's showroom, boat engines and three antique Chris-Crafts are on display: a 26-foot runabout built in 1925, a 15 and 1/2-foot utility boat from 1934 and a 19-foot runabout from 1935.

### Art of the Sea

Here you can enjoy the works of marine artists from the 17th through the 20th century. Artists whose work is on display include Fitz Hugh Lane, Montague Dawson, Samuel Walters and a number of others.

### Chesapeake Bay

No Hampton Roads maritime museum worth its saltwater would be without a tribute to this aquatic masterpiece. Here you will find interpretations of the Bay's early history, its watermen, shipbuilding industries and the maritime complexes it supports, all brought to life through hundreds of artifacts, photographs, maps and even computer games. Boats in this gallery include a Native American dugout canoe that plied local waters in the early 17th century, a deadrise workboat, a menhaden purse seine boat and a rowing pleasure barge.

---

## INSIDERS' TIP

**Each year on a Saturday in early May, the Newport News Department of Parks and Recreation sponsors Children's Festival of Friends at Newport News Park. The event runs from 10 AM to 5 PM and features food, animals, make-and-take crafts, entertainment and celebrities like Doug, Arnold and Tommie. (If you don't know who they are, ask your children!) Admission is free, but parking costs about $3. For information call 888-3333.**

## Collections

The newest of the museum's permanent galleries showcases rare, unusual and interesting artifacts from all of the Mariners' collections. Study the button from the uniform of British Admiral Horatio Nelson and check out relics from the *HMS Bounty*. While the gallery is permanent, items on display are rotated from time to time, so visitors can experience the full depth of the Mariners' collections.

## Crabtree Collection of Miniature Ships

No, they're not in bottles. This exquisite grouping of 16 miniature hand-carved vessels reflects 28 years of intensive work by artist-carver August F. Crabtree. Crabtree's labor of love depicts the evolution of the sailing ship. Most of the models are built to the scale of a quarter-inch to one foot and are constructed in the same way as their full-size counterparts. The intricately detailed carvings must be seen to be believed.

## Great Hall of Steam

Here you'll find the museum's extensive figurehead collection as well as exhibits about the *Titanic* and the Civil War battle between the *USS Monitor* and *CSS Virginia*.

## Photography

Both contemporary and historical photos are displayed in changing exhibits in this gallery.

## Ship Models

Everything from a miniature sealskin kayak made by a Greenland Eskimo to a gold and silver music box model of the Long Island Sound Steamboat Commonwealth are part of this collection. Model shipbuilders periodically demonstrate their craft in this gallery.

## Small Craft

More than 55 vessels from five continents are featured, including a gondola from Italy, canoes from Africa and sampans from China and Burma.

## "Thar She Blows!" Whaling Exhibit

Designed for the whole family, this hands-on gallery gives visitors the chance to explore a life-size reproduction of a ship's crew quarters and examine the contents of a sailor's sea chest. Kids can make a craft related to the sea's biggest animals to take home.

## "William Francis Gibbs: Naval Architect"

This gallery is dedicated to the life and career of Gibbs, who designed more than 6,000 naval and commercial vessels. Featured are re-creations of Gibbs' office, ship models and photographs.

Frequent changing exhibits also are part of the vast Mariners' experience. The museum has several changing exhibits on display and planned for the coming year.

Through March 30, 1999, is "Skin Deep: The Art of the Tattoo," which examines more than 500 tattoo designs,

Instruments, engravings, colorful illustrations, narratives, circus memorabilia and more.

Opening February 14, 1999, is "Chris Craft: The Affordable Dream." This exhibit demonstrates boat builder Chris Smith's gift to the growing American middle class: social status through owning a Chris-Craft boat. Ads for the beautiful yet affordable mahogany boats are among the artifacts, including craft, shown in this exhibit.

Opening July 1999, "Defense of Sea Power," which explores the strength and vitality of the U.S. Navy from the $18^{th}$ —century frigates to the $21^{st}$ century nuclear-powered ships, subs and aircraft carriers.

Opening in the fall of 1999, "A. Aubrey Bodine and the Chesapeake Bay," which creates a visual chronicle of the diversity and beauty of the Chesapeake Bay and the people who live along its shores, the watermen and shipbuilders.

Opening in September 1999, "It's About Time (The Millenium Exhibition)," examines how our ability to measure time, distance and our place on Earth has evolved over the centuries. It explores the importance of the development of navigational skills and instruments.

Perhaps one of the museum's biggest treasures is its research library and archives, home to more than 75,000 maritime holdings. In fact, there is no other American institution that can match the library for the size, scope and depth of its maritime collection. At last count, more than 5,000 of the library's volumes were classified as rare. The library also houses more than 600,000 photographs and negatives, 5,000 nautical charts and maps, nearly 50,000 plans to build craft from warships to pleasure boats, more than 800 ships' logs and thousands of other archival items. The library is open from 9 AM to 5 PM Monday through Saturday. If you plan to do extensive research, call ahead for an appointment.

The museum also has a gift gallery that offers maritime books, prints and sea-related gifts, and a vending area where sandwiches, snacks and soft drinks may be purchased. Throughout the year, the museum stages a number of special lectures, presentations and demonstrations. There also are a variety of programs offered for children. For information on this year's offerings, call (800) 581-7245 or write The Mariners' Museum, 100 Museum Drive, Newport News VA 23606.

After visiting the museum, explore the 550-acre Mariner's Museum Park on the Noland Trail, a 5-mile amble around Lake Maury featuring 14 pedestrian bridges, or have lunch in shady picnic areas. The park also features bike trails and boat rentals for fishing.

The museum is at the end of J. Clyde Morris Boulevard and is open daily from 10 AM to 5 PM. Current admission prices are $6.50 for adults and $3.25 for any student age 6 or older. (A college ID is required for students older than 18.) Discounts are offered for active duty military, AAA members and anyone age 60 and older. Group rates also are available.

Photo: The Mariners' Museum

Three thousand years of maritime history are chronicled at The Mariners' Museum.

Guided tours by docents are conducted Monday through Friday at 11 AM and 1:30 PM and at various times on weekends.

## The Newsome House Museum and Cultural Center
**2803 Oak Ave. (Exit 3 off I-664) • (757) 247-2360**

Built in 1899, the Newsome House is a modified Queen Anne structure that was home to Joseph Thomas Newsome, one of the first black attorneys to argue before the Virginia Supreme Court. Newsome also was the editor of a black newspaper, cofounded a Newport News church and formed the Colored Voters League of Warwick County. His home, on Oak Avenue in the city's East End, offers meeting and kitchen facilities, a park picnic area and a black history study collection. Hours are from 10 AM to 4 PM Monday through Saturday, and admission is free.

## The Peninsula Fine Arts Center
**101 Museum Dr. (Exit 258A off I-64) • (757) 596-8175**

Just across from The Mariners' Museum is Newport News' fine arts center, which offers changing exhibits that showcase works by outstanding artists to help promote education and an appreciation of the visual arts. Exhibitions change every eight to 10 weeks and feature art of regional and national interest, juried exhibitions, student shows and touring collections of historical and contemporary works.

Interest in the center, which celebrated its 35th anniversary in 1997, continues to grow. That was particularly evident in 1996, when the museum enjoyed a 46 percent surge in attendance over 1995.

**Kidstuff**

One reason for the museum's growing popularity is the attention it is paying to all the budding artists out there. In June 1997, the center opened a newly expanded permanent "Hands On For Kids" Gallery that features activities and exhibits that involve visitors in active learning about art. Among the activities first-timers to the gallery enjoyed were finger-painting with sound, creating a "goof-proof" portrait and making a flag in honor of Flag Day. The gallery, designed for children ages 5 through 13, is open daily for self-directed arts activities. There also are weekly supervised activities that change regularly. The gallery also boasts a puppet theater and a quiet area to relax with books and puzzles.

But the opportunities for kids to spread artistic wings don't end there. On Sundays, the museum offers hands-on workshops designed to enhance a youngster's involvement with and appreciation for art. Projects range from confetti pictures and kite making to tissue flowers and paper fans. The first Sunday of each month is reserved for a free "Arty Party," during which children make their own name tags, listen to a storyteller, create their own small masterpiece and enjoy refreshments. Other Sunday events include second Sunday Family Workshops, which require a $10 supply fee and involve everyone in the family; third Sunday Studios, free workshops that encourage parent-child interaction; and fourth Sunday Children's Workshops, which require a $5 materials fee per child. Most of the Sunday events start at 2:30 PM. Preregistration is required for all events except the third Sunday studios.

For art lovers ages 18 through 45, there's Young at Art, a group that supports the center and works to promote an interest in the arts among young adults. Membership in Young at Art, which is $10 for center members, offers opportunities to attend all previews, programs

## INSIDERS' TIP

**If you decide to come to the Peninsula by boat, you're in luck. Downtown Hampton recently enhanced its public docking facilities to include 24 transient slips that easily can handle 50-foot vessels. The public docks are located next to the Hampton Visitor Center at 762 Settlers Landing Road. Call 727-1276 for more information.**

and special events as well as entitling members to discounts on purchases from the museum's gift shop.

Speaking of which, the Center's Gallery Shop offers a diverse collection of fine and unique decorative objects, cards, books, silk scarves and jewelry. Best of all, admission to the Fine Arts Center is free (although donations are graciously accepted). Hours are Tuesday through Saturday from 10 AM to 5 PM and Sundays from 1 to 5 PM. The gift shop closes at 4 PM daily, and the museum is closed on Thanksgiving, Christmas and New Year's Day. Free docent-led tours are available for school and community groups.

### Peninsula SPCA
**523 J. Clyde Morris Blvd. (Exit 258A off I-64) • (757) 595-1399**

Lions and tigers but no bears . . . oh my! That's what you'll find at this popular SPCA zoo. Inside, of course, there are all those cats and dogs that need good homes, but outdoors you'll find a unique petting zoo for kids. The menagerie features everything from goats and turkeys to llamas and otters. There also are a number of jungle cats, including a lion, tiger, jaguar and cougar, but they, of course, are not for petting. Hours are Monday through Friday 10 AM to 5 PM, Saturday 10 AM to 4:30 PM and Sunday noon to 5 PM. Cost is $2 for adults, $1 for children 3 through 12.

### U.S. Army Transportation Museum
**Bldg. 300/Besson Hall, Fort Eustis (Exit 250A off I-64) • (757) 878-1182**

At this museum on an active military base, visitors can explore more than 200 years of Army transportation history including minia-tures, dioramas, experimental models and video presentations that include authentic World War II footage. Kids will enjoy checking out the truck that walks, the ship that flies and the world's only captive "flying saucer." There also is a gift shop and two parks where aircraft, trains, ships, land craft and jeeps are on display. A new exhibit pays tribute to Gen. Frank Besson, the exhibit's namesake, and a former chief of the transportation school at Fort Eustis. The museum, located just 11 miles south of Williamsburg, is open daily from 9 AM to 4:30 PM. It is closed Mondays and federal holidays. Admission is free, but donations are accepted.

### Victory Arch
**West Ave. and 25th St. (Exit 6 off I-664) • (757) 926-8451**

Since Hampton Roads was the World War II Port of Embarkation, the Victory Arch greeted our nation's armed forces during their jubilant homecoming. Its eternal flame serves as a memorial for all of the troops lost in battle. The arch was originally built of wood in 1919 and reconstructed in granite in 1962. Its inscription reads: "Greetings with love to those who return: a triumph with tears to those who sleep."

### Virginia Living Museum
**524 J. Clyde Morris Blvd. • (757) 595-1900**

Take a walk on the wild side at the fascinating Virginia Living Museum. The museum is an intriguing hybrid: part zoo, part botanical gardens, part observatory and planetarium, with native bird and aquatic life exhibits thrown in for good measure. Opened in May 1987, this multifaceted center is devoted to the pres-

### INSIDERS' TIP

The African-American Heritage Tour of Hampton is a narrated tour that explores the city's African-American history. Each tour visits sites at Hampton University, Fort Monroe and Little England Chapel. Additional commentary is provided on related exhibits at the Virginia Air and Space Center and a number of off-the-beaten-path sites. Tours are offered by limousine, van or minibus on Tuesdays, Thursdays, Fridays and Saturdays from 10 AM to 2 PM. Adult rates start at $15 per person with an eight-person minimum. For more information call 988-0015.

ervation and study of Virginia and Eastern coastal plains wildlife and flora. Inside the museum, you'll find a 60-foot living reproduction of the James River, fossil exhibits, a touch tank for hands-on learning about marine life and a two-story glass aviary with native songbirds. Younger visitors get a special thrill from putting their hands in the authentic footprints of a 210-million-year-old dinosaur or from petting a docile horseshoe crab.

Outside, walkways wind through a nature preserve where animals - everything from regal bald eagles to playful otters - can be viewed in their natural habitats. In the Wetlands Aviary, a net canopy encloses a marshy ecosystem for herons, egrets, ducks, gulls, gallinules and other birds, as well as turtles and a variety of plants indigenous to wetland areas. Every summer since 1995, the museum has staged its outdoor "Dinosaur World," a fun and fascinating exhibit that transports visitors through a time tunnel of 200 million years, back when dinosaurs ruled the earth. The exhibit features close to 20 animated Dinamation dinosaurs - including the 1997 addition of a 25-foot tall replica of Tyrannosaurus rex - that move and roar in a jungle atmosphere of misty fog and bubbling mud pots.

This is one of our favorite places to take visitors who have children. Not only does everyone love the exposure to nature and the outdoors, but the dinosaur exhibit is truly a treat of prehistoric proportions.

Back indoors, the Living Museum's state-of-the-art planetarium is your ticket to the greater universe, featuring multi-image shows and telescope observation.

Indeed, the Living Museum has so much to offer that it recently announced plans for an ambitious expansion at its current site. Plans include more space for just about every aspect of the museum - from permanent and changing exhibits to the planetarium, observatory and museum store. A restaurant, multipurpose space and library will be added as well as additional parking spaces and restroom facilities. Construction is expected to begin in 1999 with the first phase opening sometime in mid- to late 2000.

If you haven't been to the Living Museum, don't wait for the expansion to make your first trek to the wilder side of Newport News. When you come to the museum, adults should expect to pay $6 for the museum and observatory, $2.50 for the planetarium or $7 for a combination ticket. For children 3 to 12, tickets are $3.50 for the museum and observatory, $2.50 for the planetarium, $4.50 for a combination ticket. Children younger than 3 are admitted free, but only those 4 or older are allowed in the planetarium.

When the dinosaur exhibit comes to town, you'll have to pay extra to see everything (It's still a bargain!). A separate ticket to see these beasts from yester-yester-yesteryear is $5 for adults and $4 for children ages 3 to 12. A combination ticket to the dinosaur and wildlife exhibits is $10 for adults and $7 for children. Throw in the planetarium show and adults pay $11 and children $8. Area residents may want to purchase yearly memberships, which provide for unlimited visits to the museum and planetarium as well as discounts on classes, nature safari trips and on gift store purchases.

Summer hours are Monday through Saturday 9 AM to 6 PM, Sundays 10 AM to 6 PM and Thursday nights until 9 PM. Winter hours (Labor Day to Memorial Day) are Monday through Saturday 9 AM to 5 PM, Sunday 1 to 5 PM and Thursday nights from 7 to 9 PM. Planetarium shows are offered every day and Thursday evenings.

## Virginia War Museum
**9285 Warwick Blvd.,**
**Huntington Park**
**• (757) 247-8523**

This fascinating museum, administered by the Historic Services Division of the city's Department of Parks and Recreation, offers a detailed look at U.S. military history from 1775 to the present. Kids will particularly like the array of artillery on the lawn allowing for close-up looks. There are more than 60,000 artifacts on exhibit including an 1883 brass Gatling Gun, a World War I Renault Char I tank and a Civil War blockade runner's uniform. Most aspects of America's military heritage are well represented in the museum's many galleries. The primary gallery is America and War, but several minigalleries have interesting exhibits. These include "The Evolution of Weaponry," "The Black Soldier," "Women at War," "Hampton Roads - Port of Embarkation" and "Visions of War," an exhibit featuring propaganda posters from the world wars. Even though the museum deals with a grave subject, folks here prove they have a sense of humor: "Obeying the Call of Duty," an exhibit about military sanitation, is displayed where else but in the bathrooms. Modestly priced at just $2 per adult and $1 per child age 6 to 15, this is a great stop for families, especially those with school-age kids who've begun the study of American history.

Since 1996, the museum has been hard at work developing Endview Plantation in northern Newport News as an adjunct to the War Memorial property. The plantation, which briefly served as a Confederate field hospital during the Civil War, is believed to hold the remains of both Confederate and Union soldiers buried on the site. Work to develop a Civil War interpretation at the property, including Confederate and Union camps, a re-created military hospital and a variety of indoor and outdoor living history programs, probably will continue for five years, but special events relating to the Civil War will be staged at the site throughout the transformation. To learn more about historic Endview Plantation and the Civil War on the Peninsula, turn to our close-up "Civil War Survivors" in this chapter. The Virginia War Museum is open Monday through Saturday from 9 AM until 5 PM and Sunday from 1 to 5 PM.

## Hampton

Downtown Hampton enjoyed its glory days in the 1940s and 1950s. Then along came the '60s. The decade that spun the whole country into a new orbit saw the stagnation of Old Hampton - as the downtown area is called - when businesses yanked up their roots and headed out to Mercury Boulevard (to an area now called Coliseum Central), the city's new commercial district. During the last dozen years or so, city officials have struggled long and hard to turn around the fortunes of Old Hampton. The Radisson, the city's first luxury hotel, sprang up on the waterfront with a lighthouse-inspired visitors' center next door. A 14-story office tower has given downtown a legitimate claim to a skyline, and new restaurants and museums, outdoor cafes, attractive murals, a

pedestrian walkway winding along the Hampton River and a park featuring a restored 1920 carousel have contributed to the area's rejuvenation.

In 1996, the Downtown Hampton Development Partnership was formed to help revitalize the heart of the city while promoting growth through policy development, the establishment of new programs and improvements to the local environment. In its first few months, the partnership developed a new downtown logo and marketing campaign to promote downtown amenities. A monthly newsletter keeps local businesses apprised of the nonprofit partnership's progress. The partnership also produces and updates Hampton boaters' guides, trolley schedules and retail leasing information. If you would like information in any of those areas, you can call the partnership at 727-1271.

On the outskirts of downtown, a new library opened in 1987, and the former library next door was transformed into the city's first arts center. The Casemate Museum on the grounds of Fort Monroe traces that Army installation's colorful history, while the Hampton University Museum showcases an outstanding collection of African and Native American art. Hampton also is home to Langley Air Force Base, where our nation's Air Combat Command is headquartered. (Read more about Langley in the military section of this chapter.) In addition, the city boasts its own public beach, a pleasant alternative to Virginia Beach for anyone who doesn't want the hassle of traffic and crowds. And Phoebus, a tightly knit community at Hampton's eastern tip, is a must-see with its plethora of antique shops and fine restaurants.

Each year, more than a half-million visitors come to Hampton to see what the city has to offer. At least a third of that crowd is tempted to spend the night. After you read through the attractions we've detailed below, you just might want to be counted among their numbers.

## Getting Started

To begin your tour of downtown Hampton, you can either park your car in one of 3,000 public spaces and set out on foot (it's a pleasant walk when the weather is nice) or hop aboard one of the Pentran trolley shuttles that stop at clearly marked points throughout downtown and the Coliseum Central area along Mercury Boulevard and connecting commercial corridors. Trolleys operate from 10:30 AM to 8:30 PM Tuesday through Saturday and each trip costs 25 cents. (Exact change is required.) From downtown, trolleys leave the Radisson hotel on the half-hour from 11 AM to 8 PM and the Holiday Inn off Mercury Boulevard from 10:30 AM to 8 PM. You can pick up a trolley schedule at the Visitor's Center downtown.

## Air Power Park
**413 W. Mercury Blvd. • (757) 727-1163**

One place for the kids to work off a little energy is Air Power Park, which houses one of the largest civilian-owned collections of aircraft and missiles in the nation. Outdoors, surrounding the park's information center, are aircraft from various service branches, including a Nike surface-to-air missile and an F-100D Super Sabre, the first Air Force fighter with true supersonic performance. The park is open daily from 9 AM to 4:30 PM. Admission is free.

## Bluebird Gap Farm
**60 Pine Chapel Rd. • (757) 727-6739**

Not only is the 60-acre Bluebird Gap Farm a great retreat for the younger set, it's also free. Located about a 10-minute drive from downtown, Bluebird Gap Farm's four-legged inhabitants include pigs, deer, goats, sheep, cows and Charlie the blind horse, a kind of resident mascot. There also are a variety of chickens and ducks and some of the animals that farmers might see in the wilds around their property, such as wolves and owls. A playground area is perfect for picnicking, and public restrooms and vending machines are available. The park is open Wednesday through Sunday from 9 AM to 5 PM. Bluebird Gap Farm is closed Thanksgiving, Christmas, New Year's Day and Wednesdays when a major holiday falls on a Monday or Tuesday. Admission is free, but you may want to bring a couple of quarters in your pocket to plunk into food machines to feed the animals.

## Casemate Museum
**Grounds of Fort Monroe • (757) 727-3391**

Fort Monroe, which serves as headquar-

ters for the U.S. Army Training and Doctrine Command, holds the title of the largest stone fort ever built in America. Within its walled core, you'll find the Casemate Museum, which chronicles the history of the fort and the Coast Artillery Corp. During your tour of the museum, you will see the cell in which captured Confederate President Jefferson Davis was imprisoned as well as weapons, uniforms, Frederick Remington drawings and other military artifacts. You also will learn how "Freedom's Fortress" helped shelter thousands of slave refugees. Other nearby points of interest include Robert E. Lee's quarters, now a private residence, seacoast batteries and the Old Point Comfort Lighthouse. The Casemate Museum is open daily with no admission charge from 10:30 AM to 4:30 PM. It is closed Thanksgiving, Christmas and New Year's Day. Fort Monroe also is open for touring daily, but visitors should keep in mind that this is an active military base with residential areas and offices and that they should therefore behave accordingly. For more information on Fort Monroe, see our Military section in this chapter.

## Charles H. Taylor Arts Center
**4205 Victoria Blvd.**
**• (757) 722-ARTS**

On historic Victoria Boulevard, where grand old homes dominate the landscape, sits the Charles H. Taylor Arts Center. Housed in Hampton's 1926 library, where Victoria intersects Kecoughtan Road, the center displays both the work of local artists and photographers as well as traveling exhibitions. The center also is home to the Hampton Arts Commission, which stages the highly acclaimed Great Performers Series each year. If you stop in, pick up a copy of the organization's newsletter *Diversions*, which gives a comprehensive rundown of arts activities on the Peninsula. The center is open Tuesday through Friday from 10 AM to 6 PM and Saturday and Sunday from 1 to 5 PM. Admission is free.

## Hampton Carousel Park
**602 Settlers Landing Rd. • (757) 727-6347, 727-6381**

Pony up 50 cents and take a ride on Hampton's beautifully restored 1920s carousel. Housed in its own weather-protected pavilion along the city's downtown waterfront, it is one of only 170 antique wooden merry-go-rounds still existing in the United States. Hampton's carousel was originally built in 1920 by the Philadelphia Toboggan Company, once the premier manufacturer of both merry-go-rounds and roller coasters in the United States. Its 48 prancing steeds and two stately chariots were handcarved and carefully painted by German, Italian and Russian immigrants. The carousel was delivered to Buckroe Beach Amusement Park in 1921, where it delighted thousands of visitors until the park closed in the 1980s. Knowing a historic gem when it saw one, the city bought the carousel and had it painstakingly restored by R&F Designs of Bristol, Connecticut. After two years of work, the ponies - painted in elegant shades of cream, yellow and brown - were ready to be ridden once again. The carousel officially opened for business June 30, 1991. You can take a spin on one of its prancing steeds from 10 AM to 8 PM Monday through Saturday and noon to 6 PM Sunday, April through September; noon to 6 PM daily, October through November and weekends through December 15. The carousel is closed mid-December through March.

## Hampton History Museum Association
**555 Settlers Landing Rd., Ste. P**
**• (757) 727-0830**

Incorporated in 1995 with the goal of organizing the eventual construction of a permanent history museum in downtown Hampton, the association displays numerous photographs and artifacts related to Hampton's early days in its temporary office in the Settlers Landing parking garage. Visitors to museum quarters will see such relics as an antique baby carriage, woolen full-length swimsuits, a rusting coffee grinder and numerous photographs from the vast and awesome Cheyne collection. The association also offers a fall and winter lecture series, provides a speakers' bureau for local clubs and civic groups, helps catalog artifacts in the City of Hampton's collection and seeks public support for the construction of a permanent Hampton History Museum. At its current location, the museum is open to the public from 11 AM to 3 PM Tuesday through Saturday. Admission is free.

## Hampton University Museum
**Huntington Building, Frissell Ave.**
**• (757) 727-5308**

If you're still in the mood for a little cultural grooming, stop by the Hampton University campus, where you'll find one of America's most remarkable museums. Founded in 1868, the Hampton University Museum is the second-oldest museum in the Old Dominion. Its collection contains more than 9,000 objects and works of art from cultures and nations worldwide, including African, Native American and fine arts collections. Among the works housed at the museum are nine paintings by the renowned Black American artist Henry O. Tanner. In the spring of 1997, the museum moved to a beautiful, expanded facility - a former Beaux Art-style library, painstakingly renovated at a cost of $5 million - and is gradually relocating its various collections to its new home. The new Fine Arts Gallery opened in April 1997. The African Gallery, with objects from nearly 100 ethnic groups and cultures, will opened in April 1998; the Native American, with its vast collection of American Indian artifacts including everything from basketry to beadwork opened in October 1998; the Asian and Pacific, with artistry from such faraway places as Polynesia, the Philippines and Japan will open in April 1999; and the Hampton History, which traces the university's own historical contributions, will debut in October 1999. The museum is open Monday through Friday, 8 AM to 5 PM; Saturday and Sunday, noon to 4 PM. It is closed on major holidays and campus holidays. Admission is free, and free tours can be arranged. In addition to the museum, the university also is the site of six National Historic Landmarks, including the Emancipation Oak, where President Abraham Lincoln's Emancipation Proclamation was first read to the slaves of Hampton in 1863.

## Little England Chapel
**4100 Kecoughtan Rd. • (757) 723-6803**

Built in 1879 by students of the nearby Hampton Normal and Agricultural School (now Hampton University), this simple white structure is believed to be the only existing African-

American missionary chapel in Virginia. Both a state and National Historic Landmark, the chapel had fallen into disrepair until 1990, when the Newtown Improvement and Civic Club raised more than $100,000 for its restoration. Today, with its low wooden benches and pot-bellied stove, the chapel looks much as it did more than 100 years ago when black families first gathered under its roof for Bible study and community meetings. When you visit, you will see handwritten Sunday school lessons, photographs, 19th-century religious books and a 12-minute video. The chapel is open Tuesday, Wednesday, Friday and Saturday from 10 AM to 2 PM and other days by appointment. Admission is free, but donations are accepted.

### Miss Hampton II Harbor Cruise
**Hampton Visitor Center • (757) 727-1102, (800) 244-1040**

There are distinct advantages to visiting waterfront destinations. One of these is the opportunity to scope out the place while aboard a boat. Hampton offers a cruise of its own. From April through October, the 65-foot *Miss Hampton II* departs from the Visitor's Center for a 2 and 1/2 - to 3-hour voyage out of the Hampton River into the Hampton Roads harbor. The cruise sails past Fort Monroe and docks at Fort Wool for a guided walking tour. Construction of this pre-Civil War fort, built on a 15-acre manmade island, was supervised by then Lt. Robert E. Lee. The fort was active during the battle of the *Monitor* and *Merrimac* and was used to guard the entrance to the harbor during the Civil War and both world wars.

After completing your tour of Fort Wool, you will once again board the *Miss Hampton II* for a slow trip along the 2-mile waterfront of the Norfolk Naval Base, the world's largest naval installation, before heading home. A 10 AM cruise is scheduled daily from April to Memorial Day and from Labor Day to October 31. A second 2 PM cruise is available Memorial Day through Labor Day. Fares are $14.50 for adults, $8 for children ages 6 through 12 and $12.50 for seniors. Reservations are recommended, and group rates are available.

### St. John's Episcopal Church
**100 W. Queens Wy. • (757) 722-2567**

Away from the waterfront on downtown's Queens Way sits St. John's Church, the oldest continuous English-speaking parish in the United States. The church was built in 1728, but it is the fourth site of worship of Elizabeth City Parish, which was established in 1610. The tree-lined churchyard holds graves dating back to 1701, including a memorial to Virginia Laydon, one of the first persons to survive an arduous birth in the New World. Communion silver made in London in 1618 and a stained-glass window depicting the baptism of the Indian Princess Pocahontas are among the church's most prized possessions. The church is open weekdays from 9 AM to 3 PM and on Saturdays from 9 AM to noon. There are no tours at St. John's on Sunday because of services. Guided tours may be arranged by calling the church office, and admission is free.

### Venture Inn II - Whale Watching and Evening Cruises
**Downtown Hampton Public Piers**
**• (757) 722-5120, (800) 853-5002**

If you're in town during the cooler months (December through March), sign up for a scenic whale-watching expedition. As interest dictates, the *Venture Inn II* will leave the Downtown Hampton Public Piers Wednesday through Sunday at 10 AM to scout out these magnificent creatures at work and play. Each day's destination varies depending on previous sightings, known feeding patterns and a bit of captain's intuition. The cruises last five hours and are narrated by a naturalist who has studied the behaviors of whales, dolphin and other sea life. Because of the season, you are advised to dress warmly, in layers, as air temperatures typically are 10 to 15 degrees lower on the water. Rubber-soled shoes, a hat, sunglasses and sunscreen are also recommended, and it wouldn't hurt to bring along a pair of binoculars and a camera to capture your adventure for posterity. Costs of the tours are adults, $25, children, 12 and younger, $20 (the cruise is not recommended for children younger than 8); and seniors 65 and older, $22.50. Discounts are available for prearranged cruises for groups of 20 or more. Now, matie, you're all suited up and ready for some action . . . Thar she blows!

The *Venture Inn II* also offers a number of evening cruises October through April. These include fall foliage sunset cruises in October, scenic river cruises in November and March, a Holiday Harbor Lights Tour in December and both sunset and scenic river cruises in April. Cost of the tours varies, depending upon length and destination, but prices for tickets range from $15 to $40.

## Virginia Air and Space Museum and Hampton Roads History Center
**600 Settlers Landing Rd. • (757) 727-0900, (800) 296-0800**

After working off your sealegs, why not flap your wings a little. After all, the Virginia Air and Space Center and Hampton Roads History Center is just a short stroll along the waterfront, lending credence to the popular Hampton theme "from the sea to the stars." As you approach the glass, brick and steel structure, you'll notice that, appropriately enough, the stunning architecture does resemble a bird in flight. This $30 million museum, which opened to sellout crowds in April 1992 and is designated the official NASA Langley Visitors Center, is considered the piece de resistance of Hampton's revitalization.

Inside, the museum features changing exhibits relating to its "from the sea to the stars" theme. Artifacts from the visitors center's previous site at NASA Langley Research Center - such as the Apollo 12 command module, astronaut's suit and a 3 billion-year-old moon rock - are incorporated into new exhibits at the Air and Space Center, which also serves as NASA/Langley's Teacher Resource Center with classrooms and educational programs. In the 300-seat giant screen IMAX theater, visi-

tors can watch films on topics related to flight and space exploration on a 50- by 70-foot wide screen. Nineteen vintage U.S. aircraft hang from the 94-foot ceiling, including a Corsair f-106B "Delta Dart" struck nearly 700 times by lightning while flying through storms as part of NASA lightning research. A gantry that rises three stories takes visitors up for closer inspection. Both a cafe and gift shop are in the museum. Since opening in 1992, the center has hosted more than 1 million visitors and unveiled 20 major exhibits. One of the newest - and most timely - is the 1997 opening of a permanent display titled "Vision of Mars." The new exhibit marks the 20th anniversary of the Viking Project and examines mankind's historical relationship with Mars - through both fact and fantasy. The exhibit also looks at the future of Mars space explorations and has proved extremely popular in the wake of NASA's Pathfinder mission. A second permanent display that opened in 1997 is "Space Station," an interactive exhibit that focuses on the process of design and construction required to build the first international space station. Since 1995, the center also has increased its summer camp programs for children, expanded outreach efforts in local schools and introduced live science demonstrations.

In the east wing of the Virginia Air and Space Center, the Hampton Roads History Center (supported by the U.S. Air Force and the Smithsonian Institution) houses exhibits pertaining to the history of Hampton Roads, including a partial reproduction of the Bunch of Grapes Tavern, a Colonial pub that once stood on the site of the center, and a replica of a pirate's skeleton that was unearthed during the renovation of the city's waterfront. Sum-

## INSIDERS' TIP

If you're in or around downtown Hampton on a Thursday, Friday or Saturday evening during the summer, check out one of the outdoor street parties. On Thursday there's food, drinks and musical entertainment outside the Hampton Visitor Center on Settlers Landing Road. Fridays head over to Strawberry Banks near the entrance to the Hampton Roads Bridge-Tunnel for Fridays on the Bay for more of the same. And on Saturdays there's the Saturday Night Block Party along Queens Way, complete with live music and an "artscapade" entertainment area for children.

## Price Guidelines

The following price code gives a range for the cost of dinner for two. All restaurants listed accept major credit cards unless otherwise noted.

| | |
|---|---|
| $ | Less than $20 |
| $$ | $20 to $35 |
| $$$ | $36 to $50 |
| $$$$ | More than $50 |

mer hours of operation for both museums are Monday through Wednesday, 10 AM to 5 PM; Thursday through Sunday, 10 AM to 7 PM. Winter hours are Monday through Sunday, 10 AM to 5 PM. Admission prices, which include a movie in the IMAX theater, are $9 for adults and $8 for seniors, military personnel and children ages 3 to 11. Admission to just the exhibits is $6 for adults, $4 for seniors, military and children. Group discounts are available. (Note: Admission fees change periodically, so it may be wise to call ahead.)

The Air and Space Center also is the starting point for a seasonal motor tour of the NASA Langley Research Center. The tour includes a look at several of NASA's wind tunnels and a visit to the giant scaffold-works from which space capsules were dropped to simulate lunar landings. Tickets and information are available at the Air and Space Center.

# Restaurants

All this sightseeing is bound to stir up a hearty appetite. Lucky for you, there's a bounty of choices in both Hampton and Newport News. Pretty much all the bases are covered - from the ever-popular seafood and Italian eateries to those serving Japanese or Vietnamese fare. To better acquaint you with this Peninsula smorgasbord, we've pulled together a sampling of our favorites.

## Newport News

### Bodine's Hickory Smoked

### Bar-B-Que

$$ • 754 J. Clyde Morris Blvd. • (757) 596-7427

Specialties of this popular 'cue joint, open for lunch and dinner, include Texas brisket, pork barbecue and baby back ribs slow-cooked over hickory wood. The menu also features hush puppies, home fries and Brunswick stew.

### Bon Appetit

$$ • 11710 Jefferson Ave. • (757) 873-0644

This well-established restaurant in the Oyster Point area cooks first-rate French and Vietnamese cuisine for lunch and dinner. French entrees include lamb chops in herb sauce, baked half duckling marinated in cognac and veal-stuffed chicken prepared in wine and cream. Vietnamese features include shrimp, scallop and lobster specialties, stir-fried vegetables and flounder baked in black bean sauce. Desserts are, in a word, delicious.

### Carmela's Homestyle Italian Cuisine

$$ • 14501-A Warwick Blvd. • (757) 874-8421

In Denbigh, Carmela's prepares homestyle Italian dishes including a variety of pastas. Pizzas are made in a wood-burning oven. If you're a garlic lover, we heartily recommend the clams casino, some of the best we've had anywhere. Carmela's offers dinner daily and lunch Sunday through Friday.

### Cheers Unlimited Cafe & Tavern

$$ • 615 Thimble Shoals Blvd. • (757) 873-3375

This casual Oyster Point hangout is popular for its snacks, sandwiches and generous dinners. Baby back ribs are a specialty of the house. Come only if you enjoy a packed house and spirited atmosphere.

### Danny's Deli

$ • 10838 Warwick Blvd. • (757) 595-0252

If you're a sandwich lover, you're in luck. This busy lunch spot offers just about any combination your heart desires, and all are served up with an endless supply of crunchy sliced dill pickles. The deli is also open for breakfast and weekday dinners (until 7 PM). It is closed on Sundays.

## Das Waldcafe
**$$ • 12529 Warwick Blvd. • (757) 930-1781**

This longtime Peninsula favorite prepares authentic German cuisine (from the Rhineland region) including wiener schnitzel, bratwurst, knockwurst and noodle dumplings. A variety of more obscure dishes round out the menu. Specialty sausages are from New York, and the beers are German imports. Das Waldcafe serves lunch and dinner Tuesday through Sunday.

## El Mariachi
**$ • 660 J. Clyde Morris Blvd. • (757) 596-4933**
**$ • 13809 Warwick Blvd. • (757) 890-0334**

We were in Mexican heaven when we discovered this authentic eatery. Don't fill up on the chunky salsa and chips, as here you can custom order all the traditional Mexican dishes you have come to love in just about any combination. We especially liked the quesadillas and enchiladas over shredded pork. The service is speedy, and the Margaritas sparkle. But be aware: since reservations aren't accepted, on weekends you'll probably have to take a number and wait your turn. Don't worry; service is swift and lines move fast at both lunch and dinner.

## Kyung Sung Korean Restaurant
**$$ • 13748 Warwick Blvd. • (757) 877-2797**

One of a only a handful of Korean restaurants on the Peninsula, the Kyung Sung prepares inexpensive and spicy food and serves it in an unadorned setting. The house specialty is beef boolgogi, a Korean-style barbecue, but the menu also includes chop suey, several teriyaki variations, shrimp tempura, some stir-fried dishes, soups and noodle dishes. If you like food with a kick, try a side order of kim chee, a spicy Korean cabbage. We love it but admit it's an acquired taste. Both lunch and dinner are available daily.

## Johnny's Frozen Custard
**$ • 10119 Jefferson Ave. • (757) 595-3286**

OK, so it's not a bona fide restaurant, but who doesn't need an ice cream break once in awhile? And, at Johnny's, you get the real deal - cold custard treats that reach sky high. As soon as your tongue touches one of these tempting cones, you'll feel transported to another era, when bobby sox, poodle skirts and leather jackets were the order of the day, and only Elvis could be heard on the car radio. The specialty of the house are concretes, frozen custard whipped with your choice of 30 or more toppings, from M&Ms and Oreo cookies to pineapple and strawberries. You'll have to eat in your car or stand around in the parking lot - no outside or inside seating is provided - but you'll gobble it all down so quickly, you probably won't even notice. All ice cream dishes ring in at less than $3.50.

## Lucido's Pastries & Coffeehouse
**$ • 10367 Warwick Blvd., Hilton Village • (757) 596-3702**

Soups, sandwiches, pastries and coffee drinks galore are the order of the day at Lucido's. For lunch, try a Coffeehouse Rollup, in which luncheon meats, cheese, lettuce, tomato and onion are rolled up in a flour tortilla and heated. Specialty sandwiches include a chicken salad croissant and a Lucido veggie - sliced cucumber, alfalfa sprouts and basil atop cream cheese on your choice of bread. More than 30 Torani syrup flavors add pizzazz to coffee, tea or sparkling soda water. Lucido's is open for breakfast, lunch and dinner.

## Luigi's Italian Restaurant
**$ • 15515 Warwick Blvd. • (757) 887-0005**

The operative word here is Italian. The marinara sauce is to die for (try it over mussels as an appetizer), and the pasta dishes are classic. We enjoy the veal and spaghetti with a red shrimp sauce, but our friends rave about the manicotti, ravioli and lasagne. Portions are huge, and dinners are served with warm and delicious garlic knots. This is an inexpensive way to enjoy good Italian cooking.

## Manchester Grill
**$$ • 1000 Brick Kiln Blvd. • (757) 874-2600**

In a laid-back atmosphere, chow down on sandwiches, munchies and steak dishes. Buffet specials are offered, and sweeping views of the surrounding golf course add to the ambiance. Manchester Grill is open for breakfast, lunch and dinner Tuesday through Sunday.

## Mike's Place
**$ • 458 Warwick Village Shopping Ctr.**
**• (757) 599-5500**

Locals like to gather in this neighborhood tavern, which offers crab cakes, prime rib and daily specials in pub-like environs. Popular items include the Big O Burger and deviled crabs. An Irish theme prevails and, needless to say, the place is packed on St. Paddy's Day. Four wide-screen televisions ensure you won't miss weekend football games. The restaurant is open for lunch and dinner.

## Mitty's Ristorante
**$$ • 1000 Omni Blvd. • (757) 873-6664**

This Italian restaurant is in the Omni Newport News Hotel. Its menu features fine seafood and pasta entrees and individual pizzas made in a wood-burning oven. A lunch buffet is served.

## Nara of Japan
**$$ • 10608 Warwick Blvd. • (757) 595-7399**

If you like to be entertained while you dine, grab a few friends and head over to the Nara for dinner. At this lively Japanese restaurant, your waiter prepares your food right at your table. Nara specializes in hibachi steak, chicken and seafood seasoned with lemon juice, soy sauce, pepper and sesame seeds. Soup, salad and appetizer are included with your meal. This is a great place to enjoy a birthday celebration. Nara does not serve lunch.

## Not Betty's
**$$ • 10844 Warwick Blvd. • (757) 599-4915**

Listen to a bit of Broadway (recorded, not live) as you savor house specialties including lump crab cake, pasta and vegetable dishes and contemporary flatbreads. The restaurant got its name from its location - it's in space that, for decades, housed the venerable Betti Paige dress shop. Not Betty's offers its variety of culinary choices for both lunch and dinner.

## Old Virginia Brewery & Restaurant
**$$ • 12644 Jefferson Ave. • (757) 988-**

1669

Beer lovers unite. This new eatery, open for lunch and dinner, gives you the opportunity to dine in a brewery and sample any of the seven styles of beer made in the gleaming copper vats you see around you. Specialties include barbecued ribs and chicken and pizzas made in a wood-burning oven. The brewery also has a separate cigar lounge and offers acoustic entertainment most evenings.

## Port Arthur's
**$ • 11137 Warwick Blvd. • (757) 599-6474**

Housed in an impressive brick structure with elegant Oriental touches, Port Arthur is one of the Peninsula's most enduring Chinese restaurants. The eatery first opened in downtown Newport News in 1934, before moving to its current site in 1974. If you visit for lunch or dinner, you'll most likely rub elbows with a host of Peninsula regulars. Mandarin and Szechwan specialties are featured along with a complete menu of beef, poultry, seafood and pork preparations. Sodium-free dishes are available upon request.

## Red Maple Inn
**$$$ • 202 Harpersville Rd. • (757) 596-6333**

This lovely, converted 1920s home is the perfect setting for a romantic dinner for two. There are a screened-in porch and two dining rooms downstairs - the main one overlooks the beautiful maple that lends its name to the restaurant - and two smaller rooms on the second floor. The dinner menu is seasonal and features seafood, pork, lamb, poultry and beef. Recent selections include a tenderloin of lamb sliced and blackened and served with an orange mimosa chutney and a Kansas City strip marinated in bourbon, black peppercorns and au jus. As an appetizer, we recommend the Creole crab cakes, made with lump crabmeat and crawfish tails, pan-fried, then garnished with black-eyed pea relish and mango chutney. The recently constructed backyard gardens feature kitchen herb, English cottage-style and organic vegetable gardens. The restaurant is closed on Mondays.

## Sushi Yama Japanese Restaurant
**$$ • 11745-2 Jefferson Ave. • (757) 596-**

**1150**

If you love sushi (and we know there are many who do), you can order yours here with a variety of toppings from the traditional (tuna, salmon and shrimp) to the exotic (squid and eel). Other traditional Japanese dishes also are available. Lunch is offered Monday through Friday and dinner Monday through Saturday.

# Hampton

## Buckroe's Island Grill

$$ • Ivory Gull Cres., Salt Ponds Marina • (757) 850-5757

Part of the Salt Ponds development near Buckroe Beach, this eatery features burgers and sandwiches, a raw bar and steak, chicken and fresh local seafood for lunch and dinner. Children's dishes and outdoor deck dining are available. There's also an extensive selection of beers and bar drinks.

## Carmela's Pasta Cafe

$ • 2123 Coliseum Dr., Coliseum Crossing • (757) 825-5375

A sister to the Newport News Carmela's, the Hampton restaurant offers a lengthy menu that includes veal, chicken, seafood and a seemingly infinite variety of pasta dishes. Diners have the option of mixing and matching their pasta and sauces. Linguini with olive oil, white wine, garlic and mushrooms, anyone? Dinner is available daily; lunch is served weekdays only.

## The Chamberlin

$$ • Fort Monroe • (757) 723-6511

This restaurant, in the historic Chamberlin hotel at Fort Monroe, cooks steak, seafood and fresh fish. Piano music adds a relaxing note to dinner. Stop in for the bountiful Sunday brunch and soak up the sweeping view of the Hampton Roads harbor.

## Fire & Ice

$$$ • 2040 Coliseum Dr. • (757) 826-6698

Across Coliseum Drive from the mall, Fire & Ice takes the prize as Hampton's most innovative restaurant. Folks around here know it: The restaurant typically is packed for both lunch and dinner. The menu changes frequently, so there's always something new to look forward to. Some recent summer selections include veal medallions sauteed with jumbo shrimp, a mixed grill of honey-glazed chicken breast and pork tenderloin and grilled marinated tofu over braised Swiss chard. For lunch, try one of the unique flatbreads or salads.

## Golden Palace

$$ • 2234 Cunningham Dr. • (757) 825-1900

The specialty of this 300-seat restaurant with its colorful, inviting decor is an 80-item buffet and sushi bar, available for both afternoon and evening patrons. The offerings on the a la carte menu are always fresh and appealing.

## Good Fortune

$$ • 225 D-1 Fox Hill Rd. • (757) 851-6888

At Willow Oaks Shopping Center, Good Fortune has a varied menu of traditional Chinese dishes. You may think once you've tasted one wonton soup you've tasted them all, but Good Fortune's is especially delicious (and our kids can't get enough of the egg drop). A variety of steamed entrees offer a low-fat dining option. A lunch buffet is a filling mid-day repast.

## Goodfella's

13 E. Queens Wy. • 723-4979

In downtown digs vacated by Sorry Sara's, Goodfella's serves up reasonably priced pasta, seafood, beef and pizza. Live music on weekend nights pull in the crowds. Outdoor patio dining is available in warm weather months. Enjoy Goodfella's family atmosphere during lunch or dinner.

## The Grate Steak

$$ • 1934 Coliseum Dr. • (757) 827-1886

Just minutes from Hampton Coliseum, this extremely popular steakhouse adds a new twist to dining. Beefeaters have the opportunity to select the steak of their choice and prepare it themselves on a huge grill in the center of the restaurant. Steaks come in three cuts: petite, restaurant and owner's. If you select the owner's cut, there's an added bonus - you get to peruse the refrigerated display case

The red fox is one inhabitant of the Virginia Living Museum's native wildlife park.

and come away with the steak of your choice. All steaks are served with salad and potato bar as well as all the garlic bread you can eat. The menu also offers prime rib (it's delicious), pork, poultry and seafood dishes. This is one of our favorite places to go when the nights start getting chilly. We grab a beer, belly up to the grill and cook away. The Grate Steak serves dinner daily and lunch and dinner on Sundays.

### Harpoon Larry's Oyster Bar
$$ • 2000 N. Armistead Ave. • (757) 827-0600

This is the kind of restaurant you'd expect to find at the beach. Its long wooden tables, massive bar and casual atmosphere all make it a favorite after-work spot for locals. The menu includes all types of "killer" seafood prepared just about any way you can imagine. A Thursday night shrimp special - buy a half-pound and get the next half-pound for a penny - jams the place, but it's worth the wait. You might want to brave the crowds and check it out. Or, better yet, come for lunch when the lines are shorter, but the food is just as good!

### Keith's Dockside
$$$ • 38-C Water St. • (757) 723-1781

A decades-old Phoebus establishment, Keith's cooks up a wide variety of broiled, fried and steamed seafood dishes. Whenever we visit, we select the Steamboat Special, a heaping combo of steamed crab legs, shrimp and clams. Wines from the Williamsburg Winery are served by the glass or bottle. Keith's serves up lunch and dinner daily, breakfast Tuesday through Sunday.

### Ming Gate Restaurant
$$ • 3509 Kecoughtan Rd. • (757) 723-9572

Although it's off the beaten path in the city's historic Wythe section, this extremely popular Chinese eatery features a well-rounded array of Mandarin and Szechwan dishes. When you pull into the parking lot, don't be put off by the less-than-elegant exterior because the food is wonderful. One Insider we know always orders the Peking duck, which is served with scallions, pancakes and plum sauce. Our favorites include the hot and sour soup and steamed dumplings. Lunch specials are available daily.

### Mongolian Bar-B-Q Restaurant
$ • 1118 W. Mercury Blvd., Riverdale Plaza • (757) 838-3638

If you like an incredible amount of food and don't mind watching while it's cooked (it's actually part of the fun), check out this popular Hampton eatery. This is an authentic Mongolian barbecue, where you heap your plate with seasonal vegetables, meats ranging from beef to lamb and a variety of sauces that include lemon, garlic, oyster, hot oil and barbecue. There's also an accompanying salad and hot foods bar, where you can fill up on any number of Chinese entrees being offered that night. Soup, sesame bread, steamed rice (upon request) and light desserts are also part of the package. The food is excellent, and the price is more than reasonable.

### Oasis Restaurant
$ • 3506 Kecoughtan Rd. • (757) 723-5736

For a reasonably priced homestyle meal any time of day, this long-established eatery is the place. Popular with locals, the Oasis serves meals like Mom used to make. There's everything from grits and eggs to cream chipped beef for breakfast, a variety of seafood dishes and specialty sandwiches for lunch and daily lunch and dinner specials. We particularly like the roasted chicken and chicken and dumplings.

### Oyster Alley
$ • 700 Settlers Landing Rd. • (757) 727-9700

This casual outdoor restaurant is in downtown's Radisson Hotel and overlooks a marina. Sandwiches, salads and seafood appetizers are featured. Oyster Alley is open daily from 7 PM to 11 PM.

### Rooney's Downtown
$$ • Cafe 21 E. Queens Wy. • (757) 726-2614

Sister to the original Rooney's on Big Bethel Road, this casual downtown restaurant serves sandwiches, soups, salads, beef, seafood and some pasta choices for lunch and dinner daily. Outdoor seating is available on a wooden deck, and the back dining room has a pool table and dartboard.

### The Second Street Restaurant and Tavern
$$ • 132 E. Queen St. • (757) 722-6811

A sister to the popular Williamsburg eatery, Second Street opened in downtown Hampton's former post office in August 1994. The decor features nautical props and a sweeping mural of the Hampton waterfront. Lunch and dinner entrees run the gamut and include sandwiches, nine varieties of burgers, seafood, steak, chicken and baby back ribs. Seasonal patio seating and occasional indoor and outdoor entertainment make this a popular gathering spot for locals.

### Two Sergeants Inc.
$, no credit cards • 1335 N. King St.
• (757) 737-0937

There's nothing fancy about this restaurant, but the food - ribs, brisket and pork and chicken barbecue - is downright good. Everything is done up Texas mesquite style with side orders of collards, cabbage, potato salad, red beans and rice, French fries and a number of other vegetables available. For dessert, try the sweet potato pie. The most expensive item on the menu is a whole rotisserie chicken, which will set you back a mere $7. Two Sergeants is closed on Sundays.

### Victorian Station
$$ • 36 N. Mallory St. • (757) 722-4220

In a house that was built at the turn of the century by students at the Hampton Normal and Agricultural School, this Phoebus tearoom has a country store downstairs with adjacent and upstairs dining. The restaurant serves lunch Tuesday through Saturday, but we recommend you try their "afternoon tea ritual," served after 2 PM. If you follow our advice, you'll find your table laden with jam-lathered scones, fruit tarts, tea muffins or teacakes, open-faced sandwiches and a pot of the tea of your choice.

# Accommodations

Perhaps you've decided there's too much to see and do in one day in Hampton and Newport News, so you'll spend the night and devote another 24 hours to your local explorations. Or maybe you're just so dog-tired that the thought of driving anywhere - even 20 miles up the road - makes you ache with fatigue. No matter. There are plenty of options should you

## Price Guidelines

While we have included price ranges for rooms in each of the properties listed, keep in mind that rates are subject to change, particularly during times of peak demand, such as Mother's Day weekend in May and the Hampton Jazz Festival in late June. The following accommodations accept credit cards unless we've noted otherwise.

| | |
|---|---|
| $ | $31 to $45 |
| $$ | $46 to $60 |
| $$$ | $61 to $75 |
| $$$$ | $76 to $100 |
| $$$$$ | More than $100 |

decide to rest your weary head on a lower Peninsula pillow. The facilities we've listed below are well run and offer the modern conveniences you've come to expect when you're spending a night on the road. We have included 800 numbers when available, but be aware that many are for central reservation offices and will not connect you directly to the hotel.

# Newport News

### The Boxwood Inn
**$$$$-$$$$$ • 10 Elmhurst, Lee Hall Village (just off Rt. 60 near Old Rt. 238 • (757) 888-8854**

The city's only bona fide bed and breakfast, the Boxwood Inn is run by Barbara and Bob Lucas. Built in 1896, the inn originally was the home of Simon Curtis, once considered the "boss man" of Warwick County. It also has served as the Warwick County Hall of Records, a general store, a post office and a hotel for soldiers during World War I and II. Items found in the home's spacious attic have been used to decorate the house and its two rooms and two suites, each of which has a private bath. Breakfast is offered from 8 to 9 AM Monday through Friday and 8:30 to 9:30 AM on Saturday and Sunday. A "sleepy head" breakfast is an option for those who prefer to eat in their room prior to checkout. The Boxwood Inn also has its own tea room, a general store and gift shop with antiques and consignments and offers special seasonal dinner shows. The inn cannot accommodate children, and smoking is not permitted.

### Comfort Inn
**$$$ • 12330 Jefferson Ave. • (757) 249-0200, (800) 368-2477**

Adjacent to Patrick Henry Mall in Denbigh, Comfort Inn is just 13 miles from Williamsburg. It has 124 rooms, each equipped with coffee maker, iron and ironing boards. There's also an outdoor pool, and guests have free access to a local fitness club. Children 18 and younger stay free with their parents, a continental breakfast is included in the price of a night's stay, and room service is provided by both Ruby Tuesday's and The Outback Steakhouse. In 1996, the Newport News hotel was named Comfort Inn of the Year from among 1,157 properties nationwide.

### Days Inn Oyster Point
**$$-$$$ • 11829 Fishing Point Dr.**
**• (757) 873-6700, (800) 873-2369**

In Oyster Point business park, Days Inn offers 125 rooms, all equipped with refrigerators and coffee makers. Amenities include an exercise room, outdoor pool, courtesy van transportation within fives miles by appointment, same-day valet dry cleaning and complimentary continental breakfast. Microwaves are available upon request. A restaurant is adjacent to the hotel.

### Hampton Inn & Suites
**$$$-$$$$ • 12251 Jefferson Ave.**
**• (757) 249-0001, (800) HAMPTON**

Across from the Patrick Henry Mall, this hotel, built in 1995, marked the Hampton Inn chain's first foray into the suite business. The Newport News property has 90 guestrooms, 30 suites, a small weight room and an outdoor pool. Guests also enjoy a free continental breakfast, HBO and free access to a local health club. Room service is provided by The Outback Steakhouse.

## Kiln Creek

$$$$ • 1003 Brick Kiln Blvd. • (757) 874-2600

This attractive hotel is actually part of a golf and country club. Its 16 rooms overlook a golf course. A restaurant is on site, and a swimming pool and fitness center, complete with a Jacuzzi, steam and sauna rooms and locker facilities, are available. The hotel also offers an indoor tennis "bubble," a refrigerator, a coffee maker and a small safe in each room, and patios or balconies overlooking the putting green. If you're an avid duffer, ask for details on the special golf packages Kiln Creek offers.

## Mulberry Inn

$$$-$$$$ • 16890 Warwick Blvd. • (757) 887-3000, (800) 223-0404

This hotel's 162 guestrooms include some efficiencies and connecting rooms. All rooms have refrigerators. Amenities include a fitness center, guest laundry, a pool, terrace and a free continental breakfast. An extra rollaway bed is $8.

## Omni Newport News Hotel

$$$$ • 1000 Omni Blvd. • (757) 873-6664, (800) 843-6664

Another Oyster Point hotel, the Omni has 183 rooms, including four suites. Mitty's, an Italian restaurant, is on the premises. Other amenities include a nightclub, piano bar, indoor pool and health club with whirlpool and sauna.

## Ramada Inn & Conference Center

$$$-$$$$ • 960 J. Clyde Morris Blvd. • (757) 599-4460, (800) 272-6232

Redecorated in 1994, the Ramada's 219 guestrooms feature work areas, clock radios and individual temperature controls. A restaurant is on the premises. The hotel also has an indoor fitness center and heated pool.

# Hampton

## The Chamberlin

$$$$-$$$$$$ • Fort Monroe • (757) 723-6511, (800) 852-8975

This stately old hotel overlooks the water, providing a breathtaking view of the Hampton Roads harbor. A Virginia landmark, the original Chamberlin was built in 1894 adjacent to the elegant Hygeia Hotel, which was razed in 1902. The present Chamberlin was built in 1928 after fire destroyed the original structure. For modern-day visitors, this grand antique - recently restored to much of its former elegance - offers tennis courts, shuffleboard, bike riding and two pools, one of them overlooking the water. You'll also enjoy a restaurant, lounge and small museum. Tea and sweets are served each afternoon, and weekend and off-season senior specials are offered. The Chamberlin has a total of 185 rooms, including seven suites and eight junior suites, which include a sitting area as part of the single room layout. This remains a wonderful - and romantic - spot to step back in time to the Hampton of yesteryear. We particularly enjoy walking along the tiled veranda and feeling the sea breezes on our faces.

## Courtyard by Marriott

$$$$ • 1917 Coliseum Dr. • (757) 838-3300, (800) 321-2211

A moderately priced motor inn next door to the Hampton Coliseum, Courtyard by Marriott has 146 rooms, including 12 suites, a pool, a whirlpool, a mini-gym and a restaurant and lounge.

## Days Inn-Hampton

$$-$$$ • 1918 Coliseum Dr. • (757) 826-4810, (800) DAYS INN

Another Coliseum area motor inn, Days Inn has 144 units, a pool and a coin laundry. A casual restaurant is on site. Pets are permitted for an extra $6 charge.

## Fairfield Inn by Marriott

$$-$$$ • 1905 Coliseum Dr. • (757) 827-7400, (800) 228-2800

This motor inn provides economical lodging in its 134 rooms. It offers a pool and complimentary continental breakfast.

## Hampton Inn

$$$$ • (757) 1813 W. Mercury Blvd. • (757) 838-8484, (800) HAMPTON

Near an I-64 exit, the Hampton Inn has 132 rooms and pool privileges at the nearby

Holiday Inn. Teens stay free with their parents, and a complimentary continental breakfast is served each morning. Pets weighing less than 25 pounds are permitted for no additional charge.

### Holiday Inn Hampton

$$$$$ • 1815 W. Mercury Blvd. • (757) 838-0200, (800) 842-9370

One block from the Hampton Coliseum and within walking distance of a number of shopping centers, this Holiday Inn has 324 guest rooms (each equipped with coffee maker, irons and boards), indoor and outdoor pools, a fitness center, a gift shop and a jogging course. An open atrium area features the Tivoli Gardens Restaurant and Garden Court Lounge.

### Quality Inn & Suites

$$$$ •1809 W. Mercury Blvd. • (757) 838-5011, (800) 562-8090

Located a stone's throw from the city's main business district, Quality Inn, formerly the Sheraton, has 190 guest rooms (including 34 suites), an indoor swimming pool and a restaurant and lounge. A recent $2 million renovation upgraded guestrooms and bathrooms.

### Radisson Hotel Hampton

$$$$$ •700 Settlers Landing Rd. • (757) 727-9700, (800) 333-3333

The city's only luxury hotel, the Radisson is on the waterfront overlooking the Hampton River. All 172 guestrooms have floor-to-ceiling windows - a big plus if you happen to get one facing the water. Amenities include a seafood restaurant and raw bar, outdoor rooftop pool and Jacuzzi, a lounge, health club and complimentary covered parking.

### Strawberry Banks Inn

$$$-$$$$ • 30 Strawberry Banks Blvd. (Exit 268 off I-64) • (757) 723-6061, (800) 446-4088

This delightful waterfront motel, near the Hampton Roads Bridge-Tunnel, has been under new management during the past couple of years. Improvements have been made to the motor inn's 99 units, which include a number of suites with working fireplaces. The motel also features an excellent restaurant, an

outdoor swimming pool at water's edge, exercise facilities, a private beach, a playground and a fishing pier. Packages are available.

# Shopping

A little bit of this, a little bit of that . . . that just about sums up the shopping experience on the Peninsula. To make it a little easier to find your way around, we've divided our entries geographically: In Hampton, there's Old Hampton (or downtown), the old-fashioned community of Phoebus and the bustling Mercury Central corridor along newly widened Mercury Boulevard. The two main shopping areas in Newport News are Hilton Village, a charming enclave to the south, and Denbigh, a rapidly developing neighborhood to the north.

## Hampton

### Old Hampton

If you're looking for ambiance while you browse, stroll along the quaint brick and tree-lined streets in Old Hampton. Here you will find dozens of specialty shops selling everything from British imports to elaborate doll collections. Our favorites are listed below. (Those with an address of 555 Settlers Landing Road are located in the first floor of the downtown Hampton parking garage across the street from the Virginia Air and Space Museum.)

### Benton-Knight Ltd.

28 S. King St. • (757) 723-0521

Fine high-quality men's clothing - ranging from casual to formal - is sold at this downtown Hampton landmark. Service is superb.

### Black Butterfly

555 Settlers Landing Rd., Ste. J • (757) 723-2737

This unusual shop sells African-American books, gifts and art.

### Blue Skies Gallery

26 King St. • (757) 727-0028

In the past year, this popular gallery has relocated and almost doubled in size and now offers 5,000 square feet of creative work by more than 100 established artisans. Their selection includes sculpture, paintings, clothing and crafts in silver, acrylic, wood, fiber, fabric, paper and glass. You can even browse among some selections of antique books and furniture.

### Bluewater Wear
**19 E. Queens Wy. • (757) 723-5451**

New in June 1997, this store carries an ocean theme into its marine-related line of sportswear. Fabrics depict boats, fish, sailing and other water activities. Gifts with a nautical theme also are available. Bluewater Wear donates 10 percent of its profits to marine conservation.

### Brass Shop
**197 W. Queen St. • (757) 723-4523**

Don't miss this excellent shop where thousands of brass items are deeply discounted. This is a great place to stop for brass lamps, candlesticks, brass frames and trivets.

### My Doll & Toy Shoppe
**555 Settlers Landing Rd. • (757) 723-0000**

If there's a child on your shopping list, this shop is a must. My Doll & Toy Shoppe carries everything from Madame Alexander and Ashton-Drake dolls to Playmobil and Brio wooden trains.

### Old Hampton Bookstore
**555 Settlers Landing Rd. • (757) 722-1454**

This charming downtown bookstore offers a wide selection of fiction, nonfiction and children's books.

### Ole Hampton Sportswear
**55 W. Queens Wy., Ste. 102 • (757) 728-3678**

Here you can find an excellent selection of screen-printed T-shirts, sweats and accessories, including articles sporting the new downtown Hampton logo.

### The Pottery Wine & Cheese Shop
**22 Wine St. • (757) 722-VINO**

This delightful newcomer to the downtown Hampton scene sells glassware, linens, gourmet foods, gift items, a variety of freshly made sandwiches and salads, more unusual beers

and shelves and shelves of wine. The staff is knowledgeable and helpful. Grab a quick lunch and browse to your heart's content.

### Scents & Treasures
**555 Settlers Landing Rd. • (757) 727-0763**

Add a gentle touch of fragrance to your home with a purchase of potpourri, incense and other treasures from this downtown shop.

### The Smokehouse
**47 E. Queens Wy. • (757) 722-4185**

This small, 400-square-foot shop, tucked in next door to Rooney's Downtown Café, opened just as the cigar craze caught fire. The shop stocks 30 different domestic and imported brand of cigars, as well as humidors, lighters, ashtrays and a collection of magazines for the cigar enthusiast.

### The Virginia Store
**555 Settlers Landing Rd., Ste. L**
**• (757) 727-0600, (800) 633-2203**

If you want something that screams Virginia to give the folks back home, this is the place to stop. True to its name, The Virginia Store carries Old Dominion gift baskets, wines, hams, peanuts, pottery, jewelry and books.

## Phoebus

While you're in the neighborhood, you might want to make a quick detour down Settlers Landing Road to Phoebus, a quaint waterfront community that was incorporated into the City of Hampton in 1952. Visiting Phoebus is like a trip back in time, when malls were unheard of and Main Street was where everything happened. The two major streets in Phoebus - Mallory and Mellen - intersect one another and are home to a number of interesting shops and restaurants. The former New American Theater, a movie house and restaurant, has been purchased by the Charles H. Taylor Arts Center Foundation to be used by the Hampton Arts Commission as a performing arts hall. It should open sometime in 1999. For general information or brochures about Phoebus, contact the Phoebus Improvement League at 727-0808. Some of the more unusual stores in Phoebus are listed below.

### Electric Glass Co.

**1 E. Mellen St.** • **(757) 722-6600**

This attractive and unique shop carries an astonishing array of stained glass lamps and crystal chandeliers. (We guarantee, however, that one glance in the window, and parents of small children will silently recite that old quip, "Beautiful to look at, nice to hold, but if you break it, consider it . . ." well, you get the idea.)

## Free City Traders
**22 E. Mellen St.** • **(757) 722-3899**

This two-story antique mall displays the merchandise of 33 antique dealers. We made one of our favorite finds here - an antique oak pedestal mirror that once graced the inside of a department store. Free City Traders is closed Mondays.

## Mugler's of Phoebus
**123 E. Mellen St.** • **(757) 723-6431**

Established in 1898, this shop carries fine men's clothing in more than 150 sizes.

## Phoebus Auction Gallery
**16 E. Mellen St.** • **(757) 722-9210**

While not actually a shop, per se, this popular gallery pulls in big crowds every two weeks or so for its Sunday auction of fine art, antique furniture, rugs and advertised items and collectibles. A military memorabilia auction is held each November, and there's always a New Year's Day auction. The gallery often is open for browsing before each auction. Call ahead to see what's on the agenda when you plan to be in town.

## Snow's Bicycle Shop
**135 E. Mellen St.** • **(757) 723-1101**

A veritable institution in Phoebus, you can buy new or gently used bikes here or bring yours in for a quick repair.

# Coliseum Central

For all intents and purposes, this is the main business district in Hampton. Located on either side of recently widened Mercury Boulevard, the area is named after the Hampton Coliseum, just off Mercury, a highly visible landmark from I-64, as well as the Coliseum Mall, on the other side of the boulevard. In February 1997, an ambitious improvement plan was released for Coliseum Central, calling for more green and open spaces; the transformation of a part of the boulevard into "Mercury Mile," with bus shelters, better lighting and water icons at key areas celebrating Hampton's connection to its natural environment; and a new visitor center and community building near the intersection of Mercury Boulevard and Coliseum Drive, considered the primary gateway to this important business district. But these changes won't occur overnight. The Coliseum Central master plan is a 20-year blueprint for redevelopment that will be done in more manageable phases throughout the next two decades.

What you'll see right now is a busy thoroughfare crowded with stores, chain restaurants, movie theaters and some hotels. To make it easier for you to locate a store, we've divided our entries by mall or shopping center. Since most of these stores will be familiar to you, we've listed rather than described them and provided central phone numbers, when available. The area also harbors a freestanding Super Wal-Mart, that stocks anything and everything, Pier I Imports for wicker and gifts and a relatively new Target department store that sells slightly higher end merchandise.

Let's start with the most visible shrine to consumerism, Coliseum Mall.

## Coliseum Mall
**1800 W. Mercury Blvd.** • **(757) 838-1505**

Anchored by a Hecht's, JCPenney, Montgomery Ward and the newly opened Dillard's Department Store, the mall also offers more than 100 smaller stores and kiosks, including The Disney Store, American Eagle, The Art Works, Bath & Body Works, The Coffee Beanery, General Nutrition, Kay-Bee Toys, Spencer Gifts, Sunglass Hut and Victoria's Secret. If you get hungry while shopping, you can grab a bite at the 10 or so restaurants in the centrally located Food Court or enjoy home cooking at Picadilly Cafeteria.

## Coliseum Crossing
**2100 through 2159 Coliseum Dr. (odd numbers only)** • **(757) no phone**

The Crossing is a popular, fast-growing strip center that not only offers stores galore but also has plenty of restaurants and ser-

# Civil War Survivors

Close-up

It happened back in the spring of 1862: The Peninsula Campaign of the Civil War. And it temporarily turned the fortunes of the Confederacy around. It was during that time that the eyes of every American were focused on the Virginia Peninsula as Maj. Gen. George B. McClellan's campaign to capture Richmond unexpectedly came to a halt for 29 days along the Warwick River. It was the Civil War's first siege, and it would pass relatively quickly for the area once known as Warwick County, but its effects on the future of this farming community would be felt for countless generations to come.

Endview Plantation - located in what was once Warwick County but what is today the City of Newport News - is one of the survivors of that bloody time in American history. Built in the mid-1700s by William Harwood - one of the area's land-owning elite - as a symbol of his family's power, Endview happened to be strategically located on one of two roads leading from Williamsburg to Yorktown at a midpoint between the James and York rivers.

That location sealed Endview's fate. While the plantation played a lesser role in other wars fought on American soil (in 1781, the Virginia militia paused at the mansion on its way to the siege of Yorktown, and during the War of 1812, militia units camped at Endview in their vain attempts to stop the British from wreaking havoc throughout the area), the Civil War turned the plantation into a historic military campground.

At the time war broke out, Endview was owned by Dr. Humphrey Harwood Curtis, a descendant of the original owner and one of two doctors in Warwick County (later annexed by the City of Newport News). Dr. Curtis mustered his considerable influence around town and formed the Warwick Beauregards of the 32nd Virginia Infantry, a regiment that remained on the Peninsula. Endview was used by troops from both sides, first as a campground for Confederate units and a Confederate hospital, then as a hospital by the Federals when the Union army occupied the house after the South retreated on May 3, 1862. The historic mansion even was once visited by McClellan when he was on his way to the May 5, 1862, Battle of Williamsburg. The grounds are believed to hold the remains of both Confederate and Union soldiers who were buried there during the war.

Today, work is under way to preserve Endview's rich, battle-scarred history and turn the mansion and 40 surrounding acres into a living history museum. With funding through grants from the General Assembly, private gifts and a multimillion dollar capital improvement appropriation from the city, the Virginia War Museum in lower Newport News is laboring hard and long to complete the transformation. The work involves extensive architectural studies and archaeological surveys, the removal of a more modern addition and the installation of French drains underground around the foundation to catch water and make it flow away from the house and its sunken basement. Indeed, researchers digging beside the old foundation have unearthed even older bricks and fragments of discarded plaster, which lend credence to family legends that traced the building's origins back to the 1720s. Luckily, the house is in pretty good condition. "Just cleaning it up made a big difference," noted Williamsburg architect Carlton Abbott, who worked on the restoration.

Although plans for the plantation's future are far from complete, they currently call for outdoor Confederate and Union camps, a re-created military hospital, a mid-19th

— continued on next page

Photo: Courtesy of the Virginia War Museum

Endview Plantation in Newport News played a critical role in the Civil War.

century farm site, earthworks and a variety of indoor and outdoor living-history programs that will familiarize visitors with the events that took place at the site in 1862. These interpretive efforts will focus not only on military life, Civil War medicine and the plantation culture but also on the experience of the vast numbers of escaped slaves - known as contraband - who followed the movements of the Union troops throughout the South. The Virginia War Museum expects to have everything up and running within five years.

At the same time all this energy is being expended at Endview, work also is ongoing at Lee Hall Mansion, built in the 1850s by Richard Decanter Lee, a wealthy planter who financed construction after he harvested a bumper tobacco crop. During the Peninsula Campaign, the mansion, located less than a mile from Endview, was one of the headquarters for Confederate Gen. John Bankhead Magruder. A small earthen fort on the front lawn remains the only evidence of the property's military occupation. This fort was the site where the Confederates launched the observation balloon used to view Union positions during the 1862 Warwick River Siege of the Peninsula Campaign. Plans for refurbishing Lee Hall, which were opened for tours in the spring of 1998, include establishing a Civil War interpretive center with exhibits of traditional artifacts and setting up a Magruder study in one of the rooms so visitors can get a glimpse of what the military occupation of a private home looked like during the Civil War.

— continued on next page

At this time, both Endview and Lee Hall are open for self-guided grounds tours from 10 AM to 4 PM Monday through Saturday. Admission is free. Endview Plantation is located on Yorktown Road in upper Newport News. To get to the site from Williamsburg, take Interstate 64 East to Exit 247. Turn left onto Route 143 and follow it for a mile. At the first stoplight, take another left onto Yorktown Road. The plantation will be about a quarter-mile down the road on your right. To reach Lee Hall, follow the same directions, but turn right at the light onto Yorktown Road and travel about a half-mile to the mansion entrance. Special tours of the houses are available by appointment. For more information about Endview, call 887-1862. For Lee Hall, call 888-3371.

vices, including banks, a dry cleaner and a one-hour photo outlet. The main stores here include Phar-Mor, Food Lion, Marshalls (discount clothing), A&N Stores, Lillian Vernon Outlet (discounted mail order merchandise), Linen Warehouse (linens, towels and drapes), Pet World (where you can find that special toy or treat for Fido or Fluffy) and Boater's World, a discount marine center that stocks everything from deck shoes and snorkels to wet suits and water skis.

## Coliseum Square
**2040 Coliseum Dr. • (757) no phone**
Stores in this shopping center, located across Coliseum Drive from the mall, include The Ski Center, which offers everything you need for a great time on the slopes, Beautiful Bedrooms, Ames Tuxedos and 360 Communications, which sells cellular phones.

## Mercury Plaza
**2201 through 2223 W. Mercury Blvd. (odd numbers only) • (757) no phone**
Up the road a short distance and across the highway is this plaza that includes a Circuit City Store, Burlington Coat Factory and Home Quarters Warehouse.

## Riverdale Plaza
**1044 through 1118 W. Mercury Blvd. (even numbers only) • (757) no phone**
Casual Male Big & Tall, Office Depot, Sneaker Stadium, Goodwood Unfinished Furniture, a post office outlet and Farmer Jack's grocery store are among the major stores in this strip center.

# Newport News

## Hilton Village
This charming residential area in lower Newport News features a number of quaint shops, stretching from Warwick Boulevard to the James River. The village recently was transformed with an updated streetscape that included brick-patterned sidewalks and lush landscaping. Some of the shops you will find nestled amid the newfound splendor are listed below.

## Beecroft & Bull Ltd.
**10325 Warwick Blvd. • (757) 596-0951**
This long-established store is the last word in fine men's clothing and accessories. Beecroft & Bull also has a shop in Williamsburg.

## Hilton Village Goldsmith
**10345 Warwick Blvd. • (757) 599-6300**
With a gemologist and master craftsman on staff, this jeweler's is the place to go for that one-of-a-kind, custom-designed ring, brooch, pendant or bracelet.

## Pasquier House of Art
**10218 Warwick Blvd. • (757) 591-0485**
This new gallery (across the street and a block closer to downtown) stocks water color and oil paintings, art prints, hand-crafted wood items, jewelry, quilts, kaleidoscopes, bonsai plants and small furniture.

## Plantiques - Hilton Village
**10377 Warwick Blvd. • (757) 595-1545**
Established in 1978, this gift shop sells a

little bit of everything - antiques, small collectibles, candles, pewter, stained glass, sailing ship models, silk flowers and wreaths, Christmas items, skin-care products . . . well, you get the idea.

### Silverman Furs
**10301 Warwick Blvd.**
**• (757) 595-5514**

This Hilton institution has been in business since 1938, specializing in furs, leathers and outerwear. Silverman also does repairs and cleaning on site.

### Village Stitchery
**97 Main St. • (757) 599-0101**

Just around the corner from most of our Warwick Boulevard establishments, the Village Stitchery sells everything you need for cross-stitch, knitting and other creative needlework. Custom framing is available.

## Denbigh

As we mentioned in our introduction to Newport News, the Denbigh area - particularly along Jefferson Avenue - has been growing like dandelions in the spring sunshine. It has become somewhat of a retail Mecca in this long, slender city, sprouting entire new shopping centers seemingly overnight. It is also home to Patrick Henry Mall, easily accessible off I-64. We'll start there to give you our rundown.

### Patrick Henry Mall
**12300 Jefferson Ave. (Exit 255A off I-64)**
**• (757) 249-4305, 249-2338**

Anchored by Belk (formerly Leggett) and Upton's, Patrick Henry also is home to American Eagle Outfitters, Casual Corner, Express, Fashion Bug, Structure, Spencer Gifts Express, Musselman Jewelers, Radio Shack and dozens of other shops. If you work up an appetite while shopping, check out one of the eateries in the Food Court. The mall also has a movie theater.

### Crafters Mall
**12233 Jefferson Ave. (Exit 255A off I-64)**
**• (757) 249-5114**

Located across the street from Patrick Henry Mall, this retail outlet celebrates and

sells the handiwork of more than 250 crafters. Come inside and check out the ceramics, jewelry, miniatures, quilts, custom flags and porcelain dolls. The mall is open Monday through Saturday from 10 AM to 7 PM and Sunday, noon to 5 PM.

### Yoder Farms Shopping Center
**Jefferson Ave. and Oyster Point Rd.**
**• (757) no phone**

The newest entry on the Denbigh retail scene, Yoder Farms gets its name from - what else - a long-lived dairy farm that stood on the property. Just a short distance down Jefferson Avenue from Patrick Henry Mall, this 400,000-square-foot strip houses Barnes & Noble, Circuit City, PetSmart, Target and OfficeMax stores.

# Recreation

## Beaches

### Newport News

### Huntington Park Beach
**5500 W. Mercury Blvd. (foot of James River Bridge) • (757) 886-7912**

Newport News also has its own free public beach, located in the same park that is home to Fort Fun and the James River Fishing Pier (see Fishing later in this chapter). The sandy strip fronts the James River, of course, and is open from sunrise to sunset. Lifeguards are on duty from 10 AM to 7 PM daily during the summer, but at other times you're allowed to swim at your own risk. There's a nice little snackbar with a deck and picnic tables, and restrooms are available. Two swing sets and a few volleyball nets offer a couple of other diversions.

## Hampton

### Buckroe Beach
**End of Pembroke Ave. at First St.**
**• (757) 727-6347**

If you're interested in a day at the beach, there's no reason to trek all the way to the Virginia Beach resort strip. Hampton's own

Buckroe Beach is an ideal spot for a little family R and R. Bordering the Chesapeake Bay, Buckroe's gentle surf and sandy shore are perfect for family frolicking and castle building. A paved boardwalk attracts strollers and cyclists, while an outdoor pavilion is the setting for plenty of warm-weather entertainment. A bustling resort back in the 1930s, Buckroe Beach's fortunes declined when the 1957 opening of the Hampton Roads Bridge-Tunnel provided easier access to ocean attractions. In the late 1980s, the city invested millions to build Buckroe Park, complete with a stage, picnic shelters and public restrooms. During the summer, the beach pavilion frequently is the scene of free Big Band and jazz concerts, while family movies are shown on a big outdoor screen on Wednesday evenings. Lifeguards are on duty at the beach from 10 AM to 6 PM from Memorial Day to Labor Day. Nearby, pier and charter fishing are available.

To get to the beach, take the last Hampton exit from I-64 before the bridge-tunnel (Exit 268). Turn left on Mallory Street. Follow it to its end; then, turn right on Pembroke Avenue. The beach will be right in front of you. There's a small parking lot next to the beach, but on hot summer days it typically is full. Paid parking is available in makeshift lots on fields across the street.

# Fishing

If you want to get an angle on some outdoor fun, toss a line off one of the Peninsula's many fishing piers. Depending on the time of year, you'll probably pull out spot, croaker, flounder (check to make sure it's a keeper - in 1997 a flounder had to be 14 and 1/2-inches long to qualify for that "honor" - before tossing it in your cooler), bluefish and an occasional trout. No listing is needed for fishing at any of these piers (it's included in the fee), and equipment rentals are available at most of them. Some of the best places for your hook, line and sinker are listed here.

## Newport News

### James River Fishing Pier
**Huntington Park, 5500 W. Mercury Blvd.**
**• (757) 247-0364**

This popular fishing pier is located at the foot of the James River Bridge. To fish the waters beneath will cost adults $4.50 and children ages 7 through 12, $2.50. If all that casting and reeling works up an appetite - or if the fish aren't biting and you have a hankering for some fresh seafood - The Crab Shack restaurant, 245-2722, is located at the entrance to the pier. Here you can get everything from soft-shell crabs to shrimp at reasonable prices.

## Hampton

### Buckroe Beach Fishing Pier
**330 South Resort Blvd. • (757) 851-9146**

This pier at Buckroe Beach is a great spot to pick up a few spot (and croaker, trout and an occasional keeper flounder). Open round the clock, it costs $4.50 for an adult to fish and $2.50 for children ages 6 to 12 (and you can stay all day if you like). If the fish aren't biting, you can always cool off with a dip in the Bay.

### Grandview Fishing Pier
**Foxhill end of Beach Rd. • (757) 851-2811**

This is off the beaten path - you have to travel through a large portion of residential Hampton to get there - but is a superb area for fishing. Daily fishing rates are $4.50 for adults, $2.50 for children younger than 12. Call ahead for directions from where you are staying.

# Golf

While the fishermen troll the waters in pursuit of the big one, golfers might want to shoulder their clubs and tee off at one of the area's public courses.

## Newport News

### Newport News Golf Club at Deer Run
**Newport News Park, Jefferson Ave. (Exit 250B off I-64) • (757) 886-7925**

Test your skills at either the Deer Run Golf Course, an 18-hole course rated "best value" in 1996 by *Golf Digest*, or Cardinal Golf Course, a challenging, middle-length 18-hole course. Both are located in the 8,000-acre Newport News Park. The clubhouse has a snack bar and restaurant, driving range, putting greens and pro shop. The city's Department of Parks and Recreation Department manage the course. Greens fees start at $27; if you "ride share" a cart, the total cost is $36. For more information on this club and duffers' havens closer to Williamsburg, turn to our Golf chapter.

# Hampton

### The Hamptons
**Hampton Roads Center Pkwy. • (757) 766-9148**

This meticulously maintained 27-hole championship course (three different nine-hole courses) is set in a combination of woods, wildflowers, waterfalls and lakes. There's a large practice putting green and driving range, and the clubhouse offers a full-service restaurant, snack bar and pro shop. Greens fees start at $9 for 18 holes on weekdays and go up to $19 for 18 holes on weekends. Cart rentals are $4.50 on weekdays and $9 on weekends. At those prices, you could play every day. Look out, Tiger Woods!

### The Woodlands
**9 Woodland Rd. • (757) 727-1195**

Located 25 minutes south of Williamsburg, this 5,900-yard regulation par 69 course has bentgrass greens, Bermuda fairways and roughs and 52 sand bunkers to test your skills. The clubhouse features a pro shop and snack bar, and a practice putting green and seven tennis courts are available. With green fees starting at $9 for nine holes on weekdays (not including a cart), the Woodlands truly is a bargain!

# Parks

## Newport News

### Newport News Park
**13560 Jefferson Ave. (Exit 250B off I-64) • (757) 888-3333, (800) 203-8322**

This beautiful oasis in the northern tier of the city - among the largest municipal parks in the United States - has more than 8,000 acres of woodlands and two fresh water lakes. While entrance to the park is free, more than 180 individual campsites are available for rent. Each includes a picnic table and charcoal grill, 24-hour registration and security. Heated restrooms with hot showers, a laundry room, pay phones, sewage dumping station, playground equipment, ice, general store and water and electrical hookups also are available. Campsites are open year round. Rental rates start at $14.50 a night.

The park also offers 30 miles of hiking trails, a 5.4-mile mountain bike trail and a variety of trails that serve as bridle paths. For the angler in the family, there are two reservoirs stocked with bass, pickerel, pike, bluegill, perch and crappie. Boats are available for rent starting at $4 for an entire day of fishing fun (bring sunscreen).

For you history buffs, Dam No. 1, Confederate gun positions and remaining Union trenches are evidence of the present-day park's involvement in the Peninsula campaign. The park's visitors center interprets the action that took place there and offers literature on other pertinent sites nearby.

The park also hosts the annual Fall Festival in October and is the site of Celebration of Lights during the holiday season. For more information on these and other nearby festivals, turn to our Annual Events chapter.

## Hampton

### Grandview Nature Preserve
**Intersection of Beach Rd. and State Park Dr. • (757) 727-6347**

Another place sure to please the outdoor enthusiast is the Grandview Nature Preserve in northeast Hampton, with its 578 acres of marshland and beach area. Grandview is home to endangered species of birds and wildlife. It's the perfect place to stroll a 2 and 1/2-mile stretch of bayfront beach to observe all of nature's glory. Off the beaten path a bit, you get to Grandview by taking Mercury to Fox Hill. Travel Fox Hill for a few miles - past the Willow Oaks development - and turn left on Beach Road. You'll find Grandview just where you would expect - at the end of Beach. No admission fee is charged.

### Sandy Bottom Nature Park
**1255 Big Bethel Rd. • (757) 825-4657**

Hampton's newest public park is Sandy Bottom Nature Park on Big Bethel Road, which has 456 acres of woodland, two lakes, play and picnic areas, walking and interpretive trails, a wildlife area, nature center, paddleboats and concessions. The park also offers environmental education programs and special programming in astronomy, wildlife observation and environmental field-testing. To get to the park take Exit 261A of I-64 and follow Hampton Roads Center Parkway to Big Bethel Road. The park entrance will be on your left. Admission to the park is free.

# Education

There are 40 public schools in Newport News, including two new high schools that opened in the fall of 1996. Two middle schools and another elementary school also are on the drawing boards. In Hampton, 33 schools - including four high and five middle schools - serve the needs of the population, although there is continued discussion on converting the school administration center into either a middle school or a magnet high school to meet the needs of the public.

In the area of higher education, the Peninsula has two four-year institutions and a two-year community college. We have listed these here. For more detailed information on learning opportunities in and around Williamsburg, turn to our chapter on Education and Child Care.

## Christopher Newport University
50 Shoe Ln., Newport News • (757) 594-7000

This state-supported, four-year school offers more than 50 different majors and concentrations to its 5,000 full- and part-time students. It has master's programs in applied physics and education. CNU also operates SEVAnet, a nonprofit online education center that has been working to set up electronic commerce and data interchange in partnership with a number of businesses, including Newport News Shipbuilding. In 1996, the university announced it was building a new performing arts center. The center, which is being designed by the world-class architectural firm founded by I.M. Pei, is expected to be open by the end of 1999. In the fall of 1997, freshman enrollment at CNU was up 43 percent to 674 students, giving the university its largest first-year class in its 37-year history.

## Hampton University
East Hampton off Settlers Landing Rd.
• (757) 727-5000

The country's largest historically black college offers 47 bachelor's degree programs and 18 master's degree programs in fields such as architecture, business and art to its 5,700 full- and part-time students. The college also has a Ph.D. program in physics. Hampton University achieved a longtime goal in 1995, when its endowment money topped the $100 million mark. In December 1996, the University learned it had the highest graduation rate - 53 percent - among large, historically black colleges. From a historical standpoint, Booker T. Washington is one of the university's most famous graduates. A former slave, who later became a determined student and gifted leader, Washington graduated in 1875 and later moved to Alabama to launch what eventually would become the prestigious Tuskegee Institute. On Marshall Avenue on the university campus stands a statue of Booker T. Washington. In the midst of a memorial garden, the statue serves as a reminder of one man's inspiring accomplishments. The works of another Hampton University graduate, famed artist Dr. John Biggers, can be seen in the William R. and Norma B. Harvey Library on campus.

## Thomas Nelson Community College
99 Thomas Nelson Dr., Hampton
• (757) 825-2700

When it comes to two-year associate programs, Thomas Nelson Community College in Hampton has a reputation for quality. The college, established in 1967, grants associate degrees in 31 fields and more than 36 certificates in career-related areas, including administrative support technology, automotive career studies and information systems technology. In recent years, the college expanded its involvement with local businesses, frequently tailoring training programs for industries located on the Peninsula. The college is planning a permanent facility for the Williamsburg area in the near future. (See education chapter for more information.)

# Modern Military

While you're visiting the Peninsula, take a moment and look around you. A glance across the James River reveals the Navy's massive aircraft carriers. If you look up at the sky, you might see air squadrons from Langley Air Force Base flying in formation. And, if you stop off at a downtown Hampton restaurant for lunch, you'll probably see at least a few diners dressed in flight suits or fatigues. Hampton Roads, after all, is a military stronghold, a fact that becomes quite obvious once you have spent a little time here. The local military community includes all branches of the service.

When you consider the region as a whole, the Navy is dominant, with more than a dozen Navy bases spread over 36,000 acres from Yorktown to Virginia Beach and a $5 billion payroll. On the Peninsula, both the Army and Air Force prevail. Of the three Army bases in Hampton Roads, two - Fort Eustis and Fort Monroe - are on the Peninsula. Together, these installations provide jobs for more than 16,000 active duty and civilian personnel and support an annual payroll approaching $500 million. And Fort Eustis will continue to grow with the addition of another 475 jobs by 1999, when the Western and Eastern Commands of the Military Traffic Management Command consolidate and relocate from California and New Jersey to the Newport News base.

Close to 10,000 personnel are based at Hampton's Langley Air Force Base, including 7,800 active military. The payroll for that installation tops $301 million annually. What follows is a breakdown of the military installations and related properties on the middle and lower Peninsula.

# Newport News

## Fort Eustis
**Upper Newport News, Exit 250A off I-64**
• **(757) 878-4920**
In upper Newport News, this is the Army's command and training center for air, sea, rail

and land transportation. The base has 9,022 military personnel and 3,945 civilian workers with a payroll of $384 million. On post are the Army Transportation Center, the 7th Transportation Group and the U.S. Army Transportation Museum, which features more than 200 years of Army transportation history depicted through models, dioramas and life-size displays. (For more on the Transportation Museum see our Newport News Attractions section of this chapter.)

# Hampton

## Fort Monroe
**Old Point Comfort, southeastern Hampton**
• **(757) 727-2000**
At Old Point Comfort at the southeastern tip of Hampton, Fort Monroe is headquarters for the Training and Doctrine Command, the Army's main think tank. The only active moat-surrounded fort on the Army's roster, Fort Monroe can trace its history to Fort Algernourne, built on the site in 1609 to protect the first settlers. Present-day Fort Monroe was completed in 1834 and is recognized as the largest stone fort ever built in the United States. The fort has 835 military personnel, 1,794 civilian workers and a $113 million payroll. Of particular interest on the post are the Casemate Museum, 727-3391, where Jefferson Davis was imprisoned, the historic buildings dating to the early 19th century and the coastal gunnery fortifications. A seawall surrounding much of the base offers a breathtaking view of boaters on the Chesapeake Bay. A covered bandstand on the well-kept lawn next to the Chamberlin Hotel is the site of Continental Army Band concerts during the summer. It is also a popular spot for military personnel to tie the knot: If you drive by some sunny Saturday, you might just catch a wedding in progress. Fort Monroe is open to the public, and, unless a security check is in progress, you will be waved through - or saluted if your vehicle identifies you as a military officer. Speed limits range from 10 to 25 miles per hour on base and are clearly posted. We advise you to adhere to these limits. One aggrieved Insider recently let his foot rest just a tad too heavily on the accelerator and found

he couldn't talk his way out of a speeding ticket.

To reach the base, follow Mercury Boulevard through Phoebus to its eastern tip at the Fort Monroe gate. For more information on the Casemate Museum see Hampton's Attractions in this chapter.

## Hampton National Cemetery
### Cemetery Rd., Hampton University Campus • (757) 728-3131

This cemetery dates to the Civil War, with many of the fallen from both sides interred here. Burials of veterans still are conducted in both the older and newer parts of the cemetery, and beautiful and fitting tributes to the servicemen and servicewomen interred here are presented each Memorial Day.

## Langley Air Force Base
### End of LaSalle Ave. • (757) 764-9990

This base has a history of operation beginning as Langley Field in the days when the flight line consisted of biplanes; for a while, military dirigibles were housed here as well. Today it's possible to see F-15 and F-16 fighter-bombers, Stealth aircraft and other planes taking off and making their landing approaches in the skies near the base. Home base to the combat air crews active in the Gulf War, Langley is headquarters for the 1st Fighter Wing and the Air Combat Command, which oversees all Air Force combat commands. Sharing the base property is the 787-acre NASA Langley Research Center, where the Mercury missions were conceived and where air and space flight research is conducted. Although the base does not have exhibits open to the public, periodic open houses and air shows afford an opportunity to visit.

# Yorktown and York County

## Coast Guard Reserve Training Center
### End of Rt. 238 • (757) 898-3500

This facility is a key training center for the Coast Guard, providing classroom as well as shipboard instruction for men and women entering the service. Cutters regularly dock at the center's pier, which has a beautiful view of the mouth of the York River. The training center's workforce includes 52 civilians and 438 military personnel. No public tours are available.

## Navy Supply Center Cheatham Annex
### York Co. • (757) 887-7108

This bulk storage facility in York County belongs to the Fleet and Industrial Supply Center in Norfolk. It is mainly a cold storage plant for food that supplies many East Coast service installations as well as the Atlantic Fleet. The center's loading piers in the York River are visible from the Colonial Parkway just where it turns inland from the river.

## Yorktown Naval Weapons Station
### Rt. 143, Yorktown • (757) 887-4609, 887-4545

As the title suggests, this installation is where ordnance used by the Atlantic Fleet is maintained and stored. On Route 143, just west of Lee Hall, it extends much of the length of the York River between Williamsburg and Yorktown. Ships being armed can be seen at the station's piers from pullouts on the Colonial Parkway near its Yorktown end. This view will have to do, as the weapons station is a closed base.

# Index of Advertisers

Alice Person House ................................................................................................................ 56
Busch Gardens Water Country ................................................................... inside front cover
Candlewick Bed and Breakfast ............................................................................................ 49
The Cedars Bed and Breakfast ............................................................................................ 50
Colonel Waller Motel ............................................................................................................ 32
Colonial Capital Bed and Breakfast .................................................................................... 61
Colonial Gardens Bed and Breakfast .................................................................................. 51
Edgewood Plantation ............................................................................................................ 52
Embassy Suites .................................................................................................................... 27
Four Points Sheraton ............................................................................................................ 24
Holland's Lodge .................................................................................................................... 62
Inn at 802 .............................................................................................................................. 54
North Bend Plantation .......................................................................................................... 58
Patrick Henry Inn ........................................................................................ inside back cover
Shops at Carolina Furniture ............................................................................................... 168
Williamsburg Manor .............................................................................................................. 60
Williamsburg Outlet Mall .................................................................................................... 119
Williamsburg Sampler .......................................................................................................... 59

# Index

## A

Abbitt Realty Company Inc. 302
Abby Aldrich Rockefeller Folk Art Center 159, 225
Aberdeen Barn 83
Accommodations 25
Adam's Hunt 294
Aerobics Plus 273
Affairs of the Heart 166
African-American Heritage 163, 166
Agecroft Hall 256
AIDS: Peninsula AIDS Foundation 312
Air Power Park 356
Air Tours 193
Airfield Conference Center 39
Alcoholics Anonymous 313
Algonquian Indians 133
Alice Person House 48
Alliance for the Chesapeake Bay 288
Alpengeist 3
Alternative Healthcare 314–315
American Heritage Festival 234
America's Railroads on Parade 215
AMF Williamsburg Bowl 272
Amtrak 17
Amusement Parks and Minigolf 214
An Occasion for the Arts 4, 239
Anastasia's 83
Andersons Corner Motel 29
Andrews Gallery 227
Anheuser-Busch 3, 4, 8
Annual Antique Show and Sale 232
Annual Events 231–243
Annual Independence Day Ice Cream Social 236
Antiques Forum 231
Applewood Colonial 49
Archer Cottage 200
Armistead House 149
Arts 221–229
Association for Research and Enlightenment 265
Association for the Preservation of Virginia
    Antiquities 149, 191
Atlantic Waterfowl Heritage Museum 264
Attic Collections 127
Attractions 169–189
Augustine Moore House 200
AuPairCare - European Nanny Service 324
Auto Parts and Supply Inc. 126
Avalon, A Center for Women and Children 313

## B

Babysitting Services for Visitors 324
Bacon's Castle 246
Bacova Guild Ltd. 118
Bagel Bakery & Yogurt Shop 83
Bake Shop 155

Baker's Crust 262
Ball Corp. 4
Banbury Cross 294
Band Box Music & Video 120
Barnes and Noble 174
Baron Woods 294
Basketville Of Williamsburg Inc. 131
Baskin-Robbins Ice Cream and Frozen Yogurt 118
Bassett Hall 152, 153, 159
Bassett Motel 29
Bassett's Classic Christmas Shop 124
Bay Days 238
Bay Room 80
Bayou Boogaloo & Cajun Food Festival 235
Bayside Inn 254
Beckham Tours/Mississippi 18
Beecroft & Bull Ltd 118, 373
Beethoven's Inn 83
Belgian Waffles 83
Bell Atlantic 6
Belle Aire Plantation 169
Benson House of Williamsburg 47
Benton-Knight Ltd. 368
Berkeley Commons Outlet Center 128
Berkeley Middle School 317
Berkeley Plantation 170
Berkeley William E. Wood Realtors 302
Berkeley's Green 294
Berret's Seafood Restaurant & Raw Bar 84, 118
Best Western - The Williamsburg Westpark Hotel
    31
Best Western Colonial Capitol Inn 29
Best Western Patrick Henry Inn 30
Best Western Williamsburg 30
Big Apple Bagels 84
Bikes Unlimited 271
Bikesmith of Williamsburg 271
Biking 271–272
Binn's Of Williamsburg 118
Birchwood Park 294
Bistro! 263
Black Butterfly 369
Blue Skies Gallery 369
Bluebird Gap Farm 356
Bluewater Wear 369
Bob Timberlake collection of North Carolina
    Americ 119
Bobbywood 263
Bodine's Hickory Smoked Bar-B-Que 69, 360
Bon Appetit 360
Bones 84
Bones Sports Pub & Rotisserie 108
Book House 121
Bookpress Ltd. 122
Bookstore, The 174
Bowling 272
Boxwood Inn 366
Brafferton Building 141
Brass Shop 369
Bright Beginnings 317
Brush-Everard House 158
Bruton Heights School Education Center 149
Bruton Parish 144, 145
Bruton Parish Book & Gift Shop 175
Bruton Parish Church 2, 3, 142, 156, 175

Bryant Guest Home 63
Buckroe Beach 375
Buckroe's Island Grill 363
Busch Brewery 8
Busch Gardens 1, 3, 6, 9, 19, 22, 176, 213

**C**

C.W. Cowling's 250
Caddy Shack Golf Works 281
Cale Realty Company 302
Campgrounds 35
Campus Shop 118
Candle Factory Restaurant 84
Candlewick Bed and Breakfast 50
Canon 4
Canterbury Hills 294
Capitol Motel 31
Capriole 222
Captain George's Seafood Restaurant 84
Captain John Smith Inn 31
Carlton Farm 273
Carmela's Homestyle Italian Cuisine 360
Carmela's Pasta Cafe 363
Carmike Cinema 4 113
Carolina Carpets 127
Carolina Furniture 127
Carolynn Court Motel 31
Carousel 118
Carpenter's Yard 213
Carrot Tree Kitchen 122
Carters Grove Plantation 6, 142, 153, 160, 162, 170
Carter's Guest Home 63
Cary Street Bistro & Tavern 84
Cascades 29, 80
Casemate Museum 356
Casey's Of Williamsburg 118
Cattle Baron of Williamsburg 85
Cedar Valley Farm 273
Cedars, The 50
Celebrate Yorktown Festival 202, 238
Center for Marine Conservation, Atlantic Regional 288
Chamber Ballet Company 225
Chamberlin, The 363, 367
Chambrel at Williamsburg 308
Chanco's Grant 294
Charles H. Taylor Arts Center 356
Charlie's Antiques and Repairs 130
Charlottesville 14
Charly's 85
Cheers Unlimited Cafe & Tavern 360
Cheese Shop Cafe 85, 118
Chesapeake Bay 283, 285
Chesapeake Bay Foundation 288
Chesapeake Bay National Estuarine Research Reserve 289
Chez Trinh 86
Chickahominy 135
Chickahominy Haven 295
Chickahominy Watershed Alliance 288
Child Caring Connection 323, 325
Child Development Resources 324
Childcare 323–325
Children's Hospital of the King's Daughters 311

Chippokes Plantation State Park 247
Chowning's Tavern 81, 110, 157
Christiana Campbell's Tavern 81, 157
Christina's Kitchen 86
Christmas Mouse 126
Christmas Shop 118
Christopher Newport University 320, 377
Christopher Wren Association for Lifelong Learning 306
Christophers Tavern 44
Chrysler Hall 115
Chrysler Museum 260
Church Tower 193
Churches 175
Classic Amphitheatre on Strawberry Hill 115
Classic Cravats 118
Clean the Bay Day 290
Clipper Cruise Line Inc. 19
Coach House Tavern 86
Coast Guard Reserve Training Center 379
Coffeehouse, The 86
Coliseum Central 370
Coliseum Crossing 373
Coliseum Mall 370
Coliseum Square 373
College Delly & Pizza Restaurant 87
College Landing Park 270
College of William and Mary 1, 2, 3, 4, 6, 8, 9, 19, 118, 140, 148, 173, 222, 284, 319
College of William and Mary's President's House 140
College Shop 119
Colleges and Universities 319–324
Colonel Waller Motel 31
Colonial Capitol 154
Colonial Capital Bed and Breakfast 50
Colonial Children's Fair 236
Colonial Community Mental Health Center 312
Colonial Connections 18
Colonial Gardens Bed & Breakfast 51
Colonial Golf Course 277
Colonial Houses and Taverns 26
Colonial Motel 31
Colonial One-Hour Photo 119
Colonial One-Hour Portrait Studio 119
Colonial Parkway Inn 32
Colonial Post Office 158
Colonial Rent-A-Car 22
Colonial Restaurant 88
Colonial Road Runners 274
Colonial Town Plaza 129
Colonial Williamsburg Evening Tours 114
Colonial Williamsburg Foundation 149, 150
Colonial Williamsburg Golden Horseshoe Golf Course 277
Colonial Williamsburg Learning Weekends 231
Colonial Williamsburg Tickets 152
Colonial Williamsburg Visitor Center 19
Colonial Williamsburg Visitors Companion 149
Colonial Williamsburg's Company of Colonial Performers 225
Colony Square Shopping Center 122
Comfort Inn 366
Comfort Inn & Suites 32
Comfort Inn - Central 32

Comfort Inn - King George Historic 32
Comfort Inn - Outlet Center 33
Commonwealth Inn 33
Community Christmas Tree Lighting 242
Copper Top Lounge 108
Corner Pocket 88, 110
Corning Revere Factory Store 130
Country Harvest Buffet 88
County Grill & Smokehouse 69
Courtyard by Marriott 367
Courtyard Cafe 88
Coves, The 295
Covington Cruises 18
Crab Louie's 258
Cracker Barrel Old Country Store 88, 124
Craft House 119
Crafters Mall 374
Crisis and Support Groups 312–314
Cross or Crown 165
Cry Witch 165
Customhouse 200

**D**

Daily Press 339
Dale House 193
Dance, Our Dearest Diversion 165
Danny's Deli 360
d'art Center 260
Das Waldcafe 361
Days Inn - Downtown Colonial 33
Days Inn - East Williamsburg 33
Days Inn - Historic Area 34
Days Inn - Pottery 34
Days Inn - West 34
Days Inn Oyster Point 366
Days Inn-Hampton 367
Daytrips 245
Delmarva Peninsula 14
Denbigh 374
Dennys 45
DeWitt Wallace Collections and Conservation
    Buildi 149
DeWitt Wallace Decorative Arts Gallery 160, 226
Dining Room at Ford's Colony Country Club
    71, 89
Discovery 195, 246
Domestic Violence Hotline 313
Dominion Village 308
Doraldo's 89
Douglas MacArthur Memorial 260
Doumar's 263
Downtown Hampton Public Piers 358
Drucilla King Guest Home 64
Druid Hills 295
Drum House 200
Drummond's Field On The James 296
Dudley Digges House 202
Duke of York Motor Hotel 208
Dumbwaiter, The 263

**E**

E.Js Landing 38
Eastern Chickahominy 136

Eastern State Educational Program 317
Eastern State Hospital 4
Eastern Virginia School of the Performing Arts
    225
Econo Lodge Central 34
Edgar Allen Poe Museum 256
Edgewood Plantation 52, 170
Education and Child Care 317–323
Edwards' Virginia Ham Shoppe Of Williamsburg
    126
El Mariachi 361
Electric Glass Co. 370
Elms, The 64
Embassy Suites - Williamsburg 34
Emergency Healthcare 311–312
Emmanuel Ungaro 119
English Gallery 194
Environment 283
Environmental Action Council 286
Environmental Groups 286–289
Estuaries Day 289
Evelynton Plantation 171
Everything Williamsburg 119
Ewell Station Shopping Center 128
Executive Homes Realty 303

**F**

Fairfield Inn by Marriott 367
Family Inns Of America 35
Family Life Adventures 163
Family Programs 163
Farm House 131
Favorite Meals from Williamsburg: A Menu
    Cookbook 157
Felicity in Williamsburg 164
Fencing 272
Fernbrook 296
Festival Marketplace 124
Festival of Lights 243
Fieldcrest 296
Fife and Drum Corps 165
Fifty Plus 307
Fire & Ice 363
Fireside Steak House & Seafood 89
First Baptist Church 175
First Colony 296
First Colony Coffee House 263
First Landing/Seashore State Park 266
First Med Of Williamsburg 312
First Night of Williamsburg 4, 9, 243
Fisherman's Corner 252
Fishing and Hunting 272–273
Five Forks Motel and Campground 35
Five Forks Shopping Center 124
Flat Hat 340
Flood Zone 115
Flower Cupboard 121
Folk Art Center 152, 153
Food & Feasts in the 17th Century 241
For Cant Hill 64
Ford's Colony Country Club 278, 296
Forest Hill Guest Home 64
Fort Boykin Historic Park 249
Fort Cherokee Trading Post 125

Fort Eustis 378
Fort Fun 347
Fort Magruder Inn and Conference
    Center 35
Fort Monroe 378
Four Points Hotel by Sheraton 35
Fourth at the Fort 236
Fox & Grape Bed & Breakfast 53
Fox Ridge 296
Free City Traders 370
Frog and the Redneck 258

**G**

Gabriel Archer Tavern at the
    Williamsburg Winery 89
Galleries 227–229
Gallery On The Green 209, 227
Gallery Shops at Lightfoot 129
Garden Symposium 233
Gatehouse Farms 296
Gateway 2000 4
Gazebo House of Pancakes and
    Waffles 90
Geddy Foundry 142
Geddy House 151
George Washington Inn 90
George Wythe House 142
Georges Tavern 42
Ghosts of Williamsburg 114, 139
Gidi Gourmet 90
Giorgio's Pizza Shoppe 90
Giuseppe's Italian Cafe 91
Glasshouse 193
Gloucester County 13
Gloucester Daffodil Festival 233
Go-Karts Plus 214
Godspeed 195, 246
Golden Ball 158
Golden Horseshoe Golf Course
    277
Golden Horseshoe Club House
    Grille 81
Golden Palace 363
Golf 277–281
Golf Shoppe 281
Golf Supply Shops 279–281
Golf USA 279
Good Fortune 363
Good Neighbors Pass 153, 305
Good Place To Eat, A 82, 118
Goodfella's 363
Goodwin, Rev. W. A. R. 3, 148
Goswick-Whittaker Guest Home 64
Governor Spottswood Motel 35
Governors Inn 28
Governor's Land at Two Rivers 3,
    8, 133, 285, 296
Governor's Palace 3, 152, 154
Governor's Trace 53
Grace Episcopal Church 200
Grandview Fishing Pier 375
Grandview Nature Preserve 376
Grate Steak 363
Gray Line of Williamsburg 18

Graylin Woods 297
Greek Festival 234
Green Leafe Cafe 91, 108
Green Springs Plantation 297
Greenhow Store 158
Greyhound/Trailways Bus System 17
Grille at Ford's Colony 91
Grissell Hay 151
GSH Real Estate,Williamsburg Office 302

**H**

Hampton 343–379
Hampton Carousel Park 356
Hampton Coliseum 115
Hampton Cup Regatta 237
Hampton History Museum Association 357
Hampton Inn 368
Hampton Inn & Suites 366
Hampton Inn & Suites - Williamsburg 36
Hampton Inn - Historic Area 36
Hampton Inn - Williamsburg Center 36
Hampton Jazz Festival 235
Hampton National Cemetery 379
Hampton Roads Academy 318
Hampton University 136, 322, 357, 377
Hampton Visitor's Center 346
Harbor Cruise 348
Harbor Park 260
Harbor Side Restaurant 254
Harborfest 235
Harpoon Larry's Oyster Bar 364
Harrison Opera House 115
Hayashi Japanese Restaurant 91
Health and Fitness Clubs 273
Healthcare 311
Henry, Patrick 2, 147, 154
Henry Street Chocolatier 119
Heritage Inn 36
Heritage Landing 297
Hickory Neck Church 175
Hilda Crockett's Chesapeake House 252
Hilton Village 373
Hilton Village Goldsmith 373
Historic Garden Week 233
Historic Ghent 261
Historic Meals 156
History Forum 241
Hite's Bed and Breakfast 54
Holiday Inn 1776- Williamsburg 38
Holiday Inn Downtown - Williamsburg & Holidome
    36
Holiday Inn Express 38
Holiday Inn Hampton 368
Holiday Inn Patriot and Conference Center 38
Holland's Lodge Bed and Breakfast 55
Holland's Sleepy Lodge 64
Holly Hills of Williamsburg 8, 297
Homestay Bed and Breakfast 55
Homewood Suites Hotel 38
Hornsby Real Estate Co. 303
Horseback Riding 273–274
Hospice Support Care of Williamsburg 314
Hotel Colonial America 39
Howard Johnson Central 39

Howard JohnsonHistoric Area 39
Hughes Guest Home 64
Hunter's Creek 297
Huntington Park Beach 374

**I**

IHOP 91
Independence Day Festivities 235, 236
Indian Fields Tavern 72, 91
Indian Springs Bed and Breakfast 56
Indigo Park 297
Ingleside Plantation Winery 76
International Coastal Cleanup Day 290
Iron Bound Fitness Center 273
Isle of Capri 266
Isle of Wight County 5, 13, 249, 259

**J**

J. Fenton Gallery 119
J.B.'s Lounge 108
J.M. Randalls Restaurant & Tavern 92, 109
J.W.s 44
James Anderson Blacksmith Shop 157
James Blair Middle School 317
James City County Division of Parks and
   Recreation 269, 275
James City County Fair 237
James City County Library 218
James City County Parks and Recreation 218
James City County Transit 23
James City County-Williamsburg Community
   Center 213, 271, 274
James Fort 193, 196
James Geddy House and Foundry 158
James River Association 289
James River Community Center 271
James River Fishing Pier 375
James River Pie 92
James River Plantations 169
Jamestown 191–211
Jamestown Christmas 242
Jamestown Church 140
Jamestown Explorer 197, 214
Jamestown Ferry 192
Jamestown Gallery 195
Jamestown High School 317
Jamestown Island 6, 133, 192, 193
Jamestown Landing Day 234
Jamestown Settlement
   3, 4, 6, 133, 134, 136, 191, 194, 213
Jamestown-Scotland Ferry 245
Jamestown-Yorktown Foundation 213
Japanese Tea House 348
JBs Lounge 35
Jefferson Inn 92
Jefferson, Thomas 2, 142, 154
"Jefferson's Virginia" 6
Jewish Mother, The 102, 267
Jim and Pat Carter Real Estate 302
Jimmy's Pizza-Pasta Restaurant 92
Joe's Inn 258
John D. Rockefeller Jr. Library, 149
Johnny's Frozen Custard 361

Johnson's Guest Home 64
Jolly Pond Convenience Center 291
Joseph and Margaret Muscarelle Museum Of Art
   226
Jumpin the Broom 165

**K**

Keith's Dockside 364
Ken's Bar-B-Q 250
Kidsburg 213, 214
Kidstuff 213–219
Kiln Creek 113, 367
King William Inn 40
King's Arms Tavern 81, 157
Kingsgate Greene Shopping Center 124
Kingsmill Golf Club 278
Kingsmill On The James 298
Kingsmill Realty Inc. 303
Kingsmill Resort 39
Kingsmill Restaurants 92
Kingsmill Tennis Club 275
Kingspoint 298
Kingswood 298
Kiskiack Golf Club 278
Kiskiack Indians 199
Kitchen At Powhatan Plantation 94
Kiwanis Municipal Park 270, 275
Kristiansand 298
Kyung Sung Korean Restaurant 361

**L**

La Tolteca Mexican Restaurante 94
Lafayette High School 317
Lake Toano 298
Langley Air Force Base 379
Lanthorn Tour 164
Laura Ashley 119
Le Chambord 266
Le Yaca 94
Lee Hall Reservoir 273
Legacy of Williamsburg Bed and Breakfast Inn 56
Legend of Bruton Parish Vault 142
Legends at Stonehouse 279
Legends of the Past Tour 164
Lewis Guest Home 64
Lewis Tyler 151
Liberty Rose Bed and Breakfast 57
Library Tavern 109
Lightfoot Pancake and Steak House 94
Little Cheeper Car Rentals 22
Little Creek Reservoir 273
Little Creek Reservoir Park 216
Little England Chapel 357
Lobster House 94
Lodge Coffee Shop 80
Longhill Gate 298
Lucido's Pastries & Coffeehouse 361
Luigi's Italian Restaurant 361
Lumber House 152

**M**

M. Dubois Grocer 158

Mama Mia's Pizza & Delicatessen 95
Mama Steve's House of Pancakes 95
Manchester Grill 362
Manhattan Bagel 95
Maple Tree Pancakes & Waffles 95
Margaret Hunter Shop 158
Marie Bauer Hall 142
Mariners' Museum 137, 349
Marino's Italian Cuisine 95
Market Square 332
Marketplace at Kingsmill 124
Marl Inn 209
Martha's Plantation Breakfast 42, 95
Mary Dickinson Store 158
Mary Immaculate Hospital 311
Massey's Camera Shop 121
Master Craftsmen 125
Mattaponi Indian Museum 137
Mattaponi Reservation 134
Matthew Jones House 348
Maupin Tours/Kansas 18
Maximum Guided Tours Inc. 18
Mayflower Tours/Illinois 18
Meadows, The 298
Meals on Wheels 305
Media 339–341
Medical College of Virginia in Richmond 311
Mental and Therapeutic Healthcare 312
Mercantile Shops 158
Merchants Square 47, 118, 152
Mercury Plaza 373
MergeTech Inc. 4
Meridian 18
Metal Container Group 4
Metro Richmond Convention and Visitors Bureau 255
Metro Richmond Visitor Center 255
Michelob Championship Golf Tournament at Kingsmill 8, 239, 276, 277
Mid County Park 270, 275
Mike's Place 362
Milano's Italian Family Restaurant 95
Military by Night 165
Military Demonstrations 165
Military Encampment 165
Mill Creek Landing 299
Ming Gate Restaurant 364
Mini-Golf America 214
Mirror Lake Estates 299
Miss Hampton II Harbor Cruise 358
Miss Yorktown 206
Mitty's Ristorante 362
Mongolian BBQ Restaurant 96, 365
Monticello Marketplace 8
Monticello Shopping Center 126
Moore House 145
Morrison's Cafeteria 96
Motel 6 40
Mother-in-law Tree 140
Motorcoach 18
Mr. Liu's Chinese Restaurant & Lounge 96
Mugler's of Phoebus 370
Muhlbauer Inc 4
Mulberry Inn 367
Muscarelle Museum of Art 219

Museum and White House of the Confederacy 256
Museums, Native American 136–137
Museums Ticket 152
Museums, Visual Arts 225–227
Music 221–225
Music Theatre of Williamsburg 3, 112
Musical Traditions of African Americans 167
My Doll & Toy Shoppe 369

**N**

Nancy Thomas Gallery 209, 227
Nantucket Clipper, The 19
Nara of Japan 362
Nathaniel Bacon 142
National Association for the Education of Young Children 323
National Pancake House 96
Nauticus 261
Navy Supply Center Cheatham Annex 379
Nawab Indian Cuisine 97
Neighborhoods and Real Estate 293–303
Nelson House 145, 200
New England Grill 97
New Quarter Park 270
New York Deli 97
Newport House 58
Newport News 343–344
Newsome House Museum and Cultural Center 352
Newton Bus Service Inc. 18
Nicks Seafood Pavilion 207
Norfolk 8, 13, 15, 258–263
Norfolk Botanical Gardens 261
Norfolk Convention & Visitors Bureau 259
Norfolk International Airport 16
Norfolk Naval Base 261
Norfolk's Waterside 19
Norge Shoppes 130
North Bend Plantation 58
North Cove 299
Not Betty's 362

**O**

Oasis Restaurant 365
Occasional Downtown Doo Dah Parade 232
Old Cape Henry Lighthouse 266
Old Chickahominy House 97, 122
Old Coast Guard Station 265
Old Dominion Opry 3
Old Hampton Bookstore 369
Old Mill House Of Pancakes & Waffles 98
Old Virginia Brewery & Restaurant 362
Ole Hampton Sportswear 369
Omni Newport News Hotel 367
On the Hill Cultural Arts Center 209, 227
Other Half Tour 166
Our Military Heritage 331
Owens-Brockway Glass 4
Oyster Alley 365

**P**

Padow's Hams & Deli 98

Palace and Capitol Concerts 164
Pamunkey Indian Museum 137
Pamunkey Reservation 134
Papillions 44
Papillon: A Bistro 98
Paramount's Kings Dominion 257
Parents' Guide to Children's Services in Hampt 323
Parks and Recreation 269–275
Parlett's Card and Gift Boutique 121
Pasbehegh Indians 133
Pasquier House of Art 373
Pasta E Pani 266
Patrick Henry Inn and Conference Center 30
Patrick Henry Mall 374
Patriots Colony 309
Patriots Pass 152
Patriot's Plaza Outlets 127
Paul's Deli Restaurant & Pizza 98, 109
Peacock Hill Antiques 121
Peanut Shop Of Williamsburg 119
Peddler Steak House 98
Peking Restaurant 98
Peninsula Agency on Aging 305
Peninsula Biking Association 272
Peninsula Fine Arts Center 352
Peninsula Model Railroad Club 215
Peninsula SPCA 353
Pennsylvania House Collector's Gallery 127
People for the Ethical Treatment of Animals (PETA) 289
Performing Arts 221–225
Period Designs 209
Perry Ellis 119
Peyton Randolph House 141
Phi Beta Kappa Memorial Hall 221
Phillip Morris 4
Phoebus 369–370
Phoebus Auction Gallery 370
Phoenix Rising Yoga Therapy 314, 315
Physmed 314
Piano-Organ Outlet 128
Pierce's Pitt Bar-B-Que 70, 99
Piney Creek Estates 299
Piney Grove 169
Piney Grove at Southall's Plantation 60, 171
Pitchers 44
Pizzeria Uno Chicago Bar & Grill 99
Plantation Dining Room 38
Plantiques - Hilton Village 374
Pocahontas 133, 145
Polo Club Restaurant 99
Poor Potter House 200
Poplar Hall 299
Poquoson 13
Poquoson Seafood Festival 238
Porcelain Collector 119
Port Anne 299
Port Arthur's 362
Portsmouth 13
Pottery Factory Outlets 129
Pottery Wine & Cheese Shop 369
Powder Magazine at Colonial Williamsburg 332
Powell House 213
Powhatan 133

Powhatan Confederacy 133
Powhatan Crossing 299
Powhatan Indian Gallery 194
Powhatan Indian Village 195
Powhatan Secondary of Williamsburg 299
Powhatan Shores 300
Precious Gem 119
Prentis Store 158
Prime Rib House 99
Primrose Cottage, A 48
Prince George Espresso Bar & Roastery 99, 111, 119
Prince George Graphics 121
Princess Anne Motor Lodge 40
Printing Office 157
Private Guest Homes 63–65
Private Schools 318–319
Providence Hall 28
Prudential McCardle Realty 303
Public Education 317–318
Public Gaol 155
Public Hospital 148, 159
Publick Times 240
Pungo Strawberry Festival 234

**Q**

Quality Inn & Suites 368
Quality Inn - The Lord Paget 41
Quality Inn at Kingsmill 41
Quality Inn Historic 41
Quality InnColony 40
Quality InnOutlet Mall 41
Quality SuitesWilliamsburg 41
Quarterpath Inn 41
Quarterpath Park 269, 274
Queen Anne Dairy Snack 70, 100
Queen's Lake 19, 300
Queen's Lake Club Inc. 19
Queenswood 300
Quilts Unlimited 119

**R**

R. Bryant Ltd. 119
Radio Stations 341
Radisson Hotel Hampton 368
Raleigh Economy Inn 41
Raleigh Tavern 2, 3, 155
Ramada Inn & Conference Center 42, 367
Ramada Inn Central Williamsburg 42
Real Estate Companies 302–303
Recycling 286, 290–291
Red Maple Inn 362
Referral Services 312
Regency Room 28, 72
Remember Me 167
Reservation Services 25
Residential Living 308
Restaurants 79–105
Retired and Senior Volunteer Program (RSVP) 307
Retirement 305–309
Revolutionary Fun 6
Reynolds Aluminum Recycling Center 291

Richmond 14, 254–258
Richmond Children's Museum 256
Richmond Coliseum 115
Richmond Hill 300
Richmond International Airport 16
Richmond National Battlefield Park Visitor Center 255
Richmond Times-Dispatch 339
River Room 207
Riverdale Plaza 373
Riverside Adult Daycare Center 306
Riverside Hospitals in Newport News 311
Rizzoli Bookstore 120
Roberts Restaurant 33
Robertson's Windmill 213
Rochambeau Motel 42
Rockin' Robin 109
Rocky Mount Bar B-Q House 70
Rolling Woods 300
Rooney's Downtown 365
Rosie Rumpe's Regal Dumpe 112
Royal Cruise Line 18
Royal New Kent 279
Royal Odyssey, The 18
Ruke's Seafood Deck 254

**S**

S. Wallace Edwards & Sons 247
Saint Luke's Church 249
Sal's by Victor Italian Restaurant 101
Sal's Piccolo Forno Ristorante Italiano 101
Sandy Bottom Nature Park 377
Scents & Treasures 369
Science, Conjuration and Humbug 165
Science Museum of Virginia 257
Scotland House Ltd. 120
Seafare Of Williamsburg 101
Seafood 70–72
Seasonal Programs and Special Tours 163
Seasons Cafe 101
Seasons Trace 300
Second Street Restaurant and Tavern 102, 109, 365
Senior Citizens Bridge Club 307
Services for Citizens 55 and Older 306
Sessions House 199
Settler's Mill 300
Shenandoah Tours/Virginia 18
Shenandoah Valley 14
Sherwood Forest Plantation 172
Shields Tavern 82, 157
Shirley Metalcraft 121
Shirley Pewter Shop 120
Shirley Plantation 139, 172
Shoney's Restaurant 102
Sign of the Rooster 120
Silver Vault Ltd 120
Silverman Furs 374
Skimino Hills 301
Skipwith Farms 301
Skipwith, Lady Anne 141
Slave Quarter 161
Sleep Inn 42
Smith, Captain John 145

Smith Island 252–254
Smithfield 248
Smithfield Confectionery & Ice Cream Parlor 250
Smithfield Gourmet Bakery and Cafe 250
Smithfield Inn, The 250
Smithfield Station 250
Smith's Fort Plantation 246
Smokehouse, The 369
Snow's Bicycle Shop 370
Soccer 275
Soccer Club of Williamsburg 275
South Hampton Roads 13
Southern Inn 42
Southern States Cooperative 124
Spiggle Guest Home 65
Sports & Balloons In Store 121
Sports Bar and Grille 38
Sportsman's Grille 102
St. George Tucker House Donor Reception Center 149
St. George's Hundred 301
St. John's Episcopal Church 358
St. Patrick's Day Parade 232
Star Tours/New Jersey 18
Stonehouse Golf Club 8
Strawberry Banks Inn 368
Suffolk 13
Summer Breeze Concert Series 112, 222
Surrey House Restaurant 248
Sushi Yama Japanese Restaurant 363
Swan Tavern Antiques 211

**T**

Tangier Island 251–252
Tarleton, Colonel Banastre 142
Tarpleys Store 158
Taste of Olde England 82
Tazewell Club Fitness Center 26
Teaching Center and Golf Academy 277
Television Stations 341
Tennis 274–275
Texas-Wisconsin Border Cafe 258
Thanksgiving at Berkeley Plantation 241
That Seafood Place 102
Theater 224–225
Thomas Jefferson Inn 42
Thomas Jefferson National Accelerator Facility 4
Thomas Nelson Community College 322, 377
Thompson Guest House 65
Three Ships Inn 267
Tickets to Colonial Williamsburg 152
Tidewater Touring Inc. 18
Tioga Motel 43
TK Oriental Arts 122
Toano 19
Toano Middle School 317
Toano Toy Works 130
Tobacco Company 258
Top's China Restaurant 103
Touch Of Earth, A 227
Tours and Tastings 75
Town and Gown Luncheon 307
Toymaker Of Williamsburg 120

Trade Shops and Demonstrations 157
TravelodgeHistoric Area 43
Trellis Restaurant and Cafe 102, 120
Trevillian Furniture and Interiors 124
Trying to Git Some Mother Wit 167
Tucker House 150
Twentieth Century Gallery 121, 229
Two Sergeants Inc. 365

U

U.S. Army Transportation Museum 353
Undergrounds 119
United Way Community Resource Service 313
Upper County Park 270
Upper Mattaponi 134

V

Valentine Museum 257
Venture Inn II - Whale Watching and Evening
    Cruise 358
Veranda Room 35, 103
Veritat 144, 145
Vernon Wooten Studio & Gallery 122
Vic Zodda's 1776 Restaurant 38, 104
Victorian Station 365
Victory Arch 353
Victory Monument 206
Village Diner 248
Village Shops At Kingsmill 125
Village Stitchery 374
Villager Lodge 43
Vineyards Of Williamsburg 301
Virginia Air and Space Museum and Hampton
    Roads History Center 359
Virginia Beach 13, 14, 15, 115, 263–267
Virginia Gazette 339
Virginia Indian Heritage Festival 133, 235
Virginia Institute of Marine Science at Gloucester
    284
Virginia Living Museum 353
Virginia Marine Science Museum 266
Virginia Museum of Fine Arts 257
Virginia Peninsulas Public Service Authority
    286, 290
Virginia Scenic Byway, Route 5 14
Virginia Shakespeare Festival 8, 224, 237
Virginia Store, The 369
Virginia War Museum 354
Virginia Water Quality Improvement Act 285
Virginia Waterfront International Arts Festival 234
Virginia Zoological Park 262
Virginian-Pilot 339
Visitors Companion 154
Visual Arts 225–229

W

Wallace Gallery 152, 153
Waller Mill Park 216, 270, 273, 274
Walsingham Academy 8, 318
War Hill Inn 60
Washington, George 142, 155, 198
Washington, Martha 151

Water Country USA 3, 6, 8, 9, 182, 213
Water Street Landing 208
Watermen's Museum 206, 211
Watermen's Museum 226
Waterside Festival Marketplace 262
Webster's Incredible Gifts 121
Welcome South 29, 71
Welcome South Restaurant 104
Westmoreland 302
Westover Plantation 139, 140, 172
Westray Downs 301
Wetherburns Tavern 158
Whaling Company 104
White House on Washington Street 61
White Lion Motel 43
Whitehall Restaurant 104
Whitley's Virginia Peanuts and Peanut Factory 126
Wildlife Arts Festival 231
William and Mary News 340
William E. Wood and Associates Realtors 303
Williamsburg AIDS Network 312
Williamsburg Area Golf Association 8
Williamsburg Area Tourist Shuttle 23
Williamsburg Bowl 111
Williamsburg Brass, Lighting and Textiles 127
Williamsburg Center Hotel 44
Williamsburg Chocolatier Ltd. 126
Williamsburg Choral Guild 222
Williamsburg Christian Academy 318
Williamsburg Coffee & Tea 104
Williamsburg Community Hospital 311
Williamsburg Community Sentara Home Care
    Services 306
Williamsburg Cookbook 157
Williamsburg Courtyard By Marriott 44
Williamsburg Crossing Shopping Center 114, 123
Williamsburg Doll Factory 130
Williamsburg Drug Company Inc. 120
Williamsburg Drug Company Lunch Counter 105
Williamsburg Farm Fresh Shopping Center 125
Williamsburg Fencing Club 272
Williamsburg Film Festival 4, 232
Williamsburg Genesis Eldercare 309
Williamsburg Golf Club Co. 281
Williamsburg Health Care and Rehabilitation
    Center 312
Williamsburg Hospitality House 44
Williamsburg Hotel/Motel Association 25, 47
Williamsburg Inn 28, 275
Williamsburg Inn Regency Dining Room 82
Williamsburg Land Conservancy 286
Williamsburg Landing 309
Williamsburg Limousine 18
Williamsburg Lodge 28
Williamsburg Magazine 340
Williamsburg Manor 61
Williamsburg Marriott 44
Williamsburg Motor Court 45
Williamsburg National Golf Club 279
Williamsburg Outlet Mall 128
Williamsburg Pavilion Shops 129
Williamsburg Players 224
Williamsburg Pottery Factory 3, 4, 8, 129, 186
Williamsburg Professional Pharmacy 126
Williamsburg Recreation Department 269

Williamsburg Regional Commission on Growth 9
Williamsburg Regional Library
    112, 219, 221, 306
Williamsburg Reproductions Program 119
Williamsburg Sampler Bed and Breakfast 62
Williamsburg Scottish Festival 4, 238
Williamsburg Shopping Center 126
Williamsburg Soap & Candle Company 4, 130
Williamsburg Symphonia 219, 222
Williamsburg Theatre 114
Williamsburg Transportation Center 17, 22
Williamsburg Travel Inn 45
Williamsburg Urgent Care 311
Williamsburg Wicker and Rattan Shoppe 130
Williamsburg Winery & Gabriel Archer Tavern
    8, 74
Williamsburg Women's Chorus 222
Williamsburg Woodlands 29
Williamsburg-Jamestown Airport 16, 214
Williamsburg: Great Entertainer Magazine 340
Williamsburg's Grand Illumination 241
Windsor Forest 302
Winthrop Rockefeller Archaeological Museum
    6, 160, 161
Wolstenholme Towne 160, 162
Woodland Indians 133
Woodlands Grill 82
Woodlands, The 376
Woods, The 302
Worship 327–329
Wythe Candies and Gourmet Shop 120
Wythe House 141, 156

Y

Yoder Farms Shopping Center 374
York County 13
York County Division of Parks and Recreation 275
York County Recycling Center 291
York County School System 317
York River Cruises 206
York River Inn Bed & Breakfast 63
York River State Park 270
York Town Crier 339
Yorkshire Inn Restaurant 105
Yorktown 191–211
Yorktown Beach 203, 271
Yorktown Christmas 242
Yorktown Civil War Weekend 234
Yorktown Motor Lodge 209
Yorktown Naval Weapons Station 199, 379
Yorktown Pub 208
Yorktown Shoppe 211
Yorktown Tree Lighting Festivities 242
Yorktown Victory Center 3, 6, 191, 204, 213
Yorktown Victory Day Celebration 240
Yorktown Visitor Center 6, 203
Yorktown Waterfront 216
Yukon Steak Company 105